Themes
Teachers Use

Themes
Teachers Use

MARJORIE J. KOSTELNIK, *Editor*
DONNA HOWE
KIT PAYNE
BARBARA ROHDE
GRACE SPALDING
LAURA STEIN
DUANE WHITBECK

MICHIGAN STATE UNIVERSITY

Illustrated by
BARBARA ROHDE

GoodYearBooks

An Imprint of ScottForesman
A Division of HarperCollinsPublishers

GoodYearBooks

are available for preschool through grade 6 for every basic curriculum subject plus many enrichment areas. For more GoodYearBooks, contact your local bookseller or educational dealer. For a complete catalog with information about other GoodYearBooks, please write:

GoodYearBooks

Scott, Foresman and Company
1900 East Lake Avenue
Glenview, IL 60025

Themes teachers use/Marjorie J. Kostelnik, editor; Donna Howe . . . [et al.] ;
    illustrated by Barbara Rohde.
        p.   cm.
      Continues: Teaching young children using themes.
      Includes bibliographical references and index.
      ISBN 0-673-36076-8
      1. Early childhood education—Activity programs—United States—
Handbooks, manuals, etc. 2. Early childhood education—United States—
Curricula—Handbooks, manuals, etc. 3. Creative activities and seat work—
United States—Handbooks, manuals, etc. I. Kostelnik, Marjorie J. II. Howe,
Donna. III. Teaching young children using themes.
    LB1139.35.A37T54 1996
    372. 13—dc20   95-24821
                                               CIP

McDonald's® Golden Arches symbol used by permission of McDonald's Corporation.

ISBN 0-673-36076-8

 2 3 4 5 6 7 8 9 - MP - 03 02 01 00 99 98 97 96

Preface

Themes Teachers Use is filled with exciting, age-appropriate, theme-related activities teachers easily can implement in their classrooms with children ages three to eight. It serves as a follow-up to the authors' popular book entitled *Teaching Young Children Using Themes* (GoodYear, 1991). This second book complements but does not duplicate material found in the first.

Writing a follow-up to a successful thematic guide like *Teaching Young Children Using Themes* is a lot like making a sequel to a movie. On the one hand, there is great satisfaction knowing that people have enjoyed your work and found it useful. On the other, there is a concern about how to make the second volume as exciting as the first, but different enough to provide a fresh look at a familiar idea. That was the dilemma facing us when we set out to write this publication. We solved it by maintaining the elements of the original volume that readers have told us are most helpful to them. At the same time, we have changed the structure of the thematic units in order to be even more responsive to the needs of children and teachers from preschool through the second grade. We did all of this within the context of thirteen new topics—ranging from "Art and Artists" to "Math Connections" to "Dogs." The result was *Themes Teachers Use*.

What's the Same About This Volume

Among the popular elements we kept from *Teaching Young Children Using Themes* is the list of terms, facts, and principles (TFPs), the core ideas and informational background that form the basis of each thematic unit. In maintaining a holistic, integrated approach to theme teaching, we have continued to suggest a wide range of activities in every unit using materials easily obtained by educators and programs throughout North America. Again, you will find many children's books, teacher resources, field trips, and classroom visitors. And our thematic activities, which emphasize hands-on learning, remain organized around developmental domains (aesthetics, affective, cognitive, language, physical, social, construction, and pretend play).

Significant Changes

Based on reader response, there are several new as well as expanded features in *Themes Teachers Use*. For example, we have added simplifications and extensions to most of the activities in the current edition. This strategy enables teachers to accommodate the learning needs of individual children whose development and abilities vary. Although beneficial for everyone, the simplifications and extensions will be particularly useful to educators in mixed-age and mainstreamed classrooms. In addition, we have written shorter procedures, making this book even easier to follow. More activities focused on anti-bias teaching are integrated into each thematic unit. Thus, ideas for helping children develop respect for people of all ages, backgrounds, abilities, and appearances are woven into suggestions throughout all the units. In these efforts, we were careful not to repeat activities from the previous volume. On the few occasions when such activities are essential to the unit at hand, they are varied enough to give them a different feel and purpose.

Finally and most importantly, we have answered reader requests to develop novel topics and to write them in ways that make it easy to expand and combine units. With this idea in mind, we have adopted a new format for putting together each theme. In our first book, themes are presented as large topics. Although the content can be broken down into smaller sub-themes, teachers must do this for themselves, separating TFPs and activities according to their own logic. In this volume, we have done that work for you. All thirteen units are divided into two or more mini-themes, making a grand total of thirty-eight mini-themes in all.

The flexibility built into the presentation of these units, because of their organization around mini-themes, enables teachers to choose an approach that is best suited to their children's interests, abilities, and imaginations. Mini-themes may be addressed either separately, as an introduction to a concept, or collectively, to provide children with the means for in-depth study. There is another option, too. Mini-themes from more than one unit can be linked to create a theme tailored for a particular group of children. Potential combinations are numerous and varied.

Audience

Teachers in training, as well as those already working in the field, will find a host of valuable ideas in *Themes Teachers Use*. The more than 1,200 theme-related activities in this book are well suited for children in a variety of early childhood settings: nursery schools; child care centers and family child care homes; Head Start, Home Start and Chapter I programs; pre-primary special education classes; kindergarten, first-, and second-grade classrooms. Readers familiar with our first book will find new theme-related activities to carry out and enjoy. Educators encountering our work for the first time will discover theme-related ideas that are easy to understand and implement.

Having said this, readers are cautioned that we have not created a "cookie-cutter" approach to theme-teaching. We do not expect early childhood professionals to simply replicate the activities presented here without adding input of their own. Neither do we expect teachers to use all the activity ideas offered in any unit. Instead, we assume teachers will choose from among the activities provided and adapt activities to suit the children in their groups. In our view, the ideal reader is one seeking guidance and inspiration for theme-teaching, as he or she finds ways to put his or her personal stamp on a particular unit.

Age Range of Children Addressed

The thirteen units described in these pages are suitable for use with children ranging from three through eight. Each activity has been developed with four- and five-year-old children in mind. However, we have provided suggestions for simplifying most activities to meet the needs of younger children and expanding them to suit first- and second-graders.

Background

Themes Teachers Use was written for teachers by teachers. The authors and editor have had many years of experience in a wide array of early childhood programs. Currently, all of us are actively engaged in the education of young children and the people who work with them. Consequently, most of the activities described here originated in our own classrooms. We have seen first-hand how children, students-in-training, and parent volunteers reacted to our initial ideas, how clearly they understood the directions, and what variations children invented on their own. Such pilot efforts led to many revisions, adaptations, and eliminations.

Next, we expanded the field-testing to early childhood settings beyond our own. These settings included urban, suburban, and rural programs; large, medium, and small classes; public, private, not-for-profit, and profit-seeking organizations; half-day and full-day programs; preschool classrooms as well as ones in the elementary grades. Ultimately, the criteria for including a topic or activity hinged on its educational value, how practical it was for people in different settings to obtain materials and carry out the lesson, and how much children and teachers enjoyed doing it. New activities as well as novel thematic approaches resulted from child, student, teacher, and parent input. Based on the feedback we received, this book took its final form.

Content

In deciding what theme-based units to include in *Themes Teachers Use*, we considered concepts that would complement those covered in our first theme book while still offering a comprehensive array of subjects for the reader whose only source of topics is this volume. Several criteria influenced our final selections. Most important was relevance to children. Most of the themes center on the everyday phenomena that dominate children's lives: the body, food, safety, classroom pets, and backyard animals. Others deal with issues critical to children's development in the early years: communication, people living together, art and artists, and math connections. The remainder are themes about which children often express curiosity. Units are designed to answer the kinds of questions children ask: "Why do leaves change color?" (Trees), "How does that work?" (Science and Scientists), "What kind of dog is that?" (Dogs), and "Are tigers really cats?" (Cats).

Secondly, we made sure to include some of the traditional topics teachers use year after year (such as interpersonal communication, parts and wholes, where food comes from, fire safety). Less common ones were also selected (such as earthworms, working dogs, print media, bodies in action). We also considered how well each unit lent itself to the creation of related hands-on activities and selected only those with content children could experience through the direct manipulation of objects. Once this standard was satisfied, we evaluated the degree to which potential activities represented varying instructional modes. For instance, topics that prompted many craft ideas but which were not well suited to pretend play, games, or problem-solving activities were rejected as too limiting. Instead we chose themes conducive to many different activity types.

General availability of props and other support materials was a final consideration. None of the units rely on teacher access to scarce resource items. And while there are often commercial materials available that could supplement certain themes, we assume teachers will discover many of these on their own, so the activities in this book do not rely on such items. The one exception to this general rule is the inclusion of children's books, which often are identified by name within an activity. When this occurs, activities are built around selections that are easily available through libraries and other free or inexpensive sources. Books that may be more difficult to find are clustered, two or three to an activity. Teachers who cannot secure one are likely to find another of those mentioned.

Chapter Order

This book's first section offers the reader an introduction to theme teaching. It describes ways to recognize effective theme teaching in action, how to incorporate themes into one's daily schedule, and how to implement thematic units over time. Methods for accommodating developmental differences among children in the instructional process and the relationship between theme teaching and holiday festivities also are discussed. Included, too, are a variety of means teachers can use to assess their own theme planning as well as the children's interest and knowledge about each theme. This first chapter closes with suggestions for how readers might use the rest of the book.

The order of the rest of the chapters is loosely based on keeping like units together for ease of reader reference. The first is an art unit, followed by two health units, two social studies units, a language arts unit, a unit focusing on mathematics, four units highlighting science topics, and two units combining science and social studies concepts. However, readers are reminded that although the overall focus of a unit falls within a particular subject area, every unit contains activities to address all aspects of childhood development and learning. A general subject area focus (such as health or social studies) can be stressed, deemphasized, or even changed, depending on which TFPs and which activities teachers select to support the given theme they wish to address.

We caution readers not to interpret the order of the units as representing a calendar for the year. It would be a violation of developmentally appropriate practice for readers simply to work their way through the book from start to finish. Instead, readers are encouraged to move from one theme to another (such as from unit two to unit ten to unit five) as dictated by the needs of the children in their group. This means that no two teachers are likely to progress through this book in exactly the same way.

Unit Sequence

Each of the units in this book encompasses a significant thematic idea (such as "Food."). All are comprised of two or more mini-themes (such as "Food and Food Preparation," "Where Food Comes From," "How the Body Uses Food"). Collectively, the mini-themes for a particular unit offer a comprehensive approach to the concept in question. Implemented individually, each mini-theme focuses on one aspect of the overall theme. The order of each unit's mini-themes is purposely sequenced from more concrete to more abstract, from simple to more complex. All of the introductory mini-themes are suitable for preschoolers and kindergarten-age children. Those that follow may be more or less appropriate depending on the children's level of understanding and their interests. Due to their abstract or complex nature, some of the mini-themes that come last in a few of the units (such as "Personal Safety," "People Living in Communities," "Communication Through the Visual Media," "Wild Cats," and "Wild Dogs") are best used with children thoroughly familiar with the larger topic (such as "Safety," "People Living Together," "Communication," "Cats," "Dogs"). Children for whom a concept is particularly relevant due to current events in their lives may also benefit from the activities presented in these latter mini-themes.

Acknowledgements

Much of what we have learned about theme teaching has come from our continued involvement with the children, families, and students participating in the Child Development Laboratories at Michigan State University. We have also been actively engaged with a variety of school districts, Head Start, Chapter I, child care, and nursery school programs throughout the country. We therefore acknowledge our indebtedness to all of those organizations and individuals. We are especially grateful to LaVelle Gipson, a longtime colleague and educator, for challenging our thinking, giving us constructive input, and providing useful feedback throughout the life of this project. We would like to thank the following additional persons for their contributions to the content of our work: Janet Brock, Kimberly Brock, Sandy Dickman, Norma Eppinger, David Kostelnik, Joan Lessen-Firestone, Rita Luks, Karen Morrison, Joyce Parker, Gayle Renken, Anne Rice, Jill Seaman, Anne Soderman, Bob Stein, and Alice Whiren. All of them offered "food for thought" as well as encouragement, both of which were much appreciated.

Contents

Introduction 1

1 Art and Artists 15
Visual Arts 17
Performing Arts 28
Usable Arts 35

2 The Human Body 49
The Body and Its Parts 51
The Senses 62
Bodies in Action: Mobility and
  Immobility 76

3 Food 89
Food and Food Preparation 91
Where Food Comes From 104
How the Body Uses Food 117

4 Safety 133
Vehicle Safety 135
Fire Safety 150
Personal Safety 161

5 People Living Together 179
People Playing 181
People Working 194
People Living in Communities 206

6 Communication 223
Interpersonal Communication 224
Print Media 241
Visual Media 250

7 Math Connections 257
Grouping and Patterning 258
Parts and Wholes 270
Geometrical Exploration 279

8 Science and Scientists 291
The Process of Science 293
Physical Science in the Everyday World 312

9 Trees 331
Trees Are Plants 333
Variety and Changes in Trees 345
Tree Gifts 362

10 Classroom Pets 373
Rabbits 375
Gerbils 394
Fish 407

11 Backyard Animals 421
Spiders 422
Earthworms 432
Frogs and Toads 446

12 Cats 461
Introduction to Cats 462
Domestic Cats 473
Wild Cats 484

13 Dogs 493
Dogs as Pets 495
Working and Helping Dogs 508
Wild Dogs 518

**Appendix A Curriculum
Domains** 531

Appendix B List of Themes 537

Index 539

Introduction

The children in the three- and four-year-old group at the Starshine Childcare Center were studying apple trees and apples—how they grow and how they are used. On Monday, the children went on a walking field trip to a nearby orchard. There they saw apple trees and picked three different varieties of apples. Back at the center, the children and their teacher talked about the trip. The teacher wrote the children's words and read them back to the group. Throughout the rest of the week, children made believe they were picking apples in an orchard set up in pretend play. Children examined Winesap, MacIntosh, and Golden Delicious apples, noting similarities and differences. At the snack table they tasted the different kinds of apples they picked on the field trip. In the block area, youngsters pretended they were truckers moving apples from the orchard to a store they had created out of large hollow blocks. Making applesauce, choosing favorite apple products, examining apple leaves, smelling apple wood, and investigating pictures showing the growth of an apple tree from seed to fruit were some additional theme-related activities children could choose. Children also participated in activities that had nothing to do with apples or apple trees—the walking beam, puzzles, grouping and counting activities, and art activities in which they experimented with color mixing.

Jorge walked into his kindergarten classroom asking, "What are we studying this week?" His teacher invited him to look around to see if he could figure it out. Jorge's tour of the learning centers available for the morning revealed several clues. The water table had been emptied of liquid and was now filled with whole leaves and bark of different kinds of trees. There were tree silhouettes on the easel for children to paint. The reading corner had a variety of narrative picture books including *The Tree in the Wood: An Old Nursery Song* (Manson, 1993), *The Living Tree* (Hester, 1990), and *The Gift of the Tree* (Tresselt, 1992). On the science table there was a cross-cut section of a log and several magnifying glasses children could use to examine it. Many of last week's pictures on the walls of different types of birds were supplemented with forest photographs and pictures of trees of varying kinds. Jorge returned to the large rug where the children were gathering for group time. He announced, "It's going to be

'the woods' or 'leaves' or 'trees' or something like that. That's what this week's gonna be about."

Building on a district-wide required science topic, "Plants in Our Environment," the first graders in Mr. Ho's class created a list of what they knew and what they wanted to learn about trees.

What We Know

Trees have leaves.

Trees are tall.

Some people have trees in their yards.

There are trees in the city and in our neighborhood.

Some trees have leaves that fall off and some don't.

Some leaves change colors.

Trees stay in one place.

People sometimes climb trees.

Trees grow in the ground.

There are different kinds of trees.

Some trees grow out of cement.

Some trees grow fruit.

What We Want to Find Out

Are all trees plants?

What are the different kinds of trees?

How many kinds of trees are there?

What makes some trees straight and some trees twisted?

How come some trees have leaves that fall off and some don't?

Do they have trees on the moon?

How do trees get their food?

This list served as a guide to the teacher and the children for developing activities in many different subject areas aimed at helping children check out their ideas about trees. The unit of study that followed lasted three weeks, combining both teacher-initiated activities as well as activities generated by the children themselves. Throughout this period of time, the children went back over their list confirming or modifying their original notions and determining to what extent they answered the questions posed. The children also noted new, unexpected facts they discovered during their study of "Trees."

Although their participation varied, the children and teachers in these classrooms were all engaged in thematic instruction. Theme teaching involves creating an array of activities around a central idea. These activities are integrated into every aspect of the curriculum within a concentrated time frame, ranging from several days to a few weeks. As children engage in various theme-oriented experiences, they extract relevant bits of information from one activity and connect them to information gained in another. These connections prompt children to modify and expand ideas related to the theme. This, in turn, enhances children's development of more comprehensive, accurate concepts. Such linkages among activities and ideas are fundamental to theme teaching and provide the most important rationale for its use in early childhood classrooms (Kostelnik, Soderman, and Whiren, 1993). Moreover, the practice of thinking in an integrated fashion that develops from children's experiences with thematic instruction carries over into unrelated instructional activities as well. Children become more adept at making connections among the various learning episodes in which they participate. This makes theme teaching a valuable curricular tool that transcends the content of the moment.

Characteristics of Effective Theme Teaching

Teachers who wish to make effective use of themes keep in mind that children's concept development, not simple memorization, is their goal. Consequently, they integrate theme teaching with principles of developmentally appropriate practice as described by the National Association for the Education of Young Children (Bredekamp, 1988). Among these principles are:

● Providing hands-on experience with real objects for children to examine and manipulate

● Creating activities in which children use all of their senses

● Building classroom activities around children's current interests

● Helping children acquire new knowledge and skills by building on what they already know and can do

● Providing activities and routines that address all aspects of children's development—cognitive, emotional, social, and physical

● Including a wide range of activities that address variations in children's learning styles and preferred modes of involvement

● Accommodating children's needs for movement and physical activity, social interaction, independence, and positive self-image

● Providing opportunities for children to use play to translate experience into understanding

● Respecting the individual differences, cultural backgrounds, and home experiences that children bring with them to the classroom

● Finding ways to involve members of children's families.

In addition to maintaining the tenets of developmentally appropriate practice, teachers use themes effectively when they make sure that the topics they choose have direct relevance to the children with whom they are working. Relevance requires that the concepts under study be directly tied to children's real-life experiences. Themes like "Backyard Animals," "The Human Body," "Food," "Safety," or "People Living Together" are pertinent for preschoolers and early elementary-age children because they help them make sense of their lives and expand their understanding of the world around them. Such themes also can be designed to give children first-hand experiences with the concepts being taught. Some themes are inappropriate for this age group ("Gravity" or "Life in Ancient Rome" or "Penguins," for example) because the concepts they represent are too abstract and/or fall outside the bounds of children's day-to-day living. Even when children express an interest in a concept far removed from their personal experience, it is usually best to introduce the idea with a more familiar concept. Thus, second-graders interested in the penguins they heard about in *Mr. Popper's Penguins* (Atwater, 1938) might begin their exploration of the topic with a unit on birds or one on snow and ice. Consequently, the best source of thematic ideas comes from the children themselves. The things children frequently enact, discuss, or wonder about provide the strongest foundation for planning and implementing themes in early childhood programs.

Themes become even more relevant when their content is adapted to the needs of a specific group of children in a particular community. For instance, the theme "Trees" has meaning for most children no matter where they live. Yet, children growing up in the Great Lakes region would find it more interesting and appropriate to focus on red oak or white oak trees, silver maple or sugar maple trees, white pine or apple trees, rather than studying palm or piñon trees. Likewise, youngsters living in Louisiana would find it most relevant to study live oaks, magnolia, lemon, and cypress trees. In both cases, the general information offered to children about trees would be similar, but the examples would be tailored to accommodate different populations.

In each of the preceding examples, thematic relevance was determined based on the suitability of the subject matter. Another attribute of relevance is timeliness. Timely themes build on children's current interests. Teachers create units around the topics children bring up and want to know more about. They do not plan a whole year's themes in advance, nor do they simply repeat the same themes year after year. Their planning is individualized for each group of children, making the most of opportune events and shifts in children's needs.

Relevant themes also go beyond mere collections of engaging activities designed to keep children entertained and busy. They are educational in nature, enhancing children's store of knowledge. They also help to build skills such as observing, comparing, estimating, predicting, remembering, role-playing, socializing, communicating, reading, writing, and counting. To promote children's acquisition of knowledge and skills, themes must be tied to information gathered through careful research. Consequently, establishing a database of relevant facts and concepts should be a first step in effective theme planning. Using that information in providing children with theme-relevant, hands-on activities and firsthand experiences follows. When all the preceding conditions are present, theme teaching becomes truly relevant to children and, therefore, very effective.

Incorporating Themes into Daily Routines

Theme-related activities can be interjected into any classroom routine. For instance, teachers may carry out whole group instruction (the majority of the children are expected to do the same thing at the same time) during which all or part of the lesson is focused on the theme. Theme-related stories, songs, and fingerplays, as well as demonstrations during circle time, exemplify this approach. Whole group activities can create a sense of cohesiveness within the group, provide everyone with the same information at once, introduce subsequent theme-related activities, and give children a chance to verbalize what they are doing and learning. However, whole group instruction is not a synonym for lecture time. The same principles that govern any other type of activity—hands-on instruction, active involvement, variety, and balance across the curriculum—continue to play a role in teachers' planning and implementation.

Small-group activities (a few children, assigned to one of several groups, carry out certain tasks during a particular time of the day) afford additional opportunities to address the theme. Almost any activity can be adapted to a small group format. The actual composition of the group is often determined by the teacher, based on specific instructional needs. Knowing that children share a common interest may be one basis for group placement. Other small groups may be formed when certain children have or need to practice a particular skill. Still others can be created by mixing children of varying abilities so that they can help one another in the learning process. Each type of small group has its particular strengths. These can be tapped at different times throughout the day or year.

Free choice options, in which children circulate among a variety of learning centers at will, is another significant teaching strategy in the theme-oriented classroom. Effective learning centers share the following characteristics (Kostelnik, et al., 1993, pp. 295–97):

● They are organized and implemented on the basis of knowledge the teacher has about the children and their abilities and are well grounded in early childhood development and education principles.

● The activities offered to children within the centers are flexible and adaptable, not rigid or fixed.

● The array of learning centers provided to children in a day, and over time, are varied and provide a balance of aesthetic, affective, cognitive, language, social, and physical experiences.

● Children understand how to use the centers properly.

● The same learning center, at different times, is used to address different developmental domains or curricular areas.

● Teachers use the learning center period as a time to interact freely with children rather than as a time to put children on "hold" because adults are grading work, working exclusively with one small group of children the entire time, or preparing materials or activities for later use.

The most effective approach to theme teaching is for teachers to make use of individual, small group, and whole group learning activities within each thematic unit. In other words, themes should not be confined to circle time instruction or reserved for learning centers only. Instead, the theme should cut across these routines, appearing throughout the day, every day. This gives children ready access to theme-related content from the beginning of each session to the end. Moreover, within a particular time on a given day, either all or only part of each individual, small group, or whole group activity may be theme-related. In this way the time frame and format taken by theme-related activities vary from day to day, as well as from classroom to classroom.

Balance within the Theme

Balance is a key concept in thematic instruction and refers to the reasonable distribution of theme-related activities throughout a teaching plan. A reasonable distribution is one in which there are enough worthwhile, theme-related activities to support children's concept development. Teaching plans containing activities that have been contrived to fit the theme or plans including too few thematic activities undermine children's concept development. This is because farfetched activities have no perceivable link to the theme's database and offer little substance to promote children's learning. Also, when theme-related activities are insufficient in number, children don't have enough opportunities to get involved in the theme. Making the connection from one activity to another becomes difficult. To avoid these dilemmas teachers create theme-related activities that are meaningful to children and that have a clear link to the theme. They also include activities in large enough numbers to provide children with multiple experiences in a variety of domains or subject areas. When developing such a plan, teachers consider the notion of balance from at least three perspectives:

● balancing the theme across the curriculum,

● balancing theme-related and non-theme-related activities, and

● balancing thematic instruction with other required program content.

Theme teaching is not an add-on. It is not another layer to be introduced into the day's instruction, nor is it an isolated component to be added to an already bursting curriculum. Therefore, teachers who use themes do not list "theme time" as a separate part of the day. Themes are tools for integrating the curriculum. They transcend traditional subject matter and materials-based boundaries and pull together experiences carried out at different times during the teaching day.

Themes across the curriculum.

Effective themes are ones in which thematic content is addressed in each of a program's curricular domains (such as aesthetic, affective, cognitive, language, social, and physical), subject areas (such as math, reading, science, etc.), or activity areas (blocks, book corner, puzzle table, housekeeping area, and so forth). This means children's theme-related experiences should traverse the curriculum. When that kind of distribution occurs, children encounter the same pool of information through many different avenues. Regardless of whether they prefer more structured or less structured activities, active or less active means of interaction, certain kinds of materials, or particular sensory experiences, children can gain

access to the content in ways that best suit their individual learning styles. If one activity is unappealing or is not developmentally appropriate for them at a given time, children can still learn about the theme in other ways. This would not be true if the theme were presented within a narrower range of experiences.

Another way teachers balance themes across the curriculum is to choose topics over time that represent different arenas of learning. For instance, in this volume some themes are more scientific in nature, others are focused on social studies concepts, some have a mathematical orientation, and still others take on a language arts perspective. Children benefit most from a varied selection of themes rather than only having access to ones in which the same perspective dominates.

Theme-related and non-theme-related activities.
It is important to have enough theme-related activities for children to easily grasp what topic is being explored. Such activities should be spread out through the duration of the unit and should be represented within a variety of routines as well as through differing materials, curriculum areas, and activity types. In half-day programs, the minimum number of theme-related activities that seems to be sufficient is three or four, with one of these taking place during large group time. For full-day programs, an average of three activities in each half of the day works reasonably well. At least a portion of one group time should also be devoted to some aspect of the theme (Kostelnik, Spalding, and Howe, 1993).

Although it is important to have several theme-related activities each day, **not every** activity has to be theme-oriented. In fact, it is preferable to create a mix of theme-related and non-theme-related activities for children to try. If a classroom is overly saturated by a given topic, it loses its appeal for children and grown-ups alike. Some non-theme-oriented activities interspersed throughout a teaching plan provide a respite from the topic and enable teachers to address necessary skills development that bears no relationship to the dominant concept being addressed. Repeating favorite activities, reviewing past experiences, and including activities targeted toward certain of children's non-theme-related needs and skills are appropriate alternatives to consider. Teachers also should take time to create activities that introduce children to new content that might be expanded upon in the future. Such activities give teachers opportunities to gauge children's interest in untried topics and determine what children may know or not know about a concept.

Thematic instruction and other required content.
Some early childhood programs mandate that certain topics be covered during the

year; "fire safety," "animals," and "likenesses and differences" are typical examples. Teachers can address required content by incorporating such material into the non-theme-related activities they include in their teaching plan. On the other hand, required content can serve as the topic around which entire units are developed. Social studies, science, health, math, or language arts concepts all have the potential for use as the basis for theme-planning. Teachers who plan a week or more around concepts like "Parts and Wholes" or "Communities" or "Art and Artists" are able to combine previously segregated subjects or skills: math with writing, social studies with science, health with reading, or art with critical thinking, for example. This makes the day less fragmented, allowing children and teachers more time to explore topics in depth.

Theme Teaching Over Time

Teachers often ask, "How long should a theme last?" The answer is, "It depends." It depends on the children's needs and interests and on how the teacher structures the topic. As a result, themes vary in their duration from topic to topic and from group to group. For instance, a week on "Worms" might cover the subject nicely. On the other hand, three weeks devoted to "Food" might barely scratch the surface of possible information or children's enjoyment of the unit. Similarly, one class could find a week devoted to "Fruits" to be plenty. Another group of children might be so intrigued by fruits and their characteristics that week one leads to a second week focusing on fruit products and perhaps a third week concentrating on people whose work involves growing and/or selling fruit. Teachers must exercise judgment in determining what length is most fitting for their class. Based on the authors' experience with themes, here are a few guidelines to follow in making such judgments:

1. The less experience children have with a concept, the more time they will need to explore it.
2. Themes lasting less than a week are not as effective as themes lasting a week or longer. Children and teachers benefit from the natural time frame offered by a week-to-week approach to theme planning.
3. The more concentrated the distribution of thematic activities, the fewer days are necessary to carry out the theme; the less concentrated the distribution of thematic activities, the more days are necessary to implement the theme effectively.
4. Expand units if children's interest remains high, even if it means rearranging some other teaching plans.
5. Curtail themes or change their direction when children's interest is obviously waning, even if it means rearranging some other teaching plans.

Although theme length will vary with the topic and the group of children, many teachers report that it works well to plan units lasting two to three weeks, with an optional follow-up week available if needed (Kostelnik, et al., 1993). Suggestions for how units of this length might be created around the themes presented in this book are offered in each chapter's introductory materials.

How often a theme is addressed throughout the year is as important to consider as how long each unit lasts. One must recognize that the concepts children construct in association with a particular theme do not end when the unit is over. Children will continue to explore and apply their knowledge within subsequent themes. Although they do this spontaneously, it is also useful for teachers to plan some activities throughout the year that encourage children to retrieve content explored in previous units. These kinds of activities become some of the non-theme-related activities included in later teaching plans. Note, too, that some concepts may be particularly enriched when they receive deliberate attention for several days, at different times during the year. A unit on "Trees" is one such example. A tree theme could be introduced in the fall, then repeated in the winter and again in the spring, building on what children learned earlier in the year as well as contrasting trees and tree growth during three different seasons.

Themes also can be repeated from one program level to the next. That is, children may participate in a "Family Life" theme or a unit on "Dinosaurs" two or even three years in a row. Sometimes teachers and parents worry about children revisiting certain themes as they move from the four-year-old room to the five-year-old class, from the first grade to the second grade, or from year one to year two in a multiage or continuous progress program. They are concerned that children will be bored or that they will not learn anything new. When these issues surface, it helps to remember that children learn from repetition and that no one period of investigation is ever complete. Each time they encounter the same theme, children take away different information. Having opportunities to explore familiar concepts is not only worthwhile, it is the best way for children to expand their understanding by building on what they already know. Consequently, repeating some themes from one year to the next is an excellent instructional strategy (Kostelnik, et al., 1993).

On the other hand, simply rehashing the exact same material as children mature may not offer enough stimulation to hold children's interest or promote their concept development over time. To avoid this problem, teachers in the same program can plan similar themes with the idea of drawing children's attention to different facets with each repetition. A "Stores" theme in the preschool might revolve around things and people in stores, such as groceries, clothing, customers, and clerks. In the kindergarten, a "Stores" theme could be expanded to include the variety of activities that take place in stores, such as pricing items, making an inventory of goods, and exchanging money for items purchased. By the first grade, these ideas could be further developed to include the activities of marketing and advertising. Creating program-wide plans that incorporate this kind of developmental progression into theme teaching supports children's continued interest in such themes. It also enables each teacher to take a fresh approach to topics that have been addressed previously. Program-wide planning also prevents teachers from becoming "territorial" about certain topics or feeling that "all the good ideas have been used up" by the time children reach their particular program level.

Accommodating Developmental Differences Among Children

Children are not all the same. Obviously children vary in age, gender, temperament, culture, ethnicity, family contexts, and socioeconomic circumstances. Even children who share similar attributes are different from one another in their rates of development, learning styles, and interests. One challenge for early childhood professionals is how to accommodate such differences among children in theme teaching. This is true for teachers who work with children in mixed-age groups, single-age groups, and for those who work across age groups. There are three ways in which appropriate provisions can be made:

● Accommodating differences in the same activity (intra-activity)

● Accommodating differences within the theme

● Accommodating differences from one application of the theme to another

Intra-activity accommodations.

Classroom activities that encompass multiple learning objectives versus a single outcome enable children of varying abilities to experience challenge and success within the same lesson. Consequently, teachers should strive to create individual theme-related activities that cover a range of goals for children's participation. These goals, progressing from easy to more difficult, are based on the principles that development and learning proceed from:

simple to complex,

known to unknown,

self to other,

whole to part,

concrete to abstract,

exploratory to goal directed,

inaccurate to more accurate,

impulsive to self-controlled.

For example, consider this range of objectives for an activity in which children are engaged in puppet play. Children:

1. Explore the puppets by looking at them, handling them, and putting the puppets on their hands.

2. Give their puppets a name.

3. Create voices for their puppets.

4. Practice making their puppets move in different ways.

5. Practice moving the puppet in relation to an object, such as a block for the puppet to hold or a chair for the puppet to sit on.

6. Practice moving their puppets in relation to another child's puppet.

7. Act out a simple scenario with another child and his or her puppet.

Some children might focus on the first objective throughout the entire activity period. Others might begin to create a personality for their puppets by giving them a name and a voice. Still others could act out skits, either with their teacher or with their peers. While all of the children can enter the activity successfully and make progress in using the materials, their rate of progress will vary in accordance with their previous experiences and current abilities. When children have chances to participate in broad-based, open-ended activities like this, they can extrapolate experiences which are meaningful at the time. When such activities are repeated throughout the year, children have additional opportunities to practice what they have learned—to build on it and apply their knowledge and skills to novel situations. Thus, as children gain experience in handling puppets, they might eventually turn their character creating skills to more elaborate role playing with other children in the class. Perhaps they even will create simple plays with dolls or other figures.

Accommodating developmental differences within the theme.
Besides providing children with a wide range of open-ended activities that address a broad spectrum of objectives, teachers should offer children activities representing differing sensory modalities: auditory, visual, kinesthetic, and tac-

tile. It also is important to include variations in the degree of participation required of children in these activities: solitary small and large groups; more or less active; more or less self-directed. When these strategies are combined with opportunities for self-selection, children are able to find experiences in the classroom that best meet their individual learning needs.

An additional strategy to consider is to select themes with certain children in mind. Perhaps Carl talks endlessly about trains—a theme on that topic would be appropriate for all the children, but would be especially meaningful for him. Likewise, if a teacher observes several children in the class intrigued by a grackle building a nest in the downspout near the classroom window, a unit on local birds might be in order. As the year progresses, it is useful to consider whether the special interests of the individual children in the group have been addressed in some form or another. An affirmative answer helps to ensure that differences among the children also have been accommodated.

Accommodating differences across age groups. The process involved in planning and implementing themes is the same regardless of children's ages. Selecting a topic, creating a database, generating activity ideas, planning the unit, and carrying it out are steps necessary to developing every theme. However, theme teaching will vary both in terms of the concepts chosen for study and in the actual information highlighted, depending on the ages of the children and their prior experience with the concept. To make these kinds of differentiations, it is necessary to divide the information base into two categories: simple and advanced. Simple information includes that which can be observed or experienced directly by the children. Existing in the here and now, rather than in the past or future, this kind of information does not require teacher explanations for children to understand. Adult talk may reinforce children's self-discoveries, but it is never a substitute for direct experience. For instance, the theme "The Senses" could be supported by activities and classroom routines that lead children in discovering for themselves the following simple and directly observable information:

1. People use their eyes to see.
2. People hear sounds with their ears.
3. People sense tastes with their tongues.
4. People sense smells with their noses.
5. People sense touches and feel with their skin.
6. Skin covers the whole body.
7. The color of people's skin varies on their own bodies and from one person to another.

Advanced data, on the other hand, encompasses information children learn about through representa-tional experiences such as pictures or models. Such advanced information may also refer to past or future events or events that take place beyond the immediate program environment. Often this kind of information requires children to envision something in order to comprehend it. The fact that people sense touches and feel with their skin is a simple one to understand because it is readily observable and can be easily experienced in a variety of ways. The fact that nerves in the skin send messages to the brain is advanced because it can only be represented in a picture, diagram, or discussion. To understand this material, children must envision the inner workings of the body without seeing them directly. Other examples of advanced information related to the senses are listed below:

1. A special nerve in the eye sends messages to the brain about sights.
2. Sounds produce vibrations that enter the ear through the ear canal and vibrate parts inside the ear.
3. Taste buds are tiny bumps on the tongue that sense sweet, sour, salty, and bitter tastes.
4. The brain stores and interprets information about sights, sounds, tastes, smells, and touches that people use again later.

Simple information is most suitable for preschoolers and children less experienced with the concept, no matter how old they are. Kindergartners and children in the lower elementary grades will find some advanced information meaningful, especially in relation to themes with which they are very familiar. Teachers working with children whose ages and experiences cut across these conditions should plan on using a mixture of the two.

The criteria that differentiates simple information from advanced data also is applicable to themes overall (Kostelnik, et al., 1993). These differentiations influence which themes are chosen for which groups of children. Concepts that deal with the present and that youngsters can experience through numerous, direct hands-on experiences are most suitable for children whose thinking is dominated by preoperational thinking. Examples are dogs as pets, domestic cats, spiders, the senses, interpersonal communication, art and artists, families, and people at school. All of these topics are familiar to children and ones they can explore within the program. They need not rely on field trips or visitors as their only firsthand experience with the concept. Neither must children rely on memory alone or projections to think about the theme meaningfully.

Thematic units that require children to draw on memory and/or make projections are more abstract and should be considered advanced. Samples are the circus (activities depend on children remembering or envisioning a circus experience), wild dogs (children need to make comparisons between something known—domestic dogs—and something unknown—dogs in the wild), and the eye (much of the instruction focuses on models and diagrams to illustrate how the eye works). Advanced themes are best implemented with children functioning beyond the preoperational period of intellectual development. In this volume we have made clear differentiations between simple information and advanced data. These designations are described in more detail in the section of this chapter entitled "Format."

Themes and Holidays

Readers will notice that there are no themes in this volume titled "Easter" or "Fourth of July Fun." We realize that planning teaching units in conjunction with "the holiday of the month" is a common practice in many preschool and elementary school programs. It is not unusual to have weeks at a time centered around Halloween, Christmas, or Valentine's Day. For some programs, holidays are the heart of the curriculum. However, from our perspective, several potential problems may accompany these thematic designations.

First, holiday themes run the risk of being little more than convenient backdrops for classroom decorations and craft projects for children to take home. While there is nothing wrong with decorations and arts and crafts projects, there is seldom a real database associated with holiday themes that goes beyond the backdrops and artifacts. Young children usually come away from such experiences without having expanded their conceptualizations or increasing their skills across the curriculum. This is the antithesis of effective theme teaching.

Second, early childhood professionals have limited time to cover the wide variety of topics pertinent to young children. Although holidays are a valued facet of many children's lives, they are not the only or even most critical events children encounter growing up. Additionally, there are many opportunities for children to learn holiday lore at home and through the media. The same cannot be said for other concepts such as "Spiders," "Personal Safety," "Communication," or "Geometric Exploration." Limiting holiday themes allows more attention to be paid to those concepts for which early childhood programs can add richness, variety, and experiences not so easily obtained elsewhere (Deardon, 1984).

A third pitfall of the holiday-dominated curriculum is that the religious or cultural significance of certain holidays may be lost. For instance, the true significance of Christmas may be overlooked in a flurry of red and green, Santa images, and Christmas trees. Such simplistic approaches to holidays may also result in the promotion of stereotypes. For example, Thanksgiving, which is frequently depicted as a universal time of celebration throughout the United States, is a time of happiness for some, but a time of mourning for others. Many Native Americans associate the coming of the Pilgrims with the demise of Native Americans' power and dignity. Equitable treatment of the holiday demands a more accurate view that would be too abstract for most young children to absorb. Yet, promoting the traditional stereotypes of happy Pilgrims and happy Indians, with the hope that children will gain more balanced understandings later in life, is uncertain. Such modifications do not always happen. In addition, treating holidays as universal assumes that every family celebrates particular holidays in particular ways. When this is not the case, families for whom a holiday is not observed are frequently excluded from the program. None of these results are in keeping with the cultural and religious sensitivity that early childhood professionals strive to achieve. For all these reasons, the authors advise selecting concepts other than holidays as a major source for theme ideas.

Not using holidays as the primary basis for theme planning does not mean ignoring them altogether. Holiday activities may be included even though they are not directly related to the theme at hand. Also, it may be relevant to children and their families to incorporate holidays into the context of a larger concept such as "People Living Together" or "Family Traditions" or "Celebrations." Such concepts are inclusive, not exclusive. They support children's growing awareness and appreciation of the similarities as well as the differences among people. Additionally, integrating holidays such as Valentine's Day into the more global theme of "Friends," using Halloween as a way to stimulate children's interest in "Clothing," or exploring and comparing rituals in the home associated with Christmas, Hanukkah, and Kwanzaa through a unit on "Families" or "People in Communities" are all ways to acknowledge and enjoy holidays as they occur. Because they make meaningful connections between holidays and children's lives, these are the approaches to holidays that readers will encounter in this volume.

Theme Teaching Assessment

Teachers often ask, "How will I know if my theme teaching is successful?" There are two ways to answer this query. The first is to assess the extent to which a teacher's planning and implementation of the theme meets standards associated with effective theme teaching. The second is to determine how well children understand and make use of the knowledge and skills addressed within each theme.

Evaluating Theme Implementation. The evaluation of any theme encompasses an assessment of the number and quality of theme-related activities provided to the children, the extent to which children are actively engaged in the theme, the classroom environment, and parents' involvement in the theme. The authors have created a theme-teaching checklist for this purpose. (See Table 1.) Readers are encouraged to use this checklist for each new theme they create.

Theme Teaching Checklist

Purpose: To help teachers assess the effectiveness of theme implementation in their classrooms.

Directions: Put a 1 by each item that accurately depicts the classroom being observed. Total the items to achieve a final score.

Score	Level of Effectiveness
26–23	Excellent use of themes
22–20	Good use of themes; minor additions could make it better
19–17	Satisfactory start; gradually address missing items to improve
16 and below	Poor use of themes; major revisions necessary

Theme-Related Activities

1. The theme planner can articulate why the theme is relevant to a particular group of children.
2. The theme-related information conveyed to children is accurate.
3. The theme-related information conveyed to children is meaningful (of interest to them and age-appropriate in terms of vocabulary and detail).
4. Two or more theme-related firsthand experiences are made available to the children each week.
5. At least two to three theme-related activities are offered to the children each half-day.
6. Theme-related activities take place at different times throughout the day.
7. Every week at least one theme-related activity has been included for each of the developmental domains: aesthetic, affective, cognitive, construction, language, social, physical, pretend play.
8. Theme-related activities chosen are mostly ones children can do on their own. Activities are not overly dependent on adult direction.
9. Opportunities for children to apply, synthesize, and summarize what they have learned about the theme are made available throughout the week.

Child Involvement

10. Children are talking about the theme (offering information, asking questions, conversing with peers and adults).
11. Children are pretending in relation to the theme.
12. Children are creating theme-related products of their own invention.
13. Children report discussing or playing the theme at home.
14. Children demonstrate linking the theme to their past or current experiences either physically or verbally.
15. Parents report that children have discussed or engaged in theme-related play at home.
16. Children continue to refer to the theme or demonstrate knowledge of its content after the unit is over.

Classroom Environment

17. Terms, facts, and principles supporting the theme are posted or otherwise available for adult reference.
18. Children's own theme-related creations (projects, writings, etc.) are hanging up or otherwise displayed in the room.
19. Theme-related props are available to the children each day.
20. Theme-related pictures, songs, poems, books, and other such items are used to create a thematic atmosphere.
21. One circle time each day is theme-related.
22. The theme-related purpose of the circle time is made clear to the children.
23. Theme-related circle time activities include active child participation.

Parent Involvement

24. Parents are provided with information about the theme.

25. Parents are invited to contribute to the theme.

26. Parents give and receive feedback regarding children's interest and participation in the theme.

Table 1 Theme Teaching Checklist. Reprinted with the permission of Prentice Hall, Inc. from *Developmentally Appropriate Programs in Early Childhood Education* by Marjorie J. Kostelnik et al. Copyright © 1993 by Macmillan College Publishing Company.

Individual Child and Group Assessment.
The goal of theme teaching is to promote children's concept development. Consequently, early childhood professionals involved in theme teaching need to continuously assess children's understanding of theme-related concepts. These determinations inform the teaching process, enabling educators to shape their instruction more effectively. As teachers evaluate children's theme-related learning, they can make revisions and change direction in response to children's needs and interests.

Making such decisions, however, requires teachers to know what kinds of outcomes to expect. The goal of theme teaching is to promote children's concept development. Just because children repeat a few facts related to the theme does not mean they have learned anything new or that their concepts have been extended. Children may simply be echoing knowledge they possessed prior to theme implementation or reciting things they have heard without really comprehending them. The real extent to which children have increased their comprehension of the theme is revealed through their play, conversations with classmates and adults, the questions they ask, the errors they make in their explanations or experimentations, and their references in new situations to what they have learned through earlier theme teaching.

Throughout the assessment process, early childhood educators also keep in mind that even very young children enter the classroom with rudimentary concepts about themselves and the world in which they live. However, because each child's knowledge base is unique to him or her, the exact make-up of these concepts differs from child to child. Yet, all children involved in a theme should extend what they know—adding new information to their current store of knowledge, filling voids in their previous understandings, and correcting some of the inaccurate assumptions under which they had been operating. The teacher's role becomes that of helping children expand their concepts in personally meaningful ways. This results in individualized outcomes, not uniform ones for the entire group. Such outcomes make it imperative that teachers keep some individual records of children's progress as well as more general group evaluations.

Teachers who observe children carefully and who talk with them about the theme under study gain valuable information about children's conceptual understandings. Some teachers carry out this process informally, making use of *anecdotal records* to chronicle children's theme-related comments, information provided by parents about children's conversations at home, and examples of children applying what they have learned in relation to one theme in the context of other experiences. Other teachers make use of *portfolios or dated work samples* as a means for substantiating comparative shifts in children's understandings over time (Perrone, 1991). Samples may include children's drawings, paintings, maps, graphs, descriptions of constructions, charts, photographs of projects and friends, webs, written work, and projects. Portfolios are established for individual children and often include samples selected by the child as well as ones chosen by the teacher.

Another method of documenting children's conceptual development is to invite children to engage in self-evaluation (Kostelnik, et al., 1993). The children in Mr. Ho's first grade, cited at the beginning of this chapter, were illustrative of this process. They created a list of what they knew or thought they knew about the theme before their study began. The children also generated a list of questions about which they were curious. As they participated in theme-related activities, children were encouraged to confirm and adjust their original ideas as well as answer the questions they had raised. In this way, both the teacher and the children had a tangible record of changes in the group's comprehension of the concepts. Such methods can be employed with younger children as a group and with older children individually.

Now that readers are acquainted with some of the rudiments of theme teaching, it is time to turn our attention to the content of *Themes Teachers Use*. Let's begin by examining the foundations upon which the book has been developed.

Foundations

There are thirteen units in this book, each representing a significant thematic idea. Every unit is divided into two or three subunits called mini-themes. Any of the mini-themes may be treated as a self-contained topic or implemented in combination with others in the unit for a more in-depth study of the concept. Either way, readers have the choice of implementing simple, brief themes or creating more complex ones that last longer. The decisions they make will be based on the relevance of the theme to the children in their classes and on children's demonstrated interests and understandings.

All thirteen units contain both content learning and process learning. *Content learning* encompasses the factual information relevant to the theme. It is embodied in a collection of related terms, facts, and principles (hereafter referred to as TFPs). *Terms* are the vocabulary children should know to describe objects and events linked to the theme. Something known to have happened is a *fact*. *Principles* involve combinations of facts and the relationships among them.

All of the cognitive, social, emotional, and physical operations and skills that form the basis for children's experiences within the early childhood classroom comprise *process learning*. These learning processes are addressed through eight curricular domains: aesthetic learning, affective learning, cognitive learning, language learning, physical learning, social learning, construction play, and pretend play. The first six domains encompass learning processes related to major facets of child development; the latter two are the means by which these facets are integrated. Together, the entire array incorporates learning processes essential to the "whole child." These processes are summarized in Table 2. A more detailed list of the goals and objectives associated with each domain is offered in Appendix A. The reader also is referred to *Teaching Young Children Using Themes* (1991) for an in-depth discussion of how to use themes to integrate content and process learning in the classroom.

These learning processes encompass knowledge, concepts, and skills related to the development of:

Aesthetics	• self-expression through the visual and performing arts • aesthetic appreciation
Affective skills	• self-awareness • decision making • independence • instrumental know-how • appreciation of own cultural identity and heritage • self-confidence • positive self-esteem
Cognition	• critical and creative thinking • organizing, analyzing, generating, integrating, and evaluating skills • scientific understanding • mathematical understanding
Construction skills	• concrete representation through modeling, drawing, and building
Language	• effective communication through listening, speaking, writing, and reading
Physical skills	• competence in use of large and small muscles • physical fitness • care and respect for the body • appreciation and enjoyment of human movement
Pretend Play skills	• active representation through imitating, role-playing, and dramatizing
Social Skills	• internal behavior controls • successful patterns of interaction • cooperative attitudes and actions • helpful attitudes and actions • responsible attitudes and actions • appreciation and respect for individual and cultural similarities and differences • respect for the environment

Table 2 Learning Processes Essential to "Whole Child" Teaching

Format

The format for all of the units is the same and consists of the following components:

1. **Title and Introduction.** The title of the unit identifies the main idea on which it is based. The mini-theme titles represent the more specific concept around which each subunit is planned.

2. **Purpose.** The rationale gives readers an introduction to the unit as a whole and provides relevant background information. Each rationale begins with an explanation of the significance of the overall topic to children and is followed by a discussion of the direction taken within the unit as well as why certain mini-themes were chosen for inclusion.

3. **Implementation.** Suggestions for how the mini-themes that make up the unit might be implemented separately or collectively to promote children's concept development are provided in the implementation section.

4. **Terms, Facts, and Principles.** The central core of every mini-theme is the list of terms, facts, and principles (TFPs) that accompany it. As many as thirty to forty TFPs are listed for each mini-theme. Individual TFPs are categorized as simple or advanced. Simple TFPs are fundamental to children's understanding of the theme and form the foundation upon which the advanced TFPs build.

They consist of beginning definitions or facts that can be observed or experienced directly. Because they involve deduction, principles are more abstract and are seldom identified at this level. Advanced TFPs consist of more elaborate vocabulary, more complicated facts, and introductory principles. Often, they represent information that youngsters learn about indirectly through simulated experiences. Because of the complexity of advanced TFPs, children generally need more opportunities and time to grasp them than they do in order to understand simple TFPs. In assigning information to these two levels, we have worked from the known to the unknown, from the tangible to the abstract, from exploration to skill acquisition.

The designations of *simple* and *advanced* enable teachers to identify which category of TFPs to emphasize when working with a particular group of children. Simple TFPs are designed for use with preschoolers and older children who have had little experience with the theme. Advanced TFPs are more suitable for preschool children who know the theme well or for children of elementary school age. Advanced TFPs are designated with an asterisk in the list at the front of each mini-theme. This stratification makes it possible for readers to choose the subset of TFPs that best corresponds to the needs of the children in their class. Depending on the topic, the subset may be composed of TFPs representing one or both levels of difficulty.

5. **Activity Ideas.** The thirty to forty activities identified for each mini-theme provide an applied means for integrating content and process learning in the classroom. Activities have been developed for all of the curricular domains described earlier: aesthetic, affective, cognitive, language, physical, social, construction play, and pretend play. The domains are presented in each unit and contain no fewer than two sample activities each. There are more activities listed per domain than teachers will use in their planning. The idea was to provide enough variety so teachers could select those experiences best suited to the children in their class. Some activities are described in a few sentences. Others, however, require more elaborate directions using the format depicted below.

Activity Name and Procedure: The title of the activity, followed by a step-by-step description of how the teacher is to carry it out. The procedure includes descriptions of needed materials as well as directions for what instructors are to do and sometimes suggestions for what they might say.

Hints for Success: When warranted, we've supplied suggestions for how adults should structure the activity to meet the needs of children of differing ages and abilities.

To Simplify: Ideas for making the activity more suitable for three- and four-year-olds and other inexperienced children.

To Extend: Suggestions for ways to increase the complexity of the activity, making it more appropriate for first or second graders.

The activity ideas for each mini-theme include lessons that can be carried out in large groups, small groups, or with children individually. Some activities rely on direct instruction while many others focus on self-discovery. Together, they represent a variety of instructional modes: firsthand experiences, simulations, demonstrations, group projects, and indirect teaching of the theme through theme-related props.

6. **Teacher Resources.** At the end of each unit readers will find a list of resource materials. These include suggested field trips, ideas for potential visitors, children's books related to the topic, and reference books readers might use to increase their knowledge of the concepts addressed. At the time this volume went to press, all of the books listed were still in print or were readily available at public libraries.

Procedures for Using This Book

1. Choose a unit. Consider the children's interests, the relevance of the concept to the children in your group, your own comfort level with the topic, and the availability of props. If theme teaching is new to you, begin with familiar concepts and ones for which props are readily accessible. Gradually branch out into areas less well known to you and for which you may have to search for support materials.

2. Review the mini-themes associated with the unit you selected. These are arranged in order from simple to complex, from concrete to more abstract. Readers looking for the most basic approach to the unit should concentrate on the first mini-theme. Those wishing a more substantive approach can add mini-themes two and/or three successively. Another alternative is to combine mini-themes from different units into a cohesive teaching plan that covers several weeks.

3. Choose the mini-theme with which you will begin.

4. Select a subgroup of TFPs for the mini-theme you have chosen; ten to fifteen are recommended. Use the others as background information or as a reference in responding to children's questions.

5. Go through the activity ideas, selecting those that seem to support your TFPs. Be sure to pick at least one activity from each domain. Do not attempt to implement all the theme-related activities provided. Be selective, choosing those activities most suited to what you are trying to teach. Feel free to change activities to make them more suitable for the children in your class.

6. Incorporate the activities into a weekly plan. Disperse the theme-related activities over the week. Decide how long and how many times each activity will be made available to the children. Plan additional non-theme-related activities to address other learning goals you may have for children in your group.

7. Consider classroom management issues such as availability of materials, number of adults in the classroom, and special events. Make adjustments in your plan if necessary.

8. Gather your materials. Create any props you will need. Make an effort to use some of the same props for more than one activity as a way to minimize preparation time.

9. Create a thematic atmosphere. Post theme-related pictures at children's eye level. Choose songs, books, poems, and audiovisual materials related to the topic.

10. Carry out your plan. Take advantage of spontaneous events that may further children's understanding of the concept they are exploring through the theme.

11. Assess children's understanding of the theme using some of the methods suggested earlier in this chapter.

12. Evaluate your implementation of the theme. Use the theme teaching checklist presented in Table 1 for this purpose. Also, write down the changes you made in your plan and what you might do differently if you were ever to repeat the theme. File these observations with other planning materials related to this topic.

13. Consider extending the theme if children's interest is high. As children demonstrate understanding and curiosity about the concept, introduce additional TFPs and their activities or initiate a related mini-theme for children to investigate.

Summary

Theme teaching is an exciting tool early childhood educators use to promote children's concept development. Easily adapted to a variety of instructional modes, themes provide a vehicle whereby children make links among diverse bits of information. In this way children derive greater meaning from what they are experiencing. The effective use of themes requires that teachers engage in developmentally appropriate practices. The themes they choose must also demonstrate relevance to children, balance within and across the curriculum, and accommodate the developmental differences represented within children in the class. All of the themes in this volume have been developed with these principles in mind. Using the structure and content presented here will enhance teaching and learning in early childhood classrooms ranging from preschool through the first or second grade.

Finally, readers are reminded that *Themes Teachers Use* can be used in conjunction with the author's other thematic book, *Teaching Young Children Using Themes*. When the units from the two books are combined, educators have an array of more than sixty-three themes from which to choose. That provides several years of early childhood activities. The combined content of the two books is presented in Appendix B.

Children's Books

Atwater, R., and F. Atwater. (1938). *Mr. Popper's Penguins*. New York: Little, Brown.

Hester, N. (1990). *The Living Tree*. New York: Watts.

Manson, C. (Adaptor). (1993). *The Tree in the Wood: An Old Nursery Song*. New York: North-South Books NYC.

Tresselt, A. (1992). *The Gift of the Tree*. New York: Lothrop, Lee & Shepard Books.

Adult References

Bredekamp, S. (1988). *Developmentally Appropriate Practice in Early Childhood Programs Serving Children Birth Through Age 8*. Washington , DC: National Association for the Education of Young Children.

Deardon, R. F. (1984). *Theory and Practice in Education*. London: Routledge and Kegan Paul.

Kostelnik, M. J., Soderman, A. K., and Whiren, A. P. (1993). *Developmentally Appropriate Programs in Early Childhood* Education. New York: Macmillan Publishing.

Kostelnik, M. J., Howe, D. R., and Spalding, G. M. (1993). "Teaching Young Children Using Themes." Paper presented at the national conference of the National Association for the Education of Young Children. Anaheim, CA.

Kostelnik, M. J. (Ed.). (1991). *Teaching Young Children Using Themes*. Glenview, IL: GoodYearBooks.

Perrone, V. (Ed.). (1991). *Expanding Student Assessment*. Alexandria, VA: Association for Supervision and Curriculum Development.

Art and Artists

Violet, indigo, blue and green,

Yellow and orange and red.

I can paint a rainbow, paint a rainbow,

Paint a rainbow too.

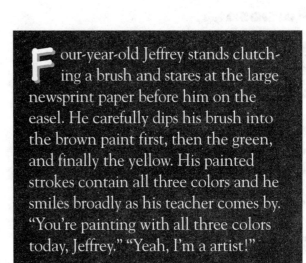

Four-year-old Jeffrey stands clutching a brush and stares at the large newsprint paper before him on the easel. He carefully dips his brush into the brown paint first, then the green, and finally the yellow. His painted strokes contain all three colors and he smiles broadly as his teacher comes by. "You're painting with all three colors today, Jeffrey." "Yeah, I'm a artist!"

Thanks to Lavelle Gipson, whose time and talent made this chapter possible.

Jeffrey is correct; he really is an artist as he explores what he can do with color, tries various ways to use a brush, and recognizes his own achievement. Young children who have experiences such as these each day grow in their abilities to control materials, express themselves creatively, and experience success in ways that might not otherwise be available to them: "Learning about the arts is learning about a rich world of personal expression . . . . Learning through the arts can enhance children's motivation to learn and to develop a more disciplined approach to learning." (National Arts Convention, 1988) Most successful teachers of young children agree it is important to offer a daily art activity in their classrooms. Since this is the case, some may wonder why we recommend focusing on art and artists as a theme.

Purpose

In general, the activities throughout this unit are intended to broaden the young child's view of art and what it is to be an artist. Taken separately, these activities may serve many purposes: 1) to provide exposure to interesting art forms that may be new to children, 2) to further stimulate creative expression in ways children may not have previously participated, 3) to expand children's aesthetic awareness and appreciation of the arts around them, 4) to demonstrate the value of diversity in our world as expressed through the arts, and 5) to provide opportunities for children to formulate judgments and preferences about the arts.

There are as many art forms as can be imagined. Creative expression can take the form of drawing, painting, sculpture, ceramics, printmaking, instrumental music, dramatics, film-making, creative movement, dance, singing, composing poetry, telling stories, humor, and so on. The list is extensive and within each art form there are many kinds and styles to explore. To make this theme manageable, it has been divided into three mini-themes that include many, but not all of the arts: visual arts, performing arts, and usable arts.

Each mini-theme has its own focus. In the "Visual Arts" section, we look at two-and three-dimensional art forms that are primarily decorative and appreciated by seeing. The "Performing Arts" section features art forms that are fleeting in nature, and often involve various recording methods to preserve them for future audiences. While children may be very familiar with some of the performing arts because they have been audience members (television or movies), there may be others that will be new to them or that they may never have participated in, such as creative dramatics, dance, or storytelling. Last, the "Usable Arts" mini-theme presents skills and crafts that produce objects that are both func-

tional and decorative. A broad unit on the arts can give children opportunities to experience many different art forms within a framework of exploration, experimentation, and acceptance.

Implementation

The "Art and Artists" theme may be carried out in a number of different ways depending on the needs of the group: a) teachers may choose to start with the foundational Terms, Facts, and Principles (see the General Information sections) and select one of the mini-themes as a single unit that could be presented by itself over one or two weeks, b) all three mini-themes could be presented in a three- or four-week art unit, or c) teachers may select activities from each of the clusters to enrich the daily classroom art experience.

This unit could lead to interest in many areas. It could be followed by a week devoted to a single artist that children are intrigued by, such as Shel Silverstein, Ezra Jack Keats, or Maurice Sendak. Their stories and paintings can encourage further exploration of visual images, as well as the performing arts of storytelling, creative dramatics, or poetry.

Some teachers may find that their classes want to explore variations in painting, to try splatter techniques like those of Jackson Pollock, Chinese brush techniques like Wang Yani's, or portraiture like that credited to Vincent Van Gogh. Still other teachers may want to follow up with a unit on paints, including different kinds of paints, uses for paint in our society, and a cooperative group project such as a mural.

Terms, Facts, and Principles (TFPs)

General Information

1. Art is a deliberate expression of feelings, mood, or a message created by a person for his or her own enjoyment and the enjoyment of others.
2. An artist is a person who creates art.
3. Anyone can be an artist; artists may be grown-ups or children, men or women, girls or boys.
4. Art is both the process (the way something is made) and the product (what is made).
*5. Art is created all over the world, in all cultures and in special ways that express ideas about that culture.
*6. Art is experienced by people in various ways; many forms of art can be seen, touched, heard, smelled, or even tasted.

Visual Arts

7. Art that people see and touch is often called visual art.

8. There are many kinds of visual art: drawings, paintings, designs, sculptures, collages, mosaics, mobiles, prints, portraits, and others.

*9. People can learn more about a visual art piece by studying its lines, colors, forms, textures, composition, balance, pattern, and contrasts.

*10. Each kind of visual art will vary with the artist's selection from a wide variety of materials, surfaces, and techniques. For example, a painting can be made using tempera, acrylic, watercolor, or oil paints on paper, plastic, wood, fabric, cork, canvas, leather, or foil. Paint can be applied in many ways including the use of brushes, fingers, feathers, rollers, cotton balls, or sponges.

11. Each artist chooses the media and techniques that he or she enjoys and that helps him or her create a unique work of art that is personally meaningful.

12. People learn about being visual artists by trying various media, watching others work, and studying examples of art made by other artists; some people go to school to study art.

13. Examples of the visual arts are found in many places: art galleries, books, people's homes, schools, train stations, churches, and so on.

*14. Some visual art pieces are very old; works of art have been found that were made many thousands of years ago (such as cave paintings).

*15. Some visual art pieces are new; many artists make art every day.

*16. Some visual art looks like things people know (realistic); some does not (abstract).

*17. People often have preferences for various visual arts; what's pleasing and interesting to one person is not always pleasing and interesting to others.

*18. Many works of visual art are given a name or title by the artist; titles often tell something about the work.

19. Most visual artists use special tools and materials when they work. For example, printmakers often use ink, brayers, paper, and scissors .

20. Many visual artists sell their art for money, some trade their art for other things, some give art away, and some keep their art for themselves.

21. Some artists keep their work in an art portfolio.

Activity Ideas

Aesthetic

1. Tour of Art

Take children on a tour through the building pointing out the variety of art on display. Look at the posters or pictures, statues, murals, or special decorations particular to your setting. Help children recognize that they have art right in their own school.

Hints for Success:

● Avoid criticizing or negatively evaluating children's art work on your tour.

● Discourage children from finding fault in other youngsters' work. Instead, keep comments positive or neutral, asking children questions that point out particular aspects of the aesthetic qualities of each art example (the colors, the kind of lines, design or layout of the subject), or ask children to tell what they like about a particular example.

2. Making Styrofoam Prints

Help children recognize their strengths as artists. Gather together flat pieces of Styrofoam (foam trays, such as those used for meat or vegetables at the store, work well—the larger the better), several ballpoint pens or pencils, two to three brayers (ink rollers), water soluble printer's ink or thick tempera paint, a movable flat hard surface such as a plastic tray, several pieces of absorbent paper (newsprint or manila), and old newspapers.

Remind children that artists can be adults or children. Invite children to be a special kind of artist called a print maker. Explain that a print is a kind of picture that can be made over and over and each picture will look exactly the same. Demonstrate the technique for children. Make and use a Styrofoam "printing block" following these steps:

a. Cut the curved edges off clean Styrofoam trays. Encourage children to draw any design or picture they want on their Styrofoam piece using a ball point pen or pencil. The lines should be fairly deep in order to print well.

b. Spread a smooth layer of paint or washable printers ink over the whole surface of the Styrofoam design using a brayer (roller) or wide brush.

c. Before it can dry, lay a clean piece of paper on top of the inked surface and help the child carefully

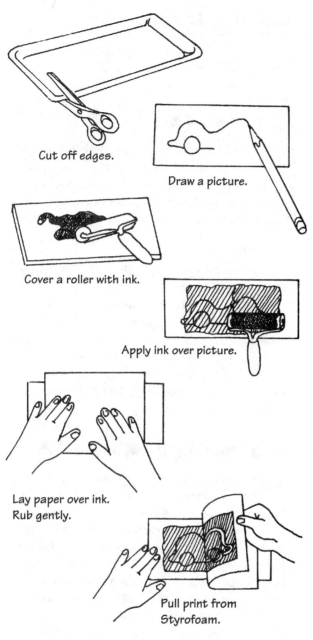

Cut off edges.

Draw a picture.

Cover a roller with ink.

Apply ink over picture.

Lay paper over ink. Rub gently.

Pull print from Styrofoam.

smooth it out with his or her fingers. Then help separate (pull) the print from the "printing block."

To Simplify:
● Instead of drawing on the Styrofoam, give children objects that they can press into the surface to make designs (such as paper clips, clothespins, cookie cutters, or potato mashers).

To Extend:
● Suggest the child re-ink his or her "printing block" with a different color of ink, or print on various colors of paper.

● Have the child think of a title for his or her print.

3. You Inspire Me

Invite a local painter to set up and work in the classroom for a day. Provide a place for interested children to watch the artist work. Introduce the artist to the children and have her or him explain the kind of work she or he does, the tools she or he uses, and something about techniques. Ask if some of the artist's work can be displayed for children to experience and enjoy.

4. Sing About Color

Learning the names for colors is an aspect of visual art that children often learn early. Teach children songs about color that they can enjoy together. The following song is about a naturally occurring color display—a rainbow. Note that the colors in this song have been arranged so they correspond to the actual sequence of the colors in a rainbow.

♫ The Rainbow Song

Violet, indigo, blue and green,
Yellow and orange and red.
I can sing a rainbow, sing a rainbow,
Sing a rainbow too.

Repeat the song, but change the ending to "I can paint a rainbow," or "we can be a rainbow." Add motions that relate to the various endings, such as gesturing the shape of a rainbow, gesturing painting, and holding hands with classmates indicating unity among children of all colors.

Another color song:

♫ Lavender Blue (Traditional English)

Lavender blue, dilly dilly
Lavender green.
When you are king, dilly dilly
I'll be your queen.

A color game:

♫ Making a Purple Stew
Tune: "I Went to the Animal Fair"

We're making a purple stew,
We're making a purple stew,
With purple potatoes and purple tomatoes,
And how about some of you?

Teach the song until children are familiar with the tune. Then have everyone sing as they stand in a circle holding hands. When singing the line, "And how about some of you?", everyone who is wearing that color steps into the middle and becomes part of the stew. Repeat, using other colors, until everyone is in the stew.

5. Paint with What?

Broaden thinking about painting and the kinds of tools artists sometimes use to apply paint by asking children to generate a list of things people paint with. Before you begin, make a collection of many things that could be used and put them in a paper bag. As children run out of ideas for their list, pull each one out of the bag and ask if someone could paint with it. The collection could include feathers, sponges, kitchen gadgets, straws, ice cubes in a sealed plastic bag, sticks, rollers, tiny brushes, squirt bottles, pencil erasers, and cotton swabs. Then challenge each child to try painting with three or four things he or she has never tried before.

Hint for Success:
● Color the ice cubes with various colors of food coloring before freezing. Keep them in the freezer until the last minute.

To Simplify:
● Provide one or two unusual things to paint with at a time.

To Extend:
● When the paintings are dry, display them along with the tools used to make each one.

6. Lines, Lines, Lines

Show children samples of real artwork that utilizes lines such as Vincent Van Gogh's *Starry Night* (1889) or Piet Mondrian's *Broadway Boogie Woogie* (1942–43). Point out various kinds of lines that each artist used in his work (straight, curved, zigzag, long, short, fat, thin, curly). Show how these lines are used to create certain feelings in designs and pictures. Ask children to make a line picture using different kinds of lines that they cut from construction paper and glue onto a dark background.

To Simplify:
● Precut a collection of lines from construction paper so children can concentrate on choosing kinds, colors, and arrangements rather than on the skill of cutting.

To Extend:
● Suggest that children think of other ways to make lines and add some of these to their design.

● Children could make another picture using a variety of methods and materials to make lines (painted, yarn, markers, string, glue with glitter, torn lines, chalk, stamp lines, and so on).

7. A Style of Painting

Point out an artist who has a particular style of painting that is obvious. A good example of this would be Jackson Pollock, whose drip method of design is unmistakable. Show children one or more reproductions of this painter's work such as *One* (Number 31, 1950) or *Echo* (Number 25, 1951). Suggest they make a painting in the same style that Mr. Pollock did. Cover a table with newspaper and offer children an opportunity to make a painting of their own. Give children bowls of thin paint in various brilliant colors with spoons for dipping and dripping. Lay their paintings to dry flat.

Hint for Success:
● Another particular style of painting can be found in the work of Chinese artist Wang Yani. See this child's technique and style explored in the book *A Young Painter: The Life and Paintings of Wang Yani, China's Extraordinary Young Artist* (1991). Suggest children paint with large brushes on wet and dry paper.

Affective

1. That's Cool

Select two or more examples of the same kind of visual art (reproductions of paintings, photographs, sculptures, and so on) to show children. Ask them to explore the examples carefully and tell which one they prefer. Ask them to tell about the reasons for their selections. Make a chart showing the choices and who liked which one best. Display the chart, pointing out that not everyone has the same opinions about art.

2. It's Done Now

Challenge interested children to begin, work on, and finish an art project that takes more than one day to complete. Examples of long-term projects are papiermâché, mosaics, or cardboard prints. Praise children for completing the task.

Cardboard Prints: Explain that artists sometimes need or want to print the same picture over and over. Using soft flexible cardboard (such as cut-up cereal boxes), cut some shapes and arrange them on another piece of cardboard to make a design. Glue the pieces down using white liquid glue. Allow the design to dry overnight. The next day, roll a thin layer of water-soluble printer's ink (or poster paint thickened with liquid soap) over the cardboard surfaces. Then, lay a clean piece of paper over the inked design and press with your fingertips. Lift the paper and see the print.

Hints for Success:

● Avoid using letters or numbers because everything prints backwards. Use a roller or brayer (roller with a handle) to apply the color.

● Work quickly so the ink doesn't dry.

To Simplify:

● Precut various shapes from cardboard and have children arrange and glue them as they wish.

To Extend:

● Encourage children to print the same design many times on the same paper, or on different papers of various colors, or print on burlap or other cloth.

● Another time, use corrugated cardboard to make the design for a more textured print.

3. I'm an Artist

As children have experiences making art in a variety of ways, offer them materials to make badges to wear that label themselves as a kind of visual artist (painter, drawing artist, sculptor, print maker, collage artist, finger painter, cartoonist, etc.). Help them select which words best describe the art they do. Encourage them to wear their badges—even more than one at a time.

4. I Can Decide

Collect each child's artwork into a simple portfolio made from cardboard with his or her name on it. Before changing the classroom art display, suggest that children look through their portfolios and choose one or two pieces to have included. Help them decide what color to mount their work on, and what to call each piece. Attach a name plate giving information about the artist.

5. Computer Drawing

Introduce children to a graphics program on a computer you have in the classroom. Encourage them to experiment with the various colors, textures, and line possibilities available. Save their pictures by printing if possible.

Some programs for young children that have drawing applications are: *Kindercomp* by Queue, Inc.,

KidPix by Broderbund Software Co., *Color Me* by Mindscape, *Delta Drawing* by Power Industries, and *Magic Crayon* by C&C Software. Encourage children to work alone or together in pairs. They could make individual pictures or designs or, if willing, could work together on one picture, with both children adding parts.

Hints for Success:

● Since a computer in the classroom can be fascinating for young children who are just getting to know what this technology is about, it may be especially difficult to manage turn-taking. Help children take turns being "users" at the computer. Make turn-taking as child-monitored and independent as possible, while allowing each person or pair to have a turn that is reasonable in length.

● Teach children how to use a sand timer or cooking timer, which is kept at the computer, so they can time each turn in case several people want to use the computer at the same time.

● Provide a "Waiting List," a sheet of paper and a pencil nearby where children can sign up for a turn; they can sign up to use the computer individually or in pairs. Either way, all turn lengths should be the same.

● When the current user finishes, he or she should cross off his or her name from the waiting list, and take responsibility to remind the next person on the list to take a turn.

● Allow children to wait nearby and watch. Many of the positive social aspects of using computers in the classroom happen as a result of the interactions of users as they watch and wait for their turn.

● If necessary, establish a "waiting chair" for the next-in-line person. This strategy physically helps youngsters remember the waiting order and shows them how close they are to getting a turn.

Cognitive

1. Seriating Brushes

Provide children with a collection of various kinds of brushes artists use (different lengths, widths, colors, shapes, and so on). Help children discover how to put the brushes in a row from longest to shortest.

To Simplify:

● Use only a few brushes with obvious differences.

To Extend:

● Challenge the child to think of other ways the brushes are different and to seriate by those characteristics. Examples may be widest to narrowest, most bristles to least bristles, oldest to newest, and so on.

2. Find Details in Art

Obtain a large reproduction of a painting, sculpture or other art. An example of a good reproduction to use for this purpose is Joan Miro's *The Tilled Field* (1923) or any painting containing many objects. Prepare a set of cards, with each card describing or showing a detail in the larger picture (for example, a small blue flower in a bouquet, or red stripes on a man's shirt). Mix up the cards and play a game in which children choose a card and find the detail it shows on the larger picture. Explore the large reproduction together first, asking children to look carefully and notice things about what they see (colors, lines, textures, objects). Have them take turns trying to find small details.

To Simplify:
● Choose obvious details. Praise children for trying, even if they are not successful.

To Extend:
● Divide the class into small groups, giving each group a different art reproduction. Have each group work together preparing a set of detail cards for that work of art. Then suggest they trade with another group, playing the game using the new materials.

3. What's Similar?

Make a collection of postcards of famous art. (Postcards are available commercially and often can be purchased in art gallery gift shops.) Spread them out on a table and ask children to find things that are similar about some of the pictures. Suggest that they make groups of pictures according to the similarities they find. Then ask them to explain the reasons for their groupings.

To Simplify:
● Begin by giving the least experienced children sets of cards that contain duplicates, asking them to match the same pictures. After this becomes easy, eliminate one of each pair, asking children to find two that are similar (or have something the same in some way).

● Use a limited number of pictures, selecting ones that have obvious features in common.

To Extend:
● Add more cards.

● Ask children to make new piles, finding different ways they are similar for each pile.

4. Buying/Selling Art

To practice establishing a sense of number, put pretend price tags on a collection of art that is displayed where children can see it. Give children play money coins (or make some out of paper) to purchase the art. Have one child assume the role of artist who is selling; others may be buyers. Encourage the children to count out the correct number of coins needed for the piece they select.

To Simplify:
● Use single-digit numbers for the prices and indicate how many you mean by placing that number of dots on the price tag.

● Ignore the value on the coins and make them each count as one.

To Extend:
● Use larger numbers and include the numerals on each price tag.

Construction

1. My Own Mobile

To help children realize the many different ways to approach a construction task, introduce them to the idea of art that moves—mobiles. Begin by showing children one or more examples of mobiles, commercial or handmade, or a photograph of a famous mobile such as Alexander Calder's *Red Lily Pads* (1956). Encourage children to make the mobile move and notice how the design changes as the pieces turn. Show children the parts of all mobiles (supports, suspended objects and connectors). Then introduce the following materials you have gathered for them to use in constructing their own mobiles:

Supports: Two or more thin dowels, two or more wire coat hangers, two to three heavy straws, or two or more sticks for each mobile.

Suspended Objects: Have children select from a variety such as cut or torn paper shapes, various natural objects (seashells, driftwood, feathers, pinecones, leaves, acorns, etc.), pipe cleaner shapes, small decorated boxes, small drawings, "yarn bubbles," corks, decorated paper cups, and so on.

Connectors: yarn, string, fish line, wire, cord.

Several tools should also be available to children: scissors, markers, glue, tape.

Tell children they can make their own kind of mobile using any of the materials. Point out the variety of choices they have within each category. Suggest they plan their mobiles and begin work. If necessary, assist children with tying strings or make suggestions on ways objects can be attached. Help them balance their mobile by adding or moving suspended objects.

Hint for Success:

● Avoid making a sample mobile using the same materials you give to the children. Once they see yours, they will find it difficult to think creatively, and most children will try to make one just like yours. Instead, offer a variety of materials, demonstrate techniques that may be challenging, and praise children's individual ideas.

To Simplify:

● Choose one method of supports and give several choices of suspended objects.

● Avoid tying by suggesting children use tape to attach string or yarn to objects.

To Extend:

● Take children on a collecting hike or suggest they gather found objects from home for their mobiles. Things to look for at home may be buttons, screws, metal pieces, keys, film containers, small boxes, wire screening, bottle caps, small Christmas tree balls, tiny plastic toys, and other lightweight and safe objects. Things found in nature could be pine cones, small sticks, leaves, acorns, pieces of tree bark, pine needles, small stones, and so on.

2. Yarn Bubbles

To make these three-dimensional yarn sculptures, blow up tiny balloons. Soak pieces of yarn or string, cut in two-foot lengths, in liquid starch for a few minutes. Demonstrate how artists wrap the yarn or colored string around the balloon, overlapping in many directions, and leaving some spaces empty. Set the balloon in a paper cup to dry. When completely dry, prick the balloon with a pin and remove it. The yarn will stay in the shape of the balloon.

3. Wood Construction

After introducing children to three-dimensional sculpture, give them an opportunity to make one using wood. Purchase or collect small wood scraps of various shapes and sizes. Give children wood glue and larger pieces for a base.

To Simplify:

● Demonstrate how to balance pieces and use the glue.

To Extend:

● When the glue is dry, suggest that children paint their sculptures and title them.

4. My Art Portfolio

Show children a real art portfolio or pouch used for storing and carrying artwork (available in art supply stores) or ask an artist friend to bring one in to show the class. Help children make and decorate portfolios of their own in which to keep selected samples of their artwork. A portfolio can be made using two large pieces of tagboard, posterboard, or cardboard fastened together on two sides with tape, yarn, or staples. Offer children decorating materials such as crayons, rubber stamps, markers, or colored pencils. Place the portfolios in an accessible storage area so children can keep their completed two-dimensional art pieces in a dust-free location.

To Simplify:

● Fasten the portfolios for the children; they can then decorate their own any way they want.

To Extend:

● Encourage children to fasten their own portfolios. Punch holes along two sides and offer children yarn to hold it together.

Language

1. Little Blue, Little Yellow

Prepare children for the story of *Little Blue and Little Yellow*, written by Leo Lionni (1959), by telling them this is a story about colors and paint. Ask them to notice what colors are in the story and what happens to them. Read the story with expression. Then, ask them to name all the colors they remember from the story. Are there more than the title suggests? (In the story, green is made when yellow and blue are mixed together.) Follow your discussion by giving children similar paints at the art table and suggesting they try mixing for themselves. Another children's book that presents similar concepts is *Mouse Paint* by Ellen Walsh (1989).

2. Talking with Artists

Introduce children to a particular living artist by looking at several examples of his or her work. Children's picture books offer easy-to-find examples. For example, show the children Steven Kellogg's illustrations in books such as *Best Friends*, also written by Steven Kellogg (1986); *Engelbert the Elephant* by Tom Paxton (1990); and *Jack and the Beanstalk,* retold by Steven Kellogg (1991). Follow this by reading the interview with Steven Kellogg in *Talking with Artists* by Pat Cummings (1992). Finally, discuss the children's own interests in art.

To Simplify:
● Paraphrase parts of the interview or just read the section devoted to telling about Kellogg's life when he was growing up.

To Extend:
● Suggest that children think of other questions they would like to ask the artist about his or her work or life. Have children write or dictate letters to an artist they admire. Addresses are usually available by writing the publisher.

● Another way to extend this activity is to suggest children write or dictate their own autobiographies as artists. Use the format on page 24.

3. You Are Invited!

Plan a special art exhibit that includes children's work, samples of art from around the world, or a combination of many kinds of art. Have children write invitations telling about the exhibit, when and where to come. Provide materials for them to decorate their invitations and envelopes for mailing. Suggest that they mail the invitations to family members or special friends.

To Simplify:
● Print an invitation with blanks that children fill in to provide the information. See above.

To Extend:
● Have children make title signs for their artwork indicating their names, the titles they have chosen, and the media they have used.

Dear _____

We are having a wonderful exhibit of artwork made

by _____

on _____ from _____ to _____.

I especially want you to see _____.

Please come.

_____

4. Art Messages

Hang several prints of famous art around the room at children's eye level. Near each one, post an open-ended question about the picture and provide a place for children to respond to the question. Ask adult helpers to read the questions to interested children and write their responses, or encourage them write their responses. After several days, read the response charts to the whole group. Possible questions include:

- How does this picture make you feel? Why?
- Why do you think the girl is sitting on the chair?
- Do you think this picture shows daytime or nighttime? Why?
- What do you think these people are doing?
- What's your favorite part of this picture?

Physical

1. Mystery Wax Resist

Encourage children to press hard with a light-colored wax crayon, making any kind of picture or design on heavy white paper. Tell children the harder they press, the better their final picture will look. Suggest they paint over their picture with very thin, dark, water-based paint using a wide brush. Wherever the wax has been applied, it will resist the watery paint and show through.

Hint for Success:
● Be sure the paint is mixed with plenty of water, and no soap has been added, as this will cause the paint to adhere to the wax.

My Artist Autobiography

My name is _____.

I am an artist because I _____

_____.

I get my ideas from _____

_____.

I use _____

to make my _____.

This is me . . .

I am a _____ artist.

To Simplify:

● Offer only white or yellow crayons, or have children draw with wax candles instead of crayons.

To Extend:

● Encourage children to try the technique using a variety of crayon colors or various colors of paint.

2. As Still as a Statue

Show children a statue of a person or animal. Let them explore it, tell them what it's made of and the name of the artist. Have them try to put their bodies in the same position as the statue. Then introduce a game in which you play music as everyone moves freely; but when the music stops, everyone stops, as still as a statue. Challenge children to be funny statues, happy statues, sad statues, and so on.

3. Rubber Band Designs

Give children geoboards (squares of wood with nails hammered in regular rows), and a collection of colorful rubber bands. Suggest they attach the rubber bands to make designs, experimenting with various combinations.

To Simplify:

● Use long flexible rubber bands and geoboards with nails wide apart.

To Extend:

● Have children try to draw the design they have created, or draw it first and then make it.

4. Slab Patterns

Show children how to create designs by pressing objects that leave interesting imprints into flattened clay slabs and allowing them to dry. Start with a ball of well-kneaded gray or red potter's clay (clay should be moist and easy to manipulate, but not sticky). If it's too dry, sprinkle water on the surface and knead; if it's too sticky, allow it to air-dry awhile. Flatten the clay ball onto a surface of wax paper or onto an individual piece of cloth (to make it easier to lift). Roll the clay out with a rolling pin or wooden dowel to create a flat smooth slab, about a half-inch thick. A variety of patterns can be created by pressing objects into the slab, leaving lines and textures in the clay. Objects that leave interesting marks include a screw, paper clip, toothpick, fork, tongue depressor, pencil, spool, twine, button, or a stone. Poke two holes near the top of the slab, trim the edges, and allow the clay to dry several days in a flat position. When the clay slab is completely dry, run a strong twine or shoelace through the holes and tie securely. The new artwork can now be displayed.

To Simplify:

● Roll the clay out for the children.

To Extend:

● If a kiln is available, fire the dry clay according to directions on the package.

● If clay will not be fired, small lightweight objects may be pressed and left in the clay to dry.

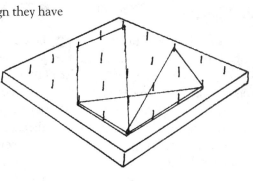

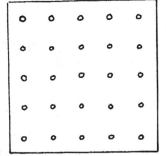

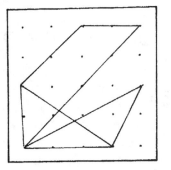

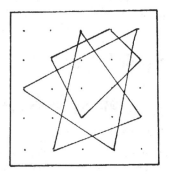

Pretend Play

1. Our Art Gallery/Museum

Help children prepare an area of the room to be a pretend art gallery. Arrange shelves, floor areas, tables, and wall areas where artwork can be displayed. Spread cloth or construction paper under and behind sculpture pieces to make the area look like a real museum. Gather examples of art from many sources (parents, friends, the children's work, and so on). Other props for a museum that children could make are tickets, guide hats, signs that say "touch" and "don't touch," and title signs for the art. Encourage children to take on roles of museum director, guide, ticket seller, visitor, or worker. Ask children to suggest a role for newcomers who want to play. Praise children for using their imaginations.

2. An Artist's Studio

Gather props suggesting an artist's studio (suggestions include an easel, brushes, pretend paints, containers, still-life arrangements, flowers, sketch pads, pretend carving materials, cardboard frames, etc.). Invite children to be part of the pretend play in this artist's studio. Explain that a studio is where some artists make and sell their art. Suggest that one child could be a pretend model for the artists to pretend sketch or paint. Encourage children to take the roles of artists, models, art buyers, visitors, and any others that they can think of.

3. Outdoor Art Picnic

After taking children outdoors to draw or paint; encourage them to pretend about that experience in the classroom. Gather props for a pretend outdoor sketching and painting excursion (such as a picnic basket, pretend food, blanket, scenery to paint, flowers to pick and/or paint, dress-ups, sketch pads, pencils, cameras, and so on). Invite children to pretend about creating art in the outdoors. Encourage children to explore the props, and take on roles as artists and friends on a picnic.

Social

1. Sticky Group Collage

Invite children to work together to make a large picture called a collage. Explain that a collage is a picture with different materials glued on to make it look interesting. Gather the following materials: a large piece of clear adhesive paper, a colorful variety of lightweight materials to attach (scraps of construction paper, tissue paper, fabric scraps, yarn, string, glitter, cotton balls, feathers).

Peel the paper backing off the clear adhesive paper and lay it, sticky side up, on a large flat surface. Show children that the paper is sticky so no glue is needed. Point out all the different things to attach. Encourage children to choose some pieces and press them onto the collage. Praise them for arranging the pieces carefully. Reinforce children for working together—by filling up the collage, and by helping each other, by making suggestions, and by listening to each other.

Hint for Success:
● Cut half-inch-wide construction-paper strips. Before starting on the collage, lay the paper strips on all four edges to form a frame around the sticky surface. The frame strengthens the edges and makes it easier to move.

To Simplify:
● Make smaller collages with smaller pieces of clear adhesive paper.

● Suggest that only two children work on each collage.

To Extend:
● When children are finished, hang their collages on the window so the light shines through.

● Have each group think of a title for its work of art. Write the title on the paper frame.

2. Friendly Portraits

Show children several portraits done by famous artists such as Pablo Picasso's *Woman with Yellow Hair* (1931). Engage them in a discussion about what they see, what the artist showed about the person, and other aspects that interest them. You may also want to show them *People* by Philip Yenawine (1993), an excellent book about portraits. Then have children choose a partner and provide them with materials to do portraits of each other. They could take turns being the model or do the portraits simultaneously.

Hints for Success:
● Young children can be very frustrated by and should not be expected to achieve an adult standard in their drawings. Therefore, teachers should remove the sample portraits from view while they draw, and allow children to approach the exercise at their present level of drawing, with complete support and encouragement.

● In addition, to make it easier to focus on the portrait rather than controlling the materials, choose a very simple medium for this task. Crayons, markers, or colored pencils work the best. Newer crayon collections are available that provide a broad array of skin and hair tone colors for those children who find this level of realism desirable.

To Simplify:

● Provide cut pieces of paper in various colors and shapes (different noses, eyes, mouths, etc.) for children to glue together for their portrait.

To Extend:

● Have the models describe themselves first; then suggest the artists use both visual and verbal cues to make a portrait of their friend.

3. This One's for You

Talk together about friendly behaviors—how to let people know we like them. Ask children to list some ways friends show they like each other, such as smiling, waiting for that person, playing together, and giving special presents. Help them think of a person they like and suggest they make a work of art for that friend. Allow children to individually plan what materials they will use and provide time and encouragement for their projects. For children who have difficulty organizing a plan, suggest several choices such as making a painting, building a sculpture, or making a puppet for their special friend.

4. Let's Name It

In a large or small group setting, display a work of art (but do not tell what its title is) and ask the children to notice things about it. Then tell them that artists often choose names for their art that tell something about it. (Demonstrate by showing them an interesting picture and tell them the title. Good examples would be *Twittering Machine* by Paul Klee (1922) or *Three Musicians* by Pablo Picasso (1921). Encourage children to generate a list of possible titles for the unnamed picture or sculpture. Record their suggestions; then ask them to think of a way they could all decide what the title will be. Children may suggest that they vote, draw a title out of a hat, or that a specific person should decide for the group. Whatever way they choose, help them carry it out and write their title on a special card that you display near the picture. Praise them for working together to decide. After they have chosen a title for the selected artwork, reveal the real title that was given by the artist.

Teacher Resources

Field Trip Ideas

1. Visit an art museum or gallery.
2. Visit an artist's studio.
3. Visit a store that sells artists' materials.
4. Visit and interview a collector of art.

Classroom Visitors

1. Invite an artist to bring some of his/her work to show the children.
2. Invite parents to demonstrate an artistic talent for the children.
3. Invite parents to bring an example of art from their culture to the classroom and tell about it.

Children's Books

Blizzard, G. S. (1993). *Come Look with Me: World of Play*. Charlottesville, VA: Thomasson-Grant.

Cummings, P. (1992).*Talking with Artists*. New York: Bradbury Press.

DePaola, T. (1989).*The Art Lesson*. New York: Putnam.

Henderson, K. (1992). *In the Middle of the Night*. London: Walker Books.

Johnson, C. (1955). *Harold and the Purple Crayon*. New York: HarperCollins.

Jonas, A. (1989). *Color Dance*. New York: Greenwillow.

Kellogg, S. (1986). *Best Friends*. New York: Dial Books for Young Readers.

Kellogg, S. (1991). *Jack and the Beanstalk*. New York: Morrow Junior Books.

Lionni, L. (1959). *Little Blue and Little Yellow*. New York: Astor-Honor.

Mayers, F. (1986). *The Museum of Modern Art*. New York. New York: Harry N. Abrams.

Mayhew, J. (1989). *Katie's Picture Show*. New York: Bantam Doubleday Dell.

Micklethwait, L. (1993). *A Child's Book of Art*. New York: Dorling Kindersley.

Micklethwait, L. (1992). *I Spy: An Alphabet in Art*. New York: Greenwillow.

Paxton, T. (1990). *Engelbert the Elephant*. New York: Morrow Junior Books.

Schick, E. (1987). *Art Lessons*. New York: Greenwillow.

Winter, J., and Winter, J. (1991). *Diego*. New York: Alfred A. Knopf.

Yenawine, P. (1991). *Shapes*. New York: Delacorte.

Yenawine, P. (1991). *Lines*. New York: Delacorte.

Yenawine, P. (1991). *Colors*. New York: Delacorte.

Yenawine, P. (1993). *People.* New York: Museum of Modern Art.

Walsh, E. S. (1989). *Mouse Paint.* New York: Harcourt Brace Jovanovich.

Zhensun, Z. and Low, A. (1991). *A Young Painter: The Life and Paintings of Wang Yani, China's Extraordinary Young Artist.* New York: Scholastic.

Adult References

Art Image Publications, Champlain, NY 12919, a source for reproductions of famous art.

Cherry, C. (1990). *Creative Art for the Developing Child.* Carthage, IL: Fearon Teacher Aids.

Jenkins, P. D. (1986). *Art for the Fun of It: A Guide for Teaching Young Children.* New York: Prentice Hall.

Lasky, L. & Mukerji, R. (1980). *Art Basics for Young Children.* Washington, DC: National Association for the Education of Young Children.

Meilach, D. Z. (1968). *Creating Art from Anything: Ideas, Materials, Techniques.* Chicago: Reilly and Lee.

National Arts Convention. (1989). *Why We Need Arts: 8 Quotable Speeches.* New York, New York: American Council for the Arts in Education Books.

School Arts Magazine. Worcester, MA: Davis Publications.

Wolf, A. D. (1984). *Mommy, It's a Renoir!* Altoona, PA: Parent Press.

Graphic Computer Programs

Color Me. (1985) Mindscape Educational Software: 1345 Diversey Parkway, Chicago, IL 60614.

Delta Drawing Today, (1990) Power Industries: 37 Walnut St., Wellesley Hills, MA 02181.

KidPix. (1991). Broderbund Software: 17 Paul Dr., San Rafael, CA 94903.

Kindercomp. (1986). Cambridge, MA: Queue, Inc.: 201 Broadway, Cambridge, MA 02139.

Magic Crayon. (1983) Wichita, KS: C & C Software: 5713 Kentford Circle, Wichita, KS 67220.

Mosaic Magic. (1989). KinderMagic Software: 1680 Medowglen Lane, Encinitas, CA 92024.

Picture Perfect. (1984). Mindplay: 3130 N. Dodge Blvd., Tucson, AZ 85716.

Easy Color Paint 2.0. (1991). MECC: 6160 Summit Dr. N., Minneapolis, MN 55430.

Performing Arts

Terms, Facts, and Principles (TFPs)

General Information

1. Momentary art presented to an audience is called performing arts.

2. There are many different kinds of performing arts such as singing, instrumental music, dance, drama, magic, and storytelling.

3. A performing artist is a person who makes art happen in a presentation.

4. The audience is made up of people who watch, listen to, and respond to the performance.

*5. Depending on the kind of art, performances may be called shows, plays, readings, concerts, recitals, ballets, operas, or musicals.

6. Sometimes a performance is done once and only once; sometimes it is repeated many times.

7. Sometimes performances are recorded so they can be viewed by audiences after the performance; recordings may be in the form of audio tapes, videotapes, compact disks, television shows, or movies.

*8. Some artists perform alone; some performances are presented by many people working together.

*9. Performances are presented all over the world, in all cultures, and in special ways that express ideas about that culture (such as Native American dances, puppet shows in China, folk music in Ireland, and so on).

10. Dancing is a performing art that is a part of many cultures around the world.

*11. Dancing is a series of steps and/or body movements, done to a beat, rhythm, or melody, that can be performed alone, with a partner, or with a group.

12. Dancers can be men or women, boys or girls.

13. Sometimes groups of people dance without an audience to express joy, have fun together, or celebrate a special event.

14. Some dances are spontaneous creations of the performer; others are designed (choreographed) by a person and learned by the dancer.

15. There are many different forms of dance (such as ballet, folk, modern, square dance, ballroom, tap, and jazz).

16. Some traditional dances in various cultures are performed to tell a story (for example, about a good hunt or a happy marriage) or to communicate special cultural values.

17. Dramatizing stories is a performing art that is part of cultural traditions found throughout the world.

18. The performers in a dramatic presentation are actors; they may be men, women, boys, or girls.

19. An actor pretends to be a person or animal in the story, using props, mannerisms, gestures, movements, and words typical of that role.

20. In order to be successful, actors practice so they can remember what to do and say before their performances.

21. Performances often lead audiences to imagine, make-believe, or think about ideas in new ways.

22. As a result of performances, people in the audience often feel and express strong emotions such as joy, fear, sadness, happiness, or pride.

*23. Performing artists frequently wear special clothing (costumes), for their performances; some wear things on their faces and heads to create an illusion such as makeup, wigs, masks, or pretend beards.

24. When a performance is over, the audience usually responds in some way to show approval by clapping, standing up, bowing, or smiling.

Activity Ideas

Aesthetic

1. This Is a Performance

Introduce children to various kinds of performing arts by showing them examples of dance, drama, and other kinds. Use pictures, parts of videos, or segments of taped television performances by real people. Prepare children for what they will see, asking them to look for particular things such as costumes, makeup, music or other characteristics. After seeing portions of various kinds of performances, ask children what they saw and then what they liked about each one. Teach them how to respond as an appreciative audience.

2. Creative Dancing

Explain that dancing is a performing art. Select several kinds of music (such as jazz, classical, and rock). Invite children to listen and respond to the music by dancing in their own ways. Dance with them, but

avoid telling children to follow what you do. Encourage them to use their own ideas.

3. Paint with Feet

Introduce this activity by reading the book *Mouse Paint* by Ellen Walsh (1989). Invite a few children at a time to take off their shoes and socks and paint with their feet on a large paper. Structure the activity with waiting chairs, a paint selection area with one or more paint cans and wide brushes to paint the bottoms of their feet, and a foot-washing area with chairs, tubs of soapy water, and towels. Assist children by holding a hand while they move, to prevent slipping. Demonstrate how their steps can be made in a variety of ways (such as on tiptoes, full foot, feet close together and far apart, in straight lines or curvy lines, etc.). Emphasize how their footsteps with paint leave prints showing how they moved across the paper. Label one or more of their footsteps so they can recall their own steps.

4. Artist Performers on the Wall

Help children experience different kinds of dancing and performing arts portrayed in the visual arts. Show them photographs or prints of paintings that depict costumed dancers, moving or resting, singers, jugglers, and so on. Some paintings to look for are:

Two Dancers, Edgar Degas, 1905

Dancer at the Café, Jean Metzinger, 1912

The Singer, Rufino Tamayo, 1950

Three Musicians, Pablo Picasso, 1921

The Dance of Life, Edvard Munch, 1899

Rehearsal on the Stage, Edgar Degas, 1879

Mezzetin, Jean Antoine Watteau, 1704

Ask children to talk about what they see and what the people are doing. Ask them to tell what they like about one of the pictures and why.

Affective

1. I Can Be a Creative Performer

Prepare a simple performance, for or without an audience. Let every child select a part in a familiar story such as "Goldilocks and the Three Bears," "The Billy Goats Gruff," or a favorite nursery rhyme such as "Humpty Dumpty." Read or tell the story first, discussing who the characters are in the story. To avoid casting problems and competition, allow each child to choose who she or he will be in the performance, even if this results in many children being a single character (many father bears, many Goldilockses, or many Humpty Dumpties). Act as the narrator, direct the action, and tell the story simply a second time, encouraging all children to behave as they think they should when you cue them. Use simple props or imaginary props (such as pretend bowls of porridge and pretend spoons). Encourage children to exaggerate their use of voice, body movements, and gestures. Involve less outgoing children by having them take the parts of inactive (but important) things such as trees in the forest or the door to the cottage. Praise all children for their performances.

To Simplify:
● Tell the story and suggest that everyone take on all the character roles at the same time. For example, in the story of "Goldilocks and the Three Bears," everyone can pretend to be Goldilocks knocking at the door; everyone can play the part of Papa Bear growling, "Somebody's been sitting in my chair!"; and every child can be the Baby Bear noticing Goldilocks still asleep in the wee little bed.

To Extend:
● Read a story children are less familiar with, such as *Caps for Sale* by Esphyr Slobodkina (1947). Help them figure out what characters are needed for the story and act out the events in sequence, using simple props and a narrator.

2. Music of My Family

Invite children to share an example of a musical performance from his or her family heritage in the form of records or tapes. Encourage families to share samples of traditional music that they or their parents and grandparents enjoy. Provide time for children to tell something about the music they bring in, and play it for the class. If possible, make a recording of a sample of the various kinds of music and make this available for children to listen to in a Listening Center area of the room.

3. The Way I Like to Move

Play various kinds of music (bouncy, smooth, sad, fast, exciting, and so on) and invite one child at a time to make up a short dance that shows how each one makes him or her feel.

Cognitive

1. Useful Props

Collect a large variety of objects that could be used in the performances of stories. Lay the objects out on the floor or on a large table and explain that these are "props" that could be used in acting out stories. Hold up one at a time and ask, "What could an actor use this for in a story?" Encourage creative ideas by assuring children that there can be many answers and by praising their inventiveness.

To Simplify:
● Use obvious common objects such as a badge, a hat, a scarf, a pair of shoes, a wig, a brush, a bowl, etc.

To Extend:
● Ask children to think of an example of a story for which each prop would be appropriate and to show how it could be used.

2. Something in Common

Collect various things that could be used as story props, such as a cup, a mug, a hat, a scarf, a boot, a wig, a brush, a bowl, or a pretend apple. Ask children to examine the objects and put them into groups according to something they have in common. Say, "Look at this _____ . Find another object that has something that's the same about it or goes with it in some way. Tell me why you put those two things together. What do you think they have in common?" Accept any answers.

To Simplify:
● Select objects that have obvious similarities (such as a cup and saucer or a spoon and fork).

To Extend:
● Add more objects to the collection.
● Have children work in pairs, with one child making groups and another child try to guess what the objects have in common.

Construction

1. Creating a Mask

In some African ceremonies, children wear masks as they celebrate their becoming adults. Masks are usually made to look like a certain animal, fish, or bird. Masks were worn by Native Americans for storytelling and as a part of dancing costumes. Provide an experience with masks showing real ones or pictures of masks that are used in special performances. Try to include some masks that are funny, some that look realistic, and others that may be exaggerations of certain features. Discuss any emotions children may feel when seeing the masks. Point out the ways masks change the look of a performer and how they were made. Ask children if they can guess what a person might pretend to be with each mask. Then suggest children use a variety of materials to create their own kind of mask. Creative masks can be made in any number of ways. Some simple masks are made from 1) a paper plate that is decorated and with eyeholes cut out; 2) a decorated paper grocery bag worn over the head with eyeholes cut out; or 3) a simple paper shape cut from heavy construction paper that is then decorated, with eyeholes cut. Select one method or demonstrate techniques of making all three and allow each child to choose the one he or she likes best. Provide paints, crayons, markers, construction paper and paste, yarn, feathers, and other interesting materials to complete the mask.

Hint for Success:
● Avoid making a mask of your own, as this can inhibit children's creativity and self-confidence.

2. Scenery for a Performance

Visit a real stage or show children pictures of a stage with scenery backdrops. Provide a simple cardboard stage for a puppet show and suggest they each make a painting for the stage scenery. Provide paints or markers and large paper that fits the stage. Avoid making an example for them to follow, since this can negatively influence their creativity.

3. My Puppet Character

After children have had experience playing with many different kinds of puppets, suggest that they make their own puppets. Finger puppets are fun and simple to make using clean old gloves or inexpensive gardening gloves. Cut the glove fingers off at the base and offer one finger to each child. Provide construction paper, glue, yarn, scissors, markers, and bits of cloth for children to use in creating their own characters. Avoid making a puppet of your own, since this can establish an adult standard that may discourage children from trying their own ideas or feeling good about their own work. When the glue dries, tell children to slip their puppets on and use them to make a show with other puppets.

Language

1. Bump-a-Deedle

To have fun with language and inspire children to move in dancelike motions teach them the song "Everybody Says" by Malvina Reynolds. This song can be found in *There's Music in the Air* by Malvina Reynolds (1976). Play or sing the song for the children first, then encourage them to get up and dance creatively as you repeat the song. Suggest they make up a substitute word for "Bump-A-Deedle" (such as "Bump-A-Noodle" or "Lump-A-Doodle").

2. My Dance Has Meaning

Gather children into a space large enough so that they can freely move. Explain that dance is movement that often expresses a meaning or feeling. Begin by warming up, moving in various ways and stretching. Play neutral background music without words. Invite children to watch and then imitate your movements; use your whole body with slow repeated gestures that convey a meaning of something obvious such as a clown juggling, a horse prancing, or an elephant moving around. Tell them what you were trying to convey with your "dance." Have children take turns showing their own dance movements and have the group imitate them. Then, ask them to tell what they were trying to communicate with their dance.

To Simplify:
● Use very concrete gestures of familiar ideas such as driving a car, eating a meal, going to sleep, or flying.

To Extend:
● Use gestures that convey more abstract ideas such as happiness, sadness, or surprise.

3. Come to Our Play

Gather a small group of children together who are interested in making posters inviting people to attend the play your class is preparing. To introduce this activity, read the book *Albert's Play* by Leslie Tryon (1992). Afterward, look through the pages together for the many signs in the story. Encourage children to make signs announcing their performance and suggest they brainstorm ideas for what information to include. Have children write or dictate their words to an adult, who writes them down so they can be copied. Then ask them to decorate their signs.

To Simplify:

● For younger children, take dictation directly onto their signs. Then have them decorate the signs.

To Extend:

● Point out the way the poster in *Albert's Play* is being made. Gather the tools children will need to make similar ones (tagboard, rulers, erasers, dictionary, colored pencils, or markers).

● Ask children to provide more detailed information about the performance.

● Help children hang the signs and posters around the room, in the school halls, and/or on an outside wall to attract an audience for the show.

4. Story Time

Model storytelling for children by telling a story without using a book. Stories can be about something that really happened, a traditional story, a familiar tale, or a fantasy. Demonstrate how you can change your voice for various characters in the story to make it a more interesting performance. Then invite children to practice and tell stories of their own into a tape recorder. Arrange a quiet place in the room where children can concentrate without distractions. Play each child's story performance back for him or her to hear and suggest it be played for others to hear.

Hints for Success:

● Ask each family to send in a blank audiotape for their child to use each time they have a story to record. Clearly label the tapes with the children's names. Store the tapes conveniently to make them handy for use.

● Keep a record or chart indicating when each child uses his or her individual tape. Suggest children put a sticker on the chart each time they record a story.

To Simplify:

● Expect very short stories from the youngest or least experienced storytellers. Ask prompting questions such as "And then what happened?" or "How did they feel when that happened?"

To Extend:

● Suggest that each child illustrate his or her story or make props for parts of the story. When they are ready, video-tape children telling their stories alone or with help from friends. Replay the tapes so they can see themselves performing.

Physical

1. Ready, Set, Action

Tell children a story that contains obvious action, such as "The Hare and the Tortoise." In a space large enough that children can freely move, suggest they act out the story, being sure to crawl like the tortoise and run or hop like the hare.

To Simplify:

● Practice the movements first, giving verbal cues "hare" and "tortoise."

To Extend:

● Act out other stories that emphasize physical movement such as "The Three Billy Goats Gruff" (trip trapping across the bridge).

2. Act Out a Stretching Poem

Have children make up movements to the poem "The Giant." Encourage them to experiment with ways to show tallness, smallness, and reaching.

The Giant (Author unknown)

Once there was a giant who was tall tall tall.
Then there was an elf, who was small small small.
Now the elf, who was small, would try try try,
To reach to the giant who was high high high.

3. Dance Game

Teach children a dance game, "Let Everyone Dance Like Me." Tell children in this game they can each make up a fun way to dance, and everyone will imitate that way. Teach the chant or make up a simple tune that goes with the following words:

♫ **Let Everyone Dance Like Me** (Traditional)

Let everyone dance like me.
Let everyone dance like me.
Come on, join into the game,
You'll find that it's always the same.

Suggest that children take turns being the leader who shows a way to move. Encourage them to be creative by praising them for their different ideas about dancing movements.

To Simplify:

● Demonstrate various ways to move the body to give children ideas: shaking shoulders, moving hips, slow swaying, fast bouncing, swinging the arms, tapping feet, twisting, and so on.

To Extend:

● Add music. Each time a child demonstrates a movement, turn on a record or tape to encourage others to join in; turn the music off when saying the chant and it's someone else's turn.

4. What's a Pas de Deux?

Read the book *Bravo, Tanya* by Patricia Gauch (1992) to introduce children to various dance positions and steps used in ballet. Show children pictures of Tanya trying different ones. Point out the way she holds her arms, legs, feet, and head. Invite children to experiment and imitate each movement that they can.

To Simplify:

● Choose two or three positions or movements that will be easiest for the children to imitate.

To Extend:

● Invite someone who has studied ballet to demonstrate the actual movements and give children the names for them. Encourage children to imitate the visitor's movements.

Pretend Play

1. Our Show

Arrange an area of the room as a pretend stage. Provide a variety of dress-up clothes that children can use to create their own costumes, and a box of props (such as scarves, pretend musical instruments, wigs, masks, tails, ears, etc.). Set up chairs facing the pretend stage where the audience can sit. Encourage children to take the roles of actors, directors, and audience members.

2. TV Studio

Gather props that could be used for making pretend TV shows. Use an old TV shell or make one using a large cardboard box. Supply the area with puppets, costumes, large signs that say "Back in a Minute" or "Commercial Break" and other props. Discuss the kinds of TV shows they watch and point out that TV programs are performances. Suggest that children make their own entertainment, news, talk, commercials, or game shows. Encourage creative ideas and various roles such as actors, directors, camera people, and so on.

3. Pretend the Story

Supply an area of the room with props related to a specific storybook that the children have heard recently. Place the book in the area, along with costumes that suggest certain roles and simple scenery for acting out the story. Stories and nursery rhymes that are appropriate for this area might be: "Goldilocks and the Three Bears" (a yellow wig, three bowls, three pillows and blankets, a table, three chairs, bear ears, or masks); "The Three Little Kittens" (three pairs of mittens, a pie, cat ears); "Humpty Dumpty" (a large white pillowcase with a hole for head and arms, a low shelf or table for a wall, a king's crown, horse ears); or "The Three Billy Goats Gruff" (horns or ears for three goats, a table for a bridge, a troll mask, or ears).

Social

1. Did You Ever See a Lassie?

Teach children the traditional song. Then have the group stand together in a circle. As the leader, encourage children to imitate your motions. Then suggest that children take turns being the leader, showing others what to do in a game. Each time the leader is a female, use the word *lassie*; when it's a male, use the word *laddie*. Help decide how many motions the leader will do before giving the lead to someone else. Have that person choose the next leader.

♫ **Did You Ever See a Lassie?** (Traditional)

Did you ever see a lassie, a lassie, a lassie,
Did you ever see a lassie, go this way and that?
Go this way and that way, go this way and that way?
Did you ever see a lassie, go this way and that?

2. You Look Very Different

Discuss with children how actors often have paint (or make-up) applied to their faces to make them look a special way and or to give them a disguise. Point out that often actors have a helper called a make-up artist put on their face paint. Provide non-toxic washable face paint and a mirror. Ask children to choose a partner and suggest they take turns painting each other's faces.

3. What a Great Audience!

Discuss the role of the audience and some acceptable behaviors for this group. Have children brainstorm ways an audience shows they appreciate the performance. Divide the group into performers and audience. Encourage the "performers" to put on a simple impromptu show (perhaps singing a song or dancing), and have the "audience" practice responding positively to what they see and hear. Then have the two groups switch roles and repeat.

4. A Tisket, A Tasket

Teach children to play a singing and dancing game that tells a little story called " A Tisket, A Tasket."

🎵 **A Tisket, A Tasket** (Traditional)

A tisket, a tasket, a green and yellow basket,

I wrote a letter to my friend and on the way I dropped it.

I dropped it, I dropped it, and on the way I dropped it.

First teach the song, so it sounds familiar to the children. Then tell everyone to sit in a circle facing the middle. As the group sings, one person moves around on the outside of the circle holding a paper letter; when everyone sings the words "to my friend . . . ," the child drops the letter in the lap of a friend. The friend stands up, holds hands with the person who gave him or her the letter, and together they dance around the outside of the circle as others complete the song. Repeating the song, the chosen friend gets to dance around alone, and then chooses a different friend. The game repeats until everyone has had a turn to dance.

Teacher Resources

Field Trip Ideas

1. Visit the costume warehouse at a local theater.
2. Visit a dance studio.
3. Visit a television studio.
4. Visit a radio station.

Classroom Visitors

Invite performers to visit the class (dancers, musicians, actors) to discuss their work and tell what they enjoy.

Children's Books

Ackerman, K. (1988). *Song and Dance Man*. New York: Alfred A. Knopf.

Gauch, P. (1992). *Bravo Tanya*. New York: Putnam.

Schick, E. (1992). *I Have Another Language. The Language Is Dance*. New York: Macmillan.

Slobodkina, E. (1947). *Caps for Sale*. New York: HarperCollins.

Sendak, M. (1963). *Where the Wild Things Are*. New York: HarperCollins.

Schwartz, H. B. (1993). *Backstage with Clawdio*. New York: Alfred A. Knopf.

Tryon, L. (1992). *Albert's Play*. New York: Macmillan.

Adult References

Abrahams, R. D. (1985). *Afro-American Folk Tales*. New York: Pantheon.

Bauer, C. (1977). *Handbook for Storytellers*. Chicago: American Library Association.

Baylor, B. (1993). *Sometimes I Dance Mountains*. New York: Scribner's.

Cole, J. & Calmenson, S. (1990). *Miss Mary Mack and Other Children's Street Rhymes*. New York: Morrow.

Mendeza, G. (1970). *The Marcel Marceau Alphabet Book*. Garden City, NJ: Doubleday.

Reynolds, M. (1976). *There's Music in the Air*. Berkeley, CA: Schroeder Music.

Yolen, J. (1992). *Street Rhymes Around the World*. Honesdale, PA: Boyds Mills Press.

Usable Arts

Terms Facts and Principles (TFPs)

General Information

1. Some art is made to be used in people's everyday lives.

*2. Some usable forms of art are found in car design, architecture, furniture design, jewelry-making, quilting, weaving, basketry, pottery, flower-arranging, doll-making, knitting, embroidery, clothing design, sewing, and rug-making.

3. People decide which usable art form they like and would like to learn to make.

*4. Beginning artists learn from other artists and by studying examples other artists have made.

5. To improve, artists practice many hours using the tools and materials needed for their art form.

*6. Artists who specialize in a particular kind of art are sometimes known by a specific title such as jeweler, carver, architect, weaver, potter, or designer.

*7. Each artist must learn to master the use of special materials and tools;
   ● basket weavers use reeds, water, and special cutters.
   ● knitters use yarn, special needles and scissors, and machines.
   ● flower arrangers use flowers, containers, anchoring materials, and wire.
   ● potters use clay, rollers, sticks, and a kiln.
   ● jewelers use metals, gemstones, wire, solder, cutters, pliers, and files.

8. Usable art is made by artists and found in cultures all over the world.

*9. The same usable form of art may be used by people in different cultures to communicate their own cultural values. For example, in some cultures beads are used for adornment or self-expression. Elsewhere, beads may indicate economic or marital status or role in society. In other cultures, beads may be used in ceremonies, rituals or for money.

10. People often have preferences for different usable art; what's useful and appealing to one person is not always useful and appealing to everyone.

11. Usable art is often found in people's homes, schools, workplaces, museums, or places of worship.

*12. The same usable work of art can be useful to many different people in many different ways for various reasons. For example, a basket can be used for displaying flowers, holding toys, carrying laundry, or transporting apples from the orchard.

13. Artists produce works of usable art which they may choose to give away, sell, or keep.

*14. Some usable art is unique (one of a kind) while some is mass-produced (one of many that look the same).

Activity Ideas

Aesthetic

1. Interesting Stuff

Bring in samples of usable art from your own home and/or request parents to send in examples. Give parents an idea of the kinds of art forms you are including in your unit, and provide a list of suggestions. Make a display of usable art objects on a shelf at a height where children can see and carefully handle the pieces. Discuss the variety of materials used for the objects and how they may be used.

2. Artists' Tools

Invite an artist to the classroom who specializes in a usable art form such as basketry, rug-making, or architecture. Ask him or her to bring a collection of tools and materials that are used for such art work and explain how each tool is used. During free choice time, offer children a pretend set of tools and materials so they can simulate what the artist has shown them.

To Simplify:
   ● For the simulation, use commercially made plastic tools that look somewhat like the ones used by the artist. For example, if the artist used wire cutters and wire, give children plastic pliers and pipe cleaners.

To Extend:
   ● Make a display of artists' tools for children to look at. Ask parents to contribute to the collection. Label each tool telling its name, who uses it and how they use it.

3. Beautiful Beads

Show children some examples of handmade jewelry that includes beads. Offer children an opportunity

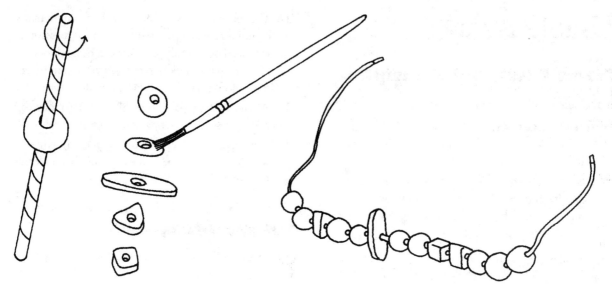

to make their own kind of beads. Make up one or more batches of cornstarch clay and demonstrate how to mold beads. Encourage children to experiment with shapes. Then show children how to push a drinking straw through each bead to make the holes. Lay their collection of beads out on a paper plate to dry, they will be dry in two days with good air circulation. Add food coloring to the dough for color. Alternatively, when the beads are completely dry, children can paint them with water-based poster paint and then coat them with shellac (if a shiny surface is desired).

Cornstarch Clay

> 2 parts table salt
>
> 1 part cornstarch
>
> 1 part water

Mix ingredients and cook over low heat until stiff. Add a few drops of cooking oil to delay drying. Food coloring also may be added. Mold and allow to dry for two days.

4. Making Flower Arrangements

Organize a variety of materials for flower arrangements and demonstrate making a simple arrangement. Talk to children as you make choices among containers, flowers, and other materials, explaining your choices, what you think will go nicely together, and so on. Invite one or two children at a time to make their own arrangement to add beauty to the classroom environment.

Hints for Success:

● To obtain flowers and other needed materials contact a florist for help in making a collection of attractive sturdy containers (vases, dishes, baskets, and so on), anchoring medium (dense plastic foam or wire netting, that is 5 cm or 2-inch size is best), and flowers (either real, silk, or plastic). Inexpensive plastic or fabric flowers may also be purchased at variety stores in different colors and sizes.

● You also could take children on a walk to a field where they have permission to pick wildflowers and grasses.

● Cut and tape the ends of plastic flowers and small branches to ensure safe handling by younger children.

To Simplify:

● Place anchoring material in each container and lay strips of strong tape across the top to secure it.

To Extend:

● Invite an artist who specializes in flower arrangements to demonstrate this art for the class. (Japanese flower arrangement, called Ikebana, has special appeal for children and extends the art form by using branches, grasses, and driftwood.) Have children make arrangements of their own and choose a place in the room to display them. Suggest that each child make a nameplate to place near her or his arrangement.

5. What a Hat!

Begin this activity by wearing a real hat and reading the children's story *Jennie's Hat* by Ezra Jack Keats (1966). Ask children to describe Jennie's hat and what they liked about it. Suggest that they could each be a hat designer and make their own kinds of hats. Select a method of making a paper hat and demonstrate it to children. Then provide them with a wide array of materials for decorating theirs any way they want: fabric scraps, yarn, glue, string, glitter, feathers, buttons, construction paper scraps, netting, cotton balls, and so on.

Hint for Success:

● Avoid showing them a teacher-designed hat as a model since this will establish an adult standard that children will want to copy and can stifle their individual creativity. (See page 38.)

Making Paper Hats

Method 1: Using a large piece of construction paper, slide two corners of the long side together and overlap them in such a way that a point is created. Staple the paper together in several places. Cut to the shape desired or fold the edges to create an individual design. Decorate.

Method 2: Cut stiff paper strips of various length (some 18", 20", 22", and 24"). Fit one paper strip around the head and fasten with a staple or tape. Fasten the other strips around the circle and across the top of the hat, weaving them over and under each other to fill in the top opening. Decorate.

Method 3: Cut a hole in a large stiff dinner-sized paper or Styrofoam plate so it fits on the head well. Punch holes and attach strings to tie it under the chin. Decorate.

Method 4: Cut a paper rectangle large enough to fold into a cylinder that snugly fits over the head. Before stapling the cylinder, measure and draw a line one inch away from the short side of the rectangle. Then cut flaps (about 2" apart) all along one edge and fold them up. Staple the cylinder together. Make a brim for the hat by cutting a hole (as large as the cylinder) in a large paper plate. Slide the cylinder into the plate hole and glue the flaps to the underside of the plate. Decorate.

Affective

1. My Usable Family Art

Promote children's individual cultural awareness by inviting them to bring something from home that their families use and value that also is an example of art from their cultural tradition. Establish a time each child can show their special object and tell others about it by explaining how it is used and why it is special.

Hints for Success:

● Send a note home or describe in a newsletter to the parents what kinds of art objects you want children to bring in. Indicate specific ways you will care for the objects and how long you will keep them.

● Invite parents to personally bring in objects that may be too fragile for children to handle. (See the sample note to parents.)

Dear Parents,

As you know, we are doing a unit about usable art at school. The children are beginning to understand more about art already. Usable art can be any object that is handmade and that you use for some purpose. We would like to have some examples of usable art to put on display in the classroom. We will keep them in a safe place and return them when our unit is completed.

Can you help us? Please look around your home for something that is useful to you, and you consider to be art. (Examples are a basket, bowl, ashtray, rug, quilt.) Perhaps it could be an item that represents your family culture or traditions. Items should be sent to school the week of _____(date). If your usable art is too valuable to send with your child, you are invited to bring it in, and tell the children about it. Please give us information by filling out the attached note and returning it by _____(date). Thanks for your help.

Signed _____

Dear Teacher,

We have a _____. We use it for _____.

It was made by _____.

We plan to send it to school on _____ with our child _____ .

We prefer to bring it on _____ to show the children.

Signed _____

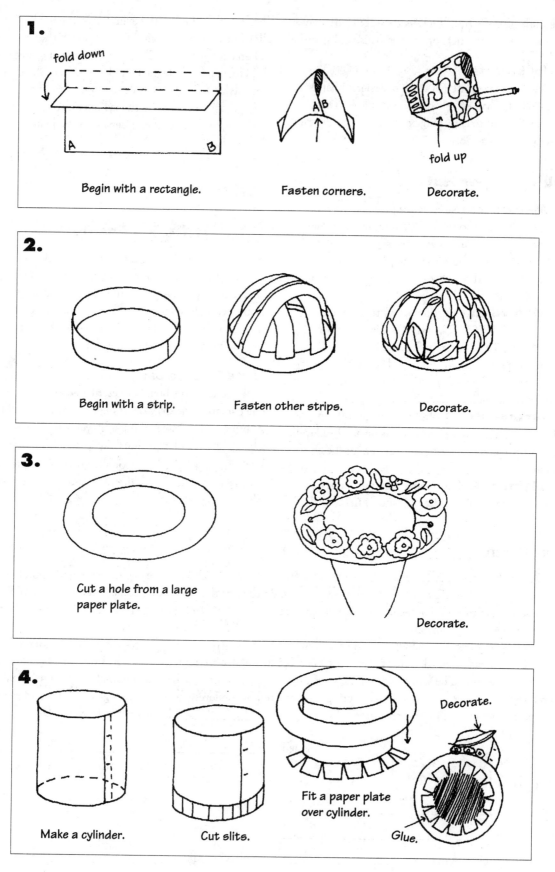

1.

fold down

A   B

Begin with a rectangle.

Fasten corners.

A B

fold up

Decorate.

2.

Begin with a strip.

Fasten other strips.

Decorate.

3.

Cut a hole from a large paper plate.

Decorate.

4.

Make a cylinder.

Cut slits.

Fit a paper plate over cylinder.

Decorate.

Glue.

2. The Choice Is Yours

Display several pictures of useful art objects or of artists engaged in making useful forms of art, or a collection of actual usable art objects (such as teapots, bowls, woven mats, baskets, and so on). Put a number on each item and make a "choosing chart" that displays the items and leaves room for indicating each child's preference. Ask the class to look over the collection of things carefully. Discuss the kinds of usable art represented. Suggest children consider the following question: "If you could learn to make one of these forms of usable art, which would you choose?" Have each child write his or her name on the chart, under the art form he or she prefers. When everyone has had an opportunity to make a choice, ask each child to tell the reasons for his or her selection.

To Simplify:
● Place pictures on the chart instead of numbers.

● Make a sticker for each child with his or her name on it. Tell children to stick their names onto the chart under the picture of the art form they like best.

To Extend:
● Use the information from this activity as an indication of the kinds of art in which children are especially interested. Search for and offer children opportunities to see real artists working in those art forms.

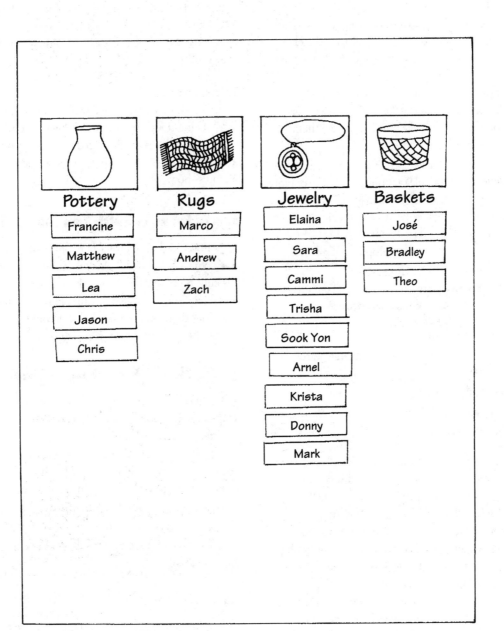

3. Designing My Own Clothes

Discuss the clothes children see people wearing, focusing on the variety of colors, styles, and fabrics used. Tell children they can be a fashion designer, too. Have them trace a simple person shape (about 8 to 10 inches tall) onto paper. Suggest they make their own facial features on the figure. Offer scissors, glue, yarn, ribbon, buttons, and a collection of fabric scraps in a variety of colors. Suggest they design the kinds of clothing that they would like to wear.

To Simplify:
● Pre-cut or pre-trace the person shapes for younger children.

To Extend:
● Ask children to bring to school a plain colored T-shirt or purchase inexpensive T-shirts for the class. Provide a variety of fabric paints in squeeze bottles for children to use in designing their own shirts to wear. Tape each shirt to a flat surface such as a tray, piece of cardboard, or table top so it is easier to work on. Display the shirts on the wall or have children model them when they are completely dry.

● Tie-dying offers another method for designing fabric. Show children a sample of a tie-dyed article of clothing. Point out how the design was made by allowing the color of the dye to touch only parts of the cloth. Explain that children who are interested may try this technique. (Those who have fairly well developed fine muscles will have better success with this process.)

Materials: nontoxic commercial dyes that mix with water or special cold-water dyes

> metal or plastic tubs or pails
> pieces of unbleached muslin or a large cotton handkerchiefs
> rubber bands or string
> mixing sticks
> rubber gloves (for adult)

Prepare several different colors of dye baths in metal or plastic tubs or pails. Mix according to directions on the package. Give each child in a small group a piece of fabric to design. Show children how to pinch a small section of the fabric and wind string or rubber bands tightly around the area, leaving a bubble knob at the end. Continue to do this until the whole cloth is covered by tied knobs. Place the cloth into the die, mixing with a stick, and leave it in until the desired color is reached. Remove and rinse with cold water, wring out and carefully cut away the strings or rubber bands. Open the fabric and help children iron it while damp to set

the color. Dyes can be saved in closed jars or can be applied with brushes, as paints, on cloth.

Cognitive

1. Watch Us Work

Take the children to a place where useful art is made such as a flower shop to watch the arrangers, a bakery to watch the cake decorators, or a ceramic studio to watch the potters. Point out the various techniques they are witnessing, and ask children to tell what they notice.

To Simplify:
● Take along enough adults so that a pair or small group of children can be assigned to each adult. Tell the adults to point out the processes they see, ask children questions, and answer questions children may have as they watch.

To Extend:
● During your visit, take pictures of the artist at work. Hang the pictures in an area where children can look at them. Ask children to dictate a group story or individual stories about what they saw and/or what the pictures show.

2. How Would You Use It?

Show children pictures of people using the same object (such as a basket) in different ways in various cultures around the world. Examine the many ways the object helps people do things. Have the children think of other ways the same object could be used. Make a list or have them draw pictures of their ideas.

3. The Art Sorting Game

Put a collection of usable art objects on a tray (for example a basket, necklace, greeting card, ceramic dish, teapot, woven mat, and an embroidered handkerchief). Ask children to examine these objects and to think of ways they are similar. Tell them to put similar objects into a group and explain what is similar. Mix the objects and repeat, finding other ways things are similar.

4. How Long Will It Take to Dry?

After making usable objects from potter's clay or play dough (such as beads, a cup, flower holder, ornament, or pendant), ask children to predict how long their objects will take to dry completely. Write their

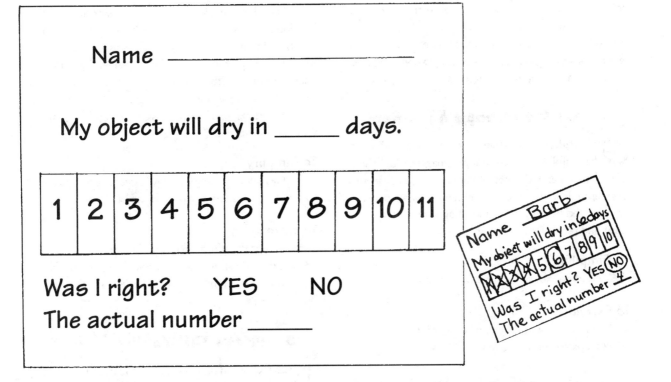

Name _____

My object will dry in _____ days.

| 1 | 2 | 3 | 4 | 5 | 6 | 7 | 8 | 9 | 10 | 11 |

Was I right?   YES   NO

The actual number _____

predictions on a group chart. Each day ask everyone to check his or her object and see if it's completely dry. Then ask children to compare their predictions with what actually happens and to explain why.

To Simplify:
● Make one kind of object and write everyone's prediction on a single chart.

To Extend:
● Provide individual prediction charts. Have children mark their charts each day to show the passage of time, and help them figure out if their predictions were accurate.

Construction

1. I Can Make My Own Usable Art

Provide experiences with many different examples of one usable art form such as jewelry. Show pictures or actual objects that vary in size, form, color, function, and design. Give children materials to design their own pieces of jewelry. Designs may be drawn on paper or actually made with clay that will harden when air-dried. Beads or pendants are easy suggestions.

Hint for Success:
● Potter's clay should be kneaded well and wedged (cut open and thrown down on a hard surface several times to remove the air bubbles) before it is used for clay pieces that will be fired.

To Simplify:
● Have children design their jewelry pieces using play dough that hardens and that can be baked in a standard oven. Poke a hole in each piece before it hardens so it can be strung and worn.

To Extend:
● If potter's clay is used, locate a kiln, and have children's pieces fired, glazed, and fired again. Alternatively, suggest they paint them when dry.

2. Homes Designed for Everyone

Show children examples of homes from all around the world. Point out that the designs and materials used relate to the needs of the people in that part of the world. (For example, houses that are built in places where it snows often are designed with steep roofs so the snow can slide off; houses that are designed for areas that are subject to flooding are often built on raised stilts; houses designed for people in wheelchairs frequently include ramps instead of stairs. Invite each child to design a home that he or she feels meets the needs of the people who will live in it. Provide materials that interest the children: wooden blocks, Lincoln Logs™, Legos™, bricks, cardboard boxes, pieces of scrap wood and glue, or a combination of many materials.

3. My Own Wrapping Paper

Give children opportunities to explore a variety of beautifully designed wrapping papers. Offer them thin plain paper and watercolor paints or sponge printing materials so that they can design their own paper. Sponges can be cut into various shapes, dipped into thin paint and pressed onto the paper.

To Simplify:
- Markers can be substituted for paints.

To Extend:
- Suggest that children make a gift for someone, select a box to put it in, and wrap it with their paper.

4. Potholder Designs

Use commercially made potholder frames and stretchy loops to make potholders. Show children how to weave the loops over and under to create designs that also hold the potholder together.

Language

1. My Artist's Badge

Make simple paper badges for children to wear that indicate what kind of artists they were today. Badges may say: "Today I was a _____ at school." Have the correct word printed on a card near the usable art learning center location. Tell children to copy the words (or dictate them to a teacher who writes on their badges) that describe what kind of art they did on that particular day. Use words such as *weaver*, *potter*, *car designer*, *architect*, and *cake decorator*.

2. An Artist's Story

Motivate thinking about being an artist. A good book for this purpose is Pat Cummings's *Talking with Artists* (1992), which provides interviews with artists including their work as children's book illustrators. Another good book to use is *A Young Painter* by Zheng Zhensun and Alice Low (1991). Select an artist whose work children have seen and read that section of the book to the group. Then read one or two of the

artist's children's books together. Discuss what the artist has done to make his or her art fit the stories. Next, suggest that children imagine themselves as an artist being interviewed by a reporter. Tell children they will have a chance to take on the roles of both the artist and the reporter asking questions. Have children brainstorm a list of questions reporters may ask. Have children interview each other using the questions.

To Simplify:
- Have adults take on the role of the reporters and let children be interviewed as the artists.

To Extend:
- Mount the interviews onto larger pages and suggest children illustrate their interviews. Then bind the pages into a large book entitled "Our Artist's Stories Book."

3. What's This For?

To give children practice expressing their ideas verbally, show them a collection of artists' tools (scissors, wire, rolling pin, frosting bag, spray bottle, pliers, etc.) and ask them to tell what they think each tool is, and how it's used to make usable art objects. Tape-record their answers.

4. Writing Labels

Show children a piece of usable art and let children watch as you make a label for it that tells the name of the piece, who made it and what it is made from. Make available a collection of usable art pieces and ask children to select one and make a label for the piece. Provide blank labels, markers, crayons, and pencils for this activity. Encourage children to write the label in any way they know how, using their own kind of letters and words. Suggest they place the label next to the objects they have chosen and then read what they have written to you.

To Simplify:
- Take dictation from children to make the label.

To Extend:
- As children make usable art objects, encourage them to make labels for their finished work and display them together.

Physical

1. Pottery

Introduce pottery-making to children. Explain that people all over the world make pottery for use and as a pleasurable activity. Show examples of pots, either in pictures or real examples from many cultures (such as Greek, Native American, Mexican, Japanese, and so on). Provide several balls of potter's clay; smocks, oil-cloth, or placemats to cover the table; small bowls of water; and plastic knives. Encourage children to work with the clay and experience its properties as they knead and explore the feel of it. Acknowledge signs of pleasure or accomplishment that are exhibited by the children. If children wish to preserve their creations after experimenting for some time, set their work aside to air-dry for several days. Children may then paint their objects with tempera paint (younger children) or acrylic paints (older children).

Hint for Success:

● To store unused clay over time without allowing it to dry out, follow this procedure: make fist-sized balls of clay, press a thumb into each ball and put water in each depression. Cover the clay with a damp cloth and keep it in a sealed plastic container.

To Simplify:

● Allow children to experiment with the clay without pressure to make or preserve any objects or products.

● Emphasize the process of using their fingers to press, punch, poke, and twist the clay while drawing attention to the fun they are having.

To Extend:

● Demonstrate one of the following simple methods to make a container and suggest children try producing a product.

Pinch Method: To make a bowl or pot, take a ball of clay that fits in one hand. Using the thumb of the other hand, make a depression in the clay. Keep the thumb inside, and the fingers on the outside, pinching and moving the ball of clay around to gradually deepen and widen the hole. Be sure that the wall of the clay bowl is even on all sides. As the clay is moved around in one hand, the other hand shapes the inside. When the bowl reaches its desired form, set it aside to dry on a paper towel. Write the artist's name on the towel and, when the bowl dries, scratch it into the bottom.

Coil Method: Begin a bowl or pot by rolling clay into a small ball, then flattening it to form the base. Roll out a coil (or snake) of clay that is even, not too thick, and also long enough to fit around the base. Lay the coil on the base and smooth the seam by molding the coil both outside and inside. Add additional coils, blending each one as it is placed. When the bowl is the desired size, set it aside to dry for a few days, marking it as described above.

Hint for Success:

● If the pot can not be finished in one day, place a damp cloth over the work "in progress" to keep it moist; place a plastic bag over the pot if possible. The next day, before adding another coil, scratch the top edge surface, and use slip (see the following "Slab and Slip" activity) to join the new coil to the old ones. This procedure will make the seams stronger and the pot is less likely to fall apart as it dries.

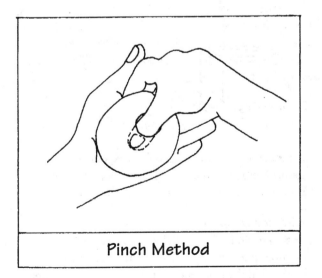

Pinch Method

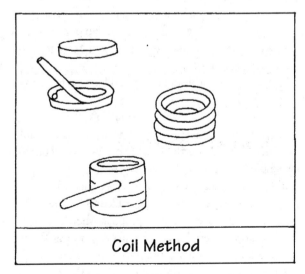

Coil Method

2. Slab and Slip Clay Method

Demonstrate a simple way of making a clay bowl using slabs of potter's clay and water. Roll out pieces of potter's clay into flat slabs about 1/4" thick.

To make the bottom of the bowl: Trace a circle in the clay and cut it out using a toothpick; lift it out and set it aside.

To make the sides: Cut out a rectangle long enough to fit around the circle, and as wide as you want the bowl to be high. (For example: with a 3" circle, make a rectangle 8" x 3".)

To fasten the parts together: Make a small bit of slip (clay and water mixed together about the consistency of glue). Scratch tiny lines in the clay with a toothpick wherever the clay will be joined (around the edges of the circle and along two sides of the rectangle) to roughen the surface. Dip a finger in the slip and apply it like glue on top of the roughened edges. Then press the parts together. Seal the seams by blending clay into the cracks. Set the bowl aside to dry.

Hint for Success:

● To prevent the potter's clay from sticking to the table, cover it with cloth (cotton or burlap) and fasten securely with tape. By using slip in this way, handles and other things that children attach are less likely to fall off when their clay pieces are dry or are being fired.

3. Using Weaving Tools

Introduce the art of weaving by showing children examples of hand-woven cloth, mats, or other samples. Ask parents if they can supply you with examples of woven goods. Show children pictures of people using different kinds of looms; weaving books have colorful pictures of this art in action. Explain that some artists weave on looms to make beautiful woven objects such as blankets, rugs, belts, and placemats. Say "You can learn how to do this, too."

Demonstrate a simple method for weaving using a cardboard loom.

Gather the following materials: a stiff piece of cardboard at least 8-1/2" x 11", scissors, strong colorful string, cardboard shuttles (4" x 2" pieces of cardboard wound with various colors of yarn, or strips of colorful cloth tied together), tape, stapler. (See page 45.)

Prepare and string cardboard looms for the children as shown. Wind several cardboard shuttles. Show children the materials and tools and demonstrate how the loom was made and strung. Demonstrate how to weave over and under the strings, using a shuttle wound with yarn or strips of cloth. Push each completed line up to the top with your fingers or a ruler. Suggest that chil-

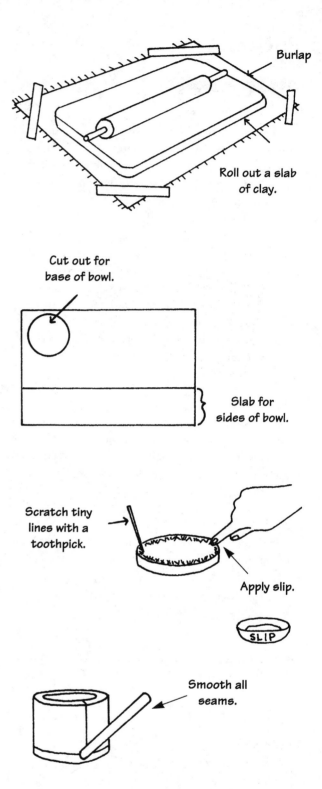

Burlap

Roll out a slab of clay.

Cut out for base of bowl.

Slab for sides of bowl.

Scratch tiny lines with a toothpick.

Apply slip.

SLIP

Smooth all seams.

dren try using the weaving tools to experience this art form. Offer help, time to work, and encouragement to those who show an interest.

Hint for Success:

● The ends of yarn or cloth can be allowed to stick out from the sides slightly. When the weaving is completed, fold the loose ends to the back and weave them into the piece or trim them off. Remove the woven piece from the loom and flatten it.

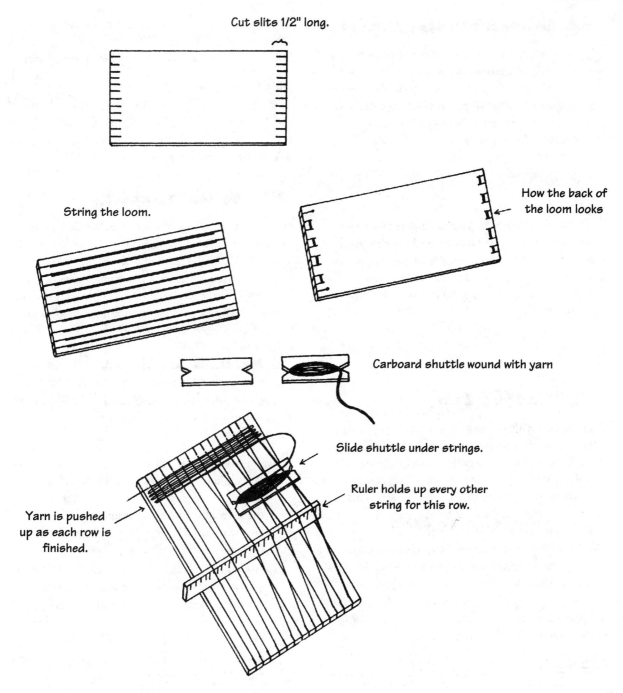

Cut slits 1/2" long.

String the loom.

How the back of the loom looks

Carboard shuttle wound with yarn

Slide shuttle under strings.

Yarn is pushed up as each row is finished.

Ruler holds up every other string for this row.

To Simplify:

● Set up only two or three cardboard looms, allowing children to take turns adding yarn or cloth strips to the design. When the piece is finished, remove it from the loom, and display it on the wall.

To Extend:

● Provide looms for each student, encouraging them to work on theirs gradually over time.

● Show children a real table loom and demonstrate how larger pieces of fabric are created using threads, shuttles, and a beater bar.

Pretend Play

1. Usable Art Store

Arrange furniture, props, and pictures to suggest a store where usable art can be sold and bought. Include a cash register, pretend money, price tags, displays of art objects (such as jewelry, hats, shoes, clothes, and so on), signs and bags. Encourage children to take on roles of buyers, sellers, store workers, and shoppers.

2. Architect's Office

Set up an area to be a pretend office where homes are designed and clients can come to meet with the architect. Include a table, large paper, rulers, pencils, photographs and drawings of homes, a telephone, and other props. Arrange chairs where customers can talk to the architects about their home design.

3. Bakery

Arrange furniture and props to suggest a bakery. Include a shelf where pretend cakes can be displayed, as well as aprons and hats, frosting bags, cardboard cakes, letter and number shapes, pictures of cakes, price tags, and other related props. Suggest children take turns being the cake decorator, the baker, the seller, and the customer.

Social

1. Our Class Quilt

Introduce the idea of quilting as a usable art form. Have a quilter come and show his or her work, or show children a quilt and pictures of quilts being made. Tell the children they will each get to help make part of a class quilt to use in the classroom. Give each child a square piece of cloth to design for the quilt. An easy way to transfer a colorful drawing is with fabric crayons. Following the directions on the crayons, have each child design a square and ask a parent to bring a portable sewing machine to school to sew all the squares together. Attach a layer of filler, a backing, and attach the layers in many places with a few stitches. Hang on a wooden dowel and enjoy as a wall hanging.

To Simplify:
● Offer markers instead of fabric crayons.

To Extend:
● Read the story *The Keeping Quilt* by Patricia Polacco (1988). Discuss how the quilt in the story tells about that family, and compare it to how the quilt the class has made tells something about the class.

2. Weaving Together

After children have had opportunities to weave something small (a belt or placemat), offer them a chance to work together on a much larger weaving that could be useful to the whole school. Take the class to an outdoor area that has chain-link fencing. Show them how strips of colorful cloth can be woven into the fence to decorate it and make a more enclosed play space. Encourage the group to work together on the project.

Hint for Success:
● An in-the-classroom group weaving can be made with fish netting suspended in a corner of the classroom. Have children bring in pieces of ribbon, lace, string, and colorful fabric strips to weave into the netting.

3. We Made Paper!

The Chinese invented the process of making paper about A.D. 105. Discuss some of the uses for paper and demonstrate the method. Ask children who are interested to participate in a group paper-making project. Follow the process step-by-step, involving the children in as many of the steps as they are able to handle themselves. Suggest their finished pieces be used for a special display.

Materials: newspaper, dishpan, water, large mixing bowl, egg beater (or electric blender), tablespoon measure, cornstarch or wallpaper paste, 4" x 4" piece of wire screen (one for each child), plastic wrap, rolling pin, food coloring.

1. One week before, fill a dishpan with 6 cups water. Ask children to help tear 3 full sheets of newspaper into small pieces (about 1/2" size) and drop them into the water. Make sure they all are covered with water and let them stand for three to four days (to break down the fibers).

2. Ask children to take turns beating the wet paper with an egg beater or use an electric blender to transform the mixture into a thin pulp called slurry.

3. Dissolve 4 tablespoons of cornstarch or wallpaper paste in 1 cup water. Add this to the pulp and stir. Let the mixture sit for a few days.

4. Dilute the slurry with 12 cups of water and stir well.

5. Show the children how to lower a piece of wire screen into the mixture horizontally and raise it, placing it on a bed of newspapers. A layer of 1/8" to 1/10" paper pulp should be on the screen. Drops of food coloring may be applied at this point for color.

6. Place a piece of plastic wrap (larger than the screen) on top of the pulp-covered screen. Roll and press with a rolling pin to force excess water out. Allow the pulp to dry; then peel off the plastic and screen.

Teacher Resources

Field Trip Ideas

1. Visit a flower shop.
2. Visit a potter's studio.
3. Visit an art gallery or museum and look for usable art.

Classroom Visitors

Invite an artist who produces usable art to visit the classroom to show his or her skills and products (a quilter, leather worker, potter, glassblower, basket maker, car designer, architect, jewelry-maker, weaver, flower-arranger, doll-maker, knitter).

Children's Books

Blood, C. L., and Link, M. (1990). *The Goat in the Rug.* New York: Macmillan.

Keats, E. J. (1966). *Jennie's Hat.* New York: HarperCollins.

Polacco, P. (1988). *The Keeping Quilt.* New York: Simon & Schuster.

Flournoy, V. (1986). *The Patchwork Quilt.* New York: Dial Books for Young Readers.

Paul, A. W. (1991). *Eight Hands Round a Patchwork Alphabet.* New York: HarperCollins.

Waddell, M., and Milne, T. A. (1992). *The Toymaker.* Cambridge, MA: Candlewick Press.

Zhensun, Z. and Low, A. (1991). *A Young Painter: The Life and Paintings of Wang Yani, China's Extraordinary Young Artist.* New York: Scholastic.

Adult References

DePaolo, T. (1977). *Charlie Needs a Cloak.* Weston, CT: Weston Woods. (Film)

Donald, E. B. (1979). *Flower Arranging.* London: Hamlyn Publishing.

Garritson, J. S. (1979). *Child Arts.* Menlo Park, CA: Addison-Wesley Publishing.

Jenkins, P. D. (1980). *Art for the Fun of It.* New York: Simon & Schuster.

Verlag, O. M. (1976). *The Reinhold Book of Art and Craft Techniques.* New York: Litton Education Publishing.

The Human Body

Head, shoulders, knees and toes,
Knees and toes.
Head, shoulders, knees and toes,
Knees and toes.
Eyes, and ears, and mouth, and nose,
Head, shoulders, knees and toes,
Knees and toes.

Children are fascinated with their bodies and the bodies of other people. From the earliest days of their lives, children hear other people name the parts of their bodies, feel the wondrous touch of skin on skin, and experience the marvelous smells of themselves and their surroundings. They begin to perceive objects around them, hear the musical magic of the human voice, and start to enjoy the pleasures of taste. Children learn about their bodies and the world through their senses.

Early pleasant sensations lead to further exploration of movement and an appreciation of the wonderful things their bodies can do. Additionally, as youngsters grow, they become more and more involved in the care of their own bodies and begin to make choices that contribute to keeping their bodies healthy. As children become more secure in knowledge of their bodies, they compare their own with others'—noticing similarities and differences, observing what others can and cannot do, and recognizing abilities and disabilities. Skillful teachers who plan meaningful experiences for children can make this period one of joyful curiosity, increased understanding, and acceptance of the diversity of human kind. Moreover, presenting a unit on the human body can encourage more positive body image, expand children's notions of the ways the body can move, and promote a healthy, active life.

While there are many interesting things to learn about the human body, we have chosen three areas of focus that we believe are appropriate and meaningful to young children: body parts, the senses, and movement.

Purpose

The mini-themes contained in this chapter emphasize the physical self. Integrated into each mini-theme are activities that address differences that children are sure to notice between their own body and the bodies of others. Activities in these mini-themes also place an emphasis on building children's recognition and acceptance that some bodies may have disabling conditions, but that everyone has capabilities. Activities are specifically designed to help children value physical diversity and the remarkable adaptations of the human body.

Our first mini-theme, "The Body and Its Parts," focuses on the names and functions of body parts, where they are located, and characteristics of body parts in typically developing people. The particular body parts chosen are those that are most meaningful to young children. Because the information is basic, this unit could be used as an introduction to the topic for inexperienced children, or it could be combined with any of the other mini-themes in this chapter to extend learning when children show enthusiasm for the subject.

"The Senses" presents the five sensory organs, where they are located, how the body uses the information the senses perceive, caring for the senses, and variations in abilities to use the senses. Activities are designed to enhance children's appreciation of their own senses and expand their understanding of disabling conditions related to the senses.

"Bodies in Action: Mobility and Immobility" deals with ways the body can move. Emphasis is placed not only on participation in various movement experiences including creative movement, but also on building recognition and acceptance of disabling conditions associated with movements of the body.

Implementation

Teachers can present "The Human Body" in many ways—from simple identification of parts and functions to an exploration of the systems working together—depending on the developmental levels in the group and based on the amount of experience the children have had with the topic. Below are a few suggestions for presenting a unit on the human body with youngsters.

Option One: Use selections from "The Body and Its Parts" to present a short unit that focuses on a limited number of body parts, starting with familiar body parts but adding a few unfamiliar ones. Follow with a short unit on the senses to build greater understanding of the ways people use some special body parts.

Option Two: Choose TFPs and activities that relate to the limbs and their appendages. Use all of the arm, leg, foot, hand, fingers, and toes activities, planning special days for each of the parts chosen. Follow this with a week or more devoted to "Bodies in Action: Mobility and Immobility" in order to extend the emphasis on movement. End with activities that expose children to one or more disabling conditions related to movement.

Option Three: Start by presenting a week or more using parts of the mini-theme "The Body and Its Parts." Use this as a springboard into a unit on food to bring in additional ways children can keep their bodies healthy.

Option Four: Focus on "The Senses" and be sure to integrate activities related to sensory disabilities. Extend these ideas by following with a theme on "Art and Artists" (see pages 15–47). Invite children to participate in creative or appreciation art activities with and without use of their senses, such as painting while wearing blindfolds.

The Body and Its Parts

Terms, Facts, and Principles (TFPs)

General Information

1. Every person has a body that belongs to only him or her.
2. Every body has parts; each part has a name.
3. Some body parts are on the outside of the body and can be seen; other parts are inside the body and cannot be seen.
*4. All of the parts of the body work together to help keep the person healthy and able to do things.

Parts on the Outside
Head, Neck, Trunk, and Limbs

5. On the outside, bodies have a head, neck, trunk and limbs.
6. Some parts of the trunk (or torso) can be seen on the outside, such as the chest, buttocks, hips, and genitals.
7. The head has many parts that help gather and use information from the environment: eyes, ears, nose, and mouth.
8. The neck joins the head to the rest of the body, holds the head steady, and enables the head to turn in different ways.
9. The limbs of the body are the arms and legs: arms have hands attached; legs have feet attached.
10. Hands have four fingers and a thumb.
11. Hands and fingers work together to do many things such as pick up objects, take things apart, put things together, reach, scratch, wave, point, and clap.
12. Legs are attached to the bottom of the trunk; they help the person move in many ways.
13. Feet are flat platforms with five toes; toes help the feet support the body when it is upright.

Genitals

14. The genitals are body parts at the bottom of the trunk that show if the person is a boy or a girl.
15. Genitals have different names; boys have a penis and girls have a vagina.
*16. Grown-up people can use their genitals to create a baby.

Skin

17. Skin is a thin, waterproof covering that protects the body; skin holds the other body parts together inside the body.
18. Skin protects the body from becoming too hot or too cold and from dirt and germs.
19. Skin comes in different colors: many shades of brown, black, yellowish-tan, reddish-brown, light or dark tan, pink, or white.
20. Skin can stretch and return to its regular shape.
*21. When skin breaks or gets cut, the body heals the break and makes new skin.
*22. Skin has tiny holes that allow the body to sweat, keeping the body cool.
23. On some areas of the body, skin has hair growing from it.

Parts on the Inside
Stomach

24. When a person swallows food, it goes to a special sack inside the trunk called the stomach.
*25. Special liquids inside the stomach help soften and break up digest foods so the body can use them for energy and growth.

Heart

26. The heart is a fist-shaped muscle inside the chest that pumps blood through the body.
27. The pumping of the heart is constant and regular, and can be heard and felt through the wall of the chest.
*28. A person's heart beats continuously; if a heart stops beating, other body parts don't get blood, and the body soon dies.
*29. The heart works harder and gets stronger when a person is active.

Lungs

30. The lungs are two large sacks inside the chest that fill up with air as the person breathes in and empty when the person breathes out.
*31. Lungs work with the heart to get oxygen to other parts of the body.

Brain

32. The brain is inside the head.
*33. The brain sends messages to other body parts through nerves that are found all through the body.
*34. The brain is important for learning new things, thinking, solving problems, remembering, and being creative.

Bones

35. The human body has many bones (206 in an adult) that make up the skeleton.

36. Bones can be felt through the skin.

37. Babies have soft bones, but they become harder as the child grows older.

38. Bones are stiff, do not bend, hold the body up, and give it shape.

*39. Bones are different sizes and shapes: some human bones are long (leg), some are short (finger), some are round (the skull), and some are very tiny (inner ear).

Joints

40. The place where two bones are connected is called a joint.

41. Some of the joints in the human body are the shoulder, elbow, wrist, knuckle, hip, knee, and ankle.

*42. Joints allow bodies to bend and twist; without joints the body would not be able to move.

Muscles

43. There are many muscles in the human body (about 650).

44. Muscles are under the skin, attached to bones and organs in the body.

*45. Muscles can relax and contract; they help the body move and do work.

Blood

46. Blood is a red liquid inside the body.

47. Blood moves through the body in blood vessels called veins and arteries.

*48. Blood carries oxygen to the body parts and helps the person stay healthy.

*49. The body needs a certain amount of blood to work well; if the body bleeds and a small amount of blood comes out, the body makes more blood to replace it.

Activity Ideas

Aesthetic

1. Sing with Me

The singing game "Head, Shoulders, Knees and Toes" has been sung and played by generations of children in this country. Versions representing different cultures can be found in several books and recordings. Here are two Euro-American and African-American versions:

♫ Head, Shoulders, Knees and Toes
(Traditional Euro-American)

Head, shoulders, knees and toes, knees and toes. (*point to body parts*)

Head, shoulders, knees and toes, knees and toes.

Eyes, and ears, and mouth, and nose,

Head, shoulders, knees and toes, knees and toes.

♫ Head 'n' Shoulders, Baby (Traditional African-American)

Head 'n' shoulders, Baby, one, two, three. (*point to body parts*)

Head 'n' shoulders, Baby, one, two, three.

Head 'n' shoulders, Head 'n' shoulders,

Head 'n' shoulders, Baby, one, two, three.

Both versions can be extended by substituting different body parts into the song. Have children take turns suggesting various body parts to use.

To Extend:

● With the African-American version, tap the head and shoulders as indicated and clap-slap (as indicated here) on "Baby, one, (rest) two, (rest) three."

(*clap -slap- clap- slap- clap- slap*)

Word changes can produce a sequence of verses. One suggested sequence is:

Knees and ankles, Baby . . .

Ankles and toes, Baby . . .

Turn around, Baby . . .

Shake a leg, Baby . . .

Do a dance, Baby . . .

Wave good-bye, Baby . . .

● If a sequence of body parts is developed, it may be reversed and the tempo speeded up toward the end.

2. Body Band

While seated on the floor, demonstrate "making music" by slapping your knees together or tapping your feet on the floor. Ask children for other suggestions and demonstrations of tapping or slapping body parts to make sounds in rhythm. Acknowledge all of the creative ways that children think of to use their bodies as music-makers. Next, introduce the "Body Band Song" as a way for children to put their body music into action.

♫ **Body Band Song**

Words by Kit Payne

Tune: "Row, Row, Row Your Boat"

Clap, clap, clap your hands.

Make a body sound!

My body makes music,

This new way I found.

Change the words as children find new ways to produce sound.

Tap, tap, tap your toes . . .

Slap, slap, slap your knees . . .

Pat, pat, pat your cheeks . . .

Hint for Success:

● Begin by using words to accompany some of the sounds children make. After a while, use only the sound in place of the verbs in this song.

To Extend:

● Provide children with bells attached to elastic bands that fit around body parts (wrists, ankles, feet, elbows) that produce a sound when that body part is moving.

3. Pressure Points

Make or obtain large balls of modeling dough for each child at this activity. Suggest that children use various parts of their bodies to produce imprints in the dough. Compare the different prints and indentations made with fingers, whole hands, elbows, forearms, even knees and feet if clothing and space permit. Also, suggest that children wrap the modeling dough around their skin to experience the texture and temperature of the dough.

4. Clap Those Hands

Use any of the following chants and songs to help children feel the beat and tempo of the words.

♫ **Clap Your Hands** (Traditional)

Clap your hands as slowly,

As slowly as can be.

Clap them very quickly,

Just like me.

♫ **We'll All Clap Hands Together**

(Traditional)

We'll all clap hands together,

We'll all clap hands together,

We'll all clap hands together,

As children like to do.

♫ **Clap, Clap, Clap Your Hands** (Traditional)

Clap, clap, clap your hands,

Clap your hands together.

Clap, clap, clap your hands,

Clap your hands together.

♫ **Let Ev'yone Clap Hands Like Me**

(Traditional)

Let ev'ryone clap hands like me (clap, clap).

Let ev'ryone clap hands like me (clap, clap).

Come on and join into the game.

You'll find that it's always the same (clap, clap).

Hint for Success:

● These chants and songs have endless possibilities. Help children suggest novel movements such as "pull your ear," "rub your chin," "scratch your nose," or "pat your elbow." Other actions that could be substituted are a sequence of human sounds such as yawn, sneeze, cough, hiccup, laugh, cry, and so on.

5. Aiken Drum

Teach the traditional song "Aiken Drum," found on many recordings by a variety of artists, using vegetable names and other foods for the various body parts. After the song becomes familiar, ask children to create new verses by using different foods for each body part.

♫ **Aiken Drum** (Traditional)

There was a man lived in the moon,

In the moon, in the moon.

There was a man lived in the moon,

And his name was Aiken Drum.

And his head was made of a cabbage,

A cabbage, a cabbage.

His head was made of a cabbage,

And his name was Aiken Drum.

And his neck was made of potato,

potato, potato.

His neck was made of potato,

And his name was Aiken Drum.

Continue in the same way, adding body parts and foods. End the song with:

And wasn't he a yummy man,

Yummy man, yummy man.

And wasn't he a yummy man,

And his name was Aiken Drum.

To Simplify:

● Provide picture cues to remind children of the food for each body part.

To Extend:

● Suggest children make their own Aiken Drum on paper, using crayons and gluing paper cut-outs or using plastic food models arranged in a body shape.

Affective

1. Same and Different

Gather posters, photographs, or magazine clippings of people of many races and ages. Include photographs of the children in your group, if possible. Tell the children that all people share certain characteristics and that every individual differs in some ways from every other. Ask children to select pictures of people who they think are very like themselves and then describe what the resemblances are. Next, ask children to choose pictures of people who differ from them in some way and explain the differences they see. Point out that there are many kinds of people in the world and that both the likenesses and the differences make us interesting to each other.

To Simplify:

● Show children one picture at a time. Ask them to identify whether the person is like them or not like them. Place each picture in one of two piles. Review their selections after they have chosen two or three that are like themselves.

To Extend:

● Challenge children to find likenesses to themselves in the pictures they chose as different from themselves.

2. This Is Me

Have a small group or pair of children look at themselves in a mirror. Give them time to notice things about their features. Then point out their skin and ask them to describe what color it is. Arrange a muffin pan with several colors of paint that could be skin tones (various browns, black, pinkish tan, yellowish tan, etc.). Use commercial skin tone paints (available from several companies) or mix your own. Compare your own skin tone to the paint, pointing out which one is like your skin. Then, ask children to point to the skin color that is closest to their own. Suggest children use these colors to make a picture of themselves on large painting paper.

Hints for Success:

● Have other colors of paint available for those who want to add details.

● The whole group could paint on one paper, or children could make individual pictures.

● Many young children are not yet drawing or painting in a representational way. Accept any attempts, even if they don't meet adult standards of portraiture.

To Simplify:

● Make simple paper body cuts-outs and have children paint in their skin tone, adding other special features if they wish.

To Extend:

● Hang the painting paper next to a full-length mirror so children can look at their whole body while they work.

3. Matching Skin and Eye Color

Give children an opportunity to recognize their own eye and skin colors and chart that information on a simple graph. Prepare two graphs, one illustrating a range of colors of eyes and a second one focusing on skin tones. Prepare two name stickers for each child—one for the eye chart and one for the skin color graph. Skin tone crayons or paints, available commercially, work well to make the chart. To point out the variety of eye and skin colors in people, use a variety of colors in both categories, regardless of how diverse or homogeneous the group is. Begin this activity by showing a number of large color pictures of different people's faces, or demonstrate variation in skin and eye color, using yourself and another adult in the classroom as examples. Find your eye color and skin color on each chart. Offer a mirror for children to check their own eye and skin colors. After children determine which colors match theirs, suggest

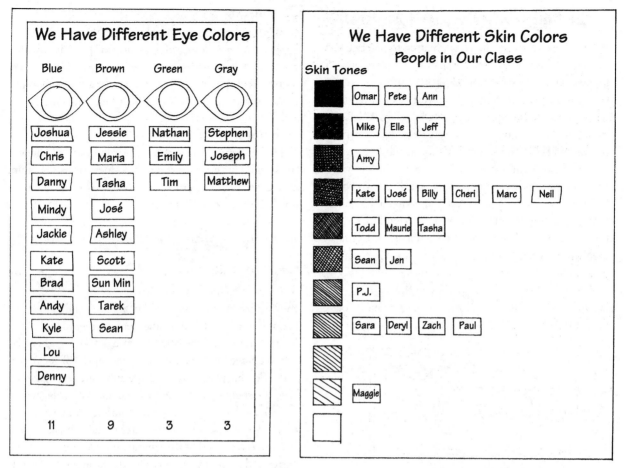

they place their name sticker in the correct columns. When all of the children's names are on the chart, ask them to look at the chart together and discuss the group findings: how many children have blue eyes? brown eyes? brown skin? tan skin? and so on. Which color has the most names? The fewest?

To Simplify:

● Create individual charts for each child rather than graphing the group.

To Extend:

● Prompt children to look for more than one skin color on their own bodies. Identify each of these on the graph.

Cognitive

1. What's a Bone Like You Doing in a Joint Like This?

Ask for a volunteer to help in a demonstration about bones and joints. First, point out some of the bones in the volunteer's body (head, arms, legs, fingers).

Suggest the other children find these same bones on their own bodies. Ask your volunteer to do some bending. Point out that every place that the body can bend has a joint. Demonstrate the fact that bones don't bend by asking your volunteer to try to bend in a place that's not possible (such as the middle of the forearm or the middle of the calf). Ask children to tell why that's impossible. Next, invite children to help make a list of all the places where their bodies can bend, "Joints We Know." Read the list aloud and count how many joints they thought of.

To Simplify:

● Suggest that each child get up and move around, investigating his or her own body's ability to bend. As children notice a bending place, they should call it out.

To Extend:

● Make or obtain a large chart of the human body. Laminate it or cover it with clear adhesive paper. Place labels on the chart indicating joints. Compare the chart to the list of joints the children made. Help them determine whether their list omitted some joints or whether some joints have names that were unknown to the children.

2. Singles, Pairs, and Multiples

The aim of this activity is for children to practice constructing a concept of quantity. Prepare the following materials in advance: a pair of shoes, a hat, a large laminated posterboard chart sectioned into four quarters (label each section: "1 One," "2 Two," "10 Ten," and "More Than Ten"), a grease pencil or wipe-off marker. Begin the activity by showing children a pair of shoes. Ask them to count the shoes and explain why there are two. Ask them to think about their own bodies and name some other pairs. As children name the pairs, write them onto the chart under the section that is labeled "2 Two." Then show them a hat; ask the children why a person needs only one hat. Encourage them to consider other body parts of which they have just one. Record their correct responses on the section labeled "1 One." Repeat the same process for each section of the chart.

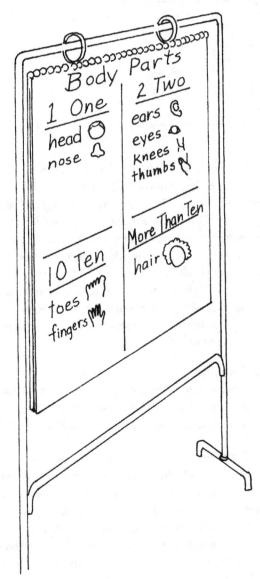

To Simplify:

● Copy and cut out simple line drawings of body parts (eyes, ears, nose, mouth, legs, arms, hands, fingers, toes, trunk, hair, teeth) or make your own. Hold up each picture as children mention that body part and ask one child to place it on the correct section of the chart.

To Extend:

● Challenge more experienced children to include internal body parts (heart, lungs, kidney, stomach, brain, etc.) on their chart. Provide reference books for them to check their answers.

3. Heart Throbs

Obtain a real stethoscope and encourage children to listen to the beating of their own hearts; encourage them to listen to their friends' hearts, too. Then talk about it as a kind of pump and demonstrate how the heart works inside the body. For this activity, gather one or more large kitchen basters, one or more 18" lengths of clear, flexible plastic tubing large enough to fit tightly over the spout end of a baster (available in hardware stores), a tub of water, and food coloring. Add a few drops of food coloring to the water to make it easier to see. Fasten one end of the tubing onto the spout end of a baster and place the other end of the tubing into the tub of colored water. Show children what happens to water when the baster bulb is squeezed, then released. Ask them to watch carefully and tell what they see—a baster that is squeezed and released pumps water through the tubing. Explain that this is similar to what happens inside us—a heart that is beating pumps blood throughout the body. Make these materials available for several days so that children can try this experiment on their own.

4. Boy Bodies/Girl Bodies

To point out that bodies have genitals, use anatomically correct dolls in the housekeeping area and encourage children to take care of the babies. Explain that some of the babies are boys and some are girls. Include several changes of clothing for the dolls so children are encouraged to dress and undress the dolls. To encourage children to consider sexual characteristics, ask them, "Is your baby a boy baby or a girl baby? How do you know?" Provide pretend baby bathtubs, washcloths and towels to encourage children to undress their babies.

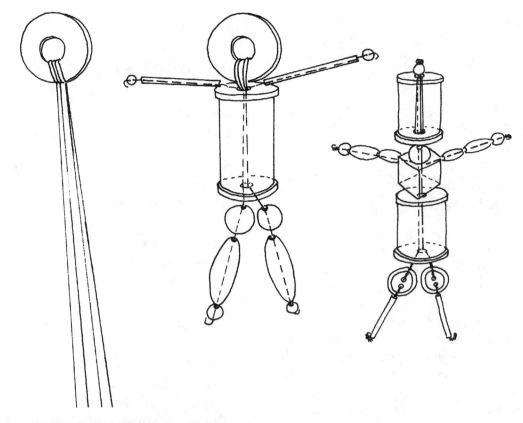

5. How Would It Be?

Encourage children to imagine changes in the human body and act them out. Write some ideas on small cards ahead of time. Have children draw one and read it aloud. Ask for children to volunteer to act out what they think would happen if . . .

> eyes were on the palms of your hands
>
> your mouth was in your knee
>
> arms grew out of your head
>
> people had wings instead of arms
>
> your nose was on the bottom of your foot

To Simplify:
● Create simpler scenarios, naming only one body part, such as: You had no nose; how would you smell? Your arms couldn't bend; how would you eat lunch?

To Extend:
● Ask children to imagine how objects we use would look different if our bodies were different. Explain that many things people use are made that way because body parts are a certain shape or can move in certain ways. (For example, glasses rest on the nose; what would they look like if people didn't have noses?) Ask them to brainstorm ideas of objects that would look different if bodies were different and illustrate their ideas on paper.

Construction

1. What Moves You?

After one or more discussions about body parts, including bones and joints, tell children they can make a "body" that moves. Explain that they can design "a person" in any way they want and that everyone's creation will look different. Set up an activity area with a collection of materials that could be used to make a body such as empty spools of various sizes (from sewing shops), metal or plastic washers and nuts (from hardware stores), drinking straws cut in various lengths, old wooden beads of various sizes and shapes, large buttons, and three or four very long pipe cleaners for each child. Point out all the different materials and encourage children to brainstorm what body parts each could be used for. Suggest that children begin by selecting one object for the head (a spool, button, or bead) and then attach several long pipe cleaners to it to provide a way to add other body parts. Show children how the pipe cleaners allow movement where the objects come together. Encourage children to explore the various materials and try different combinations for their "body creations."

To Simplify:
● Provide heads and torsos already put together. Encourage children to attach arms, hands, legs, and feet to make their "person."

To Extend:

● Add a degree of challenge by substituting yarn and long rubber bands instead of pipe cleaners as the main connecting material for this activity. Although it will be more difficult to pass them through some of the objects, they will provide stretch and tension analogous to muscle function and will add an interesting problem-solving dimension as well.

2. We'll Eat It Up, We Love It So

Encourage children to make and eat their own fruit or vegetable "person". Use fresh or canned fruits or vegetables in a variety of colors and shapes such as peach halves, pear halves, pineapple tidbits, raisins, carrot sticks, green pepper slices or rings, and so forth. Remind children of the major parts that make up a human body and that each one has its own shape. Point out that people have only one of some parts (head and torso), and pairs of some (arms and legs), and many of others (teeth, fingers, hair, and so on). Direct children to wash their hands before creating their own fruit and/or vegetable person. Give each child a large paper plate for a base and suggest they make their people any way they want. As children work, comment about how well they are using their own creative ideas. Ask each child to show her or his finished person to you and others before eating it.

Hint for Success:

● Have children begin with the largest body part, the torso. This will make it more likely that children will create a figure using amounts of food they can actually eat.

3. Assembly of People

Prepare "people" figures to be used on a flannel board. To make the figures, choose several colors of flannel that are similar to a variety of skin tones (tan, bronze, brown, pink, black). After making several flannel persons, cut them apart at the shoulders, hips, and neck. Mix all of the pieces up and invite children to put the people back together correctly.

To Simplify:

● Cut one or two people figures into only four or five pieces. Offer one person on each flannelboard.

To Extend:

● Make several more cuts, separating the figures at the wrists, ankles, knees, and neck.

Language

1. Add-On Song

Teach children one or more of the following song verses. When the words are familiar to the children, invite them to add their own ideas to create new verses about other body parts. Depending on the range of development of the group, children may take several days of practice before they are familiar with the song and can begin to make their own song verse.

♫ **The Body Part Song**
Words by Kit Payne
Tune: "The Farmer in the Dell"
(Knees)

> They only bend one way,
> To make me short or tall.
> And if they didn't work just right,
> Then surely I would fall.
> My two legs each have one,
> They're knobby and they're round.
> And it's my knees I sing about,
> The leg joints, half way down.

(Ankles)

> By bending either way,
> They make my feet flip-flop
> And fasten them below my legs,
> These joints can lift and drop.
> When I am sitting down,
> They help my feet tuck in.
> My ankles help me walk and run,
> To go and stop again.

(Tongue)

> This lays inside my mouth,
> But I can stick it out.
> It's really quite a muscle,
> I can wag it all about.
> It helps me taste my food.
> It helps me catch my sips.
> My tongue is what I sing about,
> It's here behind my lips.

When children appear ready to make up their own verse, select a body part that the class could write about. Ask all of the children to generate ideas about things this part does for the body, how it moves, or ways a person uses it. Then encourage children to think of words that rhyme with other words that were suggested. As a group, begin to put together the verse. Accept even silly suggestions and have fun trying them out in the song.

2. A Complete Joke

Prepare several copies of the following story on large pieces of chart paper. Leave spaces for illustrations to be added after the stories are completed. Divide the class into several small groups of children. Provide each group with the same completion story. Explain to children that they can make the story as silly as they like by adding words where there are blanks.

One day I was _____ down the sidewalk, waving my _____ and tapping my _____ . I heard a strange sound and looked up to see a _____ coming towards me. I bent at the _____ and ducked my _____ so that it wouldn't _____ me, but it was too late. The _____ with purple _____ just kept on _____ .

Suddenly, I had an idea. I started to push with my _____, and turned around on my _____ and away I went. The next thing I knew, my _____ was calling me. I was very glad to hear that because I needed help. I yelled, "Quick, help me _____!" So, together we solved the problem by _____ .

To Simplify:
● Take dictation and offer assistance to one child at a time, working individually.

To Extend:
● Suggest children illustrate their work after the text is inserted. Read the stories to the whole group.

3. What Do You Know?

Early in this unit, ask children to tell you some things they already know about bodies. Write their responses on a chalkboard or large piece of chart paper entitled "Things We Know About The Body." Read the list to the group, pointing out words as you read them. Next, ask children to name some things about their bodies about which they want to know more. To get them thinking, suggest something that puzzles you and write this at the top of a new list called "Things We Want to Know About the Body." Make a list of the children's responses and read it to them. Finally, brainstorm ideas about how they could learn more about the body. Ask

questions such as "Who could we ask about that?" "Where can we look for more information?" "Does anyone have a book about the body that we could borrow?" Refer back to the lists occasionally as the unit gets underway. Repeat the process at the end of the unit, comparing what was known at the beginning to what the children know at the end.

4. Anybody Got a Word Match?

Find or draw two large outlines of the body. Laminate or cover the drawings with clear adhesive paper. On one of the diagrams, label as many of the parts as you wish with single words. Prepare a set of matching label cards; laminate the cards for durability. Hang the pictures side by side, suggesting children apply labels in the correct positions to the blank body diagram. (A similar game could be made for the flannelboard. Write labels on felt strips with permanent marker.)

To Simplify:
● Encourage children to compare their label cards to the pre-labeled chart as they make placement decisions. Then suggest they try labeling the body parts without looking at the pre-labeled chart. Afterwards, they can check their accuracy.

To Extend:
● Challenge children to construct additional label cards for body parts that are not labeled.

Physical

1. Robot Parade

Gather the children in a large area. Talk about the differences between robot bodies and people's bodies. Discuss the remarkable mobility of the human body parts and some of the actions made easier by our ability to be "bendable." Explain that robots may move with fewer joints than real people. Invite children to stand up and move like a robot might (without bending their knees and with stiff arms) when you call out "Robot Walk." To help children experience the contrast, follow this by calling out "Real Person Walk." Alternate calling out "Robot Walk," "Real Person Walk," "Robot Walk" several times. Turn on some walking music and have a parade, suggesting children walk one behind the other as they listen for your call telling them which way to walk.

To Simplify:

● Focus on robot walking without changing to normal walking.

To Extend:

● Experiment with non-bending waists, elbows, shoulders, and wrists.

2. Everybody's Song

S ing a simple verse about each child in the group, inserting words for body parts and describing the ways they are attached.

♫ Everybody's Song

Words by Kit Payne
Tune: "Mary Had a Little Lamb"

Mary has a little head, little head, little head.
Mary has a little head, jointed at the neck.

Peter has two little arms, little arms, little arms.
Peter has two little arms, jointed at the shoulders.

SungYun has two little hands, little hands,
little hands.
SungYun has two little hands, jointed at the
wrists.

Leon has one little nose, little nose, little nose.
Leon has one little nose, right below his eyes.

Invite everyone to insert her or his own name and a body part they want to sing about.

3. My Lungs Can Fill Up

H ave children take deep breaths and blow air out onto a light object on a table, such as a feather, small scraps of paper, or cotton balls. Point out that the air they are blowing out was inside their lungs. Have them feel their own lungs both inflated and deflated. Set up the water table or a small pool of water outdoors. Have the children try to blow things across the water using their lung capacity.

To Simplify:

● Lay lightweight objects in the water such as an aluminum foil tart pan. Suggest that children try to blow it with or without little toy people inside. Can they do it?

To Extend:

● Help children make simple sailboats from Styrofoam picnic plates with paper sails attached to pipe cleaners. Encourage children to be aware of their lungs filling up with air and their ability to blow that air out slowly or with more force. Have them try to blow the paper sails to move the boats across the water. Ask them to tell you how they did that; where did the air come from?

Pretend Play

1. Thrift Shop

A rrange a clothing store using dress-up clothes that can be categorized by body parts. Encourage children to pretend that they are selling them to customers, and the customers want to choose clothing for different parts of their body. Make illustrated signs indicating the body part your clothing collection relates to. Examples: Head (hats, sunglasses, hoods, scarves); Legs (pants, shorts, skirts); Feet (boots, shoes, sandals, socks), and so on. Model how to shop by asking for clothing for a particular body part.

To Simplify:

● Limit the number of body parts children must deal with to only two or three (head, feet, hands).

To Extend:

● Mix up all the dress-ups and suggest children either fix the mistakes or try the clothes for the wrong body part.

2. Doctor's Office

A rrange an area of the room like a doctor's office, with a waiting room, receptionist, treatment area, and so on. Gather props that suggest various things doctors use, such as a stethoscope, a scale, bandages, gauze, or beds. Display body parts pictures on the walls and demonstrate how the doctors and nurses check the patient's body parts when they come to the office.

Social

1. Body Tracing with a Friend

W ith the help of an adult friend, demonstrate how a whole body can be traced on a big piece of paper. Ask the friend to lie on the paper on his or her back. Trace carefully around the person. As the tracer moves the crayon, the subject tells what body part he or she feels being traced. Emphasize the way the two people must work together, cooperating to accomplish this task. Divide the class into pairs, provide them with materials, and suggest they take turns being traced. When the pictures are done, suggest the partners name as many of the body parts as they can.

2. A Baby's Body

Ask a parent to bring in her or his baby for the children to see and, if possible, watch as it is given a bath. Ask the parent to point out body parts and help children figure out if this is a boy or a girl baby. If possible, allow the children to help in some way. Suggest they sit and take turns holding the baby as the bath is being prepared, play with the baby to amuse it, or hold the towel, soap, or shampoo for the baby's bath.

Teacher Resources

Field Trip Ideas

1. Take the group to visit a biology lab at a nearby middle school or high school. Request that the students explain some things they have learned about the body. Ask if the children can examine a skeleton or see some posters or models of internal organs.

2. Visit an exercise studio where people are working out on machines to strengthen their bodies.

3. Ask the doctor to show instruments used to check body parts that are inside the body, such as the heart, lungs, inner ear, and so on.

Classroom Visitors

1. Contact a local high school or college sports instructor or coach. Invite one or more student athletes to visit your classroom with the permission of their instructor or coach. Ask them to tell the children about routines they follow to prepare themselves for sporting events. Suggest that the athletes bring equipment to show the children.

2. Invite a pediatrician or children's nurse to visit. Ask that he or she bring tools and equipment so that the children can examine the visitor as they learn about the health professional's strategies for assessing and maintaining children's health.

Children's Books

Aliki. (1984). *Feelings*. New York: Greenwillow.

Aliki. (1990). *My Feet*. New York: HarperCollins.

Aliki. (1990). *My Hands*. New York: HarperCollins.

Balestrino, P. (1986). *The Skeleton Inside You*. New York: HarperCollins.

Brenner, B. (1970). *Faces*. New York: Dutton.

Cleary, B. (1987). *The Growing-up Feet*. New York: Morrow Junior Books.

Cole, J. (1992). *Your Insides*. New York: Putnam.

Cumbaa, S. (1991). *The Bones & Skeleton Book*. New York: Workman Publishing.

Joyce, W. (1985). *George Shrinks*. New York: HarperCollins.

Linn, M. (1988). *A Trip to the Doctor*. New York: HarperCollins.

Patrick, D. (1989). *Look Inside Your Body*. New York: Putnam.

Perez, C., and Robinson, D. (1982). *Your Turn, Doctor*. New York: Dial Books for Young Readers.

Showers, P. (1967). *A Drop of Blood*. New York: HarperCollins.

Showers, P. (1965). *Your Skin and Mine*. New York: HarperCollins.

Smallman, C. (1986). *Outside-In*. New York: Barron's.

Stinson, K. (1986). *The Bare Naked Book*. Buffalo, NY: Firefly Books.

Adult References

Jennings, T. (1989). *The Human Body*. Chicago: Childrens Press.

Neugebauer, B., ed. (1987). *Alike and Different: Exploring Our Humanity with Young Children*. Redmond, WA: Exchange Press.

Schiamberg, L. B. (1988). *Child and Adolescent Development*. New York: Macmillan.

Schindler, A. (1989). *Too Tall? Too Short? Too Fat? Too Thin?: A Guide to the Growth and Sexual Development of Children*. New York: Agathon.

Smoll, F. R., Magill, M. and Ash, M. (1988). *Children in Sport*. Champaign, IL: Human Kinetics Books.

Wool, D. (1986). *How Did We Find Out About Blood?* New York: Walker.

Zeller, P., and M. Jacobson. (1987). *Eat, Think, and Be Healthy!* Washington, DC: Center for Science in the Public Interest.

The Senses

Terms, Facts, and Principles (TFPs)

General Information

1. People gather information from their environment through their senses.

2. Human beings have five senses: seeing, hearing, tasting, smelling and touching.

3. Each of the five senses is associated with specific body parts called sensory organs: eyes, ears, tongue, nose, and skin.

4. Some sensory experiences are pleasant; some are unpleasant.

*5. Pleasant sensory experiences are often a signal that things are OK, while unpleasant ones often signal danger or tell the person to take action. For example, very loud thunder probably means a storm is coming and signals the need to take shelter; a food that tastes bad may mean it has spoiled and tells the person to spit it out.

Seeing

6. People sense sights or see with their eyes.

*7. Eyes can see form, color, size, surface features, distance, and the movement of objects.

*8. People's eyes need light to see and are less accurate in dim light; where there is no light, people cannot see at all.

*9. A special nerve in the eye sends messages to the brain about sights.

Hearing

10. People sense sounds or hear with their ears.

*11. Sounds produce vibrations that enter the ear through the ear canal and vibrate parts inside the ear (the ear drum and tiny bones).

*12. Some sounds are easy to hear when they are clear and distinct; some sounds are not easy to hear, especially if they are muffled or very quiet.

*13. A special nerve in the ear sends messages to the brain about sounds.

Tasting

14. People sense tastes with their tongues.

*15. Some tastes are easy to notice—they are distinctive or strong; some tastes are harder to notice—they are subtle or delicate.

*16. Taste buds are tiny bumps on the tongue that sense sweet, sour, salty, and bitter tastes.

*17. The tongue contains nerves that send messages to the brain about tastes.

Smelling

18. People sense smells with their noses.

*19. Smells enter the nose through the nasal passages and stimulate nerves which send messages to the brain about the smells.

*20. Some smells are easy to notice—they are fragrant or pungent; some smells are harder to notice—they are subtle or weak.

Touching

21. People sense touches or feel with their skin, which covers the whole body.

*22. Skin can sense hot, cold, pressure, pain, and textures.

*23. Nerves in the skin send messages to the brain about touches.

Responding to the Senses

*24. When the body senses something, the brain sends a signal to other body parts in response; for example, if skin feels something very hot, the brain tells the hand to pull away from the heat.

25. People remember familiar sensory messages (for example, ice cream is cold, sugar tastes sweet, and so on).

*26. The brain stores and interprets information about sights, sounds, tastes, smells, and touches that people use again later.

*27. People often use more than one sense at a time.

*28. People describe sensory messages using different words. For example:

   a. How something looks may be described with words such as *bright, bumpy, dull, small, tall, red, pointed, straight, curved,* or *swollen.*

   b. How something sounds may be described with words such as *loud, quiet, soft, hollow, hoarse, sharp,* or *squeaky.*

   c. How something smells may be described with words such as *sweet, musty, pungent, minty, fruity, fragrant,* or *fishy.*

   d. How something tastes may be described with words such as *sweet, sour, salty, spicy,* or *peppery.*

   e. How something feels may be described with words such as *soft, hard, leathery, rough, mushy, bumpy, sandy, gummy, sticky, smooth,* or *slick.*

*29. People like different sensations; not all people like the same *sights, sounds, tastes, smells,* or *touches.*

Protecting the Senses

30. People's sensory organs are very important parts of their bodies and should be protected from injury.

*31. People can protect their eyes against harmful rays from the sun by wearing sunglasses and avoiding looking directly into the sun.

*32. Wearing goggles while working with tools or when swimming offers protection from tiny bits of wood, glass, sand, chemicals, or other harmful objects that may get into eyes.

*33. People who work around very loud sounds can protect their ears by using earplugs or ear coverings.

*34. To protect their skin from harm people wear clothing, use lotions and wear sunscreen.

Sensory Abilities and Impairments

*35. Some people have one or more senses that are especially sensitive. Some people have one or more poorly functioning senses. Some people have a sense that doesn't work at all; they have an impairment.

*36. Sensory impairments vary. For example:

   a. Some people can see only a little; they are visually impaired. Some cannot see at all; they are blind.

   b. Some people can hear only a little; they are hearing-impaired. Some cannot hear at all; they are deaf.

   c. Some people can sense smells a little. Some cannot smell anything.

   d. Some people can sense tastes a little. Some cannot taste anything.

*37. Many things can cause sensory impairments: an illness, being injured in some way, or being born with a special condition.

38. Some people who are visually impaired use glasses or contact lenses to help them see better.

*39. Some people cannot see, even with glasses. They may use other special aids such as a cane to get around safely, braille print to read and write, or a seeing-eye dog who helps lead them safely from place to place.

40. Some hearing-impaired people use hearing aids to help them hear better.

*41. Some people cannot hear, even with hearing aids. They use other ways to help them communicate with people such as lip reading, sign language, or finger spelling.

*42. Hearing people who learn to use sign language and finger spelling can communicate with deaf people more easily.

Aesthetic

1. Vegetable Fun

Give children an opportunity to experience the sensory aspects of a variety of vegetables. Gather a small collection of fresh vegetables; leave some whole for exploring the outside parts and cut others into bite-sized pieces for tasting. For sanitary purposes, have children wash their hands before they explore the food. Then, working with a small group at a time, encourage children to touch, smell and taste the various vegetables, emphasizing their sensory discoveries. For example, how does broccoli feel in their hands or when it is brushed against their cheek, what does the shape of a tomato remind them of, how many different colors can they see in a cabbage, and so on. Ask children to tell you what they notice about color, shape, smell, texture, and taste. Give each child an opportunity to taste the vegetables if they wish.

To Simplify:
● Use only a few vegetables, choosing ones familiar to the children.

To Extend:
● Include some vegetables with which the children are less experienced. Help children record their discoveries.

2. Beautiful Sounds

Hang wind chimes near a window where breezes enter the classroom or hang them from a tree branch on the playground. Point out the pretty sounds they make when the wind blows and how lucky we are to be able to hear them. Other beautiful sounds that could be used in this activity include taped music, the sounds of birds singing, or a music box. To heighten their awareness of the sounds, suggest that children first cover their ears and try to hear the chimes, and then listen again without covering their ears.

3. Bread Day

Bake one or more loaves of bread at school, pointing out the pleasurable sensory experiences this brings about. Point out the sight of the rising dough, the smells of the bread baking, the texture of the crust, and the taste of the fresh bread right out of the oven. Discuss which sensory organ they are using to appreciate each sensation. Offer children soft margarine or jelly to spread on their slices.

Hint for Success:

● If there is no oven available, use half the recipe and bake in a portable toaster oven or bake the bread at home and bring it to school while it is still hot.

Perfect White Bread

1 package active dry yeast

1/4 cup water

2 cups milk, scalded

2 Tablespoons sugar

2 teaspoons salt

1 Tablespoon shortening

6 to 6 1/4 cups sifted flour

Soften the yeast in warm water. Combine the hot milk, sugar, salt, and shortening. Cool to lukewarm. Stir in 2 cups flour. Beat. Add the softened yeast and mix. Add enough remaining flour to make a moderately stiff dough. Place the dough on a floured surface and knead 8 to 10 minutes (till satiny). Shape into a ball. Place dough in a greased bowl, turning once to coat the surface. Let the dough rise in a warm place until it is double in size (about 1-1/2 hours). Punch down. Repeat rising (about 45 minutes). Cut dough in two pieces, shaping each into a ball. Cover and let rest 10 minutes. Shape into two loaves, placing each into a greased loaf pan. Cover and let rise about 1 hour. Bake at 400° for 35 minutes or till done. Cover tops with foil the last 20 minutes if browning too fast. Enjoy slightly warm.

To Simplify:

● Use frozen bread dough and follow package directions for baking.

To Extend:

● Prepare bread-shaped papers for children to use in dictating or listing the senses they used during this activity.

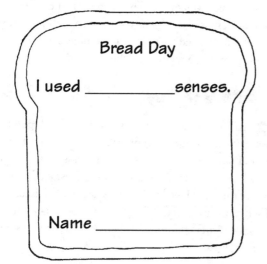

Bread Day

I used _____ senses.

Name _____

4. Popping Corn

Use the experience of popping popcorn as a way to point out the senses children use every day. Let children see and touch the kernels both unpopped and popped; point out the smell of the fresh corn as it pops. Have children listen for the sound of the kernels bursting in the popper. And finally, let them taste the snack. Then conduct a discussion of all the ways the children used their senses to enjoy this treat. A variation on this activity is to hide the corn popper as it pops the corn. Place it under a box or behind a shelf and surprise the children's senses.

5. Shaving Cream Squish

Ask children if they have ever seen shaving cream; discuss what it's used for and who uses it in their families. Squirt a dab of shaving cream on a slick table surface in front of each child so that eveyrone can explore the sound, look, texture, and smell. As they experiment, ask children questions about the various sensations they are noticing. On another day, offer two kinds of shaving cream—one that is scented and one that is not. Ask children to tell what they notice.

Hint for Success:

● Remind children that even though it looks good enough to eat, shaving cream is not food.

6. Smell This Modeling Dough

Make homemade modeling dough and divide it into several pieces, adding food coloring to make it different colors. Find liquid food flavorings in a cake decorating section of the local grocery store (such as lemon, cherry, lime, orange, and so on). Match the appropriate flavor to the colors you have chosen for the dough. As children play with the dough, ask them to use two of their senses, sight and smell, to appreciate the variations.

Soft and Easy Modeling Dough Recipe

Boil 2 scant cups water with 1/2 cup salt.

While hot, add 2 Tbsp. salad oil

2 Tbsp. alum

2 cups flour

Mix the ingredients until a firm dough forms. Turn the dough out onto a table with a light dusting of flour. When the dough is cool enough to touch, knead for about 5 minutes. Divide the dough and add food colorings; knead again. Add flavorings and knead in a few drops at a time until the odors are strong enough to notice.

Affective

1. Favorite Flavor Chart

Provide a simple food that nearly everyone likes and that comes in various flavors. Carry out a taste-testing activity that focuses on children choosing the flavor they like best. Clear gelatin can be made using various fruit juices to obtain different flavors. Cut the solid gelatin into tiny squares so children can have one of each flavor. After they taste, ask each child to place a sticker on a chart showing which was their favorite. Point out and discuss with the whole group the similarities and differences. Count how many like each flavor the best.

Fruity Gelatin Squares

Soften one tablespoon of granular unflavored gelatin in 1/2 cup orange juice (or some other distinct fruit juice). Heat 1-1/2 cups juice to boil, add the softened gelatin and stir until dissolved. Pour into small molds, dishes, or muffin tins. Chill until set.

2. My Hands Can Feel

Encourage children to experiment with all the things they can do with their hands to make them feel different ways. Suggest they try rubbing their hands together, clapping them hard, putting their hands first in very warm water and then in very cold water, and finally feeling a mixture of mud or cornstarch and water. After each part of the experiment, ask the child to discuss how their hands feel and whether or not they like that feeling.

3. Do You Like This Taste?

To encourage children to explore similarities and differences among people, select five or six foods for tasting that are interesting and vary in taste (such as apples, grapes, bananas, sour pickles, lemons, salty pretzels, potato chips, and so on). Divide the foods into individual tasting portions. Remind children that the sense of taste helps us know more about what foods are like, but not everyone likes the same taste. Tell children they are going to get to taste some different foods today and see who likes what. Proceed slowly, passing out individual portions of one food at a time. Tell children what each item is and suggest they taste it. Ask them to tell each other what they think of each kind of food. Give

children the option of swallowing or spitting out unwanted tastes onto their napkins. Help individual children notice that their opinions are similar or different from others in the group: "Jacob, you and Rosealie really like that banana. Jacob, I noticed you didn't care for the prune. Rosealie, you really liked it."

Hints for Success:

● Check your class records for anyone who has food allergies before trying this activity.

● As unfamiliar foods are passed around the circle, encourage children to try them, but do not insist that they taste everything. (Note: a small piece of bitter baking chocolate may be used for the fourth taste, but most children will not like it, so using this last is advisable.)

To Simplify:

● Use only very common foods—ones with which children are likely to be familiar. Work with a pair of children at a time.

To Extend:

● Offer foods that are likely to be new to children and repeat the exercise. To eliminate color as a way of choosing favorites, try using a variety of same colored foods (such as red foods—tomatoes, strawberries, cherries, gumdrops, and so on).

Cognitive

1. How Could You Tell?

Ask a volunteer to be blindfolded in front of the group. Give him or her an object to hold, such as an apple. Caution other children not to tell what it is. Ask the child to guess what he or she is holding. After the child guesses correctly, ask how she or he knew what it was. Point out all the senses he or she was using to identify it without seeing it. Write the name of the object and the senses that were used to identify it on a chart. Repeat the game with other volunteers and other objects.

To Simplify:

● Choose very familiar objects that have obvious distinctive textures, odors, or shapes.

To Extend:

Give each child two objects that are very similar and challenge him or her to tell which is which. Examples of pairs of similar objects are: an orange and a lemon, a ball and an egg, a pencil and a marker.

2. Texture Tubs

To give children experiences in attending to tactile sensory characteristics and distinguishing physical textures of objects, arrange a series of basins or dishpans, each containing a different kind of material. Choose materials with distinctive textures such as feathers, marbles, sand, Styrofoam pellets, cotton balls, tiny stone pebbles, and so on. Encourage children to touch the various textures with their hands. Next, highlight the fact that skin is sensitive all over the body by having children feel the textures with their elbows or bare feet.

To Simplify:

● Have only two tubs that children can touch and compare.

To Extend:

● To enhance the sense of touch, eliminate visual clues by giving children blindfolds to wear, or suggesting they close their eyes while touching the textures.

3. Smell and Tell

Create a game in which children identify objects using their sense of smell. Choose things that have a distinctive odor such as flowers, peanut butter, orange slices, chocolate, an onion, or peppermint. Find or make a picture of each of the objects. Place the samples into opaque containers with tight-fitting lids and holes for sniffing the contents; metal spice shakers or empty film canisters with small holes punched in the lids work well. Show the children the pictures, and ask that they name the objects. Then tell children that the smell of each object will help them figure out what's hidden in each container. Without opening the containers, suggest they try to match the smells to the pictures.

To Simplify:

● Use only a few very familiar items.

To Extend:

● Incorporate a greater number of smells in the activity, including less familiar ones such as rubber, wood shavings, grass clippings, or soap.

● Instead of or in addition to providing pictures, print out the names of objects on cards for children who are ready for this word-recognition variation.

● Have pairs of children work together; have one mix up the containers while the other closes his or her eyes and then makes the matches. Switch roles and repeat.

4. Seriating Textures

Give children a wide variety of fabric samples cut into pieces the same size and shape. Encourage children to touch them, exploring and feeling the various textures. After they have explored the pieces, ask one child at a time to choose a fabric sample that has an outstanding characteristic. (Children may focus on color or roughness, smoothness, holes, or other characteristics.) Since there is no one right answer, ask the child to tell you what she or he has focused on; then tell her or him to line the samples up in order from the most of that attribute to the least of it (such as most colorful to least colorful).

To Simplify:

● Demonstrate the process using a characteristic that's obvious; for example, "I noticed this one has a lot of stripes on it, so I'll put that first. Now I'll find some others that have stripes and put them in order from most to least stripes."

To Extend:

● Challenge the children to find as many different ways to seriate the materials as they can. Make a list or draw a record of all the combinations created.

5. My Senses Book

Plan the following series of sensory experiences on separate days. After each sensory observation, provide children with materials to make a page for their own "Senses Book." Provide a symbol of the particular sense to use as a header for each page, and encourage children to illustrate their accompanying sensory experience (described below). Later, laminate the pages and bind them together into individual books that focus on things children have experienced firsthand. Give children lightweight poster board to make covers for their books. Suggest they share their completed books by passing them around and reading each others' books.

a. For the "I See" page: Arrange a looking table with hand lenses, a microscope, a mirror, binoculars, color paddles, and so on, along with interesting objects such as a plant with flowers, beautiful rocks, worms in a jar, and so on. Encourage children to examine their own skin, face, clothing, or objects that are far away using the sight-enhancing tools provided.

b. For the "I Hear" page: Arrange an area with musical instruments, a keyboard, a tape recorder with tapes of sounds, and various kinds of music.

c. For the "I Touch" page: Provide a variety of textures to feel including fabrics, sand, corrugated cardboard, foil, animal fur, wood, and so on.

d. For the "I Taste" page: Have the children make a big mouth with a tongue. Give children small samples of a variety of foods to taste such as (sweet) apple, carrot or strawberry, (sour) lemon or pickle, (salty) cracker, pretzel, peanut, and so on.

e. For the "I Smell" page: Prepare a set of "smelly jars" using small baby food jars covered with adhesive paper to disguise the contents. Punch holes in the covers and place things with strong odors inside, such as pickles, onion, peanut butter, hand lotion, shaving cream, cinnamon, and lemon. Secure the jar covers with tape.

To Simplify:
● Suggest children find pictures in magazines for each page of their book.

To Extend:
● Add one or more pages called "I Use All My Senses." Brainstorm ideas from the children about places they went or experiences they have had when they used all of their senses at the same time.

● Add a page called "I Use My Senses at Home." Send the book home for children to complete with their families.

6. A Sensory Walk

Take the children on a walk outdoors to help them become better observers and to help them focus on the sensory aspects of their environment. At first, tell them to look for things with their eyes and describe what they see. Get things started by pointing out some things you see along the walk, such as the color of the sky, the clouds, the vegetation, and tiny insects. Ask the children to describe other things they see. Then, ask children to notice anything they smell; help them note the smells of the air, grass, trees, leaves, any pollution evident, and so on. Continue with all the senses in the same way. For example, ask children to listen for cars, airplanes, birds, dogs, wind, and so on. To focus on the sense of touch, choose interesting textures for children to feel—trees, grass, sidewalk, bushes, stones, and so on. The children's sense of taste can be utilized by bringing along a snack for them to eat. Plan a snack that contains things that have various tastes, smells, colors, and textures, such as fresh carrot sticks, apples, cherry tomatoes, raisins, or nuts.

7. Protection Plus

To focus on ways people protect their senses, prepare five large cards, each one illustrating one of the five sensory organs (eyes, ears, nose, mouth, an arm with hand), and a collection of protection devices, such as sunscreen, earplugs, swim goggles, working goggles, sunglasses, gloves, a shirt with sleeves, and a hat. Keep all of the materials out of sight at first. Start by telling a story about a time you didn't protect one of your senses—for example, when you didn't bring your sunglasses along on a sunny day or didn't protect your hands while using tools. Explain what happened and what you should have done to protect yourself. Ask children to tell about a time when something similar happened to them or someone in their family. Then show the children each of the sensory organ picture cards. Ask them to name the sense organ, and brainstorm ideas about ways people protect each sense: for example, "What are some ways we protect our ears so we can hear? How do people protect their eyes?" Next, show the collection of protection devices and discuss each one, demonstrating how it is used. Allow children time to look and touch. Then have children take turns placing each one in front of the correct sensory organ card.

To Simplify:
● Use only the senses that actually have objects associated with their protection—eyes, ears, and skin.

To Extend:
● Challenge children to think of other ways they protect their sensory organs, such as their tongues or their noses.

8. What a Surprise

Surprise children's senses with balls of homemade modeling dough of various colors, that have very different smells than what they might expect by looking at them (for example, red modeling dough that smells like blueberry, or brown dough that smells like lemon). Use the recipe for "Soft and Easy modeling dough" on page 64. Introduce the activity by telling children they can make things with the dough, but they should not mix the colors together. As they handle it, ask children to tell what they notice about the modeling dough. If they don't notice the different smells, suggest they sniff it. Watch their surprise! Then ask what they thought they would smell.

To Simplify:
● Choose flavors that are commonly known by young children.

To Extend:

● Make a similar game using incorrect sight and sound combinations. Gather a collection of objects that make familiar sounds (bell, drum, triangle, whistle, and so on). Take pictures of them and lay the pictures out in a row on the floor. Have the actual objects behind a flannelboard. Tell children to point to a picture, then make the wrong sound for that picture. For example, if the child points to a drum, play a bell! Ask children to tell you why they're surprised.

Construction

1. Build with Wet Sand or Snow

Bring wet sand or snow into the classroom water table or encourage children to use these materials outside. Emphasize the feel and look of the wet sand or snow and how it packs well. Demonstrate how to press it into a container (bowl, plastic freezer container, or an empty butter container) and then unmold a shape. Placing the shapes near or on top of each other makes the wet sand or snow a building medium that can be used to construct a variety of things. Suggest children use this material alone or in a group to make things. Brainstorm ideas of the things children could make stacking sand or snow shapes together (houses, cars, castles, food, monsters, mountains, islands, and so on).

2. My Touch-Tone Phone

Telephones are good examples of instruments that require people to use their senses together (hearing, touch, and sight). Introduce children to the look and sound of a touch-tone phone by bringing one from home. If possible, plug it into a phone jack in the classroom to demonstrate the sounds each button makes. If this is not possible, tape record the sounds of each button as you say the number and play the tape for the class. Point out the numerals and symbols that are on the phone—the receiver (part for listening) and the speaking part. Explain that the children can make their own pretend telephones using various materials. Provide construction paper, small boxes, paper tubes, scissors, the appropriate numerals and symbols, glue, and tape. Encourage children to use their imaginations and create the kind of telephones they want. Avoid making a model for them to copy, as this will greatly limit their creativity.

To Simplify:

● Provide simple telephone shapes that children could trace and then decorate any way they want.

To Extend:

● Discuss ways blind, deaf, or physically disabled people can use a telephone. Encourage children to add devices to their creations to accommodate the needs of people who cannot see or hear.

Language

1. All the Better to See You with, My Dear

Obtain a copy of the wonderful book *All the Better To See You With* by Margaret Wild (1992) to illustrate how things look to people who are nearsighted, a common eye problem. After the story, ask children why they think the little girl didn't realize she had a vision problem. (The busy people around her don't notice.) Turn back to the pages that show the way Kate saw before she had glasses and compare them to the pages showing the way she saw after she had glasses. Then give children an opportunity to experience poor vision by providing them with "distortion viewers" to look through. Tell them this is how things might look to some people who don't see well. Point out that glasses made Kate's vision much better, and she could finally notice things around her that she never saw before. Another book about a similar topic is Ellen Raskin's *Spectacles* (1988).

Making A Distortion Viewer

Cut a rectangle of cardboard approximately 4" x 8" and make an opening 2" x 6" on the inside of the rectangle. Tape two pieces of clear plastic wrap over the opening. Look through the opening at the world around you.

Hint for Success:

● Avoid making the viewers look or feel like glasses, as this can confuse children into thinking glasses make people's vision worse.

To Simplify:

● Make several viewers with varying degrees of distortion by using additional layers of plastic wrap. Number the viewers so you will be able to have children experience vision from bad to worse.

To Extend:

● Read Estelle Condra's *See the Ocean* (1994), about a young girl who is blind but who "sees" with her other senses.

2. This Is Braille

Demonstrate how it is not possible for a visually impaired person to read regular books. Blindfold an adult who usually reads to the children and ask him or her to read a book aloud. Discuss the problem the person is having. Then explain that a person who can't see letters and words can still read and write with special print called braille. If possible, obtain real samples of braille writing from the public library or the local association for the blind. (Braille can also be simulated by punching holes into stiff paper using an ice pick or similar sharp instrument.) Show children the samples. Demonstrate how a visually impaired reader can use the tiny dots to feel the words, just like some people use visual symbols to read words. The bumps of braille print are arranged in recurring patterns that represent letters and numerals.

Hint for Success:

● Young children who don't read may have a difficult time understanding the relationship between sight and reading, since they have never done it themselves. Demonstrate the importance of sight by showing a picture book that has the pages covered by black paper; ask children to tell what the book is about.

To Simplify:

● Use the braille alphabet to make the first letter in each child's name.

To Extend:

● Suggest each child make a kind of braille letter or numeral of their choice using a square of cardboard, a marker, and a collection of plastic-headed thumbtacks. Draw the letter or numeral carefully and show children how to press tacks into the line and pull them out, leaving holes on the bottom. When finished, they should be able to close their eyes and feel the bumps forming the shape of the letter or number. Challenge children to feel two braille letters and determine which is their own, without looking at them.

● Teach children some real braille symbols that may be meaningful. If possible, get a braille machine and make individual name cards with the children's names printed on one end and pressed in braille on the other.

3. Smell Talk

Offer children the opportunity to explore a variety of distinctive smells. Collect objects and substances that have interesting scents, such as leather, musk aftershave lotion, pine needles, cinnamon sticks, and fresh mint leaves. After children sniff the items, ask them to use a variety of words to describe these smells. Record children's ideas either by taking dictation or with a tape recorder. Invite children to add to the collection throughout the week by adding items and recording their impressions. Go over the items and records periodically, noting similarities and differences among the objects and descriptions.

To Simplify:

● A simple way to obtain a collection of interesting smells is to purchase markers that also feature smells (cherry, lemon, and so on). Younger children will give one-word responses or characterize the smell as good or bad. Encourage them to say more by using open-ended questions such as "What does that remind you of?" or "Where were you when you smelled this smell before?"

To Extend:

● Some odors are unhealthy for people to smell. Ask children to think of and make a list of things that have smells that signal danger. Suggest to parents that they talk to their children about things that may be on this list (such as gasoline, some kinds of glue, hair spray, charcoal lighter, or smoke).

4. Skinnamarink

Explain that people who can't hear usually have difficulty speaking too. Some hearing-impaired people learn to use gestures or signs to substitute for spoken words. Teach children to sing the traditional children's song "Skinnamarink." Use gestures for each of the lines in the song as indicated.

♫ **Skinnamarink**

Skinnamarink-a-dink-a-dink, (*turn hands*)*

Skinnamarink-a-do, (*change, turn hands the opposite way*)

I love you. (*point to self, cross arms, point to friend*)

Skinnamarink-a-dink-a-dink, (*turn hands*)*

Skinnamarink-a-do, (*change, turn hands the opposite way*)

I love you. (*point to self, cross arms, point to friend*)

I love you in the morning, (*cross arms, raise arms, hands touching*)

And in the month of June. (*point to calendar*)

I love you in the evening, (*cross arms, point up*)

Underneath the moon. (*form small moon with raised circle*)

Skinnamarink-a-dink-a-dink, (*turn hands*)*

Skinnamarink-a-do, (*change, turn hands the opposite way*)

I love you. (*point to self, cross arms, point to friend*)

I love you in the morning, (*cross arms, raise arms, hands touching*)

I love you in the night, (*cross arms, lay head on hands*)

I love you when I see you, (*cross arms, touch eye*)

I love you out of sight. (*cross arms, cover eyes*)

Skinnamarink-a-dink-a-dink, (*turn hands*)*

Skinnamarink-a-do, (*change, turn hands the opposite way*)

I love you.(*point to self, cross arms, point to friend*)

*Note: The gesture for skinnamarink is made by placing the left hand on the right elbow and turning the right hand back and forth. Change hands and repeat.

To Simplify:

● Sing only part of the song, at first without gestures. Repeat, adding only the turning gestures. Add more gestures as children become familiar with the song.

To Extend:

● After children have learned the song and gestures well, try humming the melody and using only the gestures as word indicators; challenge children to do the same. Sing the song fast.

● Another song that illustrates signing is "My Hat It Has Three Corners."

♫ My Hat It Has Three Corners

My hat, it has three corners,
Three corners has my hat.
And had it not three corners,
It would not be my hat.

Teach the signs for each of the major words first.

my= point to chest

hat= touch head

three= show three fingers

corners= index fingers form a triangle

Practice the song slowly, using the signs as the song indicates. After children are familiar with the words and motions, try leaving out a word, using only the gesture. Follow this by leaving out two words, then three, and so on, until the whole song is gestures only.

5. Sound Vibrations

Gather the following materials: a drum or tambourine, a sturdy inflated rubber balloon for each child, and a tuning fork. Explain that sounds are made by objects vibrating; sound vibrations enter our ears, vibrate the eardrum, and send sound messages to the brain. Ask children to pretend the drum is the eardrum inside a giant ear. Show how the drum sounds when you strike it and it vibrates. Use the tuning fork to demonstrate how sound can vibrate the eardrum in the ear. Say, "Here is something that makes very fast vibrations; it's called a tuning fork." Strike the tuning fork on your wrist and then place the handle end of it against the drum head. "If your ear is working well, the sound vibrations strike the eardrum and make it vibrate too, like this. Can you hear it?"

Use the balloons to simulate eardrums, too. Give each child an inflated balloon. Tell children to hold their balloons in front of their faces near their mouths. Show them how to make their balloons vibrate by humming on the side of the balloon. Suggest they experiment with various sounds to make the balloon vibrate a lot or a little. Try sounds such as "aaaa," "oooo," "eee," "mmmmm" and the sounds of hard consonants like B, P, T. Suggest children say words into their balloon to discover if that creates vibrations, too. Ask children to tell you what they discover.

To Simplify:

● Use one balloon and allow children to take turns making it vibrate.

To Extend:

● Have children hold their balloons on their ears, away from their mouths. Move from child to child, striking the tuning fork and bringing it near each balloon. Ask children if they can hear anything and explain what they think is happening.

Physical

1. Light Touch

Introduce the idea that our skin can sense touch all over our body, even very light touches. Use a feather to demonstrate on your own body. Ask a child volunteer to close his or her eyes and tell which body part is being lightly touched with a feather that you handle. Another variation is to have the children work in pairs, taking turns being the one who touches and the one who is touched.

Hint for Success:

● Children may not want anyone to touch them. Respect their wishes, pointing out to the group that everyone has the right to say no.

2. Parachute Listening Games

U se a parachute for group fun and to stimulate the children's sense of hearing. Remind children that to do well, they have to really listen in order to know what everyone should do at the same time.

Hints for Success:

● The games listed below are in order of difficulty and should be taught in this sequence since the signals given children in later games utilize signals taught in earlier games.

● Monitor the children's level of energy. More than two or three games can tire young children and are plenty at one time.

Cooperative Parachute Games

a. **Ripples and Waves.** Start with the children and adult assistants sitting on the floor or ground in a circle, everyone holding an edge of the parachute in her or his lap. Stretch the parachute to its fullest size. Explain that you are going to give the signals and everyone will do the same thing at the same time. The signals in this game are: Ripples = little up and down movements, Waves = bigger up and down movements, and Stop = hold the parachute still. Demonstrate the three signals. Praise children for listening well. Tell them to get ready for the game to start and to listen for the signals they know. Say, "Pretend the parachute is water. It's very calm and still; then the water starts to make Ripples, then Waves, Ripples, Waves, Ripples, Stop." Repeat the game with the group standing up.

b. **Rolling the Ball.** Repeat the game of "Ripples and Waves," but add a lightweight ball to roll around on the parachute. Use the same three signals.

c. **Popping Corn.** Teach children new signals for a game of pretend popping corn. Pop Slow = bounce the balls up and down slowly, Pop Fast = bounce the balls up and down fast. Practice the signals. Praise children's listening. Then ask children to stand and begin playing: "Let's pretend the parachute is a giant popcorn maker. It's starting to get hot. Let's pour in the popcorn (shake a number of small balls into the parachute). Pop Slow, Pop Fast, Pop Slow, Pop Fast, Stop. Now let's pretend to eat the popcorn. Yummy."

d. **Hi, Friends!** In this game the group tries to make the parachute go up so high that children and adults can look at everyone and call "Hi, Friends" before it comes down. Teach the children two new signals for this game. Way Up = raise the parachute up with arms straight over your head; Way Down = lower the parachute to the floor. Then ask children to stand and begin playing: "Let's pretend this parachute is a big balloon that we can fill up with air and float so high that we can look under it and see our friends. Way Down, Way Up, look at everybody and shout, Hi, Friends! Way Down. Stop. That was fun."

e. **Trading Places.** This game is very similar to "Hi, Friends!" except when the parachute is up, two children run under the parachute, exchanging places. Teach the group the signal: (two names) Trade Places = those two children should run under the parachute and take each other's place in the circle. Be aware that children will be excited to have their turn and some will have a very hard time waiting for their name to be called. If necessary, call four children at a time, to make the waiting shorter. Ask children to stand and begin playing: "Let's pretend that two friends live across the street from each other and want to trade houses. Way Down, Way Up (Jeff and Sara Trade Places, Philip and Michael Trade Places, Zachary and Amy Trade Places, Omar and Lennie Trade Places), Way Down, Stop. Good listening, everyone."

f. **Make a Mountain.** In this game the group makes the parachute fill up with air, as in "Hi, Friends!" above, but then they trap the air by kneeling on the edge of the parachute, forming what looks like a mountain that slowly collapses. Teach children a new signal for this game. Mountain = kneel on the edge of the parachute, trapping air inside. Demonstrate and practice. Then play: "Let's make this parachute into a great big mountain. Listen to my signals. Way Down, Way Up, Mountain. Stop. Good job!"

g. **Inside the Spaceship.** In this more difficult game, children trap air in the parachute and then bring the parachute down behind them, so everyone ends up inside the parachute. Teach the new signals: Behind the Back = bring the parachute down behind your back, Sit on it = sit on the edge of the parachute. Demonstrate and practice these two movements. Begin play with children standing: "Let's pretend the parachute is a spaceship that's getting ready to go out into outer space. We are the astronauts and have to get into our spaceship. Way Down, Way Up, Behind the Back, Sit on It, Stop. We did it!"

h. **Camping with Air Conditioning.** Children love to go under the parachute and have the adults hold the edges. If there are not enough adults to do this, allow half of the group of children to go under the parachute at a time, while the others help hold it up. New signals are: Children In = designated children may go under the parachute, Children Out = they all come out from under the parachute and hold on again. Describe the various movements, practice, and then play the game: "Let's pretend the parachute is a tent for camping. Only the (red group) will go camping this time. Way Down, Way Up, Children In, now go to sleep, listen to them snoring. Let's give them air conditioning Waves. Now wake up, Children Out. Great job, everyone. You are really using your hearing today."

i. **Parachute Sounds.** After children have had many experiences using the parachute as a group and are accustomed to hearing and responding to verbal signals, change the signals from words to sounds. Use an audio tape of sounds and teach children what the sounds mean: for example, soft music could signal moving the parachute slowly up and down (Ripples), a bell sound could signal to stand still (Stop), fast music could signal moving the parachute up and down quickly (Pop Fast), a whistle could signal holding the parachute low (Way Down), and a telephone ringing could mean holding it up high (Way Up). At first, practice the new sound signals with the added help of word commands. Play the tape and say the word signals that correspond to familiar actions. To further challenge children, play the tape without giving verbal commands, asking them to move the parachute in the way the sounds tell them to.

To Simplify:

● If no parachute is available, use a bed sheet or individual streamers made from strips of cloth attached to tongue depressors.

● Use real objects that children can see to produce the sounds.

● Limit the signals to two at the start and gradually add others.

To Extend:

● Allow children to take a turn giving the signals, while others move the parachute.

3. Movement Sounds

To stimulate their sense of hearing and make the connection between physical movement and sounds, make sound-producing objects available as chil-

dren play outdoors, in a gym, or in a rainy-day room. Give children shakers, such as maracas, tambourines, or bells. Encourage children to try shaking these objects as they walk, run, or skip. Attach noisy tin cans or aluminum pie plates with strings to the backs of tricycles; encourage children to ride fast, slow, or over various surfaces to make different kinds of sounds. Place small bells on jumpropes to make this fun toy more exciting. Make simple rhythm instruments available for experimenting and encourage children to march or dance while they play.

4. Eyes Closed Movement

Discuss what it may be like for visually impaired people to try to do things for themselves. Simulate the lack of sight by suggesting activities children could try with their eyes closed, but with others nearby for assistance. Sample activities are: challenging experienced climbers to carefully climb with their eyes closed, rolling down a slight grade with eyes closed, coming down the slide with eyes closed, rocking on a large belly ball, slowly climbing stairs with eyes closed, trying to put on a jacket with eyes closed, washing hands with eyes closed, or walking on a low balance beam with eyes closed. Limit the number of children to one child at a time so everyone can be carefully monitored.

Pretend Play

1. Let's Play Bakery

After visiting a real bakery where children have had a chance to recognize wonderful sights and smells, organize an area containing props that suggest a bakery shop in the classroom. Reserve a place to roll out the pretend dough and make a rolling pin, cookie cutters, a pretend oven, aprons, and hats available; also arrange a place where customers come and buy the baked goods, and prepare signs that tell prices. Add illustrated signs that relate to the senses and display pictures of people using their senses to appreciate the bakery. Examples of appropriate signs are: "Smell the Bread Baking," "Look Over Our Delicious Cookies," "Taste the Fresh Donuts," "Watch Us Decorate Cakes." Supply the area with paper and pencil to take orders, a cash register, and plenty of playdough for dough. Encourage children to take on roles of bakers, customers, and salespeople.

2. Sensory Restaurant

Set up tables and chairs, trays, and plastic dishes for children to serve each other in a pretend restau-

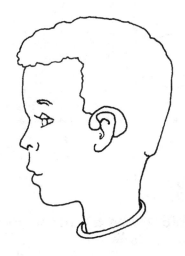

rant. Menus can be made from magazine pictures pasted onto cardboard; be sure to have pads of paper and pencils available for the wait staff to take orders from their customers. Plastic food, utensils, pictures of food on the walls, and small vases of flowers on the tables will make the area more fun and feel like a real restaurant. Demonstrate how a server might describe the tastes of various foods on the menu to customers. Encourage children to assume a variety of roles in the restaurant.

3. Audiologist/Optometrist

Describe what it's like to visit or take the class on a real visit to an audiologist or optometrist. Then arrange a simple area where the pretend audiologist can check ears and do pretend hearing tests and the pretend optometrist can check eyes and do pretend vision testing. Display pictures of the inside of an ear and the inside of an eye, a simple eye chart, a pretend hearing testing machine (earphones hooked up to a tape recorder with beeps, tones, or bells). Other appropriate props are pretend glasses and pretend hearing aids (made from cardboard) to hang over the ear. Suggest children take on roles of patient, audiologist, optometrist or assistant, and secretary.

Hint for Success:
● For safety, remind children that it is dangerous for them to put objects into anyone's eyes or ears. Make pretend glasses from cardboard. Safe pretend glasses can also be made by removing the glass from children's sunglasses. Safe pretend hearing aids can be made from cardboard that slips over the outer ear and doesn't enter the ear canal.

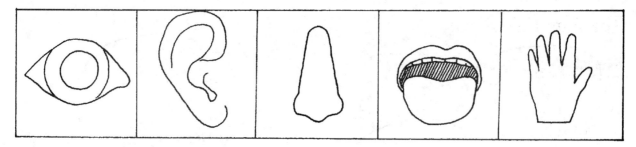

Social

1. We Write a Senses Story Together

Duplicate the picture symbols (illustrated above) indicating each of the five senses. Make several copies of each symbol, cut them apart, and place the symbols in a basket out of sight. Ask children to take turns, drawing out one of the symbols and telling a part of a group story using that sense symbol in their portion of the story.

To Simplify:

● Ask children questions that help prompt their ideas, such as "What did they see? What did the dog hear? How did it smell?"

To Extend:

● Write the story out as children make it up. Provide a glue stick to attach the sense symbols to the story paper in the appropriate places. For example:

Our Senses Story

Teacher: Once upon a time a girl and her father went on a walk together.

First child: They saw ( ) a great big dog with black fur.

Second child: They heard ( ) the dog barking.

Third child: Then they felt ( ) rain coming down.

Fourth child: The trees got wet and they smelled ( ) the leaves.

Fifth child: They decided to go to the ice cream parlor and tasted ( ) delicious chocolate ice cream. The End

2. Help Me Walk, Please

After discussing visual impairment, encourage children to help a partner move through a maze or obstacle course by holding an arm out for him or her to hold. Teach the helper to use verbal directions and ver-

bal encouragement to get his or her partner through without bumping into something. Simulate the condition of being visually impaired by offering children blindfolds to wear or sunglasses that are colored with black crayon on the outside surface. Suggest children take turns being the visually impaired person and being the helper.

3. Try to See Me in the Dark

To help children understand more about the way their eyes work better when light is present, arrange an activity in which pairs of children look at each other in a dark place. Seek an appropriately dark but safe space such as an interior hallway or an empty storage closet. If neither is available, bring in a cardboard box large enough for two children to fit in comfortably when it is closed. Once settled in this darkened place, suggest that children take turns making faces at their partner that show various emotions (sad, happy, afraid, silly, etc.) while their partner tries to name the emotion. Have children try the game again in the light. Ask what they discovered.

4. Make Juicy Pops

Purchase several flavors of frozen or dry juice mixes. Give children an opportunity to choose the flavor of juice they like; then divide the class into small groups according to the flavors they chose. Ask each group of children to help make Popsicles™ for their group to eat after they are frozen. Provide children with a tray containing: 3-4 oz. paper cups, tongue depressors, one large and one small pitcher, a large mixing spoon, juice mix (if frozen, thawed slightly), and water. Ask children to help decide how to divide up the work so that everyone participates and helps. Generate a list of tasks to help in the decisions. Talk children through the process of mixing up the juice and water in the large pitcher; you or another adult should transfer it to the small pitcher so children can help pour the juice into the cups. Put sticks in each cup and place them in the freezer. When the pops are frozen, have a treat together.

Teacher Resources

Field Trip Ideas

1. Visit a bakery shop for a sensory treat.
2. Visit the local restaurant for some looking, tasting, and smelling.
3. Visit a park for a walk and picnic; plan specific activities that focus on each of the senses.
4. Visit a hands-on museum and plan specific activities that focus on the children's sense of touch.
5. Visit a zoo, pointing out how we use our senses to appreciate the animals.

Classroom Visitors

1. Invite a person with a hearing impairment to visit the classroom to demonstrate how she or he communicates.
2. Invite a person who is visually impaired to visit the classroom to demonstrate how she or he accomplishes things.
3. Invite a vision or hearing technician to demonstrate a screening game used to check children's hearing or vision.

Children's Books

Aliki. (1962). *My Five Senses*. New York: HarperCollins.

Brown, M. (1986). *Arthur's Eyes*. New York: Little, Brown.

Brown, M. W. (1947). *Goodnight, Moon*. New York: HarperCollins.

Carle, E. (1986). *My First Book of Touch*. New York: Thomas Y. Crowell.

Condra, E. (1994). *See The Ocean*. Nashville, TN: Ideal Children's Books.

Evans, D., and Williams, C. (1992). *Me and My Body*. New York: Dorling Kindersley.

Litchfield, A. (1981). *A Button in Her Ear*. Morton Grove, IL: Albert Whitman.

Martin, B., Jr. (1983). *Brown Bear, Brown Bear, What Do You See?* New York: Henry Holt.

Pace, B. (1987). *Chris Gets Ear Tubes*. Washington, DC: Gallaudet University Press.

Peterson, J. W. (1977). *I Have a Sister, My Sister Is Deaf*. New York: HarperCollins.

Rankin, L. (1991). *The Handmade Alphabet*. New York: Dial Books for Young Readers.

Raskin, E. (1988). *Spectacles*. 2nd ed. New York: Macmillan.

Royston, A. (1993). *The Senses*. Hauppauge, NY: Barron's.

Rylant, C. (1988). *All I See*. New York: Orchard Books.

Showers, P. (1991). *Your Skin and Mine*. Rev. ed. New York: HarperCollins.

Showers, P. (1987). *Hearing*. Mahwah, NJ: Troll Associates.

Showers, P. (1987). *Smelling*. Mahwah, NJ: Troll Associates.

Showers, P. (1987). *Tasting*. Mahwah, NJ: Troll Associates.

Showers, P. (1987). *Touching*. Mahwah, NJ: Troll Associates.

Wild, M. (1992). *All the Better to See You With*. Morton Grove, IL: Albert Whitman.

Adult References

Ardley, N. (1992). *The Science Book of the Senses*. New York: Harcourt Brace Jovanovich.

Bornstein, H., and Saunier, K. (1984). *The Signed English Starter*. Washington, DC: Gallaudet University Press. (Note: Galludet University Press and Bookstores specialize in materials for people with hearing impairments. Call 1-800-451-1073.)

Butterworth, R., and Flodin, M. (1989). *Signing Made Easy*. New York: Putnam.

Cook, R., Tessier, A., and Klein, M. D. (1992). *Adapting Early Childhood Curricula for Children with Special Needs*. New York: Macmillan.

Costello, E. (1983). *Signing: How to Speak with Your Hands*. New York: Bantam Books.

Flodin, M. (1991). *Signing for Kids: The Fun Way for Anyone to Learn American Sign Language*. New York: Putnam Publishers.

Hafer, J., and Wilson, R. (1990). *Come Sign with Us: Sign Language Activities for Children*. Washington, DC: Gallaudet University Press.

Nickelsburg, J. (1976). *Nature Activities for Early Childhood*. Redding, MA: Addison-Wesley.

Orlick, T. (1978). *The Cooperative Sports and Games Book*. New York: Pantheon.

Safford, P. L. (1989). *Integrated Teaching in Early Childhood*. White Plains, NY: Longman.

Sternberg, M. (1990). *American Sign Language Dictionary*. New York: HarperCollins.

U. S. Office of Human Development Services. (1980). *Directory of National Information Sources on Handicapping Conditions and Related Services*. Washington, DC: Clearinghouse on the Handicapped.

Bodies in Action: Mobility and Immobility

Terms, Facts, and Principles (TFPs)

1. The human body is constantly in motion; even when at rest, the body is breathing and parts are working inside.

*2. Body parts (such as the bones, muscles, joints, nerves, and the brain) work together to help people be active and move.

3. People can move their body parts in many ways: bending, stretching, opening, closing, shaking, swinging, tapping, jabbing, wiggling, swaying, pointing, tightening, and relaxing.

4. Bodies can move while in various positions: laying, sitting, kneeling, crouching, or standing.

*5. People can move while in a lying position in many ways: by moving their head, arms, legs, and by rolling, twisting, bouncing, bending, twirling, thumping, shaking, squirming, and turning—alone or with someone.

*6. People can move from a sitting or kneeling position in many ways: by moving their arms, legs, or head and turning or twisting their torso—alone or with someone.

*7. People can move from a crouching position in many ways: by moving their arms, head, torso, bending, swaying, or using leg motions such as low walking, bouncing, or tapping—alone or with someone.

*8. People can move from a standing position in many ways: by moving their arms, head, or torso, bending, swaying, walking, sliding, bouncing, jumping, running, skipping, hopping, galloping, leaping, dancing, and other coordinated movements—alone or with someone.

9. People can make the same movements in different ways: fast, slow, heavy, light, strong, weak, flowing, long, or short.

10. Movements from different positions can be at various levels: for example, high waving, low waving, and middle-level waving.

11. Movements from different positions can be in various directions: forward, backward, diagonal, horizontal, and vertical.

12. Movements from different positions can be in various spatial patterns: circles, zigzags, over, under, around, through, and so on.

13. Some actions involve big movements: for example, large arm movements for pounding with a hammer, large brush strokes for painting, or wide sweeping motions with a broom.

14. Some actions involve small movements: for example, pressing fingers on a keyboard, making small marks with a pencil, or putting the cover on the toothpaste.

*15. Most people can move their bodies and learn to do active things (such as crawling, walking, jumping, running, bending, stretching, reaching and also picking up, catching, throwing, or striking objects), but some people cannot because of a disabling condition.

*16. When a person cannot move her or his body easily or at all, she or he has an impairment, a disability, or a handicapping condition.

*17. People with movement disabilities must learn to move in different ways; for example, if a person cannot walk, he or she may be able to learn to move using a walker or a wheelchair.

18. Some impairments can be changed and improved so the person's body parts work well again; some impairments cannot be changed, so the person has a permanent disability.

19. There are many different things disabled people can use to help them move and do things in their own way: braces, crutches, walkers, wheelchairs, artificial legs, artificial arms, artificial hands, mouth machines, and others.

20. People with disabilities are learning and growing have feelings and emotions, needs and desires like everyone.

21. People with disabilities want to have friends, have fun, and be treated with respect like everyone.

21. Sometimes a person with a disability wants help doing things; sometimes they want to do things by themselves.

*23. People are often curious about the ways that people with disabilities do things and use their bodies; people can learn about this by asking questions, reading about it, and watching.

24. Children can help people with disabilities in many ways: listening, smiling and being friendly, not letting others say unkind things about the person, and offering to help the person.

25. Grown-ups can help people with disabilities in many ways: making sure there is an elevator in buildings, making ramps available where there are stairs, putting special handicapped parking places close to buildings, and treating disabled people fairly.

Activity Ideas

Aesthetic

1. Artful Movement

To help children relate the idea of movement to graphic art, encourage them to move their bodies in various ways, making movements that are jumpy, bouncy, smooth flowing, sleepy, and so on. Then suggest they paint pictures using those same kinds of movements. Provide large paper, various kinds of brushes, and good clear tempera paints in various colors. Encourage children with motor impairments to participate as much as they can by suggesting various ways they can move from comfortable positions. Arrange art materials in ways that assure they can use them, too.

2. Un-Handed Art

Discuss the fact that some artists can't use their hands to draw or paint. Show some examples of mouth-painted pictures and, if possible, show photographs of the artist working. (Greeting card shops sometimes carry cards designed in this way.) Arrange for children to experience making art without using their hands. Let them think of ways to hold tools for this purpose and try out their ideas. Some ways you could suggest would be to hold the pencil (marker, crayon, etc.) between their toes, in their mouths, or in the bend of their elbows.

3. Create a Movement Dance

Explain that movements can be made in ways that show emotions such as happy, sad, afraid, angry, and so on. Demonstrate one or more of these movements. Make a tape recording of parts of musical selections without words that match the emotions you want to convey. Tape the selections so they run together and make one dance. Play the first part of the tape for the children and encourage them to move their bodies in a way the music makes them feel. Fast forward the tape to the next part and repeat the process. Continue until children hear samples of all of the kinds of music on the tape. Then, rewind the tape and suggest children move again, changing their movements when the music changes, thereby creating a dance that tells about feelings. Praise children for using their own ideas in expressing the emotions of the music.

Hint for Success:

● In making the tape, look for musical pieces that are obviously different from one another. Happy music can be light and bouncy like a music box; exciting-sounding music could be a rousing march; sad music could be played by a quiet violin or cello; angry music could be played by loud horns with crashing cymbals.

To Simplify:

● Tape only two kinds of music that contrast in obvious ways. Make the whole dance last only a short time.

To Extend:

● Use several musical selections, asking children to tell what emotion they are portraying with their bodies.

● Suggest children move in pairs with a movement partner. Give them time to plan together their movements to express various emotions.

Affective

1. Personal Exercise Plan

Discuss the importance of regular movement and of developing personal plans for stretching and exercising each day. Have children think of ways they get exercise during play (running, climbing, riding a bicycle, jumping rope, playing ball, and so on). Teach children some simple exercises such as sit-ups, jumping jacks, running in place, arm swings, and toe touches.

Make a chart that illustrates the exercises children know and suggest they set a daily goal for themselves. Set aside time for exercising at school each day. Always have children do some stretching to warm up their muscles before they exercise. Provide "smiley face" stickers to place near their names for those who reach their daily goals.

Simple Stretching Exercises

1. In a sitting position, stretch arms out to sides and reach from the waist first on one side and then the other.

2. Sit on the floor with legs together and reach for your toes.

3. Sit on the floor with legs together, point your toes, then flex your feet; repeat several times.

4. Sit on the floor with open legs; reach for the toes on the left foot and then the right.

5. Stand up, swing both arms up, and reach for the ceiling.

6. Stand with legs apart, place the right hand on the right hip, and swing the left arm up over the head. Alternate.

7. Stand with legs apart, hands on hips; crouch slightly, hold, and then stand up. Repeat.

8. Stand with hands on a wall, step back with one foot, heal up, heal down. Repeat. Change feet and repeat.

9. Stand on tiptoes, then down on flat feet; repeat several times.

2. Quiet Movement

Have children lie on the floor completely still. Suggest they place their hands on their chest, close their eyes, and feel the movement inside their own bodies. Point out how their chest is rising and falling with each breath; have them feel for the subtle movements of their heart beating and food digesting in their stomach.

3. My Right, My Left

Teach children a song about the right and left side of their bodies. This song can also be useful in stimulating children to dress themselves.

♫ My Right and Left Hokey Pokey
Words by Barb Rohde
Tune: "Hokey Pokey"

I put my right shoe on,
I take my right shoe off,
I put my right shoe on,
And I shake it all about.
I do the hokey pokey,
And I turn myself around,
That's what it's all about.

Personal Exercise Plan

I'll do ____ ☐ and ____ ☐

	Week 1	Week 2	Week 3	Week 4	Week 5	Week 6
Mon						
Tues						
Wed						
Thur						
Fri						

Name _____

Sing other verses using other pieces of clothing that go on right and left body parts, such as mittens, sleeves, pant legs, socks, shoes, or gloves.

Another chant that emphasizes left and right is:

Thumbkin Left and Thumbkin Right
(Traditional)

Thumbkin Left and Thumbkin Right, *(Hold up both thumbs)*

Saw each other late one night. *(Move thumbs together)*

Thumbkin Left said: "How are you?" *(Wag left thumb)*

Thumbkin Right said: "Fine! And you?" *(Wag right thumb)*

See them nod each sleepy head. *(Move thumbs apart, nod)*

Now each Thumbkin's gone to bed! *(Tuck thumbs under fingers)*

Cognitive

1. Jillions of Ways to Move

Show pictures of people moving in various ways. Ask children to generate a list of all the ways they can think that bodies move. Record their ideas on a long piece of paper or on individual papers that you place end-to-end in a display of movements. Invite children to imitate some of the movements.

2. Make the Difference

Suggest and demonstrate a simple locomotor movement such as walking. Then change a characteristic of that movement (such as walk more slowly, walk faster, walk on tiptoes, or walk down low in a crouch position) and ask children to tell how you changed the movement. Next, have them think of other ways to change the same movement and encourage them to demonstrate their suggestions, one at a time. Choose another locomotor movement (running, jumping, galloping, hopping, sliding, skipping, leaping) and repeat the game.

3. Movement Directions

Play a game in which children try to move in the directions the leader says. Line children up along a wall or fence. Tell the players to listen and then move the way the leader tells them to. Start with a single direction for movement; for example, tell everyone to walk one step forward, wait for the group to follow the direction, and then give another. Examples of other single directions for movements are:

> take one step backward
>
> turn around
>
> touch your toes
>
> march five steps
>
> stick out your tongue

To increase the challenge, give two directions for movements at a time, then three at a time, and so on. Examples of two directions for movements are:

> jump forward and turn around
>
> wave your hand and rub your stomach
>
> put your hands on your head and wiggle your hips
>
> clap your hands and take three steps forward

To Simplify:

● Adults give the directions to the players. Keep directions simple.

To Extend:

● Give more than two directions.

● Include movements that require coordination and consideration of left and right.

● After children have some experience with this game, invite them to take turns being the leader.

4. Other Ways to Move

Contact a doctor or other caregiver at a hospital or health clinic, requesting the loan of mobility aids used by people with handicapping conditions, such as a wheelchair, cane, pair of crutches, leg brace, and prosthesis. Invite a knowledgeable person to talk about the use of each piece of equipment with your group. Discuss guidelines for safety before inviting children to experiment with the equipment under supervision, of course. Arrange a path bordered by furniture or indicated by tape lines on the floor for children to follow as they move along using the aids.

5. Solve a Movement Problem

Select a simple task that could be accomplished in several ways (such as getting something off a high shelf). Ask children to brainstorm ideas on how a person

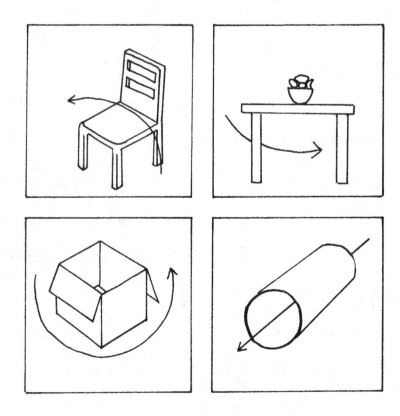

could get the object down. Make a list of their ideas. Choose a solution that is possible and safe and allow children to try it out. Then, ask small groups of children to think of all the ways the body had to move to accomplish the task. Have each group make a list of the body movements used and compare their list with those of other groups. Repeat the same activity but make it harder by not allowing children to use a body part (as if it's disabled). Challenge them to figure out a solution to this more difficult problem.

Construction

1. Make a Movement Path

Using small blocks and a doll, demonstrate a simple obstacle course that employs the movement directions: over, under, around, and through. Copy the large picture signs on page 79 (Over, Under, Around, Through), and mount them on heavy cardboard or posterboard. Show them to the children and ask them to guess what each one means. Then suggest that a small group of children arrange a life-sized obstacle course with obstacles that correspond to the movement signs. Challenge the group to select materials and create a course using furniture, large cardboard boxes, large blocks, a balance beam, and other appropriate and safe

equipment. Help them hang the signs in the appropriate places on the obstacle course; ask an adult to supervise and check their finished product for safety. Then encourage all of the children to use the obstacle course, following the directions given on the signs.

Hint for Success:
● Introduce directional words by reading *Rosie's Walk* by Pat Hutchins (1968).

To Simplify:
● Have children focus on one directional movement at a time.

To Extend:
● Suggest children move backwards through the path. Another time suggest they try moving around the course without using their hands (as if they were disabled).

2. My Moving Body Parts

To do this activity you will need construction paper of various colors that could represent skin tones, scissors, paper fasteners, and markers. Discuss the concept of joints in the human body. Have children find some of their own joints and feel the ways they can bend and move at those points. Then, using two simple con-

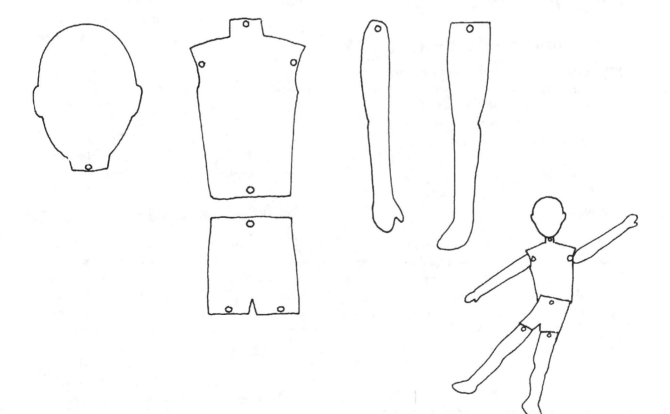

struction-paper shapes, show how paper fasteners can attach pieces that can move. Point out how these fasteners are similar to the joints in the human body (in the shoulders, elbows, knees, and so on). Encourage children to name some of the body parts that they could make and fasten together with paper fasteners (legs, arms, hands, head, and torso). Suggest that they make their own kind of person that moves. Offer children the materials and tools to make a body of their own design.

Hint for Success:

● Allow children to cut and design their own body parts using their own imagination and creativity. Avoid insisting on a realistic representation of the body. This should be their own invention, with the focus on creativity.

To Simplify:

● Prepare simple cardboard tracing forms that represent various body parts (head, torso, arm and hand, leg and foot, as illustrated on page 80).

To Extend:

● After children have designed their own person that moves, challenge them to arrange that body in a position and see if they can make their own body move like that.

Language

1. Don't Touch!

Discuss how people use their hands for many things. Then make a list of as many things as children can think of that they do with their hands. Talk about the fact that sometimes we want to handle things that we are not allowed to touch. Ask children to think of a time when this happened to them. Tell the children you are going to read a story showing what one little boy named Dan does about this problem. Suggest that they try to remember one thing he does. Then read *Don't Touch!* by Suzy Kline (1985). When you are done, ask children to recall what Dan wanted to touch but wasn't allowed to, and the various things he did with the clay; make a list of the children's ideas. Then check the book to see if they remembered them all. Follow up by providing children with clumps of modeling dough or clay and suggest that they do what they remember Dan did in the story.

2. Stories in Action

Purchase or make a set of flannelboard pieces that lend themselves to storytelling (people and objects that suggest interesting actions and movements). Include some aids that may be used by people with handicapping conditions. Ask children to play with the pieces, make up a story, and tell it to a friend. When they are ready, ask if they will tell their stories to you, and you will write them down. Ask leading questions to encourage each child to say more such as, "What are some things these people like to do? Tell me more about that. What does he/she do when that happens?"

3. Talk About Talk

Say a simple sentence to the children. Then point out all the parts of the face and mouth that move when a person talks. To emphasize how the lips and mouth are involved in communication, experiment with talking while the mouth remains closed, with the tongue laying immobile in the bottom of the mouth, or without moving the jaws. Ask children if they can understand what you are saying when you try talking in these ways. Suggest children work with a partner, one trying the different ways to talk and the other attempting to understand what they are saying. Then have them exchange roles.

To Simplify:

● Set up a mirror where children can watch themselves practice talking without moving their mouth or lips.

To Extend:

● People can talk if they are unable to move their mouth or lips by using sign language. Teach children some basic signs from the American Sign Language that are not too difficult—ones they could use with each other such as "Hello, I like you, can I play?"

4. Show Me a Story

Gather a collection of familiar objects that suggest motions, such as a hat, cup, spoon, clock, telephone, shovel, book, and so on. Place the materials on a nearby tray. Explain that you are going to tell a story using only gestures. Point to the props and ask the children to tell what each one is, and what a person can do with it. Invite children to watch and try to figure out what the story is. They should also try to recall some of the movements you used to tell the story. Demonstrate a simple short story, using one of the props in your collection.

Hello

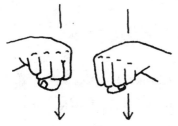

Can

I

Play

I

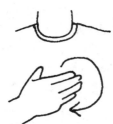

Like

You

Pretend to sleep, wake up and stretch, have a cup of coffee or tea (using the cup and spoon), eat a breakfast, wave good-bye, and leave.

Ask children to remember a movement you used to tell the story. Suggest that everyone try to imitate that movement.

To Simplify:
● Use one or two gestures to give an idea, but do not tell a whole story. Suggest that children tell the story out loud with words as they figure it out.

To Extend:
● Invite children to add to the collection of props

and volunteer to be the next storytellers. Remind the storyteller not to use words, but to simply use movements and gestures to act out the story. Praise children for participating and using their bodies to show the story.

Physical

1. Move Those Hands and Arms

Teach children songs and chants that encourage them to use their arms and hands in many ways. Encourage children to sing and move at the same time.

♫ **Swimming Song**

Author unknown
Tune: "Sailing, Sailing, Over the Bounding
Main"

> Swimming, swimming, in the swimming pool,
> When days are hot, when days are cool,
> In the swimming pool.
> Back stroke, side stroke, fancy diving too,
> Don't you wish you never had,
> Anything else to do.

♫ **Two Little Blackbirds (Chant)**

> Two little blackbirds, sitting on a hill, *(Fingers on shoulders)*
> One named Jack and one named Jill. *(Fingers wave)*
> Fly away Jack, fly away Jill, *(Fly hands behind back)*
> Come back Jack, come back Jill. *(Return hands to the front)*
>
> Two little blackbirds, sitting on a cloud, *(Fingers on shoulders)*
> One named Quiet and one named Loud. *(Fingers wave)*
> Fly away Quiet, fly away Loud, *(Fly hands behind back)*
> Come back Quiet, come back Loud. *(Return hands to the front)*

Continue in the same rhyming pattern, using opposites for the blackbirds.

♫ **My Fingers Are Starting To Wiggle**

Author unknown
Tune: "The Bear Went Over the Mountain"

> My fingers are starting to wiggle,
> My fingers are starting to wiggle,
> My fingers are starting to wiggle,
> Wiggle all around.
>
> My arms are starting to wiggle,
> My arms are starting to wiggle,
> My arms are starting to wiggle,
> Wiggle all around.

Continue in the same way, substituting different body parts that can move.

2. Going Lots of Ways

Arrange several large pictures facing each other on opposite sides of the classroom, gym, or outdoor play yard. Number the pictures so they establish a series of stations that children can move to. Tell children they are going to play a moving game, moving from one picture to the next, but getting there using various movements. Place one child at each picture and give them each a different movement to announce. For example, at the starting picture, children are told to "Walk" to the next picture; at the next picture, children are told to "Jump" to the next picture, and so on. Other movements that could be used are: hop, skip, gallop, run, and crawl. Invite the children to practice moving in various ways as they go from station to station.

3. A Disarming Game

Explain that some people don't have the use of their arms because of a disabling condition. For those who are interested in experiencing this handicap, slip a medium-sized tee-shirt over each child's clothes, keeping their arms inside to simulate the inability to use those body parts. Suggest children play and work for awhile in the classroom wearing this disabling shirt, asking for help when they need it, but doing what they can for themselves. Later, ask them to tell what were the most difficult tasks for them to accomplish and what they were able to do without assistance.

4. Funny Walks

To provide practice in the fundamental motor skill of walking, play bouncy music and encourage children to follow your lead by: walking briskly, on tiptoes, with toes in, with toes out, using baby steps, taking giant steps, stamping hard, and crouching down low.

5. The Tail Game

To encourage practice in running and other movement, teach children to play the tail game. Provide everyone with a pretend tail (a strip of cloth) that they can push into his or her waistband or back pocket, allowing most of the tail to hang behind. Explain that they are all animals moving through the forest in various ways. Along comes the fox who has lost his or her tail (a person with no cloth strip). The fox tries to replace his tail by pulling one off another animal. The other animals try to stay away from the fox, but keep moving around the forest. When the fox is successful, he or she puts the new tail in place, turns into another animal, and can move around the forest with the other animals. The person without a tail then becomes the fox and the game continues.

6. Hopscotch Jumping

Draw one or more hopscotch boards on the floor or sidewalk using sidewalk chalk or bright colored plastic tape to make the spaces. (There are many ways to make the board; variations to this traditional game can be found in cultures around the world.) Encourage children to use the board(s) to jump and play their own version of hopscotch.

Pretend Play

1. A Special Family Member

Secure a large doll into a small chair and attach pretend cardboard wheels to the chair sides with string or wire. Two large wheels toward the back and small ones near the front will give the appearance of a wheelchair. Add this to the housekeeping pretend play area. Tell children this is a family member who cannot walk because of a disabling condition. Encourage children to teach the person with a disability how to do things and care for him- or herself in the home.

2. Exercise Spa

Arrange an area of the classroom as an exercise spa with mats, pretend weights for lifting, and pictures of people doing exercises. Add tape-recorded music that encourages children to move. Hang pictures of exercise routines at children's eye level and help them interpret what the pictures tell them to do.

3. Galloping Away

To provide children with practice using a fundamental motor skill, play a pretending game in which children are horses. Talk about the way horses move when they gallop and demonstrate galloping (keeping one foot in front, draw the back foot up to the front, but not past it; then move the front foot forward again; repeat the movement). Suggest children take on roles of horses that are galloping up to the mountain top (across the room or playground), eating some delicious grass (chew like horses do), then returning to the corral (galloping back) at the bottom of the mountain. Give children verbal cues indicating when to move. Praise them for participating.

To Simplify:
- Keep distances short and focus on participation, not performing the galloping skill with accuracy.

To Extend:
- Vary the game by suggesting galloping in various ways (fast, slow, high, low). Change to other movements such as running, tiptoeing, walking, or sliding.

4. Imagine and Move

Use imagery to help children use their bodies in creative ways. Explain that people can imagine something in their minds and use their bodies to form that thought. Give a simple example, "Imagine you are as light as a feather and floating on the wind." Encourage children to close their eyes and think about the feather floating, then have them get up and move the way they think the feather would move. Remember there are no wrong ways to move—what you imagine may not be what the child imagines. Here are some examples:

a. Imagine you are . . . as heavy as a brick.
     . . . as floppy as a rag doll.
     . . . as stiff as a stick.
b. Think about yourself as a kite, blowing in the wind. Now imagine yourself as flying the kite.
c. Imagine you have a rubber band attached to one hand and one foot. Stretch your rubber band farther and farther until suddenly it snaps and breaks.
d. Imagine you are a snowperson standing straight and tall, but now the sun is coming out. You start to melt—first your head, then your shoulders, your back and stomach. Now your legs are melting—you're a puddle on the ground.

Social

1. We Meet Someone Special

Invite a person who has a disability to visit the classroom. Prepare the children before the person comes, letting them know what to expect. Ask the visitor to tell about herself or himself and the kinds of things she or he can do and not do as a result of the disability. Ask the visitor to stay and play with the children for the day, if possible, allowing the class to become comfortable with him or her as they are ready and giving children time to interact with the person.

To Simplify:

● Show the children a picture of their visitor before she or he comes. Tell them some things that the person can do well. After the visitor leaves, have children draw pictures for that person and send them to him or her.

To Extend:

● Find out what things are hard for the disabled friend to do and what would make his or her life easier. Invite the class to write a letter to someone who could make something easier or change something for that visitor. For example, if the person had a hard time coming to the building because his or her wheelchair could not move easily up a step, write the person in charge of the building; tell them what happened when your visitor came, and ask them to help.

2. Busy People

Show pictures of people doing interesting things with and without disabling conditions. (The book *People* by Peter Spier [1980] has lots.) Try to include pictures of people who vary in gender, age, and racial and ethnic origin. Display the pictures at children's eye level and lead a discussion about what the children notice—the abilities of the people and the disabilities they may have. Emphasize similarities among the people rather than differences.

3. Caterpillar Over the Mountain

Encourage cooperative movement by playing this group game. Make a "mountain" for children to crawl over by placing soft mats or a large mattress over a bench or balance beam; other mountains could be a set of low stairs or a mound of sand. Show children how to be a part of a long caterpillar by crawling on the floor and holding onto the feet of the person in front. Encourage the children to try to move their caterpillar over the mountain without unhooking any part.

4. Two in the Boat

Make cooperative movement fun with this song and game. Ask two children to sit on the floor facing each other with their legs crossed and holding hands. Tell these children they are the first two rowers in a pretend boat As you sing the simple song, invite other children to join in singing it with you and encourage the rowers to cooperatively row by leaning forward and backward in the pretend boat. Each time the song says, "Now let's add two more," select two new children

to join the others in the imaginary boat, one child to sit behind each rower, holding onto the shoulders of the person in front of her or him.

♫ Two in the Boat

Author unknown
Tune: "Ten Little Indians"

> There were two in the boat, and the boat kept rowing,
> Two in the boat, and the boat kept rowing,
> Two in the boat, and the boat kept rowing,
> Now let's add two more.
> There were four in the boat, and the boat kept rowing,
> Four in the boat, and the boat kept rowing,
> Four in the boat, and the boat kept rowing,
> Now let's add two more.

Continue adding two children until everyone is in the boat. Sing the song again, but add a surprise ending to the game by singing:

> Now we all tip over! (*Gently push the rowers over to one side.*)

Teacher Resources

Field Trip Ideas

1. Take a tour of a health club and request that the aerobics instructor or fitness trainer tell about her or his job and demonstrate some simple equipment. Ask if the children could be led through an exercise routine that is appropriate for the class age and ability range.

2. Take a tour of a center where rehabilitation work is provided for people with disabling conditions. Ask that a therapist show the children various kinds of equipment available for strengthening muscles as well as some of the ways they help disabled people live more active lives.

Visitors

1. Ask a parent or other adult who is physically active to come and show what he or she does for exercise. Encourage children to imitate his/her simple movements.

2. Invite a teacher from a special education facility to bring a group of children on a field trip to your

class. Meet with the teacher ahead of time to determine ways that you can adapt the room arrangement or materials to make them more accessible to the visitors. Plan some simple activities that all of the children can do together as they get to know one another. Follow up by having your class make pictures to send to their new acquaintances, and/or visit their classroom on another day.

Children's Books

Aliki. (1984). *Feelings*. New York: William Morrow and Co.

Ancona, G., and Miller, M. B. (1989). *Handtalk Zoo*. New York: Macmillan.

Carle, E. (1986). *My First Book of Motion*. New York: Thomas Y. Crowell.

DePaola, T. (1973). *Nana Upstairs and Nana Downstairs*. New York: Putnam.

DePaola, T. (1981). *Now One Foot, Now the Other*. New York: Putnam.

English, B. L. (1988). *Women at Their Work*. New York: Dial Books for Young Readers.

Fassler, J. (1975). *Howie Helps Himself*. Morton Grove, IL: Albert Whitman.

Gauch, P. L. (1989). *Dance, Tanya*. New York: Putnam.

Golant, M., and Crane, B. (1988). *It's O.K. to Be Different*. New York: Tor Books.

Henroid, L. (1982). *Grandma's Wheelchair*. Morton Grove, IL: Albert Whitman.

Hutchins, P. (1968). *Rosie's Walk*. New York: Macmillan.

Kline, S. (1988). *Don't Touch!* New York: Viking.

Krementz, J. (1978). *Very Young Gymnast*. New York: Dell Yearling.

Krementz, J. (1979). *Very Young Skater*. New York: Scholastic Book Service.

Krementz, J. (1987). *Very Young Rider*. New York: Dell.

Lasker, J. (1982). *Nick Joins In*. Morton Grove, IL: Albert Whitman.

Oxenbury, H. (1983). *The Dancing Class*. New York: Dial Books for Young Readers.

Peterson, J. W. (1977). *I Have a Sister, My Sister Is Deaf*. New York: HarperCollins.

Rabe, B. (1981). *Balancing Girl*. New York: Dutton.

Rosenberg, M. (1983). *My Friend Leslie*. New York: Lothrop, Lee & Shepard.

Schein, J. (1988). *Forget-Me-Not*. Toronto: Annick Press.

Showers, P. (1988). *Hear Your Heart*. New York: HarperCollins.

Spier, P. (1980). *People*. New York: Doubleday.

Stein, S. B. (1984). *About Handicaps*. New York: Walker & Co.

Adult References

Blood-Patterson, P., ed. (1988). *Rise Up Singing*. Bethlehem, PA: Sing Out Corporation.

Brehm, M., and Tindell, N. (1983). *Movement With a Purpose*. West Nyack, NY: Parker.

Cook, R., Tessier, A., and Klein, M. D. (1992). *Adapting Early Childhood Curricula for Children with Special Needs*. New York: Macmillan.

Different from You . . . and Like You Too. (1985). Filmstrip. Mendocino, CA: Lauren Productions.

Gilroy, P.J. (1985). *Kids in Motion: An Early Childhood Mevement Education Program*. Tuscon, AZ: Communication Skill Builders.

North, M. (1973). *Movement Exploration*. London: Temple Smith.

Office of Human Development Services. (1980). *Directory of National Information Sources on Handicapping Conditions and Related Services*. Washington, DC: Clearinghouse on the Handicapped.

Orlick, T. (1978). *The Cooperative Sports and Games Book*. New York: Pantheon.

Palmer, H. (1982). "Oh, What a Miracle" in *Walter The Waltzing Worm*. Topanga, CA: Music Box Recordings.

Safford, P. L. (1989). *Integrated Teaching in Early Childhood*. White Plains, NY: Longmans.

Weissman, J. (1987). *Kids in Motion*. Sherman Oaks, CA: Alfred Publishing.

Food

I wake up in the morning, at the crack of dawn,
jump up out of bed with a great big yawn!

Then I start to wonder, then I have to say,
What am I going to eat for breakfast today?

What a busy morning, filled with work and play,
sometimes feeling grouchy, sometimes feeling gay.

Then I start to wonder, then I have to say,
What am I going to eat for lunch today?

On with afternoon, songs and games and friends,
pretty soon another day is rolling to an end.

Then I start to wonder, then I have to say,
What am I going to eat for dinner today?

FOOD!

Picture a baby in her high chair. Dad brings her a dish of strained peaches. What follows is the epitome of multisensory learning. She feels it, tentatively taking a handful and squishing it between her fingers, delighting in the texture. She lifts it to her nose and smells it, then tastes it. By the end of breakfast, it's everywhere! On the tray of the high chair, on her face and shirt, even decorating the floor beneath her, rest blobs of strained peaches—and some of it has even gotten inside her body!

Children love exploring the familiar, rediscovering what is known and searching for the novel. Food is a primary arena for their exploration. And they are not alone. Because people all over the world depend on it for survival, everyone has experience with food in its myriad forms. Food provides opportunities for selection and preference, for measuring and counting, for preparing and eating, and for introducing lifelong healthful habits.

Purpose

This unit divides the study of foods into three mini-themes: "Food and Food Preparation," "Where Food Comes From," and "How the Body Uses Food." Content moves from the concrete to the more abstract. First, food and food preparation is the focus, providing a range of experiences with handling, altering and combining ingredients. Next, an examination of some of the many ways by which people produce, gather and obtain their foods is undertaken. Last, processes by which the body breaks down and uses food for fuel, repair, and growth are examined.

Many people throughout the world find it difficult to obtain enough nutritious food to maintain optimal health. For this reason, we have avoided activities that require using food for anything other than consumption. Further, we believe that many families admonish their children not to "play with their food," and so have avoided activities that give the impression of doing so. Instead, food activities have been designed to lead children to view with respect the remarkable role that food plays in good health, while deriving enjoyment and wonder from discovering the diverse ways in which people provide their bodies with food, the precious human fuel.

Implementation

Options abound in the study of "Foods." At the concrete level of learning, a unit can be planned with a focus on colors, shapes, smells, and tastes. Eventually, an exploration of the more abstract aspects of food choices and uses might focus on such concepts as nutritional quality, geographic availability, or changes induced by heat, pressure, or combining ingredients in differing ratios.

Option One: Develop single-week units that focus on foods obtained from different sources. Begin with a study of grains and plant foods. Differentiate between fruits and vegetables as well as the seeds, roots, stems, and leaves that are the edible parts of various plants. Move on to the foods we get from animals, exploring those that are continuously produced, such as eggs and milk, in addition to others, such as meats and lard.

Option Two: Undertake a study of food gathering. Introduce gardening and farming; then move on to the distribution of foods to markets, grocery stores and restaurants. Integrate a study of transportation methods that allow foods grown far away from one's home to become readily available. Discuss the fact that some foods can be gathered and then eaten with relatively few changes: carrots and apples can be consumed with only a washing. Other foods, such as wheat, often undergo many changes before consumption.

Option Three: Follow a study of the human body with an examination of the roles that foods play in maintaining health, providing energy, and enabling the body to grow and repair itself.

Option Four: The three sections of this unit are arranged in an order that begins with a concrete, hands-on exploration of the myriad tastes, smells and textures of foods—both alone and in combination. The next mini-theme takes children beyond exploration and preparation in the classroom to the fields and farms, stands and stores that provide people with food options. The last offers a mental journey inside the body that focuses on processes by which foods are transformed into their health-enhancing components. Simply select Terms, Facts, and Principles from each of the three sections around which to organize the presentation of the activities that are most suitable to the equipment, time, and space available to you and your children. Overall, we suggest spending approximately three weeks on this unit.

Food and Food Preparation

Terms, Facts, and Principles (TFPs)

General Information

1. Foods are substances that a person takes into his or her body so that the body will grow, repair itself, and have energy for movement and for vital processes.

2. There are many different foods that people eat.

3. Foods vary in their characteristics: taste, texture, color, temperature, odor.

4. People have different food preferences.

5. People's food preferences are influenced not only by experience, food availability, and allergies, but also by the appearance, smell, taste, and/or texture of food.

*6. The age, health, or beliefs of a person influence what foods he or she eats.

*7. As a person matures, his or her perception of the tastes of certain foods changes.

Food Preparation

8. Some foods are eaten in their original form.

9. Some foods must be changed from their original form to another form before they are eaten.

10. Some foods can be changed into more than one form.

11. The same food can be prepared in many different ways.

12. Foods can be combined.

13. Recipes are plans for combining and preparing foods.

14. Some food combinations preserve the original form, taste, texture, or odor of the foods used.

15. Some food combinations alter the ingredients to produce a different food.

16. The characteristics of a food can be changed through various methods of preparation: cooking, freezing, thawing, heating, chopping, mashing, grinding, tearing, blending, stirring.

17. There are several steps in food preparation:
    a. wash hands
    b. gather utensils and ingredients
    c. combine or prepare food
    d. clean up
    e. eat
    f. store leftovers properly

Food Storage

18. Some foods are eaten soon after they are prepared; others are packaged and stored for eating at a later time.

19. Foods should be properly stored to maintain their healthfulness for the body.

20. Foods can be kept for short or long periods of time depending on their ingredients and the method of storage that is chosen.

*21. Some foods should be kept cool, some should be covered or wrapped, some should be kept away from light.

*22. Foods that are improperly stored will spoil and/or lose some of their nutritional value.

*23. Eating spoiled foods can cause illness.

*24. Spoiled foods can be identified by changes in the way they normally look, smell, or taste.

*25. Some processes have been developed that preserve foods so that they can be stored longer or more easily: drying, salting, pickling, canning.

Activity Ideas

Aesthetic

1. Smell-and-Taste Party

Gather several kinds of fruits and vegetables; include a few that the children are not likely to have eaten often. Depending on your area, you might try avocados, mangoes, fresh coconut, or kohlrabi. Include nuts, too, if you wish. Clean and cut the vegetables into bite-sized portions. If possible, gather some pictures of the foods as they look when they are growing to show the children.

Talk with the children about foods that grow and the benefits they provide for people's health. Discuss, also, our amazing senses and the way that we can experience foods (and other things) by smelling, tasting, and touching, as well as by looking.

After helping all the children to wash their hands, invite them to a taste-and-smell party. Pass small plates containing one food at a time around the group. Encourage children to try a small bit of each (it's o.k. if they choose not to finish it). Children who are very reluctant to taste can still be directed to feel and smell each food. You might want to have several paper grocery bags distributed around the group area for easy collection of discards.

Discuss your own sensory reactions to the foods. Mention colors, smells, and flavors and acknowledge children as they do so. Children might enjoy deciding which foods they like the best and the least.

This activity could be carried out on a second day with animal product foods. Ascertain ahead of time whether any children's families have reservations or prohibitions against any of the food selections. Eliminate any that cause concern. Some possible inclusions are small cubes of cheese, pieces of hard-boiled egg, and perhaps pieces of tuna or meat. Mention the different source of these samples; they did not grow in the ground, but rather came from animals that first ate plants or other animals themselves.

2. Gourd Shakers

Obtain dried gourds from a farmers' market or grocery store. Alternatively, purchase fresh gourds and involve the children in observations of the drying process. Gourds can be dried in a very low oven (around 150°); however, this takes as many as fifteen hours. Simply place the gourds on oven racks, turning them occasionally, until they are hard and dry. The oven can be turned on each day and then turned off at night. A heater vent would serve the same purpose; however, it might take even longer.

Once dried, gourds can be used as musical shakers. The seeds inside the gourds will make clicking sounds when the gourds are shaken.

Play or sing familiar children's songs, such as "Jingle Bells" or "Twinkle, Twinkle, Little Star." Invite children to shake their gourds, keeping time with the beat.

3. Spice Up Your Space

Purchase a variety of spices from a grocery store. Tell children that you will be setting up a "sniffing center" in your classroom. Remove the caps from two or three different spices each day. You may want to tape around the plastic shaker insert in each jar or insert a circle of cheesecloth over the jar's opening and then replace the shaker cap. These strategies will ensure that more of the spices stay in the jars! Invite children to stop by the "sniffing center" and enjoy the new aromas each day.

To Extend:
● Invite children to shake small amounts out of the various jars and enjoy smell-testing the combinations that result.

Affective

1. Wrapping Rap

Discuss the responsibility that people have to make sure foods are stored appropriately so that they stay fresh and healthful. Ask children to tell you about some ways they package leftover foods at their homes. Next, teach the following rap, inviting children to choose a food to insert in the verse and a storage method suited to it.

♫ Wrapping Rap
Words by Kit Payne

> Had some (toast) for breakfast, didn't want the rest;
> sat and thought a minute how to store it best.
> Knew I wouldn't want it until another day,
> so I:
> (put it in a bag, a bag, a bag, put it in a bag),
> then I put it away.
> Had some (fruit) for dinner, didn't want the rest;
> sat and thought a minute how to store it best.
>
> Knew I wouldn't want it until another day,
> so I:
> (dumped it in a jar, a jar, a jar, dumped it in a jar),
> then I put it away.

Hint for Success:
● Gather some samples of food storage containers, such as jars, plastic sandwich bags, and plastic containers with snap-on tops to show the children before and during this activity. This will help them to generate and generalize ideas.

To Simplify:
● Chant several verses yourself while demonstrating with real or plastic foods and containers rather than focusing on child participation.

To Extend:
● Challenge children to make up and chant their own version of the rap for their classmates. Last, discuss where they would put away the foods they have described. Remind children that some foods are best stored in a refrigerator, while others should be kept in dark cupboards.

2. I Like It Like That

Choose two or three foods that are readily available in more than one form. Examples include apples (apple juice, apple slices, applesauce, and dried apples), potatoes (mashed, raw slices, baked, potato chips), peanuts (in the shell, peanut butter, boiled peanuts), or carrots (raw [cleaned], cooked, mashed as in baby food).

Serve small samples of these or other foods in varied forms as snack options. Encourage children to try all the variations and discuss which they like least and best. Point out to children who assert that they don't like a particular food (such as carrots) that it can taste quite different when its form has been changed.

To Simplify:

● Pass around a food in two forms during a circle time (for example, individual slices of raw potato followed by individual potato chips). Ask the children to tell ways in which the two foods are the same and different.

To Extend:

● Invite children to interview members of their families about food preferences. Tell them to bring notes to school about what they find out. Discuss or graph the differences and similarities as they relate to age groups of family members. Do younger brothers and sisters share similar preferences? Are they different from preferences that older people share?

● Follow "I Like It Like That" with the "Home Food Preference Interviews" below.

3. Home Food Preference Interviews

Prepare the following materials: the interview guidelines printed below, reproduced so that each child can take several home. Optional: a report binder or three-ring notebook, to compile the returned forms into a classroom book.

Introduce the activity with a discussion of food preferences and family food traditions. Give examples of your own: talk about foods that were (or are) served in your own family to mark special events and ones that you particularly enjoy.

Tell children that they will be taking interview forms home so that each child can carry out an investigation of food likes and dislikes and special eating practices and occasions in his or her own family. Read the form (at the right) to the children. Tell them that they may want to ask an adult in their family to help with interviews of other members. Point out that if their family includes members younger than themselves, they may need to do more writing or seek more help in determining preferences. Have each child determine how many forms will be needed (how many people live in his or her home).

Request that children bring the forms back to school in a day or two so that they can tell others what they have learned about their families.

Hint for Success:

● Print the interview form on bright paper so that it is less likely to be forgotten or overlooked at home.

To Simplify:

● Have children interview others in the classroom instead of members of their families.

To Extend:

● After children bring their interview forms back to school, have them report to others (in small groups or to the whole group) by reading or recalling the information on the form. Next, provide blank paper on which children can illustrate family members eating or preparing the foods they have identified as favorites. Hole-punch the forms and compile them in a ring binder or otherwise bind them into a classroom book.

● Guide the children through a graphing activity. Compile all the "favorite foods" that are listed on the children's interview forms on one graph and all the "I do not likes" answers on another graph. Talk about whether certain foods are frequently listed and whether some people named favorites that others identified as foods they did not like.

Interview Form: Family Food Preferences

My name is:_____

My favorite food is:_____

_____

I like to eat it for:_____

_____

I do not like to eat:_____

_____

Cognitive

1. What's My Rule?

Prepare or purchase some food picture cards for this activity. Food pictures can be cut from food packaging or from magazine advertisements or articles, then mounted on cardboard and laminated or covered with clear adhesive paper.

First, allow the children some time to explore the colorful food cards by looking through and handling them. Then tell the children that you have an idea for a game that's fun to play. Provide trays, baskets, or boxes in which to sort cards. Arrange for the children to work in teams of three to five.

Tell one of the children to first select a picture of a food that he or she really likes. Direct the child to place it in one of the sorting containers. Next, tell the sorter to choose another food that he or she believes belongs with the first one. Ask the child to tell you why he or she decided that those foods belong together. Avoid judging the reason. Answers are likely to range from "Because I like them both" or "Because they're the same color" to "Because they are both fruits." There is no one right answer to classification. Suggest that the child choose several more foods that belong in the first group. Other children may offer additional suggestions for grouping.

Next, ask the child to select a food that doesn't belong in the first group and to start a second group with it. Have the child add more foods to the second group, then explain why these belong together, instead of with the first group.

To Extend:

● Introduce a "What's My Rule" variation to sorting: as a second child begins a turn as the sorter, the other children must guess why he or she is putting particular foods together. Is it by color? kind? size? preference? Allow as many children to have turns trying to baffle their team members as would like.

2. Nose to Knows

You will need four metal spice shakers with tightly fitted, hole-punched tops for this activity. Photograph, draw, or find pictures of four different foods. Place samples of each of the pictured foods inside the cans. Examples of foods that have easily distinguished smells include peanut butter, orange slices (or orange marmalade), bananas, and chocolate chips.

Explain to the children that noses provide us with a sense of smell that helps us learn about our world. Tell them that smell will tell about what's in the cans and then eyes will give other hints. Explain that you will not be opening the cans or tasting the foods this time, just looking at pictures to help decide what the nose knows, and leaving the cans tightly covered until everyone has had turns smelling and telling.

Next, have children examine the pictures of the foods that are contained in the cans. Pass the cans and pictures around. Allow each child time to smell each can and place it on the card that they think it represents.

To Extend:

● Provide tiny tastes of some of the foods for children to identify. Put a little peanut butter or orange marmalade inside a small bun so that it can't be seen. Have children choose the can, by smell, that contains the same food they are tasting.

3. Food Riddles

Gather some foods that represent the answers to each of the riddles below, and place them in a paper grocery bag out of sight of the children. Tell them that you are going to give them some clues about mystery foods that are hidden in the bag and that their job is to guess which food you are describing each time. Remind children to keep their answers "inside their heads" until everyone has had a chance to think about the clues. Tell them that they can all call out the answer in unison after you are done giving clues. Read the riddles with emphasis on the rhyming words.

Food Riddles
Words by Kit Payne

a. Sometimes you butter this, sometimes not.
   Time in a toaster can make it hot.
   Many good things can be tucked out of sight
   between two slices, brown or white.
   Wheat can be ground, or rye instead,
   to make this food that's known as: **(BREAD)**

b. These come in many colors,
   and sizes big and little.
   They always grow on plants, and
   sometimes pits are in their middle.
   A lot of them have seeds inside,
   and sometimes outside, too.
   The seeds may be discarded,
   for some aren't good for you.
   It's not the stem, it's not the trunk,
   it's not the leaf or root. . .

The part of the plant that I'm talking about
is called the juicy (**FRUIT**)

    c. Once there was a nest,
and in it was a hen.
When we want to find this food,
that's where we begin.
This food wears a hard coat
that you have to break,
if you want to fry it up,
or mix it in a cake.
If you dropped a raw one,
it would make a mess.
Tell me what this food is;
tell me what you guess. (EGG)

    d. Some people like these
right after they dine.
If it's a little,
then that might be fine.
But if they're too much
of the food that you eat,
you might feel too full
for the ones that you need.
Remember to save them
for now-and-then treats,
the oils, and the fats,
and the sugary (SWEETS)

Construction

1. Cookbooks

Gather a few illustrated cookbooks to show to the children when introducing this project. Provide several stapled-together pieces of writing paper or construction paper, pencils, and colored markers. Explain that cookbooks contain guidelines and plans for combining foods to produce other foods. These plans are called recipes. Point out that one way to tell what the recipes make is by looking at the pictures and that cooks find it helpful to both read the plan and look at the pictures when deciding whether to try out a new recipe.

Invite children to make their own illustrated cookbooks, either singly or in small groups. Consider grouping children so that at least one member of each group is a writer, if possible. Tell children that some people may want to draw their pictures first, while others may want to begin by writing their recipes. Either way is fine. Encourage children to think about a recipe that someone at home prepares and to try to remember the ingredients and steps. Remind them that a list of ingredients and utensils that will be needed often precedes the rest of the steps. Encourage children to seek each others' help or the help of an adult, if they wish. If there is enough adult help, offer to write down the recipe plans as children dictate them.

2. Painted Toast

Fill some small plastic containers or baby food jars about half full of milk. Add food coloring to make three or four shades of "milk paint." Provide fine-tipped watercolor brushes, one per jar. Give each child one or two slices of white bread. Tell children that they can paint pictures of anything they like on the bread, using the milk paint. Suggest that children try painting pictures of other foods that they enjoy eating on bread. Next, put all the pieces of painted bread in an oven or toaster oven. Set the oven at about 325°. Watch carefully and take out the bread when it is brown and crisp. Examine the changes that applying heat caused in the bread and paint. Compare all the different pictures that children produced on their toast. Then eat and enjoy the toast.

3. Cornhusk Wreaths

Purchase or pick fresh ears of corn with the husks still intact. Have the children husk the corn and set the ears aside for eating later. Next, provide each child with a wire coat hanger. Help or direct everyone in bending the hangers into a circle shape. Next, show children how to fold a cornhusk in half, then fold the bended center over the hanger. Next, pull the ends of the husk through the loop formed by the fold until each husk is knotted tightly against the hanger. Repeat this step until the hanger is full of knotted husks. Finally, show and tell the children how to use fingers, scissors, or a large sewing needle to shred each husk, forming a fringe that surrounds the hanger.

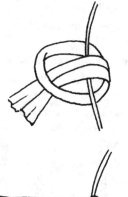

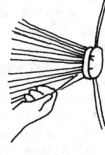

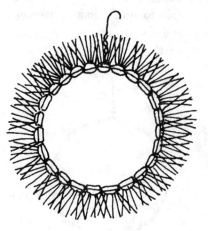

To Simplify:

● Have the children help with the cornhusking step one day. Complete the step which requires folding and knotting yourself after the children have gone. The next day, have the children complete the project by shredding and fringing.

To Extend:

● Read the book *Corn Is Maize: The Gift of the Indians* by Aliki (1976). Discuss all of the uses for corn that are introduced in this informative book. Invite the children to decide which way to prepare the corn they will be husking for the wreaths.

Language

1. Foods Grab-Bag

You will need a heavy, non-transparent plastic bag or cloth bag with a draw string closure (find a medium-sized thick rubber band—about twice the size of a child's wrist—if you cannot locate a bag with a draw string) and a variety of fruits, vegetables, and nuts for this activity. Place the foods inside the bag. Partially close the bag with the rubber band or drawstring. Have children reach inside the bag and select a food to grasp and feel. Next, direct the "feeler" to say as many words as he or she can think of to describe the food. Other children can try to guess what the food is.

Hints for Success:

● Before starting, discuss the many characteristics that make foods different from each other. Mention that some differences can be noted by smelling, tasting, or seeing. Others can be felt. Talk about texture, shape, and size characteristics.

● Pass the foods around the group to be examined before carrying out the activity.

To Simplify:

● Limit the number of foods inside the bag at any one time to two or three. Remind the child who will be describing the foods to only tell what he or she feels rather than what he or she thinks the food is.

To Extend:

● Invite the listeners to write down all the words that each describer says. Compare the word lists for similarities and differences after all the foods have been described. Add words that describe characteristics that cannot be felt (color, taste, and so on). Categorize the word lists by beginning sounds or letters.

● Choose less common foods, such as avocados, papayas, and kohlrabi, to add complexity.

2. Tastes in Nursery Rhymes

Read or tell several nursery rhymes to the children, asking them to listen carefully for foods that are mentioned. Make a list of all the foods identified on chart paper or a chalkboard. Lead a discussion of these foods. Which ones have children eaten? Which have they heard of but never eaten? Are there any that they have never heard of or tasted? Decide together whether all of the foods are real ones or whether some might be pretend. Discuss how you could find out if a food is real.

Encourage the children to guess what the foods they've never heard of might look, smell, and taste like. If possible, arrange to prepare and try one or more of the unfamiliar foods on days to come. Suggestions for nursery rhymes that mention foods include:

"Little Miss Muffet"
"Little Jack Horner"
"Jack Sprat"
"The Muffin Man"

3. Rima de Chocolate/ Chocolate Rhyme

If possible, find a Mexican chocolate beater to show the children before teaching the following rhyme. This is a wooden utensil that looks like a small, fancy baton, about ten inches long. Around the wider top are wooden rings which move freely but are kept from slipping off the end by carved ridges. This utensil is held between the palms of the hands, wide end down, and spun by rolling the palms together. As the rings agitate and the beater spins, chocolate drinks are mixed and made frothy.

If you are unable to locate a chocolate beater, you might choose to pretend to stir with a spoon as you chant the following rhyme, first in English and then in Spanish.

Chocolate Rhyme

words in English:	phonetic pronunciation:
One, two, three, cho-	(chaw)
One, two, three, -co-	(ko)
One, two, three, -la-	(la)
One, two, three, -te	(t)
Stir, stir, the chocolate. (*Twirl hands together as if using a chocolate beater, or pretend to stir.*)	

Rima de Chocolate

words in Spanish:	phonetic pronunciation:
Uno, dos, tres, cho-	(chaw)
Uno, dos, tres, -co-	(ko)
Uno, dos, tres, -la-	(lah)
Uno, dos, tres, -te	(tay)
Bate, bate chocolate.	(Bahtay, bahtay, chaw-ko-lah-tay)

After chanting these two versions of the same rhyme, ask the children if anyone knows why they sound different. Inform them, if necessary, that one is said in English and the other in Spanish. Invite children to learn the rhyme in both languages. Repeat it, one line at a time, directing the children to echo each line back. Demonstrate the counting and beating or stirring actions as you chant. Repeat the whole rhyme as many times as the children wish to practice, first in English, then in Spanish.

To Extend:

● Consider asking bilingual children or parents in your school to translate this simple rhyme into other languages for all to learn.

● Make hot chocolate on the same day as you teach the Chocolate Rhyme. Make chocolate milk with a commercial syrup for a simpler alternative. Let each child stir his or her own until blended while you chant!

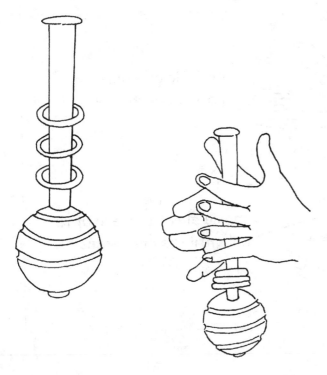

4. Rebus Recipes

Help children to gain confidence in themselves as readers and problem-solvers by providing opportunities to follow procedural steps in food preparation. Prepare your own charts by replacing the words for some steps with illustrations, as has been done with the following recipes. These can be copied and enlarged, too, of course. Consider laminating your rebus recipe chart collection so that the recipes can be used over and over, protected from spills.

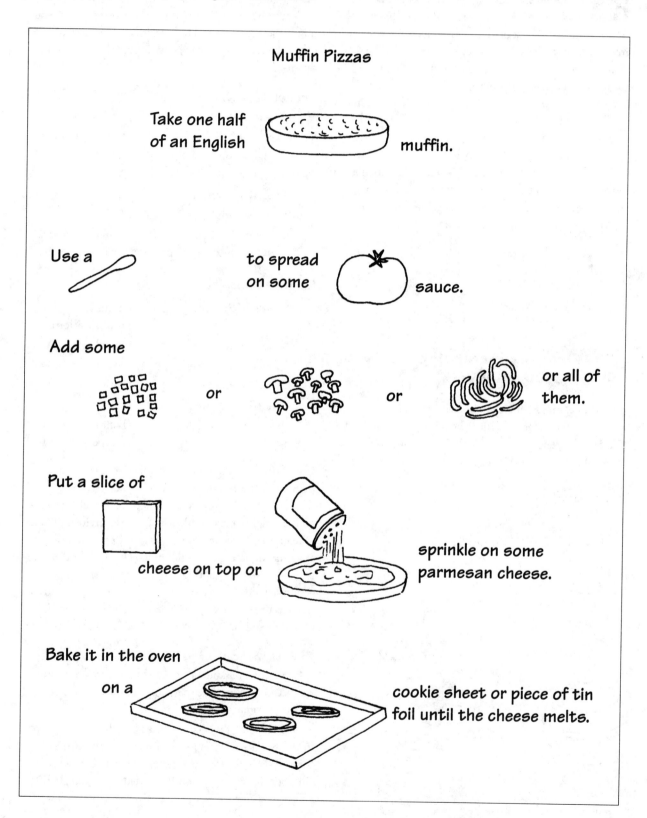

Muffin Pizzas

Take one half of an English ⬭ muffin.

Use a 🥄 to spread on some 🍅 sauce.

Add some ▫️ or 🍄 or 🧅 or all of them.

Put a slice of ◻️ cheese on top or sprinkle on some parmesan cheese.

Bake it in the oven on a ⬛ cookie sheet or piece of tin foil until the cheese melts.

Peanut Butter Balls

1 cup peanut butter

1/2 cup honey

4 cups powdered milk

Mix together with your ... in a

Roll into

Eat with your

Carrot Salad

Wash and grate a

into a

Add a scoop of Raisins

Add 1/2 cup of Yogurt

Stir it with a

Eat it with your

Physical

1. Food Tracings

Provide children with pencils or washable markers and stiff drawing paper (like manila paper or construction paper, or even cardboard). Note that thin paper like newsprint may frustrate children as they trace because it tends to wrinkle up or tear under the pencil.

Display a variety of foods that are large enough and firm enough for small hands to both hold in place and trace around: apples, bananas, cucumbers, zucchini, gourds. All of these foods can be peeled before preparing and eating so they will not go to waste after use in this activity.

Point out that each of the foods has several surfaces that could be held against the paper when tracing. An apple held upright (stem pointing up) provides a very different tracing surface than one held on its side—and is easier held in place as well!

To Simplify:
- Demonstrate and explain the procedure of tracing for novices. Tell the children that tracing works best when you hold the writing tool so that it touches the object you are tracing all the time. Mention that it is important to keep watching your pencil so that you can steer it where you want it to go.

To Extend:
- After children have experimented with food tracing, suggest that they color in and/or cut out the shapes they have traced.

2. The Sandwich Game

Lead a discussion of what defines a sandwich. Point out that there are usually two "covers," and a filling or middle. Invite children to work in groups of three, with one child standing in the middle as the filling, and the other two sandwiching him or her in with their bodies. Practice walking around in this fashion! Tell the children to switch places after a few minutes, until everyone who wishes to has had a chance to be the "filling."

3. Tools of the Trade

Introduce children to some of the many utensils used in food preparation. Provide instruction, demonstrations, and practice in using them. Although some cooking tools are potentially dangerous and should not be used by children without constant supervision (electric frying pans, sharp knives and so on), others are wonderfully interesting and safe.

Introduce hand-held mechanical beaters, and show children how holding them upright and pushing down makes it easier to turn the crank handle. Provide spatulas, potato mashers and rubber jar scrapers for experimentation with modeling dough, finger paint, and/or actual food preparation and service.

Place kitchen tongs in your Pretend Play area for use with plastic food models, or along with small manipulative toys and sorting trays. While children enjoy grasping and releasing small objects into targeted compartments like egg cartons provide, they will be practicing skills much like those used in scissor cutting! Before teaching the function of each utensil, ask children to speculate about their purposes. Elicit and list many guesses.

4. Tossed Salad

Gather a variety of plastic foods such as those used for pretend play, and a very large plastic bowl, basket or bucket. Bring the children together in a large open area of the classroom, the gym or the outdoor play area.

Discuss the meaning of the word "salad" with the children. Ask if anyone has heard of a tossed salad. Invite guesses about how the phrase "tossed salad" came about. If necessary, explain that salads are usually a mixture of foods, tossed or stirred together. Salads can contain combinations of fruits or vegetables, with pastas or meats, nuts, cheese or cooked eggs—almost any food can be found in a salad!

Invite the children to play a game called "Tossed Salad." Have them form a circle around you. Tell them that you will toss a food to a child in the circle, who will then toss it to the person on his or her right, while calling out the name of the food. The tossing will continue from person to person, with each calling out the name of the food while tossing it on. The last person can attempt to toss it into the "salad bowl" in the middle of the circle.

Hints for Success:

● Carefully specify which direction the foods should go around the circle. Walk around in the direction you specify as you talk about this rule.

● Remind children that many foods are easily bruised, and so are people. Remember to toss gently!

To Simplify:

● You can toss a food to one child at a time, naming it as you do so. Have the child toss it in the "bowl," repeating its name. Retrieve it yourself, then toss it to the next child, and so on around the circle.

To Extend:

● Start several foods going around the circle at once, and direct the children to name each one as they receive it. Of course, each child will be catching and naming one food after another, so many food names will be heard all at once! When you shout out "Salad!", everyone tosses the food she or he is holding into the "bowl" in the middle.

5. Wrap It, Snap It

Add food containers with snap-on lids, plastic storage bags with fold-over or zip-together tops, and packaged clear storage wrap to your Pretend Play area. Show children how they are used. Encourage them to practice fine motor skills by sealing plastic foods into storage bags and containers.

6. Wrap It, Roll It, Eat It Up

For more opportunities to practice chopping and other fine motor skills, have the children share in the preparation and consumption of several versions of "sandwiches" that are representative of different cultures. Some recipes follow.

Vegetable Pita Pockets (Middle Eastern countries including Iraq, Iran, and Lebanon)

12 circles (loafs) of Pita bread, cut in half to make 24 servings

Three or more of the following: shredded lettuce, grated cheese, chopped tomato, chopped avocado, bean sprouts, chopped green onion, or chopped green or red bell peppers

The pita halves will have an opening, like a pocket, at the cut edge. Have children use tongs or spoons to stuff individual pockets with the ingredients of their choice.

Vegetable Burritos (Mexico)

Flour tortillas, one per child

Three or more of the vegetables listed above, prepared in the same ways.

Soften the tortillas by warming them in a microwave oven, three or four at a time. Warm for about 12 seconds for each (36 seconds for a stack of three, 48 seconds for four). Place paper towels, napkins, or waxed paper between them. The tortillas can also be warmed in a frying pan or on a griddle on a stove burner, just until they are soft and flexible.

Show the children how to spoon a little of some of the fillings into the center of the round tortilla, then fold it in half to be eaten by hand.

Moo Shoo Vegetables (China)

Purchase Moo Shoo wrappings, which are made of rice flour and are packaged in stacks. They often are available in the produce section of large grocery stores as well as in Oriental markets. Follow the package directions for preparation. Fill and eat in the same way as the burritos above.

Pretend Play

1. Which "Weigh" to the Check Out?

Set up a mini grocery store in an area of your classroom. Include pretend models of foods, labeled empty food packages, grocery sacks or tote bags, a cash register, play money, and a weighing scale. Inform children that sometimes people pay for their food purchases by weight, rather than by referring to a price that has been stamped onto the item. While introducing this new concept, ask children for their ideas about which foods these are likely to be, based on experiences shopping with their families. Ask whether anyone recalls how the weight of such items is determined. Demonstrate the use of the scale. Then tell children that when they take a turn as the store clerk, they will want to weigh the choices of some of their customers in order to assign a price to charge. As children begin exploring the store area, visit it yourself often. Act out the clerk's role as well as the customer's role to provide children with ideas and modeling to enrich their play.

Point out that more weight usually means more money. Later, you may want to add stick-on labels and marking pens so that the weight and price can be affixed to merchandise before customers go through the check out line.

2. Preparation Pantomimes

Invite children to act out the steps one would follow in preparing and enjoying a meal or snack. Remind them of the preliminaries like washing your hands and gathering ingredients from the cupboard and the refrigerator, as well as the clean-up steps that one follows after food preparation. Other children can serve as an audience, guessing what each actor is preparing and eating.

To help children get started, demonstrate a sequence of steps yourself. Pretend to hold your hands under running water. "Pick up" an imaginary bar of soap and rub it briskly between your hands. Pretend to rinse your hands under running water, turning them this way and that. Enact putting bread in a toaster, pushing a knob down, and so on. Tell the children what you are doing as you go. As children begin taking turns, you may want to provide concrete cues at first. Suggest that the child open the cupboard door and begin getting out ingredients. Demonstrate the action that you think would be involved as the child joins you. Ask what utensils will be needed from the drawer. Say "show us how it would look when you opened the drawer." Continue modeling and prompting until the child takes over.

3. What's That For?

Send home a newsletter request asking parents to help their children select an interesting food preparation utensil to bring to school. Remind them to be selective about safety when helping their child to make a selection (no sharp blades or mechanical grinding implements). Give children opportunities to demonstrate, for the whole group or a small group, the ways in which the implements are used. Tell them to pretend they are preparing something with their spatula, egg beater, rubber scraper, garlic press, and so on, while telling the others about its use. You might want to gather utensils from your own home for use by children who do not bring one to class.

Social

1. Feeding My Friends

For each of the days of this unit, have a different small group of children participate in preparing and serving a snack to the rest of the children. The snack-team-of-the-day should first wash their hands carefully, while hearing about the importance of clean hands during food preparation.

Together, have the children decide who will do which job in preparing the snack you have in mind. For example, explain, one day, that the team will be making peanut butter and jelly sandwiches—enough for everybody in the class. Point out that they must decide who will get out bread slices, who will spread jelly, who will spread peanut butter, and who will cut the sandwiches into sections. Other children can be responsible for counting the number of finished sandwich sections, for counting out cups and napkins, for washing the blunt spreading and cutting knives, and for recapping the jars. This will result in a sort of assembly line, thus providing practice in negotiation, compromise, and cooperation. The preparation group can also be responsible for taking plates of food and paper goods around to all the snack tables.

Other snacks that children could prepare include washing and cutting up fruits and vegetables. (Use children's pumpkin carving knives here. They are serrated, but not sharp enough to cut a child, and are used with a sawing motion that allows them to pierce foods effectively.) This group could also mix up a special dip. Yogurt and spices can be stirred together or mix packets can be prepared by following package directions. Snack-kabobs could be made by skewering fruit and cheese cubes on large toothpicks (grapes, banana chunks, and strawberries are fun to skewer). "Healthful Parfaits" can be made by layering yogurt, then a dry cereal, then raisins, and a final layer of yogurt. Use transparent plastic cups so that children can see the effect of layering.

2. Cooperation Cafe

Explore the concept of assembly-line production while preparing a special class treat. Pull two or three tables together or use a length of counter top to set up a production line. Set out one ingredient every foot or so, to be added by a child who stands before it. At the first "station," set out stacks of cups. At subsequent stations along the line, place bowls of small cereal bits (like Grapenuts™), yogurt, raisins, more yogurt, and finely chopped apple. Provide a spoon or small scoop with each bowl. The first child hands a cup to the cereal-scooper, who scoops in a little cereal, then passes a cup to the yogurt person, and so on. By the end of the line, "snack parfaits" have been assembled. Remind the children to plan ahead when deciding how much of their food to scoop into the cup so there is room for everything. Remind them that working together to set a pace

is important—no one should be rushed, but no one should wait too long either. Signal shift-changes so that different teams of children have chances to participate. Try this with sandwich or salad assemblies, as well. The whole class can sit down to eat the finished products in a "Cooperation Cafe" after enough snacks have been assembled.

To Extend:

● Encourage discussion of the experience of working in a team, and ask about whether this method was faster or easier than if one person had to prepare all the food alone. Consider timing the two methods to find out!

3. Cold Garden Soup

Begin this activity by reading a version of the children's classic story *Stone Soup*. The version by Marcia Brown (1947) is simple, attractively illustrated, still in print, and available in many libraries and book stores. (Several other versions are in print, too. Any of them will work for this activity.) After discussing the tale of a hungry and resourceful young man who seeks food donations from people of a village in order to make a tasty meal, propose that your class cooperate in making soup, too. Write a short note to parents explaining this project. List some ingredients from the recipe below. Ask that they send something from the list to school with their child. Gather other ingredients yourself. (This soup should turn out to be fine with adaptations of amounts and kinds of vegetables and seasonings.)

On the appointed day, gather all of the children in a circle. Move around the circle carrying a large pot. Tell each child, one by one, that you are very hungry and could make a wonderful soup if only he or she would share what they have brought. Hold out your pot for offerings.

Take the full pot to a food preparation area in your room. Have the children work together to clean, chop, measure, and combine the ingredients. At the end of the day or on the following day, enjoy eating your group effort. Praise everyone's involvement in the delicious outcome.

Cold Garden Soup

6 ripe tomatoes, chopped (peel first, if you wish)
1/2 cup chopped green pepper
1/4 cup chopped onions
1/2 cup chopped celery
1/2 cup chopped cucumbers
1/2 cup chopped carrots

1-1/2 cups tomato juice

1-1/2 cups beef broth

2 Tablespoons vinegar

2 Tablespoons olive oil

1 teaspoon salt

1/2 teaspoon dried dill

1/2 teaspoon pepper

1/2 teaspoon garlic salt

Combine, cover, and chill for 4 or more hours.

Teacher Resources

Field Trip Ideas

1. Arrange in advance for a class tour of a pizza shop. Tell the person with whom you arrange the trip that the children are studying food combinations, the effects of heat, the uses of various utensils, and so on. Ask if the children can watch the whole preparation process, including chopping and slicing the toppings, crust making, assembly, and baking. Collect money from families in advance, if possible, so that you can purchase pizza to eat at the store or take back to school. Alternatively, arrange for pizzas to be delivered after you get back to your classroom so that the children can anticipate their arrival and witness you paying the driver, receiving change, and so on.

2. Visit a health care facility, such as a hospital or nursing home, to tour its food preparation kitchens. Request that a nutritionist employed by the facility conduct the tour. Ask this person to explain special food needs associated with people of different ages, with different preferences, and in different states of health. Perhaps the children could help to deliver some meals to the patients or residents of the facility.

3. Contact area supermarkets, seeking permission to bring children "behind the scenes" so that they can see changes that are made in some foods before they are shelved to be sold. If possible, select a place where butchers work at the store preparing meat for purchase and/or where breads and pastries are made. A market with a deli counter where personnel prepare salads and other food combinations on site would be interesting, too. Send ahead a list of the terms, facts, and principles you have selected to teach, so that the people who talk with the children have background information about the focus of your unit.

Classroom Visitors

1. Ask for parent volunteers who will come to school to prepare family-favorite recipes while the children watch. Encourage these visiting chefs to talk about special events, special feelings, or special people that their families associate with the foods being prepared. Encourage questions. How (or from whom) did they learn to make this food? Are there special ways to serve it? (If your school does not have ovens that you can use, take foods home that require cooking or baking, then bring them back the next day to eat.)

2. Invite another class in your school or a nearby school to come to a food party for which your children plan and prepare. Send child-made invitations. Plan several food preparation activities and freeze or store foods until the day of the party. Provide children with opportunities to decorate the room for the party ahead of time. Alternatively (or at another party), invite families. For example, consider having an early-morning family breakfast so that busy parents can come on their way to work.

Children's Books

Aliki. (1976). *Corn Is Maize: The Gift of the Indians*. New York: HarperTrophy.

Balian, L. (1976). *The Sweet Touch*. Nashville, TN: Abingdon.

Berry, J. (1986). *Teach Me About Mealtime*. Chicago: Childrens Press.

Brown, M. (1947). *Stone Soup*. New York: Aladdin. (There are additional versions.)

Butler, M. C. (1988). *Too Many Eggs: A Counting Book*. Boston: Godine.

Carle, E. (1992). *Pancakes, Pancakes*. New York: Scholastic.

De Paola, T. (1978). *Pancakes for Breakfast*. New York: Harcourt Brace Jovanovich.

De Paola, T. (1978). *The Popcorn Book*. New York: Holiday.

Ehlert, L. (1989). *Eating the Alphabet: Fruits and Vegetables from A to Z*. New York: Harcourt Brace Jovanovich.

Florian, D. (1992). *A Chef*. New York: Greenwillow.

Gelman, R. G. (1984). *More Spaghetti, I Say!* Big Book Edition. New York: Scholastic.

Hoban, R. (1962). *Bread and Jam for Frances*. New York: HarperCollins.

Hutchins, P. (1978). *Don't Forget the Bacon*. New York: Puffin.

Kelley, T. (1989). *Let's Eat*. New York: Dutton Child Books.

Morris, A. (1989). *Bread Bread Bread*. New York: Scholastic.

Pearson, T. (1986). *A Apple Pie*. New York: Dial.

Pienkowski, J. (1991). *Food*. New York: Simon & Schuster Trade.

Polacco, P. (1991). *Thunder Cake*. New York: Putnam Publishing Group.

Reece, C. (1985). *What Was It Before It Was Ice Cream?* Mankato, MN: Childs World.

Sendak, M. (1962). *Chicken Soup with Rice*. New York: HarperCollins.

Sendak, M. (1970). *In the Night Kitchen*. New York: HarperCollins.

Seuss, Dr. (1960). *Green Eggs and Ham*. New York: Random Books for Young Readers.

Sharmat, M. (1980). *Gregory the Terrible Eater*. New York: Scholastic.

Smalley, G. (1989). *My Very Own Book of What's for Lunch*. New York: Camex Books.

Adult References

Berman, C. & Fromer, J. (1991). *Meals Without Squeals: Child Care Feeding Guide & Cookbook*. Palo Alto, CA: Bull Publishing Co.

Christenberry, M. A,. & Stevens, B. (1984). *Can Piaget Cook?* Atlanta, GA: Humanics Limited.

Paul, A. (1985). *Kids Cooking Without a Stove: A Cookbook for Young Children*. Santa Fe, NM: Sunstone Press.

Satter, E. (1987). *How to Get Your Kid to Eat—But Not Too Much*. Menlo Park, CA: Bull Publishing.

Where Food Comes From

Terms, Facts, and Principles (TFPs)

General Information

1. Growing plants are the source of all food.
2. People's food comes from plants or animals who eat plants.
   a. Fruits, vegetables, grains and nuts come from plants.
   b. Sugar, honey and syrup come from plants.
   c. Eggs come from birds and reptiles.
   d. Meat, chicken, and fish come from animals.
   e. Milk, cheese, yogurt, and butter come from animals.
3. Many people grow some of their own food.
4. Some people who grow their own food live on farms.
5. People who grow food on a farm are sometimes called farmers.
6. Farmers may grow crops or livestock.
7. Crops are plants grown from seed and then harvested for selling, eating, or feeding to animals.
8. Livestock are animals, such as cows, pigs, or chickens, who are fed crops, then processed into meats and other animal products.
9. Some livestock food sources—eggs and milk—are continuously produced by the same animals.
10. Some livestock food sources are processed only after the animal has died: chicken, meat, lard.
11. Some people grow food in a garden, which is a small patch of land, prepared for seeds and plants, then maintained by such methods as weeding, watering, and harvesting.
12. Harvesting means to gather the edible parts of plants so that they can be prepared for selling or eating.
13. Most people buy some food that others grow.
14. Supermarkets and grocery stores, dairy stores and bakeries, fruit and vegetable stands, bakeries and restaurants are places where food is sold that others have grown.
15. Fruit and vegetable stands sell food very soon after it is harvested.
*16. Bakeries and restaurants sell food after processing or preparation.

*17. Grocery stores and supermarkets sell some foods in their harvested state, as well as other foods that have been processed or prepared.

*18. Sometimes foods are prepared or processed in the same place they are sold; sometimes foods are processed or prepared in one place, and then transported to another place to be sold.

19. People use many vehicles for transporting foods to the places that they are sold: tankers, trucks, cars, wagons, airplanes.

*20. People who sell food must store and display it in ways that enhance its healthfulness, for example, grocery stores keep some foods in refrigeration units, some in freezers, some on shelves or in glass display cases.

Activity Ideas

Aesthetic

1. Walk Around the Garden

Sing the following song with the children, encouraging them to name foods that grow as crops to replace those named in the verses provided. Walk in a circle and pretend to pick or dig up crops as you sing.

♫ **Walk Around the Garden**
Words by Kit Payne
Tune: "Ring Around the Rosey"

Walk around the garden
the crop's about to come in
lima beans, lima beans, we all pick some!

Walk around the garden
the crop's about to come in
melons, melons, we all pick some!

Walk around the garden
the crop's about to come in
potatoes, potatoes, we all dig some!

Walk around the garden
the crop's about to come in
carrots, carrots, we all dig some!

2. Garden Wash

Take large pieces of sidewalk chalk and several plant spraying bottles to the outdoor play yard with you.

Invite children to draw pictures of garden foods on the sidewalk, then spray them with water. Enjoy the ways that the colors and intensity change as the chalk becomes soaked. Use the opportunity to introduce the concept of plants needing water in order to grow and thrive. Consider adding small amounts of food coloring to the water in the spray bottles to add another dimension of color as children spray their chalk drawings.

If you have planted a school garden, children will enjoy the sensory pleasure to be had from spraying real plants, as well.

3. Discard Art

Collect the discards of foods, such as crushed egg shells, nut shells, rinsed coffee grounds, tea leaves and chicken bones to be used in collage or sculpture art projects. (Wash chicken bones in a dishwasher before using them.) Put the various food discards into individual bowls, with small scoops or spoons. Provide white glue or paste, and pieces of cardboard or stiff manila art paper. Comment on the smells, textures and colors of the various substances, as well as the designs being produced, as children work.

Affective

1. My Favorite Crop

Introduce children to the concept of crops, giving many examples of foods that are labeled in this way. Include grains, fruits, vegetables, peanuts, and so on. Show samples of some of these foods. Mention that people who study healthful eating recommend that many crop foods be included in one's diet.

Point out that many prepared foods with which children are familiar start out as crops, and then are changed by grinding, combining or cooking into common forms. Flour, peanut butter, apple sauce, and chocolate are examples of such foods. Next, prepare some samples of the foods you have discussed for children to taste.

Invite children to taste the samples, and decide which they like best and which they like least. Write down the choices on chart paper, and point out where preferences are the same and different. Note where some children prefer the same food in different forms, as with peanuts versus peanut butter, or bread versus flour. You may also find that many prefer fruits over grains, or vegetables over fruits.

3. Home Food Inventory

Prepare a home-to-school activity sheet like the one to the right to encourage children to share information learned at school with their families. Send the checklists home, along with a short note explaining the activity and/or the Terms, Facts, and Principles from this unit on food (see page 104). When children bring the lists back the next day, allow time for them to report to the group about what they have found or to compare their findings with those of two or three classmates.

Foods I Found at Home

Name:_____

Put a check by the ones you find. Write in ones that are not listed.

Crop Foods:

Carrots ____
Apples ____
Potatoes ____
Cereal ____
Bread ____

____ ____
____ ____
____ ____
____ ____
____ ____
____ ____

Livestock Foods:

Eggs ____
Butter ____
Milk ____
Beef ____
Chicken ____

____ ____
____ ____
____ ____
____ ____
____ ____
____ ____

We could not decide if these were crop or livestock foods:

____ ____   ____ ____
____ ____   ____ ____
____ ____   ____ ____

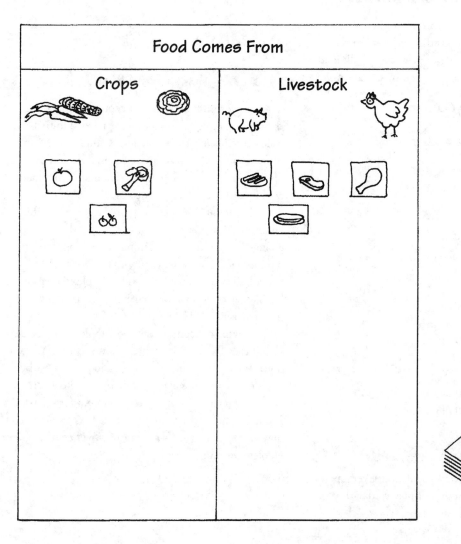

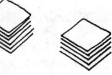

Cognitive

1. Food Source Sorting Game

Prepare a board game with small pictures of foods that can be arranged under two headings, "Crops" and "Livestock." Divide a piece of posterboard down the middle by drawing a line with a dark marker. Head one side "Crops" and draw or glue on some pictures of crop plants. Head the other side "Livestock" and draw or glue on some pictures of animals that provide foods.

Prepare some small game cards with pictures of foods by cutting another piece of poster board into two inch squares and drawing or gluing on pictures of individual foods. Laminate to make them last longer.

Turn all the food cards over, picture-side down, and place them in a pile. Direct children to take turns drawing a card from the pile and deciding where to place it on the board.

To Simplify:
● Put pictures of foods from the two categories under their headings; direct children to find ones that match from among those on the game cards and then place them on the side they represent.

To Extend:
● Assign small groups of children to create the game boards, then trade them with other small groups for different rounds of the game.

2. What Happened to That?

Introduce the concepts of food processing and packaging to the children. Show them several examples of foods that are purchased after undergoing some processing: ground beef, canned pineapple rings, shredded coconut, peanut butter, or bread.

Lead a guessing game in which children attempt to explain how each food looked in its natural form and what was done to change it to its present form. Ask such questions as: Why does that make sense? Does anyone else have a different idea? How else could you explain it? Write down everyone's replies.

Next, ask for ideas about ways to research the correct answers. Write these down, too. Finally, initiate a study of the answers to questions that the children generated. Find out if anyone has a family member with special expertise in food preparation who might be willing to speak to the class. Call a librarian and ask for references to books that you can make available in the classroom. Call local farmers to request presentations to the class. Take a field trip to a supermarket or butcher shop

to witness the process of turning a side of beef into hamburger. Summarize your studies with a discussion of what you have learned. Encourage recall of how information was learned as well.

To Simplify:
● Select foods for which the processing from one state to another can be accomplished in the classroom: peanuts to peanut butter, cream to butter, whole apples to applesauce, or cucumbers to pickles.

To Extend:
● Select foods for which commercial processes such as canning are necessary. Provide homemade examples, if possible, or visit a place in the community where such processing takes place.

3. Trucks, Trains, Ships, and Planes

This activity is best carried out with children in the first grade or beyond. Call a local supermarket to request information about foods that are sold there, but not grown locally. Make a list of foods and their geographical origins. Bring a large map of the world to the group area, along with the list of food origins.

Invite children to help you locate the places from which the foods originate on the map. Explain the colors and symbols on the map that indicate bodies of water versus land masses.

Next, make a list of possible means of transporting foods from their countries of origin to the place where you live. Could a food from Hawaii have come all the way by truck? How can you tell? How about a food from Columbia, like coffee?

How many ways can the children think of to transport a food across the ocean? How about across the country? Consider visiting a local farmers' market to interview the vendors about ways that they transported their crops.

4. What Came First?

Prepare a few series of cards that illustrate food processing or preparation steps. Each series should have at least three to five cards. One set could include peanut vines, peanuts in the shell, unshelled peanuts, peanut butter, and a peanut butter sandwich. Another could include a whole pineapple, pineapple rings, crushed pineapple, and a pineapple upside-down cake. A third set could be comprised of pictures of a wheat field, wheat stalks, flour, and bread. Also make a series that includes a whole egg, broken egg, scrambled eggs and a

chicken. Direct the children to order the cards in the way they believe the process would occur. Ask children to explain their series to you or to each other. Question why some steps (such as crushed pineapple) couldn't come before others (such as pineapple rings).

To Simplify:

● Start with only two pictures, asking the child which comes first. Then provide additional pictures, one at a time, to be placed in the series.

To Extend:

● Select a series that can be duplicated through action in the classroom. Ask children to predict the order of the steps. Then try to carry out the food processing in the way that the children think it should proceed. Discuss the results and try more than one approach to a sequence, as dictated by the children.

5. Food Book Extension

Display one or more of the many children's books that include labeled pictures of foods. After the children have had opportunities to examine the books on their own, provide each child with a chart that includes fabric swatches or paint chips, labeled with color names.

Direct the children to go carefully through one of the books, finding foods in the colors listed. Invite them to write, in their own spelling, the names of the foods that represent each color. Children could then count how many foods appear in each of the colors, and/or compare their lists with a friend's.

Construction

1. Sandwich Books

Prepare templates of several foods that might be included in a sandwich: a lettuce leaf, meats, tomato, onion, green pepper rings, a dollop of mayonnaise or mustard, and so on. Templates can be constructed of stiff cardboard, cut into desired shapes, and colored for ease in identification. You may be able to find puzzles that include single-shape foods, perhaps even some with knobs for holding them still, that can also serve as templates.

Provide the templates, along with construction paper in many colors or manila paper and colored markers. In addition, prepare "pages" produced by cutting construction paper into bread-shaped squares of equal size, with two or three holes punched along one edge. Provide scissors and glue. Help children to:

1. Trace around the food shapes the child would want in his or her sandwich.
2. Cut each one out. (Children can color them if they wish.)
3. Next, glue each food to its own book page.
4. Now assemble the sandwich and lace through the holes with yarn or pipe cleaners, tied or twisted to hold the concoction together.

2. Cases and Places

Stock an art area with the usual paper, scissors, markers, and glue. Then add tin foil, clear plastic wrap, tape, and discarded cardboard boxes (shoe boxes, gift boxes, cheese and egg cartons). Also, provide magazines with many pictures of foods.

Prior to a visit to a grocery store, discuss the many ways that food stores display the products that they are selling. Mention that some displays are designed to keep the food clean, cool, or frozen; others are designed to make it easy to help yourself to your selections. Some even have sprinklers to keep food moist, or heaters to keep food warm! Look for these display cases and places during the grocery store visit.

After the children return to the classroom, tell them to spend a few minutes looking over all the materials provided, while thinking about what they saw on their visit. Invite them to design food cases of various kinds. Children may want to draw foods inside their cases, cut and glue pictures from the magazines, or construct them from the art materials. Some may want to label or price their products as well.

3. Sensory Tubes

Collect discarded toilet paper tubes, one or two per child. Provide the children with these tubes, along with tightly woven net or cheesecloth squares and tape or staplers. Show children how to close one end of the tube by pressing the sides together and then stapling it shut. Suggest that they work in pairs, one holding, the other stapling. Alternatively, have the children press the sides together at one end, and then apply strips of tape to hold the end shut. Next, partially fill the tube with one of the substances below. Finally, fold a square of net across the open end, and staple or tape it in place.

Provide bowls of unpopped popcorn, dried beans, and uncooked barley for sound tubes; use cinnamon, cloves, garlic powder, and cumin (or some other combination of spices) for smell tubes. Point out that all these foods come from crops.

After the children have constructed one or more sensory tubes, they can challenge other children to guess

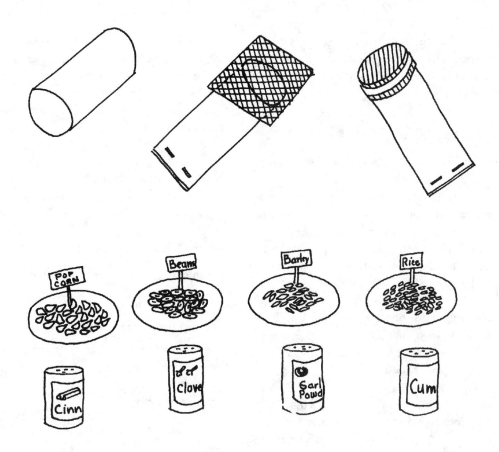

what was placed inside by shaking or sniffing. The "guesser" can match the sensory message to a visual cue, by pointing out which open bowl contains the same ingredient as the tube they are smelling or listening to or naming the ingredient from memory.

To Simplify:

● Pre-construct tubes that are closed on one end. Have children select items and pour a different kind in each of their tubes. Assist children in securing the items inside.

To Extend:

● Help children to label each of their tubes with the name of its contents to provide a way of checking later.

Language

1. Down Around the Corner

Teach children the following song, which allows each of them to name a food as well as to hear their own names sung. Begin with a discussion of the kinds of foods one might find at a produce stand and the reasons that produce provides healthful food choices. Display posters to help children with ideas.

♫ Down Around the Corner

Words by Kit Payne

Tune: "The Donut Shop" (or can be chanted)

> Down around the corner at the produce stand,
> there was one (red apple) from a farmer's land,
> along came (Ronald) who selected it, and . . .
> now there's no (red apple) at the produce stand!
> Down around the corner at the produce stand,
> there was one (orange carrot) from a farmer's land,
> along came (Alicia) who selected it, and . . .
> now there's no (orange carrot) at the produce stand!

To Simplify:

● For each child's turn, hold up a different color and kind of fruit or vegetable that you have made from construction paper. Alternatively, use plastic models of fruits and vegetables to hold up.

To Extend:

● Place plastic fruits and vegetables in a paper bag. As each child's turn comes around, invite him or her to select an item from the bag to be named in the song.

● Another alternative is to make shapes of common fruits and vegetables from black construction paper.

Also, cut out color squares from various colors of construction paper. Have children select one color and one shape (such as blue banana, red corn) to create silly combinations to name in the song.

2. Recipe Files

Lead a discussion of the purpose of recipes as food-combination plans. Show the children some cookbooks or commercial recipe cards to illustrate this concept. Point out that recipes are sometimes illustrated to give the reader more information about the plan. Mention that sometimes the necessary equipment and ingredients are listed separately at the beginning of the recipe and then the procedure steps follow.

Provide children with easel paper or construction paper and pencils or fine-tipped marking pens. Tell them that the class will work together to create a recipe file. Prepare a simple recipe in class, then have children prepare a written and/or illustrated recipe to describe what they did.

Later, invite children to choose a food that they like—perhaps one that they have observed someone in their family preparing or have helped to prepare. Suggest that they begin by drawing pictures of utensils and ingredients that would be needed if they are unsure about how to write the words. Point out that a whole recipe can be told in pictures.

As children work on illustrations, move among them, offering to write down the steps in words, or to help them to sound out spellings, if they wish. Also, suggest that children seek each other's help with this process.

A separate activity is for each child to dictate a favorite home recipe, then illustrate it as desired. Combine all the dictated recipes into a class cookbook. Expect many interesting ideas about cooking heat, cooking time and quantities! Don't worry about accuracy, unless you plan to prepare foods by these guidelines!

To Extend:
● Read the story *Too Many Eggs* by M. C. Butler (1988) before or after this activity. Discuss what happened to the main character's cake when she lost track of the quantity of an important ingredient while preparing her batter.

3. Family Food Completion Stories

Make enough copies of the following completion story so that each child can take one home to finish with his or her family. Introduce the activity with a discussion of the many ways that people gather various ingredients and prepare special recipes in honor of important days in their lives. Point out that different families acknowledge different special days, in different special ways. Later in the week, you can read some or all of the stories to the whole group or compile them into a book to add to your reading corner.

You might also consider asking families to contribute recipe cards for the foods they describe. These could be used throughout the year to prepare very special snacks. Be sure to label them with family names so that you can offer special thanks to contributors when enjoying these special foods.

In our family, we prepare a special food called
_____ whenever a
special day called _____ comes around.
We start getting ready to fix this food by gathering

_____
_____
_____
_____. We learned about this special food
from_____. Here are some other
special things that we do, or that we eat, when we share
this food:_____
_____.
When we prepare and eat this food, we feel_____.

Here is a picture of us enjoying this food:

4. Oh, Dear!

Before reading the story *Oh Dear!* by Rod Campbell (1984), collect plastic figures of the animals mentioned in this story of a little boy, searching a farm for the source of eggs for breakfast, a cow, a pig, a sheep, a horse, a dog, a rabbit, a duck, and/or a chicken. Also include some figures of animals that do not appear in the story. Place all of the animal figures in a paper bag or box.

Tell the children to listen carefully as you read the story because you will all play a remembering game when it is over. Then read the story, stopping for discussion as the children wish. Next, hold up your bag or box, telling the children that it contains animals, some from the story and some not. Pull out one animal at a time, asking whether the children think it appeared in the story. Form one set of animals that the children think did appear and one set of animals that they think did not, as you proceed.

Read through the story again, checking to see whether the sets have been formed to reflect the story.

Hint for Success:

● If you are unable to locate a copy of this book, use a version of the children's classic "The Little Red Hen" or the book *Rooster's Off to See the World* by Eric Carle (1972) instead.

To Simplify:

● Before reading the book, tell the children that you will be asking them to remember animal names.

To Extend:

● Invite the children to recall the order in which their selected animals appear before reading through the book again to check.

● Alternatively, ask the children to dictate or write more pages for the book, adding animals that did not appear and the housing in which each might be found.

Physical

1. Grinding Grains

Collect a few mortar and pestle sets for children to use in this activity. Ask families for loaners or visit kitchen stores to purchase inexpensive ones. Purchase dried corn or wheat berries from a supermarket, a farmer's market, or a local farmer.

Demonstrate the use of a mortar and pestle, emphasizing the downward pressure applied by straightening the arm on each stroke, the wrist-twisting motion that enhances grinding, and the importance of firmly gripping the pestle.

Give every child who expresses interest a turn to grind. If you have managed to collect several mortar and pestle sets, turn-taking won't take long. If there is only one set, consider using a sign-up sheet and perhaps a kitchen timer to ensure that everyone has a chance to try this grinding utensil. The ground grain can be added to any bread recipe or sampled on its own. A corn bread recipe is given below.

Mexican Cornbread

3 cups corn meal

2-1/2 cups milk

3 eggs, beaten

1-1/2 cup corn kernels

2-1/2 cups cheddar cheese

1 large grated or finely chopped onion

1/2 cup salad oil

Stir all of the ingredients together in the order given. Pour the batter into a six-cup greased ring mold or Bundt pan. Bake at 375° for 45 minutes. Unmold and slice.

2. Plucking Out the Seeds

Inform children that when people eat crop foods, they are eating parts of plants. When people eat livestock foods, they are eating parts of animals or products made by animals. One way to decide whether a food is a crop or not is to find out if it contains seeds in its raw form; all crops have seeds. Also mention that when a food is called a fruit, the seed is contained in or on the part that is eaten. Vegetables usually have seeds that are more difficult to find and that are somewhere other than in or on the part we eat. When we eat grains, we are usually eating the seed itself.

Provide the children with fruits, and perhaps some vegetables and grains, in their raw form. Direct them to use their hands to "dissect" each food, searching for seeds. Mention that seeds can be large or small, hard or soft and that some are eaten while others are not healthful for people.

Tell the children to try to separate the seeds from their foods and to set them aside for later examination. You may want to provide some magnifying glasses so that children can more easily examine the tiny seeds in bananas, strawberries, and so on.

Hint for Success:

● Choose foods that contain a variety of seed types, such as avocados, pomegranates, corn on the cob, bananas, and strawberries. This will make comparisons as well as seed retrieval more interesting.

To Simplify:

● Peel or cut up the foods ahead of time to make disassembling them easier.

To Extend:

● Add some meat product foods, such as whole sardines, canned clams, eggs, yogurt, and milk. Invite the children to break or pull apart these foods, too, to determine whether any seeds can be found.

● Plan one or more cooking activities as a follow-up experience so that the "dissected" foods are not wasted.

● Make available some reference books so that children can research where in a vegetable plant the seed would be found.

3. Shelling, Peeling, Stripping, Boning

Provide children with opportunities to carry out some of the processing steps necessary for preparing many foods. Bring in whole cobs of corn so that children can strip them of their husks and silk. Shell peas from their pods. Shell peanuts. Peel bananas and tangerines by hand. Remove the bones from canned salmon or canned crab. Point out how like kitchen utensils one's hands and fingers can be—even better than tools in many cases!

4. Grinding, Shaking, and Churning

Borrow or purchase a meat grinder that is operated mechanically by turning a handle. This machine can be used to prepare apples for applesauce, to grind meats for sandwich spreads, and to grind peanuts for peanut butter. Let the children take turns pouring in foods and cranking the handle.

Butter can be made by sealing cream tightly in small jars, then shaking repeatedly until it thickens to a spread.

Ice cream makers are available that are operated by a hand crank. Follow a recipe that includes crushing ice to pack around the freezer, as well as cranking so that the mixture blends and freezes at the same time. Let the children crush ice blocks wrapped in cheesecloth or plastic with hammers that have been washed well or try crushing ice cubes in a meat grinder.

An easy no-cook ice cream recipe is provided below. Before preparing it, show children pictures of a maple tree or take a walking trip to look at a maple tree, if this is possible in your area. Discuss the process by which people extract maple from the trees and boil it into syrup. Show a picture of a whole pineapple or, if possible, bring one in to show to the children. If you can locate a fresh pineapple, cut off the skin and let the children crush the fruit themselves. Use this instead of canned pineapple.

Maple-Pineapple Ice Cream

    1 cup maple syrup

    2 cups cream

    1 cup canned or fresh pineapple, crushed

Mix together all ingredients. Fill the container of a crank-type ice cream maker not more than 3/4 full. Place the container with the ice cream mixture in the freezer pail. Surround the container with one part salt to eight parts crushed ice, enough to fill it. Rock salt works best. Mix the salt and ice before packing the freezer. Put on the cover and turn the crank slowly until the mixture begins to freeze (you will feel resistance against the crank). Turn the crank more rapidly for twelve to twenty minutes more.

Pretend Play

1. Produce Stand

Collect all the fruits and vegetables from your program's plastic food sets. Place them in baskets and boxes on tables in a pretend play area. Provide a cash register or cash box with play money, small empty grocery sacks, and hats or aprons for salespeople to wear. Add balance scales if possible. Provide pads of paper and pencils for figuring orders and sales. Other good additions include stickers and number stamps to make stick-on price tags and sign-making materials (posterboard or construction paper, markers or crayons, tape, and so on) to designate specials. Hang a sign yourself that reads "Produce Stand" and a flip-over "Open/Closed" sign. Hang produce posters on the walls.

Inform children about the roles of shelf-stocker, delivery person, customer, and weigher/sorter/bagger, as well as the more familiar one of cashier.

2. Pizza Parlor

Make a few sturdy cardboard-circle pizzas; cover them with tan flannel or felt. Cut out felt "toppings" in a variety of colors and types: grated cheese strips in yellow and white felt, pepperoni circles in brown, green onions and peppers, gold pineapple chunks, and so on.

Set up a phone-in, order-taking desk. Provide pencils and pads. Select some hats, aprons, or shirts to designate employees.

If available, leave the pretend-area oven and refrigerator out and ready for pizza-supply storage and preparation; add cookie sheets or pizza pans and spatulas.

Small tables and chairs, plates and forks, and cups and napkins can make this an eat-in restaurant; a wagon can add a delivery service. For either eat-in or delivery, offer juice on the menu, as well (serve in empty, cleaned individual-size juice containers). Find opportunities to visit this area often. Talk about the many foods that are combined in a pizza-and-juice meal. Ask children to determine which toppings are crop foods, and which come from livestock.

Discuss your expectation that all the pizza toppings will be sorted and stored in separate containers, ready for the next day's business, at each clean-up time.

Provide several covered margarine tubs or similar containers for this purpose . . . and extra clean-up time!

3. Food Story Corner

When telling or reading traditional stories or nursery rhymes with food themes, provide children with opportunities to re-enact them. Examples of such stories include "Old Mother Hubbard," "Little Jack Horner," "Little Miss Muffet," "Stone Soup," "Jack and the Beanstalk," and "The Big, Big Turnip." To enhance the children's creative dramatics, prepare props or costumes that relate to each story. Simple stick puppets can be produced by following book illustrations, cutting out single parts, and taping them to tongue depressors. Simple "costumes" can be made by purchasing plastic headbands and taping on paper cut-outs of hat brims, animal ears, spider legs, foods, and so on. Real or plastic foods can be dropped into a basket or pot as the story "Stone Soup" is retold.

Social

1. From Farm to Market

Introduce the idea of cooperative efforts in farming. Mention the many stages involved between planting crops and raising livestock, and getting the end products to market. Ask children for ideas about ways for transporting the foods from the farm to the market place. Discuss the marketing strategies that result in selling the foods to customers. Ask the children about some of the ways they decide which foods seem best—pictures on the packages, big displays, advertisements on television, and so on.

Next, invite the children to create, collaboratively, a market place for the pretend foods available in your dramatic play area. Point out that some children may want to design display stands, while others price the foods with stick-on labels or numbers and phrases written directly on boxes used for transport and display. Some may want to construct signs that convince customers to choose their products. Some may want to serve as clerks, figuring up the total price of customers' selections. Ways of transporting the foods with wagons, boxes with rope handles affixed, and so on could be determined.

Encourage the children to seek whatever materials they think are necessary, or to ask you for help in finding them, or in adapting some other classroom equipment to fill the bill. Shelves could be turned on their sides to serve as display bins. Individual desks could be used as check-out stations. Extra food products could be made from art materials. Sign-lettering could be accomplished by copying lettering from food books.

Discuss the importance of working together in such complex undertakings as running a farm or a farmer's market.

2. Production Song

Teach about the sources of foods through an adaptation of the song, The Farmer in the Dell." To add to the fun, gather models and pictures or empty food containers for the children to hold up as they sing their verses. Give children, one at a time, a food picture or model or just the name of a food. Ask them to determine its source, and sing a verse about it, using the word "produces." Explain that this word means "provides" or "makes," and is about where the food comes from. You may want to mention that often a person finishes production, rather than the source by itself: cows don't really produce cheese without help from people, and tomatoes don't turn themselves into spaghetti sauce! They do, however, produce the essential ingredients. Start out by singing a couple of verses yourself:

> The chicken produces eggs, the chicken produces eggs,
> Heigh-ho the derry-oh, the chicken produces eggs.
>
> The cow produces milk, the cow produces milk,
> Heigh-ho the derry-oh, the cow produces milk.
>
> The tomato produces spaghetti sauce, the tomato produces spaghetti sauce,
> Heigh-oh the derry-oh, the tomato produces spaghetti sauce.

Encourage children to help each other determine production. Expect that many sources will be unknown to the children. Many will be surprised that pigs produce bacon and cows produce Big Macs™! You may have to provide the information, and then enhance children's recall by inviting them to sing about it.

3. Crop-and-Livestock-Pizza Vendors

Ahead of time, prepare a variety of pizza toppings, chopped and separated into bowls. Purchase English muffins and divide them into halves; they will be used as individual pizza crusts. Prepare an order form with pictures of each ingredient. Divide the form into crop toppings (green pepper, onion, mushrooms, tomato sauce, and so on) and toppings made by/from livestock (cheese, chopped bologna or pepperoni, ground beef, and so on).

Next, let small groups of four or five children take orders from one other small group about which toppings they would like on their pizza. Each order-taker can then prepare one other person's pizza order. After the pizzas have been baked in a toaster oven, the order-takers can serve their customers' snack. While the first group of patrons is eating, direct a third group to take orders from a fourth. Continue until everyone has had a turn as an order-taker and as an eater. You may want to carry this activity out over two or three days if there is not time in your schedule for everyone to participate on the same day.

Teacher Resources

Field Trip Ideas

1. Take the children to one or more pick-your-own crop farms or orchards. Ask the personnel to speak to the group about the care they have taken to raise the crop and about whether they also raise livestock. If so, do the livestock ever eat the same crop that you are picking for yourselves? Encourage the children to pause to examine the foods they are picking, looking for leaves, stems, seeds, and so on.

2. Take the children to visit a dairy barn. Talk ahead of time about the unexpected sounds and smells they are likely to encounter. Ask animal tenders to tell the children about what they feed the livestock and about what products they ultimately sell or consume that are produced by the livestock. Ask to see some production steps in action, if possible, such as milking cows.

3. Visit a supermarket. Inquire ahead of time about whether the children can watch deliveries being made by transport vehicles. Some large supermarkets have their own bakeries, butchers, fish counters (sometimes with live lobsters), or deli counters with salads and so on prepared on-site. Arrange to watch some of these processes in action.

   Take a walk through the store aisles, noting the many ways that foods are stored and displayed. Look for sections that contain categories of foods: the produce department, the dairy cases, the meat counter, and the cereal shelves where many grain foods are displayed.

4. Travel to a farmers' market on a market day. Prepare an interview form ahead of time so that information about distance traveled, means of transportation, and variety of products that came from the same place can be gathered. Point out the weighing scales and pricing guidelines that some of the farmers use.

Classroom Visitors

1. Invite a truck driver who transports foods to market to visit your school. Call a supermarket to seek the name or number of a milk-tanker driver or a bread-delivery person. Request that the children be allowed to look inside the vehicle. Ask the driver to tell about the trips he or she takes, the methods of unloading they employ, the problems of keeping the food in good shape during transport, and so on.

2. Find out whether any of your children are from farming families. Invite a parent to visit the classroom and discuss the many chores involved in running a farm. Ask questions about what is grown or raised, in what number, and whether the products are sold to stores, food manufacturers, or used by the family and their neighbors alone. Ask the visitor to bring pictures or tools and implements that might interest the children.

3. Invite a representative of a seed or feed company to come to your classroom, bringing samples of the products they sell for the children to examine. Ask questions about ways in which the products are packaged, transported, and used.

Children's Books

Brown, M. (1947). *Stone Soup*. New York: Macmillan.

Buckley, H. (1963). *Some Cheese for Charles*. New York: Lothrop, Lee and Shepard.

Butler, M. C. (1988). *Too Many Eggs: A Counting Book*. Boston: Godine.

Campbell, R. (1984). *Oh Dear!* New York: Macmillan.

Carle, E. (1972). *Rooster's Off to See the World*. New York: Scholastic.

Ehlert, L. (1989). *Eating the Alphabet*. New York: Harcourt Brace Jovanovich.

Ehlert, L. (1987). *Growing Vegetable Soup*. New York: Harcourt Brace Jovanovich.

Gunthrop, K. (1967). *Fish for Breakfast*. New York: Doubleday.

Kelley, T. (1989). *Let's Eat*. New York: Dutton Child Books.

Krauss, R. (1945). *The Carrot Seed*. New York: HarperCollins.

Mitgutsch, A. (1971). *From Seed to Pear*. Minneapolis: Carolrhoda.

Pienkowski, J. (1991). *Food*. New York: Simon & Schuster.

Reece, C. (1985). *What Was It Before It Was Ice Cream?* Mankato, MN: Child's World.

Smalley, G. (1989). *My Very Own Book of What's for Lunch*. New York: Camex Books.

Tolstoy, A. (1968). *The Great Big Enormous Turnip*. New York: Watts.

Adult References

Atlas, N. (1993). *Vegetariana: A Rich Harvest of Wit, Lore, and Recipes*. Boston: Little, Brown.

Christenberry, M. A., and Stevens, B. (1984). *Can Piaget Cook?* Atlanta: Humanics.

Dowden, A. O. (1979). *The Noble Harvest: A Chronicle of Herbs*. New York: Collins.

Selsam, M. E. (1981). *The Plants We Eat*. New York: William Morrow.

How the Body Uses Food

Terms, Facts, and Principles (TFPs)

General Information

1. People eat food and drink water to get nourishment inside their bodies.

2. People bite and chew some foods; some they lick or drink.

*3. Energy is stored in the foods that people eat.

*4. Energy makes the body move, grow, and repair itself.

*5. Energy is stored in the form of carbohydrates, proteins, fats, vitamins, and minerals.

6. Foods are broken down inside the body.

7. The process of breaking down food inside the body is called digestion.

*8. When foods break down through digestion, they release energy into the body.

*9. Some foods supply more energy than others.

*10. A food is seldom used up entirely by the body. Some of it eventually comes back out of the body in a process called elimination.

*11. Food is changed and combined into other substances before it is eliminated, usually through the anus, urethra, or nose.

12. There is no one food that contains all ingredients necessary for a healthy body.

13. It is important to eat a wide variety of foods.

*14. It is important to drink plenty of water since many body processes, including digestion and elimination, depend on water.

*15. People have developed guidelines that help us determine whether we are getting enough variety in the foods we eat. One such guideline is called the Food Guide Pyramid.

*16. The Food Guide Pyramid depicts foods in six different groups, all necessary for good health.

*17. Foods from some of the groups should be eaten in larger quantities than foods in other groups.

*18. The six food groups in the Food Guide Pyramid, in order of importance for good health, are:

1) the bread, cereal, rice, and pasta group;

2) the vegetable group;

3) the fruit group;

4) the meat, poultry, fish, dry beans, nuts, and eggs group;

5) the milk, cheese, and yogurt group;

6) the fats, oils and sweets group.

*19. Each food group has a special function in relation to the body.

*20. People do not have to eat all the foods in a given food group, but should eat some.

*21. People should choose foods from each food group rather than choosing all their food from one group only.

22. There are many combinations of foods that can supply the energy that people's bodies need.

*23. Many prepared foods contain a combination of foods, representing more than one group.

24. Most packaged and canned foods contain lists which describe their ingredients.

Poor Food Choices

25. Eating too many fats and sweets contributes to health problems, such as obesity and tooth decay.

*26. Tooth decay happens when substances in the mouth called bacteria combine with ingredients in some foods to produce acids that can dissolve tooth enamel.

27. Sweet, sticky foods that cling to the teeth are the most harmful.

28. Brushing teeth after eating removes food particles and makes tooth decay less likely.

*29. Eating more food than the body needs or foods that cause a person to feel full but do not provide much energy can cause weight gain that can lead to health problems. This is called obesity.

30. When people feel full, they should decide not to eat or to stop eating until they are hungry again.

Activity Ideas

Aesthetic

1. Please Pass the Senses

Pass around a variety of foods as the children sit together in a circle. Encourage everyone to smell, feel, and look at the bountiful variety of sensory cues. Examine grapefruits and oranges with fingertips, noses, and eyes. Compare them with smooth-skinned apples and bananas. Feel the ridges in pumpkins and the bumps on an avocado. Notice how nut shells feel.

2. Peels Appeal

Peel some fruits and vegetables to be served for a snack. Invite children to arrange the peels in interesting collage-type arrangements and to enjoy the effects they create in combination. Apple peels, orange rings, carrot shavings, and avocado skins all have interesting colors and textures and create pleasing designs when piled or placed together. After using the peels for artistic arrangements, add them to an outdoor compost pile or scatter them in a wooded area for critters to enjoy as snacks.

3. Top to Bottom

When serving hot drinks like cocoa or iced drinks like juice, encourage the children to be alert for the sensation of the liquids flowing through the body. Feel them moving down your throat and through the winding tube (esophagus) that takes them to your stomach. Point out that sometimes we can even feel foods being processed in the stomach or hear stomach sounds as this work goes on. The stomach then sends food into a long, curly tube (intestines) where the body sorts parts it needs from parts it does not need. Later we can feel the unneeded parts getting ready to come back out of our bodies when we use the toilet. Encourage children to take pleasure in the sensory experiences that the body provides as it carries out the process of digestion.

4. The Peanut Butter and Jelly Chant

Chant the following verses to a popular early childhood poem that teaches children about making and eating a peanut butter and jelly sandwich. The easy repetition in the verses will soon have children joining in the chanting and the fun. Act out the suggested motions as you chant.

Peanut Butter and Jelly (Chant)

Peanut . . . peanut butter! Jelly!

Peanut . . . peanut butter! Jelly!

First you find the peanuts and you pick `em, and you pick `em, and you pick `em, pick `em, pick `em.

Peanut . . . peanut butter! Jelly!

Peanut . . . peanut butter! Jelly!

Then you take the peanuts and you shell `em, and you shell `em, and you shell `em, shell `em, shell `em.

Peanut . . . peanut butter! Jelly!

Peanut . . . peanut butter! Jelly!

Then you take the peanuts and you smash `em, and you smash `em, and you smash `em, smash `em, smash `em.

Peanut . . . peanut butter! Jelly!

Peanut . . . peanut butter! Jelly!

Next you find the berries and you pick `em, and you pick `em and you pick `em, pick `em, pick `em, then you wash `em and you wash `em and you wash `em, wash `em, wash `em, then you smash `em and you smash `em and you smash `em, smash `em, smash `em.

Peanut . . . peanut butter! Jelly!

Peanut . . . peanut butter! Jelly!

Then you get some bread, and you spread it and you spread it and you spread it, spread it, spread it,

Then you bite it, and you bite it, and you bite it, bite it, bite it,

Then you swallow, and you swallow, and you swallow, swallow, swallow.

Peanut . . . peanut butter! Jelly!

Peanut . . . peanut butter! Jelly!

Note: When you get to the parts where you chew and swallow, try "talking" with your mouth firmly closed, after telling the children what you're meaning to say. This results in a sort of a humming-talk that adds to the silliness and the fun!

Affective

1. Planning for Healthful Eating

Lead a discussion about the responsibility that each person must take for his or her own health. Introduce the Food Guide Pyramid and the kinds of foods that represent each band. Discuss the importance of choosing many kinds of foods, emphasizing that no one food, by itself, provides all the body's needs. Inform the children that the pyramid is arranged so that wider bands are comprised of foods that should be eaten in greater quantity and that narrow bands have foods that people should eat less of. Point out that some people who study healthful food choices believe that by choosing foods in a variety of (natural) colors, we enhance the chances of a well-balanced diet.

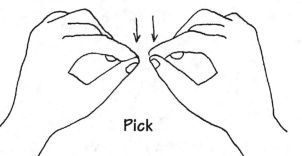

Pick

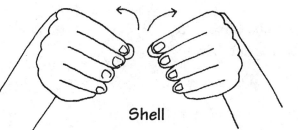

Shell

Smash

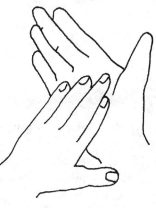

Spread

Plan for a Food Pyramid

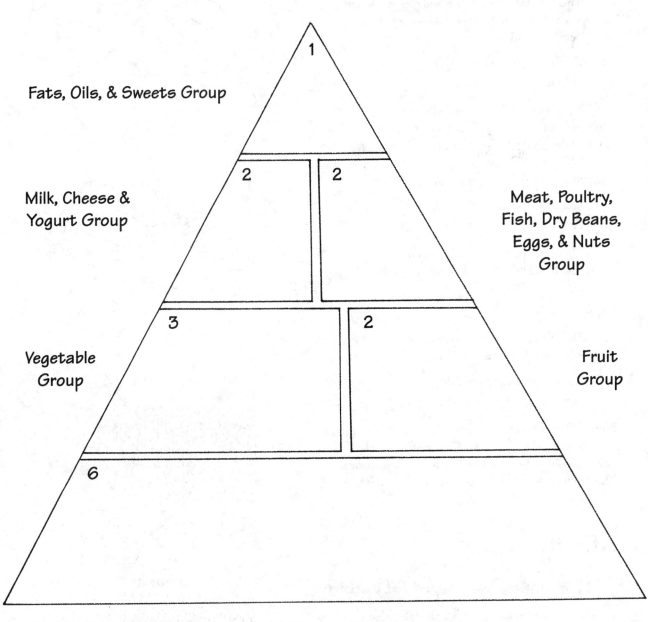

Fats, Oils, & Sweets Group

Milk, Cheese & Yogurt Group

Meat, Poultry, Fish, Dry Beans, Eggs, & Nuts Group

Vegetable Group

Fruit Group

Bread, Cereal, Rice, & Pasta Group

2. Pyramid Plan

Provide each child with a triangular piece of paper to further emphasize the meaning of the Food Guide Pyramid plan. Suggest that they write or draw food choices, or cut and paste pictures from old magazines to compile food choices.

Another option is to have children collect pictures of foods from magazines and packages in their homes, with family help. Send home a note asking for this assistance, and requesting that children bring the pictures with them to school. Tell children that it's important to choose foods that they like, but that also are good for them.

Hint for Success:

● Display pictures of the Food Guide Pyramid for children to refer to as they plan their pyramids.

To Simplify:

● Locate rubber stamps of foods for children to use to imprint pictures on their pyramids. Using either the stamps or pictures that you have collected, talk with the children as a group about which foods would be located on each band of the pyramid. Wait for the children to fill in one band before moving on to a discussion of the next band.

To Extend:

● Provide children with grocery store advertising circulars and food coupons to refer to as they make choices. Direct children who are working on math skills to price their selections, using the available advertisements.

● Provide a guideline* for children to use as they make their pyramids that specifies quantities of foods to select from each category: six kinds of bread, cereal, rice, or pasta foods; three vegetables; two fruits; two servings of meat, poultry, fish, dry beans, eggs, or nuts; two milk, cheese, or yogurt products; and one from the fats, oils, or sweets category.

* From recommendations for minimum number of daily servings, U.S. Department of Health and Human Services.

3. My Favorite Grain, My Favorite Fruit

After some discussions of foods that belong together in certain nutritional categories, have children take turns naming favorites from each category (see pyramid labels). As children name a food, add it to a master list, divided by category. Later help the children to produce graphs for the various categories. Encourage children to compare how many children chose the same favorites, how many different foods were generated per group, or how many foods are the same color, and so on.

Cognitive

1. Searching for the Pyramids

Before carrying out this activity, compile a collection of empty food packages. Ask parents for help with this step. You will find that many food containers now include a labeled illustration of the Food Guide Pyramid (source: U.S. Department of Agriculture, U.S. Department of Health and Human Services). This picture is frequently found on packages of cereal, crackers, rice, and pasta.

Display all the packages you have collected on a table. Ask children to look at them closely to see if they can find the Food Guide Pyramid. After children have had several minutes to examine these packages, ask them to discuss why they think some contain the pyramid and others do not. Read the information that accompanies the picture. Point out the different foods that are pictured on each band of the pyramid. Ask children which band is represented by the most packages that include the picture. This is a good time to discuss recommendations for various food choices.

To Simplify:

● Show children what the pyramid picture looks like. Then have them sort the collected packages into two groups—those with the picture and those without.

To Extend:

● Provide children with empty boxes that have at least some plain surfaces on which to write (shoeboxes, collapsible, solid-colored gift boxes, boxes for bars of soap, and so on). Invite them to use these containers in designing a new food package, complete with a food pyramid, product name, and illustration of the contents.

2. The Parts of the Whole

Gather some plant and animal foods that can be displayed, in whole, for the children to examine: a whole chicken or Cornish hen; a whole fish; a whole carrot with tops in place; a stalk of celery complete with leaves; a whole broccoli plant, a whole head of cauliflower with leaves, roots, and stem still intact; a small pumpkin. Tell the children that people seldom eat all of a food. Usually, we discard some parts or we cut off one part and give other parts to other people.

Allow the children plenty of time to examine and/or dissect the foods you have provided. For each plant, ask them to decide which are the edible plant parts—the leaves, roots, stems, flowers, or seeds. Ask them to name the parts of the chicken—legs, wings, neck, and so on. Look the fish over carefully, deciding if there are inedible parts (such as the bones and eyes). Wash, prepare, and eat only those foods that are safely kept away from refrigeration for long periods (not the chicken or fish, unless they are examined from a frozen state and prepared as soon as they thaw). Make sure that children wash their hands well after handling raw meats. Wash the tabletops carefully with a disinfectant after exposing them to raw meat as well. Avoid placing vegetables that you plan to eat raw on the same surfaces as the raw meats.

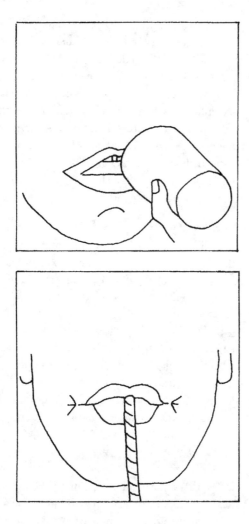
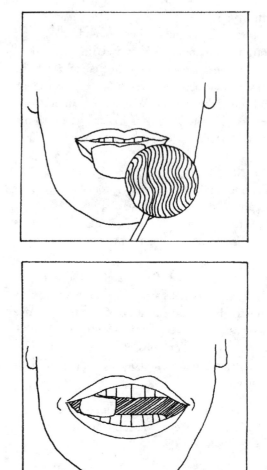

3. How Do You Eat It? Collage

Prepare large pieces of newsprint or construction paper ahead of time by drawing lines to divide the pages into four equal sections. Label the sections Chew It, Drink It, Lick It, Suck It. Add simple line drawings that depict each label. Provide grocery special inserts from newspapers, food magazines, scissors, and glue sticks.

Tell the children that there are many ways to take foods into our bodies and that the labels on their papers tell some of the ways. Have them first cut out a variety of food pictures, then determine in which section each would go. Then have children glue the pictures into the appropriate squares.

To Simplify:

● Discuss the ways that people get foods inside their bodies. Then hold up some foods or pictures of foods, asking children to tell how each one is eaten.

● Prepare four different charts, one with each of the labels mentioned above. Gather the children into four smaller groups. Assign each group to work on one of the four categories.

To Extend:

● Hang a copy of the chart described above in your snack or meal area for a week or two. Invite children to add the names of foods that are served each day to the appropriate section on the chart. At the end of this unit, count together the number of foods in each section.

Construction

1. Building Digestive Systems

Collect many clear plastic jugs that milk, juice, or cleaning supplies come packaged in. Wash them well before using. Visit a large hardware store and purchase flexible plastic tubing that is wide enough in diameter to stretch over the neck of the jugs. (Check for tubing in the plumbing section.)

Draw faces on some of the plastic jugs with permanent marker, turning the jugs upside down so that the opening represents a neck. Cut large mouth openings in the center of the jugs.

Invite children to experiment with assembling transparent bodies by stretching tubes around the necks of the face-jugs, then connecting the other end to an upright jug to serve as the stomach.

Next, provide water and small, firm foods such as dried beans and peas or peanuts, so that the children can watch the way these substances and objects travel from the mouth, down the throat and esophagus, into the stomach. Add some food coloring to the water to make its progress easier to track, if you wish. You may want to use an empty water table for a work surface, to contain spills and messes. As you work together, remind children which parts of the body the jugs and tubes represent (a picture of the body and/or a model would be helpful here).

You could also help the children to construct intestines by cutting small holes in the bottoms of the "stomach" jugs into which another piece of tubing can be inserted. (Silly Putty® makes a great sealer to prevent leaks.) The foods and liquids that start at the "mouth" can then travel all the way through and back out of the "body." Point out that this is the way elimination works.

Note: Be sure that you discuss the importance of chewing small, firm foods before swallowing them, to avoid choking. Point out that the bodies the children are building do not have teeth, but that real people would only be given such foods if they had teeth, and would then be reminded to chew them up well before swallowing (dry beans would have to be cooked first, too).

2. Hidden Ingredient Detectors

Tell children that some of the ingredients in foods are easy to find just by looking: we can easily spot raisins or nuts in a cookie or detect and count all of the vegetables in a salad. Other ingredients can be very hard to find, even if you taste the foods they're hidden in, such as eggs in cake and milk in mashed potatoes.

Mention that water is an important component of a healthful diet—perhaps the most important. People, however, don't have to rely only on drinking water in a cup to get it into their bodies. Many foods have water in them. Oils and fats, on the other hand, should only be eaten in small amounts. Too much of them can make you sick or overweight. Tell the children that fats, oils, and water are hard to detect in many of the foods that contain them. Go on to tell the children that you will help them to build detecting boxes to use in determining which foods have each of these ingredients. Work with a few children each day on this project until everyone has had a turn or recruit parent volunteers to help.

Provide each child with a rectangle of stiff paper or light cardboard. Prepare these ahead of time by drawing lines that look like little boxes in all four corners.

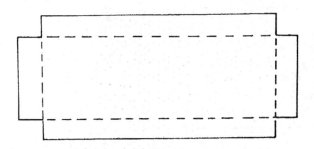

Ask children to cut out the little boxes at each corner with their scissors. Now the corners can be folded up to turn the papers into trays with sides. Show the children how to fold the sides up beside each of the cut corners, along the lengths of the paper. Provide masking tape or cellophane tape so that the children can fasten the edges of their trays together. Have each child make two trays in this manner.

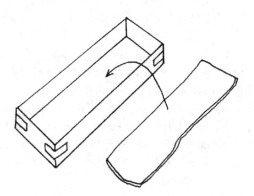

Next, provide each child with one sheet of thick, white paper towel, as well as one piece of either brown butcher paper, a cut-up brown grocery sack, or a piece of a brown hand towel. These papers should be cut to fit in the bottom of the paper trays. Direct the children to fit a piece of white paper towel into one tray bottom and one piece of brown paper into the other.

Provide pieces of food that can be placed in the trays for several minutes. Then have the children lift out the foods and look for water spots or oil stains that they have left behind.

Hint for Success:
● Fruits and vegetables, such as halved grapes, apple or pear slices, green pepper or carrot strips will leave good water spots. Many kinds of crackers and cookies will leave oil stains, especially if lard or butter are listed in their ingredients.

To Simplify:
● Give each child a small brown paper lunch or grocery sack. High-fat foods placed in the sacks will leave oil stains after a while.

To Extend:
● Line the trays with wax paper before putting the other paper liners in place so that the paper liners can be replaced over and over. Try detecting fats and water in different foods each day for a week or so. Try packaged meats, such as bacon and sliced turkey, and compare the appearance and feel of the stains they leave. Keep records of your findings.

● Add a prediction step. Try to guess by feel or taste which foods will leave water or oil spots before placing them in the detection trays. Decide if you were right or not when they are removed and their stains are examined.

3. Toothbrush Test Kits

Purchase or seek donations of small ceramic bathroom tile squares. Look for the one- or two-inch squares. Get enough for each child to have at least six squares. (They are usually packaged in 12" x 12" sheets, so one sheet would yield 144 one-inch squares or 36 two-inch squares.)

Provide each child with a piece of cardboard (or use stiff plastic if available). Draw a crescent shape that resembles a smiling mouth in the center of each cardboard. Since the tiles will represent teeth, provide a strong adhesive such as wood glue which dries fast and holds tight.

Direct each child to glue his or her set of tiles in a line along the crescent. Tell them to use plenty of glue so the "teeth" hold tight. Next, invite them to draw the rest of a face around the mouth they have made.

After the glue has had a day to dry, provide each child with a toothbrush and some samples of foods that vary in stickiness such as caramel sauce, syrup, and raisins—all sticky; and apple slices, carrot coins, and halved grapes—all less sticky. Direct children to rub the foods, one at a time, onto one of their "teeth," then to attempt to brush it off with a toothbrush. Try this with each of the food samples, comparing easy-to-remove with hard-to-remove foods.

Remind children that many foods should be brushed off right after eating since they can promote tooth decay if left on teeth for a long time.

Hint for Success:

● Demonstrate and describe the steps that the children will follow during a large group meeting. Then place your completed project, along with the materials the children will need, in a learning center.

To Simplify:

● Invite parents to visit the classroom as helpers on the day you plan to carry out this activity or assist a few children each day until everyone has had a chance to complete this project.

● Use food trays or vinyl placemats instead of tiles. Tell children that different foods are more and less easy to brush off your teeth after eating them. Have children rub some food samples onto the trays or mats, then try brushing them off. Discuss the amount of effort it takes to remove the different foods.

Language

1. Food Talk Around the World

Refer to the list below to introduce the children to some words for foods in another language. Begin by finding or drawing pictures of selected foods before beginning to teach the words. Show one picture at a time to the children, asking them to tell what it is. Next, explain that all people speak a language, but that these languages differ. People around the world use different words even though they are talking about the same thing. Tell the children that you will help them learn some words for the foods in the pictures using the Spanish language. (If there are Spanish-speaking children in your class, ask them to tell the other children the Spanish words for the foods.)

English	Spanish
rice	arroz (ah-roze)
orange	naranjo (nahr-ahn-ho)
milk	leche (lay-chay)
chicken	pollo (poy-yo)
bread	pan (pahn)
refried beans	refrites (ray-free-tays)
sauce	salsa (sahl-sah)
soup	sopa (so-pah)
meat	carne (cahr-nay)

Spanish words that are also used in English:

chili	chili
taco	taco
burrito	burrito
tortilla	tortilla

Foods to find out about, in Spanish:

Sopapillas (soap-ah-peeyahs—a fried-bread dessert)

guacamole (whuah-cah-moh-lay—a dip made of avocados)

Begin by discussing the words that the children may already know (like burrito, tortilla, taco). Then decide if any of the words describe foods that your children eat but know by a different name. Learn more about foods with which no one is familiar by finding some to taste or by inviting in a visitor who is familiar with them.

Ask your families or your school librarian to provide the words for these (or other) foods in other languages as well. Invite these resource people to visit with the children and teach them the new words and/or share descriptions or samples of the foods that they describe.

2. Word Collections

Many young children are interested in coming to understand and/or learning to write or spell unusual words. Here are some that relate to the body's use of foods. Write them on individual index cards for children to keep in a box or small accordion-type file. Add some illustrations of animals or objects that provide examples of the concepts described by the words or invite children to add these pictures as they find out more about the word meanings. Some children will enjoy using these word collections as personal dictionaries as they undertake individual writing assignments.

Herbivore: a living thing that feeds on mostly or only plants.

Examples: butterflies, sheep, cows, rabbits, some humans.

Omnivore: a living thing that feeds on both plants and animals/animal products.

Examples: flies, many birds (note that insects are animals), pigs, turtles, many humans.

Carnivore: a living thing that feeds on mostly or only animals/animal products.

Examples: mosquitoes, Venus flytraps (a plant), dogs, bears, minks, seals, a few humans.

Carbohydrate: a part of many foods, especially grains, fruits, and vegetables, that gives the body energy.

Protein: a part of many foods, especially meat, eggs, chicken, fish, dry beans, nuts, milk, and cheese, that helps the body to grow and repair itself.

Fat: a part of many foods (especially butter, some oils, and lard and foods prepared with these ingredients) that helps keep the body warm and may make the body move more slowly and need more sleep or grow plumper.

3. Food Group Books

Assign small groups of children to create classroom books that illustrate and name each of the six food categories depicted on the Food Guide Pyramid (see page 120). Convene six groups of children, with three to six children per group, depending on your class size.

If you have a very small class, consider assigning two categories to each group. The categories are as follows: the bread, cereal, rice, and pasta group; the vegetable group; the fruit group; the milk, yogurt, and cheese group; the meat, poultry, fish, dry beans, eggs, and nuts group; and the fats, oils, and sweets group.

Provide each group of children with paper, colored markers, scissors, glue or paste, and old magazines. Meet with each group separately, helping each to determine what foods they are looking for or planning to draw. Have each group prepare pages for a book about their category or categories. Direct them to design a book cover with the name and/or a collage of their food category.

Hint for Success:

● Plan this activity for some time after you have introduced this theme, so children are familiar with the concept of food categories. Provide some word cards that children can use as references as they write, unless child-constructed phonetic spelling is among your goals for this experience.

To Simplify:

● Label and illustrate book covers ahead of time; then have the children look through the magazines for food matches. Pictures can be cut out and glued on separate pages.

To Extend:

● Suggest that the children choose a text writer who will label their food pictures or ask each one of them to label pictures as they go. Provide reference books so that children can decide and describe in their texts what some functions of their food categories are in establishing and maintaining good health. Ask them to also write warnings about misuses, abuses, and preparation concerns particular to their food category.

Physical

1. Trace the Path Your Food Takes

Provide each child with one or more copies of the picture on page 127 that shows the path that foods and drinks take through the body's digestive system. Discuss the job of digestion: breaking foods down so that the parts that are needed get sent to the body parts that need them and the parts that are not needed get sent out of the body.

Provide children with tiny plastic food models, markers, or pencils (as their fine motor skills and eye-hand coordination indicates). Direct them to use the models or writing instruments to trace the route that food would follow.

Remind children that paying attention to the direction that the arrows point will help them to guide their food, marker, or pencil along the path. Watching their hand and the picture while working will be important, too.

2. Energy and Growth Exercise Song

To emphasize the roles that foods play in growth and energy, sing the following song with children while demonstrating some of the suggested actions. Encourage children to join in with the actions and to sing the words, too, if they wish.

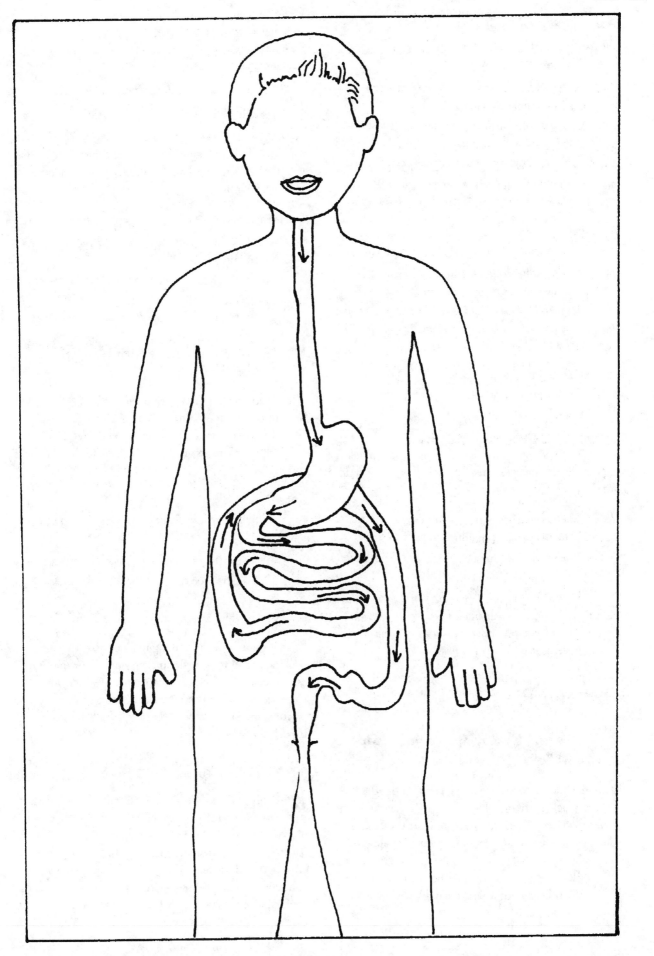

♫ **Thanks to Food**

Words by Kit Payne
Tune: "Happy Birthday to You"

I can move very slow,
with my knees bent just so.
'Cause the foods that I eat
keep me strong while I grow.

(Stand in a deep-knee-bend posture, lifting one foot after the other slowly off the floor just a little way. Notice the extra leg and back strength needed to hold this position!)

Being quick can be fun,
see how fast I can run.
'Cause the foods that I eat
turn my energy on.

(Run quickly in place, standing fully upright and lifting each leg and arm very high, as in marching, as you sing this verse.)

Though I used to just crawl,
now I stand big and tall.
'Cause of foods that I eat
I am no longer small.

(Begin on your hands and knees; then rise to a full standing stretch, on tiptoes, reaching as high over your head with your arms as you can.)

I am not very stiff,
see my joints bend and lift.
'Cause the foods that I eat
make my muscles so swift.

(Sit on the floor; then lift one thigh off the floor. Next, bend the knee to lift, then drop, the lower leg. Extend an arm; then bend and straighten the elbow. Try a similar motion from the shoulder, wrist, ankle, neck.)

Pretend Play

1. What Has It Done for You Lately?

Invite children to recite with you and act out the following action rhymes about the body's reaction to different foods. Alternatively, you can recite the words alone while the children perform appropriate actions.

Protein

When I eat foods with protein, like beans and eggs
  and meat,
my body gets some help to grow, and that seems
  really neat.
For once I was much smaller, but now I'm growing
  tall,
my arms, my legs, my feet, and hands are bigger,
  overall.

Actions: Begin by squatting down, and as you say the words, begin rising slowly to a standing position. As you finish this rhyme, stretch out your arms and legs and fan wide your fingers.

Carbohydrates

The foods with carbohydrates, like veggies, fruit,
  and bread,
are ones that give me energy. When I jump out of
  bed
I want to run and scamper; I want to jump and
  shout,
and eating lots of these foods helps me get my
  wiggles out.

Actions: Begin by sitting very still, with your head resting on your arms as though sleeping. As you recite the words, pretend to wake up and stretch. Then, as the rhyme nears its end, jump up, wiggle all over, and run in place.

Fats

I only eat a few "fat foods," like butter and ice
  cream.
Although they're very tasty, my body loses steam.
If I have had too many of the foods with lots of
  fat,
I sometimes feel as drowsy as an old and lazy cat!

Actions: Begin walking in place. Reduce your walking pace until you are in exaggerated slow-motion as you recite the words. Slow the pace at which you are reciting, too. As you end the verse, lower to a seated position and put your head on your folded arms, as though sleeping.

2. Nutritionist's Office

Set up a Pretend Play area with telephones, a desk or table and chairs, and many clippings of a variety of foods cut from old magazines. Include construction paper, glue sticks, markers, and pencils. Include some envelopes and stickers to be used as stamps. An ink pad and rubber stamps for making imprints on the envelopes could also be provided. Play money and a cash box or cash register could be added later.

Explain to the children that nutritionists sometimes help their clients to plan healthful diets. Model the role of a client when the children are first exploring the area. Approach a "nutritionist," asking for advice on menu planning. Suggest that the children help you put together a diet plan by selecting several food pictures and telling you about the benefits that some of them have for good health. Mention that foods could also be drawn if there are recommendations for which you can't find clipped pictures.

Tell the children that they can send their clients off with "picture-plans" to help them make choices when they shop. Help them decide on the fees to collect from their clients. Mention that this service could also be provided by telephone, and then you would send a bill for your expertise through the mail.

Social

1. Oh My, No More Pie!

The following echo-chant is a fine one to teach to children. The words are fun, and the procedure encourages group cooperation. Start out by providing one line at a time while the whole group of children echoes your words back. Eventually, as the children learn the words, divide the class into two groups, one to start the chant and the other to echo each line.

Oh My, No More Pie! (American Traditional)
Author unknown

Oh My	Oh My
Wanna piece of pie!	Wanna piece of pie!
Pie's too sweet,	Pie's too sweet
Wanna piece of meat!	Wanna piece of meat!
Meat's too red,	Meat's too red,
Wanna piece of bread!	Wanna piece of bread!
Bread's too brown,	Bread's too brown,
Think I'll go to town!	Think I'll go to town!
Town's too far,	Town's too far,
Better take a car!	Better take a car!
Car's too slow,	Car's too slow,
Fell and stubbed my toe!	Fell and stubbed my toe!
Toe gives me pain,	Toe gives me pain,
Think I'll take a train!	Think I'll take a train!
Train had a wreck,	Train had a wreck,
Nearly broke my neck!	Nearly broke my neck!
Oh my, no more pie!	Oh my, no more pie!

After the children have mastered the words, invite them to write new lines to add on. Start by asking whether the "complaints" might have led to less healthful versions of the foods (meat that's too red, pie that's too sweet). What other foods can be too-something—either for your health or your taste?

The lines could also be sung in two parts with a simple melody. Experiment with tunes you are comfortable carrying. Try it while clapping out the 1-2-3, 1-2-3-4-5 beat.

2. Cooperative Food Chain

You will need a ball of yarn and pictures or models of plants and animals that represent simple-to-complex levels of the food chain for this activity. For example, you could use pictures of a leaf, an insect such as a beetle that eats leaves, a frog that eats insects, a snake that eats frogs, and an opossum that eats snakes. You can also tell the children that sometimes people eat opossum meat. Gather as many children in a circle around you as you have pictures. The rest of the children could gather around them to watch or provide suggestions.

Now hand the ball of yarn to the child with the leaf picture. Have him or her hold the end of the yarn, then roll the rest of the ball to the child with the insect. The insect-holder rolls the yarn, after grasping a part of it, on to the frog-holder, the frog-holder to the snake-holder, and so on. Comment on the complexity of the yarn-crossings that result. Relate this to the many ways that plants and animals rely on each other for food sources.

To Simplify:
● Teach the same concept of the food chain by obtaining a copy of the book *Over the Steamy Swamp* by Paul Geraghty (1989). This cumulative story is about a variety of plant, insect, and animal characters who search each other out for food. After one or two readings, invite all the children to join in reciting the characters in order of appearance. Note that the final character is a human hunter. You may want to discuss the fact that some people hunt animals to eat, while other people eat animals that someone else has killed and processed for them. Still other people choose not to eat animals, although they may eat foods that animals produce continuously such as eggs or milk.

To Extend:
● Obtain a copy of one or both of the audiotapes produced by Billy Brennan (Do Dreams Music, Takoma, Maryland) that include songs about the food chain. The audiotape entitled *Romp in the Swamp* contains a song called "We're All Part of the Food Chain"; the audio-

tape entitled *When My Shoes Are Loose* contains a song called "I'm Just Hungry," which is about predators and prey. Play either of these songs, cueing children to listen carefully so that they can recall the plants and/or animals mentioned. Then have pairs or groups of children search for pictures of or draw the various characters. These pictures or drawings can then be shared by everyone to carry out the "Cooperative Food Chain" activity described above.

● *Over the Steamy Swamp* could be used instead of the songs. The illustrations could then serve as drawing guides for use in the activity.

3. Food for All the People of the World

Lead a discussion of similarities and differences in food choices that relate to age, geographical location, cultural beliefs, and health practices. Emphasize that although most people share similar nutritional needs, there are many ways to go about meeting them, and no one way is the "right" way. This activity could be launched with a reading of the book *Bread, Bread, Bread* by Ann Morris (1989), which has fine photographs (by Ken Meyman) of many people eating many kinds of bread in many of the world's countries. Alternately, you could begin by asking children what foods they like and dislike and contrast the preferences in your own group.

Tell children that some people choose only foods that grow and animal foods that the animal can produce while alive. Ask them to think about why that might be so. Inform them that some people eat only plant foods, while some people eat insects. Mention that insects are a good source of protein, which helps the body to grow and repair itself. Ask them if they can think of other high protein foods that their families eat. Talk about foods that only grow in certain climates or certain soil, adding that some people have no way to transport (or import) foods that grow far away. Review the Terms, Facts, and Principles from the unit "Where Food Comes From" (page 104) for other discussion ideas.

You may wish to discuss foods in the various nutrient groups separately, showing samples or pictures of less familiar foods, one category at a time (carbohydrates, proteins, and fats or categories designated in the Food Guide Pyramid). Help children to learn about similarities in needs as well as about unique or unfamiliar ways of meeting them.

Teacher Resources
Field Trip Ideas

1. If your children are six to nine years old, visit a hospital or nursing home where a nutritionist is responsible for planning healthful menus that cater to individual needs, preferences, and beliefs. Ask the nutritionist to discuss examples of individual diets and the reasons for designing them, as well as some of the foods that they include. Tour the food preparation and storage facilities, if possible. Look for posted nutrition guidelines. Send a copy of the Terms, Facts, and Principles for this mini-unit ahead of time to familiarize the nutritionist with the concepts that the children are studying.

2. Take the children to visit the food preparation area in your center. If you do not prepare foods on-site, perhaps a local elementary or middle school does and will let your class visit. Invite children to look in the cupboards, refrigerator, and other food storage areas. Prepare an inventory sheet ahead of time so that children can check off foods that they find on hand that meet the Food Guide Pyramid guidelines. Show the children some of the utensils, storage containers, and so on that are used to prepare and preserve foods. Emphasize foods and techniques that provide a variety of nutritional benefits. You could also invite children to examine packaged foods for the Food Guide Pyramid symbol.

Classroom Visitors

1. Invite members of the children's families to come to school for a "Balanced Breakfast." Prepare foods that represent the bread, cereal, rice, or pasta group; the vegetable and/or fruit group; the milk, yogurt, or cheese group; and the meat, poultry, fish, dry beans, eggs, and nuts group. Offer a little of the fats, oils, and sweets group. Consider making egg omelets with fillings from the vegetable and meat (or bean) group and bagels or toast with butter (fat) and cinnamon sugar. This meal includes foods from every group! Have children explain to their visitors which foods are from each category. Other serving options include peanut butter on toast (which can take the place of meat) or pancakes with toppings that include nuts (which can serve as a substitute for animal products).

2. Invite someone from your state or national dairy council office to visit the classroom. Ask this visitor to explain food choices using the puppets, picture cards, and posters that the councils make available for purchase or use in their presentations.

Children's Books and Audiotapes

Balestrino, P. (1992). *Fat and Skinny*. New York: HarperCollins.

Brennan, B. (1988). *Romp in the Swamp*. (Audiotape). Tacoma Park, MD: Do Dreams Music.

Brennan, B. (1984). *When My Shoes Are Loose*. (Audiotape). Tacoma Park, MD: Do Dreams Music.

Facklam, Margery. (1987). *I Eat Dinner*. Etna, CA: Bell Books.

Friedman, I. (1987). *How My Parents Learned to Eat*. Boston: Houghton Mifflin.

Geraghty, P. (1988). *Over the Steamy Swamp*. New York: Harcourt Brace Jovanovich.

Glyman, C. A. (1992). *Learning Your ABCs of Nutrition*. Lake Forest, IL: Forest House.

Gomi, Taro. (1994). *Everyone Poops*. New York: Kane-Miller.

Manry, I. (1979). *My Mother and I Are Growing Strong*. Berkeley, CA: New Seed Press.

Moncure, J. B. (1982). *The Healthkin Food Train*. Mankato, MN: Child's World.

Monjo, F. (1970). *The Drinking Gourd*. New York: HarperCollins.

Morris, A. (1989). *Bread, Bread, Bread*. New York: Scholastic.

Rhodes, J. (1982). *Nutrition Mission*. Carthage, IL: Good Apple.

Schwarzenegger, A. (1993). *Arnold's Fitness for Kids Ages Birth to 5*. New York: Doubleday.

Shigeo, W. (1982). *What a Good Lunch*. New York: Putnam Publishing Group.

Showers, P. (1985). *What Happens to a Hamburger*. New York: HarperCollins.

Suhr, M. (1992). *When I Eat*. Minneapolis: Carolrhoda Books.

Adult References

Parker, S. (1990). *Eating A Meal: How You Eat, Drink and Digest*. New York: Watts.

Parker, S. (1990). *Food and Digestion*. New York: Watts.

Zeller, P., and Jacobson, M. (1987). *Eat, Think and Be Healthy*. Washington, DC: Center for Service in the Public Interest.

Safety

Two little blackbirds sitting on a hill
One named Jack, one named Jill
Fly away Jack, fly away Jill
Come back Jack, come back Jill.
Two little blackbirds sitting on a hill.

The ultimate goal in teaching children about safety is that a child can venture away, do things on his or her own, make decisions, experience a broader world, meet new people, and return unharmed.

Caring adults protect very little children from harm by providing close supervision, checking environments for hazards and "child-proofing" areas so that play and learning can take place in safety. As children grow, adults begin to teach them about ways to care for their own safety. They offer frequent instructions such as "Take that out of your mouth; that's not good to eat," or "Hold on tight while I push you on the swing," or "Don't run, walk with a stick in your hand." Gradually, adults allow children to take steps into a less monitored, less protected world and to experience some of the daily risks of living in today's society. What adults choose to teach, how the information and skills are presented to children, and the amount of practice offered to children are factors that influence the effectiveness of these lessons.

Purpose

This unit offers activities that present facts and strategies useful for youngsters learning to stay safe as they move toward greater independence—spending time away from parents and being influenced to a greater degree by their peers and other adults. Mini-themes are built around the concepts of (1) vehicle safety, (2) fire safety, and (3) personal safety because these are common issues that affect youngsters' lives most directly and most universally. Care has been taken to utilize terms, facts, and principles (TFPs) that are meaningful to young children. We have striven to create TFPs that appeal to children's interests and levels of understanding and that deal with children's concerns without overly frightening them. The chapter also includes sample letters to parents giving information, soliciting their support, and suggesting ways they can become involved with the theme.

Each mini-theme in this unit is divided into sections related to the general topic of "Safety." The first mini-theme, "Vehicle Safety," takes the child's point of view. It presents activities dealing with passenger safety and being a safe pedestrian. Another cluster of activities deals with how bicycle riders can ride safely and how automobile drivers keep passengers safe. A substantial number of activities are devoted to teaching children to buckle up, cross streets safely, and interpret signs and symbols they encounter as pedestrians.

A second mini-theme is devoted to "Fire Safety." Here children learn about fire hazards, ways adults put out fires, and fire safety procedures relevant to young children. Teachers are not encouraged to demonstrate real fire at any time throughout this mini-theme. When little children see adults lighting matches, even under the safest conditions, their fascination with fire can easily overshadow any well-intentioned message about "never do this." Instead, children are unfortunately encouraged to try what they see teachers do. In this unit, fire is portrayed as useful under specially controlled circumstances by careful adults, but dangerous when people are careless. Its recreational uses are minimally explored.

Under the heading "Personal Safety," teachers will find sections that deal with defining private body parts, differentiating good touches from bad touches, and distinguishing strangers from trusted adults. While a personal safety unit cannot prepare children for every danger, specialists in preventing child abuse tell us that children are safest when they can speak up for themselves, develop the ability to make decisions in a variety of situations, know where and how to get help, and know they will be believed. Therefore, the emphasis here is on helping children learn to assert their rights in situations involving touching and to feel confident in seeking help from appropriate sources. The concept of strangers is dealt with in this mini-theme and also in the "Vehicle Safety" mini-theme to stress different safety contexts.

At the end of the chapter we present a social activity called "The Safety Land Game." It integrates concepts from all three mini-themes.

Implementation

The "Safety" theme can be implemented in several different ways:

Option One: Choose one of the mini-themes to present by itself for two or more weeks. Precede or follow the theme with a related unit from this volume: from "Vehicle Safety" branch into a week or more on "People Living Together"; from "Fire Safety" move into "Science and Scientists"; and introduce "Personal Safety" by first doing a unit on "The Human Body."

Option Two: Choose activities from all three mini-themes and create your own unit on safety, continuing for as long as the children are interested. Maintain communication with parents about your goals for this unit. Suggest ways parents can participate.

Option Three: Select one or two safety issues with which children in the group may be dealing. Without identifying individual situations, use activities that present strategies and/or help children consider various solutions to problems. Utilize several of the puppet scenarios offered here with small groups to reinforce for children the importance of being appropriately assertive in a variety of safety-related circumstances.

Vehicle Safety

Terms, Facts, and Principles (TFPs)

General Information

1. Vehicles are machines with wheels or runners that are used to carry people or things from one place to another (such as car, wagon, truck, bus, bicycle, sled, and so on).

2. Vehicles have many moving parts, may be traveling fast, may be heavy, and are often difficult to stop quickly. All of these things make it important for people to be careful in and around vehicles.

3. If people are not careful, vehicles can cause injury to drivers, passengers, and pedestrians; vehicles can break bones and even kill people.

4. There are many ways to be safe in and around vehicles.

Safe Passengers

5. Riding in a child restraint seat, safety harness, or safety shield keeps small children safer while in vehicles.

6. Wearing a safety belt while riding in the car keeps people safer by protecting them from being thrown around if the vehicle has to stop suddenly.

*7. People are safer when they ride in a protected place inside vehicles; it is unsafe to ride in the back of an open pickup truck because a person could fall out.

8. It is safer to keep hands and arms inside while riding in a moving vehicle because people might be injured by objects sticking out near the windows or doors.

Strangers

*9. A stranger is someone the person doesn't know; it is not safe for a child to ride in someone's car if that person is a stranger,to the child or to his or her parents.

*10. If a stranger offers a child a ride, the child should say "No!", get away fast, and tell a trusted adult.

Safe Pedestrians

11. Pedestrians are people who are walking, being pushed or pulled by a walking person, riding tricycles, or moving in a wheelchair near a street.

12. When people walk or play near a road or parking lot, it is safest to stay on the sidewalk and away from moving cars; people should never run into the road after a ball, a pet, or a toy.

13. If people must walk in the street, it is safest to walk at the side of the road and face oncoming traffic.

*14. When people must walk near traffic after dark, it is safest to wear white clothes, clothes with reflector strips, or bright-colored clothes because it makes it easier for drivers to see them.

15. When walking near driveways or parking lots, people must watch for vehicles coming and going. Children should play away from parked cars.

16. It is safest to cross a street at the corner.

17. Some corners have community helpers who signal when it is safe to cross; traffic police officers and crossing guards help people cross safely.

18. Some corners have crossing signals that tell when it is safe to cross; a green or white signal (some with a walking person) means it's time to WALK; a red signal (some with an open hand) means DON'T WALK.

19. Some corners have traffic lights: a green light means cars can go, a red light means cars must stop, and a yellow light means cars should slow down. Pedestrians should wait until the light changes and cars stop, look to the left, look to the right, and look left again before crossing.

20. People stay safest by waiting to cross the street until the crossing signal, traffic officer, or crossing guard indicate it is safe to cross.

21. When crossing a street, it is safest to walk between the lines painted on the street in the crosswalk.

*22. Some street corners don't have a crossing guard, police officer, or a crossing signal. People should cross only after looking both ways and listening for traffic, making sure no vehicles are coming.

Safe Drivers/Riders

*23. Safe vehicle drivers must pay careful attention to what they are doing. Passengers are helpful to drivers when they talk in low voices, stay seated, and keep their hands away from the driver's face.

24. When riding a bicycle on the sidewalk, the rider keeps safe by walking his or her bike across busy streets, slowing down when pedestrians are near, and watching out for cars turning into driveways.

*25. A safe place to ride bicycles is on a bike path; if people must ride their bicycle in the street, they are safer when they ride at the right edge of the road (in the direction of the traffic), out of the way of traffic.

26. Bicycle riders are safest when they wear bike helmets for protection.

27. Skilled bicycle riders use hand signals to be safer by letting pedestrians and drivers nearby know what they are planning to do:
    a) holding the left arm straight out to the side signals that the rider plans to turn left,
    b) holding the left arm out, elbow bent with hand and fingers pointing down, signals that the rider is stopping, and
    c) holding the left arm out to the side, elbow bent and fingers pointing up signals that the rider plans to turn right.

*28. Careful vehicle drivers keep passengers, pedestrians, and other drivers safe by following traffic rules, watching the road ahead, and listening for dangers.

*29. Drivers follow traffic rules by reading signs near the road:
    a) A red STOP sign means drivers should stop, then go when it is safe.
    b) A yellow sign showing children walking means a school is near, drivers should go slow and watch for children.
    c) A yellow sign with RXR means train tracks are ahead, watch for a train.
    d) A speed limit sign tells drivers how fast they can safely travel.

Activity Ideas

Aesthetic

1. The Car Song

Teach children Woodie Guthrie's song, "Riding in My Car," found on the cassette or CD *Songs to Grow On* or treat the words like a chant. Remind children that in this song, someone is inviting them to ride in their car, but that person is not a stranger so it is safe to accept the ride. Make up your own verses or ask children to suggest car parts and appropriate safety-related words such as:

> Wipers they go, swish swish
> Door locks they go, lock lock
> Seat belts they go, click click
> Lights they go, blink blink
> Brakes they go, slow down
> Horn it goes, watch out
> For fun end the song with the original final verse:

> Brrm, brrm, chrrka, chrrka, brrm, brrm.
> Brrm, brrm, chrrka, chrrka, brrm, brrm.
> Brrm, brrm, chrrka, chrrka, brrm, brrm.
> I'll take you riding in my car.

2. Make a Picture with Safety Colors

After introducing the traffic light and discussing the meaning of each color (red, yellow, and green), place those three colors of chalk at the easel with large pieces of black paper. Suggest children use these "safety colors" to make any kind of picture they want.

3. Paint to Stop and Go Music

Use the tape-recorded music described in the activity "Stop and Go Movements" (see page 143). Offer children large pieces of paper and paints in an area appropriate for art. Arrange the paper on the floor, on a large table, on a wall, or outdoors on a fence. Tell children that they will paint to stop and go music. They can paint when the music is going; when the music stops, their painting should halt. Then when they hear music again, they can resume their painting. Repeat. (You may want to model this activity by pretending to paint while listening to the music.)

To Simplify:
● Encourage children to simply make brushstrokes on the paper rather that making an actual design or picture. Another option is to offer markers instead of paints for making designs.

To Extend:
● Suggest that children think of things that stop and go. Encourage children to paint a picture of the images they have in their minds.

Affective

1. Safety Captain for Today

Institute a new job in your classroom to contribute to children taking responsibility and thinking about safety, too. Consider your daily schedule and the transitions your class makes in moving from one place to another (such as from indoors to outdoors, from classroom to gym, from hallway to classroom, and so on). Select a point in a daily transition where the class could use a safety captain who would urge others to go or stop. (For example, when they reach the end of a hall, the safety captain could look both ways and tell children if it's safe to turn the corner.) Teach children how to do this job so they can help keep the class safe. Have children take turns being the safety captain.

2. Cover-up Bingo

Prior to beginning this activity, collect the following materials:

a variety of small pictures of objects (see below) people might see out their car window, one-foot squares made from heavy cardboard, clear adhesive paper to cover the boards after they have

been completed, scissors, glue, one dark crayon per child, and one large, self-closing plastic bag to hold a board, a tissue, and crayon for each youngster who makes a game

Explain to the children that "Cover-up Bingo" is fun to play in the car. Show them a sample board and demonstrate how to play the game by pretending to be riding along in your car (as a passenger). Point out objects on your bingo board and mark them with the crayon.

Invite children to make their bingo game special to them by selecting objects they usually see on their way home. Explain that not everyone sees the same

things as they ride in a car. Have children cut out the pictures they have selected, and glue them randomly onto their board. Be sure children put their names on their boards. When the glue has dried, laminate each board or cover each with a piece of clear adhesive paper so they can be wiped off and used again. Put each child's finished board, along with a crayon and a tissue or two to wipe off the crayon marks, in a plastic bag. Distribute. Encourage the children to use their cover-up bingo games in their cars.

Hint for Success:
● Provide parents with the following directions so they will understand how to play "Cover-up Bingo."

Cover-up Bingo
This game is called "Cover-up Bingo." Mark each object on the card with a crayon as it is spotted through the car window. When all the objects are covered-up, call out "Bingo!" Wipe off and play again.

To Simplify:
● Provide pictures of common objects children might see, such as a tree or telephone pole.

To Extend:
● Provide pictures of less common objects children might see such as a particular kind of advertisement or mailbox, or ask children to make their own pictures..

● Also involve the parents in helping their children make a "Personal Cover-up Bingo Game." Send home a note with sample pictures on a single page. Ask parents to help their child designate pictures of objects particular to his or her route home. Remind them to send the page back to school so their child can make the game. Another way to involve parents is to collect the materials and have parents make this game with their child at a Parents' Night at school.

3. My Crossing Story

Obtain a copy of the book by Dorothy Chlad entitled *When I Cross the Street* (1982). Don't tell children the title of the story; instead, show children the pictures and have them guess what the story is about. Then read the book to see if they predicted correctly. As a follow-up, tell children to think about a street they have to cross and how they cross it. Suggest that children tell their stories into a tape recorder. Later everyone could make a picture that goes with his or her crossing story. Encourage children to show their pictures and play the stories for the group to hear.

Cognitive

1. Twinkle, Twinkle Traffic Light

Introduce the idea of a traffic light by showing either a picture of one or a model made out of cardboard and construction paper. Point out the colors and what each one means. To help children remember what each color stands for, teach them the following song.

♫ **Twinkle, Twinkle Traffic Light**
Author unknown
Tune: "Twinkle, Twinkle Little Star"

Twinkle, twinkle traffic light,
Shining on the corner bright.
When it's green, it means to go,
When it's red, it's stop, you know.
Slow when yellow, like the sun,
Makes it safe for everyone.

2. What Are Vehicles?

Show children pictures of various vehicles and ask them to tell you what they notice. Be sure to include familiar as well as less familiar vehicles. Obtain pictures of most vehicles used in a variety of regions and countries. Point out that vehicles have wheels, while others have runners or treads, and are used to move people and things from place to place. Brainstorm a list of vehicles and write down children's ideas. Discuss the meaning of the words *driver*, *passenger*, and *pedestrian* in relation to vehicles.

Hint for Success:
● Vehicle pictures may be found in newspapers, inmagazines, on calendars, in books, and on posters. Automobile dealerships, automobile clubs, and driving schools may have pictures to offer you, too.

3. Should I Accept the Ride?

Introduce the idea of who a stranger is by talking with children about people they know and people they don't know. Then tell children that you are going to tell them a story with puppets; they should watch and listen carefully. Gather three puppets: one will be a child, another will be a person the child knows, and the third will represent a stranger. Use them to act out two scenes in which first the familiar person and then the stranger offers a child a ride. Follow this by posing questions to the group to encourage them to think about the safe thing to do under each circumstance.

Scene One: Albert is walking home from school. It is raining hard. A friend's dad comes by in his car and calls to Albert.

Mr. Rodrigas: "Hi, Albert. It's raining pretty hard. Do you want a ride home?"

Albert: Albert says to himself, "This is a person I know well. He's always been nice to me and I feel safe with him." He answers, "Hi, yeah thanks." He gets into the car.

Mr. Rodrigas: "You got very wet, Albert. I'll take you right home."

Scene ends.

Talk about it:

Who was walking in the rain? Who came along? What happened? Why did Albert go with him? Was it safe to do this?

Scene Two: Albert is carrying some books while walking to the library near his house. It's a sunny day. A person drives near him in his car.

The stranger: "Hi there, sonny. You're carrying some heavy books. Your mother said you should go in my car. Come on, I'll drive you."

Albert: Albert says to himself, "I don't know this person. He's a stranger, and I don't think my mom knows him either." He answers, "No thanks." He keeps walking.

The stranger: "It's OK to get in. She won't mind. We'll get some ice cream."

Albert: "No! I don't know you. Leave me alone." (said loudly) He runs home and says to his mother, "Mom, a man tried to get me to go in his car."

Scene ends.

Talk about it:

Who was walking? Who came along? What happened? Why did Albert say no? Was that the safe thing to do? Should he take the ride if it were raining out? Why not?

Construction

1. My Own Kind of Vehicle

Show children several pictures of vehicles; a good variety can be found in the book *Things That Go* by Brenda Apsley (1984). Discuss what vehicles look like, notice their wheels, and talk about what each vehicle is used for. Suggest that children make their own kind of vehicle using any kind of connecting materials they like (such as wooden blocks, Legos™, Bristle Blocks™, Lincoln Logs™, Constructos™, Mobilos™, and so on). Encourage children to use their imaginations, making their vehicles any way they want. Provide enough materials so that the finished products can be displayed where everyone can see them. If they must be disassembled at once, take instant pictures of each construction, and display the photographs. Invite children to create a caption for their constructions, either by dictating words or by using their own form of writing. Display these with the creations.

To Simplify:

● Offer children one material in one part of the room for this project. Select a material to which wheels can be easily attached.

To Extend:

● Offer more choices of material for this project. Place soft wood pieces, round wooden wheels, hammers, nails, and goggles at a woodworking bench. At the art table, have a supply of small boxes, cardboard, scissors, markers, and glue for those children who want to use art materials for their construction.

● Encourage children to make use of the materials at several stations.

2. Our Class Vehicle

Suggest children work together in a small group to make a pretend vehicle that everyone in the class can take turns using. Discuss the parts of their vehicle and how big it should be to accommodate the numbers of children that will use it at one time. Encourage all children in the group to make suggestions and be part of the effort. Help children plan what materials they will need (such as one or two large boxes, large blocks, chairs or small benches, something for a steering wheel, wheels, construction paper, glue or tape, scissors, etc.). Help gather their materials, and be available as they begin. Assist them in dividing up the work and carrying out their project.

3. Making Seat Belts

Show children a real seat belt. Discuss its parts, how it is used, and why we are safer when we wear one when riding in a vehicle. Offer children the opportunity to make their own seat belts using strips of cardboard, cloth, or heavy ribbons. Supply a pattern for tracing cardboard buckles made in two parts so children can

Velcro® pieces

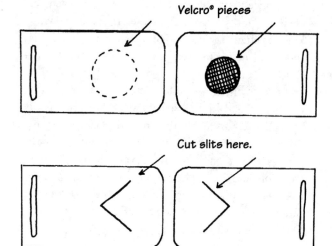

Cut slits here.

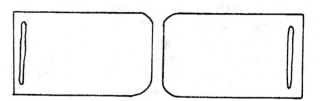

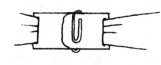

actually fasten the parts together. When their seat belts are finished, help children attach them to individual chairs which simulate car seats. Cardboard buckles may be fastened with heavy paper clips, rubber bands, tape, or interlocking slits.

Hint for Success:

● Real seat belts can often be borrowed from community automobile associations, local safety associations, or high school driver education classes.

4. Safety Helmets

Show children a real bike helmet and explain why people wear them to protect their heads while riding a bike. Ask children to tell about other helmets they know about or have seen people wearing. Offer children an opportunity to make their own pretend bike helmets. Empty plastic gallon milk jugs or get inexpensive Styrofoam cones (used to protect flowers in severe weather). Cut these to the size needed for each child. Poke holes and attach straps (shoe laces or heavy ribbon) to tie under the chin. Suggest children decorate their helmets with stickers or permanent markers.

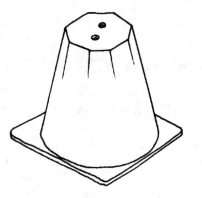

or

Language

1. A Safe Way to Cross Streets

Reinforce important safety behaviors regarding crossing the street by saying the following poem with the children. Emphasize the actions that keep a person safe. When the children are familiar with the words, have them act out the movements as they recite the poem.

Crossing the Street
Author unknown

When I reach a crossing place,
To left and right I turn my face.
I walk, not run, across the street,
And use my head to guide my feet.

2. May I Ride?

Teach children to sing a short song about being safe in a car. Write the song on a big chart and run your hand along the words as you say them. Ask children to listen for words that rhyme. Highlight these in some way. Then ask children to think of other words that rhyme with each of the highlighted words.

♫ May I Ride?
Words by Barb Rohde
Tune: "Twinkle, Twinkle Little Star"

Auto, auto, may I ride?
Yes friend, yes friend, step inside.
Switch on the engine,
We'll start slow.
Buckle your seat belt,
Away we go!
Auto, auto, may I ride?
Yes friend, yes friend, step inside.

To Simplify:
● Teach children the song using hand gestures that are appropriate such as:

Auto, auto, may I ride?
(*point to self*)
Yes friend, yes friend, step inside.
(*shake head yes*)
Switch on the engine,
(*turn ignition*)
We'll start slow.
(*move hand slowly*)

Buckle your seat belt,
(*buckling motion*)
Away we go!
(*wave*)

To Extend:
● Challenge children to make up more lines to the poem using what they know about riding in a car.

● To make it harder, number the poem lines and show children the rhyming pattern (the first two lines rhyme, and lines four and six rhyme). Suggest they make their own verses using the same rhyming pattern.

3. Safety Color Game

Teach children to say the following poem about what a traffic light looks like and what each color means. Make a large traffic signal and point to the different lights as you recite the poem. After children are familiar with the poem, have the children be part of a group traffic light; pass out small red, yellow, and green circles. As everyone says the words, have children hold up the color that matches. Mix up the circles and repeat the game.

Safety
Author unknown

Red means STOP.
Green means GO.
Yellow means WAIT,
And go real SLOW.

4. Vehicle Safety Rebus

Copy the following safety rebus story or make up one of your own using safety symbols and international traffic signs. Put your story on a piece of paper and hang it where children can see it. Explain that this kind of story is called a "rebus." In a rebus story, pictures take the place of some of the words. Read the story aloud, encouraging children to supply the words they can discover using the picture clues.

To Extend:
● Suggest that children make their own safety rebus story using words and pictures. Children can either write their own or dictate their words to an adult writer. Pictures can be easily inserted by using stickers, rubber stamps, or the safety pictures on page 135.

Danny Helps

Danny and his mom went to the store in their .

At the first corner, the was red. When it was

green, Danny said, "We can go." As they drove to the next

corner, Danny saw a , and he said, "That means

stop." They waited while some children crossed the

in front of their .

Then they heard a whistle, and Danny saw a .

He said, "Watch for a ." His mom said,

"Thanks, Danny. You're really helping to keep us safe."

Physical

1. Cutting Out Signs

Using the shapes on the next page, make patterns for children to trace various sign shapes. Trace them onto stiff cardboard and laminate them. Then carefully cut out the patterns and offer them to children along with pencils, markers or crayons and scissors. Encourage children to trace and cut out the shapes, turn them into signs using their markers and crayons, and then place them around the room.

To Simplify:

● Pretrace the shapes onto construction paper of various appropriate colors (red for the stop sign; yellow or red for yield, school, and railroad crossing; white for a speed limit sign).

● For beginning cutters make a 1/4" to 1/2" path around the outside edge of the shape; tell children to cut along the path between the lines. This is an easier task because children don't have to try to cut right on the line.

To Extend:

● Suggest children write their own words on the signs using their own form of writing. Children will approach this task from various levels: some children will scribble the words while others will use letter forms but not in any order that can be read; more advanced writers will want to know the exact letters in the words, and others, if encouraged, will write the words using invented spellings.

2. Stop and Go Movements

Tape-record some lively music that will encourage children to respond by moving. While taping, insert brief pauses every ten to fifteen seconds so the music will seem to stop and go, stop and go. When talking to the children, relate this kind of music to vehicles that must stop at a red light or a stop sign, then go again. Provide an opportunity for children to practice body control by suggesting that they get up and move to the music. Whenever the music stops, tell children to freeze until it starts again.

3. Using Hand Signals

Teach children about hand signals that tell others what they are going to do when they are riding a tricycle and provide time for practice. Then encourage youngsters to use these signals while riding tricycles. Display pictures of the hand gestures near the tricycle area and remind children what they mean. At first, suggest that children say out loud what they mean as they use a signal. For example, when children hold their arms out to the left, they should say "turning left." Praise children who remember to use signals and use them correctly.

To Simplify:

● Have children practice using their hand signals while sitting on a tricycle, but not riding it. Place blocks in front of and behind the wheels so the tricycle doesn't move.

RIGHT   LEFT   STOP

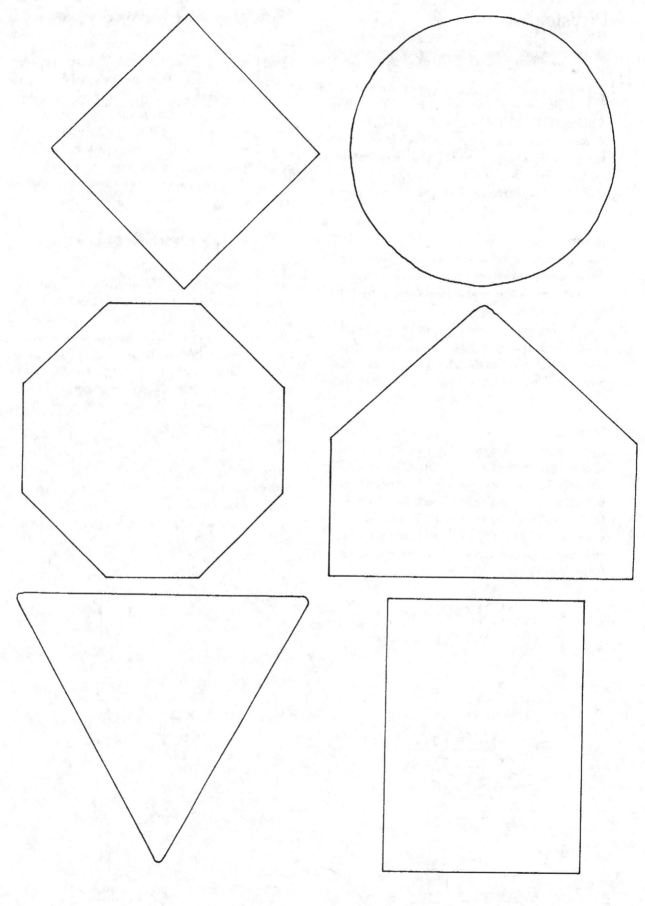

To Extend:

● After using the signals with words, suggest children use the hand signals without words and have observers tell what each signals mean.

Pretend Play

1. Our Little Street

Give children props to use in pretending about safe traffic and pedestrian movements. Arrange an area of the room with small cars, trucks, miniature people, traffic signs, streets, sidewalks, corner crosswalks, and so on. Use plastic tape strips on the floor to designate driving areas, walking areas, and so on. (Plastic tape doesn't leave a permanent residue on carpet.) Encourage small groups of children to use the area together. Stimulate their thinking by occasionally asking questions about where people are going and how they will get there. Help children decide if they need more or different signs or signals to make things safer on their little street. Encourage children to make more signs, with adult help, if needed.

2. Riding in a Pretend Car

Set up a pretend automobile using chairs, make-believe seat belts, and a steering wheel made from cardboard, lightweight tubing taped into a circle, or a lightweight wheel from a discarded bicycle. Encourage children to always buckle up before driving away. Supply the car with a doll-sized car seat made from a cardboard box or a real infant seat. Help the children feel like they are really inside the car by using a large cardboard box to make the sides of the car, cut to simulate doors that open. If children need help elaborating on their play, suggest they go grocery shopping, drive to the beach, or take a sick child to the doctor in the car.

3. Crossing a Pretend Street

Provide an opportunity for children to practice crossing a pretend street in a safe environment such as the classroom, a fenced playground, the school hallway, or in a gym. Arrange a walkway with a corner and a pretend street to cross. Tape or chalk lines on the floor or ground can be used to make the sidewalk. Use tricycles or give children cardboard steering wheels to hold as they move, simulating traffic on the busy street. Supply the area with a variety of props so that children can practice in many ways:

a. On some days provide a simple uniform for a crossing guard or a traffic police officer. Model how the guard or officer might give directions to people crossing the street. Ask children to pretend they are the pedestrians, perhaps even taking a stroller or pet dog across to the stores on the other side. Teach children to listen and watch for the guard's signals before crossing safely.

b. Other days, provide a simple traffic light that children can change that tells car drivers (tricycles) when to stop. Remind children to wait for the signal to change and for the traffic to stop before crossing the street.

c. Other days, use a WALK/DON'T WALK sign as a variation. Teach children what each signal means and to wait for the correct one before crossing.

d. On some days, explain that pedestrians will cross the street without a crossing guard, a traffic light, or a WALK signal. Help children remember to look both ways before crossing.

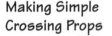

Making Simple Crossing Props

A Crossing Guard Uniform: Bring in or make a simple belt from a strip of cloth, going around the waist and over one shoulder. Fasten with Velcro® strips. Use any hat and attach a "Crossing Guard" sign to it. Make a STOP sign from heavy cardboard and attach a handle made from a tongue depressor or craft stick.

A Traffic Police Officer Uniform: White or blue gloves will help make this uniform special. Make any blue or black hat look official by adding a "Police" sign to the brim. Make a badge shape and cover it with foil. Attach to clothes with masking tape.

A Traffic Light: Use a piece of heavy cardboard or the top surface of a flat box to attach the three lights (red on top, yellow in the middle, green on the bottom). Cover these with laminate or clear adhesive paper to make them last longer. Make black covers so children can show which light is "on." (Place glue-on Velcro® patches on each light and each cover.)

A Walk/Don't Walk Signal: Make two large circles of cardboard. Attach symbols (see above) for WALK and DON'T WALK, one on each circle. Cover both circles with clear adhesive paper. Form a handle by attaching a paint mixing stick (available for free at paint stores) with glue or strong tape to the back of one of the signs. Then glue the other sign onto the back of the stick. By turning the stick, either symbol can be shown. Make another using only words.

Social

1. What Are the Rules on Our Trip?

After the class has engaged in several days' play about staying safe near traffic, plan a simple driving field trip to a real destination, far enough away that adults will have to transport children in their cars. Talk with children about ways to stay safe on the field trip. Make a list of the appropriate rules together and ask children to consider why each rule is important. Make a copy of the rules for all drivers so they can help praise children for following their rules of safety in the car and near cars.

Hint for Success:
● If your group takes field trips on a bus, ask children to generate their list in terms of how to stay safe riding on the bus, getting on and off the bus, and while standing waiting for the bus, or standing near the bus.

To Simplify:
● Divide the class into small groups according to the car in which they will ride. Ask each driver to have his or her small group think of two to three safety rules to follow in the car. Have the leaders write down the rules children think will keep them safe and report how well they followed them after the trip is over.

To Extend:
● Visit a garage specializing in vehicle maintenance. Ask that someone talk to the group and show them some ways mechanics keep vehicles safe for drivers and passengers.

2. Red Light/Green Light

Gather the children into a group. Explain that in this game they will pretend to be cars moving along the road. The cars are trying to get across the town (the other side of the room or play yard). Have the "cars" stand along a wall or on a line on the floor or the ground. Review the meanings of the two signals while showing two paper circles (red and green). Demonstrate how to be the traffic light, holding one circle up at a time and putting the other behind your back. Explain that the game is for all cars to listen and watch the traffic light carefully and to try to get to the other side without bumping into other cars. To move forward drivers must see and hear the words "Green Light" (meaning go); cars must stop when they see and hear "Red Light." Help children take turns being the cars and the traffic light.

Hint for Success:

● Avoid making this game a competition. Point out that everyone in the game will get to the other side; it doesn't matter who gets there first.

To Simplify:

● Conduct the game in a relatively small area so success will come quickly and children can take turns being the traffic light frequently.

To Extend:

● Choose a longer distance for this game. Select one child to be a traffic police officer to watch the cars as they move. If a player continues to move when the light is red, she or he is issued a pretend traffic ticket and must start over at the beginning line.

● Help children take turns being the traffic light, the police officer, and the cars.

● Another day, have the cars move in various ways such as hopping, skipping, galloping, or leaping.

3. Passenger Pull

Gather several wagons outdoors or inside a large open area. Help children decide on a route the wagons will take and ask them to think of some ways they can be safe wagon drivers and passengers. In determining what constitutes a turn, ask them to consider what's fair given the number of children and the length of the course (once around the track, twice around, and so on). Arrange a place for passengers to sit as they wait for their turn by providing a bench, chairs, or a blanket.

To Simplify:

● Limit the number of decisions children make. Ask them to determine tangible choices such as the direction of the route while you determine what constitutes a fair turn. Help children enforce these rules.

To Extend:

● Suggest children make "waiting tickets" for children who are waiting their turn—one color for passengers and a different color for those waiting to pull the wagons. As children complete their turn, the next waiting person can slip his or her ticket into a ticket box and take a place as the puller or the passenger.

4. Riding Tricycles Safely

Ask children to think of one or two safety rules they should follow while riding tricycles near others who are walking (pedestrians). Write their rules on individual signs that can be placed near the tricycle riding area. Offer children tricycles to ride while following their rules and being safe. Reinforce their attempts to be safe riders.

Teacher Resources

Field Trip Ideas

1. Plan to take the children on a walk to give them practice staying safe in real-life situations. Investigate the area immediately surrounding your school or center, looking for places to visit and appropriate routes to get there.

   a. Choose wisely based on consideration of the following factors:

   Timing. What time of day is best for the walk? When will the children be most alert? What can you expect from the weather at certain times of the day? What will you do if it begins to rain or snow?

   Distance. Be realistic about how far your class can walk in comfort. If necessary, plan to walk only in one direction. For example, arrive at your destination by car or bus and walk back to school.

   Safety. Take a look at the area through which you would be passing. Are the sidewalks safe or unsafe? Is there dangerous traffic? Are there unhealthy conditions to which children will be exposed? If so, take your walk in another part of town.

   Age-Appropriateness. Look carefully at your choices. Will the children learn anything valuable by visiting this place or is it really more appropriate for older children?

   b. Select a route that gives children practice crossing at a light, at a WALK signal, or with a crossing guard.

c. Send a permission slip home that describes your goal, tells what route you will take, and invites parents or other volunteers to come on the walk with the class.

d. Plan how you want the children to walk: single-file, as partners, holding hands, or paired with an adult. Let children know what you expect of them on the walk.

e. Before leaving the classroom, review what everyone is to do to stay safe when the class gets to a street corner.

f. Plan to take along a lightweight STOP sign for an adult to hold up in case you reach a difficult corner without crossing assistance. Ask one adult to be responsible for handling the sign whenever you need it.

To Simplify:

● Ask all of the adults to talk to the children near them about ways they are staying safe as they walk along. Upon returning, ask children to tell about one way they stayed safe on the walk.

To Extend:

● Suggest the class write a group story about things they did on their walking field trip. Encourage children to draw maps illustrating their ideas of the route they took, including any streets they crossed.

2. Plan to take the children for a ride in a bus or car to watch for safety signs. If parents can be utilized as drivers, ask each to take a different route to a location (perhaps to a park for a picnic, or around the town, returning to school at a designated time) and divide the group accordingly. Provide each car with a Sign Chart such as the one to the left, and ask a responsible child or adult rider (not the driver) to check off the signs the children see along the way. When the class returns to school, display and compare the children's sign charts.

3. Take the children on a walk in the neighborhood. Tell them to watch for safety signs, signals, and lines on the road that help drivers, passengers, and pedestrians stay safe. Follow up by suggesting that children make a picture of something they saw.

Classroom Visitors

1. Invite a crossing guard to speak to the class.
2. Invite a traffic officer to visit the class.

Children's Books

Apsley, B. (1984). *Things That Go*. New York: Preschool Press.

Broekel, R. (1981). *Police*. Chicago: Childrens Press.

Chlad, D. (1981). *When I Cross the Street*. Chicago: Childrens Press.

Chlad, D. (1982). *Strangers*. Chicago: Childrens Press.

Chlad, D. (1983). *When I Ride in a Car*. Chicago: Childrens Press.

Girard, L. W. (1985). *Who Is a Stranger and What Should I Do?* Niles, IL: Albert Whitman.

Hoban, T. (1983). *I Read Signs*. New York: Greenwillow.

Hoban, T. (1983). *I Read Symbols*. New York: Greenwillow.

Leaf, M. (1961). *Safety Can Be Fun* . Philadelphia: J. B. Lippincott.

Longman, H. (1968). *Watch Out*. New York: Parents Press.

MacDonald, G. (1944). *Red Light, Green Light*. New York: Doubleday.

McLeod, E. (1975). *The Bear's Bicycle*. New York: Little, Brown.

Shapp, M. and C. (1975). *Let's Find Out About Safety*. New York: Franklin Watts.

Viorst, J. (1970). *Try It Again, Sam: Safety When You Walk*. New York: Lothrop, Lee, and Shepard.

Vogel, C. G. (1983). *The Dangers of Strangers*. Minneapolis, MN: Dillon Press.

Adult References

Guthrie, Woodie. (n.d.). *Songs to Grow on*. Washington, DC: Smithsonian/Folkways.

Safety Steps. (1990). Princeton, New Jersey: Film Loops, Inc., P.O. Box 2233, Princeton, NJ 08540. Teaching kit for passenger and pedestrian safety education for preK-third grade: guide, a seat belt, iron-on decals, games and posters. Also includes the five-minute filmstrip Adventures of Beltman.

National Highway Traffic Safety Administration. (1985). *Andrew and the Big Kids: A Book on Traffic Safety*. Washington, DC: U.S. Department of Transportation.

National Highway Traffic Safety Administration. *The Brothers: A Book On Traffic Safety*. Washington, DC: U.S. Department of Transportation.

National Highway Traffic Safety Administration. (1985). *The Car Game: A Book On Traffic Safety*. Washington, DC: U.S. Department of Transportation.

National Highway Traffic Safety Administration. (1990). *Prevent Pedestrian Accidents: A Message for Parents of Elementary School Children*. Washington, DC: U.S. Department of Transportation.

National Highway Traffic Safety Administration. (1985). *Sharon Goes to School: A Book on Traffic Safety*. Washington, DC: U.S. Department of Transportation.

National Highway Traffic Safety Administration. (1985). *The Six Steps: A Book On Traffic Safety*. Washington, DC: U.S. Department of Transportation.

National Highway Traffic Safety Administration. (1985). *Super Scott and Super Spot: A Book On Traffic Safety*. Washington, DC: U.S. Department of Transportation.

Public Health Service. (1985). *It's Elementary for Healthy People*. Videorecording for elementary school children introducing health and safety games. Washington, DC: U.S. Department of Health and Human Services, Altman Productions.

Vandenburg, M. L. (1975). *Help! Emergencies That Could Happen to You and How to Handle Them*. Minneapolis, MN: Lerner.

Fire Safety

Terms, Facts, and Principles (TFPs)

General Information

1. Fire gives off light, is very hot, and burns things.
2. Fire needs fuel and air to burn.
3. Fire can burn many different materials such as wood, paper, leaves, fabric, skin, hair, and so on.
4. Fire can be useful or destructive.
5. Grown-ups use fire for many different purposes including:

    to cook food on a stove or campfire,

    to make a fire in a fireplace to make a room warm,

    to light a pipe or cigarette,

    to light candles,

    to make fireworks in the sky,

    to light sparklers or firecrackers.

Fire Hazards

6. It is not safe for anyone to play with fire; fire can hurt people, animals, and property.
7. A fire can start anywhere: in stores, in the forest, in offices, in the garage, in a closet, in the kitchen, in the living room, or in a bedroom.
8. A fire hazard is something inside or outside of a building that can cause a fire where fire is not wanted.
*9. Fires can start from matches, lighters, firecrackers, and sparklers; children are safer if they stay away from these things because they can be fire hazards.
*10. Fires can start from overloaded electrical sockets; children stay safe by keeping away from all sockets and telling a grown-up to fix overloaded sockets because they are a fire hazard.
*11. Fires can start from foods burning at the stove; children stay safe by keeping away from stoves and telling a grown-up if they see or smell food burning because it is a fire hazard.
*12. Fires can start from careless use of matches; children stay safe by never playing with matches because they can be a fire hazard.
13. If children find matches, lighters, firecrackers, or sparklers, it is safer to stay away from them and tell a grown-up.

Putting Out Fires

14. Grown-ups can put out a small fire, such as a campfire, by throwing dirt, sand, or water on it.
*15. When fires are in grease or oil, water will not put out the fire; grownups can smother the fire by putting the cover over a pan or throwing baking soda on grease fires to put them out.
16. When fires are big, community helpers called firefighters put them out by using a fire extinguisher, or by squirting them with water from hoses.
17. A fire hydrant is a special outdoor faucet where firefighters can hook up hoses and get water to squirt on fires.

Fire Safety Procedures

*18. If a fire starts, tell the grown-ups and go outside quickly; people should never stay inside a burning building.
19. If there is smoke in a building, stay low and crawl to the door or window to get outside.
20. If a person's clothes catch on fire, he and she should stop, drop to the ground, and roll around to put out the fire.
*21. Families are safer if they plan ways to get out of their house if there is a fire; practicing the plan helps children and adults remember what to do.
22. Families can make their house safer by installing smoke detectors that will sound a warning if there is a fire.
23. Fire alarms are loud bells or horns that sound when people are practicing how to safely get out of a building or when there is a real fire.
24. Fire alarms must be loud so that everyone in the building hears them at the same time and can get out safely.
*25. If there is a fire, a grown-up should telephone the fire department from a neighbor's house. People should never call the fire department unless there is a real emergency.
*26. If no grown-up is there to call the fire department, a child can dial 911 on the telephone to get firefighters to help put out the fire.
*27. When people call 911, they should give the address of where they are including the house number, street, and city so the firefighters know where to come.

Activity Ideas

Aesthetic

1. Fire Paintings

Ask children if they have ever seen a fire. Encourage them to describe what it looked like or what they imagine it would look like. Roll up your sleeves and put on an apron to demonstrate how to wet a large piece of fingerpaint paper with a clean wet sponge. Show children various ways to use their fingers, palms, fists, nails and knuckles to get different effects with fingerpaints. Then offer red, orange, and yellow fingerpaints for them to use to make a fire painting. Suggest children use the paints to express the way fire looks and how it makes them (the artist) feel.

2. Brilliant Art Pictures

Supply the art area with large pieces of brightly colored chalk and large pieces of manila paper (the kind that feels rough to the touch). Also make available wide paintbrushes and liquid starch (found in any grocery store) which you have poured into deep bowls. Tell children they can make brilliant colored pictures of homes, fire engines, campfires, fireplaces, or other theme-related pictures using chalk on wet paper. Invite children to dip a wide brush into the liquid starch. Show them how to brush the starch all over the blank paper; then use chalk to make a picture on the paper. When the chalk dries, it won't rub off on fingers or clothes.

Hint for Success:

● When demonstrating this process, avoid making a realistic looking picture since this will influence what children will make. To support children's creativity, show only the technique, using splashes of color but no meaningful drawings. Then encourage children to think of something they could make, using their own ideas.

3. Songs Around the Campfire

Describe how adults make a campfire for cooking and keeping warm when they camp outdoors. Encourage children to help build a pretend campfire of sticks and leaves (but not lighting it, of course) outdoors on a playground or indoors in a dramatic play area of the room. Tell the children that some campers sit near the fire and sing or tell stories together for fun. Gather the class around and sing songs they know around the pretend campfire.

Affective

1. I Have an Address

Teach children what an address is, dividing it into the parts (the number and perhaps a letter, a street, a town or city, a state, and a zip code). Ask children to find out what their address is by asking a parent or another person who takes care of them. (Give children the form outlined below to take home.) In addition, advise children to look for a number or letter on their apartment or house door, on the mailbox, or somewhere on their home, telling the address. As each child becomes aware of his or her address, hang up a house shape with that child's address and name on it.

> ## Dear Parent or Guardian,
>
> As part of our safety unit, we are learning about home addresses this week. It is important for children to be able to tell where they live if there were a fire or they were lost. Many children have never noticed the address on their house or apartment.
>
> You can help. Please show your child the address numbers (and/or letters) on his/her house or mailbox and the street or road sign, too. Then fill in the form below, and give it to your child to bring to me. You can also help your child learn his/her address by posting it where he/she will see it and where you can review it together frequently. Thanks for your help.
>
> Sincerely,
>
> _____
>
> My name is
>
> _____
>
> My address is
>
> _____
>
> _____
>
> _____

Hint for Success:

● Be aware of any child in your group who is homeless, living in a shelter, or living with relatives, in foster home, or in other temporary living quarters. Show sensitivity to this child, indicating that you understand his or her address is temporary and that's OK.

2. The Safe Thing to Do

Play a game in which a small group of children take turns responding to unsafe situations. Copy the following unsafe situations on individual strips of paper. Place them in a bowl and have children draw them out, one at a time. Read the situation, and then ask questions: "Did this ever happen to you?" and "What's the safe thing to do?" Add some situations of your own.

- You find matches on the sidewalk.
- You smell smoke when you wake up.
- A friend gives you firecrackers.
- You see a cigarette burning on the sofa.
- You notice an overloaded socket.
- The beans start to burn on the stove.
- The family is leaving a burning campfire.
- Your clothes catch on fire.
- Your house has no smoke detector.
- You are the only one who hears the fire alarm at school.
- Your neighbor helps you to report a fire and asks for your address.

Hint for Success:

● To be successful in this activity, children must have developed a basic understanding of cause and effect. Therefore, this activity is most suitable for children kindergarten-age and older.

3. I'm a Fire Hazard Spotter

After children become familiar with ways to identify fire hazards, help them feel good about what they have learned by giving them an opportunity to become a Fire Hazard Spotter. Teach them a song to sing about spotting fire hazards.

♫ Fire Hazard Spotter

Words by Majorie Kostelnik
Tune: "I've Been Working on the Railroad"

I'm a fire hazard spotter,
All the live long day.
I'm a fire hazard spotter,
'Cause I keep things safe that way.
I will never play with matches,
I'm always aware and alert.
When I look for fire hazards,
I'm safe, I don't get hurt.

4. Fire Hazard Spotter Badges

Let children know they have done a good job in learning some important things about fire safety. They have earned the right to be a Fire Hazard Spotter and wear a F.H.S. badge. Photocopy the badge shown here, cut it out or have children cut it out, and attach it with glue to a circle of construction paper in any color the child chooses. Suggest that children write their name and decorate their badge in their own way. Fasten with a large safety pin through the back of the badge.

5. Home Fire Escape Route

Tell children about your house and the way you plan to get out if there is a fire. Show children what a home fire escape route looks like (see below). Explain that people should plan two ways to escape. They should also decide upon a meeting place where everyone will go when they are out safely. Suggest that children take a copy of the Escape Route and fill it in with grown-ups at home. Encourage children to practice their route with everyone in their families so that all will know and remember how to escape safely.

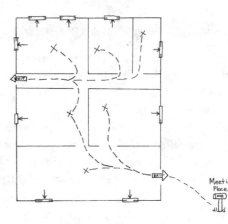

Our Home Fire Escape Route

By _____'s family

If a fire started at our home, we would leave through:

1._____

OR

2._____ .

We would all go to our outdoor "meeting place" which is:

_____ .

Here is a map of our home showing how to get out two ways:

Cognitive

1. Getting Ready for Fire Safety

At the beginning of this unit, hold a discussion with the class about fire and fire safety. Ask two main questions: "What do you know already about fire and fire safety?" and "What do you want to know about fire?" Put the questions as column headings on a large chart. As children suggest things, record their ideas under the appropriate question. Use this chart as a guide to the level of understanding some of the children have achieved and to help plan activities for particular groups or individuals. After the fire safety unit, ask children to add a third column to the chart indicating "Things we learned about fire safety."

2. Fire Is Useful

Show children a variety of pictures illustrating how fire can be useful to people. Ask them to describe what they see. Put the pictures aside and see how many uses for fire the group can recall. Write these down on large paper for future reference. Later, hang the pictures where children can see them.

3. The Fire Alarm Signal

Help children understand warning signals and be better prepared for a fire drill at school. Record a number of sounds on an audio-tape that warn people of various things. Examples could be the telephone ringing, a tea kettle whistling, the doorbell ringing, the sound of a smoke alarm going off, or a siren on an ambulance. The last sound you record should be the fire alarm bell at your center or school. Gather children together and explain that there are many signals and warnings used to help people in their daily lives. Some of these signals help people stay safe. Give an example of some signals that people use every day. Sometimes people see the signal (a red light), sometimes people hear the signal (an alarm clock). Ask children to think of other signals. Then play the tape recording of the different auditory signals and ask children to identify each one. If a signal is difficult to identify, offer clues about where it is used. End the game with the recording of the fire alarm and turn up the volume so it is close to what children would actually hear during a fire drill. Praise them for being good listeners and playing the game.

4. Fires Start Anywhere

Make a large flannelboard shape of a house. Draw lines separating the rooms inside: upstairs, downstairs, the basement, the garage, and the attic. Cut out ten to twelve small red flames and tell children they can pretend that this house has some fire hazards in it. They are to place a flame wherever they think a fire might start. To stimulate higher levels of thinking, ask children to tell why a fire could start in a particular place they have chosen.

5. Fire Hazards

After children have been introduced to the concept of a fire hazard, let them play a little game that gives them practice considering what would and would not be a fire hazard. Prepare a set of pictures of things—some that would start a fire and others that wouldn't. Cover them with clear adhesive paper or laminate them for durability. Ask children to separate the pictures, placing them on a chart that has two columns. Label one column "Safe" and the other "Not Safe." Ask children to explain the reasons for their decisions.

6. Hazard Hunt

Begin this activity by duplicating enough pictures of fire hazards so there is one for each child in the class (use the ones provided above and others you have drawn yourself). Prepare the pictures by mounting them on heavy paper, laminating or covering the pictures with clear adhesive paper to make them sturdier, and cutting them apart. Introduce the activity by explaining that these pictures of fire hazards will be hidden around the room and the children will have to find them. Tell children that when they have found one hazard picture, they should come sit in the group area. Have children close their eyes or leave the room while someone hides the pictures. Then ask children to come back and search until each has found one picture. After everyone has found one and is sitting down, ask each child to tell about the hazard he or she found.

To Simplify:

● Have children hold up their pictures, one at a time, while an adult tells the group which hazard it is.

To Extend:

● Reward children with fire hazard spotter badges to wear. Send home a copy of the hazard pictures, asking parents to help their child be a fire hazard spotter at home, checking for fire hazards.

7. Exits, Exits Everywhere!

Show children an exit sign and ask them to tell what it means. Point out that not all doors are exits; some lead to closed rooms or closets. Explain that it is important for people to know where the exits are so they could get out of a building in case of fire. Ask children to locate the exits in their classroom. Suggest that they try to find more exits in the building by taking a walk around the inside or touring the outside of the building. Have children count the exits as they find them. Challenge children to count the exits at their house and report to the class what they have learned.

Construction

1. My Own Telephone

Explain to children that telephones are tools that help them stay safe. Show children a real or realistic-looking pretend telephone. Point out the parts, particularly the dial or buttons. Then show one or more other models. Explain that while telephones can look very different in color, size, shape, and style, they are all designed to do the same thing. Ask each child to describe the telephone at her or his house. Provide the art area with materials to make telephones: various colored construction paper, markers, crayons, scissors, string or yarn, number stamps, and glue.

To Simplify:

● Supply the telephone dial. Draw a basic number pad and/or a circular dial with numbers. Photocopy and cut these out so children can glue them on the telephone of their own design.

To Extend:

● Suggest children make imaginary telephones of the future that people might have in their homes or carry with them.

2. A Home Fireplace

Show children pictures of fireplaces to help them become familiar with what they look like. Ask children to describe a fireplace they know about. Offer them a large cardboard box with an opening cut out for the fire area. Suggest that children could make a fireplace together using paints, paper, scissors, glue, and sticks. When the fireplace is dry, place it in the pretend house and add other props that make real fireplaces safe, such as a screen cover. Encour-age children to use the fireplace in their pretend play.

3. My Own Exit Sign

After looking at and discussing exit signs and how they help keep people safe (see "Exits, Exits, Everywhere," page 154), offer children materials and time to make their own exit signs. Make a word card that says "EXIT" for children who want to copy the letters. Suggest that children post their signs near exit doors only.

Language

1. What Is Fire?

To introduce the concept of fire, gather the group together and tell children you are going to read a book about something. They can guess what the book is about by figuring out the answer to this riddle:

"You have seen grown-ups use it, it can have many different colors, and it should never be touched by anyone. What is it?"

Give another clue by holding up the book *Fire* by Maria Rius (1985), which presents many aspects of fire. When children know what the topic is, ask them to listen carefully as you read. When you are finished, ask children to tell something they know about fire. Write a list called "Things We Know About Fire." Hang the list in the classroom for reference.

2. Five Brave Firefighters

Using hand motions, teach children the following poem.

Five Brave Firefighters
Author unknown

Five brave firefighters (*lay five fingers on other hand*)
Sleeping in a row. (*put hands together under cheek*)
Ding-ding rings the bell, (*stand fingers up fast*)
Down the pole they go. (*gesture sliding a pole*)
Jumping on the fire truck. (*hold fists up firmly*)
Ready to aim the hose. (*twist imaginary nozzle*)
Climbing up the ladder. (*gesture climbing*)
Out the fire goes! (*squirt imaginary hose*)

A number of activities are suggested by the poem:

Hearing the Poem. Recite the poem several times so it becomes familiar to the children. Teach them the hand gestures to increase participation.

Make and Read the Rebus. Print the words on large paper. Copy the pictures provided on page 157 and mount them on pieces of paper that are large enough to hide the words they match. Tape the pictures over the appropriate words, thus making a rebus poem. Show children what the poem looks like in rebus form. Ask them to help read the poem aloud. Run your finger along under the words as they recite them. As you get to a picture, hesitate and allow the children to fill in the words that make sense.

Picture Flipping. After reading the poem in rebus form for a few days, flip up each picture as children say the word to show them what the word looks like.

Words Only. Eventually, remove the pictures and encourage children to recite the poem using the words alone.

Find the Word. Tell children the word *fire* appears in more than one place. Show them a card with the word written on it and ask children to find and match it to the one in the poem.

To Simplify:

● Write the word *fire* in red to make it stand out. Point out the way fire is part of the word *firefighter*.

To Extend:

● Challenge children to find other words in the poem. Print other significant words (action words such as *sleeping, jumping, climbing*) and object words such as *bell, pole, truck, hose, ladder* on cards. Hold up one word at a time and ask who can find each one.

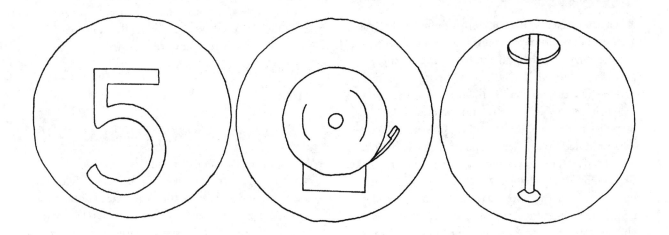

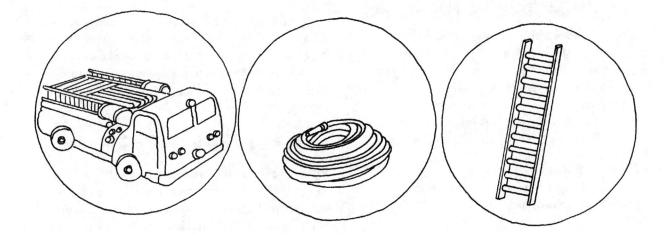

3. Telling Fire Stories

In a quiet area of the room, display fire-related pictures of firefighters in action, forest fires, and so on. Prepare a storytelling book for each child with several empty pages stapled together in book form. Invite one or two children at a time to come to the storytelling area and dictate a story about one of the fire pictures. Some children may want to use their own form of writing. If children need help getting started, point out something in one of the pictures and ask if they ever saw anything like that before. Write whatever they tell you, making sentences but using their words as much as possible. Offer pencils, markers, and crayons in the area. While one child dictates, the other can make pictures for his or her book.

4. Help! There's a Fire

Demonstrate and encourage children to practice calling 911 on pretend telephones. Remind them they should tell their address when they call. Arrange two telephones for children to practice these skills, one in the pretend house and the other in the pretend fire station. Let children know how important it is to be able to tell their address to help firefighters find the fire.

Hint for Success:
● Emphasize that people should never call 911 unless there is a real emergency.

5. Interview a Firefighter

Let the class know that they will soon get a chance to talk to a real firefighter. Propose that children think of something they want to know about being a firefighter. Have the children help plan questions to ask the firefighter and use these questions in preparing an interview booklet for the visit. Write each question at the top of a piece of paper and fasten the papers together into a booklet. The day the firefighter comes to visit (or when you take the children to visit the firefighter), arrange to have an adult read the questions the children asked and write down the answers given. Later reread the interview to the children.

6. Things We Learned About Fire and Fire Safety

Near the end of the fire safety unit, gather the children in a circle and ask them to help make a list of things they learned about fire and fire safety. Use this opportunity to demonstrate an important use for writing/recording details. Listen to what children say

and reinforce them for remembering so much. Also notice and correct any misconceptions that may result from children not fully understanding the concepts. Display your list where parents can see it.

Physical

1. Walk Fast in a Fire Drill

Review the procedures for a fire drill at your school/center. Provide a signal that alerts children to the fact that the class needs to leave the classroom. Have a route posted at each exit door which tells where to take the children in the event of a fire. Demonstrate how to walk fast—but not run!—during the fire drill. Practice a fire drill, keeping track of how long it takes everyone to vacate the building. Assign one adult to come out last, checking the room for stragglers or children in the bathroom. When you all get to your designated safe place, count the children to make sure everyone is there. Praise children for doing so well practicing in this fire safety drill and for walking fast rather than running.

2. Stop, Drop, and Roll

Teach children the safety procedure to follow if their clothes catch on fire. Show them how to stop moving, drop to the floor or ground, and roll over and over to put out the flames. Arrange a place for children to practice this skill many times. Encourage others around them to say the words out loud to reinforce the movement coordination. Play a game where children in a small group are walking around slowly. Suddenly the leader shouts, "Your clothes are on fire! STOP, DROP, AND ROLL." Repeat with another small group of children, until everyone gets a turn.

Pretend Play

1. Fire Engines Go

Prior to carrying out this activity, make or gather the following materials: make-believe fire hoses, fire extinguishers, and a make-believe blaze to put out. Play a game in which children will pretend to be a fire engine responding to a fire. Ask them to choose and wear one of the badges which indicates what color their fire engine is. Have everyone stand at one end of a large clear area, either inside or outdoors. Point to the opposite end of the area at the pretend blaze and tell children there is a building on fire down there. Explain that a "dispatcher" will call engine colors to tell which engines should go and when. When children hear their color of their engine called, they should drive fast to the fire and put it out using pretend hoses or fire extinguishers. Make yourself the first dispatcher so children will become familiar with the game. Ring a real or imaginary bell and call, "Red fire engines go." Repeat calling, "Blue fire engines go," and so on until everyone has had a turn. Then call all the engines to return to their fire stations. Select a new dispatcher and repeat.

Hint for Success:
● Make fire engine color badges by cutting out a simple fire engine shape from red, blue, green, and yellow paper. Laminate these shapes, punch two holes, and tie yarn the same color through the two holes to make a color tag to wear.

2. Mini-Firefighting

Supply the block area with small fire trucks, people, cars, and hoses for children to use in creating neighborhoods that need firefighters' help. An additional prop that will motivate fire danger play may be a small bell that children could ring as a fire alarm or siren.

3. We Are Firefighters

Provide props to help children pretend to be firefighters, fire dispatchers, or people needing firefighter assistance. Fire helmets, coats and boots, pretend fire engine hoses, several ladders, a net, a hydrant, extinguishers, face masks and plastic tools suggest many different actions and events for this kind of play. Arrange a set of chairs in a row to be the fire engine. Provide furniture (table and chairs, beds, stove), cooking equipment, telephones, and a map of the area to simulate the fire station.

Hint for Success:
● If necessary, limit the number of children allowed to play in this area at one time. Assist them in taking turns in this popular space. Set up a waiting list to help them take turns.

4. Camping Around the Fire

Gather props that suggest camping in the woods in one area of the classroom. Provide real or pretend logs to build a pretend fire, sleeping bags, pretend food, cooking pan, flashlights, animal puppets, other camping-related items, and buckets of pretend water or dirt. Help children remember what they learned about how to put out fires.

Social

1. Group Mural

Invite children to participate in a group project in which everyone makes things for one giant picture called a mural. Tell children the mural will picture many of the places and objects located in their town. Hang a large piece of paper on a bulletin board or cover part of a wall for the mural. Draw in lines suggesting roads. Provide materials such as paper, scissors, markers, crayons, and pencils for everyone to make houses, stores, a fire station, a school, and other things that are found in a town or city. Place each child's address on the house she/he makes. Suggest other objects for the mural such as signs, fire hydrants, trees, cars, street lights, traffic lights, and so on. Display the mural map about three feet above the floor so children can see and add things to it easily.

2. Don't Play with Matches Song

Start this activity with a discussion about a child who played with matches and started a fire accidentally. Show children a picture of a burnt-out building and ask them to imagine what it would be like to live there. Teach them the following song.

♫ **Don't Play with Matches**
Author unknown
Tune: "Frère Jacques"

> Don't play with matches,
> Don't play with matches.
> For if you do,
> For if you do,
> You might burn your house down,
> You might burn your house down.
> That won't do,
> Boo hoo hoo.

3. Our Escape Route

Help children plan a route out of school in case of a fire. Draw a very large but simple map of the building (your floor only) and mark all the exits, stairways, and other ways to get out of the building, including any large windows that open. Mark the two best routes on the map, one in red and the other in blue. Walk children through the red escape route one day; take the blue route another day. Practice using both of the routes in conjunction with a signal (a loud whistle or loud bell) that is used only for fire emergencies and tells everyone to come to the predetermined exit. Display the escape route map so children can trace the route they are practicing each time you hold a fire drill.

4. 911 Reminders

Talk to children about the number 911 and why it is important to remember how to use it in calling the fire department in an emergency. (If your area uses a different system, teach them that number). Teach children to help others by suggesting they make Fire 911 cards to post near every telephone in the building and to take home. Make a sample for children to copy onto cards. Assist children distribute their helpful signs to locations where they would be useful.

Teacher Resources

Field Trip Ideas

1. Visit a local fire station for a tour of the facility. Ask that a firefighter show children where the crew eats and sleeps, along with some of the equipment they use. Let the firefighters know the ages of the children and what they have been learning. Suggest some things they could show children. Be aware of children who may be fearful of loud noises; ask that the firefighters avoid sounding their sirens, if possible, when the class is there. Ask about what procedure your class should follow if an alarm comes in while you are at the station. Be sure to send a follow-up thank you from all of the children.

2. Walk to a nearby fire hydrant to inspect its parts, find out what color it is, and determine how far it is from the hydrant to your center or school.

3. Take a walking tour of the school. Have children look for fire safety items (hydrant, extinguisher, alarm box, exits, fire bell, fire hose, smoke alarm, and so on. Show children photographs of the real items before they begin their search.

Classroom Visitors

1. Invite a firefighter to come to your school, bringing equipment and gear appropriate to show young children. Ask if you can borrow any firefighting clothing or gear for children to explore.

2. Ask firefighters at a nearby station to drive a fire truck to your school or center. They could then show children the lights, hoses, gear, places to sit

and ride, and so on. Be sure to alert parents to when this will happen so they won't be concerned by seeing the truck parked at the school.

Children's Books

Beame, R. (1973). *Ladder Company 108*. New York: Julian Messner.

Brown, M., and Krensky, S. (1986). *Dinosaurs Beware!* Boston: Little, Brown.

Chlad, D. (1982). *Matches, Lighters and Firecrackers Are Not Toys*. Chicago: Childrens Press.

Chlad, D. (1982). *When There's a Fire—Go Outside*. Chicago: Childrens Press.

Maass, R. (1989). *Fire Fighters*. New York: Scholastic.

Rius, M. (1985). *Fire*. Woodbury, NY: Barron's Publishers.

Adult References

Arena, J. M. (1978). *Child Safety Is No Accident: A Parents' Handbook of Emergencies*. Durham, NC: Duke University Press.

Burger King Fire Safety Program. RLA Distribution Center, Attn: Fire Safety Order Department, 179 Saw Mill River Road, Yonkers, NY 10701. Contains film, educational games, songbook, T-shirt transfers, poster, and brochures.

Play Safe! Be Safe! Children's Fire Safety Education Program. (1994). BIC Corporation, 500 BIC Drive, Milford, CT 06460. Contains a teacher's manual, resource book, game, activity cards, and so on, for ages 3–5.

Teaching About Fire. (1977). The Hartford National Junior Fire Marshal Program. Hartford Fire Insurance Company, Junior Fire Marshal Headquarters, Hartford Plaza, Hartford, CT, 06115.

Personal Safety

Terms, Facts, and Principles (TFPs)

General Information

1. Every person has a body that belongs only to him or her.

2. Some parts of the body are private parts, meaning they are body parts other people may see or touch only with permission from the person to whom they belong.

3. To many people, private body parts are those parts covered by a bathing suit.

Touches

4. Every person has a right to keep his or her private parts protected from looks or touches.

5. There are many kinds of touches: a pat on the hand, a hug, a kiss, an arm around the shoulder, holding a hand, tickles, back rubs, and so on.

6. Some kinds of touches feel good; some touches feel neutral (not good or bad); some kinds of touches feel bad.

7. When touches feel good, they might make a person feel happy, comfortable, secure, or pleased.

8. When touches feel bad, they might hurt, or make a person feel sad, frightened, uncomfortable, angry, or confused.

9. Sometimes people want to be touched; sometimes they don't.

10. When someone doesn't want to be touched, it's best not to touch him or her.

11. When a person wants to give a hug or kiss, it's best to ask the other person's permission first; only hug or kiss people who say yes.

*12. Sometimes touches start out feeling good, but change to feeling bad.

13. When a child is touched by someone in a way that feels bad or confusing, or when a child doesn't want to be touched, that child can say "No" or "Stop" in a firm voice, and get away from the person doing the touching.

*14. If the bad touches don't stop, the child should ask for help; it's best to tell a trusted grown-up about bad touches, even if the person doing the touching said to keep it secret.

15. A secret is information that is deliberately kept by a person from another person.

*16. Some secrets are OK to keep because they cause no harm to anyone, and are usually kept for a short time. An example of an OK secret is knowing about a surprise present for someone.

*17. Some secrets are not OK to keep because they make the person uncomfortable or harm someone. If someone tells a child never to tell a secret involving touches, the child should tell a trusted adult right away.

18. Trust is a strong feeling of safety. When we trust someone, it means we believe that person will keep us safe and not hurt us.

19. A trusted adult is someone a person knows and with whom he or she feels safe.

*20. Safe touches are caring touches that help keep people safe or healthy.

*21. Safe touches don't always feel good; sometimes they hurt a little, such as when someone puts cream on a sunburn, or washes a cut.

Strangers

*22. A stranger is someone a person doesn't know, or someone a child's parents don't know.

*23. If a stranger tries to touch a child, or offers sweets or toys to a child, the child should say "No!", run away from the stranger, and tell a trusted adult or a police officer.

Getting Lost

*24. Children are safer when they stay with their trusted adults; however, if a child gets lost, she or he can look for a stranger who will help, such as a person wearing a uniform like a police officer or mail carrier, a mother with a child, another child, or a sales clerk.

*25. When children are lost and find a stranger who will help them, they should tell the adult their phone number to help find their parents.

Activity Ideas

Aesthetic

1. This Is My Body

Offer children opportunities to relate to their own body image. Set up a full length mirror in an area where children will be walking by. Encourage children to look at themselves and tell about what they see. Offer children paints, markers, or thick crayons and large paper at the easel for making pictures of themselves.

Another way to encourage children to look at their bodies closely is to offer them wipe-off markers to trace or draw directly on the mirror image of themselves.

Hints for Success:

● Remember that young children may or may not be at the representational stage of drawing. It is likely that in any group of youngsters, some will be in the scribbling stage, others will have begun to control and name their scribbles, others will be making drawings with recognizable shapes and forms, and others will be drawing representationally. It is important to accept all stages of drawing equally; ask every child-artist about his or her picture, not just the children who make recognizable forms.

● Avoid correcting "errors" in children's portraits: the wrong color for hair, missing arms, or a large head on a small body, and so on. Young children choose color for very different reasons. Often they will select colors they like, not ones that match reality. With more experience, they will relate to more body parts and begin to include them in their drawings. Pointing out forgotten parts can discourage children from showing you their work or can suggest there is only one right way to make a person in order to meet adult standards.

● Never draw on children's drawings. Respect their art as their own special work. If children ask for help drawing, suggest they think about what they are attempting to make, look at pictures, or look into a mirror for ideas. Children often respond positively with just a few words of encouragement. Remind them they can make their body picture any way they want and that you expect that everybody's pictures will be different.

2. Gentle Dance Touching

Play some stimulating music and encourage children to dance with a partner. Point out some gentle ways to touch each other while dancing. Praise children for being friendly and careful with the people around them.

3. Finger Paint on Me

Provide several colors of washable finger paints and a pan of warm water to wash the paint off. Suggest that children choose a partner, roll up their sleeves, and take turns finger-painting each other's hands. Encourage children to enjoy the gentle touches of their partner as they work, but also to say "Stop" when they want to end the experience.

4. Who Wants to Touch?

Use the song "Who Wants to Touch and Be Touched?" on Hap Palmer's record album or audio-tape, *Getting to Know Myself*. Have children find a partner and play the music, which asks questions and requires children to respond by either saying "yes" (they want to touch or be touched by their partner) or "no" (they don't). Encourage chidren to sing the song along with the recording to increase their enjoyment of the singing game, even if they don't want to participate in other ways.

Affective

1. I Like You

Give children the opportunity to explore appropriate ways of showing affection. Gather children into a group. Begin by demonstrating two ways people show others they like them. Start with a non-touching gesture, such as smiling and waving, and then use a touching gesture, such as putting your arm around someone's shoulder. Demonstrate these with a large doll or an adult volunteer (someone who won't react negatively). Ask children to think of another way to show that they like a person. Suggest they demonstrate their ideas using the doll, a teacher, or a friend. Watch for inappropriate ways and take the opportunity to talk about them as they are suggested. Leave the large doll out in the room for children to practice various ways of showing affection throughout the day.

2. My Bathing Suit

Send a letter home to parents asking that children be allowed to bring their bathing suits to the center, regardless of the season. Also ask for loans of extra bathing suits for those children who don't own one and other swimming-related props such as towels, sunglasses, etc. Explain that during part of this unit on "Personal Safety," you'll be having a pretend swimming area and that children will be encouraged to wear their bathing suits over their clothing for warmth, sanitary reasons, and easy removal. Allow children who feel comfortable to wear their suits for as long as is practical during their play day. Encourage them to take turns modeling their bathing suits for the group.

To Simplify:

● Have children model their suits all at the same time. Ask them to point to a body part that is not covered by their bathing suit. Then suggest they find a body part that is covered by their bathing suit. Repeat.

To Extend:
- Encourage children to take pretend photographs of each other wearing their bathing suits. Then suggest children draw pictures representing the photographs.

3. People I Like to Touch

Trace one of each child's hands or encourage children to trace their own hands. Then ask them to think of the names of people they like to touch. Write one name on each finger and the child's name in the palm. Cut out the hands and display them on a window, bulletin board, or along a low wall.

4. I Can Say No

Start children thinking about ways of rejecting unsafe behaviors. Say, "Sometimes in order to stay safe, you have to say "No" to another person who wants you to break a safety rule. For example, what if a friend wanted you to ride tricycles in the street? What could you say?" Teach children to say "No!" using a strong, firm voice (not shouting). Encourage everyone to try it. Then encourage children to practice this skill. Explain "I'll tell you to do some unsafe things, and you tell me 'No' in a strong voice." Begin with general unsafe behaviors that are unrelated to touches such as:

> Let's play on the railroad tracks.
> Let's cross the street without waiting for the Walk signal.
> Let's play with matches.

Praise children for using their firm, strong voices. Continue the game, using examples of unsafe touches such as:

> What can you say if somebody pushes you hard?
> Is it OK if somebody pokes you in the back?
> Is it OK for someone to keep tickling you after you say "Stop"?

To Simplify:
- Use unsafe examples that illustrate situations with which children are likely to be very familiar, especially ones that may occur in the early childhood program.

To Extend:
- Challenge children to give additional examples of unsafe behaviors. Stay involved in the game, being available to clarify ambiguous situations children may identify.

5. My Family Does It This Way

Describe your own family or someone with whom you feel close. Tell about and demonstrate an appropriate family sign of affection using a doll, a stuffed animal, or a willing volunteer: "This is one way we show 'I love you' in my family." Invite children who volunteer to demonstrate one way they show affection in their family.

6. I Want a Hug

Offer to give each child a friendly hug in turn; suggest that children either accept or reject the hug by saying "Okay" or "No, thanks." Show approval of both decisions.

7. Telephone Number Memory

Help children practice remembering their telephone numbers. Write each child's name and number in large print on a card. Have everyone decorate a "Can Do" can that has their name on it and place these cans in a special, easily accessible place in the classroom. Tell children that when they have their telephone number memorized, they should say it for you, and then they get to put their card into their "Can Do" can.

To Simplify:
- Suggest each child select a simple song he or she likes and use that tune to sing their telephone numbers to make it easier to remember.

To Extend:
- Use the "Can Do" cans to reinforce other skills the children master throughout the year, such as learning their address, being able to catch a ball, or writing their own name.

Cognitive

1. Sorting Touches

Make three kinds of paper faces: happy, neutral, and sad. Lay these out on a table and talk about what feelings each indicates. Make a pile of index cards with various ways to touch written on them, one touch per card. Play a game with one or two children at a time, asking them to point to the kind of feelings they have in response to the particular touches described. Read each "touch card" out loud. Suggest that children point to the way each touch makes them feel.

Examples for "touch cards":

tickles on your foot

tickles on your stomach

tickles on your cheek

a pat on the head from grandma

a tap on the shoulder from a friend

an arm around your shoulder from the teacher

a pinch on the cheek

a slap on the hand

holding a friend's hand

holding a stranger's hand

a hug from mom

a hug from the babysitter

a hug from a stanger

a hard poke in the stomach

a kiss from daddy

a kiss from the dog

a kiss from your brother

a hard push

a gentle push

2. Private Parts

Display pictures of children wearing bathing suits at a beach or swimming pool. Discuss what children notice about the people and point out that their bathing suits cover up parts of their bodies, the private parts. Ask children to show you some of the non-private body parts they see in the pictures as well. Use anatomically correct words for boys private parts (penis, buttocks) and girls private parts (vagina, buttocks, breasts). Remind children that they can keep their private parts private by keeping them covered and away from other people's looks or touches.

Hint for Success:

● Discuss health reasons that make it OK for some grownups to touch or look at children's private parts, such as getting children clean in the bathtub, helping children use the toilet, or examining them at the doctor's office.

3. What Would Happen If?

To encourage children to consider various responses to a touching situation, suggest the game of "What Would Happen If?" Tell children that you will describe a variety of situations involving touch. Their job will be to tell what they think would happen as a result of that circumstance. Help children take turns giving their

ideas. Use their ideas to point out good touches and bad touches and to generate alternative acceptable ways to touch. For example, the teacher could say, "What would happen if your Uncle Harry wanted to rub your cheek with his beard?" Children might say, "No, I don't like that" or "That's OK, it tickles." The teacher could respond by suggesting the child say, "Rub your beard on my teddy bear, not me" or other appropriate replies.

Sample "What Would Happen If . . ." Questions

a. What would happen if you stubbed your toe?

b. What would happen if your brother got mad and hit you?

c. What would happen if you gave your mom a big kiss?

d. What would happen if your grandma started to cry?

e. What would happen if your dad bought you a new ball?

f. What would happen if your little sister got stung by a bee?

Construction

1. Cover Me Up

Provide a cardboard tracing pattern of a body shape and suggest that children trace it on plain paper. Next ask children to "dress the body" by gluing fabric pieces on the body shape. Supply markers, paste, paper or cloth scraps. Encourage children to make a bathing suit for the person. Remind children the bathing suit should cover the private parts of the body.

To Simplify:

● Trace the body shape ahead of time for the children.

To Extend:

● Have children show their constructions to each other and tell something about them.

2. My Own Private Sign

Talk about the fact that people sometimes want or need privacy. Show children various signs that indicate privacy of space or ownership: Keep Out, Private, Hands Off, or Please Stay Out. Give children materials such as cardboard, markers, crayons, paint, glue, and colored paper scraps for making their own signs. Give assistance only if children need help making the letters.

Suggest they can make their signs any way they want to. Encourage children to display their signs on or near something of their own, or at a space they temporarily want for their own.

3. My Trusted Person

Begin by discussing the concept of trust. Show a picture of a mother and child, a father and child, or two children showing affection. Ask children, "What do you see here? How does (this person) feel about (the other)? How can you tell?" Explain that trust is a strong feeling of safety. When you trust someone, it means you believe that person will keep you safe and not hurt you. Tell children to think about someone they trust and why they trust that person so much. After the discussion, provide children with a supply of paper, crayons, pencils or markers so that they can make a picture of a person they trust. Offer to write the person's name and anything children want to tell about each person when their pictures are finished.

Language

1. Book of Hugs

Gather a small group of children together and explain that you're going to read all about different hugs people give and get. Read *A Book of Hugs* by Dave Ross (1980). Explore the pictures together and laugh at the funny parts of the book with the group. When you are finished reading, ask children to recall a hug they saw in the book.

To Simplify:
● Show children a large doll and demonstrate one or more of the hugs from the book.

To Extend:
● Using the doll, encourage children to act out each hug they recall.

2. Mama's Secret

To introduce children to the concept of a secret and expand their abilities to recognize the main idea of a story, read the book *Mama's Secret* by Maria Polushkin (1977) aloud to the group. This book tells a simple story about how a mother reveals her secret to her child. Before reading, give the children a simple definition of a secret (see TFPs 15–17, page 161). Ask them to watch, listen, and try to figure out what the secret is in the story. After the story, ask children to tell what they think the secret was. Ask other questions to get them thinking about secrets, such as "Was this secret OK to keep? Did it harm anyone or hurt anyone's feelings? Was it about touching? What should children do if someone wants them to keep a secret they think is not OK?" If they're not sure, explain that children should tell an adult they trust.

Follow this discussion by playing a game about secrets. Tell children you're going to tell them each a "secret" on their turn. If they think it's an OK secret, they should say "OK." If they think it's not OK, they should say "No" and walk over and tell another adult in the room. Tell one child at a time a secret out loud so everyone can hear it: "Now it's Jimmy's turn. It's a secret that . . ."(use the sample secrets below or make up ones more appropriate to your class). If children aren't sure what a "Not OK" secret is, help them remember the criteria for a "Not OK" secret: it harms someone or is about touching.

Sample Secrets

We are having a party soon. (OK)

I am making my mom a present for her birthday. (OK)

I'm going to surprise my dad by cleaning my room. (OK)

Sometimes my sister pinches me hard. She says not to tell. (Not OK)

My cousin pushes me when he's angry. He says not to tell. (Not OK)

I bought a present for my brother's birthday. (OK)

A friend's babysitter likes to tickle her a lot. She says not to tell. (Not OK)

3. Touching Pictures

Show children pictures of people displaying affection in appropriate ways. Encourage children to talk about what they see. Ask closed questions and open-ended questions.

Examples of closed questions are:
a. What's this? (point to an object or person)

b. Are they being friendly?

c. What are they doing?

Examples of open-ended questions are:
d. Why do you think they're hugging each other?

e. What do you think these people are saying to each other?

f. What's going to happen next?

To Simplify:

● Select one of each kind of question and ask them of one volunteer child at a time.

To Extend:

● Broaden this language experience by writing down the children's responses on large strips of paper in such a way that children can see you writing. Read their phrases or sentences back to them; be sure to tell who gave each answer. Later display the children's phrases or sentences near the corresponding pictures.

4. I Want It Too

Find a quiet area to read to a small group of children. Explain that you are going to read a special book about a problem. Ask children to listen carefully so they can discover what the problem is because when you have finished reading, you will ask them about it. Read *I Want It* by Elizabeth Crary (1982), a story about deciding how to respond to problems caused by difficulty sharing. Put much expression in your voice. Use the pictures to point out some inappropriate touches. Discuss the alternatives given for how to handle the problems the children are having in the story. Invite children to generate other ways of solving the problem.

To Simplify:

● Do one problem situation emphasizing a variety of solutions.

To Extend:

● Use more than one problem situation; suggest children act out the solutions.

5. My Own Touching Story

Let children know that you are going to be a storyteller now and that the story will have something to do with touching. Tell a simple story that has touches in it and that relates to you (such as a time you got bumped in an elevator or when your good friend came to visit and gave you a big hug). Describe your reaction to the kind of touch involved and what you did or said. Tell children they can be storytellers and when their stories are written down, they will be the authors. Tell them the touches in their stories can be good touches, neutral touches, or bad touches, or maybe all three.

To Simplify:

● Offer to write down one child's story at a time.

To Extend:

● Have children write their own story in their own form of writing. Suggest that children illustrate their stories and read them to you.

Physical

1. Show a Touch

Discuss various ways to touch in ways that are appropriate and gentle. Tell children about one way you like to touch or be touched. For example, "I like it when my father hugs me." Show them what you mean by demonstrating the hug using a large doll, a stuffed animal, or a willing volunteer. Invite children to demonstrate kinds of touches they know and like giving or getting.

To Simplify:

● Give each child a turn to demonstrate, one at a time.

To Extend:

● Give an example of a kind of touch you don't like. For example, "I don't like it when someone bumps my ankle with their shopping cart in the supermarket." Invite children to tell about some unwanted touches.

2. Pass a Hand Hug

Form a circle of children and ask them to hold hands. Demonstrate a "Hand Hug" (small hand squeeze) with a willing volunteer. Allow children to practice giving and receiving "Hand Hugs." Then play a game in which one "Hand Hug" is passed all around the circle until it gets to the original hugger. Try reversing the path, so it goes around the other way.

3. Touch and Run

Organize four or five stations in a wide open area where it is safe for children to run. Mark each station in some obvious way (a carpet square, a traffic cone, a ribbon around a tree, and so on). Place one child at each station. The "runners" run from station to station, with the "stationary children" giving the runners a gentle touch and a word of encouragement as they get to each destination. Help children think of gentle ways to touch people (pat, tap, a not-too-hard, high-five hand slap) and things they can say to runners. Play for awhile; then suggest children trade places.

4. Rig-a-Jig-Jig Game

This traditional singing game gives children lots of practice skipping, while encouraging them to touch in gentle, friendly ways. Introduce the song first; then teach the game after children are familiar with the words and tune.

Rig-a-Jig-Jig (Traditional)

> As I was walking down the street,
> Down the street, down the street,
> A friendly person I chanced to meet,
> Heigh-ho, heigh-ho, heigh-ho.
> Rig-a-jig-jig and away we go,
> Away we go, away we go,
> Rig-a-jig-jig and away we go,
> Heigh-ho, heigh-ho, heigh-ho.

The Game: Play the game with a small or large group in an area that allows lots of movement. Tell children to stand in a circle holding hands. While one person skips around the outside of the circle, the others stand still and sing the song. As the group sings "a friendly person I chanced to meet," the skipper stops behind a person and taps him or her gently on the shoulder. The two then skip together around the circle until the song is completed. The first skipper then joins the circle group, and the newly chosen child becomes the new skipper. The game continues.

To Simplify:
● Instead of skipping, have children gallop.

To Extend:
● Have the children hold hands while skipping.

5. Feather Touches

Play a light touch game in which children try to identify what body part is being touched lightly with a feather on their skin. Demonstrate on yourself or ask a child who volunteers to close his or her eyes and sit quietly, trying to feel the feather stroked gently on various places. Praise children for recognizing their body parts. Remind children that they can say "Stop" when they don't like the feeling of the touch or no longer want to be touched. Avoid touching any private body parts.

Hint for Success:
● Be quick to respond if a child says "Stop" and respond positively when a child refuses to participate, saying "That's OK. Some people don't like the feel of a feather; some people do." Reinforce children for asserting their rights not to be touched if they don't want to be.

Pretend Play

1. Swimming Together

Arrange an area of the classroom as a pretend swimming pool or beach. Provide items such as beach towels, empty suntan lotion bottles, small radio, camera, umbrella, beach ball, shovel and pail, pictures of water and sand, and other appropriate props. Set up a pretend changing room using a room divider, screen, or cardboard box to simulate an area to change into and out of their bathing suits. Place a reversible sign on the entrance that says IN USE/PRIVATE on one side and ENTER on the other side. Teach children what each sign means and how they can have privacy by turning it to the IN USE/PRIVATE side when changing into and out of their suits. Encourage children to use the pretend changing room to put on their real bathing suits over their clothes.

2. I Am Lost

Arrange an area of the room where children can practice seeking help when they are lost. Provide the area with dress-up clothes, hats, a police or letter carrier vest, a cash register, and a telephone. Prepare children for ways to seek out help from people they don't know. Demonstrate a scenario for them in which you are the lost child and they take on the roles of the strangers. Think aloud as you are deciding what to do and which stranger to approach. Be sure to give your telephone number to the stranger who then calls your parents. As children understand their alternatives and can play such scenes without you, withdraw to an observer position and allow them to create their own scenarios.

Social

1. Friendly Musical Squares

Play a musical game with carpet squares scattered on the floor. Have children move freely around, staying off the squares while the music is playing. When the music stops, tell them to find a carpet square on which to stand. Continue playing the same way until children can do this easily. Then tell children you're going to take two carpet squares away this time. When the music

stops, they should find a square to stand on with a friend. Friends can touch in friendly ways such as holding hands or giving a hug, if the person says it is OK. Continue to remove squares until three or four small friendly groups are made.

To Simplify:
● Do not remove carpet squares at all. Focus on children helping each other find a square to stand on. Clap when everyone finds one.

To Extend:
● Continue to remove carpet squares until everyone is standing together in one large group. Praise children for sharing and using friendly touches.

2. Friendly Touches

Encourage prosocial interactions by suggesting that children do things with a classmate that they usually do alone, such as setting up the easel, collecting books, feeding the classroom pet, holding the door for others, watering the plants in the room, and so on. Observe and point out ways children are using spontaneous friendly touches, such as holding hands, walking arm in arm, or sitting close together.

3. Can I Hug You?

Use two puppets to act out skits that teach children to ask another person before hugging him or her. If possible, choose people puppets that have neutral looking facial expressions (not angry or scary) and that have arms. If no puppets are available, make some from felt, as shown, or use dolls for the activity. Gather the children into a circle on the floor or have them sit in front of a simple puppet stage.

Puppet Skits: Can I Hug You?

Scene One: Carmine is playing on the floor. Annie comes in and runs over to her.

Annie: "Hi, Carmine. I'm so happy to see you!" (Annie grabs Carmine and gives her a hard hug.)

Carmine: "Hey, stop that, get away." (Pushes her.)

Annie: "But, I . . ." (Looks down and walks slowly away.) Scene ends.

Discussion: Who wanted a hug? What did she do? What did she say? What happened? How did they both feel? Why do you think that happened? Let's try another way and see what happens.

Scene Two: Carmine is playing on the floor. Annie comes in and runs over to her.

Annie: "Hi, Carmine. I'm so happy to see you. Can I give you a hug?"

Carmine: "Sure you can." (They hug each other.) Scene ends.

Discussion: Who wanted a hug? What did she do this time? What did she say this time? How did they both feel? Why do you think that happened? Sometimes people don't want a hug. Let's see what would happen if Carmine says no.

Scene Three: Carmine is playing on the floor. Annie comes in and runs over to her.

Annie: "Hi, Carmine. I'm so happy to see you. Can I give you a hug?"

Carmine: "No, I don't want a hug, but you can sit here and play with me."

Annie: "OK. (She sits down.) I really like you." Scene ends.

Discussion: Who wanted a hug? What did she do this time? What did they say this time? How did they both feel? Why do you think that happened? What's another way to tell someone you don't want a hug?

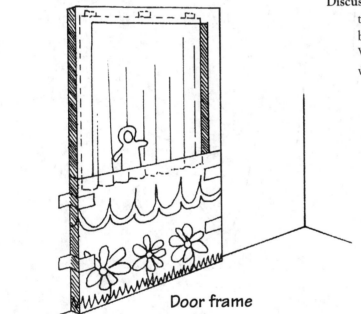

Door frame

Cardboard

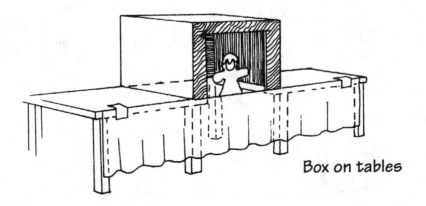

Box on tables

Hint for Success:

● A puppet stage can be made from a bench or chair draped with a piece of cloth, a large piece of cardboard with doors that open, or by using puppets on top of a room divider, low shelf, or cardboard box.

To Simplify:

● Keep the action and words minimal. When rejecting a hug, have the puppets respond with a simple "No,

not now." To practice, have the children say the exact words the puppet used to agree to or reject a hug.

To Extend:

● Have children practice this skill using their own words with the puppets or by acting out situations with a partner. Suggest children consider other expressions of affection in which asking permission would be the best practice (such as asking to hold someone's hand, asking

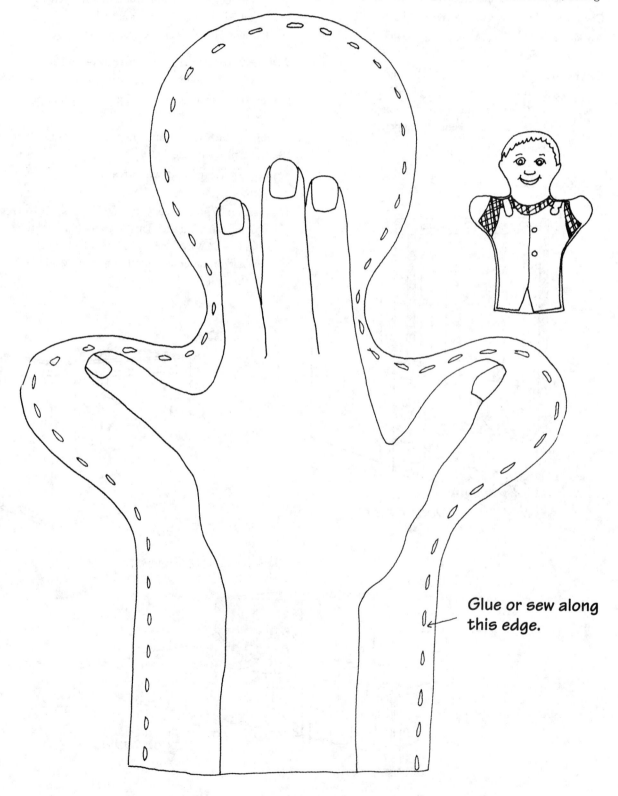

Glue or sew along
this edge.

to sit next to someone, asking to give a kiss, and so on). Encourage them to act these out using the puppets or with a partner.

Making Simple Felt Hand Puppets

To make two puppets, purchase enough felt fabric so that you have four pieces slightly larger than an adult's open hand. Choose two different colors of felt for the puppet's skin tones (black, brown, tan, pinkish, and so on). Look for colors that come close to real skin tones to make it easier for the children to relate to the puppets. Design your own puppet shape or trace the simple puppet pattern (on page 170) and cut two pieces of the same color of felt (a front and a back) for each puppet. Attach the two pieces using hot glue and a glue gun or white glue or sew the two pieces together; leave the bottom open for your hand. Use cloth scraps, yarn, buttons, beads, markers, pens, and so on to make hair, facial features, and clothes for your puppet. Allow the glue to dry completely before putting your hand inside the puppet.

4. Parents, Please Help

Write a letter to the parents describing ways they can reinforce the skills and concepts you are trying to teach in this unit. Ask them to get involved and give them ways they can teach their child to stay personnally safe. Request that they help their child learn the family's telephone number including the area code. When their child knows it, reward him or her with a special badge that says "I Know My Telephone Number."

5. Class Telephone Directory

Show children a real telephone directory. Demonstrate how you can look up any of their telephone numbers because you know their last names and the city where they live. Explain how the book is organized; the names are in alphabetical order (that is, the names that begin with A come first, all those that begin with a B come next, and so on). Tell children that the group is going to make a "Class Telephone Directory" with everyone's telephone number in it. Tell children they can each make a page for the directory and then the pages will be put together into a book. Provide markers and the directory page below. When all pages are complete, ask a child to design the front cover and another child to design the back cover. Staple all of the pages together and fasten them into the "Class Telephone Directory."

To Simplify:

● Explain alphabetizing in terms of the first letter of their first names. Use a looseleaf notebook for the directory so pages can be added later as the group expands.

To Extend:

● Alphabetize the children's names by last name and first initial.

● As pages are made, suggest that the children arrange them in alphabetical order before they are bound together into a directory.

Sample Telephone Directory Page

First Name _____ Last _____

Address _____

Telephone Number:

_____ _____
Area code   Number

This is what I look like:

Teacher Resources

Field Trip Ideas

Take the class on a walking field trip to a telephone booth or a place that has many pay telephones, such as a bus station. Show children how to make a pay call using money. If several telephones are available, divide the group of children into smaller groups, each with an adult supervisor. Give each child the opportunity to call his or her home, either speaking to someone or leaving a message on an answering machine, if one is available. As an alternative, help children call parents at work as necessary and appropriate.

Letter to Parents About Personal Safety

Dear Parents,

For the next _____ week(s) our class will be learning about personal safety. We believe children are safest when they can speak up for themselves, when they have developed the ability to make decisions in a variety of situations, when they know where and how to get help, and when they know they will be believed. You can help make this unit more successful in a variety of ways:

1. Please read the list of terms, facts, and principles attached to this note so you can see what is being discussed in the classroom.
2. Respect your child's right to say "no" in touching situations. Don't insist when your child refuses to hug a family friend or relative. Explain to the guest that your child doesn't feel like being touched, and that's OK.
3. Model assertiveness regarding unwanted touches to show that it's OK for you to say "no," too.
4. Protect your children from strangers. Give them guidelines about where they can go and how to behave when strangers talk to them. Avoid dressing your children in clothing that displays their name and explain why.
5. Play the "What If" game with your children to give them confidence in deciding what to do in various situations.

The "What If" Game

In a non-threatening, playful way, ask your child what they would do under various circumstances, such as:

- What would you do if we were shopping and you couldn't find me?
- What if someone you don't know wanted you to go home with them in their car?
- What if you couldn't find a police officer?

Add some situations of your own. However, keep your child's age and experience in mind and avoid frightening him or her.

6. Protect your children from people who are known too. Prohibit your child from entering anyone's house without your knowledge and approval.
7. Help your child learn his/her telephone number including the area code.

Please Help Your Child

Your child is trying to learn his or her telephone number (with the area code) so she/he could tell it to a police officer in an emergency. You can help with this:

- Print your telephone number on a piece of paper and hang it in a place where your child will see it.
- Some days play a fun game. Cover the first number and ask your child to recall it. Repeat, covering two numbers and so on.
- Remember it may take time to learn this long number. Be patient.
- Each day praise your child for recalling even part of the number.

We appreciate your help.

Classroom Visitors

1. Invite a police officer to come to the classroom to help children become comfortable with a person in uniform. Suggest that the officer talk about how children can get help if they become lost. Invite volunteers to tell the officer their names and telephone numbers.

Children's Books

Aliki. (1982). *We Are Best Friends.* New York: Greenwillow.

Bassett, K. (1987). *My Very Own Special Body Book.* Redding, CA: Hawthorne Press.

Berenstain, S., and Berenstain, J. (1982). *Berenstain Bears Get In a Fight.* New York: Random House.

Crary, E. (1982). *I Want It.* Seattle: Parenting Press.

Dickinson, M. (1980). *Alex's Bed.* London: A. Deutsch.

Hayes, G. (1984). *The Secret Inside.* New York: Four Winds Press.

Johnsen, K. (1986). *The Trouble with Secrets.* Seattle: Parenting Press.

Mc Phail, D. (1990). *Lost!* Boston: Little, Brown.

Polushkin, M. (1977). *Mama's Secret.* New York: Four Winds Press.

Ross, D. (1980). *A Book of Hugs.* New York: Crowell.

Van Leeuwen, J. (1982). *Amanda Pig and Her Big Brother Oliver.* New York: Dial Press.

Wachter, O. (1982). *Close to Home.* New York: Scholastic.

Wachter, O. (1983). *No More Secrets for Me.* Boston: Little, Brown.

Willis, V. (1988). *The Secret in the Matchbox.* New York: Farrar, Straus & Giroux.

Zolotow, C. (1969). *The Hating Book.* New York: HarperCollins.

Zolotow, C. (1963). *The Quarreling Book.* New York: HarperCollins.

Zolotow, C. (1975). *The Unfriendly Book.* New York: HarperCollins.

Adult References

Adams, C. and J. F. (1985). *No More Secrets.* Santa Cruz, CA: Network Publications.

Bahr, A. C. (1986). *Your Body Is Your Own: A Book for Parents and Children to Read Together* New York: Grosset & Dunlap.

Beland, K. (1986). *Talking About Touching II: Personal Safety for Preschoolers.* Seattle: Committee for Children.

Finklehor, D. (1984). *Child Sexual Abuse.* New York: The Free Press.

Freeman, L. (1984). *What Would You Do If? A First Aid Book Especially for Children.* Seattle: Parenting Press.

Kraizer, S. K. (1985). *The Safe Child Book.* New York: Dell Publishing.

Kyte, K. S. (1983). *Play It Safe: The Kid's Guide to Personal Safety and Crime Prevention.* New York: Alfred A. Knopf.

Palmer, H. (n.d.) *Getting to Know Myself.* New York:Educational Activities.

PAM/Prevention and Motivation Programs. (1985). *Good-Touch, Bad-Touch: A Major School Program Designed for Children Grades K through 6.* Available at 200 E. Mary Street, P.O. Box 5227, Valdosta GA., 31603-5227.

Sanford, L. T. (1982). *The Silent Children: A Parent's Guide to the Prevention of Child Sexual Abuse.* New York: McGraw-Hill.

Schonfield, M. *Talking About Touching with Preschoolers: A Personal Safety Curriculum.* (1984). Seattle: Seattle Institute for Child Advocacy's Committee for Children. Adapted from *Talking About Touching,* Ruth Harms and Donna James.

A Culminating Activity

Safety Land Game

This game relates to all of the parts of this chapter including vehicle safety, fire safety, and personal safety concepts. Similar to the popular game "Candy Land," the game requires no reading. Counting dots, matching pictures, and waiting a turn are skills children practice while playing this game. Help children take turns playing the Safety Land Game below:

Preparing the Game:

1. The "Safety Land Game" board:
   a. Photocopy the board and attach it to a piece of posterboard.
   b. Laminate the board to make it sturdy.
   c. Gather four different flat buttons or counters to use for playing pieces.

2. The game cards:
   a. Locate the game cards which are also illustrations throughout this chapter: "Cover-up Bingo Pictures," page 137; "Signs Chart," page 148; "Fire Hazards," page 155; and "Safety Land Game Dot Cards," page 175).
   b. Photocopy all of the cards; cut out only those that match pictures on the game board. Attach them to heavy paper, laminate and cut the cards apart. Shuffle the game cards and pile them face down on the board.

To Play: Choose a playing piece and decide who will go first. Tell children the object of the game is to get home safely. Teach two to four children to play the game by taking turns. On his or her turn, each player should:

1. Turn over one game card.
2. Count the dots and move his or her playing piece the number of dots shown, or move his or her piece to the picture shown on the card.
3. Return the game card to the bottom of the pile.
4. Play until all players have gotten home safely.

Hint for Success:

● To make the game less competitive, suggest that everyone will be a winner when she or he gets home safely and the game ends when every player achieves that goal.

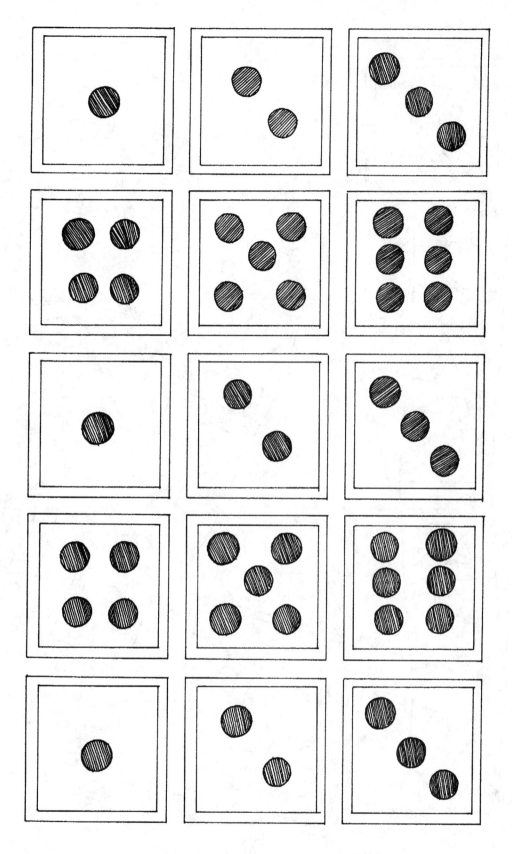

People Living Together

"The more we get together, together, together,
The more we get together, the happier we'll be!"

People need people. Both research and experience tell us that individuals in isolation from others suffer physically and psychologically. Thus, the natural human condition is to be part of a group. The family is the first place where children learn about people other than themselves. As their parents and caregivers interact with them and as they are brought into contact with other youngsters, they explore the world of play.

Play is a basic form of human activity. People of all ages and dispositions play. Adults play by having hobbies, engaging in recreational activities, and participating in sports. Children play all the time. They use their imaginations and prior experiences as they interact with other children and playthings. Children engage in playful interactions with age-mates, with older and younger siblings and friends, and with adults. No two play episodes are exactly alike and children's play has a fluid and continuous quality. Through play, children develop physical, social, language, and cognitive skills.

Purpose

Because this activity consumes so much of their time and energy, the play of children is vital to their well-being. It is an important aspect of their living with others, and consequently is the first of three mini-themes in this unit. The world of work—both children's and adults'—forms this unit's second mini-theme. As children mature, they observe adults working to care for them as well as the environments in which they live; they begin to develop some notions that most adults have job responsibilities away from home. Furthermore, they increasingly come in contact with others in the community whose work affects their lives, either directly or indirectly. We believe it is important that children understand that their home, school, and community function as the result of the labor of many individuals. Especially significant is the contribution of children themselves in this aspect of living with others. Finally, in the third mini-unit, we take a broad look at the communities of which children are a part and examine how they function. The microcosm of the classroom becomes the learning laboratory for explorations of democratic processes and decision-making. As children gain experience, we help them move beyond the classroom into their neighborhood, their town, and their city. It is in these settings that they can examine how adult society operates.

"People Living Together" goes beyond the traditional study of community helpers. It has been developed with a wide scope and a broad base. We view it as an essential social studies unit, for it encompasses the traditional social studies arenas of anthropology, economics, geography, history, human ecology, political science, and sociology. The strategies and techniques offered in the following activities allow children to learn and practice such social studies skills as negotiating, collecting data, recording, mapping, voting, and decision-making. Throughout all three mini-units, you will find activities designed to help children to recognize and embrace the diversity of people and ideas found in their world. We believe that learning about the diversity within their communities helps children develop positive attitudes about others and will encourage them to become open-minded and productive citizens.

Implementation

"People Living Together" may be presented to children as a whole or the three mini-themes may be taught separately. If you plan to cover the entire unit, plan to take anywhere from one to two months. The unit, as written, may also be used as an umbrella unit that lasts an entire year or a significant portion thereof.

We suggest that teachers begin with the mini-theme "People Playing," as this concept is one that is familiar to children. Over time, introduce the ideas of work and of children's own and others' contributions to their home and school. Some of the suggested field trips in "People Working," where children look specifically at those who help their school or child care setting function, will be an appropriate introduction to this aspect of the unit. The oldest and most experienced children will be ready for the final mini-theme, "People Living in Communities." Children who are five years old and older will most likely benefit most from this mini-theme, because the Terms, Facts, and Principles (TFPs) are more advanced and complex than those associated with "People Playing" and "People Working."

We recommend that you precede this unit with themes on self-awareness, families, friends and/or helpers in the community. An alternate idea is to intersperse portions of this whole unit with studies of self and others. Finally, aspects of this unit may be incorporated into the curriculum throughout the school year.

People Playing

Terms, Facts, and Principles (TFPs)

General Information

1. Play is fun.
2. All people play. Playing is a natural and important part of everyone's life.
3. Men and women, boys and girls, people of all ages and in every part of the world play.
4. People play alone or with others; they play actively or quietly, in small groups or large ones, and for short or long periods of time.
5. People play with people they know well or people they are getting to know; they play with family members, friends, or classmates.
6. People play with others of the same age or sex, or with others of different ages or sex.
7. People play in many different settings: streets, sidewalks, parks, recreation centers, gyms, playgrounds, vacant lots, at school, and at home.
8. People play with objects, actions, words and ideas.
9. People learn about themselves and the world through play.
10. People make choices about how, what, with whom, when, and where they play.
*11. Many factors influence people's play, including age, available materials, culture, family values, the season, weather conditions, space, people's physical abilities, their prior knowledge, their language abilities, and other people.

Play Skills

12. People show they want to play through words and actions.
13. When people want to play they say things like: "I want to play," "Let's play _____," "I'll be the _____, you be the _____," "That looks like fun," "Let's pretend."
14. When people want to let others into their play they say things like: "Okay," "Come on," "Here's one for you," "You can have a turn," and "Let's play."
15. When people don't want others to join their play, they say things like: "Not now," "I'm busy," "Wait until I'm done," "I/We want to play by myself/ourselves," or "I don't want to play with you."

16. When people want to get others to play with them they can do things like smiling, helping, offering a toy or suggestion, playing near someone else who is playing, or motioning in a friendly way.
*17. People try out different roles when they play. Sometimes people invite others to play; sometimes they accept others' invitations to play. Sometimes people lead the play; sometimes they follow someone else's lead.
18. People who play together figure out what to play and how to play. Sometimes their ideas are the same; sometimes they are different.
*19. When people have different ideas about how or what to play, they can do many things to resolve their disagreements: they can choose to play separately, decide to play according to one person's idea, take turns following each other's ideas, or combine their ideas.
20. Sometimes people like to play the same thing over and over again.
21. Sometimes people like to try new ways of playing.
22. Sometimes people choose the same playmates; sometimes they look for new people with whom to play.
*23. When people want to stop playin,g they can give their place to someone else, put their toys away, go to another area, or say things like: "I'm done," or "I don't want to play anymore," or "Good-bye."
24. When people don't know how to play, they can watch people who already know how, or they can ask for help or information.

Types of Play

25. Play takes many forms. Examples include pretend play, construction, games, hobbies, and play with words, and humor.
26. When people pretend, they make believe that they are someone, something, or somewhere else. Sometimes people pretend about things they know or have seen in books, on television, or in the movies. Anyone can pretend.
27. Many different materials can be used for construction play: clay, sand, blocks, paper, and building toys are examples. Anyone can construct things.
28. People sometimes play games. A game is an activity that usually includes rules or strategies.
29. Rules are guides for how to play.
30. Sometimes people follow set rules for games; sometimes they make up their own rules.

31. Some decisions people have to make in a game involve who will go first, who will be "it," how many turns will be played, who can play, when the game will be over, and whether or not there will be winners and losers.

32. The same game may be played differently by different people.

*33. Sports are highly organized physical games that require special rules and skills. Some sports also involve special equipment. People can participate in sports on their own or with others in teams.

*34. People often play by having hobbies. People's hobbies include collecting things, making things, or enjoying the same type of activity over and over again.

*35. People sometimes play with words and sounds. Some word play is shared; some is particular to the person creating it.

36. People often play by saying or doing funny things.

Toys

37. Objects designed for play are called toys.

38. Children all over the world play with toys.

39. Children's parents, and their parents before them, played with toys.

40. Boys and girls can use the same toys in their play.

41. Some children have favorite toys.

42. Some toys are easier for children to share than are others.

43. People who own toys must decide who else may use them, where they should be kept when not in use, and how to use them safely.

44. Toys at school or in the center belong to everyone there.

45. Toys at school or in the center must be cared for by the people who use them.

46. Some toys are designed to be used for only one purpose; some toys are designed to be used in many different ways.

47. Children sometimes use objects other than toys in their play.

*48. People use their imaginations in playing with objects or toys.

Activity Ideas

Aesthetic

1. Around It Goes

Take a round metal pie pan and cut many rounds of paper so that they just fit inside the pan. Mix tempera paint and pour a small amount into another container. Dip a Ping-Pong ball into the paint with a spoon, lift it out and put the ball inside the pie tin. Show each child how to roll the ball on the paper creating a design. When the child is satisfied, hang his or her creation up to dry or lay it flat on a surface that has been covered with paper. These make very attractive room decorations when they are suspended on a string from the ceiling or taped onto a window.

Hints for Success:

● Be sure to cover both the table and the children. Keep a sponge handy for cleaning spills.

● A simple method for ensuring that the rounds fit the pan is to hold the paper on the back side of the pie tin and press around with your finger until there is a rounded crease in the paper. Cut along the crease.

To Simplify:

● Provide one color at a time.

To Extend:

● Offer a choice of several colors. Children will find that using more than one color increases the complexity and beauty of the design they can create.

● Have two children work cooperatively, one holding the pan, and the other dipping the ball.

● Have two children grasp and tilt the pan together. Both children will have to agree on the direction the pan is to be tilted and the colors that will be used.

● Allow children to experiment with pans of diverse shapes and sizes.

2. Wordplay

Explain that people sometimes play with ideas and with words. Ask children to tell their favorite jokes. Help children write them down, compile them into a class book and make it available to the group.

To Simplify:

● Children under about 4 years old cannot understand what is funny about most "jokes." Physical humor is more to their liking. They can relate to things that strike them as incongruous, such as animals talking, or wearing silly clothes. Keep any verbal humor simple and obvious.

To Extend:

● Ask children to find and record interesting or amusing family jokes and stories, especially those having to do with themselves.

● Allow children an opportunity to share their jokes with classmates at a designated time. One or two children each day can tell their jokes or funny stories at dismissal, for instance.

3. Artplay

From art books, calendars, or storybooks, select pictures depicting groups of children playing, or of individuals—children and grownups—engaging in play. Use these pictures as a basis for discussion. Ask questions that focus on the types of play that are depicted. For example:

a. What do you see in the picture?

b. What are the people playing? Is this something you play, too?

c. Who is playing? Who is watching?

d. Do you think the people are having fun? How can you tell?

e. Could anybody play? What makes you think that?

To Simplify:

● Select pictures that show one person or a very few people in the kinds of play activities children in your group are likely to have engaged in or watched.

To Extend:

● Ask children to speculate about what activities preceded the play they see in the picture and what will happen next. Either take dictation from the children or have them write down their ideas themselves.

4. The Joy of Play

Use your local library to locate *Shake It to the One That You Love Best: Play Songs and Lullabies from Black Musical Traditions* (1990), edited by Cheryl Mattox and illustrated by Varnette Honeywood and Brenda Joysmith, or find another book in which illustrations of children at play predominate. Have children look at the illustrations and talk about the play they see. Tell them to put their bodies in the poses that are depicted. Choose one of the games that may be familiar to you (such as "Patticake, Patticake") or follow direc-

tions for "Little Sally Walker" (see "Musicplay", page 188), and have children move their bodies according to the game. Other illustrations may show such activities as doll play or checkers. Provide the appropriate props and ask children to replicate the movements shown.

Hint for Success:

● For many days or weeks preceding this activity, keep reproductions of these pictures available for children to look at. In your conversations with children, talk about the link between the actual games or activities and the artists' representations.

To Simplify:

● Choose simple illustrations and provide limited props.

To Extend:

● Encourage children to depict their own activities on paper (with paint or markers).

● Ask children to look at other illustrations and figure out the games that are shown.

Affective

1. Play Favorites

Provide a wide assortment of magazine pictures of common play objects. Encourage each child to choose a favorite object. Tape the picture on the child's shirt. Ask children to find other people in the group who have selected the same object.

To Simplify:

● Limit the pictures to three or four different objects.

To Extend:

● Divide the children into groups based on these similarities and ask children to determine the most popular play object by comparing the relative sizes of the groups. Some children may be able to compare by counting the members of each group. Others may compare the groups by lining children up next to each other and, through a one-to-one comparison, determine which group has the most people.

2. Make a Game

Provide open-ended materials from which children can create their own games. For example, provide small table blocks for children to use in designing a maze for a marble to go through. Another game that children can make is called "Concentration" or "Memory." This game is played in the following way: Pairs of pictured objects are placed in random order facedown on a table. The object is to collect as many pairs as one can. The child turns over two cards at a time. If the pictures match, the child collects the pair and takes another turn. If the two cards don't match, the cards are returned facedown, to the same spot and the next player gets a turn. Children try to remember where the pictures are on the table so they can find pairs when it is their turn to play. (For children to create this game, provide them with pairs of pictures that they can glue onto index cards or tagboard.)

Hint for Success:
● Familiarize children with existing marble maze games and present many forms of "Concentration" before asking them to create their own.

To Simplify:
● Give children sample "Concentration" cards from which to pattern their own. Begin with three or four pairs of pictures.

To Extend:
● Pair the children and have them take turns making the maze and rolling a marble through it.

● Children who are skilled in cutting may select and cut out their own pictures from magazines and catalogs.

3. Trail Mix

In preparation for going on a walk or a field trip, children can make their own trail mix. This recipe is adaptable to personal tastes, and each child may make an individual serving, or a large portion may be made for the group. Essentially, the mixture combines approximately equal portions of foods that are salty, sweet, crunchy, and soft. Nuts, raisins (or other dried fruit), pretzels, and carob chips or coconut make a tasty combination.

Hints for Success:
● Put the ingredients in separate bowls with a spoon in each. Limit the number of spoonsful each child may take from each bowl (up to two or three) so children do not overfill their own container. Within these limits, allow children to decide on their own mixture. Provide a small cup or container for the finished trail mix and, if requested, a spoon for each child.

Cognitive

1. Card Games

Teach children a simple card game so that eventually, they can play independently. Games such as "Go Fish," "Old Maid" (use a less sexist title like "Queen of Clubs"), "War" (or "Peace"), and "Hearts" (older children) are appropriate. Even three- and four-year-olds can learn to play games of "Concentration" (as described in the activity "Make-a-Game," page 183). These might be activities that can be taught by parents or grandparents.

To Simplify:
● Limit the number of cards children use in any of the games.

● Start with a game in which children simply match identical cards. When introducing a game like "Go Fish," allow younger children to show the cards in their hand rather than having to name the number or suit without looking at the other person's cards.

To Extend:
● Once children can recognize numerals, the card games may be played in the traditional ways.

● Explain that each game has its own set of rules that must be followed for the game to be successful.

2. Ball Guess

Have several children, in turn, toss a soft ball in the air and let it drop to the ground. After they have experimented for a while, ask them to predict for each toss how high the ball will go and where it will land. For variety, set up an inclined plane indoors or outdoors, with a plank and block. Add several different kinds of balls (such as varying sizes, materials, weights, etc.). After children are comfortable with the new balls, ask them to predict how fast and/or far each type of ball will roll.

To Simplify:
● Let children predict the height and distance that each child's ball will travel, in turn.

To Extend:
● Set up two inclined planes for comparison purposes. Make the slope of one steeper than the other so the balls will reach the end at different times.

● Ask children to predict how far and/or fast each ball will travel and write their predictions on a chart. Mark down what actually happens, too. Then help the children in making comparisons.

3. Playmates

Using the children's ideas, make a list of the different ways people prefer to play (alone, with a small group, with a large group, quietly, actively, and so on). Prompt their responses with suggestions if they have trouble thinking of ideas. Then ask them to make another list of games and other activities that they like to play (kickball, blocks, hopscotch, and so on). Lead them in matching these activities to the categories on the first list. An activity may fit into more than one category as different children express their preferences. Discuss these preferences with the group.

To Simplify:

- Use children's school activities as a start.

To Extend:

- Extend this activity by making a grid, such as the following:

	alone	small group	big group
sitting			
standing			
running			

Then have children place picture cards representing different activities in the appropriate squares. Categories for additional charts might be the type of

Painting   Drawing   Science   Blocks

Writing   Reading   Construction   Listening

Puzzles   Games   Music   Math

Puppets   Woodworking   Sand   Pretend

equipment needed, places or seasons for play, and so on. Use both pictographs and words to indicate the categories and the games or activities. Where possible, use actual objects, such as dominos or balls.

4. Play Teaching

Invite an older person to teach children a simple board game (such as "Chutes and Ladders®," "Candyland®") or dominoes. Find written instructions for these games as well. Show children that people learn to play games both from other people and by reading. Make some comparisons between the way the person taught the game and the written rules.

To Simplify:
● Use a picture domino game rather than dominoes with dots for children who cannot yet match the dot patterns.

To Extend:
● Once a few children have learned how to play, ask them to teach others.

5. Favorite Toy

Take a survey of the children to determine some favorite toys or playthings. Alternatively, ask children to point to favorite toys in catalogs or magazines. Cut out some representative pictures and put them on a chart. Give each child an opportunity to select his or her favorite from among the pictures, either by writing his or her name under the appropriate picture, by cutting out a matching picture and gluing it to the chart in the proper column, or by indicating a preference in any other way. When everyone has had a turn, gather the group together to analyze the graph. Help children determine which toy is the most popular, which is the least, which group of toys (such as wheeled toys, human figures, and so on) are favored, and which are not.

To Simplify:
● Give children actual examples of toys to examine before they make a choice.

To Extend:
● Carry out this activity several times during the year, and keep each graph. Ask children to compare their preferences over time.

Construction

1. Construct-a-Play

Children can make the materials necessary for their pretend play themes and use them in their play. Examples of child-made props include camping equipment (binoculars, backpacks, camping gear, food, fishing rods and fish, road maps, guidebooks, nature reference books), and physical fitness equipment (barbells, weights, and so on). Some props can be made from recycled materials, such as toilet paper rolls, boxes, scraps of material, or Styrofoam pieces.

Hints for Success:
● Set up an area for constructing props near the pretend play area so that children can move from one place to the other.
● Provide a wide variety of materials so that children's imaginations can be given free reign.

To Simplify:
● Have available models or actual props from which children can get ideas for props to make. Point out the salient features of each prop. For example, explain that exercise props such as weights or barbells must have a place for a person's hands to grasp or that binoculars have two eyepieces.

To Extend:
● Provide more durable material from which children can create their props: plastic, leather, fabric, and so on.

2. Mask Play

People use masks to pretend they are different people or animals or make-believe creatures. Children can make masks from paper plates (cut out eyes and staple the plate to a Popsicle® stick or tongue depressor). Encourage children to decorate their masks as they please.

To Simplify:
● Suggest that children make masks representing people they know or familiar story characters.

To Extend:
● Show children masks from diverse cultures (either real or pictures) and explain that often people pretend to be someone or something different from who they really are when they wear masks. Invite children to experiment with different voices, using emotional

expressions and phrases, while wearing their masks. Help them assess the reactions of others to their pretending.

3. Make-a-Toy

Precede this activity with a discussion or a demonstration of children's toys. Have children bring in favorite toys or use toys readily available in the classroom. On the day the project is to be carried out, provide a large and varied selection of cardboard boxes, dowel sticks, Styrofoam cones (or other shapes), paper towel rolls, tape, markers, scissors, diverse paper, meat trays, and wood scraps. Tell children that the object of the activity is to construct a toy or plaything that they can use. Have available pictures or actual toys that they would find appealing, such as action figures, dinosaur models, wheeled vehicles, put-together toys, and so on. Divide the children into small groups. Children may choose to work alone or with others. The teacher's task is to circulate among the children and to act as a resource person. Commend children for the effort they have put in and encourage them as they go.

Hint for Success:
● Allow ample time so children may finish their toys. If they need more time than you have planned, arrange to let them finish on a subsequent day.

To Simplify:
● Provide paper bags and material for stuffing them, so that children can be successful in making a "ball-like" toy even with minimal effort.

To Extend:
● Give children paper and pencils so they can either write about or diagram the toy that they made. Tell them to use this as a record, so they will be able to repeat the project someday or so that another person could follow their directions.

Language

1. Counting Out Games

There is a variety of chants and songs that children have used in play for generations, and you can use them to determine who goes first in a game. They are also interesting in themselves and are worthwhile teaching to children. Among a number of familiar rhymes are "Eeny-Meeny-Miney Mo" and "One Potato, Two Potato." Traditionally, the rhyme is repeated in a small group. One person points to another as each word is spoken. The child who is pointed to on the last word is "out." This process is repeated until only one child is left. As a variation, the child who is "out" simply takes a step back from the group, but continues to be involved by chanting the rhyme.

Eeny-Meeny-Miney Mo
Eeny-Meeny-Miney Mo
Catch a tiger by the toe.
If he hollers, let him go,
My mother said to pick this one.
Out goes Y-O-U.

One Potato
One potato, two potato, three potato, four
Five potato, six potato, seven potato, more.

One-Ry, Two-Ry (Georgia Sea Islands)
One-ry, two-ry , dicker-y seven,
Halli-bo, cracki-bo, ten e-leven.
Pee, po, must be done,
Twin-kle, twan-kle, twen-ty one.

"Rock, Scissors, Paper" is a more sophisticated scheme that is suitable for seven- or eight-year-olds. Customarily, it is carried out between two children to determine who goes first. Here, on a count of three, the two children simultaneously put out their right hands to represent either a rock (closed fist) or scissors (two fingers extended like scissors blades) or paper (hand held out, palm down). In this game, rock " breaks" scissors (rock wins), scissors "cuts" paper (scissors wins), and paper "covers" rock (paper wins). Usually, children play for the best of three chances.

2. Rhyming Play

Jump rope rhymes, ball bouncing rhymes, and hand clapping rhymes are all ways that children play using words to direct their actions. From the library or from your own childhood recollections, collect several rhyming chants. First teach them to the children without using the balls or ropes. Begin with simple hand clapping to the rhythm of the words and then gradually add more detail. After children know the words well, invite them to bounce medium-sized playground balls in time to the words. Show children how to bounce and catch the ball each time. Older children may also enjoy skipping rope individually as they chant each rhyme, or "dribbling" a ball in rhythm to the words. Some examples follow:

A Little Ball (China)

A little ball, a banana, a pear,
Twenty-one flowers looking everywhere.
Two, five, six, two, five, seven,
Two, eight, two, nine, thirty one.

See-Saw Sacaradown
(See-saw rhyme from England)

See-saw, sacaradown,
Which is the way to Londontown?
One foot up, the other foot down,
That is the way to Londontown.

3. Musicplay

Collect a variety of recordings of children's singing games from the library or a local music store. Include games from different regions of the United States (for example, Appalachia Mountains, American Southwest, urban areas) as well as games from a variety of culture groups. At first, play these as background music while children are engaged in their activities. Once children are familiar with the songs or chants, teach them the games. Often, singing games have been collected in both African- and Anglo-American versions. Directions for sample games follow.

Little Sally Walker
(African American version)

Little Sally Walker, sitting in a saucer,
Weeping and crying, for someone to love her.
Rise, Sally, rise. Wipe your weeping eyes.

Put your hands on your hips and let your back-
bone slip.
Shake it to the east, Sally. Shake it to the west, Sally.
Shake it to the very one that you love the best.

Little Sally Waters (Euro-American version)

Little Sally Waters, sitting in a saucer,
Weeping and crying, for someone to love her.
Rise, Sally, rise. Wipe your weeping eyes.
Turn to the east, Sally. Turn to the west, Sally.
Turn to the very one that your love the best, Sally.

Directions: These games are played identically. "Sally" kneels in the center of a circle of children who walk around her as they chant. "Sally" acts out the words. At the final line, "Sally" indicates the child who will be the next "Sally."

Hint for Success:
● If you find that boys avoid the game because the central player is "Sally," alternate with the name "Sammy" or use the child's real name.

Up on the Mountain (Euro-American version)

Up on the mountain, two by two (repeat 3 times)
Rise, Sugar, rise.
Let me see you make a motion, two by two
(repeat 3 times)
Rise, Sugar, rise.
That's a mighty fine motion, two by two
(repeat 3 times)
Rise, Sugar, rise.

Down in the Valley (African-American version)

Down in the valley, two by two, my baby,
Two by two, my baby, two by two.
Down in the valley, two by two. Rise, Sugar, Rise.

Let me see you make a motion, two by two, my baby
Two by two, my baby, two by two .
Let me see you make a motion, two by two. Rise, Sugar, Rise.

That's a mighty fine motion, two by two, my baby
Two by two, my baby, two by two .
That's a mighty fine motion, two by two. Rise, Sugar, Rise.

Directions: The directions for these games are identical. Two children stand in the center of a circle of children. During the first verse, children circle around to the right, while the couple in the middle decides on a motion. For the second verse, the group stands still, clapping in time to the chant, while the center pair do their motions. The last verse involves everyone repeating the motion while chanting. The children in the center then choose their replacements.

Physical

1. Track and Field

Hold a noncompetitive track and field event outdoors. Instead of winners and losers, everyone who wishes to gets a chance to play and children's progress in a variety of skills is measured against themselves. Long jump, high jump, obstacle courses, and relay races are easily set up and fun for all. In a standing long jump,

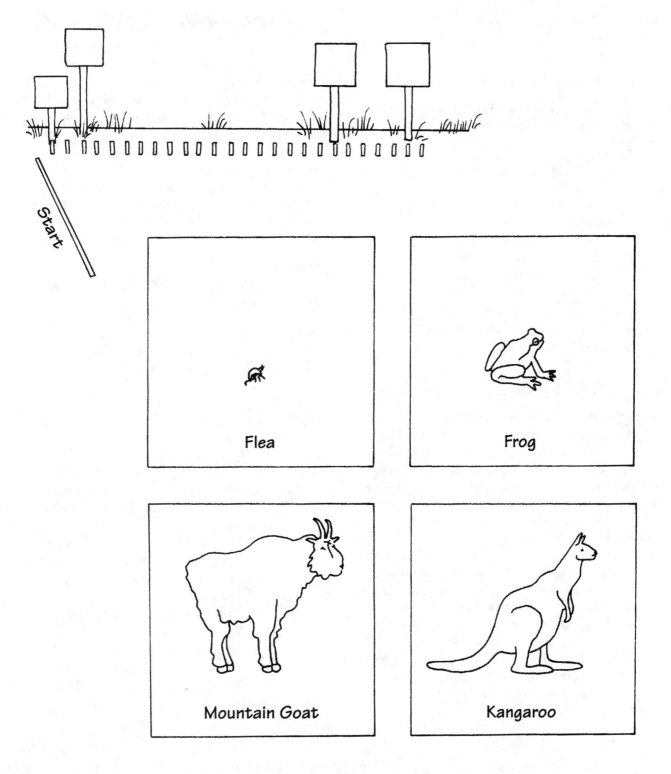

Start

Flea

Frog

Mountain Goat

Kangaroo

stand with feet in place, swing arms to improve forward momentum, and land upright. In a running long jump, run up to a starting line or mark on the floor or ground, then "take off" from this point, swinging arms forward to increase momentum. Fall forward to land.

One way to set up a long jump activity is to make small pictures of jumping animals (such as a flea, frog, mountain goat, and kangaroo). Staple the pictures onto sticks and place them in the ground at approximately the distance from the starting point that the actual animal can jump. Sample distances are:

Flea	1 foot
Frog	3 feet
Mountain Goat	20 feet
Kangaroo	25 feet

Encourage children to jump as many times as it takes to reach a particular animal's distance.

To Simplify:

● Have each child practice long jumps without the aid of the pictures.

To Extend:

● Ask children to tell you about their favorite animals. From an encyclopedia or other reference, determine the distance each animal can jump and make signs, as above, to include these in the activity.

● Suggest that children figure out how many "flea jumps" it would take to reach the frog, or how many "frog jumps" it would take to reach the kangaroo.

2. Ball Play

Everywhere in the world people play with round objects. In different countries these games have different names but they all share some elements in common. People toss the objects, kick them, hit them with their bodies or with other objects, roll them, or bounce them. Begin with rolling a ball from person to person in a circle so the ball cannot escape. Move to bouncing the ball, and then to throwing.

Games such as "Bocce" in Italy and "Boules" in France are played when balls are rolled toward a stone; the purpose is to see which player comes closest. A variant of this game can be played by children. Place a stone or other marker on a flat playing surface (indoors or outdoors). Provide children with rubber or plastic balls. In turn, have children roll their balls toward the target object. Measure each child's success by how much closer he or she is able to come to the target over time.

To Simplify:

● Begin with balls that children can hold with two hands. Demonstrate rolling the ball by propelling the ball forward from between your legs.

To Extend:

● Use smaller balls and have children stand farther from the target. Demonstrate ways to swing the "rolling" arm back in order to get propulsion and control before releasing the ball.

3. Sportsplay

Invite a local sports figure (or high school athlete) to talk with children about how he or she plays the sport, the training in which he or she must engage, and the equipment or uniforms people use while playing the sport. Other important issues include teamwork and how people communicate with each other during the play. As a follow-up, plan to introduce elements of the sport to the children in a simplified manner. For instance, use yarn balls and rackets (made from bent wire hangers with stockings stretched over the loop) as a way to simulate tennis, racquetball, badminton, or lacrosse.

To Simplify:

● Have children practice with the objects individually before "batting" balls to one another.

To Extend:

● Create a game whose object is to keep the yarn balls or balloons aloft as long as possible.

Pretend Play

1. Pretend Play Ideas

a) **Family Vacation:** Create a scenario to replicate a family vacation (camping, traveling, picnicking).

b) **Theater:** Set up a theater or a music or dance studio (with seats in rows), a concession stand, ticket booth, and a stage upon which children can "perform."

c) **Training Ground:** Develop a make-believe sports facility or sports training facility, with "weights" (made of plastic tubing and rolled paper at each end), exercise mats, and a place for aerobics (provide a record or tape player and mirrors, if possible).

d) **Recreation Center:** A recreation center with board games, card games, toys, balls, ring toss, and so on, can easily be set up in a corner of the room.

2. Figure Play

Show children a variety of male and female doll figures (superheroes, baby dolls, adult figures, and so on) used at school. Ask children which of them plays with the various dolls. Point out that both males and females are represented and that boys and girls both enjoy doll play.

To Simplify:
● Ask children to bring one doll-like figure from home.

To Extend:
● Give figures customarily used by one gender to a group of children of the opposite gender (for example, superhero figures to girls, Barbie-like figures to boys). Tell them to develop a play scenario with the figures. Watch the nature of the play that results. If the group is able, have them communicate their scenes to one another.

Social

1. Play Break

Take advantage of a real-life situation in which children's self-directed play has either interfered with the activities of others, or where some children are no longer having fun (for example, play has become aggressive). Bring the players together to discuss the incident, allowing all parties to express their feelings and also their ideas for solutions. Point out ways that children can recognize when the play has gotten out of bounds (for example, when people's facial expressions or voice tone becomes strained, or when their words indicate they are dissatisfied). Help children figure out how to express their feelings to their playmates to indicate unhappiness. Instruct children in how to express themselves when others' behavior interferes with their own play. They can say things such as:

"Stop, I don't like it when you _____ ."

"I had it first. You can play with it when I'm done."

Encourage children to establish signals to aid their communication with each other. Once children have

resolved a problem, observe their continuing activity. Review their solutions if necessary.

To Simplify:
● Adults may have to help younger children express their emotions and ideas to others. If you see a child exhibiting signs of distress, ask that child if he or she wanted the other child to, for instance, jump on top of him or her. If the child says "No," paraphrase the response: "Jim says he doesn't like it when you sit on him. Climb off." Point out the signs of distress and let children know that they don't have to put up with disagreeable behavior from others.

To Extend:
● At calmer times, engage children in discussions where they generate responses they can make to one another. Write their suggestions on easel paper and post them in the room for children to refer to when disagreements arise.

2. Family Play

Ask children to talk about the ways members of their families play together and write their comments on a chart. Compare similarities and differences by "reading" the chart and help children recognize the wide range of possible activities. Compile the various activities into a list and send copies home to the parents. Suggest that each family try a new activity and report the results. (Did the family enjoy it? What variations did the family create?) Collect the results and read them to the children at a group time later in the week.

To Simplify:
● Focus on very simple activities, such as reading stories at bedtime or going on outings.

To Extend:
● Encourage each child to report on his or her family's experience.

3. Cooperative Games

Choose a game that was originally designed to be competitive (like dominoes or a board game). Transform it into a cooperative game by having children work together to complete the task. For instance, in a board game, use only one piece and tell each child to move that one piece when his or her turn comes up. Ask children to count the number of turns it takes to move the piece to its destination. Another alternative is to give children a pegboard pattern to complete as a group using only one pegboard. Divide the labor by assigning each child one color to use or have the children take turns putting the pieces in.

To Simplify:

● Games such as "Concentration" or "Memory" can be played cooperatively by having children help each other remember where the matching cards are on the table.

To Extend:

● An interesting experiment is to ask the children to first play the game competitively and then repeat the game cooperatively. Help children compare their responses. For example, ask them to determine in which version people had more fun.

4. I Want to Play!

Children demonstrate that they want to play with others through their actions and words. Help children develop play initiation skills in the following ways.

A. Present a puppet or doll skit to a group of children that illustrates one child playing with an object and another child watching. Introduce the activity by telling children that the dolls or puppets you are using represent real children who go to a school/center just like theirs. (Be sure to use "people" figures rather than animals or cartoon characters.) Say that in this scene, one child is playing and another child wants to play. Tell children in your group that you will be asking them at the end of the scene to identify which child is hoping to play. Add that as they watch, they should be thinking of ways that the characters in the scene could be more successful. Then present the scene. Use the following script:

"Here are two children. This one is Teddy, and this one is Fred. Teddy is playing with a ball. (Show this.) Fred is watching. He doesn't say anything. The end."

Then ask these questions: Who was playing? Who was watching? Who wanted to play? How could you tell? What could Fred do or say to let Teddy know he wanted to play?

Encourage children to generate a number of possible solutions and try them out using the puppets. Ask children to evaluate the strategies they have suggested for Fred. Over time, repeat this skit using a variety of children's names, genders, and characteristics.

B. Present a puppet or doll skit following the guidelines shown above. This time, demonstrate how a child playing with an object might invite a bystander to play. Use the scripts suggested in TFP 14 or 16 (page 181). Each time you present a scenario, follow it by encouraging children to generate their own ideas of how the puppet or doll could respond to or initiate the action. As children become accustomed to watching and taking part in the skits, present unsuitable possibilities as well. For instance, one puppet might refuse to play with another. Pose this dilemma to the children for their solutions. Again, try out the suggestions they generate and then evaluate.

C. Present a puppet or doll skit using TFP 19 (page 181) as a theme. In this case, create a scenario in which two "children" are playing and they begin to disagree. Rather than resolving the dispute as a part of the initial skit, have children make suggestions as to how the puppets could come to a solution. Act out each suggestion. If children think grabbing a toy and running away with it might work, act that out as well. Ascertain by questioning whether or not the group thinks this is a viable alternative. Clearly, this is a more sophisticated formulation and should not be attempted until children are quite familiar with puppet skits.

D. Use any of the scripts in TFPs 13 to 24 (page 181) to enact play scenes that focus on play skills.

Hints for Success:

● Be sure to introduce each scene separately, as indicated above, and to let children know the scene is finished by saying, "The end." Focus on one skill at a sitting; otherwise children will become confused.

● At the conclusion of each session, tell children that the dolls have solved their dilemma and that everyone is playing happily.

To Simplify:

● Start with the simplest issues and repeat these, with variations, until children become experienced problem solvers.

To Extend:

● Once children demonstrate skill in responding to your scenarios, provide puppets or dolls and encourage them to dictate or "write" their own scripts. First determine the problem, or make sure that the children know what issue they are addressing before they begin. Record, either on paper or tape, the situations they develop and resolve. Play or read these back to the group at a later time and ask for their comments.

5. Cool Cat!

Introduce this activity by talking to children about how much easier it is to play with someone when you know his or her name. Use the following chant as a vehicle for familiarizing both teachers and children with each other's names. Establish an easy beat, adapting to children's natural walking pace by swinging your arms from side to side. Once that rhythm is well established, begin to walk to the beat. Go around the group, chanting the words. When you come to the pause after the word "down," stand still and call someone's name. That individual will then join you on the walk during the "choo choo" part. Add new people in the same manner until the whole group is moving. The chant is as follows. The syllables that are underlined indicate the strong, steady beat. The words are chanted in a syncopated rhythm that sometimes fits in between the beats, as illustrated below.

Cool Cat!

<u>Hey</u> there! ___. You're a <u>real</u> cool <u>cat</u>! You
<u>Gotta</u> lotta <u>this</u> and you
<u>Gotta</u> lotta <u>that.</u> So
<u>Come</u> on <u>in</u> and get <u>down.</u> ___

<u>Choo</u>-choo, _ <u>choo</u>-choo, _ <u>choo</u>- choo, _ <u>choo</u>- choo

Hint for Success:

● Before trying this out with children, practice the chant in private until you are comfortable with both the words and the rhythm. While you are learning it, walk the beat as you say the words until they all fit in.

6. Playful Choices

There are a large number of traditional children's games that require them to choose a partner. This can be turned into an activity in and of itself. Choosing someone from one's group is a way of acknowledging another person, and asking him or her to play is a fundamental play skill in which children improve through practice.

1. I Have Lost My Little Partner
(Swedish game)

I have lost my little partner, I must find another one.
I'll take you if you will have me, We will dance 'til day is done.

Stamp, stamp Clap, clap, clap. (Repeat 3 times.)
Turn a-round.

Directions: The leader walks around the inside of a circle of children. At the words "day is done," he or she should be standing, facing another person. The pair stamps, claps and turns around together. The chant begins again, and they each move around the circle until they have found new partners. Continue until everyone is chosen.

2. Here We Come A-Walking
(American singing game)

Here we come a-walking down the street,
Down the street, down the street.
Here we come a-walking down the street,
How are you today?

Here we come a-knocking at your door
At your door, at your door
Here we come a-knocking at your door,
Come outside and play.

Directions: Children sit in a circle with plenty of space between them. The leader walks around the outside of the circle while everyone chants the first verse. By the end of the verse, the leader sits behind another child. While the second verse is chanted, the leader taps on the floor, as if knocking on a door, and at the end, offers his or her hand to that child. Now both children get to play as everyone chants.

Teacher Resources

Field Trip Ideas

1. Go to a nearby playground to examine the equipment there. Have children discuss and record how they think children use the equipment and how their own play space might be adapted to new games and activities in which they would like to participate.

2. Visit a local high school, middle school, or professional team and watch their practice. Help chil-

dren record or make note of aspects of team play that they observe.

Classroom Visitors

1. Invite the children's family members or other members of the neighborhood to teach children the songs and games that they played as children.

2. Arrange for a professional or amateur artist, dancer, musician, poet, or storyteller to participate in the classroom. Have them demonstrate their talents or "play" with the children, as well. Before the visit, explain to children that these individuals work and play at their craft.

3. Invite a local or high school athlete to talk about his or her sport, including the preparation needed, the equipment used, and how teamwork is needed to be successful.

Children's Books

Cole, J., & Calmenson, S. (1991). *The Eentsy, Weentsy Spider: Fingerplays and Action Rhymes*. New York: Morrow Junior Books.

Larche, D. (1966). *Father Gander Nursery Rhymes*. Santa Barbara, CA: Advocacy Press.

Williams, K. L. (1990). *Galimoto*. New York: Lothrop.

Wilson, S. (1992). *June Is a Tune That Jumps on a Stair*. New York: Simon & Schuster.

Adult References

Fry-Miller, K. M., & Domer-Shank, J. R. (1988). *Young Peacemakers Project Book*. Elgin, IL: Brethren Press.

Grunfeld, F. B. (1982). *Games of the World*. Zurich, Switzerland: Swiss Committee for UNICEF.

Haines, B., Gerber, J. E., & Gerber, L. L. (1992). *Leading Young Children to Music*. 4th ed. New York: Merrill.

Jones, B., & Hawes, B. L. (1972). *Step It Down: Games, Plays, Songs, and Stories from the Afro-American Heritage*. New York: HarperCollins.

Lankford, M. D. (1992). *Hopscotch Around the World*. New York: William Morrow.

Mattox, C. W. (1989). *Shake It to the One That You Love the Best*. Nashville, TN: JTV of Nashville.

Seeger, R. C. (1955). *American Folk Songs for Children*. New York: Grosset and Dunlap.

Yolen, J. (1992). *Street Rhymes Around the World*. Honesdale, PA: Boyds Mills Press.

People Working

Terms, Facts, and Principles (TFPs)

General Information

1. Work is the effort people make toward achieving a goal, accomplishing a task, doing a job, producing an object, or providing a service.

2. All people can do work of some kind.

3. People all over the world work.

4. People of all ages work; adults and children work.

5. Men and women are capable of doing the same kinds of work.

6. Most adults spend a great deal of time doing work.

7. Sometimes people are paid for the work they do; other times they are not.

8. People who work are often called workers.

Adults at Work

*9. Work is the means by which most adults earn a living.

10. A person who works for someone else is called an employee; the person for whom others work is called an employer.

11. There are many different kinds of jobs at which adults work. Some of these include: homemaker, lawyer, health professional, teacher, scientist, computer programmer, manager, repair person, construction worker, child care provider, skilled tradesperson (electrician, plumber, and so on), student, business owner, artist, musician, salesperson, office worker, factory worker, community worker (fire fighter, police officer, postal employee), athlete, parent.

12. The location in which people work is called the workplace.

13. Adults work in a variety of workplaces (outdoors, indoors, at home, offices, factories, schools, hospitals, restaurants, studios, businesses, community agencies) depending on the kind of work they do.

*14. Some kinds of work require specialized physical abilities, specialized skills, or specialized knowledge.

*15. Work is accomplished most effectively when a person's abilities, skills, and knowledge are matched to the job to be done.

16. The work a person does often requires special training.

*17. People learn how to do their job in different ways: by going to school, participating in training programs, and learning on the job.

18. People's work skills improve with practice.

19. Some kinds of work require special tools, machines, or materials.

20. People are responsible for using tools, machines, and materials safely in their work.

*21. Workers are responsible for recycling or safely disposing of the waste materials from their work.

22. Some kinds of work require uniforms for protection or identification.

*23. Each kind of work is unique in some way.

*24. There may be common features to different kinds of work. (For example, both gardeners and construction workers work outdoors.)

*25. Some work involves single or simple tasks; other work involves many or complex tasks.

26. People vary in their ability and desire to do particular kinds of work.

27. Many people enjoy the work they do; people often find ways to make their work more enjoyable.

28. Sometimes people have choices about the work they do; sometimes they have few or no choices.

*29. Some kinds of work are done by people working alone, while other kinds require many people working together at the same or complementary tasks.

*30. Some kinds of work require that people work with other people; others require that people work primarily with things.

*31. The results of some people's work are easy to see; the results of others' work are not as obvious.

*32. Some kinds of work produce a product; some kinds of work involve people performing a service for others.

*33. People have different ideas about the importance or value of particular kinds of work.

34. All of the things we need (food, clothing, housing, etc.) are a result of the work of many people.

35. Some people work for a living outside the home while some people work for a living at home.

36. Family members do work at home to keep the family and home functioning.

*37. The kind of work people do has changed over time. Some jobs that people used to do with their hands are now accomplished by people operating machines or computers.

*38. Some adults are unable to find work. This is called being unemployed.

*39. Sometimes adults work at the same job for a long time; sometimes they change the kind of work they do over time.

Children at Work

40. Children can work at home and at school.

41. Sometimes children work alone and sometimes with others.

*42. Sometimes children help adults with their work, and sometimes adults help children with their work. Sometimes children help each other.

43. Boys and girls can both do the same kinds of work.

Activity Ideas

Aesthetic

1. Scrapwork

Collect and have available the by-products of manufacturing processes for children to use at the art table. Such materials as Styrofoam, wood scraps, telephone wire, nails, spools, and fabric are often available from sources in the community. Identify these objects for children, explaining what they are used for and people's role in the manufacturing process. Then encourage children to create their own artifacts by using these scraps as well as a variety of fasteners, such as glue, string, wire, and tape. Display their work around the classroom.

To Simplify:
● Use only material that children can glue. Provide a sturdy base for each project. Expect that younger children will build horizontally rather than vertically.

To Extend:
● Encourage children to build vertically using a variety of the materials you have provided. Show pictures of structures built out of scrap or leftover items, such as the Watts Tower in Los Angeles. This building was constructed out of concrete and leftover wire. It is decorated with shards of glass, ceramics, and imprints of tools and other objects.

2. Sing About Work

Throughout the ages, people have used music to ease the burdens of work. Introducing some of these traditional work songs to children can help them understand both the nature of the work and the means people used to cope with it. An excellent source is *American Folk Songs for Children* by Ruth Crawford Seeger (1980). It should be available both in book and recorded form from your local music store or library. Some of the work songs include "Pick a Bale of Cotton." The actions are clear from the words of the verses, and children can be encouraged to imitate them.

This song is easily done as a chant, if that is more comfortable, since even the tune is chantlike rather than being melodic. Furthermore, it can be used to encourage the group to sing or chant about such classroom tasks as putting away materials. (Example: "Me and my partner are washing the tables, Me and my partner can clean them up today.")

To Extend:

● Do some research about the job of chopping cotton in the fields and, through pictures and descriptions, tell children about it. Let them know that even in present times this kind of manual labor is needed to harvest crops.

Note: The song/story of John Henry (also included in Seeger's book) is a favorite one with children. Ezra Jack Keats retold this traditional tale in *John Henry: An American Legend* (1987). According to the legend, John Henry was pitted a miner who his hand-held hammer, against a stream drill that was newly introduced into the mine. John Henry won the contest but died in the attempt. If your group is ready for a discussion of industrialization or mechanization, this song is a good one to use.

3. Artwork

From a library or art store, get reproductions of paintings that depict food preparation, harvesting, or food manufacture. As children examine the paintings, ask them to figure out what kind of work is being done and who is doing the work.

To Simplify:

● Show each painting, one at a time, and point out the work being depicted.

To Extend:

● Ask children if they think the work shown in the picture is easy or difficult for the people to do and what the artist did to convey that idea. Ask other questions to stimulate children's imagination, such as how the people came to work, what they saw on their way, what they will do when they get home, who will be waiting for them, and so on. Record children's ideas on paper and read them aloud. Later, post them near the picture.

Affective

1. A Worker Am I

Discuss with children the jobs they have at home. Emphasize the value of the contribution they make to their home and family. Prompt them to ask their family members for ways they can be more helpful at home. Make a list of the jobs children do in their homes. Send a note home to parents asking the parent and child to list additional jobs. When these are returned to school, read them aloud. Record a master list of jobs and keep adding tasks as they become known to you over the course of the year and as children learn new jobs at home.

To Simplify:

● Cut out pictures from magazines depicting a variety of household tasks, such as setting the table, cleaning a closet, and so on. Allow children to choose the one job most closely representing their most important home responsibility and glue their choices on small pieces of construction paper for stability. Put each child's picture in an envelope and send it home with the child as a reminder to him or her about the task to be done. The picture should also serve as a message to parents that the child's job is being taken seriously.

To Extend:

● Find out children's preferences for particular jobs. Discuss with them whether the jobs they prefer can be adapted to the classroom.

2. Getting the Job Done

This activity is designed to help children work through a task from start to finish. Prior to the children's arrival, select a common activity in your classroom, such as puzzles, journal writing, blocks, easel painting, or a game. Create a chart in which the steps necessary to begin, carry out and complete the activity are listed. Use a combination of picture symbols and words to make the meaning clear. Begin with Step 1 and continue through the final step. Three sample charts are illustrated below. One depicts an easy task, one is moderately challenging, and the third is suitable for children who have had numerous experiences with this kind of activity. Post the card near the place where the job is to be done. Children may follow the steps.

Steps for getting a snack

Chart 1. cup, napkin, table

Chart 2. add juice pitcher and basket of crackers with picture of three crackers at end, cup and napkin being thrown in trash

Chart 3. add juice pitchers being taken out of the refrigerator, box of crackers being poured into basket, table being washed

Hints for Success:

● Children often enjoy a final step that involves telling someone the task is complete. Announcing, "I'm finished," or "The end," is a way that children can feel satisfied at the end of their jobs.

● Make sure to encourage children as they move from one step to another and to praise them for "getting the job done."

To Simplify:

● Choose simple activities with which children are very familiar. Require no more than three steps from beginning to end.

To Extend:

● Introduce new tasks, using only a few steps from start to finish. Gradually add more steps as the children demonstrate the ability to complete the ones you created originally.

● An alternative approach is to ask children to help create the steps for a task. Children can dictate the steps for you to illustrate or illustrate the steps themselves.

● A third option is for children to first go through a new activity, such as peeling fruit, chopping it into smaller pieces, and then eating the fruit in a salad. Next, ask children to re-create the steps in chart form. After

the charts are complete, the children can compare their interpretations of what it took to complete the task. Point out similarities and differences in what individual children chose to portray on their charts. Provide picture symbols for children to use, magazines from which they can cut out pictures for illustrations, or markers with which they may draw or write meaningful words.

● A final variation is to move this from a visual representation of the steps involved to an auditory one. Record simple steps on a tape recorder that children can start and stop themselves. Make sure to precede each direction with the words, "Step one," Step two," and so on. Also, signal completion of the task through words such as "The end."

3. Workcheck

Use this activity as a follow-up or variation on "Getting the Job Done" (above). Using the normal array of activities in the classroom, introduce a "Completion Chart" to the children. This chart lists the children's names down the left side, and across the top, depicts classroom activities, each one having its own column. These activities may include art materials, math activities, writing, manipulatives/puzzles, science, books, and so on. Place duplicate pictures representing each activity in an envelope under the appropriate column. Explain that once they have finished an activity, children may draw a picture of that activity on the chart in the appropriate column and in the row bearing their name. Plan a time at the end of the day when children can carry this out. It may be necessary for an adult to monitor this process for a few days, after which children can do it independently.

To Simplify:

● Have stickers or pictures of the areas or materials in the classroom ready for children in advance so they can see the results of the activity quickly.

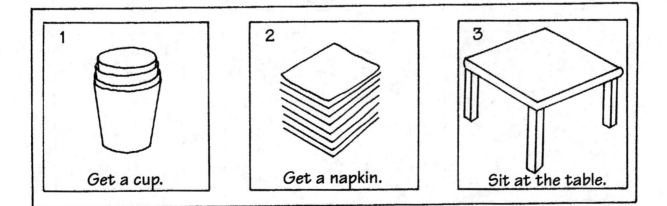

1	2	3
Get a cup.	Get a napkin.	Sit at the table.

1 Get a cup.

2 Get a napkin.

3 Sit at the table.

4 Pour a drink.

5 Take food.

6 Throw away trash.

1 Fill the basket.

2 Get the pitchers.

3 Get a cup.

4 Get a napkin.

5 Sit at the table.

6 Pour a drink.

7 Take food.

8 Wipe up spills.

9 Throw away trash.

To Extend:

● As a follow-up, count the number of times each activity was completed by the group. Compare this from week to week and keep a record. Invite children to see if the pattern changes over time or remains the same.

Cognitive

1. Our School

U se the environment in which children live and work much of the day (school, child care facility) as a laboratory for the study of work. By arranging visits and interviews, help children discover answers to the following questions:

Who works there?

What kinds of work do people do?

How does their work help children, teachers, parents?

What kinds of tools do workers use in their work?

How is the particular work of individuals related to the work of other people in the facility?

What special skills and knowledge are necessary for different people to do their work? How did people acquire their knowledge and skills?

Record the information on experience charts as the children retell what they have learned by talking with the people who work in their program. This activity should take place over an extended period of time, with each worker or specific task given attention. For instance, children may interview the office staff on one occasion and the custodial staff on another.

To Simplify:

● Concentrate initially on those people most visible to the children, such as the teacher, the lunch aide, or the bus driver.

To Extend:

● Compile the entire record of interviews that the children have carried out and arrange them in a scrapbook.

● Work with children on creating a web that depicts the interrelationships among the various workers in the school community.

2. Schoolwork

T ake photographs of the adults who work in the school or center. Mount the photos on a wall or in a book. Also prepare cut-out pictures of tools and/or machines these workers use. Ask children to match the appropriate tools and/or machines to the school worker who uses them. Be sure to include teachers, custodians, and cooks, as well as the people who work in the office.

To Simplify:

● Begin with the people with whom the children have the most direct contact.

To Extend:

● Provide printed labels indicating the title of each person's job. Have children match the labels to the workers' photographs of individuals. These identifiers may be read by an adult or a child.

3. Memories

A fter visiting other parts of the school or center, ask children to retell what they have remembered about the roles of the different workers in their school. Record these observations on paper or have children record them in their own way by drawing pictures or using their own writing. Place the children's observations near the relevant person's photograph that has been mounted on the wall or bulletin board.

To Simplify:

● To make this experience more concrete, arrange for each worker to visit the classroom a day or two after the children have visited him or her at the worksite. When the person arrives, ask children to tell what they remember about the visitor: the name, the job that he or she performs, where he or she works and the kinds of tools or machines that are used. Then ask the worker to clarify or elaborate on the children's observations.

To Extend:

● After a day or two has elapsed after the worker's visit, have children recall details of that person's job. Write their ideas on a large piece of paper and add ideas to it as children come up with additional recollections.

● Talk with children prior to a person's visit about strategies they could use to remember what they hear and see. For instance, children could repeat what they hear out loud or to themselves; they could also make a "quick" list of key words as a group or as individuals; or, they could draw a picture to help themselves remember. After the visitor has left, invite children to use one of their strategies. Following the entire activity, ask children whether or not their strategies worked.

4. Lifework

T oward the end of the study of work, make a list with children of all the jobs they have learned about. Help children identify aspects of different jobs that are alike. For instance, point out the caregiving aspects of child care professionals and veterinarians. Limit the number of jobs initially, adding more jobs as children gain experience with this task. Begin by asking children how two jobs are alike, listing their answers. Then, add another job and ask the same question about the three jobs.

To Simplify:

● Present pictures of people engaged in various occupations. Tell children to group them according to common characteristics.

To Extend:

● A more complex activity is for children to figure out that teamwork is necessary in a number of seemingly disparate jobs—for example, factory workers and athletes. Provide the same pictures as above, grouping them in advance by more abstract attributes such as "teamwork." The child's task is to figure out the common thread. The child can make note of his or her idea either independently or with help from an adult.

Construction

1. Schoolhouse

A fter the children have explored the school, have them reconstruct their notions of the structure and placement of the rooms in the building using unit blocks. Provide small people figures for children to use in their play. Take instant photographs of the structures and display these in the classroom.

To Simplify:

● Encourage children to explore the classroom first, and then have them make a representation of that familiar room in their block play.

To Extend:

● Take older children on a second tour of the building to compare their memories with reality. Then encourage children to make corrections or additions to their structures to correspond to their new observations. Take another set of photos after this second round and compare with the first.

2. Working Together

U sing a familiar material, such as unit blocks or crayons, scissors, cardboard boxes and construction paper, encourage children to work together to create a model or representation of a vehicle used by a community worker (such as a fire truck, ambulance, or mail truck). Provide large pictures or toy models of the vehicles for children to use as examples. If possible, arrange for an actual vehicle to be brought to the building. Emphasize that this construction project is to be carried out by more than one person at a time in a collective effort to complete the task.

To Simplify:

● Explain to children that a vehicle transports people and things from one place to another. Assist them, if necessary, in creating a vehicle out of the materials.

To Extend:

● Invite children to compare details and parts included on their vehicles with what they see, either on the real one or in the pictures or objects they used for reference.

● Provide pictures of the buildings that would serve the particular vehicle children are constructing (such as a fire station). Suggest that children reconstruct the buildings as well as the vehicles.

● Ask youngsters to write or draw stories or explaining about their structures.

Language

1. The Little Red Hen and the Grain of Wheat

U se flannel figures or stick puppets to tell children the familiar story "The Little Red Hen and the Grain of Wheat." The storyline is as follows: A hen finds some grains of wheat and asks several animals to help her plant the wheat, harvest it, take it to the mill, mix it into dough, and bake it. Several animals refuse her request at each step until she asks which of them will help eat the bread. All the animals offer to "help." The hen tells them that whoever worked will have the reward of eating the bread.

Introduce the story by asking children to listen carefully so that they can answer the following questions: Which of the animals did the work? Which of them did not do work? Who ate the food? Was the hen being fair? After the story is over, ask these questions again. Be sure to allow children to answer in ways that

express their true ideas, even if they differ from one another. Acknowledge each child's response with comments such as, "Amanda has another good idea," or "Sookyoung's ideas are interesting." The final question about fairness is the one likely to stimulate discussion.

To Simplify:

● Ask the children simply to focus on which animal did all the work.

To Extend:

● Sometimes children are concerned that the other animals did not get any food. This is a good opportunity to ask them to think about other ways the story could end. Write down their ideas.

2. Classroom Work Songs

Throughout history, singing has been used to make work seem easier and go faster. During the day, develop some very simple songs that fit your classroom—for transitions or clean-up or dismissal. Take a very simple melody, such as "Skip to My Lou" or "Row, Row, Row Your Boat," and put words to the tune that fit the occasion. A sample song to "Skip to My Lou" would be:

> Clean-up, Clean-up, Clean-up the room (Repeat 3 times.)
> So we can go outdoors.

Each time you use the song, it will serve as a signal for the children to get to their tasks. You will find that children sing along while they work and that they will adapt the song to fit the transition to a new activity (such as, "So we can have our snack").

To Simplify:

● Choose a different tune to represent each transition. This way, children will associate both the words and the melody with the activity.

To Extend:

● From the library, get some samples of work songs from different cultures that suit a variety of circumstances. (There are even work songs for taking care of babies.) Make these a part of the everyday rituals of the classroom. A good source for these songs are recordings made available by the Library of Congress through their Folklife Division or Folkways Recordings.

3. Mommy/Daddy Work

Read the book *Mommies at Work* by Eve Merriam (1989). Ask children in advance to pay attention to the different kinds of work women do in the book. Have them list these after the reading. Use this information to lead a discussion about the work children's mothers do while they are at school. As a follow-up, have children interview their mothers at home and record in any way they can what their mothers say they do. The next day, have children report their findings to the class. Make a chart as a permanent record. The same or a similar activity can be carried out to ascertain the work of fathers or other adults in the household. Use the book *Daddies at Work* by Eve Merriam (1980) to stimulate discussion. Below is sample interview sheet.

Dear Mom/Dad/Grandparent/ Guardian,

At school we are studying about the work people do. Please answer the questions so I will know more about your work and be able to tell the class about it.

Thanks,

I am the _____ (relationship) of

_____ (child's name).

I work at_____

(place-this could include home). Some of the jobs I

do are_____.

These jobs help our family. Here are some other

things I want you to know about my work

_____

_____

To Simplify:

● Treat the specific tasks that parents or other adults in the home engage in as work rather than focusing on a job or occupation.

To Extend:

● Carry out a discussion of what it means to be unemployed.

Physical

1. Ha Ha, This-a-Way

This is an adaptation of an old play party game originally from Kentucky. Children form a circle with one child in the center. The group circles around the child in the middle, chanting the following refrain:

> When I was a young girl (boy), young girl (boy), young girl (boy)
>
> When I was a young girl (boy), then oh then.
>
> Ha Ha this-a-way, Ha Ha that-a-way, Ha Ha this-a-way, then oh then (*Repeat 2 times.*)

At this point, the child in the center chooses an occupation and makes a motion associated with that occupation (for example, carpenter = hammering). Everyone imitates the motion and chants:

> (child's name) was a carpenter, carpenter, carpenter
>
> (child's name) was a carpenter, then oh then.

The child in the center chooses a successor, and the game continues. Each child in turn selects a new occupation and a related motion.

2. On the Line

The object of this game is for children to develop ball handling skills. Explain that some people work in factories where there is an assembly line. Describe an assembly line as a place where many people do the same sort of job, but they pass parts of the job on to others in front of them on "the line." This can be replicated using balls. Form a line of children and begin passing a ball from the beginning to the end. When the ball has reached the end, the child puts the ball in a basket. After children have shown they understand the principle of the game, begin another ball soon after the first, so children must pass one ball and then be ready to catch another one in short order.

To Simplify:

● Use one ball at a time. If necessary, begin by rolling balls along the line.

To Extend:

● As children become more proficient, quicken the pace by starting the balls closer in time to one another, thus creating a "speed-up" on "the line." Provide several stickers to each child so that each time a ball gets to the child, he or she must put a sticker on it. This will help children understand that line workers actually make changes or additions to the items that come to them.

Pretend Play

1. Play School

Transform an area of the classroom to correspond with another workplace in the school (such as the office, the nurse's room, and so on). Involve children in this pretend play setting by drawing on their experiences and memories, and having them reconstruct objects and materials used in the setting. Allow children ample time to explore the area and the tasks of the workers through pretending and role playing. Provide such props as office tools, cleaning implements, and so on, to help children play out their experiences.

2. Workplaces

Set up the classroom into work centers with each area representing a different kind of work: the art area for artists, the block area for construction workers and architects, the science area for scientists, math center for mathematicians, writing center for authors and newspaper columnists, library area for librarians and researchers, the workbench for carpenters, and so on. Provide pictures of various professionals in the appropriate areas to stimulate children's imagination. Be sure to include pictures representing different culture groups, sexes, ages, and degrees of ableness. Also include blue-collar workers as well as white-collar workers. Refer to these centers as workplaces to familiarize children with the concept.

To Simplify:

● Use easily recognized symbols to designate the areas (paintbrush = art area, book = research area, and so on).

To Extend:

● Develop descriptions with the children of the type of work to be accomplished in each workplace and post these for children to read. Add on to each list throughout the week as children come up with new ideas in response to their involvement with the materials.

Social

1. Homework

Ask children to compare specific jobs done in school with those that are carried out in their homes. Point out less obvious similarities, such as the teaching role of both school employees and parents, as well as focusing on more visible tasks, such as cooking and cleaning up. Set up a chart with the headings "The School" on one side and "Home" on the other. Record children's responses or instruct children to write or draw their comparisons in the correct column.

To Simplify:

● Provide pictures for children to tack or paste onto the chart that represent concretely the particular task or responsibility.

To Extend:

● Carry out this activity over several days or weeks. Review children's ideas periodically and note any changes that have taken place as children's understanding of the role of school workers increases.

2. Work-a-Day World

Explore the work carried out in the community by inviting several workers into the classroom to talk about and demonstrate the jobs they do. Have the visitors bring as many real objects as they can to give children firsthand exposure to the tools and uniforms associated with various trades. Some suggestions for such visitors are carpenters, mail carriers, firefighters, plumbers, electricians, telephone repairers, police officers, gardeners or landscape workers, architects, physicians, and so on. Make sure that over time, a diverse population of workers is represented and that many nontraditional workers are evident. Pay attention also to confronting gender, race, and cultural stereotyping. Look for males and females in non-stereotypic roles. Also, attempt to invite workers who use wheelchairs or other devices to help them get around. For instance, children may think that only men can be mail deliverers. When a female mail carrier is brought to the group, point out that she has all the qualifications necessary to do the job.

3. Working People

Precede or follow the "Work-a-day World" activity by exploring the genders, cultures, and abilities of working people. Collect pictures of people of both gen-

ders, varying cultures, abilities, and ages. Get a second set of pictures of objects or settings depicting different kinds of work. Put five pictures facedown in two places on a table or put each set separately in two "feely" boxes or bags. Ask children to choose a picture from each set. Then talk about whether the man/woman/boy or girl could do the job depicted. Provide "reference" books that illustrate men and women engaged in similar tasks, which children can use to "confirm" or challenge their ideas or use the Work-a-Day visitor as a resource for finding out about particular kinds of work and who can do that job.

To Simplify:

● Use pictures that depict jobs with which children are familiar or those they encounter in their everyday experience.

To Extend:

● Gradually introduce less familiar occupations or tasks as children's experiences are broadened.

4. Teamwork

After a discussion of manufacturing or factory work, set up an assembly line for a cooking activity, in which the task for each child or group of children is limited and well defined (such as adding 1 cup of sugar, or stirring the mixture). Discuss the benefits and drawbacks of this kind of division of labor (such as speed, as contrasted with pride in a finished product). Explore with them ways in which the advantages of a production team could be used to create a product in which all "workers" feel a stake. The following recipe lends itself well to this activity because of the number of assembly steps required.

Armenian Meat Pie or Lame June

Prepare the following mixture in advance, or cook the mixture in an electric frying pan in the classroom, with children adding the ingredients. Be sure the pan is on a heat-proof surface and that children are closely supervised.

1/2 chopped onion, sautéed until soft

Add and cook until no longer pink:

1/4 lb. ground lamb

1 tbsp. tomato paste

1/4 tsp. salt

2 tbsp. chopped parsley (or more, if you wish)

Cool the filling and cut English muffins in half (plan on 1/2 per child with a few extra).

Set up the work stations as follows:

1. **Crust:** Children at this station will pass English muffins to the next station.

2. **Assembling:** Children will place 1 scoop of the mixture on each muffin half and pass them to the next station.

3. **Spreading:** Children will spread the mixture around the top of the muffin half and pass it on.

4. **Readying:** Children will place muffins on baking sheets or a broiler pan.

5. **Cooking:** Depending on your set up, Lamejunes will be taken to the kitchen or they will be baked in the classroom.

If you wish to have children compare methods of assembly, set up an alternate system in which each child assembles his or her own Lamejune. In this case, have the ingredients out on a table and let children rotate around.

To Simplify:

● Choose very simple recipes that involve few steps.

To Extend:

● Older children can determine the individual tasks that comprise the cooking project and can self-select their roles.

Teacher Resources

Field Trips

Some suggested locales that specifically relate to people working include: construction sites, food stores, clothing stores, hardware stores, pharmacies, small service stores such as hairdresser or tailoring shops, restaurants, transportation headquarters (bus, subway, train), craft workshops, schools, factories, and offices. In addition, visits to places where parents work will help children become familiar with the diversity of worksites as well as give them renewed respect for the employment of parents. In some communities, a trip to an unemployment center is appropriate.

Classroom Visitors

Invite community workers of both sexes and a variety of ages and cultures, races, and abilities to speak to the class and participate in everyday activities. Parents are an important resource for this unit as well. Some specific suggestions are: cooks or chefs in local restaurants, building or construction trade workers, office workers, food handlers, and professionals such as doctors, lawyers, teachers, and the like.

Children's Books

Alda, A. (1983). *Matthew and His Dad*. New York: Simon & Schuster.

Black, I. S. (1970). *The Little Old Man Who Cooked and Cleaned*. New York: Scholastic.

Blacker, T., & Winn, C. (1987). *If I Could Work*. New York: Lippincott.

Chase, E. N. (1984). *The New Baby Calf*. Toronto, Ontario, Canada: Scholastic-TAB.

Dooley, N. (1991). *Everybody Cooks Rice*. Minneapolis, MN: Carolrhoda Books.

Florian, D. (1992). *A Carpenter*. New York: Greenwillow.

Florian, D. (1992). *A Chef*. New York: Greenwillow.

Florian, D. (1982). *People Working*. New York: Crowell.

Gibbons, G. (1983). *Department Store*. New York: Crowell.

Gibbons, G. (1983). *New Road!* New York: Crowell.

Gibbons, G. (1984). *Fire! Fire!* New York: Crowell.

Gibbons, G. (1986). *Up Goes the Skyscraper!* New York: Crowell.

Hazen, B. S. (1979). *Tight Times*. New York: Viking Press.

Keats, E. J. (1965). *John Henry*. New York: Parthenon Books.

Keats, E. J. (1968). *A Letter to Amy*. New York: HarperCollins.

Keats, E. J. (1962). *The Snowy Day*. New York: Viking.

Krasilovsky, P. (1950). *The Man Who Didn't Wash His Dishes*. New York: Scholastic.

Kuskin, K. (1982). *The Philharmonic Gets Dressed*. New York: HarperCollins.

Lasker, J. (1972). *Mothers Can Do Anything*. Chicago: Albert Whitman.

Littledale, F. (1975). *The Elves and the Shoemaker*. New York: Four Winds Press.

Marshall, J. (1989). *The Three Little Pigs*. New York: Dial Books.

Merriam, E. (1989). *Daddies at Work*. New York: Scholastic.

Merriam, E. (1989). *Mommies at Work*. New York: Knopf.

Oughton, J. (1994). *The Magic Weaver of Rugs: A Tale of the Navaho*. Boston: Houghton Mifflin.

Oxenbury, H. (1981). *Working*. New York: Simon & Schuster.

Perham, M. (1986). *People at Work*. Minneapolis, MN: Dillon Press.

Piper, W. (1961). *The Little Engine That Could*. New York: Platt & Munk.

Seuss, Dr. (1940). *Horton Hatches the Egg*. New York: Random House.

Zemach, M. (1983). *The Little Red Hen*. New York: Farrar, Straus and Giroux.

Adult References

Fields, M. V., & Hillstead, D. V. (1990). "Whole Language in the Play Store." *Childhood Education*, 67(2). Wheaton, MD: Association for Childhood International.

Nachbar, R. R. (1992). "What Do Grown-ups Do All Day? The World of Work." *Young Children*, 47(3). Washington, DC: National Association for the Education of Young Children.

Seeger, R. C. (1980). *American Folk Songs for Children*. New York: Doubleday.

Veitch, B., & Harms, T. (1981). *Cook and Learn*. New York: Addison-Wesley.

Wenning, J., & Wortis, S. (1985). *Made by Human Hands: A Curriculum for Teaching Young People About Work and Working People*. Cambridge, MA: The Multicultural Project for Communication and Education.

People Living in Communities

Terms, Facts, and Principles (TFPs)

General Information

1. All people need food, shelter, clothing, protection, human companionship, recreation, and a sense of belonging.
2. People sometimes live in communities because living together can be a better way to meet their needs.
3. The most common kind of community is a group of people living together in a particular area.
4. How people meet their needs is influenced by the environment in which they live, the resources available to them, and their culture.
5. Communities can consist of many people or just a few.
6. People in communities may live near or at a distance from one another.
7. People influence and are influenced by the communities in which they live.
8. Communities are influenced by people outside as well as inside the community.
9. People live in communities with others who are both like them and different from them.
10. When people in a community find out about the similarities between themselves and others, it helps them to better understand one another.
11. When people in a community learn to appreciate the diversity among people, it helps them develop positive attitudes about each other.
12. All people's ideas, cultural heritage, and values should be protected and respected within their communities.
13. Each person can contribute to his or her community in some way.

Community Relationships

14. Sometimes people in communities help one another. Helping means alleviating someone's distress or assisting them in their work or play.
15. People in communities learn to work together to accomplish their goals. This is called cooperating.
16. Communities require guidelines or rules in order to function. People decide on these rules and may also change them.

17. Some rules are more easily communicated and followed than are others.

18. When all people in a community know and understand the rules, they are better able to cooperate and work together.

*19. Sometimes people living in communities agree with one another; sometimes they disagree.

*20. People sometimes choose among various ways to resolve their disagreements, such as discussing, persuading, bargaining, trading, compromising, or voting.

*21. People sometimes choose unfair ways to resolve their disagreements, such as bullying, coercing, threatening, or harming.

*22. Sometimes the people in a community select leaders to represent them.

Providing for Community Needs

23. People in communities rely on one another to create and provide the goods and services the community needs. Some of these include: communication, protection, food, health care, clothing, shelter, transportation, recreation, entertainment, and education.

*24. The resources available to a community influence how the people in a community meet their needs.

*25. Sometimes communities hire people to carry out the jobs that are necessary for the community to function. These workers include teachers, hospital workers, postal employees, construction workers, bus drivers.

*26. Some of the jobs within a community are carried out by volunteers.

*27. Sometimes people contribute work and/or materials so that community projects can be carried out.

Learning About Communities

28. People learn about their communities through talking with others, visiting and exploring particular places, examining records, and sampling community produce and goods.

29. People make records of what they have learned about their community in many ways, including mapping, charting, writing, drawing, photographing, and taping.

*30. People communicate with other people both inside and outside their community to let others know more about themselves and to find out about more about how other people live in their communities.

*31. People in the present leave records of current activities for people in the future to use.

*32. Learning about the past gives people ideas about what to do now or in the future.

Activity Ideas

Aesthetic

1. Sing with Me

Teach children two versions of the same song, each from a different cultural tradition. Different versions may be found in several books and recordings. Here are the Jamaican and African American versions of a song/chant entitled, respectively, "Dumplin's" and "Cookie." "Dumplin's" is treated as a counting song.

♫ **Dumplin's**

Leader: "Cookie, you see somebody pass here?"
Chorus: "No, my friend."
Leader: "Cookie, you see somebody pass here?"
Chorus: "No, my friend."
Leader: "Well, one of my dumplin's gone!"
Chorus: "Don't tell me so."
Leader: "Two of my dumplin's gone."
Chorus: "Don't tell me so."
Leader: "Three of my dumplin's gone."
(Repeat the chant, substituting numbers in order up to six or nine.)

Cookie is treated as a substitution song.

♫ **Cookie**

Leader: "Cookie, you sure nobody pass here?"
Chorus: "No, my friend."
Leader: "Cookie, you sure nobody pass here?"
Chorus: "No, my friend."
Leader: "Well, one of my dumplin's gone."
Chorus: "Don't tell me so."
Leader: "One of my dumplin's gone."
Chorus: "Don't tell me so."
Leader: "One of my dumplin's gone."
(Substitute other objects for the "dumplin" such as food, toys, and so on.)

Hints for Success:

● These songs can be carried out at any time of the day, either at planned or spontaneous times.

● Be sure to demonstrate the motions as you sing or chant the verse; children will quickly catch on.

To Simplify:

● Begin with one version of a song until children are very comfortable and familiar with it. Then present the second version. Do only one version each day to minimize confusion.

To Extend:

● Once the songs have been taught, have children make up other verses for both versions.

2. Flower Beds

Develop a class or group project to plant flower seeds on the school grounds or on some other community property. Discuss people's responsibility in caring for and beautifying their environment. Have children sign up for turns to care for the flowers over time.

Hint for Success:

● Contact the appropriate neighborhood association or town office for permission to plant on city property.

To Simplify:

● Begin by planting seeds inside the classroom or, even more simply, by caring for commercially bought plants. Once children know how to do this, move into the outside environment.

To Extend:

● Involve the children in the planning so they have some idea about the process. Allow children to design the plot by choosing the flower seeds to be planted and arranging them in the plot in a pleasing way, using the pictures on the flower packets as a guide.

3. Sing-Along

Learn songs that represent the cultures of children in the class or neighborhood. A way to accomplish this is to send a note home inviting parents either to come in and record a song or to record one on cassette tape at home and send it to school. (Supply the tape yourself, and perhaps a tape recorder to facilitate the process.) Ask that parents send in a translation or transliteration (a phonetic pronunciation of the words) of the song on paper. Listen to the songs frequently so that you can become familiar with them. Then, with the parents' assistance, teach them to the children. Use the songs as a part of daily routines such as arrival, dismissal, and clean-up time.

Hint for Success:

● If the songs are in another language, sing the chorus or first verse only until it becomes familiar. Then gradually, over a period of days, add the remainder of the song.

4. Community Portraits

Select pictures of artworks that depict community scenes. Choose urban and rural scenes, as well as pictures depicting modern and past times. Encourage children to examine these. Ask leading questions, such as, "What are the children doing? What are the adults doing? How can you tell what the people are thinking? Was the artist portraying people as happy/sad/mad/afraid? How can you tell?"

Hints for Success:

● If possible, laminate or otherwise protect the pictures so that children may handle them without damaging or defacing them.

● Calendars or book illustrations may be used.

To Simplify:

● Use one picture at a time for children to explore. Ask them to talk about the activities depicted in the scene.

● Take pictures of the children as they are engaged in activities. Have them describe what they are doing. Write down children's responses.

To Extend:

● Post the works of art around the classroom. Provide paper and pencils so children can respond "in writing" to the scenes they see. (Print the questions noted above next to the pictures as prompts.)

● Bring out two or more pictures for children to compare. Ask the children to respond to questions such as: What is the same/different in these pictures? Are people being helpful or are they interfering with each other? How can you tell? Write down the children's ideas. Post these next to the displayed art work for children's future reference.

Affective

1. Leading Us On

As part of regular classroom procedures, choose a daily group leader. This individual may be the line leader to and from the classroom, attendance recorder, lunch counter, and so on, depending on the age of the children and your own circumstances. Be sure to rotate the leadership job among all of the class members and refrain from tying the selection to "good behavior." In this way, all children will have an opportunity to take on a leadership role with success and the activity doesn't become competitive.

Hints for Success:

● At first choose children who have already displayed some leadership abilities. They can serve as a model.

● Reinforce children's sense of pride and accomplishment, pointing out their successes both to themselves and others.

2. Community Members Collages

Following many discussions and explorations of the nature of a community, have children verbally identify the different communities of which they are a part (for example, the school community, the after school care community, the neighborhood center community, and so on). Then tell children that they will be making a special picture—a collage—of the communities of which they are a part. Show them magazine pictures (that you have prepared in advance) depicting a variety of community settings, such as schools, community centers, child care settings, towns, farms, and so on, and have children select appropriate illustrations for their individual collages. Include a photograph of the child and his or her family as a centerpiece of the collage (this can be done after the collage is completed, so as not to spoil the photographs). Next, give children opportunities to dictate or write stories about people in their communities. Use these collages and stories as the basis for a community folder each child can keep and add to over time. Invite children to include information garnered from their families as well.

To Simplify:

● Limit the selection of community settings to the home and the school program.

To Extend:

● Use these community records as classroom references and as ways to compare and contrast children's lives and experiences with one another. Display the folders, in progress and after they are completed, so that children in other parts of the program can see them.

3. Stock Exchange

Set up a toy exchange in the classroom. Ask each child to bring a toy (or book) she or he no longer wants, but that is in good enough condition to be used. Put all the items on a table or shelf and instruct children in the practice of bartering or exchanging. In other words, a child who brings an item may select a different item to use for the day. All items are to be kept at school, but children may exchange them for other things the following day. As children carry out the activity, discuss their reactions to the exchange. Find out the reasons for children's satisfaction or dissatisfaction, and elicit suggestions for modifications. Explain that in some communities people exchange goods in order to satisfy their needs.

Hints for Success:

● Inform parents about this activity in advance so they can monitor the toys their children bring to class.

● Set a regular time for the exchanges to take place. At first it may be necessary to monitor the activity; eventually, children can take responsibility to manage it on their own.

To Simplify:

● Limit the exchange to one item at a time. As soon as a child brings an item, he or she may exchange it for another.

To Extend:

● Have items on display for a period of time before opening the ""Exchange" for trading. After children have become practiced, add services as well as goods. Such services might include helping someone clean out his or her locker, or agreeing to work together on a project, or tying shoes. Set a time limit and institute a warning bell (such as is done on the New York Stock Exchange to indicate the end of the trading period).

Cognitive

1. Let's Work It Out

Identify a classroom problem and help children use problem solving strategies (see selected TFPs for ideas). Such problems may relate to health and safety (for example, blocks are falling on people during clean-up), or protection of property (for example, classroom materials are being stepped on and broken), or people's rights (for example, children are pushing ahead of others in line.) These issues can be dealt with either through whole class discussions, or immediately, as the problems arise. Encourage children to both describe the problem and generate possible solutions. A way of helping children solve a problem on the spot is for the adult to take on the role of a mediator in the dispute in the following way:*

Step 1. Identify the Problem. Separate the combatants, if necessary. Elicit from each child his or her perception of the issue by asking each one, in turn, to tell what she or he wants. Paraphrase each child's statement so that everyone develops the same understanding of the points of view. Neutralize any disputed object by holding it or setting it apart temporarily with the promise that it will be returned once the children have reached a solution.

Step 2. State the Problem in General Terms. Once you are fairly sure of the nature of the conflict, and children have had enough time to express their ideas, summarize the issue in global terms: "It sounds as if you both want the same dinosaur at the same time. We have a problem. What can we do about it?"

Step 3. Generate Alternatives. Ask each of the children, as well as any bystanders for ideas to solve the problem. Paraphrase each suggestion as it arises, checking with the disputants, in turn, whether or not the solution seems feasible. Ideas that were rejected at one point in the discussion may be acceptable at another point, so bring those back for discussion.

Step 4. Find Points of Agreement. As the discussion proceeds, look for points of mutual agreement. For instance, "You think you should both have a turn and you want the first turn." Continue to check these out with the children. When you discern that an agreement is possible, state it in positive terms. "You have both agreed to . . . . It sounds as if you have solved the problem."

Step 5. Praise Children for Coming to an Agreement. Children have worked hard to reach a solution to their problem. You can see this in their body language (fidgeting, moving away). Praise them for engaging in this problem-solving process by acknowledging their hard work and the efforts of the bystanders.

Step 6. Help Children Carry Out the Terms of the Agreement. Be sure children do as they have agreed. This may entail keeping track of time, or making sure the item is transferred. Remind them, if necessary, of the terms.

Hints for Success:

● At first, the solutions may take some time to achieve. Therefore, whenever possible, allow lots of time for discussion. While not all children will get their way every time, they generally can find an acceptable compromise. When this procedure is carried out to solve numerous issues over time, children learn to reach resolutions more speedily.

● Be sure you do not take one child's point of view as being more worthy or valid than another's, or that you indicate by word or deed that you prefer one solution over another.

To Simplify:

● Start with simple problems, such as how to decide who will have a turn at the computer. List the solutions (not more than two or three) and refer to them frequently over time.

To Extend:

● Once they are experienced negotiators, small group of classroom representatives generate a plan for solving a classroom problem and present it to the whole group. Using democratic means, such as voting or discussing it until consensus is reached, the whole group can determine whether or not they approve of the plan. If not, the small group continues to meet until its members generate an acceptable alternative. The plan is then implemented and sanctions for violation are decided upon. At a later time, children assess the strategies for their fairness and effectiveness.

**Note: A more extensive discussion of this technique can be found in the second edition of *Guiding Children's Social Development*, (1993).

2. Days Gone By

From community records, the local library, local newspapers, solicit old photos and documents of the area around your school or center. Lead children in comparing these pictures with how the area looks at present. As a follow-up, create diaries, photos, and/or experience stories of the present day.

To Simplify:

● Use the school or program environs as the basis for study. Point out changes that are occurring in the present that may influence the future look of the area (such as trees being planted or removed, road work, new houses, and so on).

To Extend:

● At the beginning of the unit, put together artifacts in a pretend "Time Capsule" that represents toys, games, illustrations, and descriptions of children's favorite activities. Open the "Time Capsule" at the very end of the school year. Discuss the items and compare what children's favorite or important things were in their lives in the "olden days" and what they prefer at present.

3. We Like to Eat

Let children sample foods that are likely to be enjoyed by the cultures represented in your classroom. Then help children compare the ingredients for similarities and differences. Use a map or globe to point out the regions of the world from which the food and people originated. Explore the different ways people have of preparing similar foods (such as wheat or rice). A short list of rice dishes from a number of countries could include: Rice Pudding (England, France, Norway, and so on), Rice Pilaf (Lebanon, Near East, Middle East), Paella (Spain, Portugal), Risotto (Italy), Basmati Rice (India, Indonesia), Rice in Seaweed (Japan, Korea), Beans and Rice (Cuba, Mexico, Puerto Rico, Africa) and Steamed Rice (China and elsewhere). Introduce children to several varieties of rice, if you can get them. For instance, bring in samples of short and long grain white rice, brown rice, Basmati rice, glutinous rice, etc. Later on, use the rice in a recipe with other ingredients.

Here are several rice dishes that are easy to prepare with children and have almost universal appeal. Refer to the book *Everybody Cooks Rice* (1991) for additional suggestions.

Rice Pudding (per serving)

> 2 tbsp. cooked rice (white or brown)
> 1/2 tsp. raisins
> 1/2 tbsp. chopped nuts (optional)
> 1/2 tsp. sugar or honey
> sprinkle of cinnamon and/or nutmeg
> dash of milk or yogurt

Mix all the ingredients together. The pudding may be served chilled, warmed, or at room temperature. If you wish, other dried fruits may be made available for children to add. Children may design their individual servings to suit their own tastes.

Chicken Soup with Rice (per serving)

> 1/2 cup chicken broth (canned or from concentrate) warmed
> 2 tbsp. rice, precooked
> 1 tbsp. cooked chicken (optional)
> pinch of parsley or dill weed

Combine the ingredients in a heat-proof cup or bowl. Children may take more or less of particular ingredients to suit their tastes. Vegetable broth may be substituted and the chicken eliminated for people following a vegetarian diet.

Arroz Con Pollo (Chicken and Rice) (per portion)

> 1/2 cup precooked rice (warm)
> 1 tbsp. chopped green pepper
> 1 tbsp. chopped tomatoes
> 1 tsp. chopped scallions (optional)
> 1/4 tsp. paprika
> 1 tbsp. cooked, diced or shredded chicken
> salt and pepper to taste

Combine the first five ingredients until thoroughly mixed. Add chicken and toss. Sprinkle on a little salt and pepper.

Arroz Con Leche (Rice with Milk) (8 to 10 small servings)

> 1 cup raw rice
> 2 cups lightly salted water
> 1/2 glass milk
> cinnamon, sugar to taste

Cook the rice and water in a covered saucepan until firm and fluffy (about 30 to 45 minutes)

Allow to cool slightly.

Serve each child a small portion in a bowl, add a few tablespoons of milk and sprinkle with cinnamon and sugar. Raisins are an additional item to offer.

Hint for Success:

● Prepare recipe cards showing the steps in pictograph form. Set out the ingredients along with the card at a table so children can prepare their rice pudding on their own. Be sure to include a preliminary step for hand washing!

4. Baseline

Have children list the things they consider to be their basic needs (that is, those things they could not live without). Help them understand that each of them needs the same kinds of things (refer to the TFPs). Help children explore the differences between "needs" and "wants," but be sure to accept children's notions of what they think they need. List the needs on a chart, leaving enough space for pictures. In small groups or as individuals, have children draw or cut out pictures of items that represent these needs and glue them on the chart in the appropriate sections.

1 Wash your hands.

2 Take 2 Tbsps. of cooked rice.

3 Take 1/2 tsp. raisins.

4 Take 1/2 tsp. chopped nuts.

5 Take 1/2 tsp. of sugar or honey.

6 Sprinkle in cinnamon.

7 Add a bit of milk.

8 Mix and eat.

To Simplify:

● Provide real items or models (such as non-perishable foods, building materials, clothing, etc.). Have children choose from among the items and group them on a table according to whether each item represents a want or a need.

To Extend:

● Make a graph based on the chart of "needs." Compare, by category, the number of different representations children were able to find. For example, compare the number of types of housing children discovered and the variety of clothing they described.

5. People Patterns

Understanding patterns is a basic mathematical skill. The purpose of this activity is for children to gain experience in working with patterns. Take individual photographs of several children in the group. Have at least four copies of each photograph printed. Lay three of the photographs out on a table, from left to right, and then repeat the pattern right next to it. Ask children, in turn, to complete the pattern using the other copies of the pictures. Use questions such as "Which picture comes next?" "Then which picture should be next?" If children are uncertain, have them directly match the photographs by placing their set on top of, above, or below the originals.

Hints for Success:

● Make sure each photograph shows only one child at a time.

● If necessary, crop the picture to eliminate background distractions.

To Simplify:

● Create a two-photograph pattern. Tape or glue the photograph pattern onto a strip to enable children to handle it without changing the pattern.

To Extend:

● Increase the number of photographs in each pattern.

● Allow children to create their own patterns for others to finish.

● Create patterns that focus on more discrete differences, for instance, "Curly Hair, Curly Hair, Straight Hair."

6. We Do It Together

With the children's assistance, identify a classroom project. This may be as simple as decorating a bulletin board, or as complex as planning a social event for parents. Help children define the tasks that are necessary for the project to succeed. Make a record of their ideas. Then, work with them in assigning responsibilities. At the conclusion of the project, help the children assess the procedure that was established and the contributions made by all concerned.

Hint for Success:

● Establish a reasonable time line for each aspect of the project. Remember that young children have difficulty sustaining interest over long periods of time.

To Simplify:

● Choose a small, short-term, concrete project such as decorating a bulletin board. Limit the deliberations and the execution to one day.

To Extend:

● A project may be carried out over several days with older or more experienced children. Record the conclusions that were reached in the discussions and help children evaluate the changes they made, if any, in bringing the project to completion. Use the information for future endeavors.

7. Of the People, By the People, For the People

To study local political life, use a local election as a springboard. First, explain in very simple terms why and how people choose others to represent them in government. Visit a polling place, arrange to have a poll worker demonstrate how the voting machines operate and allow children to try them out. Visit town or city offices and arrange to interview community officials. Prepare children to ask them about the jobs the officials do and how they do them. Encourage children to find out whether they make decisions on their own or in consultation with others. Also ascertain to whom they are responsible. Finally question the officials about the techniques they use to determine what the community's needs are. Use this information to compare with decision-making in the classroom. For example, often a needs assessment study is carried out in a community. In the classroom, carry out a "needs assessment" by polling children on their opinions about some issue—such as whether children would rather have a new classroom pet or additional plants, or whether or not to rearrange the furniture.

Note: This activity is best suited to older children.

To Simplify:

● Focus on the physical aspects of politics, such as voting booths and offices.

To Extend:

● Hold a mock election in the classroom as a follow-up activity. With older children, introduce the notion of campaigning and electioneering as efforts of individuals to influence others. Help children discuss and differentiate between those promises people can and cannot fulfill.

Construction

1. Hear Ye!

Create a classroom newspaper with the children. Explain that a newspaper is one way people have of finding out what is going on in their community. Describe the role of reporters and editorial writers. Show children actual newspapers, pointing out that there are usually different sections for different types of news. Refer also to the photographs in the paper. Section off several sheets of heavy paper. Encourage children to "write" or draw stories about the events of the school day.

Note: For a more in-depth description of newspapers, see the unit on Communication, pages 223–256.

To Simplify:

● Have each child make his or her own individual pages for the newspaper. Compile them all in a newspaper format.

To Extend:

● Keep the newspaper going over time, thereby creating a classroom archive to which children may refer in the future.

● Set aside a time when children can "read" their columns to one another.

● Encourage children to be "roving reporters" so they can "interview" various children or adults in the classroom about activities in which they are engaged.

2. Site Visit

Visit community sites, either by walking or using local transportation. Records of the excursion can be made in a variety of ways. Children can make journal entries that include drawings, writing, dictated stories, and photographs. Or, help write an experience story together of what was seen. You also can make a photo record, by taking photographs along the route; after they are developed, allowing children to place the pictures, in order, according to their walk. Retrace the route to check their recollections. In addition, provide opportunities for them to use building block reconstructions of their experience,

To Simplify:

● A first trip should be a neighborhood walk. Provide the pictures for children to use on their experience chart.

To Extend:

● As a follow-up, have children make representations of the buildings and other landmarks out of small boxes, paper, glue, fasteners, and so on. Assist children in placing what they have made on a map or diagram of the route.

● Display the representations in the classroom and add to them as children learn more about the community.

3. Playground Plotting

Use the school playground as a study territory for mapping. First, talk with the children about the unit of measure to be used—it may be a conventional one if they are well acquainted with yardsticks and the like, or it may be a unit of measure that they determine. For example, some groups of children have chosen "footprints" or the length of one child's body. Then, using a string of appropriate length, work with the children to measure the dimensions of the playground. Next, make a map of what you have measured. Children may also be encouraged to draw or even make three-dimensional replicas or representations of the playground equipment using paper, crayons, cardboard, and so on. Children can also use unit blocks to create models of the equipment.

Hint for Success:

● Decide in advance what size group is needed to make the activity meaningful. Then divide the group accordingly, spacing each small group out on the playground and provide appropriate instructions.

To Simplify:

● Choose one small area of the playground where the children normally play. Before introducing the activity, draw children's attention to the shape and size of the area as they play. Repeat this over several days.

To Extend:

● Children can construct dioramas or a bulletin board illustration of the playground or a bulletin board recreation.

Language

1. Community Clues

Take photographs of community buildings or offices (such as the post office or police station) or community workers and tape each one to a large index card. Pair children and give one child in each pair a card. Tell everyone to keep her or his card a secret at first. Explain that each child with a card will give clues or descriptions of what is on his or her card. The object is to give helpful clues so that it is possible for partners to guess correctly. Help children think of clues as the game proceeds. Some sample clues are: It's big; It's something blue; It has a door; This person wears a hat. When the children have guessed, tell them to trade cards with another pair and continue the game with the second child being the one to give "clues."

Hint for Success:

● This activity is most successful when carried out with children in first grade or older. Demonstrate how the game is to be played in advance, if necessary.

To Simplify:

● Use the most familiar locations and people.

● Do not expect all children to be able to keep secrets!

● Do this activity in a circle time. Have one child at a time offer clues, while the rest guess.

To Extend:

● Distribute cards that depict less familiar members of the community, such as a road worker, or animal control officer.

2. Pen Pals

Through your school district central office, community cooperative preschool organization, international agency, teacher's organization, magazine or personal contact, establish a pen pal relationship with a program in a different country or U.S. city or a similar program in your locale. Exchange photographs so children can have a concrete picture of the persons with whom they are corresponding. Find out as much as possible about the other school through letters and other exchanges, and

send information about yours. Even when there is a difference in language, art materials projects (such as collages) can easily be sent, received, and appreciated. When you receive the photographs and completed form (as shown below), introduce the pen pals to the class using their names, pictures, and descriptions. Post the photos and forms at children's eye level, so they can become further acquainted.

Fold a half-sized piece of white or manila construction paper in quarters.

page 1 Photograph or Self-drawn Portrait My name is _____ I live in _____ (town/city)	page 2 (leave room for drawing) In my family there is _____ _____ _____ _____
page 3 My favorite color is _____ My favorite toy is _____ _____	page 4 The things I like to do are_____ _____ _____ _____

Hint for Success:

● Choose a school that serves children and teachers from ethnic or racial backgrounds different from your own. This will add more diversity to the experiences of both your children and those in the pen pal school.

To Simplify:

● Begin with photographs, drawings, and dictated stories. Choose a local school or program. After some correspondence, a visit to or from the school will make the Pen Pal relationship more concrete and meaningful for younger children.

To Extend:

● Children can "write" to one another as they are able, using invented spelling. At times, it may be helpful to send a translation. Carry out this activity over the entire school year. If the school is fairly close by, arrange for children from both schools to visit one another. If possible, use e-mail as an effective means of communicating.

3. Little Red Riding Hood

A person's culture is often represented by the stories that are handed down through the generations. Folktales from many different cultures have elements in common. The story of "Little Red Riding Hood" appears in many lands and languages. Get several different versions of the tale from a community or school library. One such book is *Lon Po Po: A Red Riding Hood Story from China*, translated by Ed Young (1989). Read the different versions to the children. Prepare children in advance to listen for the plot of the story; they should be able to talk about who the characters are in the story and what happens to each of them when your reading is complete. After several tellings, and after a few days time, children will be somewhat familiar with the essential elements of the tale. At that point, carry out discussions during which children compare versions for similarities and differences. Write down on a large piece of paper the conclusions that the children have reached. Post in a place where children can easily refer to them.

To Simplify:

● On several consecutive days, read the different versions of the story. Ascertain whether or not the children recognize the common plot and point out the shared features.

To Extend:

● On large paper mounted on the wall, encourage children to illustrate the various parts of the story.

● Develop a classroom folk tale using the same theme as the Red Riding Hood story. This can be done by the class as a whole, by individuals or small groups. To begin, remind children of the story line. Have them suggest the characters in the new story. (Keep this very simple and concrete.) Suggest that they use some of the same characters, changing only one at a time. Other changes may include the setting (the story may take place in a city or town, rather than in the woods, for instance). Provide flannel figures, puppets, other props or "scenes" to stimulate their thinking. Make a record of what children decide on a given day so the process can be developed over time. A good strategy is to put each sentence of the story, as children tell it, on a separate sheet of paper. This allows children to change the order of the events, as they wish. When they are satisfied,

compile the papers into a book. If children have done this individually, they may take their books home. Keep group projects available for children to "read" and "reread."

● In small groups, work with children to develop their Red Riding Hood story. Give them suggestions as to character, plot, and so on. If you are able to enlist the aid of parents or other volunteers, arrange with them to help children make or bring costumes. Set aside classroom time for children to dramatize their stories for the rest of the class.

● Work with children in developing a Red Riding Hood Rap story. Divide the story into "episodes" to enable children to more easily formulate "verses" to the rap.

4. Tell Me a Story

A sk parents for stories remembered from childhood. Have them either write their stories down or tape record them. Introduce the stories to the class, one at a time, over several days or weeks. Explain where you got each story and acknowledge the child from whose family the story came. For example, "Nina's father often tells her this story at bedtime. It's one of her favorites. Her father remembers that when he was a child, his mama told it to him." Find out if any other children are familiar with the tale. Write out the short stories on chart paper, leaving room for illustrations.

To Simplify:

● Choose simple stories or ones with which children may already be familiar.

To Extend:

● Audiotape yourself (or the parent) reading or telling the story. At various times during this study of the community, give children the opportunity to draw their ideas of what the story could look like. Share these illustrations among the group.

Physical

1. Follow the Leader

B egin by explaining that in every community people choose leaders. Say, also, that leadership roles change and that each individual should have an opportunity to lead, as well as to follow. Tell children that they can practice these skills by playing the game, "Follow the Leader." Determine with the youngsters how long each "term" of leadership should last and how the transitions between leaders is to take place. Then let them play. Suggest that children focus on actions that relate to physical endurance, agility, and speed, such as hopping for a long time, running around and between stationary objects (as in an obstacle course), and racing to and from an appointed location.

Hint for Success:

● Expect that some children will be more confident as a leader than others, so be prepared to provide support and assistance when needed.

To Simplify:

● Begin the game with an adult leader, turning over the role to children only after they are familiar with the game. Arrange for frequent turnover of leadership, such as changing leaders after a certain number of "jumps," "steps," or "turns around the playground."

To Extend:

● Encourage children to try more challenging physical feats over time.

2. Clean Up Your Community

The purpose of this activity is to provide children practice in throwing. Prepare the area by using a space divider such as a balance beam, low table, or a rope tied between two poles. Form two groups of children, one on each side of the divider. Give each group a large number of yarn balls or soft round balls that are easy for children to grip with one hand. At a signal, children in each group throw their "trash" into the "dump" (or the other side of the divider). Urge them to throw vigorously and over a sustained period of time. Do not worry about accuracy. Children are to stop throwing at a signal, such as a whistle or the shake of a tambourine.

Note: This activity can be adapted to kicking. In this case, children will kick a Nerf® ball or other soft object under the balance beam or divider, rather than over it.

Hints for Success:

● Establish the signals for beginning and stopping in advance.

● Tell children they are to throw over the divider, rather than under.

To Simplify:

● Use fewer children and fewer yarn balls.

To Extend:

● Take the activity outdoors where bean bags may be used. These have more weight and are likely to go farther.

Pretend Play

1. Store Survey

Arrange to take the children on a walking or bus trip to a local clothing store or bakery. In preparation for the trip, discuss the kinds of information children will be looking for, such as what merchandise is sold, how it is displayed, where the store owner procured the merchandise, and what are the most popular items for sale. While at the store, have children count the different kinds of goods sold, observe and document in some way (through drawing or writing) how the goods are organized and displayed, and question clerks/managers about where they got or made the goods and about the work they do. When you return, re-create the store in the classroom. Help children figure out how to price and display items based upon their observations and documentation. Encourage children to assume the roles they have observed during the excursion.

Hints for Success:

● Prepare the store owner or manager for the children's visit by explaining exactly the information you are seeking.

● On the visit, children may need assistance in their observations. Point out the jobs that people in the store are doing, and help them notice the merchandise on the shelf displays.

● Prepare children in advance for the things they will see in the store.

To Simplify:

● Focus on a few items rather than looking at the entire array of merchandise. For instance, look only at shirts in the clothing store or cookies at the bakery.

To Extend:

● Provide opportunities for children to actually prepare and "sell" food items to their classmates, using "school" money or bartering services as the mediums of exchange.

2. Community Services

Visit a community site, such as a police or fire station, post office, or library. Through group discussion, help children determine in advance what information they know, and what they want to find out. For instance, children may wish to know such things as how firefighters serve the community; how they live; if there is diversity in age, sex, and race; and what kind of training was necessary to learn their job. Have them decide what techniques they will use to find out and then record information: questioning, photographing, or video-taping, and so on. For instance, children may wish to know such things as, how firefighters serve the community, how they live, whether or not there is diversity in age, sex, or race, and what kind of training was necessary to learn their job. Analyze the results back in the classroom by asking children to dictate stories, write in journals, arrange and label photographs, and/or create a bulletin board depicting the trip using a variety of materials. Use the information as the focus of future discussions about the community.

Hints for Success:

● Create a pretend setting in the classroom that matches in some ways the site children actually visited. Provide simple props such as stamps, writing pads, and envelopes for a post office; books, library cards, and "computers" for a library; old radio parts, telephones, orwriting pads and chairs in rows to simulate vehicles for police and fire stations. Encourage children to incorporate their new information in pretend play and construction activities.

To Simplify:

● Visit a site in the school, such as the school library or program office.

To Extend:

● Encourage children to create their own props. After children have pretended taking on the roles of community personnel, take a return trip to the site as a way of finding out more detailed information and confirming children's interpretation of the site and roles.

3. Home Proud

Create or purchase representations of different dwellings, apartment houses, trailers, single family houses, and so on. These can be constructed or put together from crates or boxes. Encourage children to use these in pretend play with small people figures and furniture. Be sure to include diverse racial or ethnic figures. Include pets wherever possible. As play proceeds over time, introduce community worker figures that represent a variety of occupations as well as diverse racial or ethnic groups. Make sure that both male and female figures are included in nontraditional roles.

4. International Cuisine

In the Family Living Center, make models and utensils available on a rotating basis, which represent the foods of various ethnic groups. For example, include a wok, spoons (Asian children under 8 years old rarely use chopsticks) and dishes with Asian designs; models of Hispanic food or cooking items (such as rice, beans, tortillas and tortilla presses and rice pots); and Middle East cooking utensils, such as brass pots and dishes. African American foodways could be represented by regional specialties, such as ham, corn, grits, and greens.

Social

1. Social Seniors

To explore diversity in the community, develop a relationship with a senior citizen center or nursing home. Most of these centers are eager for visits from young people and will be very receptive to your overtures. Arrange for the group to visit. Bring some activities from the school to share with the residents, such as reading a story and singing songs. Engage in some of the activities at the center, such as snack time, exercises, and so on. A very good way to "break the ice" is to have the youngsters share some hand lotion with the seniors. First the lotion is put on the child's hands and then the child rubs it on an older persons' hands. Arrange for some of the older people to visit the classroom and to participate in the normal school day. Send letters and pictures back and forth as a way to continue the relationship.

Hints for Success:

● Prepare children in advance for seeing people in wheelchairs or using walkers. Talk about older people in positive ways—they have lived a long time and had many experiences.

To Simplify:

● Begin with an retired person visiting the classroom. Choose someone who is related to one of the children in order to provide some personal connection for the youngsters in the group.

To Extend:

● Once the relationship has been established, maintain a schedule of visits (a few times a year). Each time prepare children to find out different information from the elders, such as age, number of grandchildren, and remembrances of their youth. Prepare a "memory book" that includes photos of the visits, stories the older people have told, and the children's writings and illustrations. Add to this book each time a visit is made and keep it available so children and adults may refer to it.

2. We Share

Adopt a family in the community. Find out from a local social service agency the name and composition of a family in need. Try to match the age of one of the children to that of your class. Introduce the family to the school children by name, without bringing the family into school. Through notes to your children's parents, collect clothing, food, and toys. Compare the family's needs with the children's own need for shelter, food, clothing, recreation, and so on. Discuss how people often are dependent on others in the community to help satisfy their basic needs. Talk about the values of helping and sharing.

Hint for Success:
● Carry out this project over a period of months, so children have the idea that such activities extend beyond traditional holiday charity.

3. Yesterday and Today

Introduce the activity by reading stories about "the past." Such stories might include *The Ox-Cart Man* by Donald Hall (1979) or selections from Laura Ingalls Wilder books read aloud to older children. These books are about rural, white America. Another view, although not about the past, is the rural experience of African Americans as depicted in *Big Mama's* by Donald Crews. *Aunt Flossie's Hat (and Crab Cakes Later)* by Elizabeth Fitzgerald Howard (1991) contains reminiscences of urban life in Baltimore earlier in this century. *Family Pictures* by Carmen Lomas Garza (1990) beautifully evokes, in a bilingual text, her experiences growing up in a Hispanic community in Texas.

The next step is to invite some older citizens to your class. Have the group question these visitors about what life was like for them as they grew up. Ask them to make comparisons with present-day experiences. Record their participation on audio- or videotape. Have children create booklets composed of written work, photos, and drawings based on these visits and include them in the class library.

Hint for Success:
● Remember that "the past" for children is not very long ago, and so stories of people, even the ages of their parents, are appropriate.

4. Celebrations

Choose a season or holiday time, such as harvest or winter solstice. Find out if and how different children and families in the classroom celebrate. Ask families to share food, artifacts, customs, clothing, music, and stories with the rest of the group. Integrate these into the on-going activities of the classroom once they have been introduced. For instance, Native American and Asian cultures show evidence of a special respect for elders. Help children better understand this value by including an older person in the classroom on a regular basis. Provide opportunities for children to interact meaningfully with this person during activities and use him or her as a resource to explore the past.

5. Are You Satisfied?

Explore why some people in our country eat food made primarily of rice or wheat. Bring in raw rice and wheat products for children to taste, touch, see and smell. Explain the growing conditions in their country of origin, as well as underscoring the fact that even when people move to different environments, they often carry out practices based on past necessities. People's tastes and preferences are highly influenced by familiar experiences. As a contrast, explore how people make changes when their circumstances change. For instance, people of all cultural backgrounds may eat at particular fast-food restaurants because of convenience, or because their friends introduce them to the new foods.

Hints for Success:
● Bring in actual rice or wheat dishes representing diverse ethnic heritages, such as cream of wheat, rolls, rice cakes and sushi. Provide a place in the room for children to sample these foods before you carry out the discussion.

To Simplify:
● Show children pictures of people planting and harvesting rice and wheat. Point out the different growing conditions (for example, rice is grown in flooded soil while wheat in fairly dry terrain).

To Extend:
● Survey the children to determine which kinds of food appeals to each child. Make a list. Then compare children's preferences. Point out examples of children liking similar and/or different foods. Repeat this extension activity at the end of the unit to determine if children's ideas have changed with exposure to new and different foods.

Dear Parent or Guardian,

We would very much like you to participate in our study of "People Living in Communities." Part of our work is learning how people did things in the past and how they have taught their children some of the songs, games, skills, and stories they remember from their childhood. Some examples of skills might be tying a fishing fly or playing a card game.

If you have learned something special from your grandparents or other older people and would be willing to teach it to children in our class, please send back the form below. I will call you to arrange a time. Remember, the activity doesn't have to be complicated. In fact, simple is better. We look forward to having you in our classroom.

I can come to my child (grandchild's, relative's) class to share a:

song   story   game   skill   other_____

Signed_____

6. From Generation to Generation

Send a note home to children's families requesting that the parent or guardian teach the child some skill, story, song, game, or other activity that was originally learned from a grandparent or other older relative. Provide time in the program when these can be shared or communicated to the rest of the class. Keep a record of what children have learned and, as appropriate, integrate the new skills into the classroom. Find out from parents if they have had to adapt or modify the activity in any way to account for the availability of materials and other resources. Above is an example of the message to parents.

Hint for Success:

● It is best if this activity is carried out over several weeks.

7. Help!

Maintain a classroom "Job" chart, or "Classroom Helper" chart. On it, place symbols representing the various daily tasks that need to be carried out. (Choose the tasks yourself when teaching younger children. Encourage older children to participate in that decision making process.) Sample responsibilities may include watering the plants, caring for classroom pets, signaling the end of free choice time, etc. Allow children to choose the jobs they will perform and be sure that every child is eligible for a job each week. Have a name card for each child that he or she places on the chart upon selecting a task. Make sure to remind children of their jobs, if needed, and provide a time in the day for them to carry them out.

8. Use It

The slogan for environmental awareness is, "Reduce, Reuse, and Recycle." After many discussions about renewable and non-renewable resources, set up a classroom recycling center. Use one container to hold things that can be reused in the classroom, perhaps for other purposes, and another container for those items that the community recycles such as glass or metal. Make sure these latter items are sent or taken to the appropriate recycling place in the community. This would make an excellent field trip as a follow-up activity.

To Simplify:

● Use recyclable materials in art or construction projects.

To Extend:

● Expand the idea of recycling to the school community at large. Keep track over time of any decrease in the amount of things that are thrown away.

● Have a "suggestion box" in the classroom into which children can put ideas for reusing scrap materials.

Teacher Resources

Field Trip Ideas

1. Plan visits to various community agencies or sites where children go before or after school, such as after-school care facilities or a neighborhood center.

2. Visit a local library or city office to view photographs or illustrations of the town, city, or area that were taken long ago. Help children compare what they see now with how their area was in the past.

Classroom Visitors

1. In this unit, with its focus on community, it is especially important to involve the children's families in all aspects of the study. Therefore, make it a regular practice to invite parents or other relatives to school. Many of the activities described in this chapter have suggestions for ways of accomplishing this goal.

2. Invite community leaders, such as government officials or their representatives, to the class to explain their function in helping the community.

3. If your class has formed a pen pal relationship with nearby children, arrange mutual visits.

Children's Books

Angelou, M. (1994). *My Painted House, My Friendly Chicken and Me*. New York: Clarkson Potter.

Carlson, N. (1994). *How to Lose All Your Friends*. New York: Viking.

Cheltenham Elementary School Kindergartners. (1991). *We Are All Alike. We Are All Different*. New York: Scholastic.

Crews, D. (1991). *Big Mama's*. New York: Greenwillow.

Crews, D. (1984). *School Bus*. New York: Greenwillow.

Fox, M. (1985). *Wilfrid Gordon McDonald Partridge*. Brooklyn, NY: Jabe/Miller Book Publishers.

Garza, C. L. (1991). *Family Pictures*. San Francisco: Children's Book Press.

Hall D. (1979). *The Ox-Cart Man*. New York: Viking.

Howard, E. F. (1990). *Aunt Flossie's Hats (and Crabcakes Later)*. New York: Clarion Books.

Keagan, M. (1991). *Pueblo Boy: Growing up in Two worlds*. New York: Cobblehill Books.

Komaiko, L. (1990). *My Perfect Neighborhood*. New York: HarperCollins.

Kuklin, S. (1992). *How My Family Lives in America*. New York: Bradbury Press.

Kurelek, W. (1984) *A Prairie Boy's Winter*. NY: Houghton Mifflin.

Kurelek, W. (1975). *A Prairie Boy's Summer*. Buffalo, NY: Tundra Books.

Lenski, L. (1965). *Sing a Song of People*. Boston: Little Brown.

Mathieu, J. (1979). *The Olden Days*. New York: Random House.

Provensen, A. & M. (1987). *Shaker Lane*. New York, NY: Viking.

Waber, B. (1964). *Just Like Abraham Lincoln*. New York: Scholastic.

Weiss, L. (1985). *My Teacher Sleeps at School*. New York: Viking.

Williams, V. B. (1982). *A Chair for My Mother*. New York: Greenwillow.

Young, E. (1989). *Lon Po Po*. New York: Scholastic.

Zemach, M. (1983). *The Little Red Hen*. New York: Farrar, Straus and Giroux.

Adult References

Cech, M. (1991). *Globalchild: Multicultural Resources for Young Children*. New York: Addison Wesley.

Communication

Dear _____,

    How are you? I am fine.

        Love,

        _____

    xxooxx

Extra! Extra!
Read all about it!

Stay tuned . . . . Details at eleven.

Scientific advances are having a profound impact upon our communication with others. Today, satellites allow the simultaneous transmission of television signals around the globe. It is possible to have instant communication with people all over the world via E-mail and the Internet. With a telephone and a computer, people can shop and bank from home. Adults are trying hard to keep up and adapt to these changes. The children with whom we work will probably have even more dramatic advancements with which to cope. In order to be effective communicators on a worldwide scale, it is important to first learn how to communicate directly on a person-to-person basis. It is also important to learn how to be discriminate viewer-consumers. It is our hope that this unit will serve as a beginning for such learning.

Purpose

People are social creatures. They enjoy being with other people, working, playing, laughing, and talking together. The key to satisfying social interactions is the ability to communicate effectively. In order to interact successfully, children (and adults!) must be able to recognize, interpret, and respond to the overtures of others. This unit has been developed to assist you in supporting your children as they begin to master these basic communication skills. As advancements in the world of electronics proceed at an ever-increasing rate, so, too, does the impact of electronic media. While the technicalities of these advancements are not something that can be readily understood by children, it is our hope that the activities in the media mini-themes will help your children begin to be better consumers of visual and print media.

Implementation

The "Communication" unit consists of three mini-themes: "Interpersonal Communication," "Print Media," and "Visual Media." In "Interpersonal Communication," the activities are designed to provide opportunities for children to practice communicating with others and to learn about some alternate means of communication used by special populations. It is up to you, the teacher, to provide continuous feedback to the children as they practice listening, responding, and speaking.

Option One: Some of the activities in the "Interpersonal Communication" mini-theme may be introduced early in the year and used frequently throughout the year or as a regular part of the weekly program.

Option Two: Plan a three- or four-week "Communication" unit.

Week 1 (or 1 & 2)	Interpersonal Communication
Week 2 (or 3)	Print Media
Week 3 (or 4)	Visual Media

Option Three:

Week 1	Writers, from *Teaching Young Children Using Themes* (GoodYearBooks, 1991)
Week 2	Print Media
Week 3	Visual Media

Option Four:

Week 1	Interpersonal Communication
Week 2	Visual Media with an emphasis on viewing habits and choices
Week 3	Visual Media with an emphasis on being wise consumers

Interpersonal Communication

Terms, Facts, and Principles (TFPs)

General Information

1. Communication is the process by which people share ideas, thoughts, information, and feelings with other people.
2. People communicate with each other by speaking, writing, and gesturing.
3. There are two forms of direct communication between people: verbal and non-verbal.

Verbal Communication

4. Verbal communication occurs when a person talks with or to another person.
5. Verbal communication uses words to express thoughts, feelings, emotions, and information.
6. In order to understand what a person is saying, it is important to pay attention to the speaker.
7. People know that others are paying attention if they look at them, listen quietly, and ask related questions.
*8. Speakers are bothered if listeners interrupt while they are talking.
*9. It is considered polite to wait until a speaker stops or pauses in order to comment or ask a question.
*10. If listeners do not pay careful attention to a speaker, they often do not hear or understand what the speaker is saying.

Non-Verbal Communication

11. Non-verbal communication consists of facial expressions, gestures, and body language.
12. It is often possible to determine how a person is feeling by looking at his/her face and/or the position and movement of his/her body.

13. The way in which a person moves his/her body is sometimes called body language.

*14. Some elements of body language include posture, position, and speed of movement.

*15. People move their hands and other body parts in gestures to emphasize what they are saying.

16. Sometimes people communicate ideas and feelings to others by using hand and body gestures.

17. Some common gestures include: head nods, head shakes, winks, pointing, shrugging, covering ears or eyes with the hands, and clapping.

18. People sometimes attempt to communicate with others who do not speak their language by using gestures.

Sign Language

*19. People who are unable to hear and/or speak often communicate with gestures and sign language.

*20. Many hearing and speaking people also learn sign language in order to communicate with others who are unable to speak or hear well.

*21. Some people who use sign language use the hand alphabet to finger-spell words to others.

*22. Some people use American Sign Language, which consists of signs for many words and phrases.

*23. People who use American Sign Language think that it enables people to communicate more quickly and effectively than does finger spelling.

*24. Some television broadcasts and theaters now provide signers to interpret the performance in sign language for non-hearing audience members.

*25. Many people think that people using sign language is very beautiful to see.

Activity Ideas

Aesthetic

1. Leader of the Band

For this activity you will need enough rhythm instruments for everyone in your group of children. Before distributing the instruments, tell the children what each one is called and demonstrate how it is used. Explain that you will be leading the band today and that it will be important for the musicians (children) to watch you closely for signals that tell them what to do. Demonstrate a few simple signals and practice them with the children. During the demonstration, have the

children clap their hands or slap their knees. You will want signals for the following actions:

> get ready to play (*raise hand or baton*)
> begin playing (*move hands or baton or point*)
> stop playing (*lower hands or baton*)
> instruments down (*hand in lap or baton down*)

Once the children are familiar with the signals, distribute the instruments. Direct the children to try their instruments three times and then to place them on the floor in front of them. Remind the children of the signals. Give the "get ready" signal and proceed to lead the band in using the instruments.

Hints for Success:

● Prior to using the instruments, have the children practice following the signals while they are clapping, tapping their feet, or clicking their tongue.

● To reduce frustration, have several of each instrument type or trade instruments partway through the activity so that children may try more than one.

To Simplify:

● Prior to using the instruments, have the children practice following the signals while they are clapping or tapping their feet or clicking their tongues.

● Use only one type of instrument such as bells, shakers, or rhythm sticks and introduce only start and stop signals.

To Extend:

● Allow the children to have turns as leader.

● Introduce additional signals such as softer and louder; start and stop different instruments during the "song."

2. Scarecrow Faces

Prepare a scarecrow using an old shirt and a pair of overalls or blue jeans. Pin or sew the pieces together and stuff with straw, newspaper, or cloth. For the head, insert a brown paper grocery sack stuffed with newspaper into the neck of the shirt and pin or sew in place. Attach a pair of stuffed gloves for hands. Provide every child with a large white paper plate, construction paper scraps, yarn, scissors, markers, and paste. Encourage the children to use these materials to create faces that may be used on the class scarecrow body. As the children work, engage them in conversation about the expressions on their scarecrow faces. Display the scarecrow in the classroom and use the child-created faces on a rotating basis until all have had an opportunity to be viewed.

To Simplify:

● Direct the children to draw the scarecrow faces using only markers or crayons.

To Extend:

● Obtain pictures of scarecrows for the children to explore. Provide fabric scraps, buttons, glue, and newspaper for stuffing in addition to the listed materials. Encourage the children to create individual scarecrow bodies to use with their scarecrow faces.

● Suggest that the children prepare and attach labels to explain the facial expressions on their scarecrows.

3. Sign a Song

Learn a simple and familiar song in sign yourself and practice until you are proficient, or invite a visitor to carry out this activity. Remind the children that this is a song that they know well. Sing the song through with the children once, signing as you sing. Ask if the children noticed that you were signing the song as you sang. Go on to explain that now you are going to teach them to sing the song by signing. Begin by talking through the words of the song as you sign it for the children. Sign and say the first phrase, and repeat, asking the children to sign it with you. Continue with the next phrase. Repeat from the beginning. Continue to add a phrase and repeat from the beginning until you have done the entire song. Practice the song several times over the next few days. You may decide whether you want the signing to accompany vocal singing or if you would prefer to sing silently.

To Simplify:

● Select a very short song or one that repeats the same phrase many times.

To Extend:

● Teach additional songs in sign or have a child teach a signing song to the group.

4. Silent Song

Choose a song with gestures with which the children in your group are very familiar. "Open, Shut Them" works very well to start. After singing it through once, tell the children that you have a challenge for them. The challenge is to sing the song without making any sound with their voices. Tell them that they may mouth the words and do the gestures, but they must not make any sounds. Model this for the children, using very exaggerated gestures and mouth movements. Direct them to

watch you carefully so that you all start and stay together. "Sing" the song with the children. Praise their effort. Sing your silent song frequently during the next few weeks.

♫ Open, Shut Them

Open, shut them, (*Hands extended in front of body, open and close fingers as directed in song.*)

Open, shut them,

Give a little clap.(*Clap hands together.*)

Open, shut them,

Open, shut them,

Lay them in your lap. (*Fold hands and place in lap.*)

Creep them, creep them, (*"Creep" or walk your fingers slowly up your body to your nose.*)

Creep them, creep them,

Right up to your nose.

Creep them, creep them, (*"Creep" or walk your fingers down your body to your toes.*)

Creep them, creep them,

Right down to your toes.

Creep them, creep them, (*"Creep" or walk your fingers slowly up your body to your chin.*)

Slowly creep them

Right up to your chin.

Open wide your little mouth, (*Open mouth wide.*)

But do not let them in! (*Quickly hide hands behind your back.*)

To Simplify:

● Sing the song with only the first, second, and last verses, omitting verses three and four.

To Extend:

● Choose other songs to sing silently.

● Encourage the children to help you to identify songs with many clear gestures that would make good silent songs.

5. Word and Mouth Collage

Prepare red mouth and pink tongue-shaped papers ahead of time, enough for every child to have one of each. Provide magazine pages with print, scissors, glue, pencils for names, and clean-up sponges. Direct the children to place their names on the backs of their mouth-shaped papers and to glue the tongues on the other side. Tell the children to find some words on the

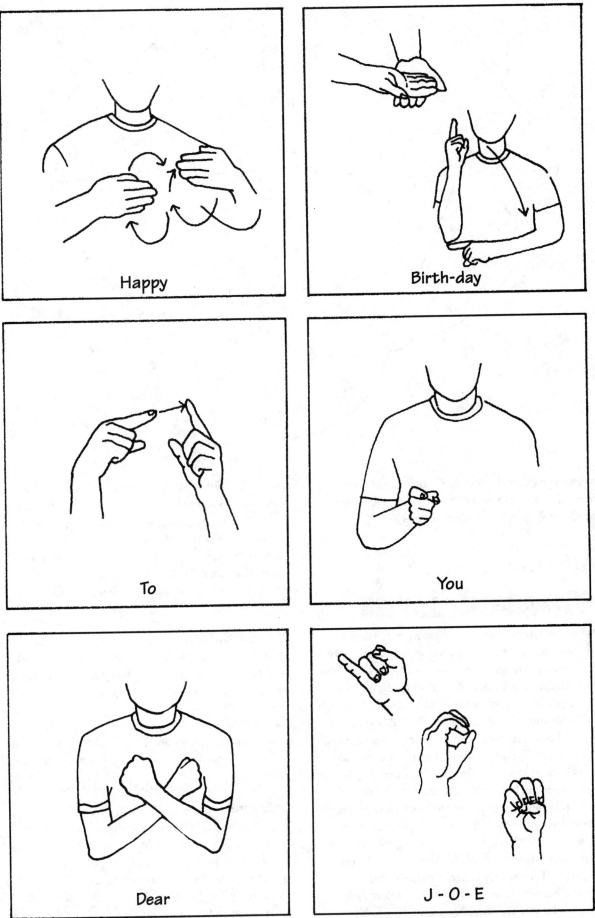

Happy

Birth-day

To

You

Dear

J - O - E

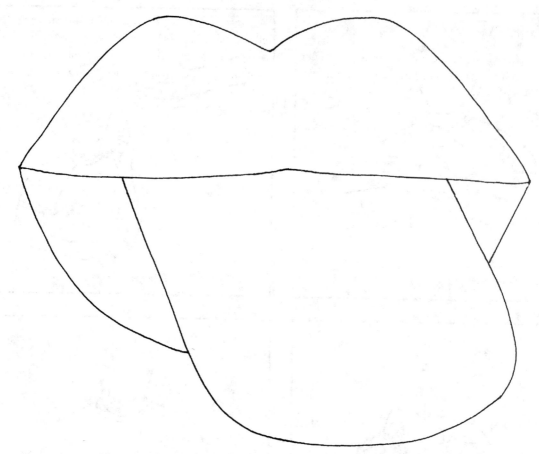

magazine pages and to cut them out and paste these on their "mouths." Stress that in verbal communication, words are spoken (come out of mouths).

Affective

1. Auction

This activity will give the children with whom you work an opportunity to develop individual non-verbal signals and to recognize signals made by other children. Gather a collection of small and inexpensive toys (perhaps a bag of party favors or small animals), enough for each child to "buy" one or two. You also will need some tokens to use as money: counters, chips, pennies, or play coins. Explain to the children that people sometimes hold auctions to sell things that many people may be interested in purchasing. An auctioneer directs the auction by describing the item to be sold and by recognizing the bids or offers that potential purchasers make. Sometimes, auction bidders use silent signals to let the auctioneer know that they are willing to pay the price suggested. Tell the children that you are going to have a pretend auction. Direct each child to think of a silent signal to let you, the auctioneer, know that he/she is interested in bidding on the item offered. Give each

child a few of the tokens and remind them that they may only bid as much as they have. Begin by holding up the first item and suggesting a price; watch for silent signals and announce the bids that you see. Sell the item to the highest bidder. Continue with other items until all are sold. As the auction progresses, tell the children to watch the others to see if they can detect who is bidding.

Hint for Success:

● If you do not wish to purchase and give toys away, auction off play spaces, classroom jobs, or other popular privileges.

To Simplify:

● Omit the tokens and conduct the auction, selling each item to the first bidder who has not yet purchased anything.

To Extend:

● Further explain that the highest bidder gets the item, but that bidders try to get items for bargain prices and so do not make their high bids until they must in order to get the desired item. Let the children know that bidders may only bid as much as they have. Distribute chips or pretend money to be used. Conduct the auction.

● Give children opportunities to be auctioneers.

2. Call Me

Prepare a book cover to be used for a class telephone directory. Draw a telephone on the cover and title it "Class Telephone Numbers." Provide a sheet of paper for each person in the class. Direct each child to write his/her name and telephone number on a paper cut to fit in the directory. Have some children assist you in putting the directory together in alphabetical order. Place the directory next to a telephone model and encourage the children to look up the name of a friend, then dial that number.

To Simplify:
● Prepare the telephone directory and make one for each child to take home. Suggest that parents allow the children to use the directories to make occasional calls to classmates.

To Extend:
● Provide blank directories and writing materials. Encourage the children to look up the numbers of friends in the class directory and to make a directory for their personal use.

3. How Was Your Day?

This activity is designed to enable the children to begin to evaluate their experiences. Introduce the activity in a total group setting near the end of a day. Use a chalkboard or wipe-off board or prepare a laminated posterboard for your evaluation sheet:

Show the faces to the children and ask them to tell you what they think they mean. Read the words that accompany the symbols and tell the children that you are going to use these faces to let them know what kind of day you have had. Talk about the things that happened to you during the day, pointing to one of the corresponding faces as you relate each experience:

When I got up and looked outside, I saw that it was raining and that made me unhappy (#2 face). I had a delicious orange with my breakfast and oranges are my favorite thing (#5 face). When I got to school, Jeffrey gave me a hug (#5 face). I saw someone hit a friend (#1 face)." Continue with other events and conclude with "All in all, today was a pretty good day so I would rate it as a good or '4 day'."

Mark your "4 day" with the appropriate marker on your sample evaluation sheet. Ask the children to think about their days and to tell you what kind of day they each have had. Record these if you wish. Later, or the next day, provide evaluation sheets for the children and have them record the evaluation of their day.

Hints for Success:
● To support the children in becoming effective evaluators, avoid over-emphasis on "5 or terrific" days. They may think that terrific days are expected.

● Also, refrain from over-reacting when a child indicates that she/he has had a terrible day. Too much attention might cause the child to repeat this. Be very

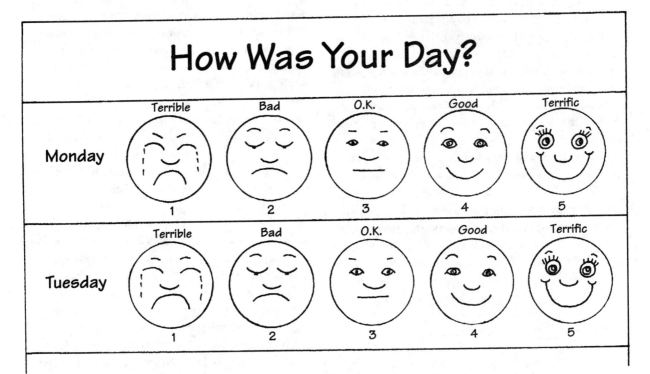

matter-of-fact and accepting, no matter how a child evaluates a day.

● If you have a child who frequently indicates that days are terrible, you may wish to discuss these feelings in private. Point out that you have a really terrific day every once in a while; most days are good or O.K.; a few are bad or terrible.

To Simplify:

● Provide only three choices: Good, O.K., and Bad.

To Extend:

● Make this an ongoing part of your daily routine. As the children become comfortable with this, vary the daily procedure by evaluating different components of the day: outdoor time, story time, the art activity, and so forth.

4. It's My Turn

To illustrate the importance of turn-taking in conversation, present a demonstration of many people talking at once. Ask five or six children to help you by inviting them up to the front of the class. Quietly tell these volunteers that you are going to be talking to the rest of the class and that you want them to be talking at the same time. Suggest that they talk loudly about anything that they choose when you give them the "go" signal (point to them) and that they stop when you give the "cut" signal (cross hands in front of your body and simultaneously move each hand quickly to the side). Address the rest of the class and tell them that you have some directions about the next activity; remind them to listen carefully. As you begin to talk softly about the next activity, point to your interrupting assistants to give them the "go" cue. Continue talking for a few moments; then give the "cut" cue. Ask if anyone has any questions about the activity. Did everyone hear the directions? Conduct a discussion about what happened. Suggest that it is very confusing when many people talk at once. Ask if the children have any ideas that would let others know when they want to have a turn to talk and be heard. Continue discussing with the group until an "It's My Turn" cue is agreed upon. Encourage the children to practice using the cue with each other. As you notice children using and responding to this cue, be sure to offer lots of reinforcing praise. Be on the alert for opportunities to use the cue yourself and to suggest its use by the children.

5. Sign Your Name

Obtain some charts with the sign language alphabet or use a book such as *The Handmade Alphabet* (1991) or *Signing for Kids: The Fun Way to Learn American Sign Language* (1991) to assist you in forming the sign language letters. Explain to the children that people who are unable to hear and speak sometimes use their hands to communicate with others. This may be done by using the hand alphabet or American Sign Language that uses signs for entire words. Tell them that today they will be learning some of the alphabet hand signals. Show the chart or book to a child and assist in forming the letters in her/his name. Keep the book or chart available in the classroom to encourage further exploration and practice.

To Simplify:

● Teach the child how to form only the first initial in her/his name.

To Extend:

● Encourage the children to learn how to sign the initials or names of other children in the class.

● Teach the children a few common words from American Sign Language.

Cognitive

1. Listen to Me!

Select a material such as colored cubes, pattern blocks, Unifix™ cubes, or small animal counters. Make a simple screen by placing a cardboard box on edge atop a table so that two children can sit across from each other and talk without seeing what the other person is doing. Put the screens aside. Pair the children, have them sit directly across from each other, and give each of them an identical supply of the material (limit this supply initially to five or six pieces per child). Direct one child in each pair to arrange four pieces in any way that he or she chooses. After the pieces are set, the person who arranged them gives verbal directions to the partner who attempts to make an identical arrangement. Stress that it is very important to give clear directions and to listen carefully. In addition, remind the children that they may *not* touch the other person's material; they may only give and receive verbal assistance. Have the children switch roles and repeat the activity. Continue, adding more pieces to the arrangements. Note that up to this point the children have been receiving verbal instruction while also being able to see what the partner is doing. Next, place the box screen

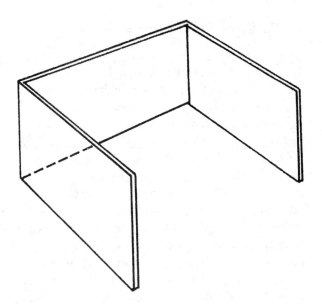

between the partners so that they cannot see each other. Have them try arranging the pieces again with only verbal cues. Start with three- or four-piece arrangements. After each arrangement has been attempted, remove the screen and have the partners compare the results. Talk with the children about how much more difficult the task is when only the verbal directions are given. Have the children continue this activity until they are able to give and follow simple verbal directions with accuracy.

To Simplify:
● Provide only three material pieces for each child.
● Give the directions yourself; have children attempt to form the described arrangement.

To Extend:
● Give pattern cards to one child on the team and ask him or her to verbally describe the arrangement portrayed on the card to the other.
● Provide large amounts of material from which the child giving directions may choose.

2. Mood Match

Collect several pictures of people with varied facial expressions. Be sure to include a representative sampling of individuals including varied ethnic backgrounds, sexes, and ages. Also collect pictures that depict a variety of events or objects. Invite a few children to join you in matching the facial expressions to the objects or events. Begin by displaying one picture of a person and three or four of the event and/or object pictures: ask the children to show you which of the pictures would cause the person to look the way shown in the picture. Prompt the children to explain their responses by statements such as "Tell me how you think this person is feeling" and "How do you think you would feel if you saw/had/did_____?" Show the children other facial expression pictures and discuss how they think the people in the pictures are feeling. When they seem ready to proceed, provide three or four pictures of people along with several object/event pictures and direct the children to match the object/event pictures with the corresponding facial expression picture.

To Simplify:
● Provide only a few pictures with fairly obvious pairings (a smile with an ice cream cone, tears with a bruise or fall, and so on).

To Extend:
● Briefly explain the task of a matching facial expression with the object or event and allow the children to independently sort, using many pictures in both groups.

Construction

1. All the Ships at Sea

Provide red, yellow, blue, white, and black construction paper; scissors; paste; and a poster or book that depicts the alphabet signal flags used by "All the Ships at Sea" (see pages 234–35). Encourage the children to construct a signal flag that depicts their own initials. Mount these signal flags on each child's cubby, locker, or chair.

Hint for Success:
● Create an initial flag of your own to serve as a model. The flags should be large: use a 12" x18" piece of construction paper upon which to mount the flag pieces.

To Simplify:
● Precut the shapes that will be needed to form the letters. Provide these shapes, backing paper, paste, and the flag letter guide. Direct the children to find the pieces needed to form their initial flags and to paste the pieces on a backing sheet of paper.

To Extend:
● Allow lots of time (several days) and encourage the children to create many letter flags to form entire names or other words of their choice.

2. No-Talk Block Structures

Announce that there will be no talking permitted in the block area today. (Use this activity only if you think that your children have the maturity to follow through.) Tell the children that they will have to communicate with each other nonverbally by using facial expressions and gestures. Suggest that they try to develop some signals or cues to let others know what they are trying to do. Visit the area frequently during play to assist in using and interpreting nonverbal communication techniques. Be sure to think of some nonverbal signals of your own to let the children know that they are doing a great job.

3. Silent Cooperation

Select a simple construction activity for this experience. Modeling dough, clay, or collage materials work well. Announce that there will be no talking in the construction area today. Discuss some possible signals with the children that can be used to ask for materials, to let someone know that you like their creation, or to ask for a work space. Limit the materials that you put out to encourage the children to interact with each other. Post a child number limit sign in the area if your children are accustomed to these. As with all activity areas, visit the area often to offer support and encouragement, nonverbally of course.

Language

1. Letter to a Friend

Read aloud a book such as C. Brighton's *Dearest Grandmama* (1991) or Pat Brisson's *Your Best Friend, Kate* (1989). Both books consist of letters written by children to important people in their lives. Then prepare multiple copies of some simple phrases that might be used in letters between friends. Some possible phrases:

> Dear _____,
>
> Yours truly,
>
> Love,
>
> How are you?
>
> I am glad that you are my friend.
>
> I like you.
>
> I hope to see you soon.
>
> Did you have fun at school today?
>
> What will you do after school?
>
> It is very warm here today.
>
> It is cold today.
>
> It is raining here.
>
> I miss you.

> I walked to school today.
>
> I rode the bus to school today.

Also provide blank paper, envelopes, scissors, paste, and pencils. Explain to the children that friends sometimes write letters to each other. Continue to explain that letters usually begin with a greeting that includes the friend's name, such as "Dear Ann" or "Dear Mike." Letters often include news about the writer and display interest in the friend's activities. Tell the children that today they will each write a letter to a friend. Show them the prepared phrases and direct them to choose some they would like to include in their letter. Make the other materials available so that the children can cut and paste the strips that they wish to use as they create their letters. Remind children to add the friend's name to the salutation and to sign their own names after the closing.

To Simplify:

- Provide a very limited choice of phrases.
- Create a sample letter using suggestions from the children. Provide copies of this sample to which children may add their personal greeting and closing.

To Extend:

- Have the children help think of possible phrases to use in a letter. Write these on the board. Direct the children to write letters to friends that include some of these phrases.

2. Sharing Day

Choose a day to be "Sharing Day" in your classroom. Tell the children that they will each have an opportunity to share one item with some of their friends at school. Model* for the group by sharing an item of your own with them:

a. Select an item to share, perhaps a family picture or one article from a collection.

b. Place your name on the item and put it in a bag. Place the bag under your chair.

c. Gather the children in a group and introduce the idea of Sharing Day. Tell them that you have brought something to share with all of them and that they will each have a chance to bring something to share with a few friends the next day.

d. Direct the children to listen and watch as you share your special item with them.

e. Show them the bag and take the item out of the bag. Hold it so all can see. Tell them what it is

---

*Use this introductory time to focus on appropriate listening behavior. Also, suggest questions to be asked and establish procedures for the children to use with each other. Provide the children with lots of cues regarding listening, attending, and waiting.

and something about it. Tell them where you got it or why it is special to you.

f. After you have displayed and described the item, give the children time to ask questions about it. Answer the questions.

g. Tell the children that you have decided to pass the item around so that everyone may see and hold it. If appropriate, state some rules about how it is to be handled.

h. Pass the item around the group.

i. Once all have had a chance to see the item, put it back in your bag and put it under your chair.

Tell the children that they may each choose one item to bring for Sharing Day the next day. Remind them to choose something that they can tell about and that they want their friends to see. The next day, divide the children into groups of five or six children and assign each group a place to meet for Sharing Day. Direct the children to place their sharing items under their chairs. Give each child an opportunity to show and describe her or his item to the children in their group. (If you are the only teacher in your classroom, establish a way to let the children know when it is time for the next person to have a turn. You might use a bell: one ding to warn of one more minute; three dings to signify time to change speakers.) Encourage children to respond to questions from others. Remind them that items should be placed under their chairs after each turn. After all children have displayed their items, they may decide if they wish to pass their items around the table. If they choose to do so, all items should be passed simultaneously to reduce waiting time.

Hints for Success:

● If a child does not bring an item to share, allow the child to select an item from the classroom.

● After sharing time is finished, direct children to place all items in their lockers, cubbies, and so on.

● Let parents know that the children will each be bringing in one item of their choice to display and to discuss with others in a sharing group. Provide some guidelines to assist parents in helping their children to select items for Sharing Day. Some suggestions include:

• All items should be clearly marked with the child's name.

• Items should not be valuable or fragile.

• Unless requested, items should not be edible.

• Weapons are not welcome.

• Items should be manageable by the child—the child should be able to carry and operate it independently.

● Parents can also help by having their children tell them something about the item before bringing it to school. Children should be able to:

• Name the item.

• Describe the item (color, shape, and so on).

• Share something about its history (where/when they got it, and so on).

• Tell something special about it (why child likes it, how it is used).

To Simplify:

● Assign each child a particular day for her/his Sharing Day. Have the child present the item to the total group with your support. To reduce group sitting time, eliminate passing the item during group time. You may wish to allow the child and/or the item to have a special place in the classroom after group time for other children to have an opportunity to see it close up and/or handle it.

To Extend:

● Have a regular Sharing Day each week.

● Designate a particular category of sharing item for each week (something red, something from your backyard, something from your bedroom, something soft, something that starts with the letter P, a favorite picture book). Ask parents to assist children in identifying items that fit in the agreed-upon categories. These categories may be theme-related if you choose. You may also wish to request items that may be used for other classroom experiences as well as for Sharing Day (five small things for a counting activity, items to graph, etc.).

3. Signal Flags

Construct ship signal flag labels for various areas in the classroom. (See "All the Ships at Sea," page 231.) Print the corresponding letters on strips of paper and fasten under the flag letters. Post these as area labels in the appropriate spots.

To Simplify:

● Choose only a few areas to label with signal flags. Leave the flags in place with the accompanying words for a long period of time.

To Extend:

● After a few days, remove the letters, but leave the signal flags in place. After the children have become accustomed to them, take the flags down and give one to each child. Direct the children to put the signal flag labels in the correct places. Make the signal flag reference guide available for use as needed.

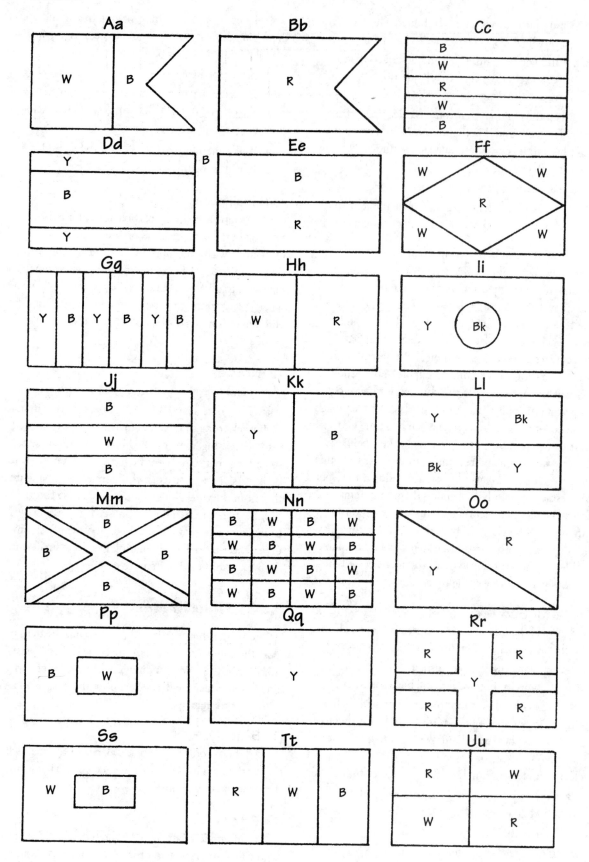

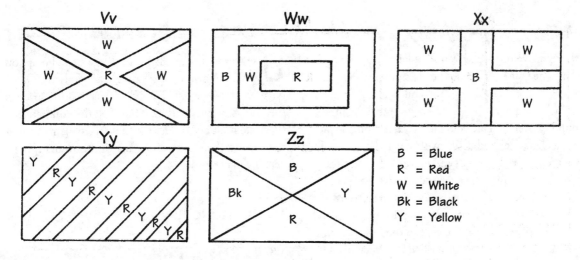

Vv
W
W R W
W

Ww
B W R

Xx
W W
B
W W

Yy
Y
R
Y
R
Y
R
Y
R
Y
R

Zz
B
Bk Y
R

B = Blue
R = Red
W = White
Bk = Black
Y = Yellow

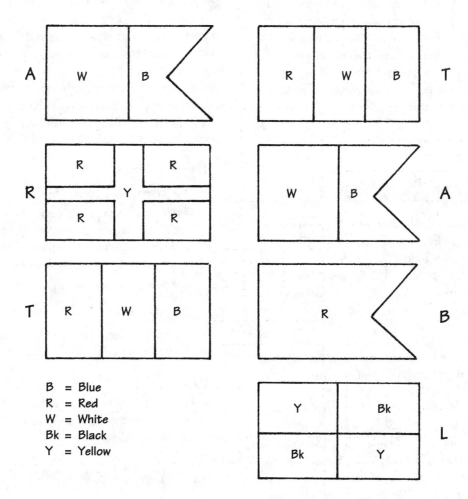

A W B

T R W B

R R R
Y
R R

A W B

T R W B

B R

B = Blue
R = Red
W = White
Bk = Black
Y = Yellow

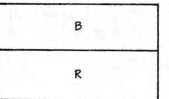

L Y Bk
Bk Y

E B
R

4. Telephone Game

Gather five or six children in order to play the telephone game (or divide the class into several small groups of five or six). Arrange the children in a circle on the floor, sitting not too close to each other. Explain to the children that you are going to play a listening game called "Telephone" and that it will be very important to listen carefully to the message. Also tell them that the person giving the message must speak very clearly so that the message may be understood by the listener. Speak a very brief message to one child in the group and direct that child to tell the message to the next person. Continue passing the message around the group until it reaches the last person who says the message out loud for all to hear. Compare the final message with the original statement. Encourage the children to evaluate their effectiveness in listening and passing the message. Try again with a different message. If the first try was not successful, encourage the children to listen more carefully in order to improve their ability to pass a clear message around the entire group.

Physical

1. Braille Letters

Ask your local or state librarian to help you locate copies of outdated magazines printed in Braille and make them available for the children in your classroom to explore. Encourage the children to gently rub their fingertips over the letters to see how they feel and to attempt to differentiate among the letters.

To Simplify:

● Simply allow the children to physically and visually explore the Braille magazines independently.

To Extend:

● Obtain a Braille printing guide and use it as a guide to form some sample Braille letters. Make your letters by arranging small dabs of glue, in Braille letter formations, onto heavy paper or tagboard and allowing the glue to dry. The dried glue forms bumps, which can be felt with the fingertips. Encourage the children to identify the letters by matching what they feel to the Braille printing guide.

● Obtain a Braille writing tool and allow the children to practice creating Braille letters with the tool.

2. The Bumps Tell Us

Use white or colored glue to create small bumps on pieces of heavy paper or tagboard. When they have dried, tape these "bumps" at each seating space on the underside of the snack table. Tell the children that there are limit cues under the table today. Direct them to feel with their fingertips to discover how many crackers they may have.

Pretend Play

1. Birthday Party

Provide a table, tablecloth, napkins; chairs; party decorations; games; dress-up clothes; invitations; and pretend cake, ice cream, and gifts. Suggest that the children hold pretend birthday parties for each other. Before beginning the party, hold a brief discussion about party activities, scripts, and behavior. Encourage the children to practice giving and receiving gifts, singing "Happy Birthday," and acknowledging each other with appropriate verbal communication.

To Prepare Props:

Ice cream-yarn pompons

Gifts-small boxes wrapped in gaily decorated paper and covered with clear vinyl adhesive (be sure to tell the children that the packages are empty and should not be opened)

Cake-a decorated box or papier-mâché

To Simplify:

● Limit the number of props provided and the number of children permitted at the party at one time

To Extend:

● Prior to the "party," involve the children in making invitations, decorating a paper party tablecloth, and preparing other party props.

2. Operator

Prepare a switchboard by using a cardboard box. Use a large nail to punch an arrangement of holes in one side of the box and place numeral stickers under each hole. Attach several lengths of heavy string or yarn to the bottom of the box and tie a small bolt on the end of each. These will be used to connect calls. Add a set of headphones to the switchboard. Also gather several telephones and place them at play spaces near the switchboard. Each telephone should have a numeral sticker that corresponds to one on the switchboard. One child serves as operator and runs the switchboard. Other children use the telephones and ask the operator to connect them to another phone.

To Simplify:

● Limit the number of phones to two or three and use single-digit numerals or an easily recognizable picture for the "telephone numbers."

To Extend:

● Provide a directory for the operator. This is a sheet of paper that is in a wipe-off folder or is laminated. Numerals corresponding to those on the telephones should be listed with a space for names next to them. Provide a wipe-off crayon to list the names of children at the telephones.

3. Post Office

Preparing for this pretend play setting gives you a chance to recycle some of your junk mail. Ask the parents of the children in your class to also save items to contribute. Some of the items that can be used include envelopes, post cards, and magazine order stamps. Gather paper, envelopes, pencils, stamps, rubber stamps, paper punches, a scale, and some small boxes. Add some large purses or grocery sack "mail bags," caps for letter carriers, and a mail box. Arrange these materials in the pretend play area. The children may serve as postal clerks, letter carriers, and patrons. Children who participate in this activity often write several letters, many to their classmates, so it is a good idea to also make available a listing of the names of the children in the class to be used when writing letters.

Social

1. Charades

Prepare several slips of paper with simple actions or an animal name on each. Place the papers in a bag or other container. Introduce the game during a whole group time by telling the children that some people like to play a game called "Charades." Explain that in this game one person silently acts out an action or the name of something that the others try to identify. No talking is allowed by the person who is doing the charade. Model by performing a charade yourself. Choose something like brushing your teeth or playing the guitar. Tell the children to watch everything that you do, because after you have finished, they will have a chance to identify the action that you were performing. Make sure to

perform all of the actions that you would use in carrying out the selected activity such as picking up the toothbrush, putting on toothpaste, turning on the water, and so on. After you complete your performance, call on children to identify the action. Give each child an opportunity to draw one of the slips out of the container and act out the named action. Allow the performer to call on people to identify the action and to select the next person to perform.

Hints for Success:

● During your modeling and the performances by the children, remind the audience to wait until the entire charade has been completed and they are called upon before making their guesses.

● Remind the children that if they draw an animal name, they must act it out silently; no animal noises may be used.

To Simplify:

● The teacher remains in charge of calling on people to identify actions and choosing the next performer.

● Provide only very simple and familiar actions such as hand-washing, eating a banana, or painting a picture.

To Extend:

● Provide paper and pencils. Encourage the children to think of their own actions and to write them down on a slip of paper before the game is played. As each child is called upon to perform, he/she gives the written slip to the teacher.

2. Classroom Signals

After introducing the idea of nonverbal communication, suggest that it might be helpful and fun to have some private signals for use only by your class. Suggest some times when it is important to communicate with the group when you are out of the classroom, and encourage the children to suggest some signals that could be used during these times. Some of these times might include: outdoor cleanup, time to line up to leave an area such as the lunchroom or gym, time for drinks of water, or rest periods. Decide with the group on some signals to use and practice them for a time. They may become part of your regular routine.

To Simplify:

● Select the times and signals and introduce them to the class one at a time. After one is firmly established, add others.

To Extend:

● Ask the children to help you think of other times when such signals might be useful and to suggest signals. Experiment using them and, with the group, decide which are helpful and should be continued.

3. Hello in Many Languages

Before presenting this activity, prepare several signs or posters with the word *hello* in a different language on each. This is a fine way to involve parents. Ask parents to help you in preparing the signs in languages with which they are familiar. Be sure to ask them to help you learn the correct pronunciation before using these greetings. Introduce the new words to the children one at a time over several days. Use these greetings throughout the day at school and encourage the children to also use them.

4. If You're Friendly and You Know It, Say "Bonjour."

Sing the familiar "If You're Happy and You Know It" song with the new words introduced in the

HELLO
English

ALOHA
Hawaiian

HOLA
Spanish

SHALOM
Hebrew

GUTEN TAG
German

BONJOUR
French

MABUHAY
Filipino

안녕
Korean

こんにちは
Japanese

你好
Chinese

activity above ("Hello in Many Languages"). Substitute "friendly" for "happy" and use greetings in the varied languages.

French:

If you're friendly and you know it,
Say Bonjour........Bonjour.

If you're friendly and you know it,
Say Bonjour........Bonjour.

If you're friendly and you know it,
Then your words will surely show it.

If you're friendly and you know it,
Say Bonjour........Bonjour.

Spanish: (*Hola* or *Buenos dias*)

If you're friendly and you know it,
Say Hola........Hola.

If you're friendly and you know it,
Say Hola........Hola.

If you're friendly and you know it,
Then your words will surely show it.

If you're friendly and you know it,
Say Hola........Hola.

Japanese:

If you're friendly and you know it,
Say Kon Ni Chi Wa........Kon Ni Chi Wa.

If you're friendly and you know it,
Say Kon Ni Chi Wa........Kon Ni Chi Wa.

If you're friendly and you know it,
Then your words will surely show it.

If you're friendly and you know it,
Say Kon Ni Chi Wa........Kon Ni Chi Wa.

Korean:

If you're friendly and you know it,
Say An NYoung........An NYoung.

If you're friendly and you know it,
Say An NYoung........An NYoung

If you're friendly and you know it,
Then your words will surely show it.

If you're friendly and you know it,
Say An NYoung........An NYoung

Also try:

Hebrew	Shalom
German	Guten Tag
Chinese	Nee How
Arabic	As-sa-la-mu A-lay-kum

5. Name Bingo

Prepare a set of Bingo cards and corresponding calling cards for your classroom. On the cards, use the names of the children in the class instead of the traditional Bingo numerals. Tell the children that they will be playing a very special game of Bingo. Distribute cards so that each child has one; also distribute markers or chips to use to cover the names called. Direct the children to look at their cards and to tell you what they see. Give each child an opportunity to share her/his observations. Place the calling cards in a container and shake them up to mix. Tell the children that they are trying to either cover the entire card or a straight line (your choice). Draw one calling card at a time and read the name. Tell the children to look at their game cards to see if they have that name. If they do, tell them to cover the name with a chip. Continue calling names until a child calls out "Bingo" or "Friends" or whatever you designate as the signal for a completed bingo.

To Simplify:

● Prepare sets of cards for small groups of five to six children. Include only the names of the children in the small group and play the game only with the children in the group.

To Extend:

● Include the names of each child in the class on each card. Vary the arrangement of the names. Everyone should win simultaneously if the children are directed to cover the entire card.

6. Silent Directions

Select a familiar activity for this experience and plan your "Silent Directions" ahead of time. (Folding a sheet of paper or coloring spaces on a sheet of grid paper works well.) Explain to the children that you are going to be using "Silent Directions" during the activity. Conduct the activity using your pre-planned "Silent Directions." At the conclusion of the activity, lead a discussion related to how simple or difficult the children found it to follow the directions. Encourage them to think of behaviors that they engaged in that made it easier or more difficult.

7. The Way You Are

Set up a two-sided art easel with paper and drawing materials, including some pencils, crayons, or markers suitable for skin tones, if possible. Select two children to work as partners on this activity. Place one child on each side of the easel and tell pairs that they will be drawing pictures that show what they have noticed about each other. Direct each child to draw two pictures of or about her or his partner. One picture should show something that the partner likes a lot—a favorite activity or item. The other picture should show something that the partner does not like at all. Tell the children that there should be no talking while they draw; they will get a chance to talk about their pictures after the drawings are finished. When the children have completed the drawing, give each child an opportunity to tell about what she or he has drawn and how she or he decided what to include. Encourage the children to discuss their ideas and observations with each other. You may have the children exchange the pictures or you may wish to display them in the classroom. For display, label pictures with the name of the subject, artist, and "Likes"/"Does Not Like" headings.

To Simplify:

● Instead of drawing, provide a large selection of magazine and catalog picture cut-outs of toys, foods, activities, and so on. and direct children to select items that the partner likes or does not like from this assortment. Choices can be glued onto a paper with appropriate headings.

To Extend:

● Provide booklet pages and covers or pre-made booklets for each child. Direct children to make books about friends or family members with a page for each person to be included in the book. In addition to the person's name, direct children to draw pictures about the person's likes and dislikes. Encourage children to share these books with the people that they have depicted.

Teacher Resources

Field Trip Ideas

1. Arrange a trip to the post office to tour the facility, see the workers, and mail a letter to your classroom or to each child's home.

2. Attend an event that includes a sign interpreter for the children to observe.

3. Visit a class that teaches American Sign Language to observe it being taught.

Classroom Visitors

1. Invite a person who uses American Sign Language to visit the classroom and teach the children a simple song in sign.

2. Invite a mime to visit and demonstrate the art of pantomime.

Children's Books

Ada, A. F. (1994). *Dear Peter Rabbit*. New York: Atheneum.

Ahlberg, J., and Ahlberg, A. (1986). *The Jolly Postman or Other People's Letters*. Boston: Little, Brown.

Brighton, C. (1991). *Dearest Grandmama*. London: Faber and Faber.

Brisson, P. (1989). *Your Best Friend, Kate*. New York: Macmillan.

Butterworth, N. (1993). *Making Faces*. Cambridge, MA: Candlewick Press.

Carle, E. (1972). *The Secret Birthday Message*. New York: Thomas Y. Crowell.

Carlstrom, N. W. (1992). *How Do You Say It Today, Jesse Bear?* New York: Macmillan.

Conrad, P. (1995). *Animal Lingo*. New York: HarperCollins.

deZutter, H. (1993). *Who Says a Dog Goes Bow-Wow?* New York: Delacorte.

Harelson, R. (1981). *SWAK: The Complete Book of Mail Fun for Kids*. New York: Workman.

Hoban, T. (1994). *I Walk and Read*. New York: Greenwillow.

Kennedy, X. J., and Kennedy, D. M. (1992). *Talking Like the Rain: A First Book of Poems*. Boston: Little, Brown.

Krauss, R. (1970). *I Write It*. New York: HarperCollins.

McNulty, F. (1990). *With Love from Koko*. New York: Scholastic.

Meddaugh, S. (1992). *Martha Speaks*. Boston: Houghton Mifflin.

Patterson, F. (1985). *Koko's Kitten*. New York: Scholastic.

Patterson, F. (1987). *Koko's Story*. New York: Scholastic.

Petersen, J. W. (1977). *I Have a Sister. My Sister Is Deaf*. New York: HarperCollins.

Rankin, L. (1991). *The Handmade Alphabet*. New York: Dial Books for Young Readers.

Ross, T. (1985). *The Boy Who Cried Wolf*. New York: Dial Books for Young Readers.

Schick, E. (1992). *I Have Another Language. The Language Is Dance*. New York: Macmillan.

Showers, P. (1966). *How You Talk*. New York: Thomas Y. Crowell.

Viorst, J. (1972). *Alexander and the Horrible, Terrible, No Good, Very Bad Day*. New York: Macmillan.

Yenawine, P. (1991). *Stories*. New York: Delacorte.

Yolen, J. (1994). *Sleep Rhymes Around the World*. Honesdale, PA: Boyds Mills Press.

Zolotow, C. (1992). *This Quiet Lady*. New York: Greenwillow.

Adult References

Flodin, M. (1991). *Signing for Kids: The Fun Way for Anyone to Learn American Sign Language*. New York: Putnam Publishing Group.

Kostelnik, et al. (1991). *Teaching Young Children Using Themes*. Glenview, IL: GoodYearBooks.

Macaulay, D. (1988). *The Way Things Work*. Boston: Houghton Mifflin.

Print Media

Terms, Facts, and Principles (TFPs)

General Information

1. Sometimes people wish to communicate information or ideas to large numbers of people. One way to do this is through print media.

2. Print media includes newspapers, magazines, flyers, and catalogs.

3. Many print media items are purchased by the people who wish to read them.

4. Some print media items are distributed at no cost by companies or organizations that wish to increase public awareness of particular products, services, or events.

*5. Many print media items include advertisements that are paid for by a company or organization that wishes to make people aware of a product or service.

*6. Sometimes people subscribe to magazines or newspapers. This means that each edition of the publication is regularly delivered to the subscriber.

7. Newspapers are often printed on a daily basis.

8. Magazines are usually printed once a week or once a month.

9. Newspapers are printed on lightweight, inexpensive paper.

10. Magazines are usually printed on heavy, sometimes glossy, paper.

*11. Newspapers are divided into sections. Some of these are: news, sports, family life, comics, and classified ads.

People Who Create Print Media

12. Many different people are needed to create magazines and newspapers.

*13. Some of the people who work to produce print media are: reporter or writer, editor, photographer, artist, cartoonist, typesetter, printer, and delivery person.

14. Reporters and writers gather information and write stories that appear in print.

*15. Editors decide what will be printed, assign reporters or writers, check what is written for errors, and arrange the material to be printed in a layout.

*16. Photographers take photographs to accompany stories and articles to be printed.

17. Artists and cartoonists draw pictures and cartoons to accompany printed words.

*18. Typesetters and printers produce the final product.

Activity Ideas

Aesthetic

1. Classroom Art Photos

Take photographs of children's artwork over a period of time. Use these photos to illustrate a classroom magazine devoted to art or create a bulletin board display in the classroom. Keep the magazine available for the children to review in the art or book area.

2. Design a Magazine Cover

Provide 9" x 12" white paper, old magazines for cutting, scissors, markers, and glue. Direct the children to use these materials to create magazine covers for their ME magazines (see "ME Magazines," at the right). They may cut out pictures and letters, write, or draw with the markers.

3. Magazine Art

Gather a collection of magazines such as *Smithsonian* or *American Heritage* that contain beautiful artwork. Make the collection available for children to examine during independent work time.

Affective

1. Help Wanted Ads

Advertise for a person to help with a routine classroom chore such as putting away blocks, table scrubbing, taking attendance, or passing out artwork or name tags. Include a "box number" in your ad. Make sure that you have a corresponding box available to receive responses. Place copies of your want ad in each child's cubby. In addition, read the ad to the entire group. Direct those who wish to apply for the job advertised to write their name on the ad and place it in your post office box. Make sure that each job applicant has an opportunity to carry out the desired chore.

WANTED: Person to assist in attendance taking. Must be able to read the names of children in the class. Apply to Box 543.

WANTED: Person to organize block shelf. Must be hard working and strong. Apply to Box 543.

Hints for Success:
● Introduce this activity only after children are familiar with advertisements and their purpose.
● Advertise for several jobs simultaneously so that all children may be successful in their "job search" within a reasonable time.

To Extend:
● Invite the children to write or dictate "help wanted" or other classified ads to include in the class newsletter. Suggest that they might advertise for a person who would like to help with a block structure, a floor puzzle, or other classroom activity. Print these ads in the classified section of the class newspaper or publish a separate classified sheet. Assist the children in making and finding a place for their own mail boxes. (See "Post Office Box," page 244.)

2. ME Magazines

Provide paper, writing, and art materials for each child to create a personal magazine. Encourage the children to include pages that illustrate their personal lives and interests such as pets, hobbies, favorite foods, family, birthdays, and so forth.

3. Portrait Session

You will need a camera in order to implement this activity. Announce to the children that you will be taking photos to include in the class magazine or newspaper. Arrange a space where the photos will be taken and take individual portrait photos of each child. Use these in the class publication at the head of stories that the children write or to illustrate stories.

4. Writing Portfolio

Prepare a folder for each child in the class. Put the children's names on the folders and store them in an easily accessible spot in the classroom. Encourage the children to file their stories, writing sheets, and any other finished work in these folders. Periodically, review the contents of each folder with the child to whom it belongs. You may also wish to discuss the contents during parent-teacher conferences.

Cognitive

1. Comics in Order

Select some comic strips and cut them into individual pieces. Mount each group on a separate color and laminate or protect with clear adhesive vinyl to extend wear. Direct the children to select a grouping and put the pictures in sequence. Encourage the children to explain their arrangements and to talk about the story portrayed.

2. Location Search

Take several photos of objects in your classroom or on the playground. As you take each photo, make a note of where you are standing with the camera. Mount each photo on tagboard and laminate. Also prepare cards to mark possible spots from which the photos were taken. Mark some cards "yes" and mark others "try again." Give a child one of the photos and place a "yes" card (with the word facedown so that the child cannot read it until it is turned over) on the spot from which the photo was taken. Place a "try again" card in another spot. Direct the child to stand on both cards and look at the object in the photo. After looking from both spots, tell the child to turn over the card that marks the spot from which she or he thinks the photo was taken. The child can then flip the card to see if the guess is correct.

To Simplify:
● Carry out this activity with a small group of children.

To Extend:
● Place an identifying numeral on each photo. Prepare some recording sheets that list the numbered photos. After each number, leave a space for the child to write a letter corresponding to the spot from which he or she thinks the photo was taken. Also prepare some letter cards (one letter on each) and place these in several spots in the room or on the playground. They should include the places where you were standing with the camera when you took the photos. Place the recording sheets on a clipboard with a pencil attached. Challenge the children to identify the spot from which each photo was taken. Give each participating child a clipboard with a recording sheet and direct her or him to select one of the photos. Ask the child to walk around the space until she or he has located the lettered spot from which the photo was taken. Have the child record the letter that marks the spot for that photo on the recording sheet. As he or she identifies one photo location, the child returns that photo and selects another, repeating until he or she has discovered all locations. Provide an answer sheet so that children may compare their responses with actual locations.

3. Page Count

The objective of this activity is for children to count in order. Provide several magazines. Direct the children to select a magazine and to count the pages.

To Simplify:
● Select children's magazines containing few pages.

To Extend:
● Invite children to estimate the number of pages before counting. Then count and compare their estimate with the actual number.

4. Photo Sort

Select several photos, either actual photos or magazine photos that you have cut out and laminated. Assign a child the job of Photo Editor and direct her/him to sort the photos into groups so that they will be ready for publication when needed. Ask the child to explain the groups and the choices made. Accept any criteria children use. Be careful that you don't determine the criteria for them.

Construction

1. Box Town Buildings

Gather an assortment of boxes such as shoe boxes and distribute them to children along with paper, glue, scissors, and markers. Direct the children to use these materials to create buildings for a Box Town. Suggest that they create houses, apartment buildings, and a post office. Use these buildings to create a Box Town for a pretend play activity (see page 246).

2. Papier-Mâché Creations

Use the small newspaper bits that the children prepare in the "Rip It Up" activity (see page 245) for this experience. Soak the paper bits in water for several hours or overnight. Pour off the water and squeeze out the excess. Add thick wallpaper paste (mixed according to package directions) to the paper. Work the paste well into the paper with both hands. The more you knead and squeeze, the more satisfactory the resulting medium will be. Involve the children in the mixing and kneading process as much as is practical. Allow the children to take a handful of the paper-paste mixture and to fashion it into anything that they wish. Place the finished creations on a thick layer of newspaper and place each sculptor's name alongside. Set these aside for a few days in a warm, dry place. Turn the pieces occasionally to hasten the drying process.

Hint for Success:

● Avoid engaging children in this activity on muggy days and stay away from damp drying areas to prevent the formation of mold before pieces dry. A sunny window is suggested.

To Simplify:

● Do the preparation of the paper-paste mixture yourself.

● Give each child only a very small amount of the mixture to reduce drying time.

To Extend:

● After the pieces are dry, provide paints, brushes, and markers so that the children can decorate their newspaper creations.

3. Post Office Box

Gather several shoe boxes or have the children bring them from home. You will need one for each child in the class. Assign a post office box number to each child and make a list to assist you in keeping track. (If you use their street numbers, this may help children learn their addresses, but it is not necessary.) Print these numbers on 3" x 5" cards and distribute to the children. Provide free access to art shelf materials such as scrap paper, scissors, glue, tape, paper punches, ribbon, and rubber stamps. Direct the children to use the materials to decorate a post office box to receive the responses to their classified ads (see "Help Wanted Ads," page 242). Remind them to place their box number on the box after decorating so that it is readily visible. They should NOT put their names on the boxes.

Hints for Success:

● Make sure that the post office box numbers used in the ads correspond to the numbers assigned to individual children.

● Make extra copies of the master box number list so that you will have ready access to it if a child forgets or becomes confused.

● Before beginning, be certain that you have sufficient space in your classroom to accommodate/display these boxes, perhaps for a lengthy period of time.

To Simplify:

● Decorate boxes and put children's names on them. Omit the box numbers.

To Extend:

● Post the master list of box number assignments in the classroom for the children to use as a reference and continue to use the boxes for messages to individual children throughout the year.

Language

1. Class Newspaper

After you have discussed and explored newspapers, tell the children that they will be creating a classroom newspaper to report news about school. During a group discussion, help the children to think of sections and articles that could be included. Some children may wish to write the sports section, reporting on playground and gym activities; another group could do the food section and report on recent snacks that have been served; social news could include reports on family news in the group; a travel section could report vacations and trips; another group might like to prepare a comic section. You and your children may think of other topics that are important to them. After this brainstorming session, help the children to decide what news stories they will work on and allow plenty of time for the reporters to write their stories. If you have a classroom computer or typewriter, the children can type up their own copy and the paper can be organized and printed. Copies can be sent home with each child. Another method is to use large sheets of newsprint divided into sections by drawing lines. Assist the children in pasting their stories into the appropriate sections and keep the newspaper available in the reading area for the children to read.

RAINBOW ROOM NEWS   April 1999

Social News

BABY SISTER SLEEPS
Matthew's new sister Alexandria spends most of her time sleeping. He likes her a lot, and sometimes he gets to hold her.

Food Section

POPULAR SNACK

All the children voted. Our favorite snack is peanut butter and jelly sandwiches. We like to make our own.

Sports

CHASING GAMES

We like to chase people on the playground. Roger runs fast. He catches everyone. Everybody has fun.

Travel News

FLORIDA TRIPS

Lots of kids went to Florida on vacation. Some kids saw Mickey Mouse. Some went swimming.

To Simplify:

● Select only a few sections for your newspaper. Provide time for each child to dictate a sentence or two related to one of the topics. The teacher does the typing or printing and all editing and publishing.

To Extend:

● Include some child editors who write the headlines and decide on the layout for the paper.

2. Plane Message

Ask the children if they have ever seen an airplane up in the sky carrying a banner. Talk with them about when they have seen the banners and the kinds of things that such banners are used for (often commercial messages or advertisements). Tell them that there will be some plane messages in the classroom during the next few days. Obtain or draw a picture of an airplane; this should be a propeller-powered plane, *not* a jet. Attach a long narrow sheet of paper to the rear of the plane and mount the plane and banner on the bulletin board. Prepare some messages for the class that will fit on the banner. Post one message per day.

Some possible messages:

"Today, at the art table: Finger painting"

"Snack: Pears and graham crackers"

"Open blocks today"

"Susie is Leader today"

"Sharing item this week: Something Green"

3. Sell It to Me!

Provide a selection of toys or other classroom materials or an assortment of product containers (cereal or cracker boxes, cans); a tape recorder; paper, markers, and other art media. Direct each child to select a product and to dictate an advertisement for the product selected. Children may also create magazine or newspaper ads by drawing pictures or cutting them out of magazines.

To Simplify:

● Provide a limited selection of three familiar classroom items from which children may choose.

To Extend:

● Invite children who have selected the same item to compare their advertisements. Carry out the comparisons in a group. Make a list of the similarities and differences among them.

Physical

1. Newspaper Fold and Roll

Gather a stack of newspapers and some rubber bands. Show the children how to prepare these for door step delivery. This is done by first folding the open paper in half, then rolling it from the open edge to form a tube. Place a rubber band around the rolled tube to hold it in place. Use these for the next activity, "Newspaper Toss."

2. Newspaper Toss

Use the folded and rolled newspapers from "Newspaper Fold and Roll" for some throwing practice. Provide large open containers such as laundry baskets to serve as targets. Explain to the children that some newspaper delivery people toss papers onto the porches of their subscribers in good weather. Encourage the children to stand back a few feet and practice their aim. As they are able to get papers into the baskets, increase the throwing distance.

3. Rip It Up

Give the children lots of newspaper. Encourage them to tear the paper into very small pieces. If you are going to use these in the "Papier-Mâché Creations" activity (see page 243), the smaller the pieces, the better.

Hint for Success:

● Make sure that the children wash their hands immediately after leaving the "Rip It Up" area to remove the newspaper ink that is sure to rub off on them.

To Simplify:

● Give each child one half of a newspaper page to tear.

To Extend:

● Give the children several thicknesses of paper to tear at once.

● Follow up with the "Papier-Mâché Creations" activity (see page 243).

● Give each participating child a container to fill with paper bits.

a. Weigh the empty containers before starting and the filled containers when the child is done.

b. Challenge the child to see how quickly he/she can fill the container. Note: Do not do this if you are planning to use the paper for papier-mâché: pieces ripped in a hurry will probably be too big.

4. The Sports Page

Plan some active experiences such as jumping, throwing, and climbing. As the children are participating in these, let them know that you will be making notes about the participants. Later, provide these notes to the class newspaper sports editor to use in writing the sports page for the Class Newspaper (see page 244). Include names, dates, and activities in your notes.

Pretend Play

1. Box Town

After the Box Town buildings are constructed (see page 243), arrange them in an orderly fashion in a large space such as the block area. Use long strips of paper to form streets for the box town. Name and label the streets and place address numbers on each building. Allow the children to use small cars and trucks to deliver mail to the addresses in town.

2. Catalog Order Desk

For this experience, you will need: a desk or counter, telephones, duplicate sets of merchandise catalogs, paper, and pencils. Some additional materials could include a set of number cards (used to determine cus-

tomer order in line), a cash register, and money. Order forms for use by the clerks are a fine additional prop. One of each catalog should be available for customer use and a duplicate set should be used for the order clerk's reference. Invite children who wish to shop by catalog to select one and to choose some items to order from the Catalog Order Desk. They may then either order in person or over the telephone. Tell them that the order clerk will ask for the following information:

Customer name
Name of catalog
Page number
Item name
Cost
Color choice and size if available

(If you prepare order forms, include these categories on the forms.)

Order clerks ask for the information and fill out the order forms as the information is provided by the customer. Remind the clerks to tell customers when their orders will be delivered and to thank them for ordering.

To Simplify:

● Use a teacher-prepared set of catalogs to limit the choices and necessary writing. Cut pictures of toys from a regular catalog and paste one picture on each page of your catalog. Code each item with a letter. The order clerk then only has to write in the letter code after the customer writes her/his name on the order form.

To Extend:

● Use the prepared order forms with lines for several items. Add calculators to the order desk. Direct order clerks to total the cost of orders that are placed.

3. Newsstand

You will need an assortment of magazines and newspapers for this activity. Ask parents to donate appropriate material. You will also need a display area (perhaps your book display rack can be used), a cash register, and play money. A jacket and cap for the seller(s) and wallets and purses for customers enhance the play. Tell children that the customers may look at the materials on display but that they should not read them until they are purchased. Encourage the sellers to keep an eye on the customers to make sure that they buy the items that they wish to read. Sellers may wish to review the items on sale so that they can assist customers in making choices. Provide potential customers with some money and direct them to visit the newsstand and purchase interesting reading material. Allow the children to switch roles to maintain interest in the area.

Social

1. Comics by Partners

Provide some Sunday newspaper comic strips for the children to read and enjoy. Discuss the elements that are present in the comic strips: characters, a situation or problem, and an action. Include some discussion about what makes a comic funny or enjoyable. Then, provide paper, pencils, crayons, scissors, tape, and other art materials. Tell the children to choose a partner or a few friends with whom to work to create an original comic strip. Allow plenty of time for the children to discuss and decide upon ideas and to work on the comic. Each pair or group may read its finished comic to the class and choose a place where it will be displayed.

2. Opinion Poll

Select a topic for your poll and prepare some Opinion Poll sheets for recording. The topic may relate to your classroom, the school or the neighborhood. Some classroom possibilities include: a name for a classroom pet, a book choice for the next read-aloud book time, or a subject for the class bulletin board. Explain to the group of youngsters that you would like some help in making a decision about _____ (the selected topic) and that an Opinion Poll will give you some information about the ideas that others have. Tell them that newspapers and other organizations often ask people to share their ideas about current topics by using Opinion Polls. Display the Opinion Poll sheets and tell the children that these will be available in the writing center. Request that each child record his/her ideas sometime in the next few days. After a few days, collect the sheets and see what kind of responses you have received. If you have only a few different ideas, next hold a vote to choose the most popular (for voting procedure, see "Our Next Feature activity," right). If you have several relevant ideas, share them with the group and ask the children to help you decide how to choose.

To Simplify:

● List two or three possible choices and direct the children to place a check mark next to the one that they prefer.

To Extend:

● Provide multiple Opinion Poll sheets and request a few volunteers to interview class members and record their ideas.

● Keep a supply of blank Opinion Poll sheets in the writing center so that the children can think of their own topics and conduct independent polls.

3. Our Next Feature

Conduct a class vote to select the topic for the next class magazine. Explain to the children that when a group of people wants to decide something, they sometimes vote to find the most popular choice. Add that today the children are going to vote to decide on the topic for the next class magazine. This means that each person has a chance to tell her or his choice and that the one that is chosen by the most people is the one that will be used. Present a choice of three or four possible topics. These may be selected by you, suggested by the children, or taken from suggestions gathered from a class Opinion Poll (at the left). The vote may be conducted in a number of ways. Choose the method that is most appropriate for your group of youngsters (these methods eliminate the problems that occur when a child casts more than one vote, something that happens frequently until children really grasp the one person-one vote rule):

a. Stand and Be Counted: Print each choice on a separate piece of paper and post on the bulletin board with space between them. Read the choices to the children and direct each child to stand near the topic for which she/he wishes to vote. Count the number of children in each group and write the total on the title paper. Have the children assist you in identifying the largest number.

b. Use Objects: Print the choices on separate pieces of paper and place on a table. Read the choices to the children. Give each child a marker (inch cube, bingo chip, or any other small object). Direct the children to place their markers on the one for which they wish to vote. This method of placing an object to indicate choice may also be used with a floor graphing mat with each possible choice having one or two rows on the graph.

c. Voting Chart: Prepare a voting chart for your classroom. This may be made by listing children's names in a row down the left side of a posterboard and adding columns for recording votes. Cover with clear adhesive vinyl and use a wipe-off marker so that the chart may be used for recording many different votes.

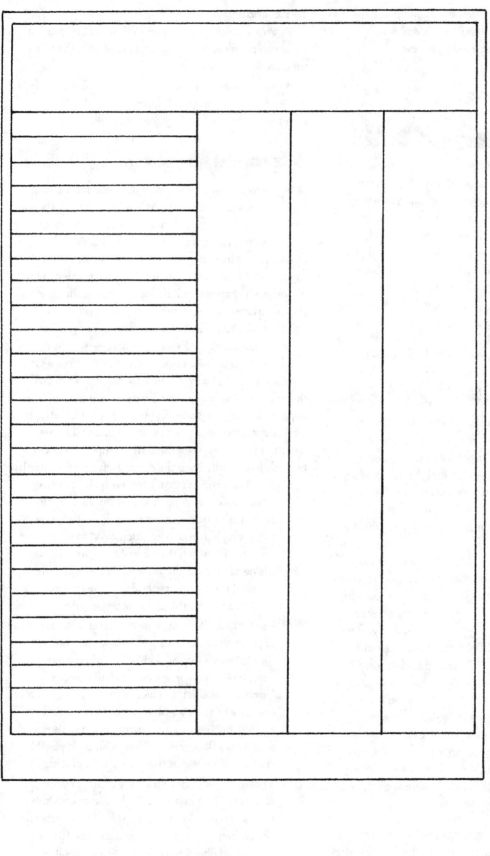

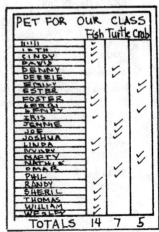

PET FOR OUR CLASS

	Fish	Turtle	Crab
BILL			
BETH	✓		
CINDY	✓		
DAVID	✓		
DENNY		✓	
DEBBIE	✓		
EMILY			✓
ESTER	✓		✓
FOSTER	✓		
GERRI		✓	✓
HENRY	✓		
IRIS			
JONNIE		✓	
JOE		✓	
JOSHUA			
LINDA	✓		
MARY			
MARTY			
NATHAN		✓	✓
OMAR		✓	
PHIL			
RANDY	✓		
SHERIL	✓		
THOMAS	✓		
WILLIAM	✓		
WESLEY			
TOTALS	14	7	5

Teacher Resources

Field Trip Ideas

1. Visit a newspaper office to see the reporters and editors at work. If possible, observe an editor working on a page layout.
2. Tour a printing plant to see a newspaper or other publication being printed.
3. Visit a photography lab to see photos being developed, trimmed, and finished. Arrange to have a photo of the group of children developed as they watch.

Classroom Visitors

1. Invite a photographer to visit the classroom and demonstrate how to take both posed and informal photos. If the photographer is willing to work with the children, permit the youngsters to practice taking photos with a camera that you provide.
2. Invite a reporter to discuss his or her job and interview you as the children observe and listen.

Children's Books

Broehel, R. (1986). *I Can Be an Author*. Chicago: Childrens Press.

Cohen, M. (1977). *When Will I Read?* New York: Greenwillow.

Craig, J. (1990). *What It's Like to Be a . . . Newspaper Reporter*. Mahwah, NJ: Troll Associates.

Drescher, H. (1983). *Simon's Book*. New York: Lothrop, Lee & Shepard.

Fleisher, P., and Keeler, P. A. (1991). *Looking Inside Machines and Constructions*. New York: Macmillan.

Forbes, R. (1979). *Click: A First Camera Book*. New York: Macmillan.

Jeunesse, G. (1993). *The Camera: Snapshots, Movies, Videos, and Cartoons*. New York: Scholastic.

Keats. E. J. (1968). *A Letter to Amy*. New York: HarperCollins.

Kehoe, M. (1982). *The Puzzle of Books*. Minneapolis: Carolrhoda Books.

King, D. (1994). *My First Photography Book*. New York: Dorling Kindersley.

Leedy, L. (1990). *The Furry News: How to Make a Newspaper*. New York: Holiday House.

Petersen, D. (1983). *Newspapers*. Chicago: Childrens Press.

Scholastic Reference. (1995). *How Things Work*. New York: Scholastic.

Stolz, M. (1988). *Zehmet, the Stone Carver*. New York: Harcourt, Brace & Jovanovich.

What's Inside? Everyday Things. (1992). New York: Dorling Kindersley.

What's Inside? Great Inventions. (1993). New York. Dorling Kindersley.

Adult References

The Eyewitness Visual Dictionaries: The Visual Dictionary of Everyday Things. (1991). New York: Dorling Kindersley.

How Things Work. (1983). New York: Simon & Schuster.

Howe, D. (1991). "Writers." *In Teaching Young Children Using Themes*, M. Kostelnik, ed. Glenview, IL: GoodYearBooks.

Macaulay, D. (1988). *The Way Things Work*. Boston: Houghton Mifflin.

Parker, S. (1991). The Random House *Book of How Things Work*. New York: Random House.

Rohde, B., and Kostelnik, M. (1991). "Storytelling." In *Teaching Young Children Using Themes*, M. Kostelnik, ed. Glenview, IL: GoodYearBooks.

Visual Media

Terms, Facts, and Principles (TFPs)

General Information

1. Visual media includes television, movies, and video tapes.
2. Visual media may be received by anyone having the appropriate equipment such as a television set, cable hook-up, or VCR.

People Who Create Visual Media

3. Many different people are needed to produce a television broadcast or film.
4. Some of the people who work in visual media are: writers, engineers, directors, camera operators, and performers such as actors, musicians, dancers, anchor persons, reporters, announcers, disc jockeys, and meteorologists.
5. Performers are the people who are heard and/or seen in a movie or on a television show.
6. Writers write scripts that are read or performed.
7. Engineers operate the electronic equipment such as sound equipment, lights, and cameras.
8. Directors are in charge and let people know when to speak, move, show film, run commercials, etc.
9. Camera operators run the cameras used to broadcast television pictures or record film performances.
10. Some television shows and movies show actual people and animals in real situations.
11. Many of the characters and situations portrayed in television shows and films are not real.
12. Actors and cartoon characters can do things that real people cannot do.
*13. Sometimes it is difficult to tell the difference between real and make-believe situations shown on television and in films.

Advertising

*14. Television networks and stations sell advertising time to sponsors who broadcast commercials designed to encourage people to try their products or services.
*15. Commercials are designed to persuade people that the items advertised are worth purchasing.
*16. Commercials often exaggerate the importance or appeal of items advertised.

*17. Consumers are sometimes disappointed when items purchased are not as good as they appeared in a commercial.
*18. It is important for consumers to make independent judgments as to the value of items featured in commercials.

Activity Ideas

Aesthetic

1. Musical Director

Choose a familiar character or story and tell the children that they will be in charge of selecting the music to accompany this choice when it is taped or filmed. Explain that music is often used to make stories more interesting when they are filmed or to accompany the appearance of a character in a film or television show. Play two musical selections and ask the children to tell you which they would select if they were the musical director of the show. Encourage them to explain their choices.

To Simplify:
● Select music with extreme differences.

To Extend:
● Provide a tape recorder, a tape with three or four choices of music (including introductory commentary and identifying numbers before each selection), headphones, and recording sheets with space for children's names and numerals that correspond to the musical selections. Direct children to listen to the musical selections and to record their choice for the production.

2. Options in Song

In order to help children develop some strategies to use in becoming more discriminating TV viewers, introduce the following song. Talk with the children about what it means. Ask if they have other suggestions for alternate activities. Incorporate their ideas into the song.

♫ **Change the Channel**
Tune: "Row, Row, Row Your Boat"

Change, change, change the channel
If you don't like the show.
You can even turn it off,
And read a book*, you know.

*Other possible activity suggestions:

play a game, clean your room, ride your bike, call a friend

Affective

1. I Don't Like It

Ask the parents of your group to help their children identify something purchased, because of a commercial or television show, that was disappointing in some way. Some suggestions might include food items that were not as tasty or toys that did not perform as expected. Give each child who brings in a disappointing product an opportunity to share his or her experience with the class. Encourage each disgruntled consumer to tell why the product was desired, what was expected based on the commercial, and why the purchase was disappointing.

2. It's Up to Me

Hold a discussion about favorite television programs with the youngsters in your class. Ask them to identify the things that they like about these favorite shows. Record the comments on a large sheet of paper. Remind the children that everyone has the right to make up his or her own mind about the things that she or he likes or doesn't like. Explain that the variety in people's taste is the reason that there are so many choices available. Be sure to allow each child an opportunity to share during these discussion times. Next, suggest that the children talk about programs that they do not like. Again, record a list of the things they dislike about these shows. Point out that some things that are favored by some people are not liked by other people.

To Simplify:

● Prepare a list of program characteristics ahead of time and simply ask children to express whether they find each of these pleasing or displeasing. Some that you may include: cartoon characters, actors, puppets; shows about people, about animals; shows with music; pretend stories, nature shows, fantasy, sports, news.

To Extend:

● Encourage the children to think of actions that they can take if they do not like something that is on a show. If they do not come up with some of the following, you may wish to suggest them: change the channel, turn the TV off, leave the room, and find something else to do.

● With the children, compile a list of alternative activities that can be pursued instead of watching TV. Have this duplicated and sent home with the children. Encourage the children to report which of these they tried.

3. My News Story

Invite children to share a brief news story about something that has happened to them recently. Provide a Class News Program time each day for these stories to be reported to the group.

4. TV Time

Prepare and distribute a weekly log, to be used by children and parents, to keep a record of the time each child spends watching TV. Include a space to record the program and the names of family viewers. Send the logs home and ask parents to assist children in filling them out accurately.

To Simplify:

● Prepare only a three-day log, perhaps for a weekend.

To Extend:

● Send the logs home at the beginning of the teaching unit and again at the end.

● Add columns for rating shows (Excellent, Average, Poor).

● Add a column to indicate if the entire show was viewed or if it was replaced by another show/activity.

TELEVISION VIEWING RECORD

for _____
   (name)

Show: Time: Watched with:
_____

SATURDAY

___minutes

SUNDAY

___minutes

MONDAY

___minutes

TUESDAY

___minutes

WEDNESDAY

___minutes

THURSDAY

___minutes

FRIDAY

___minutes

_____Total viewing time

Cognitive

1. A Commercial Pause

Prepare a short "commercial" to present to the children during a group situation. Select a very familiar product for your commercial and direct the children to listen carefully. Explain that you are going to try to make the product sound very exciting as you try to convince them to try it. Tell them that after the commercial, they will have an opportunity to identify the things that you did in your commercial to make them want to buy and to note any exaggerations. Following is a suggested commercial presentation:

Use a drum or whistle and put on a crazy hat or outfit when you present your commercial. Put your product (I'm selling a stapler) in a fancy box with bright paper, ribbons, and glitter to make it look appealing. Begin with lots of noise and movement. Add music if you wish. Talk in a fast, loud, and excited voice.

"Hi, children! Have I got a wonderful gadget for you. I know that everyone will want to get one right

away because this is such a fantastic item. Look at this beautiful box! See how bright and shiny it is! I wrapped mine myself. You can put yours in a fancy box, too! You can use this to make books or to make presents for your friends. You can even use it to fasten papers together. It is something that you will use every day for lots of things. (At this point, you may open the box and reveal the contents.) Look at this! That's right—it's a stapler! See the way it opens and closes. Have you ever seen anything like this? Watch as I demonstrate how it works. (Staple two pieces of paper together.) Isn't that fantastic? Don't you want one right away? Hurry to the store and buy a stapler!"

Conclude with more music and noise/movement.

After the commercial, lead the class in a discussion of what they saw, heard, and felt as they watched and listened. As each child offers ideas, point out that everything that you said was true, but that you managed to make the product appear better or more exciting than it actually is. Tell the children that this is what many advertisers do when they prepare commercials for TV shows.

2. Voice Predictions

Gather some videotaped stories of classic children's books and copies of the corresponding books (see page 256 for suggestions). Read one of the books to the children. Encourage them to discuss how they think the characters in the story would sound if they could hear them. Suggest that the children try creating appropriate voices for each of the characters. Play the video version and compare predictions to the voices heard on the tape. Did the characters sound as the children expected? How were they different?

Construction

1. Character Art

Provide assorted paper, markers, crayons, scissors, paste, and other art materials with which your children are familiar. Direct the children to use these materials to create their own versions of their favorite TV or movie characters. Label these with the names of the characters and the artists. Display them in the classroom.

2. Design a TV Camera

Show children a real TV camera or camcorder. Provide a variety of cardboard boxes, tubes, and tape. Encourage the children to use these materials to construct television cameras for use in the pretend play TV studio.

3. A Microphone of My Own

Often tape recorders have separate microphones that children can use to record their own voices before creating pretend microphones. Provide the children with small pieces of wood; short, thick dowels (for handles); black felt-tip markers; and duct tape. Encourage them to use these materials to create microphones for individual use.

4. Puppet Folk

Provide small paper plates or lunch-sized brown bags, yarn, buttons, scissors, construction paper scraps, glue, tape, ribbon, and markers. Also make a very simple puppet of your own ahead of time to demonstrate how to create a mouth with either the plate or bag. Invite the children to use the materials to construct puppets of their own design to use in one of the class TV productions.

Language

1. Buy This!

Ask the children to choose an item that they would like to "sell" to their classmates. These may be items found in the classroom, brought from home, or selected from a grouping that you provide. Tell them that it should be something with which they are familiar so that they can provide information about how it is used and why it is important for everyone to try it. Provide time for each child to present a TV "commercial" for the product selected. Remind children that they may exaggerate but must tell only true things about the item.

2. On the Air!

Use a tape recorder to record the children as they respond to questions about activities at school, plans for a holiday or trip, or reactions to a field trip or visitor. Explain to the children that the recording will be a pretend radio show that they will be able to listen to in the language area. Place the finished tape in the language corner so that it may be heard and discussed many times.

To Extend:

● Prepare a list of simple questions and assign a specific child to interview each participant. Review the questions ahead of time during a "rehearsal" with both the interviewer and the interviewee.

3. Press Conference

Tell the children that the president and other people in the news sometimes give press conferences where they speak briefly about a particular topic and then answer questions from reporters. Also tell them that these press conferences are often carried on television as they are occurring. Explain to the children that today you are holding a press conference about a particular topic (your choice or give the children a few topics from which to choose; some suggested topics include your family, home, hobby, vacation, pets, an appropriate movie that you have seen, a favorite story). Tell them that at your press conference they will ask questions and that you will answer them. Remind them that it is important to listen carefully to the questions and answers to avoid repeating questions that already have been answered. Suggest that the children take turns asking the questions. Give a brief opening statement: "I went to the movies last night" or "My family had an interesting experience on our vacation last summer." Tell the children to raise their hands if they have a question. Call on a child and answer the question asked. Continue until no other questions remain.

Hint for Success:

● As the questions are asked and you respond, provide some helpful feedback to the children. For instance, if a child begins to tell you about a related experience, say "You have a really interesting story to tell us about your _____. Right now it is time for me to answer questions. Another time, we will give you a chance to be interviewed." If a child asks an already answered question, say "You're asking me about _____. I've already talked about that. Maybe you can think of a different question."

To Simplify:

● Respond to a set number of questions in order to limit the sitting and listening time for the children. Try a three- to six-question limit initially.

To Extend:

● After you have modeled how to respond to questions, select a child to hold a press conference. Give many children opportunities at various times. Early in the school year, this activity could become part of the daily routine. Each day a different child could be interviewed. Rotate through the class and then repeat with a different topic.

Physical

1. Exercise Show

Ask the parents of the children in your class to send them to school wearing shorts, leotards, or T-shirts and gym shoes or to send these items so that the children can change for this activity. You should also have an exercise outfit to wear. Gather the children in a large, open area and tell them that it is time for "The Exercise Hour." Explain that some of them will have opportunities to be exercise demonstrators on the show while others will be exercising viewers, and that everyone who wishes will have a chance to be on the show. Select a few children to stand in front of the group and join you in demonstrating a particular simple exercise. Direct the "viewers" to imitate your actions. Switch demonstrators and viewers for each exercise. Remember to always start the "show" with stretching to get everyone warmed up and to end with relaxing activities.

2. How Do You Sit?

Prepare the setting for this activity: obtain an old TV set or draw a "screen and control knobs" on an appropriate-sized cardboard box; place some classroom chairs close together and cover with a blanket to form a sofa; add chairs (one very close to the "set") and a small rug for the floor. Invite children to the area and ask them to pretend that they are watching TV. Pay close attention to where and how they sit. Point out that sitting too close to a TV set is not safe. Use two yardsticks or a six-foot piece of string to show children the safe viewing distance. Also, look for any "frog sitters," children who sit with their legs pulled back and to the sides. This position causes too much stress on foot and leg muscles and can lead to problems. Tell the children that they should always sit with their feet in front of them, either forward or crossed (to support your anti-bias curriculum, avoid telling them to sit "Indian" style).

3. TV Snacks

Provide an assortment of snack foods that the children can combine to create a healthy "TV snack" of their own. Include some of the following: small cheese crackers, non-sugared cereals, raisins, pretzel sticks, and peanuts. Provide a serving spoon for each of the foods. Give a small bowl to each child. Direct the children to choose the foods that they wish to try and to place a scoop of each in their bowls. These may be eaten at the snack table or while the children are viewing a class "TV show." Other healthy TV snack foods could be featured at the snack table during this unit. Consider apples, popcorn, carrot and celery sticks, cheese cubes, and bananas.

Pretend Play

1. TV Meteorologist

Many teachers have children talk about the weather as part of a daily routine. Expand upon this familiar activity by inviting the children to carry it out on pretend TV. You may also choose to carry out this activity after a visit from a TV weather person or following an opportunity to view a videotaped weather report. Use the television cameras and microphones that the children have constructed. Add a weather map and weather symbols. For these you may either attach a map to a metal surface and use magnetic tape on the back of laminated weather symbols or cut a map shape of your state out of felt, glue it onto posterboard, and use felt weather symbol cutouts. Place the weather map on an easel. Recruit a director, some camera operators, and a meteorologist to carry out their roles. Encourage other children to listen as the weather report is broadcast.

To Simplify:

● Use an adult-constructed TV camera and omit the separate microphone.

To Extend:

● Add a laminated chart for temperature, humidity, and wind information to be filled in by the meteorologist as the report is broadcast.

2. TV at Home

Add a "television set" to the pretend playhouse area. This may be a discarded set or one that is made by gluing a paper "screen" onto a large box. Encourage the family in the home to pretend that they are watching and discussing favorite shows. Remind the parents to assist the children in choosing alternative activities for most of the day and to monitor the shows selected.

To Simplify:

● Add the "set" and allow the children to conduct their usual home play. Comment upon how pleased you are to see that they are finding lots of other things to do instead of watching TV.

To Extend:

● Add a "TV guide" with brief program descriptions written by you or the children. Encourage the family members to discuss the available shows and to decide how much TV time there will be and which shows to watch.

● Also provide pretend healthy snack foods to be prepared and served while engaged in TV viewing. These could include wooden or plastic fruits and vegetables, orange cube block cheese cubes, or a tasty snack mix made by measuring and combining assorted cereal "foods" such as Styrofoam and cardboard packing bits, Tinkertoy® "pretzels," and button "raisins." **Note:** Avoid any small parts for younger children or with children likely to actually put them in their mouths.

3. Puppet Production

Use puppets that the children create or commercially made puppets for this activity. Add a puppet stage or hang a curtain between two supports. Encourage the children to use the puppets to act out familiar stories. Add TV cameras and a camera crew to broadcast these puppet shows.

Hint for Success:

● Before presenting the puppet shows, be sure that your children are familiar with the proper way to use puppets. Practice with the whole group in the following way. Provide each child with a puppet or have the children bring puppets that they have made to the group area. Direct the children in the following steps:

   a. Examine the puppet to see how it works: where the operator's hand fits and how the puppet can speak, move, and so forth.

   b. Think of a name for the puppet.

   c. Give each child an opportunity to introduce the puppet to the group using the puppet's special voice.

   d. Next, give each puppet a chance to tell something about itself to the other puppets (if time is a problem, each puppet may speak to the puppet sitting next to it).

Throughout this experience, you should model how to use your puppet, how to create a suitable voice, and how to control the puppet's actions. It is very important that you do not use your puppet to bite or attack and that you make it clear to the children that such actions are not permitted. If you fail to establish this, your puppet shows may consist simply of puppets physically attacking each other with limited or no dia-

logue. Stress the use of the puppet to communicate with a voice and words, rather than with actions.

4. You're On!

Set up a "TV studio" area with child-created TV cameras, lights, and microphones. Add a desk for news reports or a curtain backdrop if desired. Encourage the children to take on the roles of performers, newscasters, announcers, directors, and camera people.

To Simplify:

● Provide cameras and other equipment that you have constructed.

● Assign children to the various roles and give them specific scripts such as familiar nursery rhymes to use in the broadcasts.

● Create a stage where children can perform songs or dances. Have some "camera operators" to record their actions.

To Extend:

● Provide paints, brushes, a white sheet or large piece of cardboard (an appliance box), and cleanup materials. Suggest that the children prepare the scenery for the broadcast.

Social

1. Commercial Team

This activity is best suited for older, more experienced children. It also works well in a multiage classroom where experienced children can support less experienced ones. Assign a product to each of several small groups of children. Direct the children in each team to work together to develop a TV commercial for their product. Implement this activity over several days.

Day 1: Have children describe the positive characteristics of their product and record them on a list that the children dictate or write themselves.

Day 2: Have children think of three things they want to say about the product and record as in Day 1. Call this the "script."

Day 3: Have children select roles. Who will direct and speak? Who will be in charge of props? Have children practice these roles.

Day 4: Give children more opportunities to practice and change roles, if desired.

Day 5: Present commercials to the whole class, if children wish. This should be optional.

2. Critic's Choice

Gather and preview an assortment of short video stories that are suitable for the children in your group. Establish a regular daily or weekly video time when one of these will be viewed. After each showing, encourage the children to critique and rate the show. Select one or more of the following story elements to discuss: characters, plot, setting, real vs. fiction. Also, help the children to agree on a rating for each show using a five-point scale (1 = terrible, 2 = not very good, 3 = OK, 4 = good, 5 = excellent), explaining that the highly rated shows will be seen again.

To Simplify:

● Conduct a vote on the ratings, with each child voting for one rating. The final rating will be decided by the category receiving the greatest number of votes. (See "Our Next Feature" activity, page 247, for hints on voting procedures.)

To Extend:

● Prior to deciding on the group rating, encourage the children to explain their ideas to each other.

● After viewing and rating all of the shows, show the "5" shows again and vote on the "Best of the Best," with children having time to discuss and campaign for their favorites.

Teacher Resources

Field Trip Ideas

1. Visit a movie theater to tour, not to view a film. Arrange to see the projection room and other behind-the-scenes areas.
2. Arrange a trip to a television station where your children can see a studio. If possible, have the children view themselves on camera. (Local access cable stations are sometimes more agreeable to showing young children how things work.)
3. Have children observe artists at work in a graphic arts studio.

Classroom Visitors

1. Invite a local television weather reporter to visit your class and explain his or her job.
2. Arrange for a television camera operator to film your classroom and then show the children the result. You may invite someone from your local cable access company or a parent or friend with a video camera to do the filming.

Children's Books

Barrett, N. S. (1985). *TV and Video*. New York: Franklin Watts.

Benedick, J., and Benedick, R. (1976). *Finding Out About Jobs: TV Reporting*. New York: Parents' Magazine Press.

Binder, L. (1991). *Eyewitness Books: Invention*. New York: Alfred A. Knopf.

Hautzig, E. (1991). *On the Air, Behind the Scenes at a TV Newscast*. New York: Macmillan.

Morley, J. (1994). *Screen, Stage, & Stars*. New York: Franklin Watts.

Oleksy, W. (1986). *Video Revolution*. Chicago: Childrens Press.

Platt, R. (1992). *Eyewitness Books: Film*. New York: Alfred A. Knopf.

Scholastic Reference. (1995). *How Things Work*. New York: Scholastic.

Turvey, Peter. (1992). *Inventors and Ingenious Ideas*. New York: Franklin Watts.

Story Videos

Children's Circle (Weston, CT 06883; 1-800-KIDS-VID) produces several videos of children's books that would be appropriate for use with this mini-unit. These include The Maurice Sendak Library; *Mike Mulligan and His Steam Shovel*; *Happy Birthday, Moon*; *Strega Nona*; *Tikki, Tikki, Tembo*; and many others.

Adult References

The Eyewitness Visual Dictionaries: The Visual Dictionary of Everyday Things. (1991). New York: Dorling Kindersley.

How Things Work. (1983). New York: Simon & Schuster.

Howe, D. (1991). "Stores." In *Teaching Young Children Using Themes*, M. Kostelnik, ed. Glenview, IL: GoodYearBooks.

Macaulay, D. (1988). *The Way Things Work*. Boston: Houghton Mifflin.

May, C. P. (1978). *Publishing Careers, Magazines and Books*. New York: Franklin Watts.

Parker, S. (1991). *The Random House Book of How Things Work*. New York: Random House.

Rohde, B., and Kostelnik, M. (1991). "Storytelling." In *Teaching Young Children Using Themes*, M. Kostelnik, ed. Glenview, IL: GoodYearBooks.

Stevenson, J. (1985). *Visual Science: Telecommunications*. Morristown, NJ: Silver Burdett.

Math Connections

One potato, two potato
Three potato, FOUR!

One, two,
Buckle my shoe.

This old man,
He played one . . .

A square peg in a round hole . . .

Purpose

We have included this unit to support teachers in their efforts to help children develop a basic understanding of some fundamental mathematical operations and processes. The unit contains three sections, each related to basic mathematical operations and understanding: "Grouping and Patterning," "Parts and Wholes," and "Geometrical Exploration." According to Piaget, children and adults use ordering and sequencing operations to help them to better understand and organize the world. For children to be successful in mathematics, it is also necessary that they be able to recognize and create patterns. An understanding of parts and wholes is required to conduct mathematical operations such as adding, subtracting, multiplication, and division. The "Parts and Wholes" mini-theme also serves as an early introduction to fractions. The mini-theme of "Geometrical Exploration" focuses on spatial awareness and shape, with an emphasis on the importance of exploring and recognizing solid forms as well as two-dimensional shapes.

Implementation

This unit contains many concepts and experiences that are fundamental to more advanced mathematical experiences. You may wish to plan a specific time period to focus on one of the mini-themes in this chapter. However, since many of the concepts require time and repeated exposure for children to internalize, the activities in this chapter should be incorporated into your ongoing program, with repeated and continuous opportunities for exploration and practice.

Grouping and Patterning

Terms, Facts, and Principles (TFPs)

Grouping

1. Sometimes people place objects that are similar in some way together in order to form a group.

2. People use grouping as a way to figure out similarities and differences.

3. People use grouping as a way to organize objects, actions, ideas, events, thoughts, and feelings.

4. Things can often be grouped or ordered in many different ways.

5. Attributes are the individual properties of an object. Size, color, shape, scent, tone, use, weight, and texture are examples of attributes.

6. Matching is the operation of pairing or grouping objects or events that are identical.

7. Classification is the operation of grouping objects according to similarities and differences.

8. Objects and events can be sorted into groups so that the objects/events in each group share at least one identical attribute.

9. The same objects and events can be sorted in many different ways by the same person or by different people.

10. An object cannot be included in a group if it has no attributes in common with the other members of the group.

*11. Objects and events can be sorted into groups so that the objects/events in each group share at least two identical attributes.

*12. When grouping/classifying by two or more attributes, it is sometimes helpful to first sort the objects by one attribute or property.

*13. A group of objects can be broken down into subclasses of objects.

*14. Subclasses of objects can be combined to make supraclasses of objects.

15. Sometimes people put the objects in a group in order from most to least of a particular attribute. This is called seriation.

Patterning

16. A pattern is an arrangement of objects, numbers, or events that repeats.

17. A pattern is predictable: given a complete example of a pattern and a partial repetition, it is possible to correctly identify the next element in the incomplete pattern.

18. A design is the purposeful or inventive arrangement of parts or details.

19. A design may be arranged to form a pattern.

20. Designs may be repeated to create a pattern.

21. Some ways that patterns can be represented and observed include: appearance, touch, and sound.

22. People who use numbers (mathematicians) look for patterns.

23. When a pattern occurs naturally, it helps people to predict.

24. Sometimes we use patterns to help other people.

25. People use patterns as a way to familiarize themselves or others with ideas, objects, or events.

26. Patterns are easier to remember than unrelated arrangements.

Number

27. A group of objects is called a set.

28. A set may contain any quantity of objects.

29. People count to find out how many objects are in a set.

30. Sets are sometimes compared.

31. When compared to one another, sets may contain the same quantity of objects or one set may contain more or less than the other.

32. Some words used to describe comparisons of quantity are *more than*, *less than*, and *the same as*.

33. If the number of objects in two sets is the same, the sets are said to be equal.

34. If the number of objects in two sets is not the same, one set has more objects or is greater than and one set contains fewer objects and is less than.

Activity Ideas

Aesthetic

1. Beat It

Use clapping patterns frequently with the children to provide experiences with both rhythm and patterns. This may be done for a few moments at the beginning of each group time as a method of gaining attention and settling the youngsters before moving into other planned activities. Begin by clapping a simple pattern such as "clap, clap, pause, clap, clap, clap, pause, clap, clap, pause, clap, clap, clap." Repeat the pattern four or five times and encourage the children to listen and join in the clapping as they recognize the pattern. Cue them to "Listen carefully to this pattern" and switch the pattern to "clap, clap, clap, pause, clap, clap, clap, pause, clap, clap, pause, clap, clap, clap, pause, clap, clap, clap, pause, clap, clap." Continue with other simple patterns for the children to imitate. Be sure to let the children know that they are doing a great job of "listening to the pattern" throughout this experience.

To Simplify:
● Choose one simple pattern per sitting for the children to imitate.

● Accompany the clapping by counting verbally as you clap:

"1-2, pause, 1-2-3; 1-2, pause, 1-2-3."

To Extend:
● Provide more time for pattern clapping and invite children to take turns clapping a pattern to be copied by the group. Be sure to use these opportunities to help the children to identify what is and what is not a pattern: "Jay, you're having fun clapping. It's hard for me to recognize a pattern. Count it for us as you clap" or "That was a very clear pattern. I could hear it and copy it."

● Distribute rhythm instruments (rhythm sticks, guiros, rain sticks, triangles, drums, maracas, or tone blocks) to the children and encourage them to listen to and repeat beat patterns that you model using the instruments.

2. Colorful Tunes

For this activity, you will need an instrument that can be color-coded. Some instruments (xylophones, tone pipes, bells) come with each tone already identified with a color, but you can also add small color dots to piano or keyboard keys by using self-adhesive stickers or removable tape on which you have placed marker or construction-paper spots. If you are marking an instrument, use the same method that you will use to create the "music" so that the colors will match. Prepare the music by selecting a simple, familiar one-octave song (such as "Jingle Bells" or "Row, Row, Row Your Boat") and assigning a color that matches the notes on the instrument to the corresponding notes in the song. Paste the appropriate color spots in a row on a paper in the correct order; write the song title at the top of the paper. Demonstrate for the children how to strike the notes in the order on this paper to create the tune. Encourage the children to try following the pattern on the music to create the song themselves. Stress that it is important to follow the pattern of the tones exactly in order to hear the song.

To Simplify:
● Prepare some "music" that contains only one line of a very familiar song.

To Extend:
● Provide a large supply of small construction-paper pieces in colors that match those on the instrument. Also make available long narrow strips of paper (cash register tapes work well) and paste. Direct the children to create a tune pattern with the instrument and to then paste the "notes" on a paper strip in the order in which they are to be played. Suggest that children invite others to try playing their pattern.

● Obtain color cubes in colors that correspond to the tones on your instrument and direct the children to construct a row of cubes and to then play the resulting tune.

3. Everyone's a Critic

You will need a musical/rhythm instrument such as a xylophone, bells, resonator bells, or tone pipes for this activity. Select an instrument with clear tones that will produce an accurate musical scale. Play a musical scale for the children and tell them to listen carefully to its pattern. After repeating the scale two or three times, play it again, but this time play two tones out of order. Ask the children if this sounded like the other scales. Continue playing both accurate and inaccurate scales for the children to identify.

To Simplify:
● Play only a sequence of three or four notes instead of the entire scale.

To Extend:

● Accompany your initial scale-playing by singing "Do-Re-Mi-Fa-So-La-Ti-Do" as you play the notes. Encourage the children to join you. Later, identify the misplayed tone notes by name.

4. Find the Pattern

Gather some examples of arts or crafts that use patterns. Be sure to include works from a variety of cultural groups. Consider pottery pieces, rugs, or jewelry. Display these in your classroom and encourage the children to find the patterns that are used to decorate them.

5. How Does Your Garden Grow?

Gather a large assortment of artificial, dried, or fresh flowers. These should vary in size, color, and stem length. Use these for a classification experience (see the Classification guidelines on page 264).

To Simplify:

● Select one attribute that varies (color, stem length, flower variety) when selecting the flowers to be used for this activity. Direct the children to sort their flowers by that attribute.

To Extend:

● Prepare some garden bases that can be used to hold the artificial or dried flowers. The bases may be Styrofoam pieces or trays layered with modeling dough. Tell the children that gardeners often plant their flower gardens with a planned pattern in mind. Direct the children to arrange their flowers in patterns in their garden bases. Give each child an opportunity to explain her or his garden pattern.

6. Hue View

Obtain a large quantity of paint chip samples from a local paint store. If large sample chips are not available, cut apart some paint sample reference sheets. Make sure that you have a wide variation of shades of each color. Ask the children to help you to sort these by color.

To Simplify:

● Give each participating child chips of only two colors to sort.

To Extend:

● Give a child five or six chips of the same color but widely varied in color intensity and ask her/him to show you the lightest and the darkest. Then ask the child to put all of these paint chips in order, from lightest to darkest in hue.

● This activity may be further extended by presenting additional paint chips and asking the child to show you where they belong in the order.

7. Notes in Order

Prepare a set of six to eight musical glasses by gathering identical glasses and placing water in each one. Vary the water levels. Provide a striker (short piece of dowel or a pencil) and direct the children to gently strike the glasses to create sounds. Point out that each glass produces a different tone or musical note. Challenge the children to place the glasses/notes in order from lowest to highest pitch.

To Simplify:

● Provide only three to four glasses.

To Extend:

● Arrange glasses on a tray. Add a pitcher of water and a striker. Encourage the children to pour varying amounts of water into the glasses and to then strike the tones and place the glasses in order.

Affective

1. Mood Sort

Prepare a posterboard chart with four columns labeled "happy," "mad," "sad," and "afraid." Also gather an assortment of situation pictures (people on a picnic, an ambulance, people hugging, a broken toy, an injured child or animal, a child climbing a tree, and so on). Direct the children to look at the pictures and decide how they would feel if they were part of the picture. Tell them to put each picture in the appropriate column on the board.

To Simplify:

● Use only two labels on the board: "happy" and "sad."

To Extend:

● Select a situation picture from the board and show it to a child. Say, "This is a situation where someone is feeling (state the mood). Tell me what happened to make that person feel that way."

● Select a situation picture and ask a child to help you think of other words to describe the ways a person might be feeling in that situation.

2. People Patterns

This activity is carried out as a total group experience. Choose four to six children to stand at the front of the group. Place them in some sort of order (tallest to shortest, longest hair to shortest hair, biggest buttons to no buttons, and so on) or in a pattern of your choice (tie shoes, Velcro® shoes, tie shoes; red shirt, blue shirt, red shirt). Describe your arrangement. Be sure to state if you are placing the children in order or if you are creating a pattern. Next, call on additional children, one at a time, to find where they belong in the order or pattern and to join the group.

To Simplify:

● Sort the children into two groups (long sleeves and short sleeves, straight hair and curly hair, buttons and no buttons, and so on). Give each child an opportunity to find the group to which he or she belongs.

To Extend:

● Tell children whether your arrangement is a pattern or is in order, but do not explain your organization to the group. Encourage the child observers to look carefully at how you have arranged the group and to figure out the order or pattern. You may extend this further by asking children to whisper their ideas to you and directing them to join the group if they have successfully recognized your method of organization.

● Select five or six children to come to the front of the class. Tell them to decide how to organize themselves in order. You and the rest of the class figure out the attribute that they are using.

● Select five or six children to come to the front of the class. Tell them to arrange themselves in a pattern that they decide upon. You and the rest of the class attempt to figure out and join their pattern.

3. What Comes First?

Prepare a set of picture directions for a classroom activity or self-help skill. Put each step on a separate piece of paper. Give the picture steps to a child and direct her or him to put them in order from first to last step.

To Simplify:

● First, introduce only the first and last steps and ask the child to tell you which is first and which is last. Introduce other steps, one at a time, and have the child show you where each fits in the order.

To Extend:

● Give the child only some of the step pictures. Direct the child to place these in order and to tell you what steps in the process are missing.

● Post a set of these picture directions in appropriate classroom areas so that children can refer to them when engaged in the corresponding activity.

Cognitive

1. Animals on Parade

This is a seriation activity. The goal of seriation experiences is for children to be able to recognize and order attributes. This activity may be carried out with a large or small group of children. Present an assortment of six to eight animal figures to the youngsters. Tell them that the animals have decided to have a parade but cannot decide on the marching order and would like some suggestions from them. Tell them, also, that the animals have decided that the animal with the most of some characteristic is to go first, with the others in order behind the leader. The animal with the least of the attribute will be at the end of the parade. Ask for suggestions and select one for the parade. Place the animals in order from most to least as directed by the children. As you work, continue to remind the children of the agreed upon criteria and to verbally describe how the animals are being placed.

Hints for Success:

● Be sure that the animal figures used in this activity are familiar to the children. If needed, allow some exploration time before conducting the activity so that the children are able to attend to the seriation task.

● In order to tell you how to place the animals, the children should also know the animal names.

To Simplify:

● During initial seriation activities, the teacher provides the criteria to be used in ordering the objects. After introducing the idea of the animal parade, tell the children that the animals have decided that the shortest or darkest or fattest or wildest (pick one) animal is to lead the parade, with the others following in order. Ask the children to help you put them in order.

● Use only three or four animals initially. Add others, one at a time, after the children have ordered the first group.

To Extend:

● After the initial group of animals is arranged, introduce a different animal and ask the children to show you where it will belong in the order. Ask them to explain the reason for this placement. Continue adding new animals.

● After the animals are arranged, ask the children to think of another way to put them in order. Continue until several parades have been arranged. Note: Some of the attributes that we have seen children use include: tail length, ear size, loudness of voice/roar, neck length, fierceness, leg length, most to least liked by children,

color intensity of coat, number of spots/stripes, and perceived climbing ability.

● Give each child an individual set of animals to seriate independently. Encourage the children to explain their arrangements to you or the other children.

2. Fancy Fabrics

Ask the parents of children in your class to send in patterned fabric swatches for use in this activity. Cut some of the larger pieces into smaller pieces, being sure that each smaller piece contains more than one example of the pattern. Make these pieces available for the children to use in a sorting activity.

To Simplify:

● Place large fabric swatches on a table. Direct the children to select a swatch and identify the pattern.

To Extend:

● Place large fabric swatches and markers on the table. Direct the children to use a marker to draw around one example of the pattern.

● Suggest that the children count the pattern repetitions on one large fabric swatch.

3. Put It There

Here is a sample procedure to be used in introducing patterning. Many materials may be used to construct patterns. It is probably best to start with very simple materials such as colored inch cubes. Then follow these steps:

1. Construct a simple pattern (ABABABA) and say: "Today we are going to make patterns. A pattern repeats. Look at my pattern. It is red-blue-red-blue-red-blue-red. Tell me what comes next."

2. Wait for the child's response. Then say, "Good, you knew that blue would come next! Tell me why you thought that it would be blue." After the child responds, say, "You have discovered that a pattern is predictable."

3. Give a block to each child. "What color will be next?" (Wait for children's responses.) "Let's continue my pattern across the table. Decide where your block belongs in the pattern." Support the children in accurately placing the blocks. If a child makes an error, gently guide her or him in correcting it: "You put the red block next to the other red block. Help me read our pattern. Red, blue, red, blue, red . . . . Tell me what comes after red. Great! You know that blue is next. Put it there!"

4. Give each child an equal number of two different items. "Here are some blocks for each of you. Arrange your blocks in a pattern."

5. "Read" each child's pattern. "Green-yellow-green-yellow. I can read your pattern. It repeats. It is predictable."

6. Model another pattern (such as AAB) and say, "Look. This pattern is different. It is red-red-blue-red-red-blue."

7. Repeat the procedures described above.

Hints for Success:

● Provide ample opportunity for the children to explore and become familiar with the materials before asking them to perform specific tasks such as patterning. Without prior exploration, it will be difficult for children to concentrate on the task because they will be distracted by their need to investigate the new materials.

● Provide multiple opportunities for the children to see and recognize patterns prior to presenting patterning activities. Some possible examples may include:

- Use patterns in decorating your classroom; choose borders with patterns for the bulletin board; arrange pictures with an eye to patterns (for example, using alternate background colors).

- Use two different numeral designs on the classroom calendar. Initially, arrange them in a simple AB pattern and after several pattern repeats, ask if the children can predict what picture will be on the next numeral tag. Use an AAB pattern the following month.

- Look for and point out any patterns in your classroom as they occur. Encourage the children to seek and report any patterns that they observe.

- Once children have grasped the idea of patterns, they will probably begin to form them spontaneously as they manipulate materials. Take advantage of these opportunities to challenge children to extend, copy, and "read" patterns that they create.

To Extend:

● Encourage children to construct a pattern for you or others to copy.

● Provide paper, glue sticks, and paper pieces that correspond to your patterning materials and direct the children to record their patterns by arranging these on a paper and then gluing them in place.

4. Sort Them Out

Children's (and adults') ability to recognize similarities and differences is crucial to academic learning. As a teacher, you will find many opportunities to model these sorting functions; for example, as you organize your classroom, you probably are grouping like items together (perhaps you haven't even been considering that this simple housekeeping strategy is actually a grouping activity). Talk with children about what you are doing. Also, encourage children to perform their own grouping activities each day. Children must be able to accurately and consistently match pairs of identical objects before they are ready to move into classification. Consider the following activity possibilities:

Matching Activity Format:

1. Gather an assortment of object pairs. Present these to the children and say, "This is fun. Look at (listen to, smell, touch, taste) what I have here. You can play with these, too."

"Find two that are exactly the same."

2. "Show me (find, touch, point to, pick up) the one that looks (sounds, smells, and so on) just like this one."

or

"Find two that are not the same."

3. "Show me (find, touch, point to, pick up) one that doesn't look (sound, smell, and so on) just like this one."

Sorting Activity Format:

1. Explore the objects. Say: "This is fun. Look at (listen to, smell, touch, taste) what I have here. You can play with these too."

2. "Put the ones that are the same together."

3. Point to one item in a group and say: "Tell me why you put this one here."

4. Pick up an object, point to a group and say: "Tell me why this one doesn't belong in this group."

5. We've Got Class

Classification experiences are an extension of the ability to perceive likenesses and differences. Ultimately, children should be able to explain their reasoning for classifying in a particular manner and to create subclasses and supraclasses.

Classification Activity Format:

1. Model how to examine the objects and then say: "This is fun. Look at these. You may play with them too."

2. Pick up one object and say: "Show me one that is somehow like this one."

3. Ask, "Why are these two alike?"

4. Follow with, "They're both (here repeat the attribute the child has named, such as slick)."

5. "Put all of the ones that are (slick) together in a group."

6. "Now you have two groups—objects that are slick and objects that are not slick. Think of a way to put the objects that are not slick into groups."

7. "Tell me about the groups." After children's responses, say, "Good, you have objects that are

slick, some that are rough, and some that are bumpy."

Hints for Success:

● Don't tell children how they should classify or seriate. Do allow children to choose their own criteria.

● Don't tell children they are wrong. Instead, reflect whatever children have done or said.

● Help each child recognize and correct his or her errors.

● Don't focus on social-conventional categories only. Do allow children to construct their own categories even if those categories don't fit typical groupings.

● Don't use close-ended questions, such as the yes/no variety: "Can you show me one that matches?" Use open-ended questions and do-it signals.

● Don't forget to give children a chance to talk about what they have done. Give children plenty of opportunities to talk.

● Don't push children too hard when they demonstrate that they can't think of another way to classify or seriate or when they can't describe what they have done. Use this as an opportunity to vary the experience, focusing on the steps the child has successfully achieved.

Construction

1. Blocks in Order

Tell the children to watch as you construct a simple block structure using a variety of blocks. Direct the children to build one just like yours. Remind them that it is helpful to place the blocks in the same order that you did.

To Simplify:

● Give each participating child an identical supply of blocks. Keep a supply for yourself. Tell the children to watch carefully and to do just what you do. Build a simple block structure, pausing after each block is placed to allow the children to imitate your action. Verbally describe your work as you place each block.

Sample Script:

"I am starting with a double-unit block. I am placing it flat on the floor in front of me. Now you put a double unit block on the floor in front of you. Good, our structures are started. Next, I am placing two single unit blocks on top of the first block. You do it." Continue adding and describing blocks until a satisfactory structure is created.

To Extend:

● Encourage the children to imitate a structure built by another child.

● Make some picture patterns of block structures for the children to copy.

● Photograph a group block structure before it is dismantled. Give the photograph to the children on another day and challenge them to duplicate it using the photo as a guide.

2. On the Border

For this patterning activity, you will need: 12" x 18" construction paper for each child, lots of one-inch construction paper squares in several colors, paste or glue. Tell the children that they are going to construct a border on the paper. Give each child a sheet of the construction paper and place containers of the small pieces within easy reach. Direct the children to select three colors and to take several squares of each color. Tell the children to create a color pattern around the outer edge of the construction paper with the squares. Check the patterns and have the children "read" you their patterns ("red-yellow-blue-red-yellow-blue") before giving the children the paste. Once a child has created a pattern, provide the paste and direct the children to paste their patterns in place and to continue the pattern around the entire paper edge. The finished border sheet may be laminated and used as a place mat or may be used to frame a piece of the child's art work.

To Simplify:

● Provide smaller base paper (6" x 9" or 5" x 8").

● Provide only two or three square colors; direct the children to choose only two colors for their patterns.

To Extend:

● Add small rectangle and/or triangle shapes to the squares to allow children to select pattern pieces based on both color and shape.

3. Pattern Walls

Use unit blocks and begin a pattern wall by placing blocks on edge in a pattern. Start with a simple AB pattern such as single unit, column, single unit, column, single unit. Encourage children to continue the pattern as far as space or the block supply allows.

To Simplify:

● Sort the blocks ahead of time and only make available the blocks needed to continue the pattern.

To Extend:

● Encourage the children to construct AB pattern walls of their own.

● Create pattern walls using increasingly more complex patterns: ABB; AABBBAABBB; ABCCABCC.

Language

1. Haiku

Gather some simple pictures of beautiful things, such as a flower, a bird, a rainbow, a mountain, and a cloud. Read a sample of haiku poetry to the children.

> Above the meadow
> A skylark, singing, flies high
> High into silence.
> > Author unknown

> Beautiful flower
> Growing tall in the garden
> Reaching for the sun.
> > Donna Howe

> High above green earth
> Lovely arch of varied hues
> Bending out of view.
> > Donna Howe

Explain that haiku is a very old form of Japanese poetry that often describes something in nature. Traditionally, there is a pattern of seventeen syllables in haiku: five syllables in the first line, seven in the second, and five in the third. Challenge the children to write a haiku poem using the five-seven-five syllable pattern. They may write about the objects in the pictures or choose some other natural object.

2. Story Patterns

There are patterns (repeated phrases or events) in many stories for children. Select several of these stories and read one each day for a week. Before reading each day, cue the children to listen carefully for the pattern because they will have a chance to talk about it after you finish reading. Some suggested stories with patterns: *Alexander and the Horrible, Terrible, No Good, Very Bad Day* by Judith Viorst (1972); *Barnyard Banter* by Denise Fleming (1994); *Brown Bear, Brown Bear, What Do You See?* by Bill Martin, Jr. (1983); *Bringing the Rain to Kapiti Plain* by Verna Aardema (1981); *The*

Gingerbread Man (Many versions are available.); *Goldilocks and the Three Bears* (Many versions are available.); *The Little Red Hen* (Many versions are available.); and *Why Can't I Fly?* by Rita Gelman (1986).

To Simplify:

● Before reading, tell the children that there is a pattern in the story. Tell them to listen for (here recite the pattern; for example, "I can fly, I can fly, I can FLOP!" or "Who will help me _____? Not I.") and to signal in some way that you designate (hand on top of head, cover their ears, and so on) when they hear it.

To Extend:

● After listening to and identifying story patterns, suggest that the children create stories of their own that include patterns. These may be done individually, in pairs, or in small groups. The stories may be written and included in a class book or recorded on tape and played for the class.

3. What Comes Next?

Prepare a set of word cards or use the children's name cards from your writing center. Give several cards to a child and direct her/him to put them in alphabetical order.

To Simplify:

● Initially, provide only three or four cards with widely separated beginning letters. Once the first cards are correctly alphabetized, give additional cards to be added to the order.

To Extend:

● Encourage each child to create personal word cards and to keep the words in alphabetical order. These may be words that the child identifies as special in some way: names of friends, words the child is able to read or learning to spell, a favorite list of some type, and so on. Children may store these words in an envelope or small box with a rubber band or paper clip to keep them in alphabetical order.

Physical

1. Action Patterns

Model and verbalize some action patterns for your children to imitate. Try: 3 hops, 2 jumps, 3 hops, 2 jumps; 2 jumps, 2 spins, 2 jumps, 2 spins; or jump, spin, hop, jump, spin, hop.

2. Movement in Order

Tell the children that you are going to tell them some movements to do in a particular order. Caution them to listen carefully to the whole order before moving. Try these: 3 jumps from long-longer-longest; walk, trot, run; stretch high-higher-highest; bend low-lower-lowest.

3. Nesting Toys

Provide a selection of nesting toys for your children to explore and master. Introduce these by providing only the largest, middle size, and smallest parts first. Tell the children to start by finding and putting together the two smallest pieces first. When these are connected, tell them to find the next size and to put the smaller one inside before completing the connection of the two middle size pieces. Continue by putting the mid-sized piece into the largest pair of pieces. Once the children are familiar with how these toys fit together, provide the additional pieces and encourage them to put the pieces in order from smallest to largest before assembling the entire set. Remind them that in order to be successful, they must always start with the smallest pieces and work in order to the largest pieces.

Pretend Play

1. Five-and-Ten-Cent Store

Gather several collections of small items (math counters, small animal figures, buttons, keys, inch cubes, and so on). Add a cash register, money, purses, wallets, and small bags. Set up a five-and-ten-cent store with separate containers for each collection of objects. Shoppers can purchase an assortment of items to sort. Store clerks will keep objects organized, count out purchases, and restock the display bins.

To Simplify:

● Provide only two containers for goods. Mark these with prices—5 cents and 10 cents. Decide on a single criterion (color, size, and so forth) to be used in deciding prices. Direct the children to sort items based upon this criterion.

To Extend:

● Direct the children to decide how items should be sorted for display.

● The children can also make signs for each container.

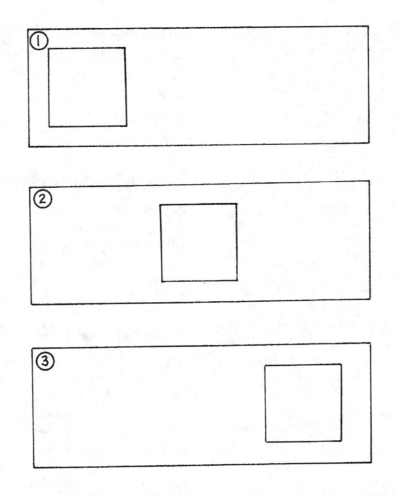

2. Paper Factory

The major activity in the paper factory will be to manufacture border paper. In order to do this, you will need long, thin paper (cash register tape works well); a simple design stencil; crayons; rubber stamp and ink pad; thick tempera paint in a low container and a printing object such as a pencil with eraser or small sponge shape; placement stencils (see above); smocks; clean-up sponges and water; a ruler; pencils; and scissors. Make the placement stencils ahead of time by deciding what shapes will be stamped on the paper and planning the pattern. Make a sample and allow it to dry. Cut three tagboard strips the same size as the paper strips to be used. Use one tagboard strip for each stamping design. Cut holes in the strip that correspond to the placement of that design element on the finished sample. Number each placement stencil to prevent a mix-up on the line. Also add arrows to assure that the stencil is placed on the paper with the correct orientation. The layout artists will lay the placement stencil over the paper and use a pencil to mark the places where the holes are to indicate where the printer should place each design.

Set up an assembly line by arranging the materials on a long table or low counter top in the following order: 1) paper, ruler, pencil, and scissors; 2) first placement stencil and pencil; 3) first set of printing materials (design stencil and crayon); 4) second placement stencil and pencil; 5) second set of stamping materials (rubber stamp and ink pad); 6) third placement stencil and pencil; 7) third set of stamping materials (paint and printing object). There should be a drying rack or space at the end of the assembly line. Tell the children that today they are going to be factory workers manufacturing some border paper to use for a class bulletin board display. Also explain that when people first created factories, each worker did one job. The jobs today are:

1. **Paper Starter:** This worker measures and cuts a piece of paper and gives it to the next worker on the line.

2. **Layout Artists:** These workers place their placement stencil over the paper and use a pencil to lightly mark the spot on the paper that should be stamped.

3. **Printers:** These workers each place their design in the appropriate place on the paper as indicated by the mark placed by the layout artist.

4. **Dryer:** This worker takes the completed paper strip and arranges it in the drying area.

5 **Supervisor:** This person directs the workers by telling the Paper Starter when to begin a new paper, checking on the Layout Artists' and Printers' spot placements, and providing a clean-up sponge for any paint drips.

Assign workers to each task and line them up at their work stations in the following order: Paper Starter, Layout Artist 1, Printer 1, Layout Artist 2, Printer 2, Layout Artist 3, Printer 3, Dryer. The Supervisor will be moving along the line throughout the activity. Begin by having the Supervisor direct the Paper Starter to measure and cut the first piece of paper. Support the Supervisor in directing the movement of the paper along the assembly line. As the children work, stress the importance of each person performing her/his task with care so that the pattern is reproduced as planned. After the border papers have dried, have the children assist in placing them on a class bulletin board.

Hint for Success:
● Alternate roles after each few paper patterns are completed if children are anxious to try particular tasks.

To Simplify:
● Use only one printing technique, either rubber stamps or crayons and stencils, and two printers.

● Prepare the paper strips with the design spots indicated (use a different colored pencil for each design element) ahead of time. Include only printers on the assembly line.

To Extend
● Create a complex pattern for the border paper and add more Layout Artists and Printers to the assembly line.

● Suggest that Layout Artists get together and plan a new pattern. Show them how to create the layout stencils so that the new pattern can be produced.

Social

1. Mystery Line Up

Prepare several bags of six to ten small items (cars, farm animals, wild animals, insect models, pom-pons, and so on). Give a child one of these bags. Direct the child to ask a friend to help her/him put the items in order from most to least of an attribute.

To Simplify:
● Provide only a few items in each bag.

● Identify the attribute by which items are to be ordered.

To Extend:
● Place unrelated items in the bags.

2. Pass the Shoe Game

"Pass the Shoe" is a cooperative game that involves passing one or more shoes in an interesting pattern to the rhythm of a song. It is described in Edgar Bley's *The Best Singing Games* (1973). An action to a music game such as this gives children experience with beat and tempo as well as with action patterns.

3. Tell Me

Prepare some "screens" by cutting cardboard boxes so that only three connecting sections remain. Also provide a simple patterning material such as colored cube blocks. Direct the children to work in pairs, sitting across a table from each other. Give each child an identical selection of blocks. Arrange a screen around the work space of one child. Direct the child whose work is screened from view to construct a simple pattern with the blocks. After this original pattern is complete, have the child verbally direct the other child to construct an identical pattern. Remind the children that it will be important to give clear, simple directions so that the other person can be successful. Encourage the children to trade roles and to continue to work together.

Teacher Resources

Field Trip Ideas

1. Visit an art museum or exhibit and look for patterns in the artwork on display. Your visit may be enriched by providing simple sample patterns for the children to look for during the visit. Give one of these samples to a small group of children and challenge them to find a similar pattern at the museum.

2. Visit the produce department of the local grocery store to see how items are grouped for display. Take along some money so that the children can help you select items for a snack at school.

3. Visit a library or bookstore to see how books are arranged in categories.

Classroom Visitors

1. Invite an artist, such as a potter or weaver, to visit the classroom to show some samples and demonstrate how they were created. Ask the artist to focus on patterns displayed on the finished pieces.

2. Invite a parent who sews to bring a sewing machine to class to assist children in assembling fabric squares into a classroom quilt. Children can participate in preparing the pattern squares by gluing fabric pieces onto base pieces or by using fabric crayons on paper. These pictures must then be ironed onto the squares by an adult.

3. Invite a collector to bring part of his or her collection and to explain how it is organized so that it is possible to find a particular item. Some possible collections might include stamps, coins, shells, insects, or rocks.

Children's Books

Aardema, V. (1981). *Bringing the Rain to Kapiti Plain*. New York: Dial Books for Young Readers.

Brett, J. (1989). *The Mitten: A Ukranian Folktale*. New York: Putnam.

Fleming, D. (1994). *Barnyard Banter*. New York: Henry Holt.

Flournoy, V. (1985). *The Patchwork Quilt*. New York: Dial Books for Young Readers.

Gelman, R. (1986). *Why Can't I Fly?* New York: Scholastic.

Lankford, M. D. (1992). *Hopscotch Around the World*. New York: Morrow Junior Books.

Lionni, L. (1959). *Little Blue and Little Yellow*. New York: Astor-Honor.

MacDonald, S. (1994). *Sea Shapes*. New York: Gulliver Books.

Martin, Bill, Jr. (1983). *Brown Bear, Brown Bear, What Do You See?* New York: Henry Holt.

Russo, M. (1986). *The Line Up Book*. New York: Greenwillow Books.

Turner, A. (1994). *Sewing Quilts*. New York: Macmillan.

Viorst, J. (1972). *Alexander and the Terrible, Horrible, No-Good, Very Bad Day*. New York: Macmillan.

Yeoman, J., and Blake, Q. (1995). *The Do-It-Yourself House That Jack Built*. New York: Atheneum Books for Young Readers.

York, J. et al. (1991). *My First Look at Sorting*. New York: Random House.

Young, E. (1992). *Seven Blind Mice*. New York: Putnam.

Adult References

Bley, E. S. (1973). *The Best Singing Games: For Children of All Ages*. New York: Sterling Publishing.

Charlesworth, R., and Lind, K. (1990). *Math and Science for Young Children*. Albany, NY: Delmar.

Kostelnik, M., et al. (1993). *Developmentally Appropriate Programs in Early Childhood Education*. New York: Macmillan.

Kostelnik, M., et al. (1991). *Teaching Young Children Using Themes*. Glenview, IL: GoodYearBooks.

McDonald, D. T., and Simons, G. M. (1989). *Musical Growth and Development, Birth Through Six*. New York: Schirmer Books.

Parts and Wholes

Terms, Facts, and Principles (TFPs)

1. To be whole means to be complete. That is, all the parts of an object fit together or work together as one.

2. A part is a portion or piece of a whole object.

3. Some objects have only one part.

4. Some objects have more than one part.

5. A whole is larger than any one of its parts.

6. Sometimes the parts of an object can be combined in different ways to make the object whole.

7. Sometimes the parts of an object can be combined in only one way to make the object whole.

8. Some whole objects can be divided into parts.

9. Some whole objects cannot be divided into parts.

10. Some whole objects are divided into parts that are equal in size and shape.

11. Some whole objects are divided into parts that are unequal in size and shape.

*12. The parts of an object can be represented using numerals.

*13. To divide a whole in half means to divide it into two equal parts.

*14. To divide a whole into thirds means to divide it into three equal parts.

*15. To divide a whole into quarters means to divide it into four equal parts.

16. The same object may be divided into parts in different ways or in different combinations.

17. Different objects may be divided in the same way or in similar combinations.

18. The way in which parts are combined can affect the outcome.

19. Sometimes you discover the whole by piecing together the parts.

20. Sometimes you know what the whole is before its parts are put together.

*21. Sometimes people put together the wrong parts and create a whole that is not a true representation.

*22. Sometimes people put the parts together in an incorrect way and are unable to correctly identify the whole.

Activity Ideas

Aesthetic

1. Mosaic Art

Provide 9" x 12" white paper, black markers, glue, small colored paper bits, and tweezers. Direct the children to draw a simple picture with a marker. After the pictures are drawn, tell the children to glue the paper mosaic pieces in place, using a different color for each part of the picture. When the mosaic art is complete, admire and display the whole pictures. Encourage the children to point out the parts that make up the whole of their picture.

2. Round and Round

Teach the children a song that may be sung in rounds such as "Row, Row, Row Your Boat" or "Brother John." Once the children know the song well, introduce the idea of singing it in rounds. Explain that one group or person will start the song and the next group or person will start after the first group sings the first line. Explain further that the second group will finish the song after the first group is done. Tell the children that it is very important to concentrate on their own part to avoid getting confused. It may be easier to introduce singing rounds by having the children sing first while you join in with the second part.

3. What's Missing?

Choose a familiar song that has gestures such as "Open, Shut Them" or "The Eensy, Weensy Spider." Tell the children that the song has three parts: the words, the melody, and the gestures. After singing it in the usual way, tell the children that now you are going to try singing it with one of the parts missing. First, sing the song with no gestures. Next, try singing it without the words by humming the melody while doing the gestures. Finally, tell the children that you are going to try "silent singing" so that two parts will be missing (see page 226 for complete directions). In silent singing, the words are silently mouthed and the gestures are performed; no sound is made. Tell the children that it is important to watch you carefully so that everyone stays together while singing silently. Mouth the words clearly and use exaggerated gestures as you lead the children in silent singing.

Affective

1. All About Me

This activity provides you and the class with an opportunity to learn about the parts that make up the whole of one class member and to consider each individual as one part of the whole that constitutes the class. Select one child each day to be interviewed by the group. Support the children in asking questions that will provide information about the selected child. Start by having the child state her/his name and age. Suggest that she or he tell who lives in her or his home; ask her or him about any pets and about a favorite story, food, TV show, and so on. After the children have finished asking questions, ask the child if we now "know all about you." Encourage the child to think of something else to tell. Point out that although you have learned much (or about many parts), there will probably be more to learn about each person.

To Simplify:
● The teacher conducts the interview while the children listen.

To Extend:
● Record the questions and responses in writing. Give this to the child and suggest that she/he add to it and make a book.

● Prepare booklets for the children to complete with information about themselves. Include the following pages:

1) My name is _____. I am _____ years old.
   My birthday is _____.
2) I live with _____.
3) My favorite things are _____.
4) Blank page for child's ideas

Provide book covers for the children to title and decorate. Give each child an opportunity to read her or his "All About Me" book to the group.

2. All of Me

This activity will take several days. Prepare and save a body tracing of each child in the class. When all of the children have been traced, tell the children that they are going to be finishing their pictures, one part at a time. Begin by providing markers, yarn for hair, colored paper for eyes, and a variety of skin-colored crayons for faces. Add scissors and glue to the available materials. Direct the children to decorate the faces on their pictures. Then ask if the pictures are whole yet. Follow by asking what else is needed. Divide work over several days, adding parts suggested by the children each day. Provide markers, colored construction paper, scissors, glue, and fabric pieces as needed. Continue adding parts until all agree that the pictures are complete or whole.

3. Complete My Collage

Provide paper, paste, scissors, and magazines. Direct the children to select pictures from the magazines to cut out and paste on the paper until they have completed a whole collage. Congratulate the youngsters on finishing the whole task.

4. Parts Make a Whole Salad

This activity gives children an opportunity to make choices and to create a healthy snack or meal for themselves. Set up a salad bar for a snack or lunch treat. Include a bowl of washed and drained lettuce pieces, tomato slices, carrot slices, green pepper strips, zucchini slices, peas, grated cheese, and croutons. Add salad dressing and other in-season vegetables as you desire. Provide plates, forks, and napkins. Invite the children to choose the parts they like to create a whole salad. Point out that although each person selected different parts, each created a whole salad of his or her own.

To Simplify:
● Give each child a bowl of prepared salad (lettuce, tomato, and other vegetables). Allow the children to select other parts from three or four additional toppings such as cheese, croutons, carrots, and raisins.

To Extend:
● Involve the children in washing and slicing vegetables for the salad parts.

● For a lunch main dish, add turkey, ham, or chicken strips, and hard-boiled egg for extra nutrition and additional part choices.

5. A Puzzle of My Own

Gather an assortment of used greeting cards with pictures of animals, toys, children, and flowers. Also provide pencils, scissors, and envelopes. Direct the children to select a card and to draw cutting lines on the back with a pencil to divide the card into three, four, or five parts. Tell the children to cut their card carefully into the parts that they have drawn to make a puzzle of their own. Challenge the children to turn the pieces over and to put the parts of their puzzle together to create the whole picture. Use separate envelopes to store all of the parts of each puzzle.

Cognitive

1. Estimating Jar

Place several (15 to 30) similar items in a clear plastic jar. Use small animal figures, inch cubes, paper clips, or any other small item of your choice. Show the jar to the children and ask them to guess (or estimate) how many parts (or items) make up the whole set that is in the jar. Write these estimates down where all can see the numerals. After all of the children have guessed, ask how you can find out how many there really are. If the children don't suggest it, tell them that you are going to count the parts one by one. Do so. Look at the recorded estimates and circle those that were close.

To Simplify:
● Place a very small number of items in the jar (less than ten).

To Extend:
● Use items that are similar except for color. Include three or four colors in the jar. As each child gives an estimate of the number, have the child also state the color that is most used in the jar. After counting the total, count each color subset.

● Instead of counting, place the colors on a graph to see which has more.

2. Halves and Half Not

Gather an assortment of pictures of familiar things. Present these to the children and ask them to identify those things that can be divided into halves and those that cannot be halved. Encourage them to give reasons for their ideas. "Tell me what would happen if you cut a _____ in half." Include pictures of food items, animals, furniture, plants, and toys.

3. Incomplete Pictures

Prepare the pictures for this activity ahead of time. Use a black felt-tip marker to draw some simple outline pictures on lightweight 8-1/2" x 11" white paper. Place another paper over your drawing and trace most, but not all, of the picture. Place another sheet of white paper over this second partial picture and trace part of that. Continue until you have five or eight partial drawings of each original picture. Invite the children to be seated where they can see. Tell them that you have made some pictures and that you want them to try and guess what is in each picture by seeing only parts. Present the first picture in a set. (Keep the other pictures in a folder or otherwise out of sight.) Wait for guesses. Have the children explain their ideas. Present the next picture in the set. Wait. Continue the process until the children have correctly identified the object pictured. After they succeed in identifying the picture but before you reveal the final drawing, congratulate them on being able to recognize the whole while only seeing parts.

Hints for Success:
● The next to last picture should reveal enough information so that the children may successfully identify the object by seeing only parts before seeing the whole picture.

● If you desire assistance with the drawing, refer to a simple coloring book for sample pictures.

● Code the pictures with light pencil on the back to help you keep them in order. Assign each set of drawings a letter and add a numeral starting with 1 for the least complete picture. For example, you will then have A-1 to A-8 for the airplane set and B-1 to B-7 for the butterfly set, and so on.

● Store each set in a separate folder.

4. Peek-a-Boo Pictures

Cut some simple pictures of familiar objects out of magazines and mount on sturdy paper. Identify four to six important parts of each picture. Place a sheet of tracing paper over the picture and mark the important parts on the tracing paper. Cut holes in the tracing paper that correspond with the important parts and place the tracing paper on a separate sheet of heavy paper. Mark the placement of the important parts by drawing square or rectangular "windows" on the heavy paper. Remove the tracing paper and discard. Cut three sides of each window to create a flap that may be lifted and closed. Fasten the heavy window paper over the original picture. Lift each flap gently to be sure that the desired part of the picture is revealed. Number each of the flaps to indicate the order in which the parts should be revealed. Make these window sheets for each picture. Tell the children that you have some peek-a-boo pictures for them to see. Show them how to carefully lift the flaps in order to see the parts underneath. Encourage them to try and identify the whole by looking at the parts revealed by the flaps.

Hint for Success:
● To extend the life of the cover sheets and flaps, replace the paper flaps with separate pieces of heavier paper or light cardboard taped in place.

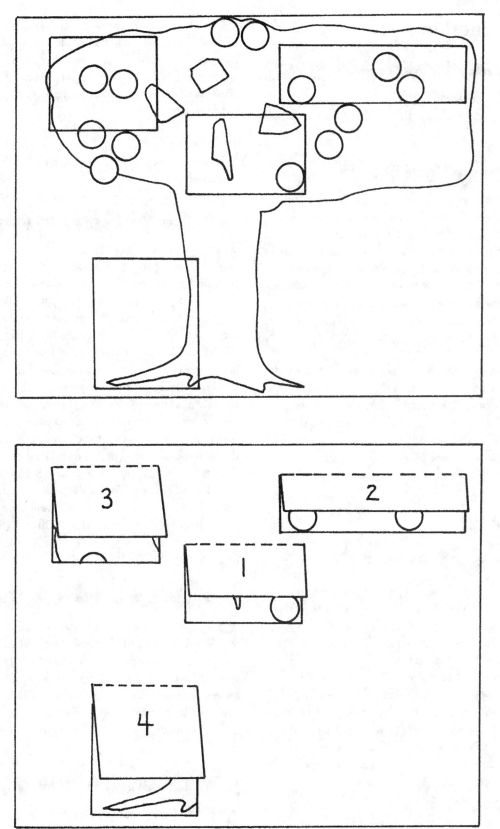

Construction

1. Crazy Word Creations

Suggest that the children use art shelf materials to construct a sample of their "Crazy Word" activity (below).

2. Funny Halves

Provide an assortment of simple pictures that have each been cut in half. Place the picture halves face down on a table and suggest that the children select two halves and put them together to form a whole. Because the selection will be random, the resulting pictures should be strange indeed. Later, challenge the children to match the halves to recreate the original pictures.

3. Gear Boards

Provide some commercially made gear boards for the children to explore. Encourage them to experiment with whole or complete arrangements, with one gear connected to another so that all of the gears on the board turn. Next, have the children remove one of the gears so that the arrangement is not whole because one of the parts is missing.

Language

1. Crazy Words

Gather an assortment of pictures that illustrate compound words such as *fingerprint*, *tablecloth*, *see-saw*, *fingernail*, *firecracker*, *waterfall*, *drawbridge*, *upstairs*, and *spareribs*. Show these to the children and ask them to name the things seen in the pictures. If the children don't point it out, tell them that all of these words are made up of two words. Ask them to think of other words that are made up of a combination of words. Write the words on the board or on a large piece of paper as they are suggested. Next, ask the children to suggest two words that can be combined to make a crazy word—words that are a combination of two words but that don't make any sense. Record these words also. For example, if a child suggests "bear" and "water," the resulting word could be *waterbear* or *bearwater*. As words are recorded, underline each of the parts.

To Simplify:
● Introduce a puppet named Frodo to show some pictures to the children. As Frodo presents the pictures, tell the children that Frodo sometimes gets mixed up and may need some help from them in naming the pictures. Have Frodo reverse the words as the pictures are shown: *fallwater*, *crackerfire*, and so on. Allow the children to help Frodo get the word parts in the correct order.

To Extend:
● Have children write their own compound or two-part words.

2. One Part of the Picture

Use a black marker to prepare a large simple line drawing of an object or animal. Select four to six parts of this picture and trace the outline of each of these on a separate piece of tracing paper. Present this activity to a small group of children or divide the class into several small groups. Give one of the picture parts to each child or group, making sure that no child or group sees what is on any other picture. Direct each child to verbally describe what is on his or her picture part. Remind the children that they are not supposed to guess what the picture is but instead just tell what they see. Tell the children to listen carefully and to try to decide if the part being described is like their part. After all of the parts have been described, tell the children that they all have one part of the same picture. Show the complete picture to the children and have each one match her or his part to the whole. This activity is a fine introduction or follow-up to the book *Seven Blind Mice* by Ed Young (1992).

3. Place That Word

Prepare some slips of paper with one word on each slip. Put the words in a basket or bowl and direct each child to select three of the slips. Assist in reading the words as needed. Challenge the children to create short stories incorporating the words as follows: use the first word in the first sentence, the second word in the second sentence, and the third word in the third sentence.

4. Something Is Missing

Make up a simple story and read it to the children. Tell them to listen carefully because something is missing. As you read, omit blends. Read the story and ask what was missing. Help the children to recognize that you left off all of the blend sounds in the story. Read it again, stopping for the children to provide the missing parts of words. Following is a sample story:

Once upon a time, a young (ch)ild was (pl)aying in (th)e park. (Sh)e was having fun wi(th) a ball. (Th)en (sh)e went over to (th)e (sl)ide. (Sh)e (cl)imbed up and went down very fa(st). Next, (sh)e looked for her (fr)iend and a(sk)ed him to (pl)ay wi(th) her.

To Simplify:

● Post a list of possible blends for child reference as they listen to the story.

● Instead of omitting blend sounds, substitute a simple story with rhyming words and have the children supply the missing rhyme.

As I was playing, on the run,
Up in the sky shone the (sun).
It beat down with heat on me,
And I looked for shade under a (tree).
As I was sitting, on a log,
Along came my playful little (dog).
He was frisky, he was quick,
He soon found a throwing (stick).
When I was too tired to roam,
I turned my feet and headed (home).

To Extend:

● Encourage the children to write a missing blend story of their own to present to the group.

Physical

1. It's a Puzzlement

Teach your children how to be successful in assembling the parts of a jigsaw puzzle to complete the whole. The following steps are suggested:

● Look at the assembled puzzle before taking it apart. Notice the picture, the shapes of pieces and how they fit in the puzzle, and where colors are placed. (With an unassembled floor puzzle, show the children how to look at the picture on the box.)

● Take the pieces out, one at a time, and place them face up on the table/floor. Put pieces that go together near each other. (*Do not* allow children to "dump" puzzles out of frames. "Dumping" does not allow time to examine the whole or the parts and increases the difficulty of the task.) With an unassembled puzzle, show the children how to look for corner (two straight edges) and edge (straight side) pieces.

● Suggest that children start a puzzle by doing the corner and outside edge pieces first.

● Teach children how to gently "wiggle-wiggle" a piece if they think that they have the right piece but it doesn't go right into place.

● Suggest trying another piece or spot on a puzzle if it is difficult to find the place for/or a particular piece.

Hints for Success:

● Begin puzzle experiences with simple puzzles; a puzzle with a few large pieces or a frame with individual spaces for pieces are easiest for beginners.

● Make sure that puzzles are complete. If a piece is missing, ask children to search for it immediately.

● Try the puzzles yourself before presenting to the children so that you are familiar with them and can offer needed assistance.

● Provide a variety of puzzles so that all ability levels may be satisfied.

● Alternate the puzzles, leaving a few familiar ones in place, every week or so.

2. Modeling Dough Cut-Ups

Provide modeling dough, rolling pins, plastic coffee can lids, and plastic knives. You may also wish to give each child a small tray or placemat as a work surface. Tell the children that today they are going to be bakers. Give each child a portion of dough and model how to roll the dough out flat with a rolling pin. Use a coffee can lid to cut out a circle of dough or trace around the lid with a knife to cut out a circle. Remove the excess dough. Describe your actions as you work and direct the children to imitate making a dough circle. After everyone has a circle, give each child a knife to use in cutting the circles into two pieces. Look around the table and see if the pieces look alike or if they are different. Tell the children to also look and to tell you what they notice. Point out that everyone started with a similar circle but that after cutting, everyone had something different. Repeat the dough rolling and cutting, but vary the number of pieces that are cut. Continue to see how many different ways a circle can be divided into pieces.

To Simplify:

● Provide several precut, small dough circles for each child.

● Instead of coffee can lids, provide small, round cutters for each child.

To Extend:

● When cutting, tell the children to cut circles into equal pieces. In this case, the parts should look similar. Introduce the idea of halves, thirds, and quarters.

● Instead of cutting flat circles, provide only dough and knives and direct the children to construct dough cylinders before cutting.

● Using dough cylinders, ask the children to see how many circles they can cut from their cylinders.

3. Pour and Tell

Provide clear plastic jars, pouring cups, funnels, and rice, colored sand, or paper confetti. Give each participating child a container, funnel, cup, and a supply of the material to be poured. Tell each child to pour some into his or her container and then to tell how full it is—one-half, one-third, one-quarter, and so on.

To Simplify:

● Place rubber bands around the outside of the containers to indicate the various levels. Point to the rubber band that marks "one-half" and tell the child to pour to that line. Then say, "Now, your jar is half full."

To Extend:

● Provide measuring cups and spoons and a small bowl for each child in addition to the other materials listed. After the child has stated how full the container appears, direct her/him to use the measuring cups to measure the amount in the container and to return this amount to the container. Then, direct the child to measure into the bowl the amount that she/he has predicted as the balance needed to fill the container. For instance, if the child said that the container was half full, say, "Measure the amount in the container, return it to the container, and then measure an equal amount; pour this into the bowl and then add it to the original amount in the container. Is there just enough, too much, or too little?" (If one-third was the original amount, add two equal amounts or two-thirds; if one-quarter was the original amount, add three equal amounts or three quarters.)

4. Tong Transfer

Gather an assortment of containers, several pairs of kitchen tongs, and some yarn balls or small plastic figures. Show the children how to use the tongs to move one item at a time into a container. Give each of the children a pair of tongs and a container. Tell them to use the tongs to move the items, one at a time, into their containers until they are half full. Direct them to predict how many more items will be needed to fill the containers. The children should then count out that

number of items and move them, one at a time, into the container. Ask them to evaluate if their predictions were accurate or too high or too low.

5. Tops and Bottoms

This activity gives the children an opportunity to explore parts and wholes while preparing some healthy snacks. Provide some vegetables such as carrots, radishes, celery stalks, pepper, broccoli stalks, and beets, as well as plastic knives. Direct the children to wash their hands and to help cut the vegetables. Begin by cutting into two pieces—tops and bottoms. Place the tops and bottoms in separate serving bowls. When children come to snack, direct them to select a top or bottom and to cut it into bite-sized parts to eat. Encourage the children to tell which part they choose, a top or a bottom.

Hint for Success:

● Parboil the vegetables briefly to make cutting with plastic knives easier. Chill before cutting and serving.

To Simplify:

● The teacher precuts the vegetables into tops and bottoms. Challenge the children to select a top and bottom of the same vegetable to eat. Have them explain their choices.

To Extend:

● Direct the children to cut the vegetables into tops, bottoms, and middles.

Pretend Play

1. Costume Shop

Many dress-up items such as shirts, skirts, capes, dresses, jackets, vests, hats, jewelry, scarves, wigs, and gloves will be needed for this activity. Be sure to include items suitable for both boys and girls and items from a variety of cultures. Add a cash register, money, bags or boxes, and mirrors. Shop personnel will assist customers in assembling a complete costume outfit. Encourage the children to carefully consider if each outfit is whole or if more pieces are needed before packing the completed costume into a bag or box and completing the sale.

2. Parts and Wholes Restaurant

Prepare a pizza restaurant set-up in the pretend play area that includes tables, chairs, range, refrigerator, sink, dishes, cake pans, cash register, money, pizza boxes, and menus. Also construct some "pizza" dough by gluing beige felt onto cardboard circles (use circles that fit inside the cake pans). Cut each dough circle into four equal pieces. For pizza "toppings," cut small felt pieces to resemble cheese (orange or gold); pepperoni (one-inch magenta circles with black dots—use a permanent felt-tipped marker); mushroom slices (tan, cut in mushroom shape); green pepper (green strips); olives (olive green circles with red "pimento" circles glued in center); and onion (white strips). Place each topping in a separate container. Arrange the cake pans, dough circles, and toppings on a work counter in the kitchen area of the restaurant. The food servers will take orders and pass them on to the pizza makers. The pizza makers will place enough dough circles in a pan to make a whole circle and will then place toppings on the pizza to fill the customer's order. Encourage the food servers to check each order to be sure that it is complete before serving or boxing the pizza for the customer.

To Simplify:

● Reduce the materials available to children by gluing pizza toppings on the dough circles ahead of time. To work on parts and wholes, have children focus on setting the table with all of the appropriate items for each setting and on making a complete pizza with the prepared slices.

To Extend:

● Involve the children in cutting the pizza toppings.

● Add spaghetti and meatballs and salad selections to the menu items. Use white yarn and brown yarn pompons for the spaghetti and meatballs. To make salads, use small paper plates with varied shades of green tissue paper lettuce, orange construction-paper carrot strips, and red paper tomato slices glued in place. Continue to focus on having the children decide when meals, salads, and so on, are complete or whole.

3. Repair Shop

Provide a construction toy such as Mobilos®, Tinker Toys®, Bolt 'n' Play®, or snap blocks. Also provide a shop counter, cash register, paper order pads, and pencils. Encourage some of the children to build partial or incomplete machines or toys with the building materials. These incomplete items are then taken to the repair shop to be finished by the workers there. The customer taking the item in for repair should give the shop clerk information regarding the intended purpose or missing parts. These instructions may be recorded on the paper to assist repair workers in their work. Shop personnel add the missing parts and charge the customer for the

work. Of course, the customer should be satisfied that the work has been completed and that the finished item is now whole and ready for use.

Social

1. Class Rainbow

Plan several days for this activity to be completed. First, ask the parents of the children in your class to send in small (1" x 2" or 2" x 2") fabric pieces. When you have a good assortment, sort the fabric pieces into seven color containers: red, orange, yellow, green, blue, indigo, and violet. You might also have a container of pieces that could go in any color band. Prepare a large sheet of heavy white paper by drawing rainbow arc lines and label each arc with a single color name in several places. (Note: The colors in a rainbow go from violet at the bottom to red at the top.) Make each arc 2 to 4 inches wide. Provide children with glue and the presorted fabric pieces and direct them to glue the fabric pieces on the rainbow until it is finished. As the children work, discuss each color arc and have the children decide when each arc is completely covered with fabric—in other words, whole. When all of the arcs are covered, the rainbow will be whole. Hang it in your room as a wall decoration. When it is time to take it down, cut it into rainbow strips from top to bottom and give each child "one part of our rainbow" to take home.

To Simplify:

● Give the children one color of fabric pieces at a time. Show them where those pieces belong and have them tell you when that arc is whole. Continue with one color at a time until all of the arcs have been covered and the rainbow is whole.

To Extend:

● Before presenting the paper and glue, have the children sort the fabric pieces, deciding into which container each should go.

2. Do the Parts Make a Whole?

Provide pita bread and tortillas; American or Swiss cheese slices; clean scissors, plastic knives, and cutting boards; and small serving bowls and plates labeled with the numerals 2, 3, 4, 5, 6. Direct the children to wash their hands before helping to prepare snacks for the class. Tell the children that they will be cutting the breads and cheeses into parts for snack. Have each child decide and tell how many parts (2, 3, 4, 5, or 6) he or she will be cutting before starting to cut. Have the child put the resulting parts into the corresponding bowls (bread) or on the plates (cheese). At serving time, direct the children to take the number indicated from a serving dish and to try fitting the pieces together to form a whole. Encourage them to discuss the results.

To Simplify:

● Omit the numeral markers. Direct children to cut the breads and cheeses into a specific number of parts (three or four).

3. The Other Half

Gather a set of simple pictures (cut from magazines or coloring books) and mount them on paper. Cut each picture into halves. Give each child in the group one-half of a picture and challenge everyone to find the person who has the other half. Once the matches are discovered, direct the children to work together to paste the halves together on a larger sheet of paper to make a whole picture and to write their names on it. Display the completed whole pictures in the classroom.

To Simplify:

● Use a different colored paper for mounting each picture pair to provide a color clue as children are seeking matches.

To Extend:

● Do not mount the picture halves on paper; simply give the children the picture halves.

● Instead of halves, cut each picture into three or four parts and direct the children to find the people who have the corresponding parts.

Teacher Resources

Field Trip Ideas

1. Plan a trip to a shopping center or mall where children can see and discuss parts and wholes. Consider the total number of stores that are each one part of the whole mall and the kinds of stores that are put together to create a shopping mall. Arrange with the manager of one store to visit the store and see all of its parts: merchandise, display areas, storage areas, dressing rooms, and the sales counter.

2. Arrange a visit to a restaurant for a tour or a simple meal. Before the trip, talk about the different parts that make up a whole meal, such as salad, beverage, entree, and dessert. During the visit, pay special attention to the various areas where these

different parts are prepared.

3. Visit any workshop or factory where separate parts are assembled to create a whole. Inquire if your local high school has a shop class that would allow youngsters to visit, preferably to watch simple toys such as wooden trucks being assembled.

Classroom Visitors

1. Arrange for a chef or baker to visit and prepare a simple dish that contains many parts, such as a pizza, casserole, or salad. If possible, plan for children to create a similar dish with the visitor or following the visit.

2. Invite a parent who sews to demonstrate how to make a simple garment using several parts to create a whole.

3. If a visit to a workshop is not possible, invite a worker to bring in some parts and demonstrate how these are put together to make a finished whole.

Children's Books

Barton, B. (1981). *Building a House*. New York: Greenwillow Books.

Carle, E. (1976). *Do You Want to Be My Friend?* New York: HarperCollins.

Carle, E. (1970). *Pancakes, Pancakes!* New York: Alfred A. Knopf.

Flournoy, V. (1985). *The Patchwork Quilt*. New York: Dial Books for Young Readers.

McMillan, B. (1991). *Eating Fractions*. New York: Scholastic.

Pekarik, A. (1992). *Sculpture Behind the Scenes*. New York: Hyperion Books for Children.

Pfister, M. (1992). *The Rainbow Fish*. New York: North-South Books.

Turner, A. (1994). *Sewing Quilts*. New York: Macmillan.

Yeoman, J., and Blake, Q. (1995). *The Do-It-Yourself House That Jack Built*. New York: Atheneum Books for Young Readers.

Young, E. (1992). *Seven Blind Mice*. New York: Putnam.

Adult References

Bley, E. S. (1973). *The Best Singing Games: For Children of All Ages*. New York: Sterling Publishing.

Charlesworth, R., and Lind, K. (1990). *Math and Science for Young Children*. Albany, NY: Delmar.

Kostelnik, M., et al. (1993). *Developmentally Appropriate Programs in Early Childhood Education*. New York: Macmillan.

Kostelnik, M., et al. (1991). *Teaching Young Children Using Themes*. Glenview, IL: GoodYearBooks.

McDonald, D. T., and Simons, G. M. (1989). *Musical Growth and Development, Birth Through Six*. New York: Schirmer Books.

Geometrical Exploration

Terms, Facts, and Principles (TFPs)

1. Objects have different shapes.
2. The shape of an object is determined by its form. The shape of an object is independent of its color, size, texture, consistency, volume, and weight.
3. People use particular words to describe shape.
4. Some shapes are two-dimensional (flat); they have height and width.
5. Some two-dimensional shapes are circles, squares, triangles, rectangles, hexagons, pentagons, crescents, diamonds, and arches.
*6. Some shapes are three-dimensional (solids); they have depth as well as height and width.
*7. Some three-dimensional (solid) shapes are spheres, cubes, and cones.
*8. Some shapes are regular, meaning there are rules that determine their form.
*9. Some shapes are irregular, meaning there are no rules that determine their form.
10. Some objects have a shape of their own.
*11. Some objects take on the shape of their container.
12. People use particular words to describe or compare locations.
13. Some of these location words are *over, under, beside, between, near, far, beneath, on, off, right, left*.

Activity Ideas

Aesthetic

1. Arty Shapes

Provide an assortment of shapes cut out of construction paper or tagboard at the art table. Also make available paste or glue and art materials such as ribbon bits, confetti, glitter, and stickers or rubber stamps. Color glue is also a popular decorating choice. Invite children to select and decorate the shape(s) of their choice. Display the completed shapes around the classroom by placing on bulletin boards or punch a hole in the shapes and suspend from the ceiling with fish line.

To Simplify:

- Provide only large (9" x 12") shapes.

- Instead of cut-out shapes, provide paper with shapes drawn with thick black permanent marker for children to decorate.

To Extend:

- Provide fairly small shapes (two to four inches).

- Add shape templates and scissors to the available materials. Invite children to draw or trace and cut their own shapes to decorate.

2. Far and Near

This activity is designed to help children become aware of distance perspective in artwork. Collect a few examples of art prints that illustrate things that are far and near. Show one of these to the children and lead a discussion about how far and near the objects in the print appear to the viewer. Ask the children how the artist is able to accomplish this. Point out that the placement in the picture and the size of the object seem to create this perspective. Present other prints and encourage the children to discuss what they notice about the placement and size of the objects in those as well.

To Simplify:

- Before presenting an art print, give each child two small balls that are identical (Ping Pong balls work well). Direct the children to hold one ball in each hand (demonstrate how to hold a ball with your thumb and fingertips). Hold one ball close to your eyes and extend the other arm as far as possible. Direct the children to imitate this position. Ask which ball appears larger—the near ball or the far ball. Direct the children to slowly bring the far ball closer to their eyes and to tell you what they notice.

To Extend:

- Tell the children that they will be drawing pictures of things that are far and near. Talk with the children about things that they are able to draw. Tell them to decide what they will draw and which things will be large and low on the paper and which will be small and at the top. Provide drawing materials such as paper and pencils, crayons, or markers. As children complete their drawings, allow them to display and describe their work with an emphasis on the distance perspective.

3. Flat or Not?

Gather an assortment of pictures or prints that include shapes, both flat and solid. Challenge the children to find and name the shapes within the pictures and to state if the shapes that they see are flat or not flat.

Hint for Success:

- Carry this activity out only after the children are familiar with basic shapes and their correct names.

4. The Rest of the Picture

Cut a shape such as a three- to four-inch circle, square, rectangle, or triangle out of each sheet of easel paper (18" x 24" newsprint) that you plan to use at your easel for the next few days. The shapes should be cut somewhat toward the center of the paper but not exactly in the middle. Tape a smaller piece of paper on the back of the large easel paper to cover each shape hole. Use the cut-out papers at the easel. Challenge the children to incorporate the shapes into their pictures as they paint. For instance, a circle might become a sun with rays painted out from the edges or the center of a flower with petals painted around the circle; a square might become a window in a house; a rectangle may become the body of a truck, and so on.

To Simplify:

- Instead of cutting out the shapes, draw them on the easel paper with a black marker.

To Extend:

- Provide shape templates and encourage the children to select, trace, and cut their own choice of shapes before painting.

5. Shape Hunt

Select a shape such as a square, circle, rectangle, or triangle. Present an example of the shape to a group of children and ask them to tell you what they notice about it. Once they seem to recognize the characteristics of the shape, direct them to look around the classroom in a hunt for similar shapes. Acknowledge correct responses. Point out why a suggested shape does not match the designated shape when children give incorrect responses. Repeat with other shapes.

To Simplify:

- Present only one shape per day.

- Before presenting the activity, place lots of examples of the shape around the classroom to ensure that the children will be able to find them easily.

To Extend:

- Present and discuss several shapes at once. Then give each child several tags with shape names printed on them. Direct the children to place their initials on their tags. Begin the "Shape Hunt" and tell the children to place a tag with the correct shape name on each shape that they spot.

● Conduct a "Solid Hunt" instead of a "Shape Hunt." Show the children a solid such as a sphere, cube, or cone and allow them to examine and handle it. Discuss the characteristics of the solid and challenge the children to find other examples of the solid in the classroom.

Affective

1. Back in Place

Here's a classroom management technique that will make block area clean-up easier for you and the children. Trace outlines of the blocks on your block shelf on construction paper and laminate or use self-adhesive vinyl (you may wish to coordinate this with other items in the classroom). Cut out and mount these block shapes in the appropriate spaces on the block shelves to serve as guides during clean-up time. Encourage the children to match blocks to the outlines and to place blocks back in place on the correct shelves as they dismantle their structures. Be sure to compliment the clean-up crew on a job well done!

Hints for Success:
● Be sure that there is sufficient room for all of the blocks of one type in the space that you label for that type.

● Place the block shapes high enough on the shelf so that they are easily seen when the children are working.

To Extend:
● Instead of tracing the block shapes, print out shape-name labels (cubes, cylinders, single units, arches, double units, boards) to mount in the block spaces on the shelves.

● Rather than mounting shapes on the shelves, make a diagram of the block shelf with block shapes indicated in the appropriate spaces. Post this so that children may refer to it when looking for particular block shapes.

2. Find the Shapes on Me

Conduct this activity during a small or large group time. Invite a child to stand in front of the group and direct the other group members to look carefully and point out and name any shapes that they observe on him or her.

To Simplify:
● Prepare a supply of varied shapes cut out of paper. As you observe a shape on the child, hold up the corresponding shape and tell the children to look carefully for a triangle, for example.

To Extend:
● Prepare a supply of varied shapes cut out of paper and a recording chart (posterboard divided into columns and rows, with each child's name listed in a row in the far left-hand column). As a shape is observed on a child, give a corresponding paper shape to the child to place on the recording chart. After each child has been observed and recorded, you will have a graph of "Shapes on Me" to discuss, post, and use for future reference.

● Use a piece of paper and marker to record the shapes and where they were observed on each child.

Christopher

Shirt - 4 circles	(buttons)
2 squares	(pockets)
Jeans - 2 triangles	(stitching)
Shoes - 4 cylinders	(shoelace tips)

Keep these papers until all of the children in the group have had an opportunity to be observed for shapes. Give each child his/her recording sheet and blank paper and pencil. Direct the children to draw a self-portrait and to include the shapes observed on them in their drawing.

3. Shapely Tags

Prepare a variety of small (two- to four-inch) construction-paper shapes in a variety of colors. Also provide paste or glue sticks, markers, round paper punches, and 34-inch lengths of yarn. Direct the children to select two or three shapes for a name tag. Tell them that the shapes may be arranged and glued together in any way that they wish. After the shapes have dried, direct the children to print their names on their tags, punch holes, and insert a length of yarn. Knot the yarn ends together so that the tags may be worn as necklaces. As children are wearing their Shapely Tags, ask them to tell you about the shapes that they used to make them.

To Simplify:
● Provide only one shape in varied sizes and colors. Refer to the completed tags as your circle (or square or triangle) tags.

To Extend:

● Provide only very small (one- to three-inch) shapes, including many circles and triangles, and suggest that the children use the shapes to construct a shapely picture tag.

Cognitive

1. Describe a Structure

Take a walk around your school building or another building and look for examples of shapes on the building. Look at entrances, windows, trim, chimneys, and walls.

2. Find a Solid

Challenge the children to search the playground for examples of solid shapes. These may be found in balls (spheres), sand toy funnels (cones), and tunnels and slides (cylinders).

3. Homey Shapes

Gather a collection of common household objects such as kitchen utensils, food containers, and cleaning tools. Allow the children to explore these for a while. Ask them to show you any shapes that they find on the items. Point out that they have found many shapes on things that might be found at home. Suggest that they look for more shapes when they go home.

4. Measure the Edge

Gather an assortment of solid shapes and allow the children to explore them. Ask the children to show you the edges of each shape. (This may prove very challenging! Proceed only if children are able to identify the edges. If they are unable to identify the edges, go to the activity simplification below.) Provide string, scissors, and small pictures of each shape. Suggest that the children use the string to measure the edges of each solid. Direct them to cut a string that represents the edges and to attach it to the small pictures. Compare the resulting string lengths.

To Simplify:

● Omit the string. Have the children watch as you trace the edge of a shape with a fingertip. Provide corresponding solids for the children and direct them to trace the edges with their fingers. Repeat with other solids.

To Extend:

● Before measuring the edges, ask the children to predict which shape will have the longest edge and which one will have the shortest edge. Record these predictions on a class chart with pictures of the shapes along the top row and the children's names down the left-hand column. On the chart for each child, write L under the shape he or she predicts will have the longest edge; write S for the predicted shortest edge.

5. Shape Walk

Arrange to take the children on a walk around the school, playground, or neighborhood. Before embarking on your walk, tell the children that you are going on a Shape Walk. Everyone should be on the look-out for shapes. Suggest that they shout out "I spy a shape" when they see a shape so that they can show their discovery to all of the class.

To Simplify:

● As you spot a shape, call children's attention to the location and give hints to assist them in successfully finding shapes.

● Before taking the children on the hunt, scout out the area to be certain that there are many shapes to be found. If you do not see many, "plant" a few by posting some shape cut-outs where they are clearly visible.

To Extend:

● Record the shapes observed during the hunt. Take along a bag of paper shapes with pencils on the walk. Write the location on the corresponding paper shape as each is spotted.

● Direct the children to hunt for solid geometrical forms such as spheres, cylinders, and cubes instead of flat shapes.

Construction

1. A Shape of My Own

After the children are familiar with common shapes, provide colored construction paper and scissors and suggest that they make an original shape of their own design.

To Simplify:

● Omit scissors. Provide lightweight paper and have the children tear a "Shape of My Own."

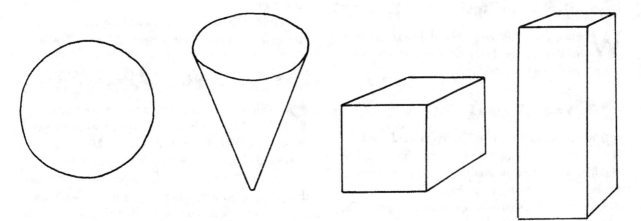

Which Shape Has the Longest Edge?				
Ashley	S		L	
Joey	S	L		
Marek	L	S		
Megan		S		L
John		S		L
Jimmy			S	L
Paolo			S	L

To Extend:

● After the children have created their shapes, suggest that they each give their shape a name. Give each child a piece of 9" x 12" white paper and direct them to trace their shapes on the white paper. Tell the children to print their names on the papers and to also write the name of their shape; assist with printing as needed. Prepare a cover for a class "Book of Shapes" and assemble the book using your cover and the shape pages that the children prepared. Place the book in the math or reading center so that the children can look at it frequently.

● Challenge the children to make smaller or larger versions of their special shape. Use these to create a class bulletin board display. Include the shape names in your display.

2. Build and Tell

Whenever the children build with blocks, encourage them to describe their block constructions using correct shape names.

3. Solid Shapes

Provide an assortment of lightweight cardboard or tagboard pieces, tape, and scissors. Challenge the children to use these materials to create solid shapes. Explain that a solid shape has three dimensions (height, width, and depth), so their shapes must not be flat. They may construct standard solids such as cubes or cones or shapes of their own design.

4. Terrific Towers

Cover the blocks on your block shelves with a cloth or paper curtain, leaving only the cylinder and cube blocks accessible. Tell the children that today they are to build Terrific Towers using only cubes and cylinders. Challenge them to think of as many tower arrangements as they can.

To Simplify

● Prepare two containers of blocks: place only cubes in one container and only cylinders in the other. Tell children to choose a container of solid shapes and to use the cubes or cylinders in their container to create a Terrific Tower by stacking the blocks as high as they can.

To Extend:

● Provide paper and pencils and suggest that children draw pictures of their completed Terrific Towers.

5. Geometric Sculptures

Provide a variety of geometric wood shapes and wood glue. Give each child a piece of waxed paper to use as a work surface. (Write each child's name on a piece of masking tape and affix to the waxed paper.) Tell the children to select some wood shapes and to use the wood glue to connect the shapes making sculptures of their own design. Remind the children that wood glue takes some time to set and that they may have to hold the pieces in place for a few minutes after applying the glue. Allow the sculptures to dry on the waxed paper.

Language

1. Shapely Letters

Cut a large supply of small (one inch or smaller) construction-paper circles, squares, rectangles, and triangles. In addition, print out a name card for each child using letters of the same approximate size as the shapes. Give each child her or his name card and a supply of shapes. Direct the children to find shapes that fit the letter shapes in their names and to place them on the letters. Give each child an opportunity to discuss the shapes that were found in his or her name.

To Simplify:

● Prepare an alphabet chart that shows the shapes in each letter for the children to use as a reference in identifying the shapes in their names. Use color shapes on the chart to make the shapes more easily seen.

To Extend:

● Direct the children to look at the letters in their names and to try to create the letters using the shapes. They may then paste the shapely letters on a paper.

2. Shape Story

Prepare some shapes, distribute them among the children, and ask them to hold the shapes as you tell the following story. Assign a sound to each shape: circle, "Hmmmm"; square, "click" tongue; rectangle, clap hands; triangle, stamp feet. Model the sounds and have the children practice each one as you hold up a sample of the corresponding shape. With this preparation complete, direct children to listen carefully for either their shape name or for something that might look like their shape and to make their sound when the shape appears in the story. Remind them that several sounds may be needed at the same time.

One day when the round *sun* was shining, two children played in front of their *house* with a *box* of musical instruments. They had *drums*, *triangles*, and *bells*. They were having lots of fun making music and marching when suddenly they heard a loud siren. A fire *truck* was coming down their street with lights flashing and the siren blaring! The children were very surprised when the fire *truck* stopped right in front of their *house*. The firefighters jumped off of the *truck* and began to rush to the *door* with *hatchets* in their hands. Just as they were about to hit the *door* with the hatchets, Mother opened the *door* and said "Stop! The fire is out." The firefighters walked into the *house* to check on the fire and Mother walked over to the children. "There was a fire in the kitchen," she said. "Something in a *pan* caught fire. I called the fire department and then I threw some baking soda on the *pan*. The fire is out and everything is fine." The children played a tune on the *instruments* as the firefighters walked back to the *truck*.

Sun = circle

Box = square, rectangle

House = rectangle (windows), square (house), triangle (roof)

Truck = circle (wheels, lights), rectangle (truck body)

Drum, bells, instruments = circle

Triangle, instruments = triangle

Hatchets = triangle

Pan = circle

The children may also assign shapes to the people.

To Simplify:

● Prepare simple drawings of the shape pictures to hold up as they are mentioned to provide a visual cue.

To Extend:

● Encourage the children to think of new stories for the class to sound out.

3. Shape Talk

As your children build with unit blocks, introduce correct shape names to describe the blocks. You may refer to these by either the two-dimensional or three-dimensional names: triangle, rectangle, cube, cylinder, cone, arch. Encourage the children to also use these names when describing or requesting blocks.

Physical

1. Lace a Shape

Cut some shapes out of heavy cardboard, Styrofoam, or plastic. Print the name of the shape on each one. Punch holes an inch or so apart and a half-inch from the edge of the shape. Tie a shoelace or yarn piece with a masking tape tip to each shape cut-out. Direct the children to lace the yarn/shoelace through the holes to form the shape. Be sure to direct the children to lace around the edges from one hole to the next and not across the shape.

2. Move to the Shape

Cut several large shapes out of colored posterboard and print the shape name on each one. Laminate these to extend their usefulness. Use these for gross motor activities in a gym or outside. Tell the children to listen carefully to some shape directions. Place the shapes on the floor or ground and direct the group of children to move in particular ways to a specific shape: hop to a square; roll around a circle; jump around an oval; gallop to a rectangle; jump three times on a triangle; and so on.

3. Over, Under, In Between

This activity is designed to teach and reinforce location descriptions such as *over*, *under*, *between*. Give each child two small colored blocks and a small animal or person figure. Allow a few moments of exploration time. Direct the children to watch you and do just as you do with your materials. Perform the following actions and accompany your movements with verbal description as you work:

1. Place the red block **above** the blue block.
2. Place the figure **next to** the blue block.
3. Place the figure **in front of** the blue block.
4. Place the red block **beside** the figure.
5. Place the figure **behind** the red block.
6. Hold the red block **over** the figure.
7. Hold the figure **under** the blue block.
8. Hold the red block **up.**
9. Hold the blue block **down.**
10. Place the figure **between** the blocks.

Once these location words are mastered, add additional blocks so that the children can construct a simple walled enclosure and practice *inside*, *outside*, *near* and *far*.

To Simplify:
● Introduce only a few directions at a time. Review previously introduced location words before teaching new words.

To Extend:
● Encourage the children to place a block or figure and to use the accurate location word to tell where they have put it.

Pretend Play

1. Shape Bookstore

Gather an assortment of shape books to stock the shelves. Add a cash register and some play money, a telephone, and some bags for purchases. Post a "Shape Bookstore" sign in the area. Suggest that a few children work as clerks to assist customers in finding shape books to purchase. Encourage the children to use correct names for the shapes as they work and shop in the store.

Hints for Success:
● Present this activity only after you have introduced the shapes and many of the children are familiar with them.

● Decorate the Shape Bookstore with some shapes that have the correct names printed on them.

To Simplify:
● Select books that include only two or three basic shapes.

To Extend:
Provide shape stencils or templates and pencils or markers; precut shapes and glue sticks; 5-1/2" x 8" paper; and a stapler. Suggest that children make books to display and sell in the Shape Bookstore.

2. Sign Shop

Provide an assortment of shapes made of tagboard or posterboard, markers or crayons, pencils, rulers, cash register, play money, a telephone, and some paper for taking orders. Arrange the available shapes in an interesting manner. Tell the children that the sign shop will make signs to order. Explain that the customers will choose a shape from those on display and will tell the clerk what the sign is to say. The customer and clerk will prepare an order form that will be given to the sign makers. The sign makers will then create the signs that have been ordered. Customers may return to pick up and pay for their signs.

To Simplify:
● Provide only two or three shapes for signs.

● Before introducing this activity, prepare some pre-printed words for use in the signs. Your prepared words might include the names of all of the children, several each of "This room belongs to ____," "This chair is reserved for ____," and "Please save—this belongs to ____." Sign makers will then find and glue the appropriate words on the signs as they are ordered.

To Extend:
● Provide tagboard, rulers and/or large shape templates (cut from posterboard), pencils, and scissors. Encourage the sign makers to draw and cut the shape ordered for each sign.

3. Pack and Wrap Shop

Provide an assortment of boxes, a variety of objects to be packed, newspaper comic sections or other large lightweight paper, scissors, and tape. Tell the children that the shop workers must decide what box is needed for each object, pack the items, and then use the paper and tape to wrap the boxes. Suggest that they try placing items in boxes until they find a good fit. Remind them to consider the shape of the object and the box and that the box shouldn't be too big or the object will bump around in it. Support the children as they explore and experiment with shapes and sizes. Encourage the children to help each other in cutting and wrapping the paper around the packages.

To Simplify:
● Omit the paper. Direct the children to find boxes of the appropriate shape and size for the items to be packed.

To Extend:
● Add pictures of the items to be wrapped to the materials for this activity. Challenge children who did not wrap a package to examine the pictures of objects and try to guess what is in each box. Encourage the children to give reasons for their predictions. Open the packages and see if they predicted accurately.

Social

1. Books for Babes

For this activity, you will need magazines with lots of varied pictures, white and colored construction-paper shapes (circles, triangles, and squares), scissors, glue sticks, a paper punch, reinforcement rings, and binder rings. Invite the children to use the materials to create shape books that will be used by younger children. Provide each child with a pair of colored paper shapes to use as book covers and several corresponding white shapes to be pages. Direct the children to look through the magazines for pictures of objects that are shaped like the book that they are making and to cut some out to paste on the book pages. Once all of the pages have shape objects on them, assemble the books and punch a hole through all of the pages and covers. Place reinforcement rings around each hole and fasten together with a binder ring. Add a title such as "My Triangle Book." The finished books may be given to younger siblings or may be donated to a group of younger children.

Hint for Success:
● Laminate the pages before assembling the books to extend their usefulness.

To Simplify:
● Provide precut pictures and pre-assembled books so that the children simply select and glue shapes on the book pages.

To Extend:
● Suggest that the children write simple descriptions on each page and/or number the pages.

2. Circle Band

Gather a selection of rhythm instruments that feature circular shapes, such as tambourines, cymbals, and drums, and put them in some circular containers. Arrange the children in a circle, seated on the floor, and tell them that today they are going to be members of a Circle Band. Point out that they are seated in a circle and that all of the instruments have circles on them. (Be sure that the formation is a circle if you call it that.) Pass out the instruments; direct the children to look for circles as they see the instruments. Lead the Circle Band in some rhythmic activities.

3. Friendship Circle

Before beginning this activity, gather the children and show them a circle. You may use a hula hoop, embroidery hoop, or any other circle to which you have access. Ask if anyone can tell where the circle begins and ends. Since they shouldn't be able to do so, point out that this is one of the things that makes a circle special. Once it is formed, it is not possible to see the beginning or end. Arrange the group of children in a circle; include yourself in the formation. (Be certain that the shape formed is a circle.) Have the children join hands. Tell the children that this is a Friendship Circle and that you are going to pass some love around through the whole group. Explain that the love will move from one person to the next and that you, the teacher, will start the love moving by gently squeezing the hand of the person next to you. That person will pass the love to the next person by gently squeezing that person's hand, and the love will move around the entire circle until it comes back to you. Further explain that if everyone watches the hands, it is possible to see the love move. Remind the children that love does not hurt, so it is important that all hand-squeezing be done gently, not too hard. Begin passing the love by squeezing the hand of the child next to you and verbally cueing children as needed to keep the love moving. When the love gets back to you, comment that the children did a great job of passing the love around the entire circle so that it came back to where it started. Point out that although you selected a particular point on the circle to start and end the passing of the love, a complete circle has no beginning or end. The love in your circle could have started at any point and still would have been able to travel the entire way around.

4. Hokey Pokey

The "Hokey Pokey" is a frequently used, and sometimes misused, action game. When you do the "Hokey Pokey" with your class, avoid teaching misinformation. Combining verbal descriptions with physical action reinforces the information, so if children are saying "right" and moving left, they may have difficulty in later learning the correct labels. For instance, if you tell the children to stand in a circle, be sure that it is a circle. Better yet, tell the children to join hands and spread out. The result will be close to a circle, but doesn't require the circle label. When you sing the words, omit the "right" and "left" labels. Instead say, "You put your hand in" and "You put your other hand in." If you want to use the "Hokey Pokey" to teach right and left, pay careful attention, and immediately and gently correct any child who puts the incorrect side in. A special cue also helps. Try stamping a red rabbit on the right hand of each child or put a rubber band on each right wrist and ankle. Point out that one hand has company, the "red rabbit or rubber band right" and one is alone, the "lonely left." As you sing refer to the "red right" and "lonely left." If you have never heard the "Hokey Pokey," the words (as revised) go as follows:

You put your hand in,
You take your hand out.
You put your hand in,
And you shake it all about

You do the Hokey Pokey,
And you turn yourself about
That's what it's all about!

You put your other hand in,
You take your other hand out.
You put your other hand in,
And you shake it all about.

You do the Hokey Pokey,
And you turn yourself about
That's what it's all about!

Repeat with leg, shoulder, hip, knee, and other body parts. End with "your whole self."

Teacher Resources
Field Trip Ideas

1. Visit an art museum or exhibit and look for patterns or shapes in the artwork on display. Your visit may be enriched by obtaining postcards or photographs of some of the pieces on display and introducing these to the children before your visit. Give one of these pictures to a small group of children and challenge them to find their pattern or shape at the museum.

2. Take a Shape Walk in the neighborhood around your school. Look for shapes as you walk. You should be able to see many examples of circles, squares, rectangles, and triangles if you look carefully at the buildings, vehicles, and signs along the route. You may also wish to try a Shape Walk around your school to find three-dimensional shapes. If you look carefully, you should see many cylinders, cubes, and spheres.

3. Visit a sporting goods store to see how many different kinds of spheres you can find. If possible, purchase some of these to use at school.

Classroom Visitors

1. Invite an artist such as a potter or weaver to visit the classroom to show some samples and demonstrate how they were created. Ask the artist to focus on patterns displayed on the finished pieces.

2. Invite a musician to demonstrate some percussion instruments of varied shapes such as a triangle, cymbals, and wood blocks. Arrange for the children to have opportunities to explore the instruments.

Children's Books

Baker, A. (1994). *Brown Rabbit's Shape Books*. New York: Grisewood & Dempsey.

Barner, N. N. (1995). *Space Race*. New York: Bantam Doubleday Dell.

Burns, M. (1994). *The Greedy Triangle*. New York: Scholastic.

Charles, N. N. (1994). *What Am I? Looking Through Shapes at Apples and Grapes*. New York: The Blue Sky Press.

Freidman, A. (1994). *A Cloak for the Dreamer*. New York: Scholastic.

Lankford, M. D. (1992). *Hopscotch Around the World*. New York: Morrow Junior Books.

MacDonald, S. (1994). *Sea Shapes*. New York: Gulliver Books.

Micklethwait, L. (1993). *I Spy Two Eyes: Numbers in Art*. New York: Greenwillow Books.

Murphy, C. (1992). *My First Book of Shapes*. New York: Scholastic.

Oliver, S. (1990). *My First Look at Shapes*. New York: David McKay.

Rann, T. et al. (1990). *My First Look at Shapes*. New York: Random House.

Schwager, I. (1993). *What's Different?* Lincolnwood, IL: Publications International.

Turner, A. (1994). *Sewing Quilts*. New York: Macmillan.

Voss, G. (1993). *Museum Shapes*. Boston: Museum of Fine Arts.

White, S. (1993). *Baby Bop Discovers Shapes*. Allen, TX: The Lyons Group.

Yenawine, P. (1991). *Shapes: Museum of Modern Art*. New York: Delacorte Press.

Adult References

Charlesworth, R., and Lind, K. (1990). *Math and Science For Young Children*. Albany, NY: Delmar Publishers.

Kostelnik, M., et al. (1993). *Developmentally Appropriate Programs In Early Childhood Education*. New York: Merrill.

Kostelnik, M., et al. (1991). *Teaching Young Children Using Themes*. Glenview, IL: GoodYearBooks.

Science and Scientists

Who? What? Why? Where? When? How?

Introduction

Children come into the world curious and eager to learn—this is the source of their survival. They display a sense of wonder and delight at the natural phenomena that surround them. Very early, they pose many of life's ultimate questions: How? Why? What if? and Why not? These are the same kinds of questions that adult scientists ask. Children, thus, are natural scientists. The role of the adult is to encourage children's curiosity, to promote their scientific inquiry, and to expand their understanding of the world around them.

In trying to help children find answers to their questions, adults sometimes shy away from explanations that involve the physical sciences because they lack familiarity with the content or because they are uncertain about how to explain these aspects of the world in ways that children can grasp. Furthermore, they are often unsure about where to begin. This unit is designed to address that dilemma.

Rationale

The unit "Science and Scientists" is exemplified by this educational maxim:

"I hear, and I forget,
I see, and I remember,
I do, and I understand."

In teaching youngsters, we know it is not sufficient merely to tell them how the world works, nor is it enough to give them demonstrations or ask them to learn about things from books. Children require direct, first-hand experiences in which the whole body is engaged to truly learn. This unit provides the ultimate in a hands-on study of what might otherwise seem an abstract set of disciplines—the physical sciences.

"Science and Scientists" is presented in a logical continuum, such that the skills and knowledge that children acquire in the first mini-theme, "The Process of Science," are applied to actual life experiences in the second mini-theme, "Physical Science in the Everyday World." Thus, through active involvement in the activities, children will explore materials, forces, and ideas in ways that will help them develop an understanding of the fundamental processes and principles of the physical sciences (physics and chemistry). Both mini-themes also emphasize that things happen for logical reasons. Often, because of their inexperience or level of cognitive development, children view the manifestations of science as "magical events," without discernible cause. Keeping that in mind, the activities in which they will be engaged promote the notion that while one may not always know why something happens, it is important to seek answers. This can be done by sharpening one's powers of observation and one's thinking skills. Furthermore, it is imperative to help children generalize their observations and the information they glean from their experimentation. To accomplish this, adults should draw the parallels among activities by reminding children of what they have discovered in the past and relating it to what they are observing in the present. Providing the means and opportunities for children to summarize their findings and the time to refer to these summaries is essential in this aspect of children's learning.

Finally, one of the primary goals of education in a democratic society is to help people develop critical thinking skills so they can make informed decisions about social and political issues, ranging from the environment and the allocation of natural and human resources to the space program and the development of new technologies. A unit such as this one gives children practice in critical thinking by offering numerous experiences in observing and evaluating phenomena and ideas, helping them learn how to obtain new information, and teaching them to apply this knowledge to solving new problems. These are skills that can be applied to all areas of life. Due to their essential nature, critical thinking skills pervade all aspects of both mini-themes.

Implementation

In this unit, children become familiar with the processes by which scientists find out about things. Through involvement with these processes, children work on acquiring key scientific skills:

● They learn to use their senses to gather information (explore).

● They practice determining quantity by observation and the use of instruments (measure).

● They make changes in objects and substances and observe the effects (manipulate/experiment).

● They decide which elements should be studied, which should be varied, and which should be controlled for further experimentation (define and control variables).

● They have experiences in analyzing data by comparing (recognizing similarities and differences), classifying (grouping by categories or attributes), seriating (sequencing from the most of something to the least and viceversa), and enumerating (numbering in some order).

● Children also learn to record and communicate their results by describing what they observe and think and making a record of it in a way that helps them and others understand and remember.

● Children learn to recognize patterns based on categorizing observations and giving them some meaning (infer/hypothesize), and they begin to use patterns to determine what might be expected to happen (predict).

● Finally, children are given opportunities to test their predictions and to formulate conclusions about the accuracy of their predictions. It is these processes that form the basis for the mini-theme "The Process of Science."

The experiences in the second mini-theme, "Physical Science in the Everyday World," allow children to use this scientific process to better understand the world in which they live. In this section, children explore the effects of heat, light, air, and sound. They then move on to the more abstract ideas of gravitational and magnetic forces. Here, too, all of their activities provide concrete experiences, rather than depending on analogy or symbolism—representations that are too abstract for most youngsters to understand.

"Science and Scientists" may be carried out in several ways. However, we strongly suggest beginning with the first mini-theme in order to establish foundation skills before embarking on any sub-unit in the second mini-theme or any of its activities.

1. Begin with a one- or two-week study of the "Process of Science" and then move on to "Physical Science in the Everyday World" for another one or two weeks.

2. If your time is limited, restrict your study to the first mini-theme.

3. Begin with the first mini-theme and move on to one or two of the elements of the second. For example, focus only on heat and light or on magnetism.

4. Certain aspects of this unit may be incorporated into other studies. As suggested in the activity, "Messing Around," a science exploration area should be included in every classroom in the same way as is a book or art area. By varying the tools or props, children can be encouraged to apply their observational, recording, and thinking skills to a number of different themes.

The Process of Science

Terms, Facts, and Principles (TFPs)

General Information

1. People are naturally curious about the world.

2. People learn about the world by observing, examining, exploring, manipulating, thinking about, and asking questions about the things in the world.

3. Scientists are people who study, in a systematic way, things and forces and how they interact.

4. Scientists think about objects and forces based on their past experience.

5. Scientists solve problems that they or other people pose.

6. A fundamental belief of scientists is that events occur as a result of some cause or reason.

7. Scientists try to answer such questions as: How? Why? What if?

8. Some of the problems scientists try to solve include: Why things happen, how things happen, what is happening now, what will happen next, and what will cause something different to happen?

9. Anyone can be a scientist: people of all ages, men and women, boys and girls, people from all over the world.

10. Scientists sometimes work alone and sometimes with others.

11. People use the results of scientific work to solve practical problems.

12. In order to study things, scientists:

- Collect Data: observe/explore (use their senses to gather information); measure (determine quantity by observation or the use of instruments); manipulate/experiment (make changes and observe the effects); and define and control variables (decide which elements should be studied or controlled for further experiments).

- Analyze Data: compare (recognize similarities and differences); classify (group by categories or attributes); seriate (sequence from the most of something to the least or viceversa); enumerate (number in some order); and recognize anomalies.

- Communicate Results: communicate/record (describe what they observe and think and record it in a way that helps themselves and others understand and remember).

- Formulate Conclusions: infer/hypothesize (recognize patterns based on categorizing observations and giving them some meaning using "If . . . then . . ." statements) and predict (use patterns to determine what might be expected to happen).

- Test Predictions: observe the situation for which a prediction was made; compare the observed and the predicted behaviors; formulate conclusions about whether or not the predictions were correct; record conclusions; and, if the predictions were incorrect, begin the process anew.

Gathering Information

13. Scientists gather information by: observing, examining, comparing, experimenting, and estimating.

14. Observing means to look at things, smell them, touch them, hold them, play with them.

15. Examining means to inspect, explore, look at closely, manipulate, and/or change.

16. Scientists may examine objects just once or more often; their examinations may be conducted in a day or two or over an extended period of time.

17. Scientists sometimes change objects and forces to find out: how they behave, what will happen next, and how they interact. This is called experimenting.

18. Scientists sometimes use tools to help them examine objects and forces. Tools aid in examining things accurately.

19. Some of the tools scientists use include: measuring tools (rulers, scales, thermometers, clocks, measuring containers), magnifiers, microscopes, telescopes, light bulbs, cameras, graph paper, prisms, weights, magnets, simple machines (inclined plane, pulley, lever), calculators, and computers.

20. Scientists often make estimates as a part of their study.

21. Estimating means to thoughtfully develop an idea of the amount without actually measuring. Estimating is done by visual or sensory examination and then making a guess based on that examination as well as past experience.

22. When people estimate, they use such words and phrases as: about, almost, nearly, approximately, similar in quantity to, like something else, and so on.

23. Based on their estimations, scientists can make a more thorough examination using formal tools and/or processes.

24. Sometimes it is important to be exact; sometimes an approximation is enough.

25. Scientists sometimes know in advance what they are looking for; sometimes scientists are not sure.

26. Sometimes scientists are surprised at what they find.

27. Scientists compare their investigations and findings with other people and with their own examinations over time.

28. Scientists become familiar with things by paying attention to details.

29. Scientists' examination skills improve with practice.

30. Scientists record the information they gather to help them remember and to let others know what they have observed.

31. Some ways of recording are: writing, drawing, photographing, recording electronically, telling it to someone else to write down, making symbols.

32. It is important that scientists compile records that are accurate and complete.

Formulating New Ideas

33. Scientists try to understand what they have observed.

34. Scientists draw conclusions based on the information that has been gathered by themselves and others.

35. Scientists act on the belief that events occur as a result of some cause or reason.

36. Scientists look for patterns in the information they gather.

*37. Scientist study patterns to determine the cause or reason for the observed behavior.

38. Scientists compare information by looking for similarities and differences.

39. Scientists classify information into categories by their attributes.

40. Scientists often arrange information into sequences. They may, for example, order things according to how much or little there is of something, or they may use chronological order. Sometimes these sequences are numbered.

41. Scientists think of many reasons to explain why something happens.

42. Scientists communicate their ideas to other people, both scientists and non-scientists.

*43. Scientists sometimes agree with one another and sometimes they have conflicting ideas about the conclusions they have reached.

Predicting and Testing

44. Predicting means to think about what will happen next.

45. Scientists make predictions based on their prior experiences, current knowledge, and their ideas about how things work.

46. Predictions are often based on patterns of events or sometimes on apparent anomalies. Over time, scientists discern patterns in how objects react in different circumstances. Scientists use these patterns to determine what might be expected to happen.

*47. Scientists have a better chance of predicting accurately when they understand the causes and reasons (how and why) a certain type of event occurs.

48. The only way to know if a prediction is correct is to test it. Scientists test predictions by comparing what is actually happening with what they thought would happen.

49. The tests scientists do based on their predictions are called experiments.

*50. Sometimes scientists observe the "real thing," and sometimes they observe the results of simulations.

51. More than one test is required to get an accurate confirmation.

52. Scientists make detailed records of their predictions and tests.

53. Sometimes scientists' predictions turn out to be correct; sometimes they are incorrect.

54. Scientists gain valuable information from the test, whether or not their predictions were right.

55. Based on the test or verification, scientists may change the way they do things in the future or they may decide to continue doing as they have done.

Activity Ideas

Aesthetic

1. Up, Up, and Away!

Provide scissors, glue, 12"x 18" sheets of white or colored paper, and several magazines from which children may cut pictures. Instruct children to cut out and glue pictures of any airborne objects they find onto the paper. A variation is to provide an even larger surface or bulletin board on which children can glue or staple the items they select. Title the collage "Up, Up, and Away." The collage will likely represent a mixture of natural and person-made items that share the common property of using air to stay aloft.

Hint for Success:

● Buy or collect magazines that focus on flying or airplanes, as well as nature magazines. These specialized publications are likely to depict a variety of appropriate objects from which children may choose.

2. Graph Crafts

Graph paper is a common tool used by scientists, and children can have fun experimenting with it.

Provide children with several different kinds of graph paper (such as different-size squares, various colors, and so on). Suggest that they use the special paper as a background for drawing or coloring with markers or watercolors.

Hints for Success:

● Choose markers or paints that are translucent so the lines on the graph paper can be seen through the drawings.

● Provide enough paper so children can experiment freely.

To Simplify:

● Give children one kind of graph paper at a time and vary it over a few days. Begin with paper that has large, well-defined squares, about 1/2" to 1" on a side. If necessary, draw large-sized grids yourself using a ruler and make copies for the children.

To Extend:

● Bring in pictures of tessellated or tile mosaics. Demonstrate how children can create their own mosaics by coloring the squares of the graph paper.

● Show children how to cut out their colored squares and glue them onto construction paper in random or planned designs. Begin with large squares and gradually, over time, introduce smaller squares as children's cutting abilities improve.

3. I'm Forever Blowing Bubbles

Bubbles are a fascinating source of experimentation and wonder. The primary scientific information about bubbles is that they are composed of a film surrounding air; they are round because a sphere is the shape that takes up the least amount of surface area with the maximum amount of volume. Children can directly observe and experience such phenomena as: all bubbles are round, bubbles are formed by a "skin" or film surrounding air, and the film of bubbles reflects the colors of the spectrum. For these experiments you need Bubble Mix (see the recipe below) and store-bought or homemade wands.

Bubble Mix (Recipe 1)

1 part liquid dish soap

1 part glycerin (or light Karo® syrup for younger children)

20 parts water

Mix the ingredients and allow to stand overnight.

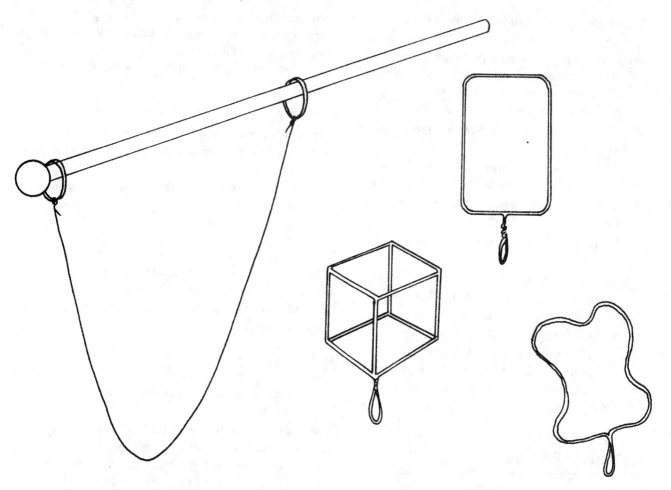

Bubble Mix (Recipe 2)

Mix liquid dish soap (Dawn® works best) with water until it is soapy. The more soap, the more stable the bubbles.

Bubble Wands

Make large bubble wands by following the diagrams above. For each wand you will need a thick wooden dowel, yarn or thick string, two small plastic hoops or rings, and a small nail.

Small bubble wands may be purchased. However, it is sometimes difficult to find ones that are not round. To create square, rectangular, or free-form shaped wands, twist thin wire into the desired shape or tie loops of string or yarn. Remember to include a handle.

Experiment 1: Show children how to dip an array of wands into the bubble mix and blow through the wand to produce bubbles (or wave the wands so the wind does the job). Pose such questions as: "Tell me what you see when you blow/shake the wands. What would happen if you used a wand in the shape of a square, triangle, oval, or other shape? Where do you think the bubbles went?"

Experiment 2: Use the large wands and a thick bubble solution to enable children to observe and examine the skin of the bubbles. Ask them to figure out what the skin is made of and how they know. Have them pop bubbles with their hands and examine the residue. Suggest that they try to push the bubbles out of shape without popping them. This will work if children dip their hands into the bubble mix until they are covered with film before touching the bubbles. The film on the wand and the film on the hand mix and create a continuous film. Have children experiment with dry hands, also, and remark on the differences they experience.

Experiment 3: On a sunny day, take the bubbles outside to avoid making a mess indoors. Use big bubble makers and have children practice until they can create gigantic bubbles. Dip the bubble maker into the mix, pull it out, and let the air push the film out. Encourage children to look at the film and describe what they see. The colors of the spectrum should be visible.

Hint for Success:

● These experiments require a lot of bubble mix, so be sure to make enough for everyone to have many refills.

To Simplify:

● Provide straws and cups of bubble mix for children to blow through to create their own bubbles. Be sure to demonstrate how to blow, rather than suck up, the mixture! For health reasons, provide each child with an individual straw and cup. Keep extra mix handy.

To Extend:

● Provide thin, flexible wire for children to create their own bubble-maker shapes. Explain to older children that air inside the bubble is pushing outward, and air outside the bubble is pushing inward.

● Encourage children to look closely at the colors on the bubble film and to describe them. Tell children that the colors appear because the light from the sun is being broken up into its individual colors and that the bubble lets us see those colors. Ask if children have ever seen a rainbow. (Provide photographs, if necessary.) Explain that in a rainbow the colors are clear and on the film they are not as clear but that the principle is the same.

Affective

1. Messing Around

Several famous scientists have promoted the notion of "messing around" with science. They have said that some of their most profound insights have been the result of free exploration of ideas and materials together with time to further play with those ideas. Just as you have a book/literacy and an art/creative area in your classroom, also provide a place where children have free access to scientific tools and materials. Include as many of the following items as you can gather:

aluminum foil

ball

beaker (plastic pitcher with a pouring lip)

binoculars

blotting paper

bulb-shaped basters

camera

containers (measuring)

diffraction grating

dish pan

electronic recording devices

eye droppers

film

filters (from fine coffee filters to wire mesh)

flashlight

fulcrum

graph paper

inclined plane ·

interlocking gears

level

lever

light sensitive paper

magnets (different shapes)

magnifying glasses

microscope (twin-lensed microscopes work well
    for young children)

periscope

plastic bags (small, self-sealing)

prism

pulley

ruler

scales

scissors

spinning top

sponges

string

telescope

thermometer

timers

weights

wire

Also, provide a variety of reference books and give children recording devices, cameras, pens, paper, pencils, and markers for recording their observations and findings, if they so desire. On a rotating basis, provide objects and substances for them to experiment with and upon.

Note: Recording is a key part of "messing around" because children, in their excitement, tend to run through many things in a hurry and then cannot remember what they did or the results of their experiments. Therefore, include some sort of routine recording even if it is a picture of the child doing something with the materials or a brief caption describing the experience. Older children may make journal entries by completing such statements as: "Today, I saw/learned . . ." or "I wonder . . ." or "If I do . . . then . . . happens."

Hints for Success:

● Keep this area open to children throughout the year, independent of the theme that is being studied. Expand it as the needs and desires of children change and develop.

● Provide a place where experiments that are in progress can be kept safe from interference. Hold a group discussion to help children decide how these should be labeled so others will know to leave them alone.

To Simplify:

● Younger children may be overwhelmed by too broad an array of implements, so limit their selection at first to the simplest and most familiar tools (such as magnifiers, magnets, or prisms).

To Extend:

● Encourage children to bring in objects and substances about which they are curious and have them add these to the "Messing Around" area.

2. Port-a-Kit

This activity is designed to familiarize children with some of the tools used by scientists in their investigations. Once they have had opportunities to use the tools, children may, on their own, examine objects in their school or home environment. Purchase or find a plastic box or tub with a tight-fitting lid and a handle. Place in it some of the science tools listed in "Messing Around." Be sure to include recording materials, as well, so that children may draw pictures of, write down, or dictate lists of what they want to investigate, check off items on a list as they gather their materials, and keep track of their findings. Take the Port-a-Kit on field trips, outdoors to the play area, and when you take walks around the building or in the neighborhood. Encourage children to use the tools to examine and observe the objects and environments they encounter. Include self-sealing plastic bags or ones with ties so that children can bring back to the classroom things they wish to study more closely.

Hint for Success:

● Children may use the Port-a-Kit either individually or in small groups. In the latter case, help children as a group decide what to include in the Kit and what materials they are going to explore.

3. I Am a Scientist

Everyone is, or has the potential to be, a scientist. This activity helps children understand how their natural investigations of the world around them are part of the scientific process. Prepare a booklet for each child containing about four pages each. On the front cover write the words "I am a scientist." On the inside, head the pages with sentences such as the following: "I am

curious about . . . (or I wonder about . . .)," "Some ways that I find out about things are . . . ," or "Some tools I can use to find out about things include . . . ." Leave room for children to write down their ideas themselves, dictate them to an adult, record them, or draw pictures of their ideas. At a group time, ask children to report by "reading" their books aloud to their classmates or by playing the recordings.

To Simplify:

● Provide pre-cut pictures of objects or events, such as storms or boats floating and so on. Give children an opportunity to choose one or two illustrations to paste or glue into their books.

To Extend:

● Use children's ideas as a basis for study. Encourage them to try out their ideas and to report or record the results of their work.

Cognitive

1. Look, Touch, Record

Through this activity, children are encouraged to develop their observing skills. Gather several like objects (such as gears, rocks, shells, and so on) that vary in one or more of their properties, such as color, size, shape, or texture. Make these available for children to examine closely in a designated area of the room. Provide paper, and markers, crayons, or pencils as well. Invite children to observe and handle the objects for the purpose of gathering information about them. Encourage them to remember some of the things they discover. Remind children that drawing, making other marks on a paper or writing are all ways to preserve their memories. Later, discuss with the children in a group what they found out. Make a master list of observable characteristics and help children compare their observations with one another's. After the list has been generated, ask children to reexamine the items, looking for things they might have missed the first time.

Hint for Success:

● Change the items in this area daily as a way to pique children's interest in the activity.

To Simplify:

● Provide only one object for observation at a time.

To Extend:

● Give each child a small "observer's" notebook in

which to record his or her findings over time. Periodically, compare observations made early on with later ones. Draw children's attention to the fact that their observations are becoming more detailed with practice.

2. Plumb the Depths

A plumb line is used to assess vertical direction—the up- and down-ness of something. By using a plumb line, children will gain firsthand experience with the force of gravity pulling on objects. To make a plumb line, tie a small weight, such as a metal nut or fishing line sinker, to the end of a 12" or 18" piece of string. When the string is not moving, the plumb bob (the weight) will hang straight down toward the center of the earth, as a result of gravity. This tool can be used to measure the true depth of something. For example, children can measure the depth of water, as sailors and riverboat captains do. After children have had opportunities to experiment with plumb lines (in closely supervised situations), fill several containers of different shapes and sizes with water and place them on the floor of the classroom or playground. Mark each container with a colored piece of tape. Direct children to hang the plumb line over the container until the plumb bob reaches the bottom of the container. Place a corresponding colored piece of tape on the string to mark the place where the top of the water comes. Children can compare the relative heights of water in the different containers by observing which color tape is the highest on the string.

Hint for Success:

● This activity may be preceded by a fishing activity, where children use poles with strings and magnets at the end to "fish" for items that contain iron. In this case, the magnet acts as a plumb bob.

To Simplify:

● Use one container and have several children, in turn, measure the water depth. Compare their results.

To Extend:

● Ask children to assess, by visual inspection, which of the containers has the deepest water. Then encourage them to test out their observations using the plumb line.

● Take children to a natural or constructed body of water (lake, stream, swimming pool). Using the same principle as above, instruct children to measure the depth of the water. Longer plumb lines may be needed for this experience. Children can make guesses as to the depth of the water and then test out their ideas using the plumb line.

3. All Fall Down

This activity illustrates the principle that all things fall toward the earth, even when thrown in the air. It encourages children to use their observing and describing skills. Provide an assortment of balls of different materials, weights, and sizes. Outdoors, provide children times to practice throwing the balls in the air and to each other. After some period of time, ask them to describe what happens to the balls when they are thrown. Ask children what they think it would take to keep the balls from falling back down. Finally, ask them whether the type of ball they were using made any difference in its behavior.

To Simplify:

● Use balls that children can handle easily, such as textured, soft, or small ones.

To Extend:

● Use a parachute to launch the balls in the following way. Have children stand around a parachute, holding onto the edge. Place one or two balls in the center and, on the count of three, tell children to raise the parachute forcefully and to watch what happens. Try the activity using other soft objects, such as teddy bears or clothing (gloves, hats, or jackets).

4. Water, Water Everywhere

Scientists act on or change objects or substances in order to discover more about them. While this activity uses water as the medium of discovery, children will be able to apply the same process while studying other elements, such as sand or soil. Set up a "Water Experiment Station" in the room or on the playground, using a water table, portable trays/tubs, or a sink with a stopper. Explain to children that they will use their bodies and their senses to study the water. First, have them look at, listen to, and smell the water as it is standing still. Then instruct them to stir the water and observe its circular motion; then ask them to make waves with their hands. Provide containers, pitchers, funnels, sieves, and cloth of various weaves and encourage children to pour water, drip water (listening to sounds), drop objects into the water to see, hear, and feel the splashes, and so on. Ask them such questions as: "What do you think will happen if you pour water through the different pieces of cloth or from a variety of heights?" or "What will happen if you drop a pebble into the water?" or "What will happen if the water is heated?" Use the phrase "What will happen if . . . ?" to excite children's curiosity. Have them try out their ideas. Children will come up with unique and interesting experiments. Encourage older children to share their discoveries with their classmates through verbal discussions, written records, or drawn summaries of their experimentation.

Hints for Success:

● When using water, make sure children's clothing is protected with plastic aprons or smocks and that you provide sponges, mops, and toweling for spills. An absorbent carpet remnant makes an effective floor covering under a free-standing water table or beneath water tubs on a table.

● Limit the number of children permitted to engage in the water experiment at a given time so children don't interfere with one another's work.

5. Condensation Sensation

This activity gives children practice in the entire scientific problem-solving sequence. To make this experience meaningful to children, you will have to assemble a number of items and have them available in the event they are called for during the process described here. The items include: a hot plate, electric fry pan (with cover), aluminum saucepan (with cover), enamel saucepan (with cover), small metal fry pans (with covers), food coloring, aluminum foil, plastic cover (large enough to almost cover the pots or pans), and a pitcher of water. Gather the children into a group. Make sure they understand safety rules in the presence of hot pots and boiling water, such as staying a certain distance from the experiment and keeping their hands away from hot items. Explain that they are going to participate in a scientific experiment that requires them to watch closely and to think hard. Introduce the activity with a short, made-up story to capture their interest. A sample of such a story follows:

"One day when I was going to have lunch, I decided to cook some soup. The first thing I needed was to boil water in a pot. So I put some water in the pot and turned on the stove. Then I began to read my book. I forgot that I had something on the stove! Oh, oh. All of a sudden, I looked up and saw that there was hardly any water in the pot. Where had it gone, I wondered? I looked all around, but all I could see was some water drops on the ceiling. So, I decided to do an experiment to find out. You are going to help me with my experiment. Watch closely and we are going to figure out what happened to the water."

Put a small quantity of water in a pot and heat it over the hot plate. Encourage children to remark on what they see, hear, feel, and smell (water bubbling, hot plate glowing, steam rising, and so on). Ask them where they think the water went. Accept all ideas as valid, and

paraphrase all their comments with such remarks as "Jon has a good idea," "Phyllis has a different good idea," and so on. Ask children what they think will happen if the pot is covered. Follow the same procedure as above, showing children the underside of the lid. They should see water droplets because the steam condenses on the cooler lid. Then, ask children what they could change in the experiment to change the outcome. Take the opportunity to change as many variables (the heat source; the size, shape, material of the pot; the color of the water; the covering; the initial temperature of the water) as they suggest. If they get stuck, make suggestions for other variables. Be sure to make only one change at a time. Each time a change is made, say "I wonder what will happen if . . ." or "Frank wonders what will happen if. . . ." Then say "Let's experiment and find out." At every step, ask children to describe what they see, feel, smell, and hear. Prepare a chart or take down in writing their observations to help children compare their predictions with what they observed. Help them evaluate these comparisons. For example, did using an ice cube make a difference? Did using a red pot yield a different outcome than using a yellow one? What about the color of the water? Did more blue water evaporate than red water?

Hint for Success:

● Safety is the most important issue in this experience. Give children specific guidelines for where to sit by either having them sit on chairs, on carpet squares, or behind lines made from masking tape on the floor.

To Simplify:

● Limit the time of the experiment to account for children's attention span.

● Reduce the number of variables considered to the most obvious (for example, the type of pot or the color of water).

To Extend:

● Prepare charts that children themselves can fill in to summarize the results of the experiments.

● Carry out this process with other experiments. For example, in experimenting with buoyancy, use variables such as the colors of objects, their weight, their composition (metal, wood, plastic), their shape, the amount of water, the salinity of the water, and so on.

6. Roll and Race

The goal of this activity is to give children practice in ordering or sequencing. Obtain or make a 2' x 6' piece of paper. Lay this flat on the floor in an open area.

At one end, place a ramp (inclined plane) made of a board held up on one end or a triangular-shaped large block. Gather several small cylindrical blocks or small cars (metal or wooden). Allow children ample opportunity to experiment with the inclined plane and the objects. Hold a discussion with the children during which you ask them to make predictions about which object will travel the farthest on the paper after rolling down the ramp. Then allow each child, in turn, to select an object and roll it down the ramp. Have each child mark off on the piece of paper where his or her object stopped rolling. Draw a line from the starting point to the finish point for each car or cylinder. Place a sticker or picture of each object on the appropriate line, to make identification more certain. Alternatively, ask each child to put his or her name on the line representing their object. Discuss with children the meaning of the graph and how they can determine the distance each object traveled by looking at the relative lengths of the lines. Then have them assess which object rolled the farthest, which the least far, and which ones ranked in between.

Hint for Success:

● When using objects that are likely to roll a distance, carry out this activity in a hallway. Mark the places where the objects stop with masking tape on the floor.

To Simplify:

● Use objects that are very dissimilar, such as a ball, a car, a paper towel roll, and so on. This will produce gross differences in the results, making it easier for children to observe.

To Extend:

● Change the angle of the ramp by adding to or subtracting from the height of the block.

● Try other changes as well, such as lengthening the ramp or using a different material or pushing the objects, using more or less force, as they are released. Ask children to determine which of the changes they made in the experiment affected their results, and in what ways.

● Another option is to give each child a different colored crayon. Ask them, one at a time, to make a mark on the paper identifying where they think their object will stop rolling. Test the objects, making a mark where each one actually completes its roll. Compare the children's predictions with the actual results.

7. Slide It

The object of the activity is to provide children with practice in guessing and verifying guesses through experimentation. Use long triangle blocks to create parallel inclined planes. (See the activity entitled "Roll and Race," page 300, for a detailed description of how to construct an inclined plane.) Place these at the edge of a table or other surface that is above the floor or ground. Put a bucket or basin underneath the end of the table (on the floor) to catch objects that are falling from the inclined planes. Encourage children to roll a variety of unbreakable objects down the inclined planes, such as marbles, toy cars, pieces of wood, crayons, paper balls, cubes, triangles, and so on. Take two objects that are the same or similar size and shape, but different mass or weight (such as a plastic ball and a ball bearing). Ask the children which they think will reach the bottom of the bucket first. Then, roll the objects down the inclined planes. (Both objects should hit the bottom at the same time.) Instruct children to tell you what they observed. Compare the results with their guesses. Next, choose two items that are the same shape, but different sizes. Follow the procedure as before. (Again, the objects should reach the bucket at the same time.) Finally, take two objects with different shapes. Now, the children should be able to discern differences. Have children summarize what they learned and write their comments on an "Idea Board" that is posted at their eye level in the room.

Hints for Success:

● Remind children that when scientists don't know what will happen next, they make guesses based on familiarity with the materials and on past experiences. Tell them that scientists find out whether their guesses are correct by doing experiments and that the more they play with things they are learning about, the more likely their guesses will be correct.

● Remember to remove objects from the buckets after each test so children can hear the objects hit bottom.

To Simplify:

● Start with round objects that will roll down the inclined plane easily.

To Extend:

● Let children experiment with objects that they find in the classroom or bring from home. Ask for their ideas about why the phenomena occurred. Accept all explanations and respond positively to children's ideas by paraphrasing their reasoning.

● Another variation is to have children rely on one sense only to determine outcomes. Provide earmuffs for children to block the sound of the objects falling in the buckets. Tell them to use their eyes only to see which object reaches the bottom first. Later, have the children remove the earmuffs, turn their backs and listen for the sounds of the objects. Ask children which way was easier to figure out the answer. Give children another chance to use their senses together. Ask them "Does this approach make the task easier or does it make no difference?"

8. Prediction Walk

Looking for patterns is a fundamental scientific process. Understanding the pattern of events means that one can predict what will happen next. Children can gain practice discerning patterns by going on a prediction walk. On the first day, take the children on a walk around the building. Stop each time you reach a door. Don't give any explanations, but respond to children's observations with phrases such as "You're wondering why we are stopping" or "You noticed that we . . . ." The next day (or later the same day), follow the identical route and the same routine of stopping at each door. At about the midpoint in the journey, ask children what they think will happen when they reach the next door or ask them to tell you the next time they are to stop. In this way, you can ascertain whether or not they have figured out the pattern of the excursion.

To Simplify:

● Take the walk with a small group of children. Go only to places the children have been in the past so that the novelty of the location isn't distracting. Once you have repeated a pattern several times, ask the children questions as indicated above.

To Extend:

● Allow children to create their own Prediction Walk. Encourage them, in turn, to lead a small group around the classroom or playground. Caution them to choose one pattern at a time and to be consistent so others can predict what they are to do next. They may need help figuring out how to create a pattern for others to follow.

9. Drop by Drop

This activity will familiarize children with the prediction-verification process. In a large plastic tub, set up several clear jars or plastic cups with about 1" of water in each. Mix weak solutions of watercolors, tempera paint, or food coloring in the primary colors.

Provide eye droppers or medicine droppers for each color. Encourage children to "mess around" with the colors for a while. Then rinse out the used containers and put fresh water in them. Ask children what they think will happen when one drop of a particular color is put in the water. Then, try two drops in another container, and so on. At each step, ask children to describe what they observe, noticing similarities and differences. Move on to other colors, treating them in the same fashion. Finally, have children mix the colors in one container, one drop at a time.

After some exploration, encourage children to chart or graph their experiments and the outcomes. Provide clipboards and graph paper or a larger wall or table chart for this purpose. A drop of the resulting color placed on the chart can be the indicator, rather than using symbols.

Sample charts are illustrated below.

COLOR MIXING

BLUE	YELLOW	RED
O (one drop)		
OO (two drops, etc.)		

COLOR INTENSITY (OR DARKNESS)

O
OO
OOO (and so on)

Hints for Success:

● This activity is most successfully carried out after children have had many experiences using paint at easels or tables.

● The activity may also be done outdoors, where spills are not an issue. Remember to provide smocks, floor and table covering (newspaper), and sponges for the indoor experiments.

To Simplify:

● Use one or two colors at a time and eliminate the charting procedures.

● Provide a separate set-up for each child to avoid difficulties. Limit the number of children experimenting to four at a time.

To Extend:

● Explain that scientists must have more than one verification before they can be certain of their conclusions. Try changing the medium, using hot water or ice, or substituting oil or vinegar for the water and see what happens. Ask children how they can make the colors brighter, paler, more intense, and so on. Let them experiment. In all cases, encourage children to compare what they thought would happen with what they observed happening.

● Keep records of the experiments and in a few days or weeks, try them again. Compare the charts for children to determine if they got the same results the second time.

10. Balancing Act

B y engaging in this activity, children will gain experience in experimenting and observing the results of their experimentation. Purchase or otherwise obtain several kinds of balance scales. If possible, hang two small buckets or trays from the ends of the balance scale. Provide numerous small items for children to work with, such as coins, plastic counters, small rocks, shells, or small cars. Also keep on hand very light items such as cotton balls or feathers. Give children many opportunities to explore the balance scales and the items. Be alert for signs that the children are drawing conclusions from their experiments by listening to their conversations and observing their play. Request that children try to balance some of the items on the scale; in other words, find out whether they can make the ends even. Ask them such questions as "What will happen if you put a rock on one side and a car on the other?" Wait for them to

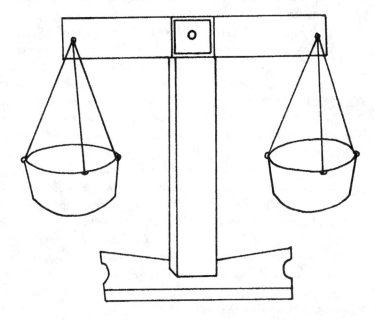

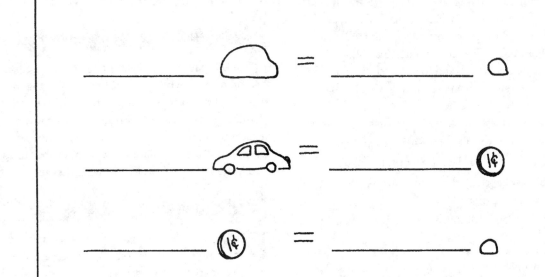

try and find out what they have observed. Pose other questions such as "What do you have to do to balance five coins or two cars?" "What happens when the items are placed side by side or on top of one another?" After some time, introduce new items, such as the cotton balls, and encourage children to explore those.

To Simplify:

● Use only a few items at a time as children may become confused with a large amount of material to consider.

● Limit the number of children permitted to work at any given time to two or three.

To Extend:

● Suggest to children that they make marks on paper to record their findings. Such marks may be hatch marks or drawings of the objects presented in an equation form. Prepare these forms in advance, as illustrated on page 303.

11. Above or Below?

This is a variation of the traditional sink and float activity. Its focus is on children changing or acting upon objects to make them sink or float. Children will be able to apply the principles they are using to other experiments. Provide a clear, deep tub or water table and allow several days of water play during which children have chances to experiment with a variety of objects and containers in water. Introduce the activity by making sure children understand what sinking and floating looks like. Then explain that they are going to experiment with certain materials by changing, adding to, or taking away from them in ways that will make floating objects sink and sinking objects float. Present an assortment of materials that includes: a lump of clay, aluminum foil, coins, or washers, Styrofoam trays, marbles, a piece of wood, and a set of clothespins. Allow children to explore the materials and to play with them in and around the water. Then pose the following kinds of questions:

What can you do to the clay to make it float/sink?

What can you add to the wood to make it sink?

How can you make the Styrofoam sink?

If you clipped all the clothespins together, what would happen?

What could you add to the marble to make it float?

Encourage children to test out their ideas. Also, invite children to think of their own questions by asking them what they want to find out. Write these questions down or have children write them. Provide time so that they can find the answers. Extend this activity by asking children to find items in the room upon which they wish to experiment.

Hint for Success:

● Give children plastic smocks or aprons to wear; cover the floor with newspapers and provide sponges and towels for cleaning up spilled water.

12. Collection Box

This activity focuses on children learning about differentiating and quantifying properties of objects, and on recording results. In shoe boxes, make collections of a variety of things, such as pebbles, shells, string or yarn, kitchen items, plastic toys, feathers, and so on. Present these to pairs of children, along with magnifying glasses, scales, a small amount of water, rulers, prisms, and other scientific tools. Ask children in each pair to examine their collection in order to find things that are the same about the items and things that are different. Tell children to seriate them in a variety of ways—in other words, to sequence them from the most of an attribute to the least and viceversa. They may use any of the tools to find out about the items. Suggest that children write down, draw pictures of, or tape record their findings (provide the appropriate materials for them to do this). One child in each pair may act as the investigator, while the other is the recorder. Then encourage them to switch roles. At the end of the information-gathering phase, arrange for children to report their findings to the group at large.

Construction

1. Fans of Mine

To demonstrate the effects of moving air, help children construct fans in one of the following ways. The simplest fan construction is to staple or tape a Popsicle® stick onto a paper plate. Another way to make a fan is to accordion-pleat a rectangle of paper and staple one end. Show children how to move the fan back and forth. Ask them to describe what they feel.

2. My Parachute

Dropping or tossing objects from a height using a parachute illustrates some of the properties of air (it takes up space, it slows down moving objects) as well as the essential principle of gravity—that all things fall to earth. Children five years and older can construct their own parachutes. Show children pictures or photographs of actual parachutes or bring one into the classroom. Point out that parachutes used for pleasure or competition vary in pattern or color to distinguish them from each other.

Provide the following materials for each parachute:

1' square of cloth (or larger)

4 lengths of 1' string

1 heavy washer

markers or water colors, for decorating

Draw the following steps in pictograph form, separating the steps so children can easily follow the instructions:

1. Select your materials.
2. Tie a piece of string to each corner of the cloth.
3. Decorate the parachute.
4. Gather the ends of the string together and then fasten the washer to them.

Find a safe place where the parachutes may be stored for use over the course of the unit.

Hint for Success:

● Some children may require help with tying. Suggest that they first ask their friends to assist them, and then, if they still need help, adults may step in.

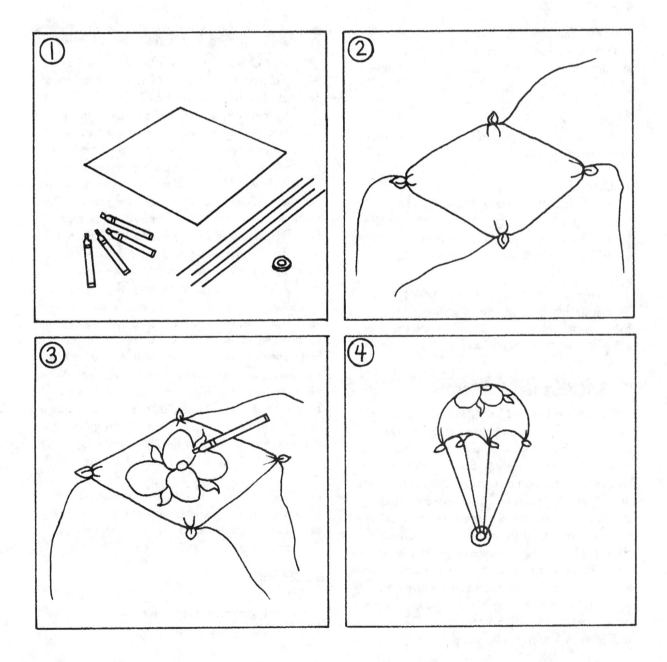

Language

1. I Spy! Part I

Use the popular children's game "I Spy" to sharpen children's awareness of the world around them. In this game, one person (the leader or the "spy") looks around, chooses an object, and, without saying the name of the object, tells the rest of the group something about it. For instance, "I spy something pointy." The rest of the group must guess the object. Children take turns being the "spy." As children become more proficient at the game, finer and finer distinctions may be used. Suggest a variety of attributes that children may focus on as they play. Use the extensive list in this unit's TFPs for guidance.

Hint for Success:
● This is a wonderful activity to do when children are waiting. With enough variation, they hardly ever tire of it.

To Simplify:
● Help children choose relatively obvious attributes, such as shape or color.

To Extend:
● A variant of the game is to describe an object or force that is not immediately visible and that children have used in experiments. An example might be: "I spy something that changes when it is heated" (ice cube or water).

● Give children a time limit to name or point to all the objects they spy that have a common attribute. Examples would be all the red things or soft things or things smaller than a child's hand.

2. "Ask the Scientists"

This activity is geared for children who are able to verbally express their ideas in sentences. The focus is teaching children to take turns in conversations. Find out if children have seen quiz shows on television and pattern this game after that genre. Select, or have children self-select, a panel of science "experts" (three or four at a time is an appropriate number). Seat them behind a table with pretend microphones in front of them. (These can easily be constructed from paper towel rolls, Styrofoam spheres, and tape.) Place a row of chairs for the "audience." Children from the audience may take turns questioning the panel on any aspect of physical science about which they are curious. The questions may be written down in advance or may be spontaneous.

Members of the panel take turns answering the questions. One child may take the role of a moderator, choosing the questioners and making sure each panelist has an opportunity to speak. Children may or may not know the answers, and panelists should be instructed that if they aren't sure, they can say things such as "Let's find out" or "Let's ask someone else." After a few rounds of questioning, the panel members may be replaced by children in the audience.

Hint for Success:
● Children may require help in thinking up questions to ask the panel or in figuring out how to answer them, so prepare several sample questions and stay nearby until children have mastered the structure of the game.

3. A Backwards Story

Once children have become familiar with properties of objects, substances, and forces, they are able to discern what is true from what is false in regard to those objects, substances, and forces. This activity prompts them to apply the knowledge they have acquired and to think critically based on that knowledge. After children have had many experiences posing questions, thinking about what would happen if, and experimenting to find out, they will enjoy creating a "Backwards Story." This is a story where everything is the opposite of the truth. At first, create a story of your own and ask children to tell when things and incidents in the story are true, as they have experienced it, or not true. Make the story as ridiculous as possible. A sample story follows:

"Once upon a time, there was a girl named Alice. Alice was a backwards person. One day, Alice went out to have adventures. She wore her sunglasses in the nighttime so she could see better. She loaded her boat full of rocks so it would float on the water. Next, Alice blew some square bubbles to use for a sail. The wind blew and blew, but her boat didn't move. She touched the sails with her dry hands, but the square bubbles didn't even burst. After a while, Alice got hungry and tried to catch some fish. She tossed her fishing line in the air, but it stayed up and caught some stars instead of fish. Suddenly, Alice's boat began to rise into the air. Up it went until it was out of sight of land. Alice's boat never came down. What do you think happened to Alice and her boat?"

To Simplify:
● Create a story using simple principles that children have experienced directly, such as those associated with air, light, heat, and sound.

To Extend:

● Over time, introduce more abstract principles, such as gravity or magnetism, being sure that children have had the relevant background experiences. Encourage children to incorporate these principles into their own backwards stories, too. Record the stories in some way and keep them for children to refer to again and again.

● An alternative is to build a round-robin story, with each child adding a successive sentence.

4. Hot or Cold?

Introduce children to a heat source, such as an oven, a radiator, an electric blowdryer, or a light bulb that has been on for a while. Very carefully, one at a time, have children move closer and farther away from the heat source. Ask them what they noticed about how it felt to be closer or farther away. Then encourage children to play the game called "Hot or Cold." In this game one child hides his or her eyes while an object is hidden in the classroom. Then, as the child seeks the item, the rest of the group tells whether the child is coming closer to the item ("Hot," "You're getting hotter") or is moving farther from it ("Cold," "You're getting colder," "You're freezing!"). The object is not to trick the child, but to give helpful instructions so the item can be located.

Hint for Success:

● Show children the item before it is hidden. Once children learn the game, they can play it on their own, either indoors or out.

To Simplify:

● Keep the item hidden in the group or circle area. Make sure the item is easily recognizable.

To Extend:

● Talk with children about camouflage and the trick of "hiding" an object in plain view. Thus the object of the game takes on the aspect of the "seeker" sharpening his or her observation skills, as well as following directions.

Physical

1. Happy Hat

Purchase several child-sized straw or cotton hats that can be tied or held securely onto children's heads. Make sure they have brims reaching beyond children's faces. Tie a plumb line onto the front brim of each hat so that it dangles at about chin level (about 4 to 6 inch-es long). Rather than using a heavy weight which might injure a child, tie a yarn pompon ball at the end of the string. As they wear the hat, encourage children to make the plumb line move in various directions by wiggling, nodding, or swaying their heads. See if they can set up a pendulum motion. Have children describe how they have to move their heads to create this motion. Then ask them to observe what the plumb line does when their heads are not moving. Ask them what they think will happen if they lie on a climber or other platform off the ground and then dangle their heads off the edge. Encourage the youngsters to experiment and to determine if their predictions were accurate.

Hint for Success:

● Provide at least five hats initially and be prepared to discuss with the children a method for taking turns. Children can decide upon an equitable arrangement themselves, or the teacher may choose a means, such as a sign up sheet and a time limit in advance. (Note: For suggestions on how to engage children in social problem solving, refer to the unit "People Living in Communities," pages 179–221.)

To Simplify:

● Give children many chances to explore the plumb line hats phenomena. As children discover the motions that can be made, have them try to imitate one another.

To Extend:

● Point out the scientific principles that are being demonstrated by the plumb line hat. Use the term pendulum, as the plumb line swings from side to side or back and forth. Compare this motion with that of a playground swing in order to illustrate the similarity. Ask children how they think the motion would change if the line were made longer or whether it would change at all. Have children try out such an experiment to determine if their ideas are correct.

2. Fresh Fish

Object control and the opportunity to explore both magnets and plumb bobs is the aim of this experience. Make several "fishing poles" in the following way. Attach a 3' length of bias tape or shoelace to a wooden or bamboo pole, approximately 1-1/2' in length. To the free end of the string attach a small donut-shaped magnet. Cut out a dozen or more fish shapes from tagboard and laminate them or cover them with clear adhesive paper. Attach a paper clip to each one. Provide a space that is designated as the "pond" or the "lake" and encourage children to "go fishing." Tell children to experiment with the poles and the fish. Have them try to "catch" fish with the poles. Find out from them which end of the fish they were able to attract with the magnet. You can adapt several games from this procedure. For example:

1. Direct children to catch fish all of one color or of a specific shape.
2. Ask children to catch a certain number of fish.
3. Provide some fish without magnets and ask children which fish they are able to catch with the magnet and which they are not.

3. Keep Your Balance

Balancing is an essential motor skill, as well as an example of the force of gravity. Purchase or construct several balance boards that are designed for one child at a time. These are simply 8" x 18" planks of wood with wooden cylinders as the fulcrum. Demonstrate how to achieve balance by standing on the board that is resting on the cylinder and by putting one foot on either side of the cylinder. This demonstration will create delight among the children. Encourage them to try it. Point out that one side or the other often goes down as children work on getting them even. As they become more proficient, children may be able to keep their balance while, at the same time, moving the board from side to side. As they attempt to do this activity, ask them what it feels like and how they have to move their bodies to shift their weight in order to balance. Suggest that they also watch others attempt to balance and make observations about what they see.

Hints for Success:

● Choose a level surface to increase chances of success.

● Less experienced or less physically able children will require an adult's hand to steady them.

4. Leveraged "Pull Out"

Pound six or seven nails into several pieces of 2" x 4" pine boards. Vary the depth of the nails. Provide children with several tools, such as a hammer, pliers, saw, sandpaper, magnet, weights, kitchen tongs, and rubber gloves. Ask children how they can get the nails out of the wood, using their hands or the tools. Have them experiment. Ascertain the strategies that were successful and under what circumstances (such as nails that were shallow could be removed with fingers, while deeper set nails required tools). Urge children to explore the idea of leverage; in other words, encourage them to use

the claw end of the hammer to pry nails loose or to try the pliers to twist the nails or to wear rubber gloves to provide more friction.

Hints for Success:

● Be sure to provide goggles for each child.

● Allow only as many children to attempt the task as there are materials available. Provide a sign-up sheet or other means of encouraging children to take turns.

Pretend Play

1. Our Science Center

Set aside a part of the classroom as a Children's Science Center in which children can pretend to be scientists. Encourage children to bring in items they wish to examine and provide some yourself as a start-up. Give children white shirts to use as "laboratory coats," an unused computer or typewriter keyboard, plenty of paper and pencils for them to record their findings, and surfaces (such as tables) upon which to work. Have "reference books" available in one corner that is set up as a research library and post relevant pictures of scientists at work around the walls. Make sure that these pictures represent people of both genders, of all ages, of many racial and cultural groups, and people of differing physical abilities.

2. Bubble Dance

After many exposures to blowing and observing bubbles, encourage children to participate in a bubble dance. Play some soft and flowing music, such as "The Dance of the Sugar Plum Fairy" from Tchaikovsky's *The Nutcracker Suite*. While demonstrating, ask children to pretend to blow up a balloon or blow a pretend bubble, showing the outline with their hands. Some may wish to make large bubbles, some small. Have them show, by moving their bodies, how the bubble would respond to a gentle breeze and then to a strong wind. Encourage them to show what happens when the bubble bursts. Emphasize that each person's bubble is unique and is an expression of one's own style and personality. If children are comfortable, ask them to show their bubbles to one another. Add rainbow-colored strips of cloth or paper to further children's interest.

To Simplify:

● Some children may have difficulty imagining bubbles. In that case, provide balloons with which children may dance. Be alert to popping balloons and remove any shreds immediately. An alternative, especially if the activity is carried on outdoors, is to blow some bubbles with a wand so children have direct, immediate experience with bubbles before pretending.

To Extend:

● As soon as children have defined their own bubbles, ask them to "toss" bubbles to one another or to change the shape and size of their bubbles as they dance.

3. Five Senses Museum

Create a hands-on museum in an area of the classroom. Provide collections for children to examine, science tools and objects for children to explore, and "unknown" items for them to investigate. Place each set of things in separate areas, on shelves or tables, and display them as if in a museum. Encourage children to act as museum guides or curators to the "visitors" that come to the museum. As this is a hands-on museum, children should be prepared to become actively involved in the museum displays. Make sure that all the five senses are stimulated during the experience; in other words, provide things for children to listen to, touch, smell, taste, and feel. If possible, play a videotape that illustrates some aspect of science exploration. Often, these may be rented from a local library or science center.

Hints for Success:

● With the children, establish guidelines for using the museum and post these at the entrance. These guidelines may include such statements as "Please touch the exhibits" and "Please return the materials to their place so others may enjoy them."

● Set a limit on the number of visitors allowed at one time.

Social

1. What in the World?

This activity helps children increase their awareness of the classroom environment in which they work and play and to work cooperatively toward a shared goal. Several days in advance of the activity, prepare children by telling them that they are going to work with their friends to find out everything they can about their classroom by tallying or inventorying all of the things it contains. Alert them to begin looking at the objects and surfaces. On the day or days of the study, divide the children into several small groups. Give each one a specific feature or attribute of the room to look for and record. For example, one group will look for and tally all of the

wooden objects and surfaces, one group will concentrate on the metal things, and so on. Use the list of the attributes of objects referred to in the TFPs for this unit as a guide, adapting it as appropriate to your particular situation. Carry out this discovery process several times over a period of days or weeks, changing the attributes that are being examined.

Hints for Success:

● Explain to children that they are discoverers and investigators; therefore they should keep a record of what they find in order to tell others about their discoveries.

● Provide each group with a clipboard and pencil and show children how to make a tally mark or slash mark for each object or surface they discover.

To Simplify:

● Choose attributes with which children are already familiar or those, such as hardness and softness, that they can discover immediately by using their senses.

To Extend:

● Select attributes that are not immediately apparent and that require some experimentation because they are not obvious from visual inspections, such as weight, hardness, and so on. Ask children to figure out in advance how they would find out about that particular property.

2. Bubble, Bubble, Pop!

The focus of this activity is on children learning to take turns. It is a variant of the popular children's game "Duck, Duck, Goose." In this game, children sit in a circle, while It walks around the outside tapping each child's head, in turn. As It taps, he or she calls out "bubble, bubble," and so on. At some point, whoever is It says, "Pop!" and runs around the circle, with the other child in pursuit, until reaching the empty spot on the floor or ground. The new It repeats the game; continue in a similar fashion until all have had a turn. This method of playing eliminates much of the competition contained in the original game. In this version, everyone can be cheered on to run faster! **Note:** This game can be played by children in wheelchairs or by those who are only slightly ambulatory. In such circumstances, the objective would be to move into an empty spot in whatever way possible.

3. Tower Topple

Provide children with a varied assortment of wooden unit blocks. Be sure there are enough so children can build or stack them as high as their shoulders. Give children many opportunities to explore and experiment with the blocks, without asking them to construct anything in particular. After a while, explain that the object of the day's building is to make a tower as tall as possible, without it falling down. Suggest that more than one child work on each project and give them ideas about how to negotiate the use of space and materials. As they build, comment on their use of particular blocks, how they are stacking them, what they discover about balance and stability, and how they are able to work as a team. Point out some principles to them after they have experimented, such as: "You've discovered that a broad base is more stable than a narrow one" or "You found out that blocks piled on top of round blocks tend to tumble down" or "Both of you were able to work together to build the tower. It pleases me when children cooperate" and so on.

To Simplify:

● Younger and less experienced children will pile blocks rather than build with them; it is sometimes useful to demonstrate or illustrate vertical building, but don't expect these youngsters to build tall structures.

To Extend:

● A follow-up activity is for children to deliberately build towers that fall down right away. Treat these as new discoveries, just as you did the stable towers. Once they have mastered the skill of building stable structures, children enjoy the joke of building unstable ones.

4. You, Too, Can Be a Scientist

The purpose of this activity is to help children recognize and confront potential stereotypes. Provide an assortment of photographs or small models of people that represent both genders, many ages, a variety of racial, ethnic, and cultural backgrounds and those with varying abilities (some people in wheelchairs, on crutches, or with seeing eye dogs or canes). One at a time, show these pictures or figures to children, in small groups or all together, asking the following questions: "Tell me what you notice about this person. Could this person be a scientist? Why do (don't) you think so?" Each time the children respond, paraphrase what they say. For example, "You think this person can/cannot be a scientist because . . . . Let's look more closely at what this person can do." Remind children of the varying ways individuals learn about the world: by using all of their senses, by seeking information from others, by guessing and experimenting, and so on. Elicit opinions from many children and discuss the similarities and differences in how they perceive other people. If and when

you come across stereotypic attitudes, confront these directly by providing accurate information about real scientists. Use these attitudes as a guide for further research on your part and as a cue for choosing specific visitors to invite to the classroom.

Hint for Success:

● Plan this discussion at both the beginning and end of the unit. Compare children's attitudes at these different points to ascertain whether or not children's opinions have changed based on new knowledge.

Teacher Resources

Field Trip Ideas

1. Arrange a visit to an industrial, university, high school, or middle school chemistry or physics laboratory. The purpose is for children to see the tools that scientists use in their investigations and to see an actual scientific setting. Arrange for a scientist, science teacher, or advanced science student to demonstrate how the equipment works by doing simple experiments. Talk with the individual in advance to help him or her gear the experiment and the explanations to the level of the children's development and experience. If possible, borrow some piece of equipment that children may use in the classroom or center. As a follow-up, provide children with open-ended craft materials back at the program and encourage them to construct their own versions of the equipment and tools they saw.

Classroom Visitors

1. Take a survey of the parents in your program to determine if any of them are engaged in scientific work or if they know anyone who is. Invite these individuals to talk with children about what they do. Prepare the visitors in advance by describing the activities in which the children have been engaged and help them plan appropriate presentations given the age and experiences of the children. Urge the visiting scientists to bring in as many actual objects as possible for children to handle and explore. These may include specialized tools such as microscopes, centrifuges, petri dishes and the like. In addition to the tools, have the scientists focus on the process of scientific exploration by describing how they observe, hypothesize, and test out their predictions. Older or more

experienced children will derive further benefits from the experience by being given an opportunity to generate questions in advance about what they want to know. Record these in some way as a reminder and have children pose their queries to the visitor.

2. Through a local magicians' organization, high school club, or community center, seek an amateur magician (of any age) to demonstrate "magic" tricks for children. Children should be urged to watch the magician very closely during the demonstration to determine whether they can discern how the tricks worked. At the end, the magician should reveal the secrets of the "magic" and should explicitly promote the notion that there is a scientific or logical explanation for even mysterious phenomena. An important follow-up to this experience is for children to be taught one or two simple "magic" tricks that depend on scientific principles, such as creating static electricity by rubbing a glass rod with a piece of chamois cloth.

Children's Books

Cobb, V. (1990). *Why Can't You Unscramble an Egg?* New York: Dutton.

Hoban, T. (1988). *Look, Look, Look.* New York: Scholastic.

Marzollo, J. (1992). *I Spy.* New York: Scholastic.

Noll, S. (1990). *Watch Where You Go.* New York: Scholastic.

Wildsmith, B., & Wildsmith, R. (1993). *Look Closer.* New York: Scholastic.

Wilkes, A., & Mostyn, D. (1983). *Simple Science.* London: Usborne Publishing.

Wyler, R. (1986). *Science Fun with Toy Boats and Planes.* New York: Julian Messner.

Adult References

Charlesworth, R., & Lind, K. K. (1990). *Math and Science for Young Children* Albany, NY: Delmar.

Cliatt, M. J. P., & Shaw, J. M. (1992). *Helping Children Explore Science* New York: Macmillan.

Cobb, V. (1989).*Why Doesn't the Earth Fall?* New York: Dutton.

Holt, B. (1977). *Science with Young Children.* Washington, DC: National Association for the Education of Young Children.

Katz, L. G., & Chard, S. C. (1989). *Engaging Children's Minds: The Project Approach.* Norwood, NJ: Ablex Publishing.

Lindberg, D. H. (1990). *"What Goes 'Round Comes 'Round: Doing Science." Childhood Education,* 67, pp. 79–81.

Macaulay, D. (1988). *The Way Things Work.* Boston: Houghton Mifflin.

Sprung, B., Froschl, M., & Campbell, P. B. (1985). *What Will Happen If...?* New York: Educational Equity Concepts.

Taylor, B. I. (1993). *Science Everywhere: Opportunities for Very Young Children.* Ft. Worth, TX: Harcourt Brace Jovanovich.

Physical Science in the Everyday World

Terms, Facts, and Principles (TFPs)

Explaining the World

1. Science is a part of everyday life.

2. Science activities can be carried out everywhere: in the home, school, and work place, indoors and outdoors.

3. Understanding scientific facts and processes helps people solve problems.

4. Plumbing, heating, cleaning, food preparation, cooking, lighting, transportation, entertainment, communication, and building all involve physical science.

5. The physical world is made up of many objects and forces.

6. Everything has properties. Some properties of objects include:

   size

   shape

   weight

   volume (how much space it takes up or can contain)

   color

   texture

   mass

   density (the amount of material in a particular space)

   brightness (how much light it gives off or reflects)

   transparency (how much light can be seen through it)

   hardness

   temperature (how hot or cold it is)

   flexibility (how much or little it can bend)

7. A force is a push or a pull. Examples of forces are gravity and magnetism.

8. Forces have properties. Some properties of forces include strength, direction, and the objects forces affect.

9. Objects begin to move, speed up, slow down, change their direction of motion, or stop moving when acted upon by a force. Objects keep moving until a force stops them.

10. People exert forces on objects: they push and pull things, lift and drop things.

*11. A force cannot be seen, but its effects can be experienced.

*12. When you make a change to one property of an object or force, there is an effect on other properties.

Light

13. Light is one of the fundamental things in the universe.

14. Every hot object produces light.

   a. Light is produced by the sun.

   b. Light is produced by burning fuel (gas, wood, coal).

   c. Light is produced by electricity flowing through such things as light bulbs, stoves, toaster coils.

   d. Batteries produce electricity.

15. Nothing can be seen without light.

*16. People can see an object that does not produce its own light because the object reflects some light from another source. That means that light bounces off the object and goes to people's eyes.

17. Light travels in a straight line called a beam.

18. Objects cannot be seen around corners, except when the direction of a light beam is changed by a reflective surface.

19. Light travels easily through some things (transparent objects), somewhat easily through others (translucent objects), and not through others (opaque objects).

20. Lights appear brighter when people are close to them; lights appear dimmer when people are farther away.

21. Shadows are made when objects block the light source.

*22. Light is a mixture of many colors.

*23. Light beams bend when they pass from one s ubstance to another, such as from air to water. When light beams get bent, they make objects look different.

24. People use the properties of light to create tools and machines that make things easier to see, such as flashlights, film projectors, and lighthouses.

Sound

25. Sounds are made when something vibrates, that is, when the object moves in the air.

26. Sound travels through many materials and substances. There are some materials and substances through which sound cannot travel.

27. Sound travels in many directions.

28. Sounds are fainter when they are made far away.

29. Distinct sounds are produced by objects of different sizes, lengths, thickness, and composition.

30. Sounds may be distinguished by their pitch (how low or high), by their volume (how loud or quiet), and by their resonance or timbre (the particular quality of the sound).

31. People use the properties of sound for communication: to talk, create music, send signals, and so on.

Heat

32. How hot or cold something is can be measured by taking its temperature.

33. Objects or substances that are heated feel hot or warm to the touch; their appearance may change, as well.

*34. Heat is produced when things rub against one another (friction as in sawing wood), or when things burn or are affected by electricity or chemicals.

35. Heat can be transferred from a hotter object to a cooler object, making the second object warmer (such as heat from a burner can cause water to boil in a pot; heat from the sun can make us feel warm in its light).

36. People use the properties of heat to cook food, warm themselves, shape objects, produce electricity, and power cars, trains, and airplanes.

Air

37. Air is everywhere on earth.

*38. Air is real, although it is invisible. Air takes up space.

*39. Air presses on everything on all sides.

40. Moving air pushes things.

*41. Air slows down moving things.

42. People can feel air when it is moving.

*43. Hot air is less dense than cold air. This is why heated air causes things, such as balloons, to rise.

44. People create machines that use the properties of air (e.g., fans, hair dryers, clothes dryers, windmills, furnaces, airplanes, and vehicles).

Gravity

45. Gravity is a force.

46. Gravity pulls everything toward the earth.

47. Gravity makes things fall to the earth. Gravity explains why water flows downhill and why objects roll down an incline.

48. People always feel gravity.

*49. The farther something falls, the faster it moves, except in the case of a very light object that is held back by air.

50. Some objects sink in water (they fall to the bottom), and some objects float (they stay on the top of the water).

*51. Objects sink if they weigh more than an equal volume of water; objects float if they weigh less than an equal volume of water.

*52. Objects rise in the air if they are filled with a gas lighter than an equal volume of air (such as a balloon filled with helium).

53. People use the properties of gravity to: move water (such as drain water from a sink), construct buildings, make boats, swim, play with balls, play on a swing, measure the depth of things.

Magnetism

54. Magnetism is a force.

55. Magnets attract (pull) some things and repel (push away) others.

56. Magnets attract and repel things that are all or partly made of iron.

57. Magnets cannot attract or repel through some materials (insulators).

58. Magnets are made in many shapes and sizes.

*59. One magnet may be used to make another object magnetic

60. Magnets are strongest at their ends.

61. Each end of the magnet acts differently in terms of its pull, with respect to other magnets.

62. People use the properties of magnetism to pick up things, lift loads, move things, and sort things.

Activity Ideas

Aesthetic

1. Puff

These activities give children pleasurable, sensory experiences using the air in their bodies or in other objects to move paint. Children may use the same principle to move other liquids, illustrating a property of moving air and the fluid that is being moved. Mix paint to a watery consistency and put three or four colors in separate tins or shallow pans. Provide children with 3" to 4" lengths of straw and sheets of construction paper. Show them how to use the straws to put a drop or two of paint onto their paper. Instruct them to blow through the clean end of the straw to move the paint. Have children blow harder and more gently, noticing the differing effects. Encourage them to use other colors in combination with the original one. A second activity is to use medicine or eye droppers or bulb-shaped basters to move the paint. Children will have to squeeze the droppers or basters to achieve the desired effects. A third alternative is to mix a bubble mixture into the paint until it is viscous in consistency. Carry out the experience as above. When the bubbles pop, they will leave designs on the paper.

Hint for Success:
● Cover the table with newspaper or provide trays on which children may work. Be sure to give each child a smock or shirt to protect clothing.

To Simplify:
● Begin with one color at a time and give children ample opportunity to explore before adding other colors.

To Extend:
● Once children have had chances to create random designs, suggest that they direct the streams of air in predetermined directions to create planned designs.

2. Playing with Light

These collages give children experiences in exploring a property of light, as well as in investigating materials for their capacity to allow light to shine through.

1. Provide square- or rectangular-shaped pieces of clear sticky paper. In small containers, have available an assortment of small paper pieces, shiny metallic shapes, confetti, and other similar materials for children to stick onto the paper. When each child has completed the picture to his or her satisfaction, cover the creation with another piece of clear, sticky paper.

2. Use pieces of waxed paper instead of the sticky paper. This time, provide glue to secure the items onto the paper. When each project is finished, place another piece of waxed paper over the top and iron it together with a warm iron. Be aware of necessary safety precautions.

3. Encourage children to glue the assorted materials onto construction paper. Cover each picture, as in the other activities, with a second piece of paper—this time, construction paper.

The final step in this experience is to hang the pictures on a classroom window and ask children to compare how well or poorly the sunlight shines through

them. Use the appropriate terms *transparent, translucent,* and *opaque* when labeling the pictures. At another time, use flashlights to study the same phenomena.

To Extend:
● Take the pictures into a dark closet to determine if anything can be seen in the absence of light.

● Suggest that children take a flashlight around the room to determine the translucent properties of other objects.

3. Scrap Iron

The properties of magnets may be used to create artistic sculptures. Collect an assortment of items that are all or in part composed of iron or steel. These could include, but not be limited to, bottle caps, wire, pipe cleaners, orange juice caps, washers, nuts, and paper clips. Provide a sturdy base of Styrofoam, plaster of paris, or clay. Introduce the activity by showing children pictures of some sculptures by Picasso and other artists who have used "found" objects in their artwork. Explain that children, too, are artists and that they may use all of the items to create scrap iron sculptures. If you wish, provide magnets so children can make sure that the items in their creations are made of iron. Children may choose to work individually or in small groups. Display their sculptures on a table or shelf. Alternatively, have children experiment with constructing a scrap iron sculpture that can hang from a magnet.

Hint for Success:
● A note home to families asking for the items listed above will usually result in an ample supply of things with which children may work.

4. Musical Glasses

The focus of this activity is for children to explore vibrations in water. Children may apply what they have discovered to other objects such as drums, sawing wood, and so on. Purchase or collect a variety of glasses, such as thick- and thin-walled, tall and short. Have ready a plastic pitcher of water and a metal rod or spoon. Place the glasses inside a rubber or plastic tub or inside an empty water table. Tell children to pour a little water in each of the glasses and to gently strike the side of the glass. Ask them what they see and hear. Focus their attention on the movement of the water in the glass, explaining that this movement is showing that the glass is vibrating, thereby producing sounds. Allow them to experiment with the amount of water they use in the various glasses. Explain that the goal is to produce pleasing, musical sounds.

Hints for Success:

● Limit the number of children to one or two at a time. Have a sign-up list to facilitate turn-taking.

● Provide a medicine dropper to aid in removing or adding water to each glass.

● Stress the importance of gentle tapping.

To Simplify:

● Provide two or three glasses of the same type at a time so children don't get distracted by too much variety.

To Extend:

● Once children have experimented, ask them to sequence the glasses according to pitch.

Affective

1. I Am a Problem Solver

Prepare several 8" x 12" posters each of which depicts in graphic form a particular problem situation (examples follow). The object of the activity is for each child to solve the problem in his or her own way, using one or more of the scientific principles included in this unit. Children may depict the solutions that they arrive at either in writing (or dictation) or by drawing their ideas on paper.

Examples of problem situations:

1. A narrow pipe with some washers or thumb tacks stuck in the elbow joint.

2. A metal car in a deep hole.

3. A wooden block in a long pipe.

4. Finding a lost dog/person in a maze or forest.

5. Picking out the red scarf in a dark closet.

2. Light Up My Life

Provide each child with a shoe box (and its lid) and cut out a small (1") hole in one short side. Make available a variety of materials, including spools, paper, markers, colored Styrofoam peanuts, paint (with thin brushes), glitter, and glue, paste, or tape. Instruct children to make a three-dimensional construction by gluing the materials to the floor of the uncovered box in ways that create a "scene" or design of their own. When children have completed their boxes to their satisfaction, cover each shoe-box with a lid and ask children to look inside. Find out whether or not they can see their collage. Problem solve with them to determine a way for them to see what they have created. Help them understand that they will need a way for the light to enter the

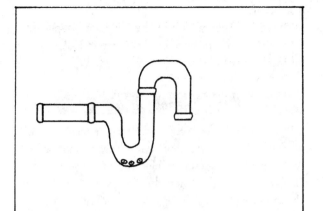

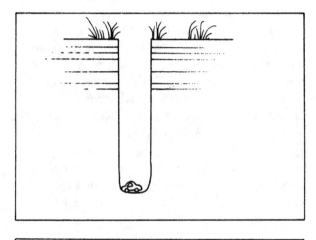

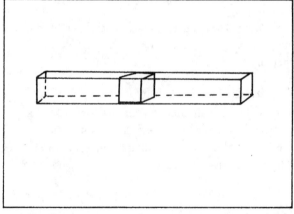

box before their eyes can see anything. They may think of a number of ways to let in the light. This activity demonstrates the principle that light from a source hits an object and bounces to someone's eye.

Hint for Success:

● Provide scissors, paper punches, or sharp implements for making holes in the boxes.

To Simplify:

● For safety, only adults should make holes in the boxes.

To Extend:

● Once children have reached solutions, display the boxes on a table and encourage children to look into each other's light boxes.

3. Sound Emotions

Sounds are often a cue to events that occur around us. In addition, certain sounds trigger emotions within people as a result of their associations with particular happenings. Explore these ideas with children in the following ways. Prepare a tape recording of various sounds heard commonly in the environment. Such sounds might include a doorbell, a siren, a baby crying, a door closing, traffic noises (for children living in towns or cities), farm noises (for children living in the country), and so on. As you play these, ask children to talk about what they think the sounds are and how they know. Follow this up by giving every child a four-page booklet entitled "Sound Emotions." Label each page with the following headings: "When I hear a _____, I feel_____ ." Ask children to fill out the pages over the next few days, concentrating on familiar sounds that conjure up in their minds specific emotions. For example, "When I hear a doorbell ring, I feel excited."

To Simplify:

● Instead of using a book, record children's thoughts and expressions of emotion on audiotape. Play it back to them if they so desire.

To Extend:

● Encourage children to write in their booklets in any way they know how or else take dictation from them. Each child's booklet will be unique and will be a reflection of his or her experiences and thoughts.

Cognitive

1. Ball Blast

The object of this activity is for children to try an experiment with a simple machine to determine whether or not they can make balls stay aloft. If one is not readily available in your play yard, make a teeter-totter or seesaw using a board balanced on a cylinder. Place a ball at the end of the seesaw that is resting on the ground. On the count of "three," have one or two children rapidly and forcefully push the other end of the seesaw down so the ball flies up. Urge the children to watch what happens. Try this same experiment using a variety of balls and ask children to first predict what will happen and then to observe the phenomena as they occur.

Hint for Success:

● Be sure the playing area is large enough so that balls do not go into a street. If this is a problem, use only balls that do not bounce very high, such as cloth balls, Ping Pong balls, or under-inflated balls.

To Simplify:

● Have some children carry out the experiment while others watch. This will make it easier for the observers to see what is happening.

To Extend:

● An explanation of why rockets can escape the earth's gravity would fit in well here, especially if the idea is brought up by the children. Rockets operate by using a powerful thrust from specialized fuel that takes them beyond the earth's gravity very fast. Explain that many rockets still circle the earth because they go just fast enough to keep them from falling to earth, but not fast enough to push them entirely beyond the force of the earth's gravity.

2. Solutions to the Problem

This activity provides children experiences with dissolving. It illustrates an important property of water (that some objects dissolve in it, some remain suspended, and some do not dissolve), as well as exploring the properties of other materials. Gather a wide selection of rounded objects such as small stones, smaller pebbles, sand, rock salt, sugar, powdered gelatin, uncooked rice, marbles, and navy beans. Place each material in a separate dish or open container into which children can reach. Prepare clear plastic jars or bottles about half full of water. Ask children to examine the materials in the containers: touch them, hold them, rub them, squeeze them and look at them using their eyes and with magnifying glasses. Then bring out the water containers and ask children to predict whether or not particular materials will dissolve in the water. Explain that dissolving means that the object can no longer be seen in its original form. Tell children that the only way to find out is to experiment or to try it out. Using one material at a time, have children place the object (or some of the object) into the water. Give children spoons or stirrers and tell them to mix up the water to try and get the substance to dissolve. Have them record their findings on paper, into a tape recorder, or in dictation to an adult or another child. An alternate suggestion is for children to put a marker on a chart to indicate their prediction. Have them do a self-check to determine how close their

Does It Dissolve?

Pebbles | Yes | No

Salt | Yes | No

Pepper | Yes | No

Rocks | Yes | No

Sand | Yes | No

prediction was to the actual event. For instance, develop a pictoral chart, on which the children glue small samples of the actual items being tested under an appropriate heading. Then ask children to look at the chart to summarize which of the items dissolved and which did not.

Hint for Success:

● For several days before carrying out the formal experiment, allow children to play with the materials in and out of water.

To Simplify:

● Use objects or substances with which children are already familiar, such as salt, pepper, sand, and so on.

To Extend:

● Develop one or more formal recording procedures that children can use to document and remember the results of the experiments.

● Explore the principle of suspension. An object or substance is suspended when it neither dissolves nor drops to the bottom. Rather, it remains suspended in the liquid, causing the liquid to change color or become cloudy.

3. Magnetic Mates

The objective of this experience is for children to examine their near environment for things to which magnets are attracted. Give children a variety of magnets to use. Direct them to find all the things in their classroom that the magnets will attract. Suggest that they go into the bathroom to test the sinks and toilets, that they try such things as the window frames and the toys and games on the shelves. Children may be surprised to discover that some items that do not look as if they contain iron actually do, such as cast iron sinks covered with porcelain. Take this opportunity to point out that scientists do not always know in advance what they will find. Provide paper and markers or pencils for children to write down or draw pictures of the items they discover to be attracted by the magnets.

To Extend:

● Children can also find any toys or classroom objects that contain magnets within them such as refrigerator magnets, magnet strips on the wall, toy trains, and so on.

● Another extension of this activity is to have children predict in advance what the magnets will and will not attract. Record their predictions and compare them with what the children actually discover.

4. Magnetic Attractions

This activity is designed to help children understand that magnets attract iron objects through some barriers and not through others. Provide several magnets of different strengths and shapes. Also have available paper clips, iron filings, or small and large metal washers, small nails, sheets of paper, Plexiglas®, a clear plastic or glass drinking cup, a china cup, several wooden sheets of varying thicknesses, plastic and metal lids, and an assortment of metal and Styrofoam trays. Begin by encouraging children to explore the magnets and the other objects. Show children how to hold a washer on the inside of a cup by using a magnet on the outside. Encourage children to follow your example and to further experiment with moving the washer by sliding the magnet along the side of the cup. Repeat this using other materials between the magnet and the iron objects. Pose some problems to the children such as:

Through how many sheets of plywood can the magnet still attract the paper clip?

Does it make a difference if the tray between the magnet and the washer is metal or Styrofoam?

Which magnets are the strongest and how can you tell?

Watch the magnets move the iron filings from underneath the sheet of Plexiglas® and describe what you observe. Will magnets attract things through your skin?

Give children paper and pencils or markers so they can write about or draw the things they discover.

To Simplify:

● Limit the materials so children will not be confused by too great a variety.

● Allow two children at a time to experiment.

To Extend:

● Explain to children that sometimes people want to know where the nails are in their walls in order to find the upright studs so they can hang pictures. Find out whether children can figure out how to use the principles they experimented with in this activity to solve the problem.

5. Is It True?

Discuss with children how carpenters and builders use the properties of gravity to help them build walls that are vertical or "true." Explain that the children will have an opportunity to determine how successful the builders were who constructed the school or center building. Provide children with several plumb lines (See the activity entitled "Plumb the Depths" on page 299.) Rub the strings with chalk. Instruct children to hold the free end of the plumb line high on a wall close to a corner, allowing the plumb bob to dangle freely. Help them snap the chalk line, until it makes a chalk mark on the wall. Inspect these marks with the children. Compare them with the near wall. Have children estimate by visual inspection whether the walls are vertical.

Hint for Success:

● Determine in advance what variation, if any, there is. Variations of less than 1" may be too small for children to see or to measure.

To Simplify:

● Demonstrate the activity, or have one child do so while the other children observe. This will help them focus on the essence of the activity, rather than being distracted by playing with the plumb bob.

To Extend:

● To confirm the observation, use a ruler to measure the distance between the wall and the chalk line at several points along the wall. Tell children that the wall is "true" or vertical when the measurements between the wall and chalk mark are the same all the way along it.

6. Blowing in the Wind

To illustrate that air moves even though the air itself cannot be seen, have children tie several 12" pieces of ribbon or light string to a wire clothes hanger and hang it at their eye level. Tell children to observe the ribbons and describe their motions. Then suggest that they wave handmade or purchased fans near the ribbons. Have children describe what they observe and ask them why they think the ribbons are moving faster or in a wider arc when they wave their fans. Bring in an electric fan (making sure the blades are covered by a safety grid) and direct the air flow toward the ribbons. Ask children to describe the effects of this strong wind. Change the force of the air stream by setting the fan on low, medium and high and elicit observations from the children as to any differences they notice. As a follow-up, take children outdoors on a windy day to feel and see the effects of moving air. Similarly, on a still day, ask them to try to feel the air moving.

7. Good Vibes

This activity illustrates the relationship between sound and vibrations. To introduce this principle, tell children to put their fingers over their vocal cords and begin to hum. Have them describe the sensations. Then ask them to make other sounds such as "aaaaaa" or "ooooooo" or "bbbbbbbbb." Again, ask for descriptions. Explain that parts of their bodies vibrate when they make sounds. Next, place a glass of water on top of a radio or tape recorder. Ask children to tell you what they see. Turn the radio on, and have children touch it and find out what they notice. Reinforce the connections between the sounds and the vibrations. As a follow-up, instruct children to make note of all the things in their classroom that make sounds.

To Simplify:

● Bring in several machines such as a hand vacuum, a blender, and a hair dryer. Encourage children to touch the machines, under supervision, and to experience the sound and vibrations simultaneously.

To Extend:

● Have children pretend that they cannot hear (they may cover up their ears to heighten the effect). Then ask them whether they could still tell if something made a sound and how they would know. Have them do a classroom search without using the sense of hearing for items that vibrate. Encourage them to use all their other senses to help in their search.

8. Straight as an Arrow

Light travels in straight lines and changes direction only when it bounces off a reflective surface. Sound, on the other hand, travels around corners. This activity gives children some exposure to those attributes of light and sound. Elicit from children a list of all the sources of light they can find inside the classroom or outside. Find out how they think the light travels from the source to their eyes. Provide paper towel tubes or lengths of garden hose, and suggest that they look through the tubes at electric lights or flashlights. Ask them to experiment by bending the hose and looking at the light and figuring out what they have to do to see the light source. They will discover that they must be looking directly at the light in order to see it.

Next, try this experiment with sources of sound. Put an audiotape, CD, or record on a player and ask children from where the sound is originating. Ask such questions as "Where do you have to be in order to hear the sound? Which directions must your ears be pointing to hear the music?" Ask children to go into a nearby cloak room or closet. Can they still hear the music? Contrast the experiences with light and with sound. Draw or write children's observations and the conclusions to which they come.

9. Eclectic Electric

After a discussion of how electricity is used in the everyday world, send children in small groups on an electric hunt. This entails finding everything in the room that is powered by batteries or plugged into a wall socket. Provide paper and pencils or markers so children can write about or draw pictures of the items they discover. Compile the various lists into a master list that you hang at children's eye level in the room. At a later time during discussion, work with the children to categorize the various items by their function. Help them determine that we either get electrical power from batteries or from a building's electrical system.

A follow-up activity is for children to look for battery or electrically powered items in their homes. Send a note home to parents explaining the project and enlisting their aid in helping children formulate lists or illustrations of the items they find

10. Kitchen Chemistry

What happens to individual ingredients when they are mixed together and heated in some way is part of the amazing world of Kitchen Chemistry. Prepare uncooked and cooked versions of the same recipes with children (examples follow). In each case, help the youngsters observe similarities and differences between the cooked and raw ingredients by looking, smelling, tasting, and touching. Make charts or diagrams to enable children to summarize their findings and, therefore, to remember them. Encourage children's experimentation with mixing and cooking ingredients (within the bounds of safety) and chart these results, as well.

To carry out these simple cooking experiences, you will need a heat source (stove, oven, microwave oven, electric fry pan, or hot plate) and the appropriate receptacles, stirrers, knives, and so on.

Suggested cooking experiences:

1. **Apples and Applesauce.** Take several apples, some water, and a few teaspoons of sugar. Cut up (or allow children to cut up) one or two apples, sprinkle with sugar, and provide a cup of water. In a saucepan or similar pot, put other cut apples, sugar, and water, and heat until bubbling. Stir the cooking apples until they are mushy and have lost their original shape. As the applesauce is cooking, elicit comments from children about what they are seeing and smelling. Once the apples are cooked, perform a taste comparison test of cooked and raw ingredients with the children. Make note of their observations as indicated above.

2. **Fruit Salad and Fruit Compote.** Gather a variety of fresh and dried fruits, including raisins, apples, plums, and apricots. Follow the same procedure as for Apples and Applesauce.

3. **Vegetable Salad and Vegetable Soup.** In similar fashion, put together a salad composed of tomatoes, carrots, string beans, green peppers, celery, and other available vegetables. Take the same ingredients and cook them until they form a soup. Have children taste, smell, and touch the salad and soup and compare them.

4. **Berries and Berry Pudding.** Wash and hull strawberries or raspberries and encourage children to taste them. Have a small amount of arrowroot powder to taste as well. Then cook some of the berries according to the following Norwegian recipe called "Rodgred Med Flode."

   Mash three pints of berries in a food processor or food mill. Cook in a pan over medium heat, stirring, until mixture boils. Remove from heat. Make a paste of 1/4 cup of cold water and 2 Tbsp. arrowroot powder. Add to berry mixture and put back on low heat. Cook until thick, but do not boil. Cool and add a little sugar or honey to taste. Serve the pudding warm or chilled, plain, or with cream and slivered almonds.

Hints for Success:

● Provide small paper or plastic plates, bowls, spoons, forks, and napkins so that children may try their creations.

● Provide sponges and paper toweling to wipe up spills, as well as aprons for children to wear while they cook.

● Make sure children wash their hands thoroughly before cooking and eating.

11. There's Music in the Air

Through this activity, children will explore how sounds vary when they are produced by different means and materials. Bring in a wide variety of musical instruments, borrowed from a local music store, children's families, or a high school or middle school in your area. Be sure to include stringed instruments, percussion instruments, and woodwinds or brass. Familiarize yourself with the instruments and try to get some sounds out of each. Allow children, under supervision, to explore the instruments. Ask them to figure out how the instruments make their sounds. Question children about the similarities and differences they detect among the various instruments. Elicit their ideas and write them on large paper for all to see. Point out the fact that sound is produced by something vibrating, whether it be a string, a column of air, or a drum head. As a follow-up, invite musicians to play actual melodies on the instruments. Have them point out how they change the pitch (highness or lowness of the sound) by shortening or lengthening the vibrating part of the instrument. (Note: See the activity, "Vibrating Strings," page 323, for follow-up projects.)

12. Sound as a Bell

The purpose of this activity is for children to explore how sound travels. Introduce the activity by having children sit very quietly and listen to the sounds around them. After about one or two minutes, ask children to name and discuss all the sounds they heard. Make a list of the sounds they mention. Help children distinguish those sounds emanating from inside your room (such as a clock ticking, people breathing, paper rustling) from those sounds that come from outside the room (doors slamming in the hall, car horn honking, people passing). Explain that sounds travel through the air and also through some materials, such as the walls of a building. Send one child outside the classroom and have him or her ring a small bell. Instruct the child to move farther and farther away, making the same sound at the same volume. Ask the rest of the group to listen for the bell sounds, raising their hands when they can no longer hear them. Ask children such questions as "What did you notice about the sound of the bell when _____ moved down the hall? Did you have to see him/her in order to hear it?"

Next, try similar experiments with light. Give a child a flashlight. Tell the youngster to turn it on in the classroom and then go into the hall, keeping the flashlight on as he or she goes. Ask children to watch closely and to raise their hands when they can no longer see the flashlight. Ask the group questions similar to the ones above. Finally, instruct a child both to keep the flashlight on and ring the bell as he or she moves farther from the classroom. Ask children what they noticed this time. At the conclusion of these experiments, assist children in summarizing on paper their observations about sound and light. This may be done through dictation, drawings, or writing.

13. Temperature Trials

The purpose of this activity is to enable children to explore what happens to objects and substances as a consequence of temperature changes. Try all or some of the following experiments. In each case, ask children to predict what will happen when the object or substance is heated or cooled. Write or record their ideas and compare them with what actually occurs.

a. **Crayons:** Melt crayons in a saucepan. While they are still soft, give them to children to use for drawing. Then put them in the freezer. In advance, ask children whether the crayons will retain their shape when heated or when cooled. Encourage them to observe what happens when crayons of several colors are melted in the same pan. Have children try to draw with the frozen crayons. Ask them to describe the two (hot and cold) experiences.

b. **Ice Cream:** Make or purchase ice cream. Keep some in the freezer, some in the refrigerator, and some in the room. Hold a taste test to determine whether or not changes in temperature affect the taste as well as the appearance of the ice cream.

c. **Finger Paint:** After children have used finger paints, put some in the refrigerator. Once hardened, give them to children to use for painting. Find out from them what they observe.

14. Flash!

Gather at least six or seven flashlights of different sizes and appearances (color and shape), and requiring a variety of battery sizes. Present them to children, asking them to predict which flashlights will shine brightest, farthest, or stay on the longest. Record children's predictions on a chart and then try the experiments. Ask children at each step of the trials what they observe. Help them compare their predictions with what they discover. As a follow-up, encourage children to seriate the flashlights by a number of attributes.

Hint for Success:
● Use a long hallway to determine which flashlight shines the farthest.

Construction

1. Paper Gliders

Show children pictures or photographs of gliders in flight. Explain that these craft fly through the air as a result of air moving around them. Tell children that they, too, can construct an aircraft that will glide through the air. Demonstrate how to fold a sheet of typing paper (or other stiff paper) in half. Then bend the sides to form wings.

Explain that this is one type of glider and that children should examine the pictures to determine those

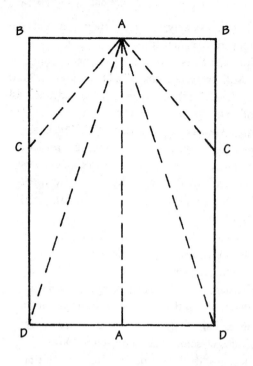

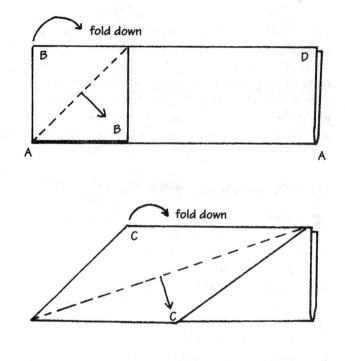

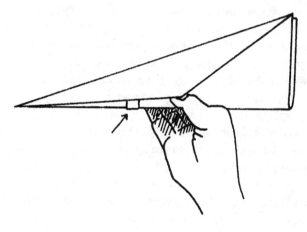

attributes the gliders have in common. Point out the body and the wings. Then provide sheets of typing paper to the children and encourage them to make gliders in their own way. Tell the youngsters that they will have an opportunity to fly these in the hallway or on the playground. Encourage children to decorate their gliders in any way they wish. Later in the day, allow children to fly their gliders. Help them decide which ones are successful flyers and why.

To Simplify:

● Draw lines on the paper to guide the folding process.

To Extend:

● Have the children experiment with different kinds of paper, varying the texture, weight, color, and stiffness.

2. Shadow Puppets

Introduce puppets to children by showing them a variety of types. If possible, bring in hand puppets, stick puppets, marionettes, Muppets®, and the like. Encourage children to play with them before asking them to construct their own.

Provide the following materials with which children will make puppets:

shapes (cut out of tagboard or used file folders) that represent heads, torsos and other body parts of people or animals.

paper fasteners

Popsicle® sticks or tongue depressors

Directions: Demonstrate to children how to construct a puppet using the pieces provided. Help them connect the parts with paper fasteners. Use the sticks to hold the puppets up and to attach to the limbs. Children may use the sticks to make the limbs move.

Explain to children that they will be making puppets to use in shadow plays. Show them how to use the fasteners to put any of the parts together in whatever ways they choose. Thin Popsicle® sticks may be attached to arms or legs to enable children to move them. See the activities "Shadows on the Wall" (page 326) and "Shadow Stage" (page 327) in this mini-theme for ways children can use their puppets in pretend play.

Hints for Success:

● Keep the parts of the puppets simple and free of detail.

● Give children time to practice moving the puppets before using them on a stage or in a show.

3. Vibrating Strings

Show children some examples of actual stringed instruments, such as a guitar, violin, cello, banjo, or mandolin. Encourage them to examine and try out the instruments. Then ask children what they think they would need to create a stringed instrument of their own. Have available such materials as boxes of various shapes and sizes, rubber bands, yarn, string, wood, nails, tape, paper, scissors, glue, and fasteners. Encourage children to use these, or other materials, in their construction. Provide support, as well as back-up materials. Give children opportunities to "play" their instruments for their friends. They will also enjoy being part of a marching band outdoors or in another large area.

4. I See the Light

Procure strips of diffraction grating (available from scientific catalogues) and cardboard photographic slide holders (available from camera stores). Cut the grating to the same size as the cardboard slide holders. Slip each piece of grating in between the cardboard of the holder in such a way that the holder becomes a frame around the grating. Encourage children to look through the diffraction grating at electric lights in the classroom, flames from a gas stove (if possible), and sunlight coming through a window. (Make sure children do not look directly at the sun, as this is dangerous!) Ask children what they notice, with particular reference to the differences they perceive looking with their naked eyes and through the grating. Have them describe the colors. Then provide paints that are the colors of the spectrum (blue, green, yellow, orange, red, and violet) along with thin brushes and paper. Suggest that children use these materials to recreate the colors and lines they have seen through the diffraction grating.

Hint for Success:
● Provide enough grating slides for several children to use at a time, as this is likely to be a popular activity.

Language

1. I Wonder as I Wander

The sense of wonder is the underpinning of all scientific endeavor. Help children become aware of their own curiosity and wonder by carrying out the following activity. As a group or as individuals, encourage children to generate a list of the things about which they wonder or are curious. To stimulate their discussion, bring in some things, such as a clock or a radio, turn on a faucet, demonstrate with some magnets, blow up a balloon, or point out objects or forces in the classroom and ask if these are things about which children want to know. Write children's queries on a large piece of paper or, if children are able, have them write or draw their own lists. Extend the discussion by asking children to think how they could learn about each of the items on the list. Emphasize all of the TFPs in this unit that relate to scientific processes, such as observing, predicting, experimenting, and so on. Look for common ideas or concepts and use these as a basis of future inquiry. Later on, go back to the original list and check off the ideas that have been explored during the unit. This will serve as a reminder to children about what they have learned.

2. I Spy! Part II

Show the children the book *I Spy: A Book of Picture Riddles* (1992) written by Jean Marzollo and Carol Carson, with photographs by Walter Wick. The photographs are of common articles and natural materials with directions for finding specific pictures. These instructions are written in riddle form. Readers are asked to pick out the designated objects from among a greater array in order to sharpen their visual acuity. After children are familiar with the book and its format, provide them with booklets, magazines from which to cut pictures, glue, and pencils. Instruct them to glue a variety of pictures on every page. When these are complete, have them write down or dictate which items other people are to look for on each page. Provide opportunities for children to trade books with each other or to "read" them to another child who then searches for the indicated items.

To Simplify:
● Provide pre-cut pictures, so children can concentrate on the real objective of the activity and not become side-tracked by the cutting process. Choose pictures that represent objects in the children's immediate environment.

To Extend:
● Encourage children to write or dictate rhyming riddles on each page. Use examples from the book to demonstrate how it can be done.

3. My Shadow

Read the poem "My Shadow" by Robert Louis Stevenson. Repeat the poem over several sessions until children are familiar with the content. One strategy for helping youngsters remember the words and the images is the following: after repeating the poem many **times**, say it again, leaving out the last word of alternate **lines** for children to fill in, speaking as a chorus.

On a sunny day, take the children outdoors and reenact the verses of the poem, relating each segment to children's experiences with their shadows. For instance, use the line "He is very, very like me from my heels up to my head" to encourage each youngster to stand where he or she can see his or her shadows clearly. Ask all children to compare their shadows with their actual selves. When the words talk about the shadow changing size quickly, have children move about until they can make their shadows grow larger or smaller. Make use of the verse about the shadow going behind and before to explore this phenomenon with the children directly. Suggest that children run and jump in an attempt to rid themselves of their shadows. Ask children how successful they were. The final verse of the poem describes the person waking before the sun is up and looking for his shadow. Ask children to try this before they come to school and to report their findings.

Hint for Success:

● Post the poem in the classroom on a large chart or paper for easy reference.

To Simplify:

● Try imitating only one or two ideas suggested by the poem at a time.

To Extend:

● Provide opportunities for children to write or dictate individual or group stories about their experiences with their shadows. Post these in the classroom as well. Encourage children to illustrate their stories.

4. Poetry for Scientists

Collect poems with content that relates to scientific principles or materials in their content or subject matter. Write each poem on a tagboard chart and hang it at children's eye level. Include photographs or illustrations (perhaps some made by children) that depict the content of the poems. Memorize two or three short poems and introduce them to children by reciting them at appropriate times. For example, as children move back and forth on swings, recite the poem "The Swing" by Robert Louis Stevenson. (This poem is included in *A Child's Garden of Verses*; several editions are available.) Show the written poster to children upon returning to the classroom. Read each verse, running your finger

under each line as you read. On another occasion, or at the same time if children are interested, read one line and then leave out critical words in the next. Encourage children to supply the missing words. As children become more familiar with the poem, omit additional words, leaving more for children to speak. "Swing Song" by A. A. Milne (in *Now We Are Six*) is another poem about going up in a swing. Poems about the wind abound. Some examples are: "Wind on the Hill," by A. A. Milne, "Who Has Seen the Wind?" by Christina Rossetti, and "The Wind," by Robert Louis Stevenson. Related to these is the poem "To a Red Kite," by Lillian Moore. A brief poem about shadows is "8 A.M. Shadows," by Patricia Hubbell. Refer to books in the Teacher Resource section of this unit for additional sources of poetry.

To Simplify:

● Select one poem at a time on which children will concentrate.

To Extend:

● An extension of this activity is for children to recite the poems in a choral speaking format. You may wish to select different groups of children to do each poem. Hold a choral speaking festival during which time children share the poems they have learned with other members of the group or other groups in the program. Invite parents to this festival, as well.

Physical

1. Make a Magnet

Many materials that contain iron can be magnetized so they exhibit the properties of magnets for brief periods of time. Demonstrate how to make a magnet by stroking a long nail or piece of wire in one direction only with an actual magnet. Give each child a magnet and a nail or wire and encourage everyone to follow your example. Caution children to avoid stroking in a circular or back and forth motion, as this will not result in magnetizing the object. (You may decide to experiment with this principle, allowing children to stroke in any way they wish, and then compare the results.) The procedure takes patience and endurance, as it requires about 50 to 60 strokes for an iron object to be magnetized. Provide such items as paper clips, small screws, or iron filings for children to test the magnets they have made.

Hints for Success:

● A rigid wire may be created by straightening out a large-sized paper clip. Iron filings can be made by snipping a steel wool pad into tiny pieces.

● Be sure you provide a container or small tray to keep the metal objects and filings off the floor.

To Simplify:

● Children may need help stroking the nail or wire. Pair children so they can take turns, making sure they are both stroking in the same direction!

● Indicate the direction of the stroke by putting a red dot of nail polish on the end of the nail they are to stroke toward.

To Extend:

● This is a good opportunity for children to explore the relative strengths of their magnet with the one provided by you. Ask them to find out how many paper clips each magnet can pick up. The strongest magnet is the one that can pick up the greatest number of items.

2. Blow Up

This activity helps children develop endurance. Purchase or borrow an air mattress and a foot pump. Give children opportunities to practice using the pump, encouraging them to feel the air being pumped out the end. Be sure they also examine the flat air mattress. Attach the pump to the air mattress and begin to inflate it. Use the mattress in children's play areas so they can experiment with bouncing on it, bouncing items off it, and lying down or sitting on it. At a later time, deflate the mattress, allowing children to feel the air rush out of the mattress. Consider bringing to the classroom smaller, plastic, inflatable toys for children to blow up and play with.

Hint for Success:

● Because this activity requires a great deal of pumping, encourage children to take turns. One idea is to limit each child to five pumps per turn.

3. Attractive Creatures

Attach a paper clip to the feet of cardboard people and animal figures as illustrated on page 326. Create a stage out of a shoe box or larger, thin-walled carton by placing the opening toward you and the closed side outward. Place the figures on top of the carton and show children how to manipulate them using magnets on the inside of the box.

To Simplify:

● Give children individual boxes to work with initially and provide one figure at a time.

To Extend:

● Have several children work at once, using a larger stage. Provide materials so children can construct their own figures out of spools, clothespins or dowels. Hammer a thumbtack at the bottom of each figure. Encourage children to decorate their figures.

● An additional extension is for children to enact favorite stories using the creatures propelled by magnets.

4. Boat Float

Precede this activity with discussions and experiments related to sinking and floating. As part of the experiment, suggest to children that they create their own boats to carry a number of items that might otherwise sink. Children can make these out of Styrofoam trays by simply placing articles on the trays and setting them in the water. Have them try to sink the trays as well as keep them afloat.

Pretend Play

1. Push and Pull

The function of this activity is to help children better understand the ideas of "attract" and "repel" through creative movement. Gather children into a group and explain that they are going to behave like magnets First, demonstrate how to clasp your hands together while calling out "Attract." Direct children to do the same. Then, have them move their hands apart, calling out "Repel." After a few minutes of practice, pair children and tell them to place their palms together and to lean in toward one another. Explain that when they do this, they, as magnets, attract. Each pair should then practice the command "Repel" while moving apart. Give them several chances to work out these procedures. On the days that you carry out this activity, provide actual magnets in the classroom for children to explore. As they work with them, point out the actions of the magnets on various materials, using the vocabulary indicated above.

To Simplify:

● Spend several days helping children become accustomed to playing "Attract" and "Repel" with different parts of their own body, using their hands as one "magnet." The directions will be such statements as "Attract your tummy" or "Repel your toes."

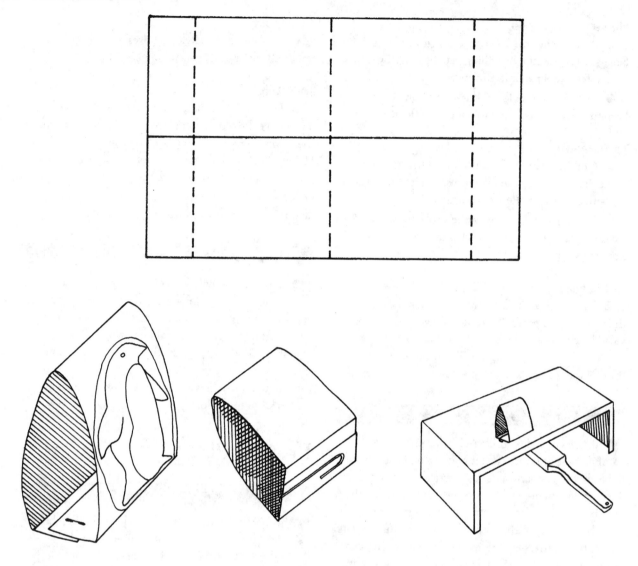

To Extend:

● A follow-up activity is to play a version of the game "Freeze." The game is played in the following way. Tell children you will play music (use an audiotape or record). They are to pretend to be magnets. When the music stops, the magnets will attract each other. To do this, children will quickly find a partner and attract one body part to a different body part of the other child (such as hip to knee or shoulder to hand). This illustrates the principle of opposites attracting. When the music begins again, the body parts will repel, and children will move away from one another until the music stops.

2. Shadows on the Wall

Set up a source of light and direct the beam toward a blank wall. Encourage children to stand in the path of the beam and to twist their bodies in a variety of ways or move their hands to create shapes and figures.

Direct children's attention to the shadows that are created on the wall. Once children have had individual turns to pretend, pair the youngsters and ask them to create animal or object shadows with their bodies. Monsters tend to be popular. Caution children to confine their pretending to the area within the beam of light and help them figure out how to take turns.

Hint for Success:

● A high-intensity lamp or a film strip projector make excellent light sources, as their beams are narrowly focused and bright. The activity is most successful in a somewhat darkened room or area where the contrast between light and dark is pronounced.

3. Shadow Stage

Set up an area of the classroom as a theater. Include seats for the audience, a ticket booth, and a concession stand. Create a shadow stage in the following way. In a darkened area of the room, hang a sheet from the ceiling or frame. Place a strong light behind the curtain, leaving enough room for children to play act between the light and the curtain. Encourage children to put on simple plays, create dances or other creative movements, or interact with puppets.

Hint for Success:

● Give children chances to be both performers and audience so they can see the effects of the shadow movements. Encourage them to modify or change their physical movements based on what they observe.

To Simplify:

● Begin by having children perform one at a time. Sit with the rest of the children in the "audience" area. Point out what is happening. For instance, direct children's attention to the ways children are moving their bodies and to the effects they are creating.

To Extend:

● A classic, silent comedy can be reenacted behind the shadow stage by older children. This pantomime is called "The Doctor" or "The Operation." The play shows doctors preparing for surgery with instruments that may include spaghetti tongs, a saw, and a drill. The quaking "patient" is brought in and is put on a covered table. The doctors begin to operate. In the process they appear to remove all sorts of ridiculous things from the patient's body, such as a rubber chicken, string of sausages, another person, and so on. Of course, these items appear to come out of the patient's body, but are, in reality, kept under the table. Once they understand the special effects that can be created by a shadow stage, help children make up their own silly plays.

4. Pretend and Real

During the science study, adapt several traditional pretend play scenarios to feature science:

1. **Housekeeping:** Include appliances that use scientific principles for their operation, such as: sink (gravity), refrigerator and cabinets (magnetic catches on doors), stove, toaster, microwave oven (heat and light), vacuum cleaner (moving air), hair dryer, clothes dryer (heated, moving air). Have the children label these items and then use them for make-believe.

2. **Store:** Include scales for weighing "produce."

3. **Restaurant:** Include cooking implements, as well as raw and cooked models of food. Encourage children to explore, in pretend ways, the processes of applying heat to food.

Social

1. Clean Up the Mess!

Solving practical problems is one of the applications to which scientific principles and discoveries may be put. Present a clean-up problem to children in the following ways and encourage them to use the scientific information they have gained in order to solve it. Procure a large tray or, alternately, a large table surface and cover it with small, metal objects (either paper clips, thumbtacks for older children, washers, or nails) and other objects such as marbles or small wooden cubes. In addition, sprinkle soap powder over the entire collection. Present this to children in a group as a problem for them to solve: "Look at this mess! How are we going to clean it up quickly so we can put snack on the tray/table? We have to do it in a way that helps us sort each kind of object into its own container so we can use them another time. Let's think about some ways we can do this." Elicit suggestions from children, paraphrasing their ideas and writing them down or recording them in some way. Help children focus on the unique properties of the objects—this may require that they think of one set of things at a time. For example, prompt them into figuring out how to use what they know about gravity to clean up the marbles or magnetism to take care of the paper clips and what they know about things dissolving in water to clean up the soap powder. Once the children have had a chance to generate ideas, combine their thoughts into three or four possibilities. Help them decide how the cleanup will be done. Will all the children do all of the jobs? Will the tasks be divided among the group? Then let them carry out their plan. Help them to evaluate the outcome of their cooperative efforts at the conclusion.

To Simplify:

● Present children with one dilemma at a time—for example, a tray full of marbles.

● Provide several trays and divide the group up so fewer children are required to work together at a time.

To Extend:

● Each time you carry out this type of activity, add another dimension for children to consider. You could, for example, put dark squares of paper or sandpaper on a similarly colored tray and provide children with a flashlight to distinguish the objects. Or take advantage of the properties of buoyancy to float objects to the surface when cleaning up a tub full of objects.

2. Two-Way Cookies

Cookies created from the following recipe may be eaten baked or unbaked! This offers children another experience in comparing cooked and raw ingredients. Divide the children into groups of between five and eight children each. Give each group the recipe and the ingredients. Ask each group to decide whether they will bake the cookies they make or let them chill in a refrigerator. Explain that whatever their decision, they will be required to choose a friend with whom to share their cookies. Discuss with children how to divide the work of preparing the cookies. Elicit suggestions from the group and then help them carry out their plan.

Ingredients

1 stick butter or margarine

3 cups oatmeal

1 cup honey

3 tbsp. unsweetened cocoa powder

3/4 cup powdered milk

1/2 tsp. salt

2 tsp. vanilla

1/2 cup raisins

Directions: Melt the butter over low heat. Stir in the oatmeal. When thoroughly mixed, add the rest of the ingredients. Mix thoroughly with your hands. The dough will be very stiff. Wet your hands in a bowl of water before shaping the cookies into little balls or snakes. Put half the cookies into a refrigerator for a while to harden. Put the other cookies on a lightly buttered cookie sheet, flatten them, and bake for 10 to 12 minutes in a preheated 350° oven.

3. Reflections

Collect a variety of small pieces of shiny paper, such as aluminum foil, colored foil, and wrapping paper. (These are sometimes available in sheets or in pre-cut shapes.) Sort the small pieces by color and put them in small tins or bowls on a table. A few containers of glitter will add to the reflections. Provide one or two glue sticks for the project, as well. Place a large piece of shiny paper in the center. Explain to children that they are to work together to create a reflecting collage and that they will have to share the materials, as there aren't enough materials for everyone to have his or her own supply. Remind children that they can ask someone to pass things to them and that they can respond to the requests of others. If necessary, give children practice in asking and responding. When the project is complete, give children flashlights to shine on their collages in order to see it sparkle.

4. Me and My Shadow

On a sunny day, take children outdoors to measure their shadows. Provide sidewalk chalk, carpenter's rulers, tape measures, pencils, and pads of paper for recording the results of the measurements. Have children self-select a partner. Explain that for this activity children are required to work together to accomplish their goals and that each child will have a turn. Have children spread out on the pavement and instruct them to stand so that they can see their shadows. One child in each pair will "pose" while the partner draws the outline of the shadow on the pavement. Once both children's shadows have been drawn, the two will collaborate on measuring the shadows using standard units of measurement (rulers, etc.) or units they devise (such as hand span or footprint). Move from group to group as they work, assisting when necessary. If children are able, encourage them to write their results on the paper you have provided. Another option is for children to write with chalk directly on the shadow outline.

Hint for Success:

● Demonstrate how to draw a person's shadow without your own shadow getting in the way. This could be a source of much merriment as shadows overlap and shapes become distorted.

To Simplify:

● Simply have pairs of children trace their shadows on the sidewalk without measuring them.

To Extend:

● Follow up on this activity by bringing outdoors several familiar objects, such as chairs, globes, scissors, and so on, and encourage children to outline and then measure these shadows.

Teacher Resources

Field Trip Ideas

1. Investigate a store or farm stand in the vicinity of the program. Ask the proprietors for permission to bring balance scales to weigh produce that you and the children will purchase. Plan with the children in advance how much of each item to buy. Do this by using a predetermined quantity of wooden inch cubes or other weights on one side of the balance scale. When you get to the store or

produce stand, balance the other side with the produce to be bought.

2. Visit a commercial kitchen, either in a restaurant or at a school. Arrange the trip so children will see food being cooked. Have available the raw ingredients as well as the cooked food for children to sample. Spend enough time so children can observe the cooking process—the heating and cooling of foods and the mixing of ingredients. Tasting the raw and cooked products will help children better understand the process.

3. Take children to a nearby building site and point out the machines and tools that are being used. Explain how these depend on the use of physical principles, such as levers, balances, gravity, inclined planes, and so on.

Classroom Visitors

1. Invite parents or other community persons to do cooking projects with the children. Suggest that they plan to cook favorite family recipes or ones that represent their cultural heritage. Provide the equipment and set up the experiences for large-group instruction or small-group participation. Obtain the recipes in advance so you can prepare pictorial directions for children to follow.

2. Invite one or more representatives of the building trades and building industry to demonstrate for children how they depend on gravity and other natural physical phenomena in their work. Have them demonstrate some of the tools they use, such as plumb lines, levels, hammers, saws, and so on. You may find that some parents are skilled at home repair and would be willing to share their expertise with the children.

Children's Books

Ardley, N. (1991). *The Science Book of Light*. New York: Harcourt Brace Javanovich.

Branley, F. M. (1987). *Air Is All Around Us*. New York: HarperCollins.

Brown, M. (1947). *Stone Soup*. New York: Macmillan.

Cobb, V. (1990). *Why Can't You Unscramble an Egg?* New York: Dutton.

Crews, D. (1981). *Light*. New York: Greenwillow.

de Regniers, B. S., ed. (1988). *Sing a Song of Popcorn*. New York: Scholastic.

Deen, M. (1976). *The Know How Book of Experiments with Batteries and Magnets*. New York: Grosset and Dunlap.

Gore, S. (1989). *My Shadow*. New York: Doubleday.

Hoban, T. (1990). *Shadows and Reflections*. New York: Greenwillow.

Isadora, R. (1985). *I Touch*. New York: Greenwillow.

Jonas, A. (1987). *Reflections*. New York: William Morrow.

Lloyd, P. (1982). *Air*. New York: Dial Books.

Marzollo, J., & Carson, C. (1992). *I Spy: A Book of Picture Riddles*. New York: Scholastic.

Milne, A. A. (1926). *Now We Are Six*. New York: Dutton.

Newman, F. R. (1983). *Zounds! The Kid's Guide to Soundmaking*. New York: Random House.

Paul, A. W. (1992). *Shadows Are About*. New York: Scholastic.

Santrey, L. (1985). *Magnets*. Mahway, NJ: Troll Associates.

Silverstein, S. (1974). *Where the Sidewalk Ends*. New York: HarperCollins.

Simon, S. (1985). *Soap Bubble Magic*. New York: Lothrop Lee & Shephard.

Sky-Peck, K., ed. (1991). *Who Has Seen the Wind?* New York: Rizzoli.

Smith, N. E. (1981). *Wind Power*. New York: Coward, McCann & Geoghegan.

Stevenson, R. L. (1981). *A Child's Garden of Verses*. London, England: Penguin Books.

Tompert, A. (1984). *Nothing Sticks Like a Shadow*. Boston: Houghton Mifflin.

Watson, P. (1982). *Light Fantastic*. New York: Lothrop, Lee & Shepard.

Watson, P. (1982). *Liquid Magic*. New York: Lothrop, Lee & Shepard.

Adult References

Barr, G. (1959). *Outdoor Science Projects for Young People*. Mineola, NY: Dover Publications.

Diebert, L. (1991). *Science for Me: Individual Recipes for Young Children*. Carthage, IL: Good Apple.

Discenna, J., ed. (n.d.). *Recipes for Science*. East Lansing, MI: The Science Theatre, Michigan State University.

Harlan, J. (1992). *Science Experiences for the Early Childhood Years*. 5th ed. New York: Macmillan.

Sources of Science Materials (Catalogs)

Arbor Scientific
PO Box 2750
Ann Arbor, MI 48106-2750

Edmund Scientific
101 E. Gloucester Pike
Barrington, NJ 08007-1380

Oriental Trading Co., Inc.
PO Box 3407
Omaha, NE 68101

Pasco Scientific
10101 Foothills Blvd.
PO Box 619011
Roseville, CA 95661

Small World Toys
PO Box 3620
Culver City, CA 90230-6515

Trees

Oh, in the woods,
Oh, in the woods,
There was a tree,
There was a tree,
The prettiest little tree,
The prettiest little tree,
That you ever did see.
That you ever did see.

The world is filled with a marvelous variety of trees.

Oak	Fir	Poplar
Birch	Pine	Willow
Maple	Spruce	Redbud
Palm	Cherry	Tulip
Beech	Apple	Cedar
Aspen	Dogwood	Cyprus
Sequoia	Redwood	Chestnut
Magnolia	Live Oak	Hawthorne

These are just a few of the more than 140 kinds of trees and a thousand different species found in North America alone. Trees are a distinctive part of every region of the world and even the youngest children have experienced firsthand the benefits of sharing the planet with these, the largest of plants. Thus, a unit on trees is an ideal way to further children's enjoyment and appreciation of the natural world.

Purpose

We wrote the "Trees" unit with three ideas in mind:

1. To promote children's understanding that trees are plants.

2. To increase children's awareness of the diversity among trees.

3. To enhance children's recognition of the important role trees play in our daily lives.

Each of these ideas is the basis for one of this unit's mini-themes. The most basic mini-theme is the first, "Trees Are Plants." Its TFPs focus on the parts of the tree and how they function. Children studying this topic for the first time will concentrate on the most visible parts: roots, trunk, and crown. More experienced children could delve into less obvious functions of the cambium, the heartwood, and the leaves. In either case, children find fascination in discovering that these large specimens have parts and functions in common with the flowers, houseplants, and garden plants with which they are most familiar.

The second mini-theme, "Variety and Changes in Trees," is designed to broaden children's awareness of the many variations among trees as well as with the changes in the same type of tree over time. In this portion of the unit children have a chance to explore different species of trees, noting distinctions in bark, leaves, and flowers—in color, shape, size, texture, and smell. Children's attention also is drawn to the fact that trees look different at each stage in their life cycles and, in some cases, at different seasons of the year. Such variations provide excellent opportunities for children to hone their observation skills and experience directly both the aesthetic and scientific aspects of nature.

The third mini-theme, "Tree Gifts," concentrates on the tangible contributions trees make to human and animal life. Shade, beauty, wood products, food, and protection are all visible means by which animals and people benefits from trees. All of these "tree gifts" are ones children can find out about firsthand. Children need not rely simply on hearing about these benefits nor is their discovery confined to pictures. Rather, the actual examination of trees in their natural habitat promotes the idea that trees add great value to our lives. The importance of trees to the air we breathe is a logical extension of these initial understandings. However, because transpiration is an invisible process, children tend to learn about it primarily through discussion and symbolic representation. These latter methods are more abstract than those we have included throughout *Themes Teachers Use*, thus transpiration is not addressed in the activities offered here.

Implementation

We expect that teachers will explore the world of trees using examples common to their locale, thereby enhancing the relevance of the learning experiences for children. Although the "Trees" unit is self-contained, it repeats little of the information and activities found in the "Plants" unit presented in *Teaching Young Children Using Themes* (1991). That unit presents activities related to photosynthesis as well as multiple activities demonstrating plants' needs for water, sunlight, and minerals/nutrients. With this in mind, we suggest that the concept of trees be presented to children following an introductory study of plants. The foundation provided by talking about plants and how they grow will make the material in this unit more comprehensible to young learners.

Within the framework of this unit, several options for the study of trees are possible:

Option One:

Week 1: Provide a general introduction to tree parts and their functions.

Week 2: Focus on different kinds of trees.

Week 3: Explore the products people derive from trees.

Option Two: Select one topic (such as kinds of trees) to focus on for a week or two. Introduce this theme in the fall, then repeat it in the winter and spring, building on what the children have learned each time. Contrast the same trees across the three seasons.

Option Three:

Week 1: Provide a general introduction to trees.

Week 2: Focus on broad-leaved trees.

Week 3: Concentrate on needle-leaved trees.

Option Four:

Week 1: Talk about tree trunks and the ways in which people and animals use this part of the tree.

Week 2: Examine tree fruits and how people and animals rely on these products.

Week 3: Focus on the work people do that is related to trees.

Trees Are Plants

Terms, Facts, and Principles (TFPs)

General

1. Trees are living things.

2. Trees are the largest of all plants.

3. Trees are tall, woody, perennial plants with one dominate stem.

   ● **Tall:** By definition, tree species grow ten feet tall or higher.

   ● **Woody:** There is a hard, fibrous substance beneath a tree's bark.

   ● **Perennial:** Trees grow from one year to the next.

4. Trees use air, sunlight, water, and minerals/nutrients from the soil to make their own food.

5. Trees are found in most areas of the world.

6. Trees cannot move from place to place.

7. We call the place where several trees grow together a woods or forest.

8. Trees have a great influence on the kinds of birds, wildflowers, and animals that live in the same area.

9. Trees have different parts that work together to keep them alive—a crown, a trunk (stem), and roots.

Tree Parts
The Crown

10. The crown of a tree includes branches, twigs, leaves, and flowers/fruit.

11. Branches and twigs support the leaves, the flowers, and fruit.

12. Leaves are where the tree makes its food.

*13. Leaves contain a substance called chlorophyll that helps turn water, air, minerals, and light energy into food for the tree.

*14. While the food is being made, the leaves breathe out tiny droplets of water and a gas called oxygen. Oxygen in the air helps people and animals breathe.

15. Leaves are attached to branches and twigs by a stalk.

16. The tree's food travels down the stalk and through the branches and trunk to the rest of the tree.

17. Flowers and fruits produce trees' seeds. New trees grow from seeds.

*18. The tree's fruits develop from its flowers.

19. Some fruits contain only one seed; some fruits contain hundreds of seeds.

The Trunk

20. Tree trunks are strong and woody—strong enough to support the crown.

21. Water and minerals move up through the trunk from the roots to the branches and finally to the leaves where they are made into food for the tree.

*22. The combination of water and minerals that flows through the tree is called sap.

23. A hard outer covering of bark covers and protects the trunk and branches.

*24. On some trees the bark offers protection against the damage caused by insects, damage from drying out in the sun and the wind, and/or damage in forest fires.

The Roots

25. Roots hold trees in the ground. Without their roots, trees fall down.

26. Roots carry water and minerals from the ground up into the trunk of the tree.

27. Trees often have one large root called a taproot along with many smaller roots.

*28. Tree roots grow as the tree grows, branching out sideways in the ground.

Activity Ideas

Aesthetic

1. Tree Art

Show children pictures of paintings and drawings. Such reproductions can be obtained through commercial art supply companies or on decorative calendars. Try to obtain works that encompass different cultural interpretations, as well as representational and abstract art forms. Discuss the picture(s) with the children. Consider such points as: a)how the trees are similar to and different from other plant life in the picture, b) what the painting would look like if the tree were not there, c) what might be behind the trees pictured, and d) which animals or people might live nearby. Encourage each child to choose a favorite picture, telling what he or she likes about it.

To Simplify:

● Select only one painting on a given day. Repeat the same kinds of questions each day.

To Extend:

● Encourage children to draw or paint a tree picture of their own that could be displayed in the classroom near the original artwork. If possible, offer children materials similar to those used by the artist (such as watercolors, paste and paper for collage, chalk, and so on).

2. Tree Part Painting

Gather the following materials: twigs, leaves, pine cones, bark, seed pods, and other tree parts; easel paper; thin tempera paint or watercolor paint. First, have children explore the tree parts, feeling the texture of each one. Talk with them about where each item can be found on the tree. Next, demonstrate dipping a twig or leaf in the paint and stroking, rolling, or brushing it across the paper. Ask children to describe the resulting effect. Invite children to make their own paintings using a variety of tree parts and to experiment with the different ways they can make marks on the paper.

To Simplify:

● Offer children stiff tree parts such as twigs and pine cones that are easily grasped.

To Extend:

● Provide a drawn outline of a tree on a large sheet of butcher paper. Include roots, trunk, branches, twigs, and leaves. Invite children to use the corresponding tree part to mark the paper.

3. Tree Trough

Put cedar mulch, wood shavings, or sawdust in an empty water table along with small objects such as cars and trucks or measuring cups, funnels, and spoons. Talk with the children about the smell and texture of the natural material and discuss its origin. (Try to find pictures of wood or tree cutting that also show the sawdust that is created.) Have pictures of trees on the walls

nearby so the children's attention can be drawn to them during play. Encourage children to explore and play in the material. A variation on this activity is to fill several dishpans, each with a different wood product. Encourage children to play in the different materials and compare how they look, smell, and feel.

To Simplify:

● Give each child a dishpan filled with shavings or sawdust of his or her own to explore. Periodically have children trade pans as a way to experience the varying materials.

To Extend:

● Help children make their own sawdust or wood shavings using a saw or plane.

Affective

1. Tree Crowns

You will need the following materials: construction-paper leaf shapes and branches, three-inch-wide paper strips at least 18 inches long, scissors, markers, and tape, glue, or a stapler. For each child, cut a three-inch-wide strip of construction paper that is a little longer than the circumference of the child's head. Connect the ends of the strip with tape or a staple. Provide each child with a variety of leaf shapes and branches. Eventually these will be glued or taped on the crown. Begin by explaining that the crown of the tree is the part including the branches and leaves. Tell children that because this part of a tree is unique, people use it to identify a tree by name. Then explain that the children will use their tree crowns to help people identify things about them. Ask children to describe themselves, what they look like, whether they are a boy or girl, and where they live. On each leaf, write one of these ideas as children name them. After each child has a collection of three or four leaves, invite everyone to glue the leaves on his or her personal leaf crown. Complete the project by putting each child's name on the band of the crown so people can identify the child by name. Invite children to wear their crowns throughout the day.

To Simplify:

● Focus on children's physical characteristics and the objects with which they like to play.

To Extend:

● Ask children to talk about what activities they like to do and to make comparisons between themselves and someone they know well. For example, "Are you taller or shorter then your sister?"

2. Tree Seed Names

This activity works well in the spring when tree seeds are plentiful and can be gathered easily from the ground. Provide each child with a supply of tree seeds and a strip of manila paper on which her or his name has been printed in block letters. Provide glue sticks or small squeezable glue bottles. Have the children glue the seeds to their names for a textured effect. Encourage children to trace the letters with their fingers afterwards to experience how their names feel.

Hint for Success:
● Give children a chance to collect the seeds they will use.

To Simplify:
● Use seeds that are flat (such as maple seeds) from which the seed coat has been removed.

To Extend:
● Ask children to write their own names as a pattern for their seed designs. Remind them to write big enough so it is easier to glue the seeds on each letter.

● This activity could also be varied using other tree parts such as twigs, bark, or leaves.

3. Trees Like Me

Arrange to visit a nursery, tree farm, or natural area where the children can see trees of varying heights and ages. First, help each child find a tree that is similar in height to him or her. Work with the children in making comparisons. Record pertinent information for later reference such as the kind of tree, its age, its circumference, and other characteristics (texture of bark, shape of leaves, color of flower if applicable, and so forth). If possible, take a picture of each child next to the tree he or she has selected. Have someone at the site available to provide information about how old the trees are. Next, look for trees that are the same age as the children. Also, find older and younger trees. What are the vital statistics for these trees? How do they compare to the information gathered for trees similar in height to the children?

To Simplify:
● Focus on one attribute only, either age or height.

To Extend:
● Back in the classroom, create a life-sized graph on which each child records her or his age and height as well as that of the tree she or he selected. Also, discuss what trees need to grow and compare these necessities with what children need to grow.

Cognitive

1. Measure by Measure

Select a number of trees in a nearby area for children to measure. Using a tailor's measuring tape, help children measure various parts of the tree. For example, measure the circumference of the trunk, measure the length of a branch and a twig, or count the buds of leaves on one branch. Record these measurements on a drawing representing the type of tree measured.

To Simplify:
● Measure one tree only. Ask different children to help measure the various parts.

To Extend:
● Before measuring anything, ask children to guess what some of the measurements might be. Compare the children's guesses with the actual measurements taken.

● Estimate the height of the tree by using the following estimation procedure. Walk away from the tree. Stop at different intervals, bend over, and look back through your legs at the tree. When you have reached a distance where you can see the top of the tree when bending over comfortably, stop. Measure the distance to the base of the tree. This should equal the approximate height of the tree.

● Children can measure the diameters of several trees using string. Cut each string to match the diameter of the tree being measured. Compare the string lengths in the classroom. Use words such as *longer, longest, the same as, shorter,* and *shortest* throughout this discussion.

2. Tree Part Examination

Provide the children with a variety of tree parts to be examined. These might include pieces of roots, a stump, trunk, branches, twigs, leaves, seeds, fruits. Peel away layers of these parts to get a better look at the inside. Provide magnifying glasses so children can see the items more clearly. Discuss information contained in the TFPs as children explore the materials. Talk about what the various parts are, where they are found in trees, and their function.

3. Sticks, Sticks, Sticks

Explore the ground with the children looking for sticks of varying kinds. Collect all types of sticks for the children to examine. Challenge children to look for a straight stick, a stick with many curves, a long stick, a short stick, a stick with branches, and so forth. Display the sticks together. Compare and contrast the sticks according to their differing characteristics. Point out, for example, how a stick that is short in comparison to one stick can be long in comparison to another. Invite children to make their own comparisons. Place labels near particular sticks or bunches of sticks identifying how they compare to the rest. Repeat this activity on different days, creating new groupings and comparisons each time.

Hint for Success:
● This same activity can be implemented another time using leaves.

To Simplify:
● Ask children to find the longest stick or the shortest one from within a group of sticks.

To Extend:
● Once children have created their groups and made their comparisons, introduce a stick that has not yet been considered. For instance, if a child decides that one stick is the "curviest" from among three or four, offer another one asking the child "which stick is the curviest now?"

4. What's Up?

Take the children to the second or third floor of a building whose windows look out over a nearby trees. Ask the children to name all of the things about the tree they can see by being up that high. Write down all of the children's responses. Next, go down to the base of the tree and repeat the same questions. Talk with children about the difference between the two perspectives. Help them determine what things are the same on both lists and how these parts looked different from each vantage point. Find out if some things could be seen best from one perspective or another.

To Simplify:
● Ask children to simply label what they see from one point of view or another.

To Extend:
● Invite children to draw pictures representing each of the perspectives they observed. Do not insist on accurate representational drawings. Instead emphasize that children think about how the tree looked from the top down and from the bottom up. Then ask them to draw those two ideas in their own way.

5. Uprooted Discoveries

In some places it is possible to find trees that have been uprooted by a storm or some other force of nature. If such a resource is available, use it as an opportunity for children to explore the roots firsthand. Also, provide each child with a small paper lunch sack, labeled with his or her name, to use for storing bits of materials to examine more closely back in the classroom.

6. Supporting Roles

Teach children the following song to emphasize how tree parts work together. Use a flannel board with appropriate pieces to help everyone remember the order.

♫ **Tree Supports**

Words by Grace Spalding
Tune: "Them Bones, Them Bones, Them Dry Bones"

Chorus

Those roots, those roots, those anchoring roots,
Those roots, those roots, those anchoring roots,
Those roots, those roots, those anchoring roots,
Grow deep down in the ground.

Verse

Oh, the roots connect to the strong trunk,
The strong trunk connects to the branches,
The branches connect to twigs and leaves,
All to make a tree.

Chorus

Those roots, those roots, those anchoring roots,
Those roots, those roots, those anchoring roots,
Those roots, those roots, those anchoring roots,
Grow deep down in the ground.

7. Tree Part Chart

Make a large diagram of a tree similar to the one illustrated here. Over the week, ask children to identify different parts of the tree. Label these. As children gain more information, invite them to tell you their ideas about each part and its function in relation to the tree as a whole. Record the children's ideas on the

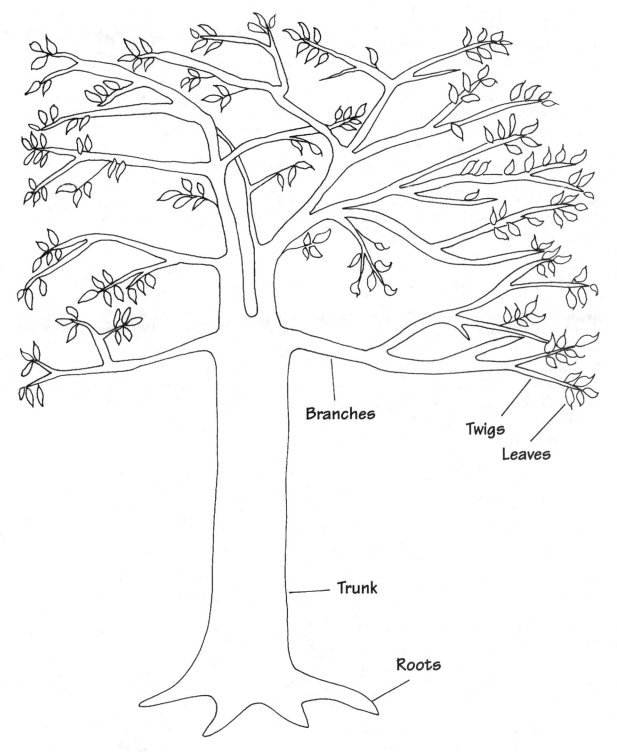

Branches

Twigs

Leaves

Trunk

Roots

chart for all to see. A variation on this idea is to create a flannelboard consisting of an outline of a tree and tree parts made out of felt. Invite children to put the tree together as they dictate or write out their ideas about the trunk, leaves, branches, and roots.

8. Tree Census

Provide the children with a chart like the one illustrated here.

	Number
Bushes	
Small trees	
Medium trees	
Large trees	
Logs or fallen trees	

Give each child his or her own chart and clipboard. Take the children outdoors to locate all of the trees on the playground or in another designated place. (If it is not possible to go to a place with enough trees and bushes, you can use a painting or photograph as a source for tree counting, but make sure there is enough detail for children to differentiate one tree from another.) Discuss which plants might be bushes and which are trees. Count all of the trees and record the numbers on the charts. Add challenge to the activity by making charts in which specific kinds of trees are identified (such as fruit trees, evergreen trees, trees with round leaves, trees with pointed leaves, and so forth).

Construction

1. People Trees

Trace an outline of everyone's body by having each child lie on a large sheet of butcher paper, legs together and arms outstretched. Tell children to paint or color in the outline as if it were a tree. Talk about the tree parts as the work continues. Arms = branches, fingers = twigs, legs and body = trunk, toes and feet = roots.

2. Paper Towel Trees

Gather the following materials: 8-1/2" x 11" pieces of construction paper, brown paper toweling (the kind that comes on rolls), green tissue paper, glue, and glue applicators. Pass out a piece of brown paper toweling, about 12 to 15 inches long, to each child. Demonstrate to the children how the paper can be ripped in sections of different sizes and then twisted to make a trunk, branches, and roots. Invite children to glue these to a piece of construction paper. Next show them how to add leaves by gluing crumpled pieces of tissue paper to the branches.

Language

1. Adjectives Under the Arbor

Prior to introducing this activity to the children, make several tree-shaped booklets using construction paper for the cover and standard paper for the pages. Print the following information on each page.

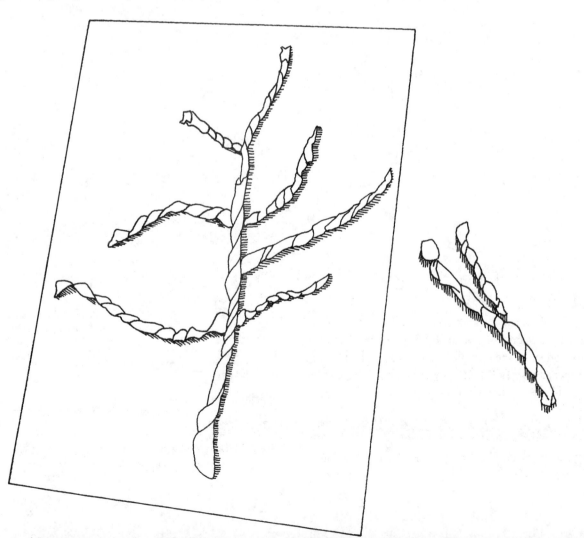

Title Page:
My Tree Book by (write child's name here)

Page 2:
I found a pretty part of my tree. It is _____.

Page 3:
I found a smooth part of my tree. It is _____.

Page 4:
I found a rough part of my tree. It is _____.

Page 5:
I found a large part of my tree. It is _____.

Page 6:
I found a small part of my tree. It is _____.

Page 7:
Trace a leaf shape from your tree here.

Page 8:
Make a bark rubbing from your tree here.

Give each child a book and go outside so that everyone can select a tree for use as a source for his or her descriptions. Children may describe the same tree or different trees. Write down the children's words as they dictate them or have children record their observations in their own form of writing. Some children will want to work through their entire book in one day, some will complete their booklets over several days.

To Simplify:
● Give children choices of adjectives to select in describing their tree. For instance, "The leaves on my tree are big or small," "The bark on my tree is rough or smooth," and "The leaves on my tree are jagged or rounded." Ask every child to select the adjective that best describes his or her tree for each item listed.

To Extend:
● Consider making pages for other adjectives such as sticky, wet, dark, light, sharp, soft, and hard.
● Create pages that ask children to supply a descriptive word to fit a variety of circumstances. For example, " The bark is _____." "The branches are _____."

2. Touch Talk

The materials for this activity include a variety of tree parts such as twigs, acorns, pine cones, seeds, bits of bark, blossoms, leaves, and short branches; a purchased "feely box" or a box closed on all sides with a hole cut in one end through which a child's hand could pass; a

brown paper bag to conceal items held in reserve; easel paper and a marker. Before putting anything into the feely box, let children explore the tree pieces by handling them. As the children explore, ask them to talk about how each object feels. Once the items have been thoroughly explored, conceal them in a paper bag. Put one or more items in the feely box without anyone else seeing what they are. Invite the children, one at a time, to discover what's in the box using their sense of touch only. Encourage each child to describe how the object feels. Write down the words children use. Periodically read the list aloud to remind children of their discoveries. After a few items have been described, remove them from the box and report their descriptors as you pass them around the group. Point out the variety of words used to describe each part of the tree.

To Simplify:
● Give children choices of words to consider as they feel what's inside the box. For instance, "Is that a rough thing or a smooth thing? Does it feel hard or soft?" Write down their choices.

To Extend:
● Ask children to guess what the item is and to tell where it may be found on a tree.
● Place several objects in the feely box. Give children a specific kind of item for which to search. For instance, "Find something that is small and hard," or "Find something that has smooth parts and rough parts at the same time."
● Ask children to find a particular tree part from among several hidden in the feely box. Once children have made their choices (without looking), ask, "How do you know that's the _____?" Focus on children's rationales and descriptors versus whether or not their answers match your own.

3. Tree Echoes

Adapt the song, "The Green Grass Grew All Around," to help children learn some parts of trees and to practice good listening skills. Gather the children in a group. Explain that you will teach them a song by saying the lines one at a time, which they must repeat or echo each time you pause. Remind children to listen carefully so they will know what to say when it is their turn.

♪♫ The Green Grass Grew All Around
(American Traditional)
Tune: "How Dry I Am" (If you don't know the tune, treat this as a chant.)

Oh, in the woods, Oh, in the woods,

There was a tree, There was a tree.

The cutest little tree, The cutest little tree,

That you ever did see, That you ever did see.

Chorus

Oh, the tree was in the hole, and the hole was in
    the ground and the green grass grew all around,
    all around, and the green grass grew all around.

And on that tree, And on that tree,

There was a branch, There was a branch,

The cutest little branch, The cutest little branch,

That you ever did see. That you ever did see.

Chorus

And on that branch, (echo)

there was a twig, (echo)

The cutest little twig, (echo)

That you ever did see. (echo)

Chorus

And on the twig, (echo)

There was a leaf. (echo)

The cutest little leaf, (echo)

That you ever did see. (echo)

Chorus

And on that leaf, (echo)

There was a bug, (echo)

The cutest little bug, (echo)

That you ever did see. (echo)

Create a flannelboard to match the sequence
depicted in the song. Make the pieces available in the
language area for children to put in order. Create a new
song or chant based on the sequence of events depicted.

To Simplify:

● Use a flannelboard with corresponding pieces as
you go through the song or chant to help children
remember the words.

To Extend:

● Once children have learned the song or chant
well, read the storybook *The Tree in the Wood: An Old
Nursery Song,* adapted and illustrated by Christopher
Manson (1993). Talk about the use of alternate words
for the tree parts in this traditional song. Encourage children to look closely at the illustrations, and help them
discover the many details.

4. Tree Facts and Fiction

Introduce this activity after children have had ample
time to become acquainted with the TFPs in this
mini-theme. Obtain a copy of the book *I Am a Tree,*
one of the Who Am I Series of books published by
Santillana Publishing (1975). It contains some segments
that are fact and some that are fiction. If you cannot
find this book prior to working with the children, make
up some sentences about trees—some of which are true
and some of which are false. Put these sentences on
individual strips of paper to read aloud. Make some of
the items obvious (such as "Trees can fly," "Trees have
roots," "Trees are plants") and make some of them more
subtle (such as "Trees move," "Trees are alive"). Begin
the activity by talking to the children about the difference between fact and fiction. Next, ask them to generate a list of what they know about trees. Write their
comments on a large sheet of easel paper and post nearby for later reference. Then ask children to listen carefully as you read parts of the book or the individual
strips. Discuss which ones are true and which are fantasy. Refer to the children's list to help clarify which is
which. If you are using your own sentences, consider
posting them in the appropriate column of a chart
labeled "fact" and "fiction" or "true" and "not true" as
children talk.

Physical

1. Puzzling Trees

Paste magazine pictures that include trees on posterboard. Cut the board into pieces according to the
parts of the tree (such as roots, trunk, crown; or roots,
trunk, branches, flowers). Make these available for children to examine. Store individual puzzles in two-gallon
plastic self-closing bags.

To Simplify:

● Cut the pictures into equal halves. Cut some
lengthwise and cut others across the width. Add challenge by making the two parts unequal in size.

To Extend:

● Increase the number of pieces.

● Cut the pieces into irregular shapes.

● Help children to make their own tree puzzles.
Provide plenty of opportunities for children to practice
cutting their puzzles in a variety of shapes.

2. Tree Tag

Play the game of tag with one person being It. Use trees as safe spots that children can hang on to with both hands periodically throughout the game. As children become more experienced with the game, give a time limit such as a count of ten for staying at each safe spot, or have only one type of tree serve the safety function. This will keep the game moving and It will not be frustrated by not being able to tag anyone.

3. Log-istics

Bring a log (minus any branches) to the playground for children to balance on or leap over. Use the log as a balance beam. Invite children to walk along it, arms outstretched at their sides. For variation, ask children to hold their arms in different positions—outstretched before them, upright over their heads, or hugging their bodies. An alternative is to put two logs together parallel to each other with about eight inches of space between them. Ask children to walk carefully—heel, toe, heel, toe—between the logs.

To Simplify:
● Assist children as they walk across by holding one hand or placing your hand on the small of a child's back.

To Extend:
● Encourage children to practice leaping over the log from a running start as well as doing a standing broad jump over it. A running leap requires children to gauge distance before taking off from the ground as well as spreading their legs to jump. The broad jump requires more attention to arm movement as a way to propel oneself over the log. It also requires balance as children land on two feet. Add challenge by using a variety of logs, differing in length and circumference.

4. Water Relay

Talk with the children about the fact that trees need water to live and what happens if a tree gets too little water. Introduce the activity by saying that most trees get their water in the form of rain. Today, however, children will provide water to a tree in a very special way. Have young children line up at a spot 10 to 15 feet away from a tree outdoors; older children will do better 10 to 15 yards away from the tree. Provide a bucket of water and assorted tablespoons and serving spoons. Have the children transport the water from the bucket to the base of the tree. Emphasize moving quickly while still balancing the spoon well enough to get some water to the tree.

To Simplify:
● Use one-cup measures rather than spoons.

To Extend:
● Carry out this activity in relays. Emphasize the cooperative nature of each person helping to pass water or a spoon on to the next individual. Do not turn this into a competitive activity between teams.

● Have the children estimate how many spoonfuls of water are in the bucket, then count how many trips they need to make to move the water from the bucket to the tree.

5. Firmly Rooted

Remind children that tree roots hold the tree upright, even when the wind blows. Tell children to "plant" their feet firmly on the ground like tree roots. Carry out a series of bending, swaying, and stretching exercises. Encourage children to move their bodies in flexible positions without lifting their feet or moving from the spot in which they are "rooted."

Hint for Success:
● Music makes a nice addition to this activity after children have tried it once. Select music representing different moods. Selected music could inspire visions of trees swaying in the breeze as well as trees standing up to mighty winds.

Pretend Play

1. Shadow Climbing

Find a place where a tree shadow is easily distinguished; it is best if the shadow is long. (This will happen either early in the morning or later in the afternoon). Talk with the children about how difficult it is to climb a tree and how careful a person must be when climbing. Tell the children that today they are going to pretend to climb a tree by climbing a tree's shadow. Invite children to try a variety of movements such as lifting their arms and legs in a climbing motion, ducking to avoid branches, hanging on as if the wind were blowing, sitting at the top of the tree looking out over the land, climbing down backwards, and/or jumping down to the ground. For variation, ask children to repeat their actions in such a way that their own shadow is the one doing the climbing. This version requires a more advanced awareness of both one's body in space and of perspectives.

2. Apple Orchard

Create an apple orchard in the classroom for the children by making large-sized (about four or five feet tall) construction-paper trees with trunks and leaf crowns. Fasten these to the wall within children's reach. Cut many apples out of red or green construction paper. Cover the apples with clear plastic adhesive. Attach one-inch squares of Velcro® to the backs of the apples. Also, attach one-inch squares of Velcro® to the branches of the tree. Add apple trees to the orchard by placing dead tree branches in coffee cans filled with sand. Fasten paper apples to these trees by punching a small hole in the stem of the apples, then tying a loop of yarn through each hole. Hang the apples on the tree branches by placing the loop over a twig.

Provide children with canvas bags, boxes, and/or baskets to put the apples in as they are gathered. Invite the children to be workers in the apple orchard. Explain that their job is to carefully pick the apples from the trees and place them in the gathering containers without bruising them. Make available a housekeeping area where children can take the apples and pretend to prepare them for meals. Once all the apples are off the trees, put the apples back on the branches so the play may continue.

To Simplify:
● Provide children with only one type of the trees described above, not both at once.

To Extend:
● Have different kinds of apples on each tree: green apples (Golden Delicious or Granny Smith), large red apples (Red Delicious), and smaller-sized red apples (Empire or Northern Spy).

3. Fruit and Seed Store

For this activity, you will need the following materials: plastic fruit, seed catalogs, make-believe packages of seeds for fruit trees as well as other tree varieties, two or more cash registers, a table or counter for the cashiers, another table for displaying wares, and perhaps a third table for catalog sales, bags and baskets, labels for making price tags, markers or pencils, inventory sheets and small clipboards children can use to count and list the items in the store, scales for weighing the fruit, boxes or cartons for holding the fruit on display, order forms and envelopes for catalog sales. Help children set up a market where they can sell fruit and seeds. Encourage children to take turns being fruit pickers, salespeople, or customers.

Hint for Success:

● Place produce shelves far enough apart so children can restock them easily.

Social

1. Tree Shadows

Find a place where the shadows from nearby trees are visible on a concrete area. Provide chalk for small groups of children to work together to trace the outline of the trees' shadows. Offer children additional chalk to color the shapes they have created from the shadows. Stand back and admire each group's handiwork when the task is done.

2. Hand Trees

Divide the children into pairs. Have the children in each pair trace an outline of their partner's hand (with the fingers slightly spread) and lower arm on a piece of construction paper. Give children prepared leaf shapes, or leaf-shaped sponges and paint for printing, or torn pieces of tissue paper to use in decorating their tree branches with leaves. Encourage children to help one another as opportunities arise. If it is a time of year when the leaves are changing colors, then adjust the colors of the materials accordingly. If it is a time when leaves are on the ground, suggest that children take that into consideration.

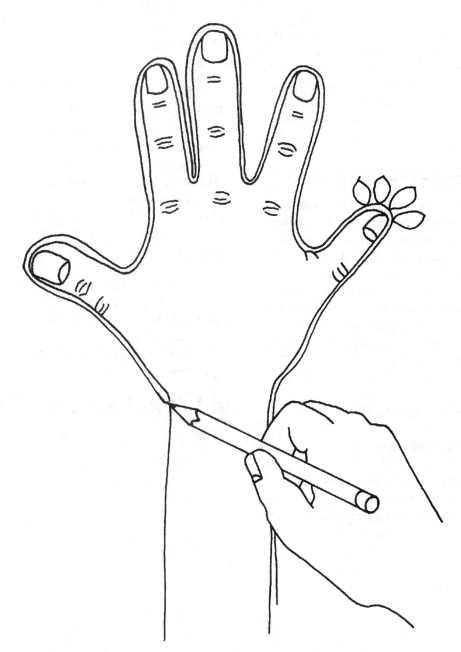

3. Forest Bed Collage

Provide the children with one large sheet of butcher paper and objects collected from the ground in a wooded area. Such objects may include pine needles, pine cones, leaves, twigs, acorns, small sticks or branches, bark, and moss or lichens. Using a mixture of school paste and wood glue, have the children glue the objects to the paper. Throughout the entire process emphasize the importance of working together to create a project the whole class can enjoy.

Hint for Success:

● Emphasize the collaborative nature of this project by having the children help collect the forest bed materials in one of three ways. One way is to gather materials from under any trees that might be in the program's play yard. Or, if a wooded area is accessible from the school grounds, then a field trip to collect things would be valuable. Hand out lunch-sized paper sacks and have the children look for small things on the ground under trees. As a third option, send a note home asking parents to assist their children in collecting things under a tree near where they live. Be sure to emphasize that the items desired are natural ones rather than ones made by people.

To Simplify:

● Provide objects that are not too difficult to attach to paper such as twigs, leaves, and pine straw. Bulkier objects such as acorns and pine cones are more difficult to attach and may frustrate some children.

To Extend:

● Offer children bulkier objects to work with as well as string, tape, thin wire, and yarn with which to attach them to their collage. Such projects are best created on cardboard or another heavy paper.

Teacher Resources

Field Trip Ideas

1. Take a nature walk through a wooded area.
2. Visit a natural history museum in which trees are used as part of the displays.

Classroom Visitors

1. Ask someone from a tree nursery or tree farm to show children a sapling whose roots are exposed. Examine the various parts of the tree while your visitor answers children's questions.
2. Invite an artist who works with a particular tree part (such as the leaves, the wood, and so on) to show his or her work to the children and to explain what he or she looks for in selecting the tree parts used.

Children's Books

Cooper, E. K., and Cooper, P. (1972). *A Tree Is Something Wonderful*. San Carlos, CA: Golden Gate Junior Books.

Day, J. (1975). *What Is a Tree?* New York: Golden Press.

DeBourgoing, P. (1989). *The Tree*. New York: Scholastic.

Florian, D. (1990). *Discovering Trees*. New York: Macmillan.

Frost, R. (1978). *Stopping by Woods on a Snowy Evening*. New York: Dutton Children's Books.

Hester, N. (1990). *The Living Tree*. New York: Franklin Watts.

Jaspersohn, W. (1980). *How the Forest Grew*. New York: Greenwillow.

Manson, C. (1993). *The Tree in the Wood*. New York: North-South Books.

Padendorf, I. (1982). *The True Book of Trees*. Chicago, IL: Childrens Press.

Patrick, D., and Ingoglia, G. (1987). *Look Inside a Tree*. New York: Putnam.

Udry, J. (1957). *A Tree Is Nice*. New York: HarperCollins.

The Who Am I Series. (1975). *I Am a Tree*. New York: Santillana Publishing.

Adult References

Cowle, J. (1977). *Discover the Trees*. New York: Sterling Publishing.

Variety and Changes in Trees

Terms, Facts, and Principles (TFPs)

Kinds of Trees

1. Trees come in many varieties.
2. Each variety has distinctive physical characteristics—silhouette, leaf shape and formation, color, fruit, flower, and bark.
3. Some trees (such as the pine, fir, and spruce) keep their leaves all year long. These trees are called evergreens.
4. Some trees (such as maple, oak, birch, and ash) shed their leaves once every year, usually in the autumn. These trees are called deciduous.
*5. Evergreen trees can have leaves shaped like needles (pines, firs, spruces, larches, and others), scales (cypresses), or awls (junipers). These leaves many grow singly or in clusters.
*6. Deciduous trees have flat, broadleafed leaves. These leaves may be single (one leaf per stalk) or compound (several leaves per stalk). Compound leaves may have individual leaflets that grow in an opposite pattern (directly across from one another) or grow in an alternate pattern.
*7. Another difference between deciduous trees and evergreens is that evergreen trees have seeds that grow inside of cones. The hard outer covering of the cone protects the seeds. Such cones come in many shapes and sizes.
8. Different kinds of trees grow in different environments. Climate, soil type, amount of rain, amount of sunlight, and other plant growth determine the kinds of trees that will grow in a given area.
9. Each kind of tree has a common name and a scientific name.

Changes in Trees Over Their Lifespan

10. Trees only produce seeds of their own kind. A tree produces seeds that will, in turn, only produce the same kind of tree.
*11. Seeds are scattered by nature in many different ways. Some stick to animal fur and are dropped, some are blown by the wind, some seeds scatter as their cases pop open, some seeds are eaten by birds and excreted elsewhere, some seeds are buried by animals and then begin to grow.

*12. Some seeds fall on fertile ground and begin to grow into new trees, some seeds fall in places where they cannot grow so no new tree grows.
13. Sometimes people plant tree seeds in order to grow new trees.
*14. How well people care for the tree seeds they plant affects whether or not a new tree will grow.
15. A nursery or tree farm is a special place where people plant and care for tree seeds and young trees. The people who work there are called nursery workers, tree farmers, or foresters.
*16. A seed sprouts by pushing one shoot up toward the sunlight (this will become the trunk of the new tree) and one shoot down into the soil (this becomes the tap root).
17. Over time, branches, fruits, and leaves begin to form as the tree becomes taller and bigger.
18. Some trees live for only a few decades. Others live for hundreds of years.
19. Trees grow taller and wider and leafier each year until they reach maturity. Then their growth slows down.
*20. Trees begin to die when they are infested by bugs or fungus, when insects eat too many leaves or eat away at their trunks, or when polluted air or rain damages them so they cannot produce leaves, fruits, and seeds.
21. When trees die, they stop making leaves, fruits, and seeds. Their branches eventually fall off, they rot, and finally the tree becomes part of the soil.
*22. A tree's age can be determined by counting the rings of wood in a cross-section of its trunk. Each ring represents one year of growth. The age of an evergreen tree can be determined by counting the number of branch layers from top to bottom. Each layer represents one year of growth.
23. People who study trees and how they grow are called botanists.

Seasonal Changes

24. All trees grow most quickly in the spring.
25. Each spring the tips of a tree's branches and leaf buds (the shoots) push upward and outward. The new growth is often a brighter green than the old growth.
*26. Each spring the tree's trunk gets thicker as a band of new wood forms under the bark and each spring the tree's roots push deeper into the soil.
*27. During the summer months, growing trees make food to become stronger and bigger and mature trees make food to stay alive and produce seeds.

28. Deciduous trees stop making food in the fall. Their leaves change from green to orange, red, yellow, and/or brown.

*29. When the leaves of deciduous trees stop making food, the green chlorophyll in the leaves goes away. This allows other colors to show through such as yellow, red, or orange.

*30. Deciduous trees lose their leaves in the fall. When the earth around the tree gets colder, there is less water for the tree to use and it begins to store moisture for the winter. The tree grows a layer of cork at each leaf stem to block water from leaving the tree through its leaves. The leaves dry up and the wind blows them to the ground.

*31. During the winter months, deciduous trees are dormant. They continue to live, but they do not produce food or seeds, and they do not grow taller or wider or leafier.

32. Evergreen trees lose some of their leaves a few at a time. They do not lose their leaves all at once at any time during the year.

Activity Ideas

Aesthetic

1. Chalk, Stencils, and Templates

This activity provides children with a different approach to stenciling and builds on the leaf stenciling activity described on page 356. Before introducing it to the children, get some old file folders or squares of posterboard, scissors, chalk, soft paper towels, or facial tissues. Cut one leaf shape from each file folder. Vary the leaf shapes you create. You will have a stencil (a piece of cardboard from which the leaf shape has been cut) and a template (the shape that was cut from the stencil). Provide the templates and the stencils to the children. Show them how to lay a stencil or template on a piece of paper, then rub the side of the chalk across the outline. Remove the stencil or template to see the design that has been made.

To Simplify:

● Provide simply shaped stencils and templates that are at least eight inches across. These will be easier for children to handle.

To Extend:

● Encourage children to make patterns using their stencils and/or templates.

● Have children experiment with overlapping shapes.

● Have children trace around the inside of the stencil or the outside of the template. Remove the cardboard and use a tissue or paper towel to gently brush the edges, creating a shadowy effect.

2. Leaf Castings

After children have gathered a variety of leaves fallen from trees, ask them to select one from which to make a casting. Use plaster of Paris poured in small aluminum foil pie tins, one per leaf, following the directions on the box. Have each child press a leaf in the plaster. Allow the castings to dry and pull away the leaf to reveal the imprint. Invite children to compare the impressions made by the different leaves. Add challenge to the activity by offering additional real leaves for children to explore. Ask them to look for leaves that are similar to the ones made into castings.

3. Tree Lines

The aim of this activity is for children to experiment with a variety of techniques for applying paint to paper using brushes and sponges. The materials needed are poster paints or watercolors (including black or brown), a variety of art papers (construction paper, easel paper, manila paper, oaktag, and so forth), household sponges cut into different abstract shapes and widths, paint brushes of varying widths, newspaper to cover a table, and smocks for the children and yourself. Show children how to make four or five lines on their papers using a light brush stroke of black or brown paint. These strokes represent the branches of a tree. Leaves can be created using colorful splotches of paint made by quickly dabbing a brush or sponge several times on top of or on either side of each line. Encourage children to experiment with different widths of lines and varying ways to make the leaves.

Hint for Success:

● Provide samples of Japanese-style tree paintings. These illustrate how trees can be depicted using very few lines.

To Simplify:

● Reduce the number of materials available. Put out only one kind of paint, although a variety of colors is still desirable.

To Extend:

● Make available both watercolors and poster paints simultaneously. Encourage children to compare the varying effects they can achieve with the different kinds of paint on the paper. Offer varying shades of green paint in both mediums, as well as "autumn" colors. Ask children to think about how their branches might look in the sun or shade or with a little of both on the same branch.

Affective

1. Birthday Rings

*G*ather the following materials: long strips of corrugated paper or corrugated cardboard cut in three- to five-foot lengths that are six to eight inches wide, markers or pens, tape, and one or more cross-cut sections of a tree trunk in which the rings of the tree are clearly visible. Remind the children that each tree ring represents one year of a tree's life. Talk about how trees

change as they grow older. Invite the children to count the rings to see how old the tree was before it was cut. Next, explain that today they will get to make a pretend set of tree rings to match how old they are. Help the children cut lengths of the corrugated paper, one for each year they have lived. Demonstrate how to cut a short length to represent the first year, a slightly longer length for the second year, and so forth. Help the children to assemble their tree trunk sections. Show them how to make the strips into rings by attaching the ends to make a circle. Nest each smaller ring inside the next larger one. Label each set with the child's name.

To Simplify:

● Precut the strips and simply have the children assemble them in nested rings.

To Extend:

● Before the children assemble their tree rings into a tree-trunk shape, invite them to dictate or write on each ring, respectively, something that describes what they were like or could do at the age represented by that ring. That is, ask children to explain what they could do or

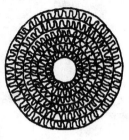

what they were like when they were one year of age, what they were like at age two, and so on. Talk about how the children have changed as they have matured.

2. Tree Photo "Ops"

All of these activities require access to a camera, either by you or by children's families. If such access is not available, consider using other forms of representation, such as drawings or written descriptions.

Home Trees. Ask parents to provide a picture of a tree near their home for their child to bring to school. This might be a tree in their yard, on their street, or in a place they visit as a family. As each picture comes in, place it on the child's locker or cubbie along with the child's own photograph. Talk with the children about the location of the tree and what it looks like. Invite children to look at one another's trees. Talk about how they are alike and different. Refer to the trees as "Juan's tree" or "Marcia's tree." Keep these pictures on display for several weeks. Ask parents to send in a second picture of the child's tree, taken at another time of year, so the children can see the changes in their own trees and in each other's trees.

Home Tree Index. After the children's tree pictures have been displayed for several weeks, take them down and mount each one on an index card. Provide resource materials children can use to find out the common/scientific name of the trees they have selected. Print this information on the back of each card along with children's verbal descriptions of their trees. Fasten the cards together into a resource file using a large notebook ring, hooked through a hole punched in the upper left-hand corner of each card. Encourage children to tell each other about their trees and to "look up" their classmates' trees by each child's name as well as the tree name.

Reflections. Encourage each child to dictate or write a story about what they like best about their tree. Display these stories with the corresponding tree picture.

Cognitive

1. Adopt a Class Tree

The purpose of this activity is for children to observe changes in one tree over time. Select a tree on program grounds if possible. Otherwise, find a tree nearby that groups of children can visit safely. Before visiting the tree, talk about things people can do to help them remember things. Discuss strategies like looking closely and slowly; talking about what they see, hear, or smell; drawing pictures; dictating or writing words about their experiences. Photographs and bits of evidence such as a leaf or some tree bark also are good reminders. Visit the tree as a group, taking along some tools such as magnifying glasses, paper, markers, and plastic bags to use in the observation process. Remind children that the bits of evidence they collect should not harm the tree in any way. Ask children to dictate or write notes about the tree. Collect all of these things in a scrapbook to keep in the book area for children to look at throughout the year. Include some blank pages so children can add information over time. As the year progresses, repeat the observing, collecting, and recording processes, documenting changes in the tree. Observe any animals, birds or insects found near or in the tree. Include this information in the scrapbook. Periodically, in newsletters sent home to families, include a class tree update.

2. Tree Part Comparisons

Collect a variety of tree parts (seeds, bark, leaves, fruits, flowers) from various trees common to your area. Make these available to children, focusing on one tree part each day. For example, provide tree seeds in individual bowls, with one kind of seed in each bowl. Encourage children to explore all aspects of the seeds, including peeling the seed covering apart and examining its inner parts. Help children compare the similarities and differences among the various tree types. Show a diagram of how a tree seed splits open and begins the growth of the tree. Put a few seeds of each type into individual self-sealing plastic bags with a moist paper towel. Put these near a window and check daily to note any changes that may occur. On another day, draw children's attention to variations in tree bark. Note differences in color, texture, thickness, and consistency. Continue in this manner for a week or more.

To Simplify:
● Offer only a few materials at a time. Provide objects in which significant differences are evident.

To Extend:
● Help children create descriptive labels for the various items they are examining.

3. Tree Part Groupings

Using some of the same materials you collected for the previous activities, provide children with one type of tree part such as leaves. Put these in one big pile on a table. Get the activity started by encouraging children to explore the items. Then give each child a pile of leaves and say, "Now you make some groups of leaves of your own. Put together the leaves that are alike in some way." Be careful not to tell children how to group their leaves. Instead, give children plenty of time to put the leaves into piles of their choosing. Once this has been accomplished, ask children to tell you why they divided their leaves as they did. There will be no one set of correct answers. Your goal is to encourage children to think about the criteria they used. Afterwards, invite children to recombine their piles and then try dividing them again in a different way.

To Simplify:
● Provide three or four pairs of items from a few different trees (such as two oak leaves, two pine needle clusters, two ginkgo leaves, and two beech leaves). Put out one item from each pair. Place the others in a paper bag. Invite children to reach in, then match the item to its mate on a tray or table.

To Extend:
● Hold a few items in reserve out of the children's sight. After the children have established their piles, introduce another item. Ask the children into which piles it might fit. Also, ask into which piles it doesn't belong. Remember to focus on the children's rationales rather than whether or not they group the items in a way that matches your own criteria.

4. Leafy Graphs

Prior to introducing this activity, make a large posterboard graph at least eight squares across and eight squares down. Have markers and paste or tape available for children to use. Keep these in reserve until the children are ready to begin graphing. Take the children outdoors to a place in which a variety of trees are available. Ask each child to find a leaf to bring back to the classroom. Remind children that trees need their leaves to live and so it is not a good idea to strip a branch of its leaves. Tell each child to select his or her leaf from a tree which no one else has chosen. Better yet, if leaves are on the ground, encourage children to choose from among them. Back in the classroom examine the leaves the children have found. As a group, create a graph depicting the differences among the leaves by shape. One procedure for doing this is to have a child place his or her leaf on the top square on the left side of the graph. As each new child brings his or her leaf to the graph, ask her or him to decide if the leaf is similar to or different from the others previously placed. If it is similar, it will be placed in the column below the one it resembles. If it is different, then the child starts a new category by placing the leaf at the top of an empty column. Continue until all the leaves have been categorized. Have each child paste his or her leaf in place. Label the tops of each column as designated by the children. Ask them to summarize the information represented on the graph (such as three pointy leaves, four rounded leaves, two needle-shaped leaves, and so on). Write this in a visible spot nearby.

Hint for Success:
● Wait to have the children paste their leaves in place until the graph is finished. Sometimes children change their minds about an object's placement based on the addition of new items.

To Simplify:
● Carry out this project in small groups so children do not have to spend much time waiting.

● Paste the items yourself after the graph is complete so it can be displayed easily.

● Have children compare their leaves to one you have chosen. They could then place their leaves in one of three columns labeled "smaller," "same size as," and "bigger."

To Extend:
● Help children create a second graph using pictures to represent the leaves they found. This could involve symbols (such as $\wedge$ = pointy; $\circ$ = rounded, and so on) representing the various categories chosen by the children, or paper leaves cut in a similar shape to the ones on the original graph. A third-stage follow-up would be to use paper squares (such as red squares for pointy, blue squares for rounded, and so on) to represent the various leaf categories. In both cases, it would be important for the children to dictate a description of the meaning of the graphs. This series of graphs could be constructed all in one day or on subsequent days.

5. Tree Silhouettes

Using the models provided on the next page, create outlines of tree shapes on heavy posterboard. Make

Pointed	Curved	Needle	Multiple	Long	Round	Chewed	

Pointed	Curved	Needle	Multiple	Long	Round	Chewed	

Norway Spruce

Poplar

Sugar Maple

Weeping Willow

Cabbage Palmetto

Live Oak

two of each. Cut the posterboard into individual cards with a drawing on each card. Invite the children to examine the drawings. Talk about the distinctive nature of the trees' shapes and the differences among them. After children have had ample time to explore the pictures, lay them facedown on a table. Ask children to find pairs of trees that look the same by turning one card, then turning a second card looking for a matching silhouette. If the child is unsuccessful, he or she turns the cards facedown again, trying to remember where each one is. This signals the next child's turn. Play continues, with each child attempting to make pairs by remembering where specific cards have been turned down on the table.

Hints for Success:

● In this version of the common memory game, give each child a chance to make only one pair at a time. This makes it more likely that every child will have one or more pairs when the game ends. Also, emphasize simply using up all the cards, not who gets the most pairs.

To Simplify:

● Play the game with the cards faceup.

To Extend:

● Make one set of cards as silhouettes and a second matching set as trees with their leaves. (These may be found in magazines or plant catalogs.) Another variation is to make one set of silhouette cards and a second set of cards on which the corresponding tree name is printed.

6. Leaf Logs

This activity is most effective when carried out using trees that are about to change color and whose branches are at children's eye level. Take some chart paper and a marker outdoors with a group of children. Have the children select a tree to observe. Ask them to look closely at the leaves, then to describe what they see. Write down the children's observations and read their words back to them. Post their descriptions in the classroom. Repeat this process every two or three days until the leaves have fallen from the trees. Refer to the different observations children made throughout the two or three weeks it took for the leaves to change from green to brown. Discuss the changes that occurred.

Hint for Success:

● Attach a sample leaf to each description to provide a visual reference to the children's words.

● Date or number the descriptions so the sequence of time is easy to maintain.

● Read aloud to the group their previous observation before they make the current one. This will give children a frame of reference from which to make new discoveries.

To Simplify:

● Carry out three observations, one week apart. Significant changes will have taken place between each one.

To Extend:

● Ask children the same questions each time to guide their observations. For instance: "Is your leaf all one color or different colors?" "How does the top of the leaf compare with its underside?" "Touch the leaves. What do they feel like?" "Describe the shape of the leaves."

7. Wood Samples

Collect samples of different varieties of wood from a lumber mill, frame shop, cabinet shop, or other woodworking enterprise. Make these available for the children to examine, group, and compare. An interesting variation is to get two samples of each kind of wood. Leave one set natural and apply a clear wood finish such as shellac to the other. Allow these to dry completely, keeping them away from the children. Invite children to try to match the natural wood samples and the treated ones. This activity can be further enhanced by providing pictures of the trees represented by the samples.

8. Tree Bingo

Using catalogues from seed and plant suppliers, create bingo boards depicting six to nine varieties of trees. Make a matching set of cards for a "caller" to use. Provide children with one bingo card each and buttons or other markers to cover the trees called. Support the children as they play "Tree Bingo."

To Simplify:

● Make this into a lotto game in which children match a single tree card directly to a tree depicted on their lotto board.

To Extend:

● Write the name of the tree variety on the back of each card and underneath the pictures on the bingo board. Ask the caller to "read" the name aloud (or do this job yourself) before showing the picture to the children. Another variation is to create verbal clues, such as "a tree with heart-shaped leaves" or "a tree that loses its leaves in the winter" or "a tree that grows at our school."

Ask children to cover trees on their bingo cards that correspond to these cues. Noting that more than one tree might fit an individual cue, advise children to cover up only one tree per clue.

9. Tree Seed Count-Up

Purchase a variety of tree fruits in which the seeds will be clearly visible (such as apple, pear, orange, mango, papaya, pomegranate). Some should be familiar to the children in your area and some may be unknown to them. Have available smocks, a cutting board, a knife for cutting fruit open as necessary, plastic bowls for holding each fruit after it is opened, individual saucers for holding the seeds of each fruit as they are extracted, a large piece of chart paper, and a marker. Place the fruits in a bag out of the children's sight. Before starting this activity, make sure children and adults wash their hands. Gather the children in a large or small group. Show them a tree fruit. Pass it around for children to examine more closely. Elicit observations from the children about the fruit. Name the fruit if the children do not know its name and explain that inside there are seeds. Ask the children to guess how many seeds there are. Record their guesses on the chart paper in a column under the fruit's name. Open the fruit. Count the seeds. Record the accurate number beside the children's guesses. Repeat this process for each item in your bag. Display each fruit in a bowl with its corresponding seeds in a saucer adjacent to it. Later, use the fruit for a Tree Salad and dry the seeds for the extension activity described below or for other counting activities.

Hint for Success:
● This activity is most beneficial to children when they can be actively involved rather than mere observers. Make sure children have things to do besides watch. They may help peel fruit, count the seeds in a particular fruit, mark the guesses on the chart, as well as participate in the original examination of each fruit before it is cut.

To Simplify:
● Use only a few fruits and select those that are familiar to the children.

To Extend:
● Combine the seeds and count the grand total. Alternately, create a bar graph using the actual seeds found in each fruit.

Construction

1. Seed Collage

Provide children with a thin piece of wood or heavy posterboard to serve as a base for the seeds. Make available a variety of tree seeds including acorns, pine cones, pods, nuts, and so forth. Provide wood glue for children to use in gluing the seeds to the wood base. Encourage children to make a design of their choice using the items provided. As the children work, talk about the differences among the seeds. This activity could be repeated with other tree parts as well. A third variation is to provide tree parts from one tree variety each day. At the end of the week have the children compare the parts on each collage for the differing trees.

2. Forest in a Box

Select a box about 12" x 12" in size or larger. Provide materials such as toilet paper tubes, construction paper, paper towels, paint, crayons, and tape. Explain to the children that they will be using these materials to make individual trees that will be combined to create a forest in the box. Brainstorm with the children about how different trees could be represented. Be sure to follow the children's lead rather than showing them how you might represent each tree. As children complete their trees, display them in the forest box.

Hint for Success:
● Bring in pictures of a variety of trees to remind children what they look like.

3. Tree Stars

Prepare in advance the following materials. Cut several sheets of 8-1/2" x 11" paper in half horizontally. On each half draw an outline of a deciduous tree— one with a leafy crown and one with its branches bare. Make several of these.

Fold each illustration in half vertically and round-off the top (using scissors) as illustrated on the next page. Unfold the pages and lay them flat.

For each child, take two pages with leafy crowns and two with bare branches. Label one bare-branched tree "winter," one bare-branched tree "spring," one leafy tree "summer," and one leafy tree "fall." Staple the pictures, end to end in the order of the seasons. Attach the last two open ends to make a square. Make sure the tree drawings are facing outward.

Push the folded halves of each page together in the center and fasten with a staple about two-thirds of

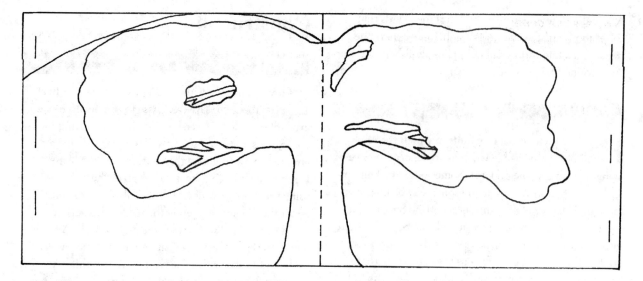

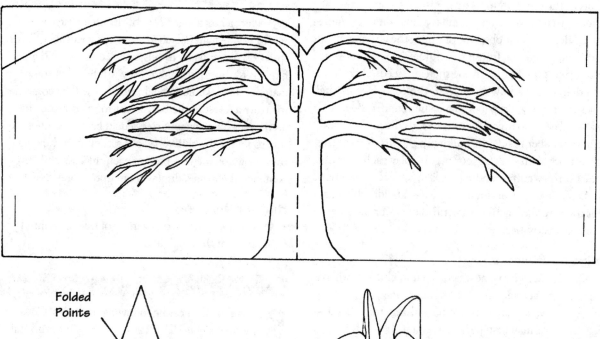

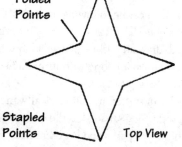

Folded
Points

Stapled
Points   Top View

Summer

Finished Tree Star

the way from the bottom. This will produce a starlike shape, with a tree for each season. Make enough of these tree stars for each child to have one or more. Gather crayons, markers, construction paper, and glue for children to use in decorating each tree according to its seasonal variations. Put these aside for the moment. Introduce the activity by reading aloud Gail Gibbon's book *The Seasons of Arnold's Apple Tree* (1984), which describes the changes that occur in an apple tree every spring, summer, fall, and winter. Next, show children an undecorated tree star. Explain that each child will create a tree star depicting the changes trees undergo during each season. Show children how to lay the star flat while they decorate each side. Invite them to use the materials provided to make their own creation. Display the finished products for all to see.

Hint for Success:
● Enlist the help of adult volunteers, parents, or older students in preparing the materials for this activity.

Language

1. Name That Tree

The purpose of this activity is for children to attach meaning to print. Learn what trees are common to your area and what they look like. With the children, conduct a survey of the playyard or a place in which a variety of trees can be found. Identify the trees by name and make a list. Back in the classroom, provide materials for children to make individual signs to identify each tree by name. Use heavy posterboard or Styrofoam meat trays. Punch two holes in the top of each one and weave a string through the holes. Tie the string in a loop. Invite children to decorate these tree name tags using crayons, chalk, or scrap materials. Return to the outdoors and have the children attach signs to the trees so people will know what variety each one is. Whenever you visit the area, ask children to use the name tags to help in remembering the different tree varieties.

2. Tree Encyclopedias

The aim of this activity is for children to observe the variety among trees and to recognize the use of books as informational resources. Carry out a process of observing, collecting, and recording similar to that described for the "Adopt a Class Tree" activity outlined on page 348. However, this time invite children to work in small groups, with each group focusing on a different tree variety. Explain that each group will create two or three pages to be combined into a tree encyclopedia for the class. Provide the necessary materials for children to use in documenting their discoveries such as paper, markers, magnifying glasses, and glue for adhering bits of bark or seeds. Use the children's book as a tree identification resource the rest of the year. Provide opportunities for children to review the information they have collected and to compare the trees they have catalogued.

To Simplify:
● Ask each child to make one page for the tree encyclopedia.

To Extend:
● Provide a number of illustrated books about trees that children can use as they create an entire resource book of their own.

3. Tree Biographies

This activity will help children increase their ability to recall the sequence of a story. Several children's picture books focus on the life cycle of trees. Some of these are *Tree* by Althea Braithwaite (1988), *A Tree Is a Plant* by Clyde R. Bulla (1960), *Red Leaf, Yellow Leaf* by Lois Ehlert (1991), and *Once There Was a Tree* by Natalia Romanova (1989). Make one or more of these available in the library corner. Create flannelboard pictures that coincide with the story you have chosen. Then read the book aloud to the children. After you have read it once, tell them you will read it again. This time their job is to listen carefully for what happens first in the story, what happens in the middle, and what happens last. Following the second reading, show children the flannel pieces you have made. Have them identify what came first, what happened in the middle, and how the story ended. Another day, ask the children to remember more of the life cycle and to put the pieces in order accordingly. An alternative is to read the story, then put the major incidents in a scrambled order that you ask the children to correct. Show children how to go back to the story to check the accuracy of their memory. A third approach is to depict events that never happened in the story and mix these among the true events. Ask children to discover the episodes that don't belong.

Hint for Success:
● Fabric stores carry medium-weight lining material that can be used to create flannelboard pieces painlessly and quickly. Obtain a yard or so of this fabric in white or beige. Trace the pictures in the book and color them with permanent markers and cut them out. They will easily stick to your flannelboard.

4. Tree Haiku

This activity is most suitable for children who are becoming interested in word sounds in their speaking, listening, reading, and/or writing. (This tends to involve children five years of age and older.) It is an excellent follow-up to "Tree Lines" found on page 346. Haiku is a form of unrhymed three-line poetry, with five syllables in the first line, seven in the second, and five syllables in the last line. Some examples of haiku created by children are:

The sun is so high,
A leaf is red and yellow,
My heart sings a song.

My autumn leaves fell,
And had different colors,
The colors are nice.

Leaves dance in the wind,
When the moon glows in the leaves.
Look! They seem happy.

After children have heard many examples of haiku, have them dictate or write their own haiku to go along with their tree painting. This is a great way to talk about word sounds (syllables) within a meaningful context. Children will need help counting syllables at first, but even those who are not writing yet can listen for the parts of words.

Hint for Success:
● Write some practice haiku poems as a group before asking children to try any on their own. As with any composing task, whether children are dictating their words or writing them in their own form of writing, they will need many opportunities to practice and refine their ideas.

● A children's book that features haiku (but does not focus on trees) is *Shadow Play* by Penny Harter (1994). In this book, a variety of haiku patterns are presented. Once children are comfortable with the form of haiku suggested above, try some different poetic forms using other syllable patterns, such as three syllables in the first line, five in the second, and seven in the third or a pattern of four syllables, then two, then four.

Physical

1. Paint a Tree

Draw outlines of various kinds of trees on newsprint or other art paper. Make the outlines simple in shape and large enough to fill most of the paper. Keep these available on the easel or at the art table. Encourage the children to paint inside the tree shapes. After the paintings are dry, have the children cut out the trees and tape them to the walls around the room making a classroom forest.

2. Leaf Stencils

Make your own leaf stencils using thick plastic container lids. Draw a leaf outline on the plastic. Cut out the leaf shape using a craft knife. Give the stencils (the cut out lids) to the children to use in making outlines on paper. Demonstrate how to hold the stencil with one hand while drawing with the other. Once children have had a chance to practice the technique, give them a large outline of a tree with branches on which to draw. Encourage them to fill out the crown of the tree and then color in the shapes.

To Simplify:
● Use simple leaf shapes with rounded edges. Provide only one kind of leaf shape at a time.

To Extend:
● Make the leaf stencils more difficult by providing ornately shaped leaves and ones that have pointed edges. These will require greater fine motor skill to transfer to the paper. Also, consider providing children with stencils representing different varieties of trees. Make sure to provide separate tree outlines for each variety.

● Have children make compound leaves using a single stencil and tracing around a long leaf stem.

3. Tree Bark Rubbing

Take the children outdoors. Help each child select a tree with bark that is interesting to him or her. Supply plain paper and old crayons from which the paper has been removed. Demonstrate how to hold the paper against the bark while rubbing over the paper and bark with the flat side of the crayon. This process should bring a relief picture of the tree bark on the paper. Encourage the children to make more than one rubbing on one sheet of paper or on separate sheets. Label the picture with the child's name and the type of tree, if known. Attach to the paper bits of bark that might be found at the base of the tree. Display the rubbings in the classroom. Have children compare rubbings from the same tree and from different trees.

Hint for Success:
● Thin paper works best for most trees. If the bark is rough then a slightly thicker paper will be necessary.

To Simplify:
● Tape the paper to the trunk of the tree to not only keep the paper from slipping, but also to avoid children having to coordinate two hands at once.

To Extend:
● Encourage children to try different rubbing techniques such as holding the crayon in different ways or trying thin and thick crayons to vary the effect.

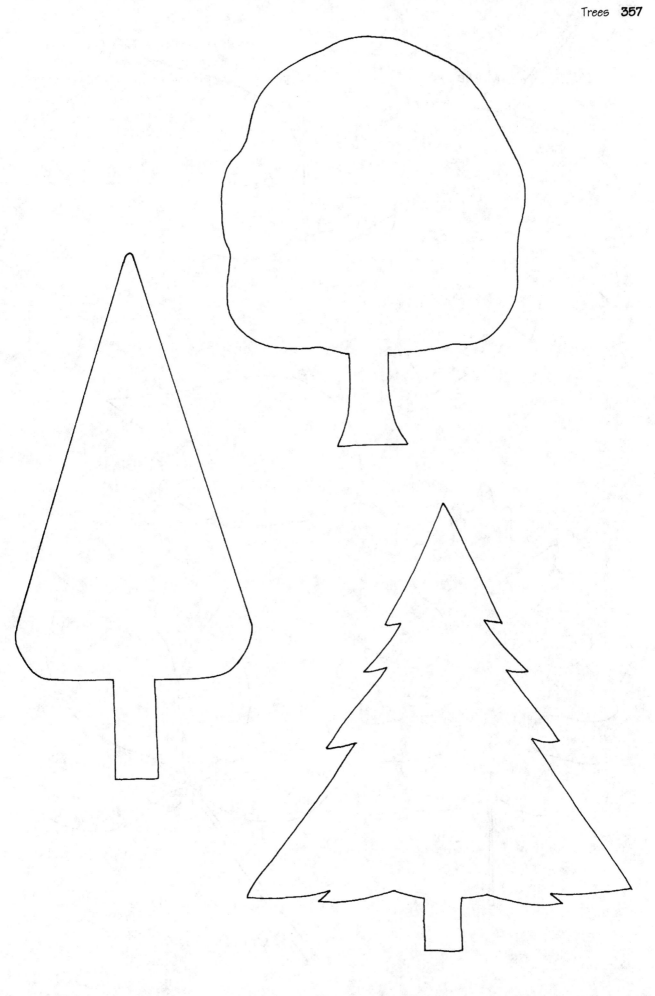

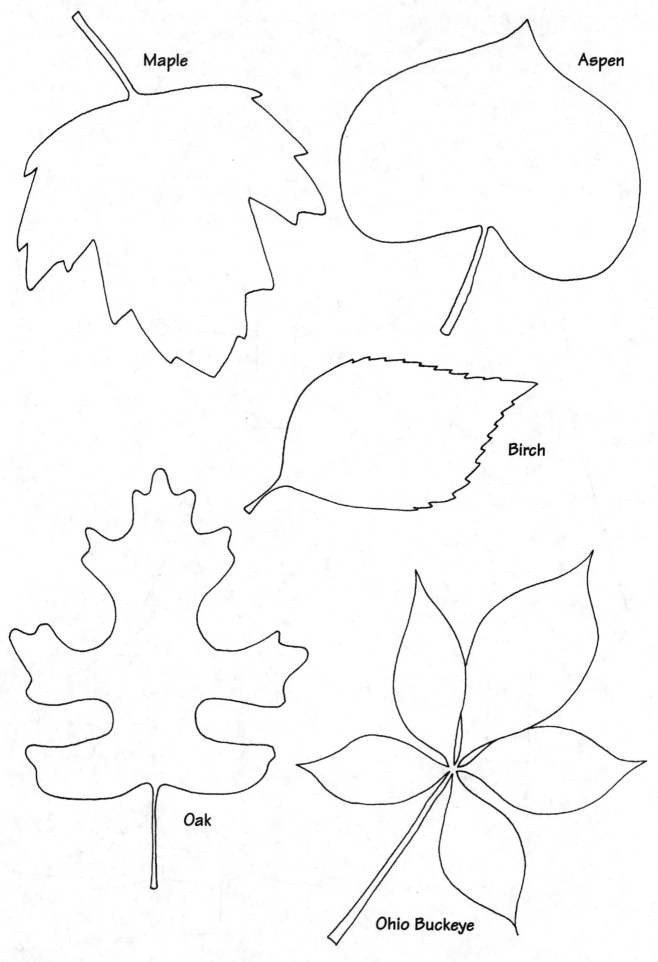

Maple

Aspen

Birch

Oak

Ohio Buckeye

4. Nutty Tools

Collect a variety of tools that could be used to open nuts—nutcrackers, rubber mallets, hammers, rocks, and hard blocks. Provide each child who participates with gloves and safety goggles as well. On a table covered with newspaper, put out a variety of tree fruits and seeds with hard outer coverings such as pine cones, walnuts, hazelnuts, and so on. Ask children to use the tools to figure out how to get inside the fruit or seed. As children experiment, talk about what part of the tree the item they are working on comes from and the different kinds of trees represented by the plant materials on the table.

To Simplify:

● Provide children with plant material that smashes easily.

To Extend:

● Make available pictures of the different trees whose parts are represented on the table. Help children match the seed or fruit they have chosen to the tree from which it came.

Pretend Play

1. Raking Leaves at Home

This activity works best in the fall in a geographic area where the leaves fall from the trees. Set up a pretend house outdoors or extend the indoor housekeeping area to include a make-believe yard. Provide piles of real leaves, small rakes, bushels, and bags. Encourage children to rake their "yards" and gather all the leaves. Some children will also enjoy sorting the leaves into huge piles by type or color.

Hint for Success:

● One way to contain the delightful mess that results from children's raking indoors is to cover the floor of the pretend yard with a tarp or other non-slip covering. Such a covering will contain the leaves while being heavy enough to remain on the floor and not come up with the children's rakes.

2. Tree Artists

Post several pictures of many different types of trees in the pretend area of the room. Cover the floor with newspaper and provide easels, smocks, poster paints, and a drying rack for children's paintings. Explain that many artists choose to include different kinds of trees in their paintings. Today the children will pretend they are artists doing the same thing. Encourage the children to put a tree in their paintings if they choose; however, do not insist that this be the case. Once the artists have completed their work and the paintings are dry, display them in a tree art gallery for others to enjoy. Consider adding a cash register and pretend money for youngsters who wish to ply their wares to potential customers in the classroom.

3. Tree Orchard/Nursery/Arboretum

This activity is similar in setup to the "Apple Orchard," described on page 342. However, it involves varying the fruit on each tree—peaches, cherries, pears, and various nuts. Another option is to create a tree nursery or arboretum where some trees have fruits and some do not. Children playing out this scenario could serve as visitors, guides, or workers taking care of the trees. Workers might pretend to sort plants, sort seeds, prepare seed beds in a water table filled with soil, check the outdoor temperature before moving plants "outside," label trees, prepare brochures or planting guides, sell trees, and give tours of their worksite.

Social

1. Cooperative Tree-Mural

Provide the children with paper cutouts of many trees that differ in shape, color, and size, a large piece of background paper with pictures of forest animals on it, and a limited amount of glue or paste in a single container. Put the trees in a tray at one end of a long table and put the glue/paste at the other end. Explain that the only way for children to get the materials they need is to ask for them and pass them to the people who need them when asked. Children cannot simply walk around the table to get something; they must ask for help from someone else to get it. Have children work together gluing or pasting the trees on the paper, sometimes hiding the animals, sometimes leaving them in the open. Encourage children also to layer trees over trees. Keep a record of how many trees of each type were used. Create a legend on the paper, indicating the types of trees depicted and their quantity. Make sure that every child has his or her name displayed on the final product. Emphasize the importance of creating a mural that is mutually satisfying. Praise children's attempts at cooperation and group decision-making.

2. Worldwide Trees

Gather pictures of trees from around the world with which the children are unfamiliar (such as a banyan tree, a rubber tree, baobab tree, ginkgo tree, and so on). Divide the children into small groups. Show them the tree pictures and ask each group to choose one tree they want to learn more about. This will require some group decision-making and negotiating. Once the group has made a selection, have them collect information about the trees and the area in which they grow. Offer book resources such as *The Tree of Life: The World of the African Baobab* by Barbara Bash (1989) for children to use. Other potential references are listed at the end of this mini-theme. Once the children have some information with which to work, ask each child to select his or her favorite tree fact related to the group's choice. Take the children's dictation or have them use their own writing to record these on sentence strips. Fasten the strips together to make a group resource book on each tree type. Provide opportunities for the children to listen to each small group's creation.

To Simplify:

● Carry out the above process focusing on trees that are familiar to the children and for which they can gather information through firsthand experience.

To Extend:

● Supplement the children's explorations with some items that come from a specific type of tree such as cinnamon, which is made from the inner bark of the laurel tree or cacao seeds which are dried, roasted, and ground into a paste, then used in making chocolate.

3. Tree Search

Carry out this activity after children have had some experience with blindfolds. Find an outdoor place in which trees of different varieties or sizes are available for children to explore actively. Gather the children into a circle or small group. Explain that they will have a chance to touch, smell, and hug a tree nearby. Add that the children will do all of this blindfolded. Escort a blindfolded child to a tree. Encourage the child to explore the tree as thoroughly as he or she can without seeing it. Then, take the child back to the group. Remove the blindfold. Ask the child to find the tree he or she explored. A variation of this activity is to have the children work in pairs, with one child serving as an escort to a blindfolded child. Once the first child's tree has been identified, the partners can switch roles.

Hints for Success:

● Remind children as they put on the blindfolds that someone will stay with them and keep them safe throughout the activity.

● Be sure to keep children from walking too far blindfolded.

● For children who feel uncomfortable with a blindfold, simply ask them to close their eyes.

4. Tree Treasure Hunt

Give a small group of children several tree-related things to find. Use a log sheet similar to the one illustrated below, adapted to your environment. Find the following things:

If you are in an environment where children are allowed to collect these items, give each group a clear plastic bag to store what they find until their return to the building. When you get back, ask each group to show what they found for each category or ask them to tape or paste the items to their log sheets in the corresponding place. Work with children to compare what they found, discussing the similarities and differences among objects.

Teacher Resources

Field Trip Ideas

1. Visit a tree farm, nursery, or garden store at which trees are sold. Look for trees of different varieties and examine them carefully.
2. Take the children on a picnic in a wooded area.
3. Visit an arboretum or nature center in your community. Look for trees of different kinds. Also look for trees that are the same variety, but different ages.
4. Visit an orchard at different seasons during the year. Record what you see. Compare the children's observations from one time to the next. Create a classroom record of the various observations made.

Classroom Visitors

1. Invite someone who has made a leaf collection to show the collection to the children and talk about the different kinds of trees represented.
2. Invite a naturalist to come to the class with cross sections of tree trunks for children to examine. Count the rings and talk about the different kinds of trees represented.

Our Tree Treasures

3 Tiny Things	Something Red	Something Yellow
A Rounded Leaf	**Something Sticky**	**A Pointed Leaf**
Something Hard	**Something Soft**	**Something with More Than One Color**

3. Invite a florist to bring one or two tropical trees to the classroom for children to see. Have children compare these trees (such as weeping fig, palm tree, or rubber plant) with the trees children see in their own community. Identify the similarities and differences. For children who live in a very warm climate, compare the small trees brought in by the florist with the larger varieties found outdoors.

Children's Books

Bash, B. (1989). *The Tree of Life: The World of the African Baobab*. New York: Little, Brown.

Braithwaite, A. (1988). *Tree*. Chicago, IL: Dearborn Financial Publishing.

Bulla, C. R. (1960). *A Tree Is a Plant*. New York: Thomas Y. Crowell.

Coats, L. J. (1987). *The Oak Tree*. New York: Macmillan.

Ehlert, L. (1991). *Red Leaf, Yellow Leaf*. New York: Harcourt Brace Jovanovich.

Gibbons, G. (1984). *The Seasons of Arnold's Apple Tree*. New York: Harcourt Brace Jovanovich.

Harter, P. (1994). *Shadow Play: Night Haiku*. New York: Simon and Schuster.

Maestro, B. (1992). *How Do Apples Grow?* New York: HarperCollins.

Romanova, N. (1989). *Once There Was a Tree*. New York: Dial Books.

Adult References

The Audobon Society Pocket Guides. (1988). *Familiar Trees of North America, Eastern Region*. New York: Alfred A. Knopf.

The Audobon Society Pocket Guides. (1988). *Familiar Trees of North America, Western Region*. New York: Alfred A. Knopf.

Cornell, J. (1979). *Sharing Nature with Children*. Nevada City, CA: DAWN Publications.

List, A., and List, I. (1977). *A Walk in the Forest: The Woodlands of North America*. New York: Thomas Y. Crowell.

Zim, H. (1991). *Trees: A Guide to Familiar American Trees*. Racine, WI: Golden Press.

Tree Gifts

Terms, Facts, and Principles (TFPs)

1. Trees produce food that people and animals eat.

2. Trees provide wood, which is used to make objects and products people want and need.

*3. Trees provide products other than wood, such as sap, that people use.

4. Trees provide shade from the hot sun.

5. Trees provide shelter and protection for many kinds of animals.

6. Trees hold down the soil with their roots and keep it from washing away in the rain.

*7. Trees hold rainwater in the ground and keep the land from flooding.

*8. Trees send oxygen into the air for people and animals to breathe.

9. Trees are beautiful to look at.

10. Trees are often pleasant smelling.

11. Wind moving through the crowns of trees makes sounds as leaves, twigs, and branches move and rub together.

12. People go to forested areas to relax and enjoy nature.

*13. Trees need some of the same things people and animals need—clean air, sunlight, water, nutrients, and a safe place to live.

*14. People's actions often affect whether trees struggle or thrive, live or die.

*15. Caring for trees and making sure there are trees on the earth for people and animals to use and enjoy is everyone's responsibility.

16. People can learn how to better care for the earth's trees.

Activity Ideas

Aesthetic

1. Children's Block Prints

Children can make an effect similar to that created by other artists using a woodblock technique. You will need glue, woodblocks (5 inches square) made from scrap lumber, heavy cardboard (consider using parts of old cardboard boxes), scissors or an X-Acto® knife, poster paint in containers that won't tip, paintbrushes, heavy rolling pins, newspaper, smocks for yourself and the children, and large sheets of construction paper for each child. Before the children arrive, cut out cardboard shapes and glue each one on a separate block of wood. Allow these to dry completely. Cover a table with newspaper, put out two or three colors of paint, and provide brushes of different sizes. Invite children to put on a smock and join you in making woodblock prints. Show them how to brush paint on a shape, then press it down on construction paper either by hand or by pressing it down with a rolling pin. Encourage experimentation. Display and enjoy.

Hint for Success:

● Gather some pictures or illustrated books demonstrating woodblock prints for children to examine and enjoy. Two excellent book examples are Christopher Manson's *A Farmyard Song* (1992) and *The Tree in the Wood: An Old Nursery Song* (1993). Japanese woodblock prints are also notable examples that may be obtained through calendar art or local libraries.

To Simplify:

● Provide one color of paint at a time.

To Extend:

● Provide materials for children to make their own woodblocks using stenciled shapes they cut out themselves.

2. Sweet Wood Sounds

Show children a variety of wooden musical instruments such as a recorder; wooden flute, fife or pennywhistle; guitar and mandolin; bongos and drums; violin or cello; oboe or clarinet; autoharp; dulcimer; Chilean rainstick; castanets; zither or West African balaphon; temple blocks or woodblocks or claves or Mexican guiro; marimba. Talk about the fact that each instrument began as a piece of wood. If possible demonstrate how the instruments are played or have a musician come in to play them for and with the children. Note that some instruments are ones people blow into, some are ones people hit or strum with their hands, and some are ones people touch with another object. Invite children to touch the instruments and examine them carefully. Encourage them to try out as many as possible.

3. Beautiful Wood Products

Gather several objects made of wood. Some may be practical such as a wooden salad bowl, wooden box, wooden spoon, or picture frame. Others may simply be wooden items that are lovely to look at and to touch, such as carvings or sculptures. Make these items available for children to examine. Display them somewhere in your classroom. Add labels that describe what the item is, to whom it belongs, and from what kind of wood it is made, if that is known. Add objects made from other tree parts, such as paperweights or paintings that use leaves or tree flowers as decorations.

Affective

1. Symbolic Trees

Most North American states and provinces, and even some countries have a type of tree that has been chosen by the people or government to symbolize that place. For example, in the book *State Trees* by Sue R. Brandt (1992), trees are illustrated and discussed for all fifty of the United States. This would be a good resource if your class is in the USA. If you live outside of the United States, contact your local tourism agency to find out about resources related to a designated official tree for your area. Talk to the children about this particular tree and what makes it unique or valuable to your community or region. Use this tree as a symbol for your group—on children's name tags, in children's lockers or cubbies, or as a "check-in tag" to identify personal possessions brought to the classroom for brief periods (such as Show and Tell). Such tags can be attached to items with string looped through a hole punched in the top or bottom of the tree.

2. Personal Paper Inventory

This activity will help children see how many paper products they use in a classroom each day. Materials needed include a large piece of chart paper and a marker, individual sandwich-sized plastic bags (one for each person in the room), and a box of large safety pins. Gather the children in a group. Talk about paper as a product of trees. Ask children to think about the different kinds of paper they use each day in the classroom. Make a list of their ideas and post it in the classroom for all to see. Give each child and adult a plastic bag to pin at their waist. Explain that as they go through the day, instead of throwing any paper away, they are to put the paper in their bag. Remind children of this procedure periodically as you move through the daily routine. At the end of the day, have a group discussion in which class members show the paper products they used. Compare these to those the children had named earlier.

Hint for Success:

● Use this activity to supplement "Recycling Tree Products," described below.

3. Recycling Tree Products

The purpose of this activity is to help children develop a sense of responsibility and empowerment regarding their role in conserving the earth's resources. It is an excellent follow-up to the "We Made Paper!" activity (see page 46). Before you begin, get three or four dishpans or small wastepaper baskets to use as recycling bins, index cards to use for labels, and markers. Talk to the children about trees being the source of much paper. Also remind children about how they used bits of paper to make new paper. Explain that there are people in the community who reuse paper in that same way to make new paper products; this process is called recycling. Ask the children to help you create a paper recycling center in your classroom. This will be a place to collect the different kinds of paper people use throughout the day. Discuss where it should be located. Take a tour of the room to identify all the different kinds of paper products that people use there (such as napkins, paper cups, scraps of construction paper, and so forth). Determine what paper categories you will assign to the recycling bins. Set up your center and begin using it. Consider adding a recycling captain to your job chart. This child's role is to check the bins each day to determine when it is time to transfer items to a program-wide or community recycling center.

To Simplify:

● Put all paper products in one bin, located near the art area or snack table for this purpose.

To Extend:

● Supplement this activity by reading the Dr. Seuss book *The Lorax* (1971). Discuss its message with the children.

● Have some bins with materials to be recycled outside the classroom (such as used napkins or cups) and some bins with materials that can be recycled inside the classroom (such as newspapers and art paper scraps). Encourage children to visit the internal recycling bins to get materials for projects they are creating.

● Consider expanding the recycling center beyond tree products.

4. Taste Tests

Give children practice making choices. First, offer them an array of food items made from the same fruit to taste. For example, at the snack table make available raw apple slices, apple juice, applesauce, and pieces of a baked apple. Offer children tiny tastes of each food. Stress that all these items come from apples and that apples are tree products. Next, ask each child to select a favorite. Their choices could be recorded on a chart. Such a chart would have the children's names down the lefthand side and the names of the apple products across the top. After children have finished the taste tests, give each child one sticker to put in the column of his or her choice across from his or her name. Later in the day, compare the numbers of children who chose each of the different items.

Hint for Success:

● Allow children to try any and all of the items; however, do not insist that a child try something if he or she does not wish to do so.

To Simplify:

● Provide fewer choices or choices in which the original form of the apple is easily discernible such as raw apple slices and cooked apple slices.

To Extend:

● Develop a graph depicting the children's choices. A second option is to continue the taste tests over several days, featuring a different tree product each day (such as maple syrup, maple candy, maple-flavored cookies; orange slices, orange juice, orange-flavored sugar-free gelatin squares, and so on).

Cognitive

1. Tree Detectives, Part I

Explain to children that today they will be tree detectives. Their job is to look for signs of animal life in and around trees in the playyard or in a place nearby where you will walk for this purpose. Talk about what children might look for such as nibbled leaves, holes in the tree's bark, empty seed casings, holes in the ground, birds' nests, or actual animals such as insects, chipmunks, and birds. If you wish, give each child a "tree detective" badge like the one illustrated above. Accompany the children outside and begin the detective work. Discuss the children's findings as they occur. Make a list of the tell-tale signs of animal life children observe. Review these on your return to the classroom.

Hints for Success:

● Gather the children in a group and read aloud *Forest Log* by James R. Newton (1992), *The Gift of the Tree* by Alvin Tresselt (1992), *Once There Was a Tree* by Natalia Romanova (1989), or *The Tree* by Naomi Russell (1989). After you have finished reading, go back over the story, pointing out all of the animals and insects that benefitted from the tree. Use this reading as a prelude to your walk outdoors as plant detectives.

To Simplify:

● Select a likely tree specimen in advance. Point out the signs of animal life to the children. Invite them to find similar clues in nearby trees.

To Extend:

● Give each child or small group of children a pad of paper for their detective work. Ask them to record their observations on-the-spot, either by writing or drawing, in order to help them remember when they are back in the classroom.

● Have children predict what signs of life they will see, then compare their predictions with their actual observations.

● Give children small, clear plastic self-sealing bags to use for collecting small bits of rotted wood, leaves on which insects have laid their eggs, or leaves on which insects are eating. The clear plastic will allow the children to see the insects as they eat and tear apart the wood or leaves while keeping them confined. Release these creatures after a few minutes of observation.

2. Tree Detectives, Part II

As a follow-up to the activity described above, ask children to look for animals who benefit from trees as depicted in photographs or paintings. Obtain some large nature paintings that include trees and animals. Have the children identify the visible animals. Write a list of all of the animals the children identify. Ask them to think of others that might also live in the same area, but which might be hidden from view. With the children, compare what they see in each picture with their real-life experiences as tree detectives outdoors.

To Simplify:

● Only ask children to talk about the birds or animals visible in the pictures. Focus more on finding them, then on naming what they are.

To Extend:

● Offer pictures representing a variety of geographic areas, those with which the children are familiar as well as less familiar ones.

3. Tree Chart Grouping

Make a posterboard chart consisting of four columns labeled: 1. Food, 2. Clothing, 3. Shelter, 4. Things We Use. Entitle the chart "How We Use Trees." Provide children with paste, a variety of magazines, and scissors. Ask children to find and cut out various products that match the categories at the top of each column.

4. Tree Tags

Make a large number of tags that are shaped like trees and have the words "tree product" printed on them. Children can attach the tags to objects in the room with tape or by using strings that have been looped through holes punched at the top of the tags. Walk around the room with the children looking for objects and materials that are tree products. Make a list of all of the things that have been labeled by the children. Keep available additional tags and add to the list as children find new objects to label throughout the week.

5. Sawdust Counting

Get enough sawdust to fill a water table half full. Also, purchase at least 50 plastic ants or other small insects at a hobby store. Such insects are relatively inexpensive to buy. However, if you prefer, make your own ants by drawing simple ant figures on stiff cardboard and cutting them out. (It is easier to cut the cardboard into small squares on which ants are depicted singly, rather than trying to cut around the legs.) Mix the insects into the sawdust. Invite children to find the insects, counting them as they do so. One variation is to have the children count in unison as each ant is found, regardless of who finds it. Another option is to give children a time period within which to find ants, then have each child count the number in his or her pile. Be sure to emphasize how many were found altogether by the group. Do not turn this game into a competition among each child. A third approach is for each child to look for a certain number of ants during his or her turn. Finding that number marks the end of a turn, with play moving on to the next child.

To Simplify:

● Use large insect models. Have children look for five or fewer.

To Extend:

● Introduce numerals by having children select a numeral card from a pile of cards placed facedown. The numeral will tell them how many insects to find on each turn.

● Number the cardboard insects from 1 to 50. Ask a group of children to find the insect with a certain numeral which will vary on each turn.

Construction

1. Wood Sculptures

Provide each child with a piece of flat wood about 5 inches square to use as a base, wood glue, and a variety of wood scraps and wood turnings from which to choose. Encourage children to create sculptures of their own invention. These may be left natural or painted after they are completely dry. Once the children have competed their projects, invite them to title their sculptures. Put the name of the work and the sculptor's name by each creation.

2. Stick Houses

Gather small sticks and twigs from the ground underneath trees. Do this on your own or with the children. Reserve these items for later use. Talk about how people use trees and wood products to make homes. Show the children the pieces that you (or they) have collected. Ask them to think about the kind of house they could make using sticks. Help them find ways to cut or break the sticks in order to get pieces in the sizes they want.

Hint for Success:

● Many children are more successful creating a stick home using a cardboard box (sizes may range from an aspirin package or tissue box to a larger cardboard carton) as a base on which to glue their twigs.

To Simplify:

● Use a large cardboard carton such as those that canned goods come in as a base. Have the children work together on their project and use tape rather than glue or paste to attach the sticks they have found.

To Extend:

● Have children make a written plan or rough drawing of what they want to include in their house or what it might look like. Help them gather additional natural or scrap materials to make their idea a reality.

3. Boats from Trees

Tree products are used by people all over the world to make watercrafts—ranging from rafts, to canoes and row boats, to ocean-going ships. Acquaint children with some of these vessels through stories, pictures, and models. If you live in an area where pleasure boats or smaller working boats are available, arrange a visit so children can see firsthand examples of wooden boat construction. Make available materials for children to use in constructing their own watercrafts to float in the water table. Try to get woods from different kinds of trees. Some wood will float (such as oak, pine, balsa, or cork); some wood in its natural state will sink (such as ironwood). First, encourage children to experiment in the water table with the wood samples to figure out which ones will float. Next, provide other wood products such as toothpicks, craft sticks, and paper as well as wood glue for children to use in creating boats of their own invention.

Hint for Success:

● Balsa wood can be shaped by using a vegetable peeler to take off small strips of surface wood. This is best accomplished when children are under the supervision of an adult or more experienced peer.

Language

1. Simple Pleasures

Read the book *Hello, Tree!* by Joanne Ryder (1991) while sitting under a tree. Read it a second time, this time having the children do some of the things the author talks about, such as reaching for the tree's branches, touching the leaves and trunk, sitting in the shade, feeling the coolness of the ground underneath the tree, listening for tree sounds, and watching the shadows and patches of light.

2. Tree Letters

Assist the children in writing a letter to a friend, parent, or grandparent about the tree activities in which they are involved. This serves as a good way for children to review what they have learned and to indicate what has been important or enjoyable for them. Ask each child to dictate their ideas, or have them draw pictures representing what they have learned, or ask them to write down their ideas in their own form of writing. Mail these letters to the intended recipients and include a return address.

Hints for Success:

● Children enjoy including some tree questions for the person receiving their letters to answer. If such an answer is desired, it is useful for teachers to include a note to this effect along with the address of the program so the recipient knows where to send a reply.

● As an alternative, have children write their questions to a local university extension agent or park office. Such individuals are likely to send a response to the children's queries. They may also be good candidates to visit the group to answer questions in person.

3. Tree Nut Narratives

Purchase several kinds of nuts that are products of trees. Examples might include almonds, Brazil nuts, cashews, chestnuts, filberts, hazelnuts, macadamias, pistachios, and walnuts. Offer these to the children to examine. Talk about the color, shape, texture, and hardness of the nutshells as well as the sounds they make when rolled together or on a table. Provide magnifiers for children to use in getting a closer look. As the children explore these items, ask them to describe their discoveries. On a large piece of chart paper, write down the children's descriptions. You may choose to record the actual phrases children use or just the adjectives. Read back their descriptions periodically. Encourage them to keep adding to the list as they find new properties of the nuts or as new people join the activity.

To Simplify:

● Draw children's attention to a particular property such as color or shape to get them started.

To Extend:

● Keep a master list, but identify by name the children who contribute various ideas. For instance: "Josh said, 'They're hard, groovy, one is cracked, and one has two colors.' " "Seandra said, 'One feels heavy, the others are light. Some are big, some are small. One has two colors.' " Don't be concerned that children repeat some of the same descriptors. Later, go back and circle each different item that was mentioned or count how many times a particular word was used. Once a master list of "nutty" vocabulary has been created, invite children to dictate or write a brief narrative using any of the words listed.

4. Tree-Nut Butter Recipes

For every four to six children, you will need: one cup of nuts out of the shell (such as almond, cashew, macadamia, pecan, pistachio, walnut), 2 tablespoons of salad oil, a dash of salt, a dash of sugar, crackers or whole grain bread, a large plastic or wooden bowl, a mixing spoon, and a potato masher. The activity also requires a blender, smocks for you and the children, two or three large pieces of chart paper, and a marker.

Prior to carrying out the activity, make sure children wash their hands thoroughly. Carry this out with small groups of children individually or with the group as a whole. Before presenting any materials, explain that today children will get to make tree-nut butter. Their job is to remember the steps they follow from start to finish. At the end of the activity, you will ask them to help you remember the steps everyone went through to make tree-nut butter. For each recipe, provide children with a cup of nuts to mash in a bowl using a potato masher. The result will be lumpy, but some mashing will have occurred. Have children add the oil, salt, and sugar to their mixture, in that order. Stir. Blend the batches more thoroughly, a little at a time, in the blender. After you empty the tree-nut butter from the blender container, returning it to the original bowl, children can spread the mixture on crackers and eat. Talk about each step of the process as it occurs. After everyone has had a turn to try their tree-nut butter, gather the children in a group. Ask them to help you remember each step of the tree-nut butter-making process, from the beginning to the end. Prompt their thinking by saying something like, "What did you do first?" Write each step down as the children describe it, leaving some space between items. Periodically read the steps back to the children to see if they agree with the sequence. Use arrows and numbering to help you remember what step occurred when. Once everyone has agreed on the order, rewrite the process and post it for future reference.

Hints for Success:
● Even when treated as a whole-group experience, it is most effective when the children participate in some aspects of the mashing, pouring, and mixing themselves.

● The emphasis for this language lesson is on remembering a sequence of steps, not the amounts of the ingredients. The sequence may be as simple as saying:

1. We mixed up the nuts.
2. We mashed them in the blender.
3. We ate the snack.

To Simplify:
● Carry this out as small-group projects throughout the week, making one batch each day. Provide a pictograph of the steps for children to refer to as they are describing the process.

To Extend:
● Prior to carrying out the activity, ask children to think of ways to help them remember. Later, refer to these methods as children recall the tree-nut butter making procedure. Offer children paper on which to draw or write the steps they carried out.

Physical

1. Rhythm Sticks

Gather the children in a group and hand out two wooden rhythm sticks to each child. Tell the children that the sticks are made of wood and encourage them to experiment with the sounds they can make by tapping or rubbing the sticks together or beating them gently on the floor. Another day, ask children to imitate a simple sound pattern you demonstrate with your sticks. Keep the pattern simple (three or four sounds at a time). Eventually, extend the patterns and make them more varied. Also, have children take turns being the rhythm stick leader who creates sounds for others to imitate.

2. Squeezing Orange Juice/ Making Lemonade

Have at a table a knife, a cutting board, several hand juicers, a pitcher of water, paper towels for cleanup, and a bag of juice oranges (such as Valencia oranges or other varieties having a thin peel), lemons, and sugar, if making lemonade. A bowl, measuring cup, spoon for stirring, and small paper cups for tasting are also necessary. Cut the fruit in half yourself or allow children to do the cutting under your supervision. Examine the fruit carefully—touch it, smell it, look at its

different parts. Talk about how these fruits are products of trees. Show children how to place a fruit half fruit-side-down on a hand juicer that has been situated over a bowl to catch the juice. Squeeze out the juice using a twisting motion. For orange juice, allow each child to fill his or her cup with the juice of one whole orange. For lemonade, add a little water and sugar to taste to the juice of one lemon. Some children enjoy the combination of one orange half with the juice of one half lemon, a little water, and a dash of sugar.

To Simplify:
● Give children orange quarters with the peels on. Invite them to peel the oranges and eat them rather than using the squeezer.

To Extend:
● Teach children this simple Mexican song, the title of which, "Naranja Dulce," means "sweet orange." Regulate the children's turns with the juicer by having each turn last one verse. Although the song does have a tune of its own, the words also can be sung to a variety of traditional tunes. "Twinkle, Twinkle, Little Star" works well with the Spanish words.

Naranja Dulce	Sweet Orange
Na-ran-ja dul-ce,	A sweet orange,
li-mon par-ti-do,	a slice of lemon,
da-me un a-bra-zo	give me a hug,
que yo te pido.	and say goodbye.

3. Sawdust Sculptures

Gather the following materials: smocks for yourself and the children, newspaper, sawdust, wheat paste, water, mixing bowls, wooden spoons, measuring cups, and paper plates. Cover a table with the newspaper. Wear a smock and have the children put smocks on too. Invite the children to help you make sawdust modeling dough. Using hands or wooden spoons, mix the following ingredients together:

4 cups of sawdust
1 cup of wheat paste
2-1/2 cups of water

Encourage the children to explore the sticky mixture with their hands. Note how the mixture can be shaped and mounded. Give children a portion of the mixture with which to work. After each child has created a shape that is pleasing to him or her, allow the shapes to dry and harden. Another day, provide paints for children to use in decorating their sculptures. Display each one on a paper plate base labeled with the sculptor's name.

Pretend Play

1. Shady Picnic

Plan a simple picnic for the children to take place outside under a tree. Use a blanket to define the sitting space. While eating, talk with the children about the shade the tree gives and why this spot makes a good place to eat. Have the children look for insects that come around looking for food. Back inside the classroom, set up a picnic area in the pretend play corner. Provide a blanket, a picnic basket, dishes and utensils, plastic food, and maybe some pretend insects. Encourage children to recreate their picnic indoors under a make-believe tree.

2. Carpenter Shop

Provide woodworking benches, drawing tables, pencils, safety goggles, and pretend or actual tools for the children to use. Find blueprints from woodworking magazines to have enlarged and placed around the area. Squares and rules are also useful. Invite children to set up shop and pretend to be carpenters creating beautiful products for people to use or architects designing homes and buildings made out of wood.

3. Poster Shop

Set up an area where children can create posters telling people about the importance of trees or describing tree-based products. Provide construction paper for signs, markers, crayons, magazines, scissors, and paste for the poster makers to use. Consider having a cash register and pretend money children can have access to in "selling" their signs after they have made them.

Social

1. Tree Salad

Send a note home with the children asking families to send to the center or school one food item from a tree that could be used in a group salad. Offer some examples for families to consider, such as an orange, an apple, an apricot, a banana, some pineapple, coconut (flaked variety), walnuts, pecans, cinnamon, nutmeg, and so forth. Have on hand some additional items for

youngsters who do not bring something from home. During a large group time, go over the items collected for the salad. Make a list of these and discuss how each relates to a tree. Later, as part of a small group or learning center time, have children peel, chop, or grate the items, as appropriate, and combine them into a salad. Eat and enjoy!

2. Cooperative Tree Web

Making a tree web is an excellent culminating activity for this mini-theme. Its purpose is to give children an opportunity to work toward a common goal and to synthesize what they have learned as a group. To carry out this plan, you must have a good-sized picture of a tree pasted to the center of a large piece of mural paper. Explain to the children that they will have a chance to create a weblike chart showing how trees are used by animals and people. Begin by brainstorming ideas related to each tree part. Ask children questions such as, "How do people or animals use the leaves of the tree?" or "How do people or animals use the branches of the tree?" From each tree part draw several large oval shapes. Show the connection between the individual parts and their corresponding ovals either by drawing a line between the two or using a piece of yarn to connect them. Provide children with magazine pictures to insert in the part of the web depicting who or how that part of the tree might be used. Add words as necessary to explain the children's ideas. For example, "Leaves give shade. Leaves are food for insects. Leaves provide a covering for birds." Have the children work in teams of two or three for each part of the web. When it is finished, congratulate the group on everyone's hard work and cooperation.

3. Town Trees

Turn the block area into a whole-group effort at making a town. Supply children with several homemade or ready-made trees that can be included as part of their plan. Encourage the children to work together to create a make-believe town in which they incorporate trees as well as houses, vehicles, roads, people, and other accessories.

4. Barn Raising

Explain that people often work together to make a difficult job easier and more fun. Building a large structure like a barn is one of those kinds of jobs. Provide a variety of wood-based materials for the children to use such as large hollow blocks and planks, long cardboard strips or squares of posterboard, masking tape,

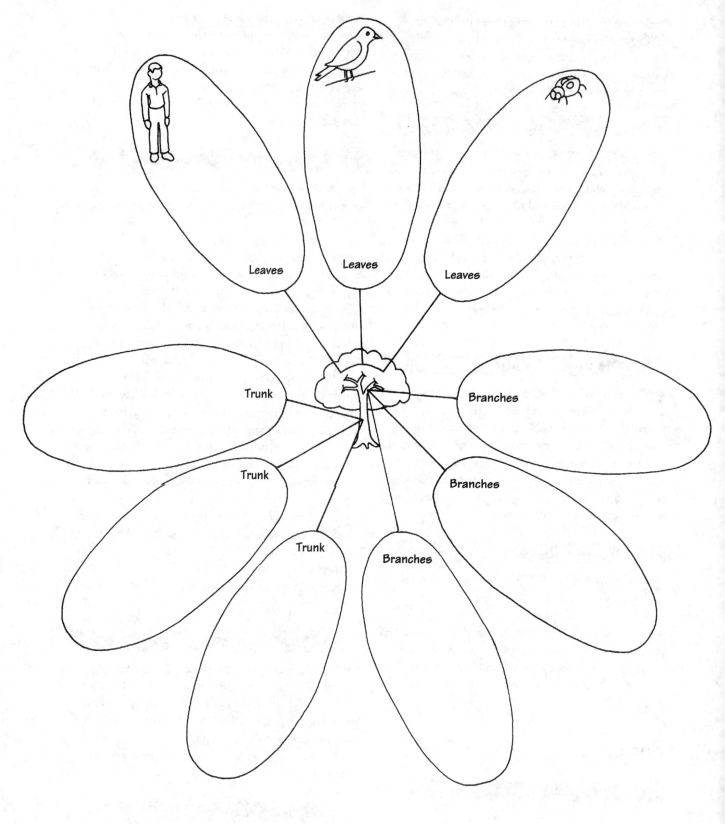

Leaves

Leaves

Leaves

Trunk

Branches

Trunk

Branches

Trunk

Branches

and string. Encourage the children to work together to construct a barn or other building with which they might be familiar using the wood products provided. An alternative to using the large wooden blocks is to offer children smaller building logs with which to make constructions in groups of two or three children.

Teacher Resources

Field Trip Ideas

1. Visit a lumberyard.
2. Explore a furniture store. Look for furniture made from wood and examine different kinds of wood items.
3. Go to a construction site during the time when the beams and wood support pieces are being put in place.
4. Visit an art studio or carpentry shop in which people work with wood.
5. Take a trip to a grocery store looking for products that come from trees.
6. Take a trip to a wooded area in your community. Look for evidence of animal life.
7. Visit a logging site or paper mill to see the raw materials that come from trees and how they are obtained or transformed.
8. Visit a recycling facility. Focus on how paper products are reused.

Classroom Visitors

1. Invite one or more of the following people to talk about how they use trees or wood products in their work: carpenter, artist, wood carver, cabinet maker, home builder.
2. Ask a forest ranger or firefighter to talk with the children about things they can do to preserve natural areas.

Children's Books

Bellamy, D. (1988). *The Forest*. New York: Clarkson N. Potter.

Cherry, L. (1990). *The Great Kapok Tree: A Tale of the Amazon Rain Forest*. New York: Harcourt Brace Jovanovich.

Greene, C. (1989). *I Can Be a Forest Ranger*. Chicago, IL: Childrens Press.

Kalman, B., and Schaub, J. (1992). *How Trees Help Me*. New York: Crabtree.

Lavies, B. (1989). *Tree Trunk Traffic*. New York: Dutton Children's Books.

Manson, C. (1992). *A Farmyard Song*. New York: North-South Books.

Manson, C. (1993). *The Tree in the Wood: An Old Nursery Song*. New York: North-South Books.

Newton, J. R. (1980). *Forest Log*. New York: Thomas Y. Crowell.

Romanova, N. (1989). *Once There Was a Tree*. New York: Dial.

Root, B. (1992). *The Singing Fir Tree*. New York: Putnam.

Russell, N., (1989). *The Tree*. New York: Dutton.

Ryder, J. (1991). *Hello, Tree!* New York: Lodestar Books.

Schwartz, D. M. (1988). *The Hidden Life of the Forest*. New York: Crown Publishers.

Seuss, Dr. (1971). *The Lorax*. New York: Random Books for Young Readers.

Tresselt, A. (1992). *The Gift of the Tree*. New York: Lothrop, Lee & Shepard.

Adult References

Better Homes and Garden Wood. (1993). *Weekend Toy Projects You Can Make*. Des Moines, IA: Meredith Corp.

Brandt, S. R. (1992). *State Trees*. New York: Franklin Watts.

Bridgewater, A., & Bridgewater G. (1991). *Carving Totem Poles and Masks*. New York: Sterling Publishing Co.

Denning, A. (1994). *The Art and Craft of Wood Carving*. Philadelphia, PA: Running Press.

Struthers, J. (1991). *Decorating with Wood*. New York, NY: Crescent Books.

Classroom Pets

When it's time for us to share, we can balance our regrets
if we focus, in the giving, on the joy the other gets.
As we learn to care for others, without tallying the debts,
an ideal way to practice is adopting classroom pets.

The benefits to children of animals in the classroom are numerous and valuable. A natural fascination with other living things leads to opportunities for children to develop the skills of observation and description, especially when animals are close at hand. When pets are in a classroom, children can learn about being responsible for the health and well-being of others.

Responsive animals in the classroom allow experiences in assessing the effects of one's own behaviors on other beings. Participating in the care of these animals leads to knowledge of routines, and to a deepening respect for the needs that all living creatures share: food and water, a clean and sheltered environment, and caring companionship.

Purpose

Though many animals are worthy candidates for classroom pets, some are more suited to the busy and bustling world of young children in groups. The best candidates are active in the daylight hours, relatively gentle and patient, and comfortable with noise and movement. Moreover, they are clean and rely on their hosts for a moderate rather than continuous amount of care. This unit explores three kinds of classroom pets that meet the above criteria.

Rabbits

Many children are curious about rabbits, perhaps because it is likely that they can easily spot these gentle creatures. By glancing out a window on a mild spring day, they may see one scurrying into a bush. By looking around a snow-filled field, they could see another—a swift and shadowy figure. We can spot them crossing country roads, just before dusk at the "bunny hour." Although they are all around us, rabbits are so quiet and private that we almost think they were only there in our thoughts.

Rabbits, because of their quiet, gentle, and clean natures, make ideal classroom pets. Although the noise and bustle of children at work may concern them at first, if adopted when young and treated with patience and love, they soon learn to return the love they are given.

Rabbits can teach us to be still, stay alert, and learn about the wonders of the world in this remarkable way. Rabbits can teach us to eat what's fresh, keep ourselves and our homes clean, and spend a few minutes in private when we're feeling upset. Rabbits can teach us to respect routines, and to frolic about with glee when the mood strikes. And rabbits can teach us to withdraw with dignity, rather than fight.

Gerbils

The social little gerbil is an expert at the skills of interaction and cooperation when sharing its cage with a same-sex sibling. Leaning on a nearby counter, the young observer will be fascinated with the gerbil way of life: scurrying in and out of hiding places, scampering up and down ladders, joyfully munching on snacks.

Gerbils, like children, are active in the daytime, play lead-and-follow games with their companions, and like to be held and touched as long as you're gentle and considerate.

Some of the mysteries of life that children ponder, such as reproduction and death, can be introduced over gerbils' two- or three-year lifespan. With careful planning and preparation, teachers can turn these natural events into valuable learning experiences, if they so choose.

Fish

Through the looking glass of an aquarium, a world quite unlike our own is revealed. Gliding in and out of rocks and plants, tails twitching, scales shimmering, its inhabitants move. During long moments at absolute rest, fish afford us tranquil opportunities to observe them.

Adopting fish as classroom pets introduces children to the importance of research. Some fish, suited to life in a classroom aquarium, must have a saltwater home, while others need fresh water. Some fish are docile and friendly toward fish unlike them, while others are unwilling to share their space with all but their own kind. Fish need diversions, just as children do: hiding places and bubbles, rocks and plants, and snail helpers to keep their homes tidy.

Much fish care revolves around the provision of a suitable watery home, kept clean, and of adequate amounts of appropriate food.

This makes them ideal as classroom pets when minimal investments of upkeep seem important to the teacher. While a rabbit can wander the classroom, and a gerbil can be held and stroked, fish are best suited to observation and contemplation.

Implementation

This unit is an ideal one to introduce if you are planning to adopt a pet for your program. Carefully consider these three candidates. Teach the children about their unique qualities and needs. Learn about the many different breeds of rabbits, and their particular personalities and appearances. Have gerbil owners or experts visit

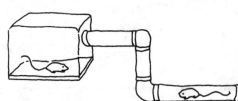
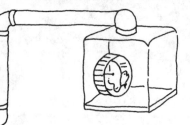

your classroom to answer questions. Visit a pet store to observe the many kinds of fish and to learn about the aquarium setups that would be suitable for your setting.

If you already have one or more of these pets who reside with the children in your program, plan this unit as an opportunity to learn more about what will keep them happy and healthy. Spend a good deal of time observing the animals carefully. Focus your observations on physical traits, as well as skills and temperamental characteristics. Learn to read the many cues that animal friends give about their needs and wants. Learn to be their friends, and they will become a friend to all of you, in return. When children are introduced to their first "up-close-and-personal" pet encounter, follow these guidelines for a successful experience:

1. Remind children that most animals have concerns about loud noises and quick movements, until they learn what they are all about. This means it is best for people to sit still and talk quietly when they are observing classroom pets.

2. Suggest that children allow a gerbil or rabbit to let them know when it is eager to be touched: the animal will nudge their hand or move toward them. When this happens, children should touch the animal with their hands open, fingers extended, so it doesn't fear it will be grabbed. Remind children that fish do not like to be touched, and that their water must be kept very clean; great care must be taken before dropping anything into the aquarium. Tell the children that they must always seek your help and advice before offering food or objects to fish.

3. Tell children that just as animals sometimes hesitate to touch people they don't yet know, sometimes people hesitate to touch animals they don't know, as well. The pet won't be bothered if anyone would rather look than touch!

4. Show the children that there are special ways to pick up and hold rabbits and gerbils. Encourage them to observe you or another expert for awhile before attempting to hold an animal themselves.

Following these guidelines will help your classroom pets as well as the children to feel more at ease with each other. Just as with people, making friends with a classroom pet requires respect and affection. Other suggestions for implementing "Classroom Pet" themes are:

Option One: If you don't yet have a classroom pet, spend two or three weeks exploring possibilities. Contrast the housing requirements, care, and amount of physical contact possible if you were to choose fish, gerbils, or a rabbit. Borrow representatives from other programs or classrooms, or seek visitors representing pet stores to bring animals for the children to meet and observe.

Option Two: Focus your "Classroom Pet" studies on an animal that you already have or plan to get. Develop a multi-week unit:

Week 1   Breeds and/or Characteristics

Week 2   What Our Animal Friend Needs (Space, Food, Safety)

Week 3   What Our Animal Friend Likes (Friends, Plants, Toys, Games)

Option Three: Our Classroom Pet in Literature: Fact and Fiction

Rabbits

Terms, Facts, and Principles (TFPs)

General Information

1. Rabbits are small furry mammals with long ears and short tails.

*2. Rabbits are a type of mammal called a *lagomorph*, as are hares.

*3. Rabbits differ from hares in that they have ears no longer than their heads, they prefer living in groups, and their babies are born blind, deaf, and hairless.

*4. Lagomorphs differ from rodents in that they cannot pick up things between their forepaws, they stretch their bodies like cats, and they have more incisors (sharp teeth).

5. Rabbits are peaceful and avoid fights by running to hide when frightened.

6. There are many breeds of rabbits—about 50—that differ by size, color, ear length, and body, length, and texture of fur.

7. Rabbits grow to their full size by about 18 months of age:

    a. Dwarf breeds weigh between 2 and 3 pounds (1 to 1.5 kgs).

    b. Small breeds weigh between 3-1/2 and 7-1/2 pounds (2 to 3.5 kgs).

    c. Medium breeds weigh between 7-1/2 and 12 pounds (3.5 to 5.5 kgs).

    d. Large breeds weigh between 12 and 16 pounds (5 to 7 kgs).

8. Rabbits can be solid colored or multicolored, and their colors include gray, white, black, brown, tan, and red. Most rabbits have tails with a white underside.

9. Some rabbits have ears that stand upright or that droop over; drooping-eared rabbits are called *lops*.

10. Rabbit ears vary in length from 2 inches to 7.5 inches (5.5 cm to 19 cm).

11. Rabbit fur can be smooth or kinky, and short or long.

12. Some long-haired rabbits (Angoras) have fur that must be shorn (cut) regularly.

13. Rabbits have teeth that continue to grow throughout their lifetime.

14. Rabbits walk on all four of their feet; they also push off with their strong rear legs, both at the same time in a hopping motion, when they run.

15. Rabbits have eyes that are set far up on the two sides of their heads.

16. Rabbits can see all around them without moving their heads.

17. Rabbits see better far away than close up, and in dim light than in bright light.

18. Rabbits are active at night.

19. Rabbits have ears that are shaped like long funnels and that can turn independently of each other.

20. Rabbits can hear all around them without moving their heads.

21. Rabbits have nostrils in their noses that move and twitch all the time; they can detect odors extremely well.

22. Rabbits can smell other rabbits and decide whether they have met before, whether the other rabbit is a male or female, and the age of the other rabbit.

23. Male rabbits are called *bucks*; female rabbits are called *does*; baby rabbits are called *kittens*.

24. People have discovered that different breeds of rabbits have different kinds of personalities:

    a. Belgians and Tans are known to be curious and lively.

    b. Lops are known to be stubborn.

    c. Angoras are known to be gentle, quiet, and affectionate.

25. Most rabbits live for between 4 and 10 years.

Rabbit Care and Handling

26. Rabbits must have many chances to chew on hard substances like wood to keep their teeth from growing so long that they have problems chewing food. The best woods for rabbits to chew are hardwoods from fruit trees, willow trees, firs, or spruce.

27. Sometimes, pet rabbits must have their teeth trimmed by veterinarians because they haven't been given enough things to chew.

28. Rabbits have four claws on each paw that continue to grow; therefore, they must have many opportunities to dig with their claws, or have them trimmed, to keep them from getting too long.

29. Rabbits are very social and may get lonely unless they live with other rabbits, or with people or other animals who like them and treat them kindly.

30. People who live with rabbits must learn about what they need and want to be happy and healthy, and make sure that those needs are met.

    a. Rabbits need fresh water every day, and several kinds of food, to grow and be healthy.

    b. The foods that rabbits need include hay, grains, vegetables, and some fruit now and then for a treat.

    c. Not all vegetables are good for rabbits. Vegetables that are good for rabbits include carrots, radishes, celery, peas and pea pods, corn kernels, kohlrabi, and cauliflower greens. Vegetables that are not good for rabbits include potatoes, lettuce, and cabbage.

    d. Rabbits should not eat green vegetables until they are four months old.

    e. Rabbits need opportunities to run and play every day in order to stay healthy.

    f. Rabbits like to be picked up, stroked, and talked to, except when they are eating or resting.

    g. Bucks do not enjoy living together, especially if they are older than four months.

    h. Does do enjoy living together, especially if they are sisters.

    i. Pet rabbits need cages or hutches that are large enough to stand up in, and that have a dark, secret place where they can hide or sleep when they want to.

    j. Rabbits are annoyed or frightened by loud noises and the sound of birds chirping.

    k. Rabbits should be eight to ten weeks old before they leave their mothers or come to live with people.

31. A pet rabbit should be picked up by using one hand to grasp the fur between its shoulder blades firmly, then quickly putting the other hand under its rear end, and holding it close against your body.

32. A rabbit should never be picked up by its ears or its trunk.

*33. Rabbits eat some substances that are produced by their own bodies:

  a. the wax from their ears, which contains vitamin D to help their bones grow strong;

  b. a special kind of feces that looks like wet and shiny tiny clusters of grapes, and contains protein and vitamin B1, to help keep the rabbit healthy.

34. Rabbits like to chew on everything; it is important to protect them by keeping unsafe objects like electrical and telephone wires and plastic toys away from where they live and play.

35. Rabbits keep themselves clean by licking parts of their bodies with their tongues, or licking their paws and then using them to wash their faces and ears.

36. Some rabbits and guinea pigs enjoy playing together; however, they do not eat the same foods nor do they enjoy sleeping in the same cage.

37. Rabbits can get ill very quickly if they are not eating healthful foods, are too hot or too cold, are living in dirty cages, or are very lonely or bored. It is important to take a rabbit to a veterinarian right away if it seems ill.

Rabbit Communication

38. Rabbits seldom make any sounds unless they are very frightened, very angry, or very hurt.

39. When rabbits do make sounds, they may sound like a mutter, a growl, a squeak, or a scream.

40. Rabbits communicate mostly with their bodies:

  a. A rabbit stands up on its haunches when it wants to look around.

  b. A rabbit drums or stamps its feet when it senses danger and wants to warn other rabbits.

  c. A rabbit presses its ears back along its head, sticks its tail straight back, and pushes its neck forward when it is angry: watch out, it may bite!

  d. A rabbit licks your hand when it is saying thank you or that it likes you.

  e. A rabbit nudges you with its nose when it is saying that it wants to be held or petted.

  f. A rabbit rolls around on the ground when it is happy.

  g. A rabbit rubs its chin against objects when it is saying that a place or object is its private property.

Activity Ideas

Aesthetic

1. All the Colors of the Rabbits

Gather several sponges in a variety of textures. Cut them into irregularly sized pieces that are about the size of a child's fist. Fill small tin pans with paint in several rabbit-fur colors: gray, brown, white, tan, black, and red or rust. Cut several sheets of easel paper into the shape of a large rabbit silhouette. Invite children to dab paint on the rabbit shapes, creating either solid-colored or multicolored rabbits.

To Extend:

● Display pictures of different breeds of rabbits. Have children determine which color combinations look like different breeds of rabbits.

● Make a large template of a rabbit that children can use to trace a bunny silhouette on easel paper. Suggest that each child cut out her or his rabbit with scissors before clipping it to the easel and painting it.

2. The Rabbit Hop

Teach the children this simple rabbit song, and sing it together while acting out the suggested motions.

♫ The Rabbit Hop
Words by Kit Payne
Tune: "I'm a Little Tea Pot"

> I'm a little rabbit, called a lop.
> Tail on my bottom, droop-ears on top.
> When I'm feeling frightened,
> Then I STOP.
> Look round and listen,
> HOP, HOP, HOP!

Explain to the children that a rabbit called a lop has ears that flop over. Put your hands beside your head, folding the fingers over, to demonstrate and suggest a motion. Put one hand at your bottom, wiggling the fingers, to suggest a tail. When feeling frightened, stretch upright, with a startled, wide-eyed expression. Hop together when singing the last line.

3. Sharing Our Snack with a Rabbit

Tell the children that rabbits enjoy eating many of the same vegetables that people do. However, people often trim off and discard the very parts that rabbits like the best. Provide the children with carrots, radishes, and cauliflower that still have the greens attached. Help them to clean, trim, and slice the vegetables, reserving all the greens for a rabbit. Invite the children to eat the vegetables, and watch the rabbit enjoying the greens that have been trimmed away.

Hints for Success:

● When feeding vegetables (and fruits) to rabbits, always provide fresh rather than cooked or frozen ones, which may cause a rabbit intestinal distress.

● Always remove the leftovers from the rabbit cage after fifteen minutes or so. Whatever the rabbit has chosen not to eat will begin to wilt or spoil and lose its nutritional value if left out too long, making it no longer a healthful rabbit food.

4. Rabbit Rhymes and Finger Plays

Enjoy reciting and performing the motions for some of these fingerplays about rabbits with the children. Mention that sometimes people call rabbits *bunnies,* and that these words mean the same thing.

Here Is a Bunny
Author: Unknown

> Here is a bunny
> with ears so funny,
> *(Make a fist, holding up two fingers to represent ears.)*
>
> and here is his
> hole in the ground.
> *(Form the other hand into an open circle, fingers touching thumb.)*
>
> When a noise she hears,
> she perks up her ears,
> *(Stretch "ear fingers" straight up.)*
>
> and jumps in her hole
> with a bound.
> *(Stick "ear fingers" in hole in circled fist.)*

Breakfast in the Garden
Words by Kit Payne

Once there grew a garden,

with carrots, peas and corn. (*Stand; gesture around with your arms.*)

Near it hopped a rabbit, (*Hop in place.*)

early in the morn.

What is there for breakfast? (*Shrug your shoulders.*)

That was on his mind. (*Point to head.*)

Then he spotted all those vegetables,

and flopped on his behind. (*Sit down on floor.*)

First I'll have a carrot. (*Pretend to pick and eat each vegetable, in turn.*)

then I'll have a pea,

Then I'll have an ear of corn,

and that's enough for me! (*Rub your stomach.*)

Rabbit Messages
Words by Kit Payne

I'm a friendly rabbit

when I lick your hand. (*Pretend to lick own hand.*)

There's a sight to see

when I try to stand. (*Sit up tall, knees bent, legs tucked under.*)

I'm a worried rabbit

when I stamp the ground. (*Drum feet rapidly against the floor.*)

I'm a happy rabbit

when I roll around. (*Lie curled on side; roll back and forth.*)

I'm an angry rabbit

when I stretch my tail and head. (*On knees, stretch head forward and behind back.*)

I'm a sleepy rabbit

when I creep off to my bed. (*Lie across own knees, head on hands, eyes closed.*)

Affective

1. How to Choose?

Carry out this activity when undertaking to adopt a pet rabbit for your program, or as a hypothetical exercise in the event that some of the children's families may someday decide to adopt a rabbit as a family pet. Its purpose is to familiarize children with rabbit characteristics and to give children opportunities to make choices. First, lead a discussion about the many ways that rabbit breeds differ from each other. Show pictures of some of the 50 different breeds of rabbits that have been classified. Inform the children that rabbits differ in color, size, ear type, fur length and texture, amount of care they need, and even personality. Using chart paper or a chalkboard, begin lists that are headed by the characteristics given above. Under the heading COLOR, begin listing all the colors that the children think rabbits may come in. Show some pictures of rabbits to generate ideas. Accept all ideas at this point, whether you believe they are representative of rabbit breeds or not. Continue in this manner, beginning new lists with EARS, SIZE, FUR TYPE, and so on. Elicit children's ideas about variances that belong under each heading. Next, invite the children to approach the lists later in the day, making check marks beside one characteristic under each heading that indicates their personal preference. Tell the children that they can ask you or a classmate for help reading the headings, if they wish. Later, bring the lists back to a class meeting, and discuss similarities and differences in the children's preferences.

To Simplify:
● Prepare a chart ahead of time, with line drawings or magazine photo clippings to illustrate the word headings for each list.

● You can also photocopy illustrations from an informational book about rabbit breeds, such as *Rabbits: A Complete Pet Owner's Manual* by Monika Wegler (1990). Cut out the pictures, adding color with markers as necessary, and paste them to the chart. Provide children with sticker dots to apply under the characteristics to indicate their preferences.

To Extend:
● Prepare a smaller chart that can be reproduced so that each child has one. Explain the activity in the same way as above. Then invite each child to complete his or her own preference chart. Later, allow time for children to meet in small groups to compare their preferences, or to bring their charts to a large group meeting to explain to classmates.

2. Rabbit Greeting Cards

This is an ideal activity to carry out if you adopt a rabbit as a classroom pet with your current group of children. If your program already has a rabbit or if you

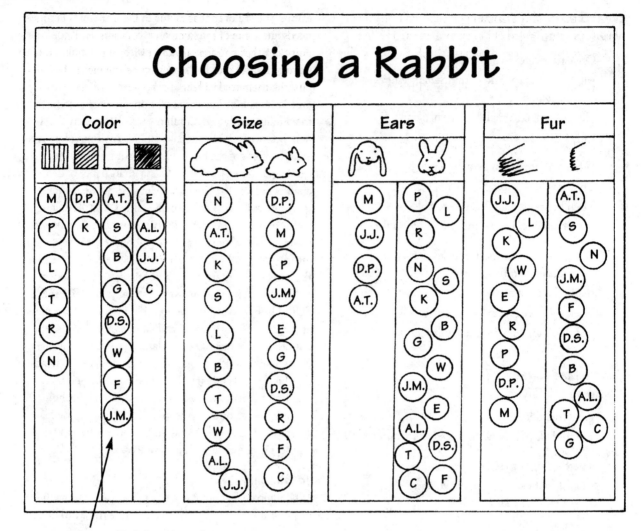

Choosing a Rabbit

indicate children in class

can provide temporary "foster care" for a program family's rabbit while teaching this unit, this activity would be a fine introduction to rabbit care. If you are unable to locate a rabbit that can visit, introduce this activity with a discussion that centers on pretending that a rabbit has been adopted. Begin by leading a group discussion about the special wants and needs that rabbits have. Refer to the Terms, Facts, and Principles at the beginning of this unit. Tell the children that many greeting cards include text that wishes something good to the recipient: wishing a fun-filled day, wishing a lot of luck, wishing a speedy recovery, and so on. Encourage the children to think about all the things that a rabbit might wish for. Then invite the children to prepare greeting cards for a rabbit. Provide folded construction paper, with the phrase "Wishing You" pre-printed on the inside. If they are not yet able to write, the children can dictate a sentiment to an adult or another child who is a writer. Next, invite the children to add a picture to the outside/cover of the card. Finally, have them sign their

names under the inside text. Hang the finished cards on a wall near the rabbit cage for the children and the rabbit to enjoy.

Hint for Success:
● Prepare a set of flannelboard figures to illustrate your discussion, including two or three rabbit figures, a cage or hutch, some food, a water bottle, and so on.

3. Carrot Cake

The purpose of this activity is for the children to follow a sequence of steps through to completion, while gaining experience with cooking implements and procedures. Prepare an illustrated chart detailing the recipe that follows. Provide some discussion and demonstrations of the uses of measuring cups and spoons. Fifteen children, all together, could measure one unit each: two for the two cups of flour, and so on. If there are more than fifteen children, include such steps as grating the carrots, greasing the pan, beating the mixture, and washing the pans and utensils. Pour the mixture into a well-greased oblong pan. Bake at 350° for 40 to 50 minutes. After the cake has cooled, encourage the children to talk about the results of their many individual contributions to its success. Discuss which of the ingredients rabbits would enjoy as you eat!

4. Like Me/Not Like Me

Collect a variety of pictures of rabbits for the children to refer to as they participate in this activity.

Inform the children that rabbits have many of the same needs and some of the same physical traits as children. Point out that children are also different from rabbits in many ways. As the children examine the pictures of rabbits, ask them to decide what about themselves is the same as a rabbit. Encourage identification of differences too. Additionally, ask children if there are rabbit traits that they wish they shared. Ask, "What would it be like to have fur?" "What kind of hat would you need if your ears were that long?" "How would you let your friends know what you wanted to do, if you weren't able to

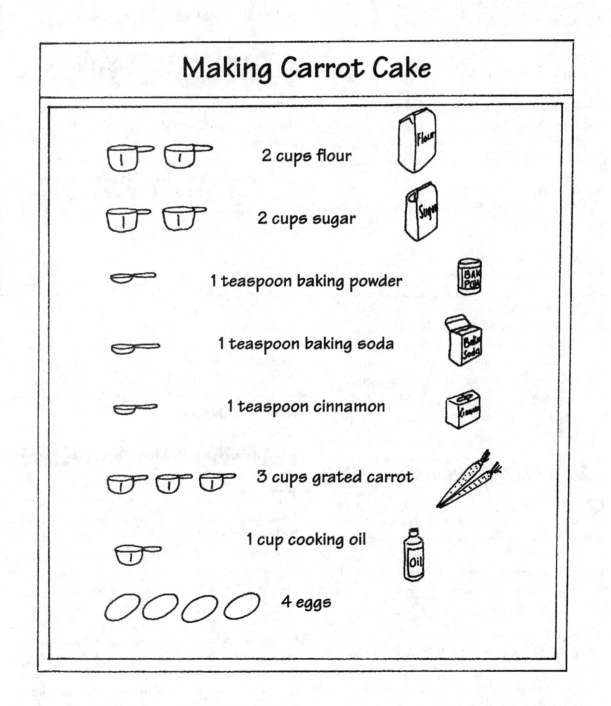

Making Carrot Cake

2 cups flour

2 cups sugar

1 teaspoon baking powder

1 teaspoon baking soda

1 teaspoon cinnamon

3 cups grated carrot

1 cup cooking oil

4 eggs

talk?"

Cognitive

1. Rabbit Lineup

D raw or photocopy and cut out a variety of rabbit shapes in different sizes. Include rabbits with varying ear sizes, as well. Invite the children to examine the many rabbit cutouts. Select three that vary considerably in size. Ask a child to decide how they would be arranged if the smallest rabbit were going on a walk and the largest following after. Then ask where the third one would go if the smallest rabbit was always first and the largest rabbit always last. Hand the child a few more rabbits, suggesting that they all decided to join the parade, arranging themselves in size so the largest rabbit was always at the back, looking out for trouble. If the children chose other ways to arrange the rabbits, ask them to tell you about the reasons for their series. Avoid suggesting that there is only one right way to seriate.

To Simplify:
● Prepare a series of five or six rabbits that vary only in size. Make the differences at least half-inch gradations.

To Extend:
● Color the rabbits in lighter-to-darker shades of the same color. For example, prepare a series that varies from light tan to darker tan to light brown to dark brown, or from white to pale gray, to darker gray to black. Make sure that the color shadings progress in a different way than the size variations, so that there is more than one way to arrange the figures in a series.

● Another variation is to prepare a series of rabbit figures with ears that progress from flopped to completely upright and touching.

2. Weighing Rabbit Food

P rovide the children with balance scales, measuring cups, and commercial rabbit-food pellets. Provide another set of objects, such as unit blocks or marbles. As the children experiment with the scales, encourage nonstandard measurement concepts. For example, help the weigher count the number of unit blocks it takes to balance a cup of rabbit pellets.

To Simplify:
● Omit the blocks or marbles. Have the children experiment with obtaining a balance across the sides of the scales by simply adding to and taking away from piles of food pellets on the two sides.

To Extend:
● Record the numbers of objects necessary to balance differing quantities of pellets on a form provided for this purpose.

● Add platform scales and teach children to read the weights that result as they vary the mass of pellets.

● Discuss the average weight of different breeds of rabbits (see Terms, Facts, and Principles, page 375). Have the children determine the amount of pellets necessary to reach the same weights. Pour the pellets into plastic bags after determining their weight in order to experience how heavy different breeds of rabbits would feel if you were to hold them in your hands.

3. Bunches and Bunches of Bunnies

O btain a copy of the book *Bunches and Bunches of Bunnies* by Louise Mathews (1991). (Note: This is available as a Big Book). In this book, lots and lots of bunnies are arranged across the pages in ways that encourage an understanding of addition. As you read the book, have the children help you add the number of bunnies that appear. Point at rabbits, one at a time, as the children help you count.

To Simplify:
● Count the number of colors of rabbits that appear on the book pages.

To Extend:
● Note the number of bunnies on each book page on chart paper after the children help you count them. After reading the whole book, add up these subtotals, two pages at a time, until you determine the entire total of bunnies in the book.

4. Fact or Fiction?

G ather some children's books about fictional rabbits, such as *The Tale of Peter Rabbit* by Beatrix Potter (many editions are available), *Mister Rabbit and the Lovely Present* by Charlotte Zolotow (1962), and *The Runaway Bunny* by Margaret Wise Brown (1942). In addition, make a copy of the Terms, Facts, and Principles from the beginning of this unit to use as a reference for yourself. Display a few informational books about rabbits for the children to look through. Begin by telling the children that you will be reading them some stories about rabbits and that you would like them to listen very carefully in order to decide whether these rabbits are real or pretend. Add that when you are finished reading, you will ask them to describe what things hap-

pened in the books that helped them decide. Then read the fictional books, one at a time. Pause after each book to lead a discussion of factors that prompted children to decide between real and pretend. Use the informational books or the list of Terms, Facts, and Principles to find out what a real rabbit would do or look like in similar circumstances.

To Simplify:

● Read only one fictional book. Ask the children to tell you or show you how a real rabbit would differ from the one in the story. For example, if you read *Mister Rabbit and the Lovely Present*, ask the children whether a real rabbit would walk on his two back feet. Then, ask the children to show you with their bodies how a real rabbit would walk.

To Extend:

● Make all the books you have gathered, both fictional and informational, available in the classroom for reading and reference. Suggest that children keep a list of things that the fictional rabbits do, say, and look like. Then have the children look for facts in the informational books that confirm their fictional findings.

5. Do You Hear What I Hear?

Tell the children that rabbits have very remarkable ears. They are shaped like long funnels, and can be turned independently of each other, so that rabbits can hear all around them without turning their heads. Tell the children that when they see a rabbit holding its body very still, they may be able to spot its ears turning, if they look very carefully. Then invite the children to practice hearing like rabbits: by keeping their heads very still, eyes straight ahead, and listening very carefully. Point out that although they cannot turn their ears like a rabbit can, they can still hear very well if they stay very still and listen carefully. Next, walk to some different places in the classroom, reminding the children not to look at you but instead to keep their heads very still. Challenge the children to decide what you are making sounds with, and where you are making them from. For example, ring a bell from one corner of the classroom. Ask the children to tell you what made that sound and ask where in the room they think you are. Remind them again to keep their heads still and use only their ears. From another spot, beyond the children's view, tap a pencil against a piece of furniture. Ask them what and where questions again. If there is a sink in your room, turn on the water, and ask what and where. Repeat with other sounds from other locations.

6. See It, Smell It, Feel It

Fill a texture tub with pellets of commercial rabbit food. Invite the children to explore its look, smell, and texture. Encourage them to twitch and wiggle their noses, like a rabbit would, as they smell the grain pellets. Provide cups, scoops, and funnels to experiment with size and volume. Tell the children that many of the foods in rabbit pellets are also used to prepare some foods that people like to eat, like bread. If children are curious, tell them that the pellets are made of compressed grains, hay, seeds, vitamins, minerals, and amino acids. These pellets are not harmful if eaten by children, so if the children are exploring with clean hands, you could allow each child to taste one pellet, if you wish.

To Simplify:

● Lead a group discussion about the foods that rabbits eat. Point out that although special pellets are available for feeding rabbits, their diets should be supplemented with fresh vegetables and a little fruit (see Terms, Facts, and Principles, page 375). They also enjoy some wild plants like yellow (never red) clover and dandelions. Pass a cupful of rabbit pellets around the circle for children to look at, smell, and touch.

To Extend:

● Acquire some of the whole grains that are processed into commercial pellets (hay and alfalfa are the most common). Compare their appearance, smell, and texture with the compressed pellets.

● Pass around samples of other foods that comprise a healthful rabbit diet (see Terms, Facts, and Principles) along with the pellets.

Construction

1. Making Rabbit Ears

For this activity you will need a cardboard template of a rabbit ear (or two—one for a lop ear, one for an upright ear). Prepare this by tracing an ear shape (or two) on a piece of heavy cardboard, then cutting around it with sturdy scissors or a box cutting knife. Use the template(s) to trace many ears on construction paper. You will also need strips of construction paper (long enough to reach around a child's head with a bit left over), a stapler, and several pairs of scissors for the children to use. Tell the children that they will be making rabbit ears to wear. Give each child tracings of two ears and with which scissors to cut them out. After the ears are cut, provide a strip of paper to each child, and help him or her hold it around his or her head to determine

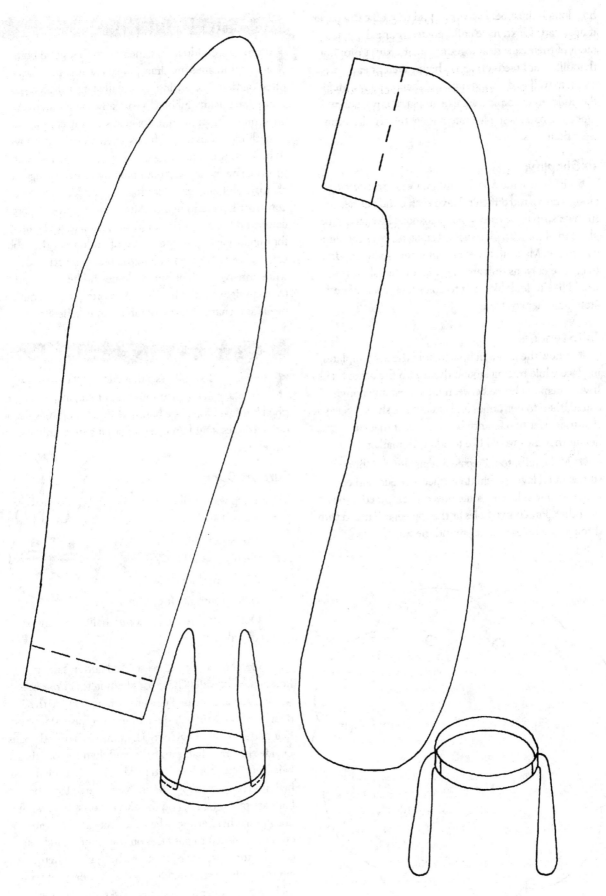

how long it must be. Have the child trim off extra paper, if necessary. Next, have children determine the placement of their ears: near together or far apart? Point out that different breeds of rabbits have different ear placement, as well as differing sizes and shapes of ears. Help the children to staple their ears in place, if necessary. Once the band is stapled into a loop, the children can wear their ears.

To Simplify:

● Pre-cut some ears for children who find cutting along a curve too difficult. Have each child cut her or his own strip to be used as a headband. The ears can be glued in place with glue sticks if staplers prove too difficult to use. Make all the ears white, and invite children to choose crayons that are the color of the rabbit they would like to look like, and to color their ears before attaching them to bands.

To Extend:

● Show the children how to hold the ear templates in place while tracing around them with the other hand. Invite them to choose between lop-eared and upright-eared, then to both trace and cut out the shapes. Suggest that they refer to reference books to see if there are other details that they would like to add with markers.

● Make tails, too. Prepare a template of a short, stubby tail. Have the children trace, cut out, and color white on one side with some other rabbit fur color on the other. Punch two holes at the top edge. Thread yarn through the holes and tie around the waist.

2. Rabbit Hutches

Inform the children that the homes that pet rabbits are kept in are sometimes called *hutches*. Hutches are often outdoor homes and are usually larger than cages. Sometimes, many rabbits live together in a hutch. A good hutch has a private, covered sleeping corner, with something soft to lie on. It has a place for food and water to be kept. It is tall enough so that the rabbit can stand up on its haunches without bumping its head. Suggest that the children use your program's wooden blocks to construct a pretend hutch. Alternatively, provide large cardboard boxes, and/or tables and blankets to be used for hutch-making. Invite the children to wear the rabbit ears and/or tails (described in the previous activity), while inhabiting their hutch. Some children may want to make signs for the hutch that inform others about the needs and characteristics of rabbits in hutches.

3. Currant Bun-nies

The recipe that follows will guide you through the process of making currant buns. In addition, the finished buns will look like bunnies! By adding a few decorative edibles, children can produce a bunny unlike anyone else's.

Currant Buns

    1 cup warm milk

    1 envelope yeast

    1 teaspoon salt

    2 tablespoons butter

    2 1/2 cups flour

    1/2 cup currants (or raisins)

Optional: shredded coconut, halved pecans or walnuts

Combine milk and yeast. Add butter, salt, and flour, and mix well. Knead for 8 minutes. Let rise in a warm place in a greased bowl for 1 hour. Divide the dough in half. Mix half the currants (or raisins) into one half of the dough. Divide this half into lots of little balls. Divide the other half into balls, and then roll out these balls between your hands to make "ears." Let the dough balls and "ears" rise for 1 hour. Assemble so that the balls are rabbit heads, and the ears are on top. Press the dough together between the head and ears. Use more currants (raisins) to put faces on the rabbits. Add some coconut fur or whiskers, if you wish. Decide whether to put some nuts in the middles of the ears, or whether to fold your ears over to make lops. Bake the bun-nies at 425° for 15 minutes.

Language

1. And Bunny Was Her Name, Oh . . .

Sing a version of the song "B-I-N-G-O," substituting the following lines about a bunny. Emphasize the spelling of the word bunny by constructing a song chart with one letter missing, then two, then three, and so on, in each successive line. Explain the way the song is sung to the children: with pauses to represent missing letters. When they are familiar with this activity, introduce humming, hopping, or clapping in place of each missing letter.

♫ **B-U-N-N-Y**

Words by Kit Payne
Tune: "B-I-N-G-O"

There was a pet with floppy ears, and Bunny was her name, oh;
B-U-N-N-Y, B-U-N-N-Y, B-U-N-N-Y, and Bunny was her name.

There was a pet with fluffy tail, and Bunny was her name, oh;
__-U-N-N-Y, __-U-N-N-Y, __-U-N-N-Y, and Bunny was her name.

There was a pet with twitchy nose, and Bunny was her name, oh;
__, __, N-N-Y, __, __, N-N-Y, __, __, N-N-Y, and Bunny was her name.

There was a pet with shiny eyes, and Bunny was her name, oh;
__, __, __, N-Y, __, __, __, N-Y, __, __, __, N-Y, and Bunny was her name.

There was a pet with soft, soft, fur, and Bunny was her name, oh;
__, __, __, __, Y, __, __, __, __, Y, __, __, __, __, Y, and Bunny was her name.

There was a very quiet pet, and Bunny was her name, oh;
__, __, __, __, __; __, __, __, __, __; __, __, __, __, and Bunny was her name.

To Simplify:

● Repeat the first line "There was a pet with floppy ears . . . " for each verse, varying only the number of letters that are left out each time. Thus children need only attend to the difference in missing letters.

To Extend:

● Invite children to suggest other characteristics of rabbits as pets that can be used to substitute for the ones given above.

● Invite children to take turns standing by the song chart and pointing out the words and silent pauses as they are sung or acknowledged.

● Prepare letter cutouts that attach to the chart with Velcro®; teach children to add and remove them, as called for in the song.

2. Rabbit Communication

Lead a discussion of ways in which rabbits use their bodies and gestures to communicate. Equate this with the many ways that people supplement their messages with facial expressions, gestures, postures, and so on. Refer to the Terms, Facts, and Principles for specific examples of rabbit communication cues. Demonstrate some of these with your own face and body. Invite children, one at a time, to act out messages as though they were rabbits. Encourage the other children to guess the meanings that are being conveyed. Help children to recall the meanings of gestures or postures as necessary by reading a few (three or four) of the statements provided in the Terms, Facts, and Principles again. Then suggest that a volunteer choose one to enact.

To Simplify:

● Choose four or five examples of rabbit communication from the list. Act them out yourself, one at a time. Invite the children to mimic your actions after watching you. Point out the probable meaning of these actions, telling a little story about each: "You're all thumping your foot very rapidly. You must be very worried about danger! Maybe you've spotted a big dog, sneaking up on your friends, and you know that a dog can get very excited around rabbits and scare them."

To Extend:

● Invite the children to create books of rabbit messages. Suggest that they draw illustrations of rabbits in various postures. Write down dictated labels that describe the message being conveyed, or encourage children to label their own drawings in their own forms of writing.

3. Rabbit-Care Guides

After several days of talking about rabbits and their needs, lead a group discussion of daily, weekly and monthly tasks that must be undertaken to ensure safe and sanitary conditions for pet rabbits. Ask the children to help generate lists of what these tasks should be. Introduce information yourself that may have been missed by the children (such as providing food and water daily, carefully examining objects that may be within chewing reach of rabbits, removing wilted foods if the rabbit has not eaten them, replacing bedding weekly, thorough cage cleaning monthly, and so on).

Tell the children that other people who are thinking of adopting rabbits may need some help deciding what they would have to do to care for their pets. Show and/or tell about guidebooks, pamphlets, and charts that have been developed for this purpose. Invite children to work singly or in small groups to create books, pamphlets, or charts that detail rabbit care. Point out that both pictures and words are good ways to inform others. Provide posterboard, lined and unlined paper, a variety of pens, pencils, markers, or crayons, and rulers or yardsticks to be used to section off the charts, if children have chosen that option. Mention that books about rabbits, available in the room, would be good references. Children may want to look at the pictures to get ideas for their own illustrations, or read or have read to them some of the information. Encourage children to help each other with spelling, drawing, line drawing, and so on. Move among the children yourself, acknowledging the strategies they are using, and responding to requests for help. Set up a classroom rabbit reference section, stocked with the children's work.

To Simplify:

● Prepare blank books ahead of time by folding a few sheets of paper together, with construction paper covers folded over them. Staple these near the top and bottom of the fold. Also prepare a few pieces of posterboard, to be made into charts, by drawing bold lines to divide the space into four or six squares. Children can then choose which format to work on and illustrate and label their guides.

To Extend:

● Assign small groups to develop guides for specific aspects of rabbit care, such as "To Keep Rabbits Well Fed," "To Keep Rabbits from Being Bored or Lonely," and "To Keep Rabbits' Homes Clean." Alternately, assign "Daily Rabbit Care," "Weekly Rabbit Care," and "Monthly Rabbit Care," or "Guide to Buying the Best Breed of Rabbit for You." Have the groups do some research about their topic by referring to other books in the classroom, or by questioning pet store personnel, a rabbit breeder, or a veterinarian. Then help the children decide who in the group will be responsible for different aspects of the project: an illustrator, a printer, an editor, a cover-maker, and so on.

4. The Tale of Peter Rabbit

Acquire a copy of this famous story by Beatrix Potter. The versions available through libraries and bookstores are often too small to be read to a large group of young children. However, this tale of mischief and woe to a young rabbit who disobeys his mother's warnings about exploring a tempting garden, and who then suffers some fearful consequences, is so fascinating to children that you can tell it, after learning it well, and expect rapt attention. After becoming very familiar with the story, prepare to tell it to the children by creating some flannel figures that represent the main characters (rabbits and Mister McGregor) and the setting of a large garden. Another alternative is to prepare paper props and mount them on craft sticks, to be manipulated like puppets. Tell the tale of Peter Rabbit with much expressiveness, pausing often for children's comments. Encourage prediction by asking the children to discuss what they think will happen next at particularly suspenseful moments in the story. Continue with the tale, commenting on whether predicted events occur. Use the props to teach about aspects of the story: point out that the garden is called a setting, and that the rabbits and Mister McGregor are called characters. Tell the children that stories have problems, and that you would like them to listen carefully for the problems in this story. After you have told the story, using your props to illustrate characters and events, invite the children to take turns retelling and reenacting it. Distribute the stick puppets or flannel figures to as many children as there are figures. Help them get started by offering to narrate as they move the characters. Gradually, encourage children to assume the jobs of both narration and manipulation. Make sure that all of the children who want turns get them. Comment on the children's memory for details from the story. Point out aspects of characters, setting, plot, problem, and so on, as they retell the story. Acknowledge creative embellishments: "You thought of a new problem that could have happened," or "You thought of a way to change the setting."

Hint for Success:

● Consider using this activity as an introduction to a related pretend-play, like the one described in the "The Cottontail Household" activity on page 391. Add these Peter Rabbit props to the area.

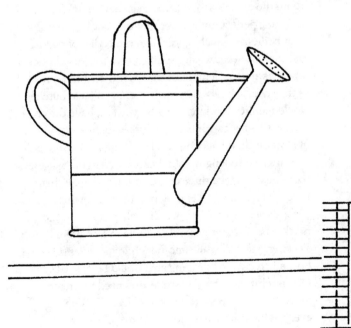

Physical

1. Shearing Rabbits

Prepare for this lacing and cutting activity by cutting rabbit shapes out of posterboard or cardboard, one for each child. Use a hole punch to make many holes all over each rabbit cutout. Cut a skein of yarn into pieces approximately four inches long. Gather several pairs of scissors and several glue sticks. Tell the children about long-hair breeds of rabbits, such as Angoras, that require occasional shearing because their fur continues to grow and becomes tangled and matted if not trimmed now and then. Show some pictures of Angoras, if possible. Tell the children that they will have a chance to practice shearing a rabbit, but they will have to make the rabbit first. Give each child one of the rabbit cutouts. Show everyone how to thread two or three lengths of yarn at a time in one hole and out a second hole. Instruct them to use the glue sticks to make the yarn stick to the back side of the rabbit where it crosses from one hole to the next. Continue in this manner until lots of yarn-ends are poking out of the holes, all over the rabbit. Next, provide the children with scissors. Tell them that they can trim the yarn/fur to whatever length they would like. Move among the children, helping them to choose different ways of holding the scissors, with first one hand and then the other, experimenting with different ways to become more adept at handling scissors. Offer to hold the rabbit for children who would like you to, or suggest that children help each other in this manner.

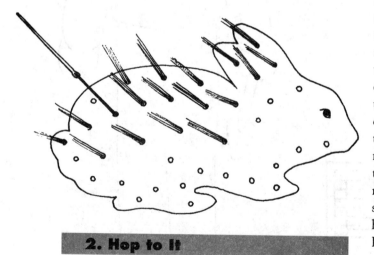

2. Hop to It

Tell the children about the unique way that rabbits have of hopping when they are in a hurry to get from place to place. Mention that they walk, much like a cat or dog, on all four feet when they are not in a hurry. Add that they have very strong hind legs, howev-

er, and that they use them both at once to push off and hop when they are hurrying. Let your classroom rabbit loose for children to observe, if possible. Allow the rabbit plenty of time to explore an open space in your room; watch for and discuss its varying gaits. After returning the rabbit to its cage, explore with the children different ways of using their own bodies to hop like a rabbit. Point out the ways that they can crouch to get more power from their hops. Caution children to remain aware of each other's movements as they explore hopping. Play some lively music to accompany the children's hopping, if you wish. Help the children relax by suggesting that the rabbits are getting tired, and are slowing to a walk, then creeping to a quiet place to sleep. Curl up together for a few minutes of rest.

3. A Hutch for Us

Discuss the meaning of the word *hutch*: a pen or coop for an animal; a place where a rabbit can live, protected from other animals that might scare it by playing too roughly (or wanting to eat it!). Tell the children that many kinds of animals are more comfortable when they have homes of their own where they can find food and water, shelter and privacy, and toys to play with or chew on. Inform the children that rabbits prefer hutches that are tall enough so that they can sit up on their haunches without bumping their heads on the roof, and long enough so that they can walk around. Rabbits also like a dark place in which to hide or sleep, undisturbed. Invite the children to imagine that they are rabbits, designing perfect hutches for themselves. Point out that their bodies are much bigger than the bodies of rabbits, and so their needs would be different. Provide yardsticks, tape measures, or lengths of string for the children to use as they decide how much space their own ideal hutches would require. Working in pairs or teams, have the children experiment with body positions, such as sitting upright on their haunches, and then use measuring tools or string, cut to length, to indicate roof height. Suggest that one child take three or four steps, while another notes the starting and ending point. Measure this distance to decide how long a child-rabbit hutch would need to be. Direct the children to lie in a comfortable sleeping position, while another child measures to see how much covered sleeping area would be needed. Discuss children's height, stride, and need to stretch, move, and curl up for comfortable sleep. Talk about every living thing's need for space to call its own.

To Simplify:

● Use yourself as the hypothetical "rabbit." Have the children measure around you with string, then cut it to length, as you demonstrate different postures and gaits. Label the strings as you tape them to a chalkboard or piece of chart paper. Use masking tape on the floor or a sidewalk later to mark out your hutch dimensions. Cut a piece of wooden dowel or a stick to show height.

To Extend:

● Call local appliance stores, or elicit the help of families, to acquire discarded packing cartons of large dimensions. Provide the children with the cartons (and extra adult help if possible) so that they can create their own hutch designs. Emphasize ideas about the amount of space their bodies take up in relation to the dimensions of their hutches. Talk about how many children could, or would want to, get in the hutches at one time. Leave these structures available for exploring spatial relationships. Use this activity to introduce measuring tools. After using string to determine dimensions, show the children how the lengths equate to marks on yardsticks and measuring tapes. Then use these measurements to learn about the size of the cartons, or to change the size of the cartons, using sturdy scissors or box knives in the hands of adult demonstrators.

Pretend Play

1. The Cottontail Household

After the children have heard the story of Peter Rabbit and his Cottontail friends, add some props to an existing housekeeping area representing the spaces outside their household. Create a garden with large pieces of packing Styrofoam, foam rubber, or flat cardboard crates. Purchase some plastic fruits, vegetables, and flowers with wire stems. Push the wire stems into the foam or cardboard bases. Purchase decorative, colored pompons from fabric or craft stores to represent berries.

Invite the children to bring the rabbit ears and tails that they made earlier (see "Making Rabbit Ears," page 384), or construct some ears by mounting cardboard shapes on plastic headbands. Fold over the wide edge of the ears and staple them around the bands. Add a flannelboard and some rabbit story characters, rabbit puppets, or stuffed rabbit toys. Find a hat that can serve as Mister McGregor's hat. Add a watering can or two. Make available one or more copies of books about rabbits, such as *The Tale of Peter Rabbit, The Tale of Benjamin Bunny, The Tale of the Flopsy Bunnies*, and *The Story of a Fierce Bad Rabbit*, all by Beatrix Potter, which you can read aloud or which children can read for themselves. These stories also can serve as sources for more play themes.

2. Pet Shop

Set up a pretend pet shop in your classroom. Include toy rabbits, animal carrying cages, empty pet food containers, water dishes, and pet toys. Include special hats or aprons for store personnel to wear, and play money for customers to carry. Invite the children to make name tags that describe their jobs in the store: manager, animal feeder, cage cleaner, clerk, or rabbit expert. Add a cash register, telephone, note pad, and pencils. Hang a few posters of pets, including plenty of rabbits. Make, or invite the children to make, signs that describe store hours, special sales, OPEN and CLOSED designations, and a name for the store that the children agree on. Suggest that the children make posters describing breeds and characteristics of rabbits and other pets. As the children complete other projects from this mini-theme, such as rabbit care guides or pictures of rabbits, suggest that they display them in this area.

3. Rabbit Charades

After the children have had opportunities to become familiar with many fictional stories about rabbits, suggest that they act out scenes from some of them while other children watch and attempt to guess which story they are seeing a scene from. Provide props, such as those listed in "The Cottontail Household" lists (at left), as well as a basket and some plastic fruit for the story *Mister Rabbit and the Lovely Present*. Examine some of the other books you have read for ideas about simple props.

To Simplify:

● Act out a story yourself first, challenging the children to guess which one it is. Then invite one or two children to act one out while you guess. Next, suggest that children act out stories for each other.

To Extend:

● Develop a multi-day small group experience wherein groups of children choose stories to enact on day 1, negotiate and rehearse roles on day 2, and create costumes and props on day 3. On day 4, help children through dress rehearsals, using the props and costumes. Spend day 5 creating invitations and tickets to the performance. Send these home, with a note of explanation, to families. Put on performances early the next week, with families joining you as an audience. You may want to provide another day or two of practice early in the second week so that the children can become comfortable in their roles again, and decide on last-minute changes. Expect to serve as a coach and cue master as the children perform their stories. Many of them may hesitate and forget with others watching. Praise all attempts at recall, and respect the preferences of some children to join the audience rather than the performance troupes. Reluctant actors may want to help with setup, costume donning, or ticket collection instead.

Social

1. Searching for Rabbits

Remind the children that you have all been learning a lot about rabbits, and that the room is full of evidence of that fact. There are child-produced pictures and projects, posters, books, and more that would let classroom visitors know what you have been studying. Tell children that the purpose of this activity is to work together, searching for evidence of rabbits. Organize the children into groups of four or five members. Give each group the following checklist and, if possible, a clipboard on which to carry it. Make sure that each group has a pencil. Then, challenge the groups to move around the room, either all at the same time, or one after another for some period of time, looking for the things they must find to complete their checklists. When all of the groups have completed their searches, invite group members to tell others in the class about what they found and where various things were.

To Simplify:

● Have just one group at a time work on this project. Go with that group, helping them to determine what each statement says. Allow the group members to take turns checking off items as they are found. Write locations as children dictate, or skip this step. Provide colored crayons for the children to mark on the lines that indicate rabbit colors, rather than having them write a color name. Help the children decide whether they can all agree on a favorite rabbit, or whether they would like to record more than one favorite. Repeat these steps with each group until all groups have had a chance to complete the activity with your help.

Rabbit Search Checklist

Group Members' Names:

_____

_____

_____

_____

_____

We found a:	Where?

Floppy-earred rabbit_____

Upright-earred rabbit_____

Angora rabbit _____

Doe rabbit _____

Rabbit kitten _____

Food that a rabbit eats_____

We found rabbits in all these colors:

_____

_____

_____

We counted this many pictures of rabbits:

_____

We decided that the following object would be a safe toy for a rabbit:

_____

We decided that the following object would be a dangerous toy for a rabbit:

_____

We agreed that our favorite rabbit was:

_____

(After studying this list yourself, either add to the room anything that is missing, or adapt the list to your own circumstances before distributing it to the children.)

2. Rabbit Garden Mural

Remind the children that if a rabbit could go anywhere it wanted to, many rabbits would choose gardens. Discuss all the good things a rabbit might find in a garden. Provide the children with one or more long strips of roll paper that have been taped to a wall or laid on a long table. Provide multiple colors of construction paper, markers or crayons, glue sticks, and scissors. Add pipe cleaners, yarn, tissue squares, cotton balls, and other art objects. Invite the children to work together to create a rabbit-garden mural to decorate the classroom. Tell them that they can choose to use the materials in any way they think of to add to the group garden. Suggest that some children may want to make rabbits, while others make garden foods, soil, plant leaves, and so on. Mention that some people may want to make things and then glue them to the mural, while others may choose to draw right on the mural paper. Remind them to respect other people's space, but that everyone will be contributing and sharing the space. Remind children that the final product will belong to everyone together. Praise helpful and cooperative behaviors as you observe them. Make suggestions about ways of working together: some children may want to draw foods or rabbits for others to cut out and glue in place. Some children may want to make carrot bottoms for other children's carrot tops.

3. Soft as a Bunny

After a discussion of the many textures and types of rabbit fur that represent various breeds of rabbits, invite children to enlist the help of their families to find something in their homes that is as soft as a bunny. Send a note home with the children explaining that you have asked them to bring something to school that reminds them of rabbit fur to share with their friends. Assure the families that you will all try to be careful with the objects that come, and to send them back home after enjoying them. Collect a few soft objects yourself to offer to children who may forget or be unable to find an object that they are interested in sharing. On the following day, set aside some time for the children to show and tell about what they have brought. If you are concerned that children in your group will grow restless as everyone shares, then have the children form smaller groups so that only five or six children are taking turns in each separate location.

Hint for Success:

● At the outset of the activity, encourage the children to decide whether others may handle their objects, or whether they are just to look and ask questions, or perhaps touch them briefly as the owner retains custody.

Teacher Resources

Field Trip Ideas

1. Visit a pet store, either to select a rabbit for your program to adopt, or to look at a variety of rabbits. Ask the store personnel to tell you some things about different breeds of rabbits, and to describe the daily care that their rabbits get. Request a tour of the store, with concentration on pets that are similar to and quite different from rabbits. Ask questions about similar and different needs and preferences among the pets that live in the store.

2. Visit a rabbit breeder. Look in the Yellow Pages™ under "Livestock"; call any numbers listed, asking if they breed rabbits or know anyone who does. When contacting the rabbit breeder to arrange your visit, ask if there are kittens (baby rabbits) available to look at and, if not, when they are expected. Send a list of the Terms, Facts, and Principles ahead of time so the breeder will be aware of the focus of your study. You may want to inquire about whether the breeder's business is growing meat rabbits (as a food for grocery stores or individuals). If so, decide whether to explain to children ahead of time that some people eat rabbits.

3. Visit a meadowland or wildlife area where rabbits live. Tell the children that although rabbits live there, they are very careful animals and may decide to stay hidden during your visit. Remind the children to keep calm and alert if they hope to see rabbits. If no rabbits appear, draw the children's attention to the features of the environment that attract rabbits to make their homes there.

Classroom Visitors

1. Send a letter to families with children in your program, requesting that anyone with a pet rabbit bring it to visit your classroom. If you find no volunteers, call local pet stores, farms, or livestock breeders to see if any have rabbits and are willing to visit your program with one or more of them. If you have 4-H programs or Future Farmers of America (FFA) clubs in your area, they may also be sources of information about local rabbit breeders.

2. Invite a veterinarian to visit your program. Inform him or her that you have been learning about rabbits as potential pets and would like information about proper care. Ask the vet to bring tools or equipment, such as nail clippers, to show to the children.

Children's Books

Bate, L. (1988). *Little Rabbit's Loose Tooth*. New York: Crown Books for Young Readers.

Brown, M. W. (1942). *The Runaway Bunny*. New York: HarperCollins.

Heyward, D. (1974). *The Country Bunny and the Little Gold Shoes*. Boston: Houghton Mifflin.

Hunter, S. (1986). *Hop to It*. Hauppauge, NY: Barron's.

Mathews, L. (1991). *Bunches and Bunches of Bunnies*. New York: Scholastic.

Piers, H. (1992). *Taking Care of Your Rabbit: A Young Pet Owner's Guide*. Hauppauge, NY: Barron's.

Potter, B. (1989). *The Complete Tales of Beatrix Potter*. London, England: Penguin Group.

Royston, A. (1992). *See How They Grow: Rabbit*. Photographs by Barrie Watts. New York: Dutton Children's Books.

Wells, R. (1979). *Max's First Word, Max's New Suit, Max's Ride*. (A series of simple board books about a little boy/rabbit character.) New York: Dial Books for Young Readers, 1979.

Zolotow, C. (1962). *Mr. Rabbit and the Lovely Present*. New York: HarperCollins.

Adult References

The National Research Council. (1977). *Nutrient Requirements of Rabbits*, 2nd ed. Washington, DC: National Academy Press.

Sandford, J. C. (1986). *The Domestic Rabbit*. London: Collins.

Vriends-Parent, L. (1989). *The New Rabbit Handbook*. Hauppauge, NY: Barron's.

Wegler, M. (1990). *Rabbits: A Complete Pet Owner's Manual*. Hauppauge: NY: Barron's.

Gerbils

Terms, Facts, and Principles (TFPs)

Origins

1. Gerbils are tiny tamed rodents.

2. Gerbils' ancestors came from Mongolia (part of China).

3. The name *gerbil* means jerboa-like; gerbils were given this name because they are similar to a larger rodent (jerboa) in Mongolia, Middle East, and North Africa.

*4. In the wild, gerbils live in very dry places called *deserts*, and hibernate in underground burrows when the weather is cold.

*5. Gerbils were brought to the United States for use as laboratory animals for scientific experiments. When people saw how easily tamed gerbils are, they began to keep some gerbils as pets.

Physical Characteristics of Gerbils

6. Gerbils are male or female.

7. Fully grown gerbils are between three and four inches long, have four legs, furry bodies, and long, fur-covered tails.

8. Gerbils come in various colors: black, white, silver-grey, brown, lilac, and several color combinations.

9. Healthy gerbils have large bright eyes, glossy coats, dry noses, excellent hearing, and filled-out bodies.

*10. Gerbils have been described as looking like tiny kangaroos because their front legs are short and their back legs are larger and very strong.

*11. Gerbils are grown up when they are three months old.

*12. Gerbils usually live until they are between two and three years old, then they die.

Behaviors of Gerbils

13. Gerbils build nests for sleeping and for protecting their babies.

14. Gerbils are often active during the daytime and sleep at night.

15. Happy gerbils are curious and explore their environment by climbing, running, standing on their hind legs, jumping, and playing.

16. When gerbils are frightened they hide, try to escape or bite in self-defense.

*17. Like other rodents, gerbils have front teeth that keep growing all their lives; to keep their teeth from getting too long, they must gnaw things.

18. Gerbils eat very little food; they need a simple diet of grains, seeds, and bits of fresh clean vegetables and fruits.

19. Gerbils drink a tiny bit of water (perhaps a thimble full) every day.

20. Gerbils eat foods where they find them, carry them back to the nest, or hide their food by covering it with bedding material.

*21. Gerbils are social animals and prefer to live with other gerbils from their litter (their brothers and sisters); gerbils that are not from the same litter usually fight with each other.

*22. Male gerbils mark their territory (home turf) by rubbing special glands located on their bellies over the area. This behavior is called *skimming*.

*23. If a grown male and a female are kept together, they can produce a litter of baby gerbils by the time they are four months old.

*24. Gerbils usually have four to five baby gerbils at one time.

*25. Gerbil parents share the care of their babies. This is unlike most other rodent parents in which the female cares for the young alone. A gerbil mother feeds her babies by giving them milk through tiny nipples on her belly; father gerbils can help with other jobs such as rearranging the nest, washing the babies, returning strays to the nest, and keeping the babies warm.

Handling and Caring for Gerbils

26. Caretakers for gerbils can be adults or children.

27. Gerbils may be handled gently for short periods of time.

*28. The best way to pick up a gerbil is for the person to slowly place a hand near the gerbil, let the animal see and sniff it, then lift the gerbil using thumb and forefinger at the base of its tail (near the body), while cupping his or her other hand under the animal's body. The person should curl his or her hand loosely around the gerbil's back and place thumb and fingers around its neck, holding the gerbil gently without squeezing.

*29. Gerbils react to handling in various ways. At first the gerbil usually cooperates and tolerates handling for a short time; it may enjoy scratching behind the ear or petting on the back. Before long it becomes more nervous and seeks to escape; the gerbil may move quickly, scratching with tiny claws or biting if it feels afraid, has been held too long, or is held too tightly.

30. Caretakers should provide gerbils with a home that is clean and escape-proof, that is kept at a moderate temperature, that is dry and free from drafts. Satisfactory homes can be made from an empty, dry fish aquarium with a cover that allows for air circulation, a wire cage, or a commercially made plastic labyrinth with air holes.

31. Caretakers should provide dry bedding material to absorb moisture and help the gerbils move about in comfort. Satisfactory bedding may be two to three inches of ground corncobs, shredded wood shavings, wood chips, sawdust, or processed alfalfa. Caretakers should avoid using newspaper for bedding because ink stains the animals. Any bedding that has become damp should be promptly replaced, and the entire cage should be cleaned out every two to three weeks.

32. Gerbils need nesting materials such as white paper, paper towels, cardboard tubes, clean strips of cloth, or cotton batting.

33. Gerbils need a continuous supply of gnawing materials such as pieces of soft wood, cardboard, twigs, or dog biscuits.

34. Gerbils need a supply of fresh water; caretakers should attach one or more water bottles with drinking tubes to the side of the cage and change the water frequently.

35. Gerbils need exercise and breaks from the monotony of life in a cage; caretakers should offer an interesting, safe environment in which to explore and play.

36. Caretakers should feed gerbils dry food once a day.

37. Occasionally caretakers should give gerbils a special treat such as clean dandelion greens, clover, shepherd's purse, yarrow, mealworms, low-fat cottage cheese, a dog biscuit, or tiny branches from beech, maple, willow, or fruit trees.

*38. Gerbils are curious about new objects and surroundings. They respond to training using food rewards and can learn many things such as how to come when called by name, take food from a caretaker's hand, approach when they hear a particular signal, climb a designated object, or enter a specific opening.

*39. Caretakers should keep gerbils safe from dangers in the classroom such as: falling from high places, chewing on dangerous objects (such as electric wires, stained or varnished woods, or poisonous plants), attacks by other pets, or accidentally being stepped on, dropped, or squeezed too tightly.

*40. Since gerbils can produce many babies very quickly, it is best for caretakers to keep grown male and female gerbils in separate cages to prevent them from mating.

*41. When mating is desired, caretakers can place one male and one female together when they are about nine weeks old; the gerbils will gradually get used to each other, mate, and stay paired for their whole lives. In these circumstances, caretakers should provide additional nesting materials and a secluded nesting place (a small box or flowerpot turned on its side).

Activity Ideas

Aesthetic

1. Gerbil Pictures

After children have had many opportunitites to see the gerbils in the classroom for a few days, point out some of their body parts and behaviors. Then encourage children to make pictures of their ideas of a gerbil using markers, pencils, chalk, or crayons on paper. Organize the drawing materials near the gerbil cage so children have models to watch as they are drawing. Tell them to make their pictures in their own ways, encouraging them to use this activity to express something they notice, feel, or think about the gerbils. Display their drawings in a prominent spot in the room.

Hint for Success:

● Accept all kinds of drawing, including scribbling if children have not reached a realistic stage in their art. Avoid drawing for the child since this indicates to him or her that there is only one right way to draw gerbils, the teacher's way. If a child needs help getting started, talk with him or her about the parts of the gerbil that can be seen and how those parts fit together; then leave the child to create his or her own kind of picture. Check in with children later and, rather than giving your opinion of what they have produced, comment on the amount of effort they have put in, the colors they have chosen, and/or the techniques they decided to use.

To Simplify:

● Provide children with one medium (pencils, markers, chalk, or crayons) with which to make their pictures.

To Extend:

● After children have made one or more drawings of the gerbils, invite them to use paint, clay, or modeling dough to make a three-dimensional representation of a gerbil.

2. Make It a Gerbil Song

Sing a song (or say familiar rhymes) that include mention of a rodent (mouse, rat, squirrel, hamster, chipmunk, etc.) and substitute the word *gerbil* for the animal. Have fun with this activity, changing other words or phrases in the song as necessary to help support the rhyme or rhythm. Examples of rodent songs with which to experiment are: "Hickory Dickory Dock," "Three Blind Mice," or "The Little Grey Mouse."

♫ **The Little Grey Mouse (Traditional)**

There was a little grey gerbil,
In a little grey house,
As lonesome as he could be.
So the little grey gerbil,
In the little grey house,
Invited company.

♫ **Hickory Dickory Dock (Traditional)**

Hickory dickory dock,
The gerbil ran up the clock.
The clock struck one,
The gerbil ran down,
Hickory dickory dock.

To Simplify:

● Do not assume children are familiar with the traditional form of each song. Select a song and teach the original words and tune first. After the class knows it well, suggest changes to make it a gerbil song.

To Extend:

● Have children look up the definition of a rodent, then make a list of as many as they can discover. With an expanded idea of rodents, ask children to suggest other songs that contain the name of a rodent; compile a list of songs that could be used for this game.

3. Gerbil Food Designs

Invite children to make pictures or designs using glue and a variety of gerbil foods arranged in a way that is pleasing to them. Provide pieces of cardboard, construction paper, or paper plates for a background and white glue for sticking on the items. Show children a variety of dry foods that gerbils like to eat and suggest they use them to make beautiful designs. Explain that some artists use many different kinds of materials, including parts of plants that rodents like to eat. Examples of this kind of collage art made with natural materials can be

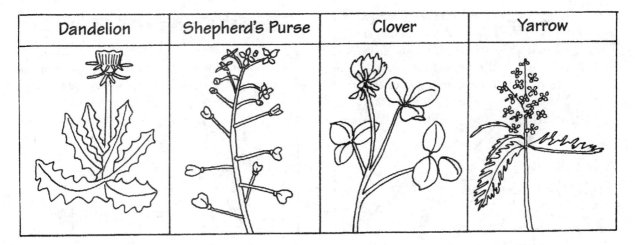

| Dandelion | Shepherd's Purse | Clover | Yarrow |

found in folk art books (such as *Folk Art of Asia, Africa, Australia, and the Americas* by Helmuth Bossert, 1990). Encourage children to use these materials to create their own kind of art in their own ways. Demonstrate how to apply glue to an area on the background and arrange the seeds and other materials in the glue. Allow the children's designs to dry laying flat.

Hint for Success:

● Purchase a commercially packaged gerbil mixture of seeds and grains, or look for individual items appropriate for gerbils to eat, such as various grains (for example, wheat, oats, barley, corn), and seeds (sunflower and other medium-sized seeds). Choose items that offer various colors and textures; feed some to the gerbils.

To Simplify:

● Limit the selection of gerbil foods to those that are easiest to handle.

To Extend:

● Introduce children to various foods for gerbils that people find in the outdoors, such as dandelion greens, clover, shepherd's purse, and yarrow. Show them pictures or samples of the weeds and point out ways to identify them. In the spring, take children on a walk outdoors to a nearby field or vacant lot to look for and gather these treats for gerbils. Wash the weeds and feed some to the gerbils; dry some between sheets of paper towels laid under heavy books for several days. Then use the weeds to make beautiful designs.

Affective

1. Me and the Gerbil

After children have seen the classroom gerbils for several days, tell children they are going to think about and compare what gerbils are like to what they (themselves) are like. Place a gerbil in a clear viewing box near a mirror where one child at a time can focus on making the comparison. Provide a tape recorder and an empty audiotape for children to use to record their thoughts. Suggest that children consider the statements: 1) I am like the gerbil because we both . . . . and 2) I am different from the gerbil because . . . .

To Simplify:

● Take dictation from each child, prompting children verbally and writing their responses on paper.

To Extend:

● Provide a response form using the statements above for children to fill in with their comparative ideas. After children have focused on the physical characteristics that they have or do not have in common with gerbils, encourage them to focus on behaviors. Add statements to their response form such as: 3) One thing gerbils do that I do too is . . . . 4) One thing gerbils do that I don't do is . . . .

2. I Can Care for the Gerbils

To enhance children's development of responsibility, include them as caretakers of the gerbils. As a group, brainstorm a list of jobs that are necessary to keep the gerbils happy and healthy each day. Make a "Gerbil Care Chart" to record how frequently children help pro-

Give Food

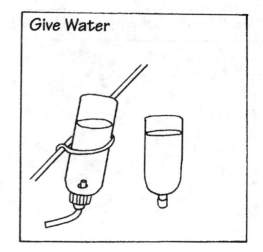

Give Water

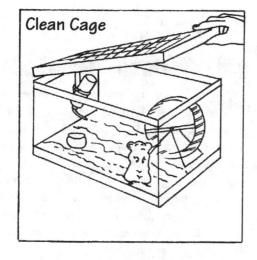

Clean Cage

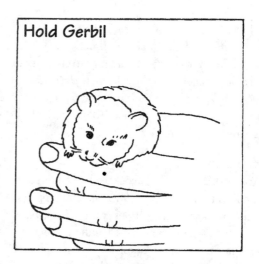

Hold Gerbil

vide care for the classroom pets. Write each child's name along one edge of the chart and record the jobs across the top; color code the jobs to correspond to a particular color sticker. Tell children that each time they do one of the care jobs, they can place that color sticker near their name. Plan a system of taking turns doing the various jobs, so each child gets an opportunity to share responsibility for the gerbils; teach the children how to do each task. Be sure to thank children when they do their job.

To Simplify:

● Place only one or two jobs on the chart. Use pictures next to the jobs to help children interpret what each one is. Assist children in carrying out their tasks until they can do them without your help.

To Extend:

● Challenge children to include the jobs that are done weekly, and occasionally. Expand the "Gerbil Care Chart" to include these two categories of jobs and plan particular days that these tasks will be carried out. Mark those jobs on a class calendar.

3. Chewy Things from Home

Help children feel proud about making a contribution to the care of the gerbils by suggesting that they bring something from home that helps gerbils. Point out the fact that gerbils, unlike people, have special teeth that keep growing all their lives; they need things to chew on so their teeth won't get too long. Show children examples of good chewing items that they may occasionally bring to school, such as a small twig from a tree, a cardboard tube (toilet paper or paper towel roll), or a small bit of soft wood. Show the children a sign you'll place near the gerbil cage that says

I Brought One Chewing Thing for Our Gerbils Today

Leave a space at the bottom for children to write their names. When children bring in items for this purpose, suggest that they sign their name and allow them, if possible, to place the chew item into the cage. Encourage them to watch as the gerbils go to work chewing the new materials.

Hint for Success:

● If many items are brought on the same day, it will be necessary to limit the number of chewing items placed into the cage at one time so the gerbils aren't overwhelmed. A good way to manage this is to decide ahead of time how many things can be added to the cage at a time; place a box or basket nearby to hold any extra items. Be sure to allow children to give their contribution to the gerbils as soon as possible after they bring it. Help extend the learning to home by sending a note to parents giving them information about what's requested, how frequently it will be needed, and why.

Sample Note to Parents

Dear Parents,

We have some gerbils in our classroom to teach children about caring for a pet and about things that animals do. Gerbils are small, tame rodents that are fun to watch and easy to care for.

YOU CAN HELP.

Gerbils need to chew on things to keep their teeth healthy and trim. Our gerbils will need daily chewing items for this purpose. Your child could occasionally bring to school one of the following:

- an empty cardboard tube (toilet paper or paper towel roll)
- a small bit of soft wood (untreated pine is best)
- a small twig from a beech, maple, willow, or fruit tree

Please do *not* allow children to bring treated wood, stained or varnished wood, or dangerous pieces of wood containing nails or staples.

Thanks for your help in keeping our gerbils happy and healthy.

To Simplify:

● Suggest only one chewing item such as paper tubes.

To Extend:

● Ask children to observe the gerbils' chewing habits to see which kind of chewing items they seem to like the best. Next, ask children, either individually or as a group, to compose a second note home, telling parents what they have discovered and requesting more of that item.

Cognitive

1. Observing the Gerbils

Give children practice carefully looking and noticing things that happen in the gerbil cage. Explain that when they do this careful looking or observing, they are behaving just like scientists. Place the gerbils at eye level so children can see them easily. Encourage youngsters to closely observe the animals by modeling this behavior yourself. Show them how to watch, point out something you saw, and write it on paper. Then, place several clipboards with paper and pencil near the gerbil cage for children to record what they observe.

To Simplify:

● Write children's observations for them or suggest they write their own in any form of writing they can. Later, ask them to read what they wrote to you. Make a note that you can attach to the back of the child's note.

To Extend:

● Compile all of the children's observations into a notebook about the gerbils entitled: "What We Observed About Our Gerbils." Read notebook entries to the group and ask the children questions based on the information they recorded. For example, if several children noticed the gerbils chewing on paper tubes and none chewing on the piece of wood in the cage, questions to ask could be "Why do you think the gerbils aren't chewing on the wood? Is that a problem? What can we do about that?"

2. Tiny Kangaroos?

For several days before this activity, give children time to become familiar with the gerbils in the classroom. Encourage them to watch the animals' behavior and notice what they can do. Next, place one or more pictures of kangaroos near the gerbil cage. Explain that people have compared gerbils to kangaroos. Tell children to continue watching the gerbils and see if they can notice any similarities to kangaroos. After children observe, ask them to tell what similarities they noticed.

To Simplify:

● Leave a large piece of paper near the gerbil cage to record children's observations as they notice similarities. Write the name of the observer and what she or he saw.

To Extend:

● Encourage experienced children to learn more about kangaroos and gerbils. Suggest they consult books, ask knowledgeable people, or look for other pictures. Using this new information, suggest that the children look for both similarities and differences between gerbils and kangaroos.

3. All About Rodents

Introduce children to the concept of rodents by reading one or more realistic stories to them about a rodent that is not a gerbil (such as a mouse, chipmunk, squirrel, or hamster). Two good books for this activity are Thomas Ulrich's *Applemouse* (1971) and Brian Wildsmith's *Squirrels* (1987). Before reading the stories, explain that they are about a kind of animal called a *rodent*. Ask children to listen carefully so that they can remember something about the rodent in the story, either the way it looks or how it behaves. After reading the books, ask children to tell what they remember, generating a list of rodent characteristics. Suggest they compare this list to the gerbils in their classroom to see if they think gerbils are rodents, too.

Hint for Success:
● Avoid selecting stories in which the rodents act like people by speaking, wearing clothes, or otherwise behaving in unrealistic ways.

To Simplify:
● Instead of several stories, select one story to read about a rodent.

To Extend:
● Suggest children find other books about rodents to share with their classmates. Request books from home, or take the children to a library to look for books about rodents, including gerbils. Place a number of resources about rodents in one area of the room. Provide time for interested children to investigate the topic and encourage them to report new things they learn about rodents by writing, tape-recording their findings, or telling the group.

4. Will They Eat It?

To involve children in the scientific process, ask them to predict if their classroom gerbils will eat a new kind of food. Using the list of occasional foods (see TFP 37), select one food item that the gerbils have not tried (such as mealworms, low-fat cottage cheese, or dandelion greens). Show this new food to the children; suggest they act like scientists and do an experiment with the gerbils. Explain to them that they should first

watch the animals eating their regular food (observe), then guess if they will like the new kind of food (predict), and tell why they think that (hypothesize). Write down everyone's prediction and their reasoning on a large piece of paper. Then, give the new food to the gerbils and encourage children to notice what the animals do with it (test out). Ask them to consider whether their predictions were correct or not (evaluate) and ask them to say why.

To Simplify:
● Use only one gerbil for this experiment; place the pet in a clear container so children can see it easily.

To Extend:
● Repeat the experiment another day in small groups (using a different food for each group). Help children write their predictions on an individual prediction sheet called, "An Experiment About Gerbils and Foods They Will Eat." Ask each child about her or his reasoning before the experiment and again after seeing the result. Have children report to the whole class about their predictions and the results of their experiment.

An Experiment About Gerbils and Foods They Will Eat

My name _____

The food _____

My Prediction (What Will Happen?)
☐ YES   The gerbils will eat it.
☐ NO   The gerbils will *not* eat it.

Why Will This Happen?
_____
_____

What Happened?
☐ They ate the food.
☐ They did *not* eat the food.

Why Did This Happen?
_____
_____

● As a follow-up to the food experiments, make a Gerbil Food Graph showing the various foods your class gave the gerbils and whether they ate it or not.

5. Counting Gerbils

Use small counters such as Unifix® cubes, stones, or shells to play a counting game. Give each child a "gerbil nest" (a three-inch paper circle). Each player in turn rolls one die and takes a corresponding number of "gerbils" (counters) to place in his or her nest. Players should count their gerbils at the beginning of their turn and announce how many they have before rolling the die. Players continue to add to their nest until the nest is full. When their nest is full, they say, "My nest is full." On their next roll, they start to take "gerbils" out of their nest corresponding to the number on the die, and continue in this same way on each turn until the nest is empty. At that time the player should say, "My nest is empty," and begin to fill it on the next roll. Play continues as long as interest continues.

6. Gerbil Patterns

After children have had other experiences making patterns, gather children together and introduce making patterns with paper gerbils. Show the children a collection of small paper circles of various colors (black, grey, brown, white, and lilac). Explain to children that you are pretending these circles are gerbils. Point out the fact that the colors are real colors of gerbils. Encourage children to play with the paper "gerbils" for a few minutes. Have children make piles of each color and set them aside. Then say, "Now we'll pretend these gerbils are walking in a line going home in a special way, forming a pattern. Watch me first." Line up nine circles on the floor creating a pattern with two black, then one grey; repeat in the established pattern: black, black, grey; black, black, grey; black, black, grey. Read the pattern aloud, saying the names of the colors as you point to each one. Ask children to help you read the pattern. While pointing to the empty space at the end of the line, ask, "What color comes next in the pattern?" Then tell each child to take six circles of one color, and three of another color; they are to make the same pattern using different colors in front of them and to read it aloud when finished. Next, encourage them to put their circles back and take different ones to make another "gerbil" pattern of their own choosing using a different color combination. Ask them to read aloud any pattern they complete and tell what color gerbil would come next.

Hint for Success:

● Children will have more success with this activity if you provide daily opportunities to work with rhythmic patterns as well. Use sound/motion cues with your hands in a pattern such as:

clap, clap, slap (*on legs*); clap, clap, slap; clap, clap, slap; and so on.

Continue making the pattern and invite children to join you. When children can repeat this simple pattern, change it slightly:

clap, clap, snap (fingers); clap, clap, snap; clap, clap, snap; and so on.

clap, clap, wave (hand); clap, clap, wave; clap, clap, wave; and so on.

To Simplify:

● Make a simpler pattern to begin, such as: black, grey; black, grey; black, grey.

To Extend:

● Place the materials at the math learning center for a week or more. Suggest children make up their own patterns by rearranging the two colors or using more than two colors. Later add another dimension to their thinking by supplying the area with a new size of paper gerbils (tiny). Give an example such as: small white, tiny white, small black; small white, tiny white, small black. Challenge children to use these materials to make other patterns.

Preparing the Materials: Laminate several sheets of each color (black, grey, brown, white, and lilac) construction paper; cut as many circles as your class will need so each child will have at least nine circles at a time to use. (For example, for a group of twenty-five children, cut twenty-five two-inch circles.) If different sizes are needed to extend the activity, cut ten one-inch circles of each color.

7. Gerbil Numbers

Help children develop problem-solving skills using gerbil facts.

Gerbil Games: Teach children that gerbils like to live and play with other gerbils. Using counters of some kind (such as Unifix® cubes, buttons, or paper "gerbils"), ask children to show a group of three gerbils. Then ask them to figure out how many gerbils there would be: 1) if one more came to play, 2) if two went back to the nest to sleep, or 3) if two more joined them.

Litter Numbers: Teach children that gerbil babies are born in a litter that usually has four babies. Using counters of some kind (such as Unifix® cubes, buttons, or paper "gerbils"), ask children to make a litter of four baby gerbils. Then ask them to figure out how many babies they would have in two litters, three litters, or four litters.

Gerbil Age: Teach children that gerbils are born, grow up, get old, and usually die when they are three years old. Using counters for years, have the children each make a line that shows how old they are right now. Then ask them, "If a gerbil were born today and lived for three years, how old would you be when it died?"

To Simplify:

● Focus on the "Gerbil Games" only, using very small numbers.

To Extend:

● Use slightly larger numbers for the problems. Challenge interested children to make up problems of their own. Write the problems and their solutions, displaying them in a special place.

8. Life in the Desert

Discuss the fact that wild gerbils live in the desert. Ask children what they know about the desert, listening to each child's ideas. Then explain that you are going to read them a story about a man who lives in the desert. Suggest that children notice as many things about the desert as they can. Read the book *Alejandro's Gift* (1994) by Richard Albert to the class, showing children the pictures as you read. When the story is finished, ask children to tell something they noticed about the desert. Write down what they recall, and prompt more thinking by asking about the animals, plants, and what kind of weather they heard about or saw in the story. Did they see a gerbil in the desert? Did they see an animal that looked a bit like a gerbil? Suggest that children make pictures of what they think a desert is like. Provide crayons and large paper for this activity.

To Simplify:

● Focus on easy-to-recall characteristics such as the animals that came to drink water.

To Extend:

● Ask children to contribute to learning more about a desert by bringing in objects related to this part of the world. Suggest they arrange an area of the room with real objects one might find in a desert (rocks, cactus, sand), pictures of deserts, and books about deserts; add a globe of the earth with large deserts marked in some way. Suggest that interested children locate information about the Mongolian, North African, and Middle Eastern deserts where gerbils live in the wild.

Construction

1. Gerbil Nests

Point out the way the gerbils pull materials together to make a sleeping place. Encourage children to watch as the gerbils work on this task. Then provide children with a variety of materials to use to build their own kind of nest for a pretend gerbil. Paper bowls, paste, torn bits of paper, wood shavings, twigs, strips of cloth, cotton balls, string, and yarn can be used for this project.

2. Gerbil Toys

Make a "playground" for the gerbils from a plastic wading pool. Spread a layer of bedding material on the bottom of the pool and place one or two gerbils at a time in the playground for children to watch. Provide an exercise wheel for running and a small cardboard box for them to climb on, over, under, and through. At a nearby table, challenge children to make a toy with which the classroom pets could have fun. Provide paper tubes, masking tape, wooden dowels, paper, small cardboard boxes, scissors, oatmeal boxes, and other safe materials to make tunnels, low bridges, steps, slides, swings, a seesaw, or a maze for the gerbils.

3. My Own Kind of Gerbil

Show children a large picture of a gerbil. Ask them to name some of the parts of a gerbil they notice, such as the body, head, feet, tail, and ears. Explain that everyone can make his or her own kind of gerbil from different materials around the room, such as modeling dough (or clay), wet sand, craft sticks with glue, building blocks, or other available construction materials. Encourage the children to choose a material and begin working. Offer help when children are ready to label and display their creations, such as "My gerbil, made from wood, by Emily." If children have used a material that cannot be permanently displayed such as Legos® or other building blocks used each day, take a picture of their constructions before they are dismantled. Display the pictures in a special place where children can see them. Help children label their picture.

Hint for Success:

● As children make their gerbils, avoid giving them advice or insisting they make realistic-looking creations. Instead, comment about the materials they have chosen to use and how they are working.

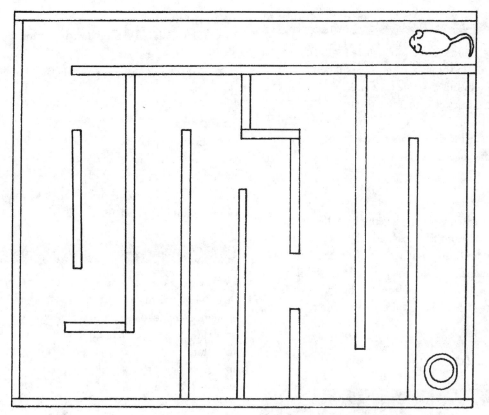

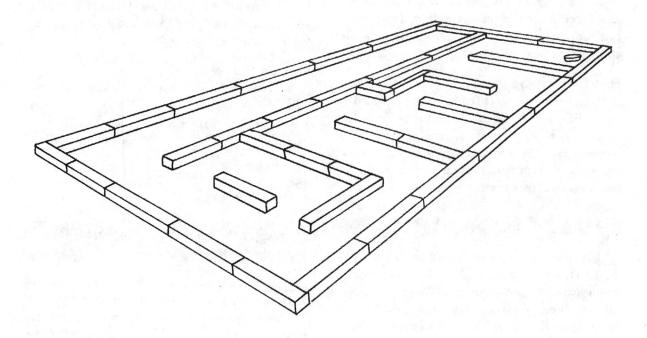

4. Amazing Gerbil Maze

Challenge children to create a maze for the classroom gerbils to run through. Introduce children to the idea of a maze by drawing one on a large piece of paper. Give them a paper gerbil to move through the maze to practice getting from the start to the finish. After children have played with the paper maze, suggest they use blocks to work together to create a real maze for the gerbils.

Hint for Success:

● Before actually placing a gerbil into the maze, avoid having to hunt for a lost gerbil by checking the construction for openings where an excited rodent may be able to escape. Also, for the pet's safety, establish guidelines for how close children may be and how they should behave when the gerbil is in the maze.

Language

1. Words That Tell About Gerbils

Offer children an opportunity to hold a gerbil with adult supervision. Afterwards, ask them to suggest words that describe what the gerbil was like. Have the children take turns holding an animal and then tape-record their descriptive words (adjectives). Later, play back the tape for the group and write a list of the words children used to describe the pet.

Hint for Success:

● Show children how to cup their fingers around the gerbil's body without squeezing it too tightly. To protect the gerbil from being hurt in a fall, hold it over a soft surface such as a lap, a towel on a table, or a cushioned box in case it jumps away. Hold each gerbil for a limited amount of time; then return it to the safety of its cage.

2. My Gerbil Book

Help children make an individual book about a gerbil that they can read. Suggest they make page one: a picture of a gerbil, page two: what gerbils like to eat, page three: something gerbils like to do, and a last page showing the best thing about gerbils. As children complete each page, urge them to compose a caption for that page, writing the words in their own form of writing. Provide a simple cover for each book and bind the pages together with yarn, staples, or notebook rings.

To Simplify:

● Give children several days to complete their books, one page each day.

● Take dictation from individual children and write their words on each page as they complete it.

To Extend:

● Encourage children to make up a title for their books. Urge them to write the title on the cover along with their name as the author.

● Ask children to read their book to you and to other children in the class.

3. Our Gerbil Story

Give children an opportunity to participate in a creative writing experience as a group by creating a sequence story about a gerbil's day. Working with one small group of six to eight children at a time, ask them to dictate a creative story about what happens to a gerbil in a given day. Prompt children with a lead sentence such as "Once upon a time, there was a gerbil who lived in a . . . ." Have children take turns telling a sentence or two of the story. Write down what they say, using their exact words whenever possible. If a child gets stuck, ask questions such as "And then what happened?" or "Then what did the gerbil do?" Write large enough for the children to be able to see the words clearly. Read the story back to the small group and then to the whole group. Display each group's story. Later encourage the writers to try reading the stories to each other.

Hint for Success:

● Focus on children being creative in this activity rather than accurately depicting what gerbils do. Allow fantastic implausible happenings to be used in their stories.

Physical

1. The Right Way to Hold a Gerbil

Give children many opportunities to practice picking up and holding a gerbil correctly. Demonstrate the skill using one or more stuffed pretend gerbils with which children may practice. Teach them to follow the steps below:

a. Move your hand slowly near the gerbil.

b. Grasp the base of the tail near the body.

c. Lift the gerbil up, cupping your other hand under the gerbil.

d. Hold the gerbil loosely around the neck and back.

After children demonstrate success with the pretend gerbil, allow them to hold a real gerbil. Place a gerbil in a small box such as a plastic dishpan or shoe box. Have the child sit on the floor with the box in front of him or her. Supervise the gerbil holding until children become skilled and comfortable doing it alone.

Making a Stuffed Gerbil: Stuff a small child's sock (or the toe of an adult sock) with cloth scraps or tissue paper; tie off or sew the end closed, and securely attach a yarn tail. Draw simple eyes and a nose on the front. Attach small paper ears.

2. Tunnel Crawling

Show children the way gerbils like to crawl through paper tubes and other tunnel-like tubes. Encourage children to have fun with this same kind of movement. Arrange one or more tunnels for children to crawl or move through in various ways. As children experiment with the tunnels, remind them they are moving like rodents do.

Hint for Success:

● Tunnels made of hard plastic, cloth, or pressboard are available commercially. Some sections of indoor or outdoor climbing sets are tunnel shaped. A tunnel can be made by draping one or more sheets or blankets over a rope that is suspended between two points, or over chairs or low tables that are arranged in a row.

3. Moving Through a Maze

Arrange a simple or complex maze for children to move through, either indoors or outdoors. A maze can be constructed using room dividers, cardboard cartons, furniture, sawhorses, climbing equipment, large hollow blocks, or similar large items to act as separators of space. Establish a beginning and an end. Encourage children to run, walk, crawl, skip, gallop, or move in other ways through the maze.

To Simplify:

● Instead of using large dividers for the maze, make a simpler one using standard wooden unit blocks laid end to end on the floor to form a sidewalk. Another kind of maze can be created by unravelling a ball of heavy string onto the floor forming a curvey line for children to walk on while moving around the room.

To Extend:

● Include parts of the maze that are dead ends, or offer choices of two or more ways, forcing children to make decisions about which way to go in order to get to the open end.

Pretend Play

1. Life in a Gerbil Cage

Arrange an area of the classroom with props that support children's pretending to be gerbils in a cage. A large appliance box or indoor climber would simulate a cage and accommodate two or three make-believe gerbils at a time. Provide children with, or suggest children make, simple gerbil "costumes" such as ears and tails to help them assume the roles of rodents. Encourage children to eat, build nests, drink from a pretend water source, climb, and move like gerbils do in their environment.

2. Pet Store

Encourage children to help set up and manage a pretend pet store that includes rodent pets. Arrange boxes for cages supplied with stuffed animals for pets. Include other props such as empty pet food boxes and cans, dog and cat toys, gerbil and hamster bedding bags, and a cash register. Children can make signs for the walls, place price tags on items, and pretend to be salespeople and customers.

Social

1. Naming Our Gerbils

Help all of the children share in the selection of names for the gerbils. Begin with a discussion of why people name their animals. Listen to children's ideas, helping them listen to each other. Generate a list of suggestions for names for the gerbils. Many very young or inexperienced children only know "people names," and may want to name the gerbils using their own names. Help the group decide if "people names" are acceptable for the pets. Ask children who have pets at home, or know someone's pet, to tell about the names they were given. Make suggestions of your own. Next, as a group, decide a fair way the decisions will be made.

Possibilities include:

    a. Everyone votes for her or his favorite name; most popular names win.

    b. Names are pulled from a hat.

    c. Children pick a person who chooses the names.

    d. Names are randomly eliminated using a street rhyme such as:

      "My mother said to pick the very best one; And you are not it."

      or "Monkey, monkey, bottle of pop; On which monkey do we stop?"

Hints for Success:

● Some children may feel it desirable to differentiate which gerbil has which name. If your gerbils look similar, challenge children to find some small way to recognize each one, and assign them the names chosen. Avoid the pitfall of having different groups of children name the pet(s) differently, (for example, morning and afternoon kindergarten groups). By assigning half of the gerbils to each class to name, unnecessary confusion can be avoided.

2. Turn-Taking with Gerbils

Help children take turns playing with the pet gerbils in their "gerbil playground." Decide how many children can safely be in the area at one time without over-stimulating or putting the gerbils at risk. Place a sign-up list near the area for children who wish to play with the gerbils as they get daily exercise. Encourage children to write their names on the list (or make a mark that means their names). Select an appropriate time limit for each turn and set a timer as a reminder to children. When one person finishes his or her turn, have the child tell the next person on the list that it's his or her turn to play with the gerbils.

3. Keeping Our Gerbils Safe

After children have had some experience with the gerbils, discuss the ways the class is keeping them safe. Ask children to contribute to a list of class safety rules about the pets. Hang the Gerbil Rules in a place where children can refer to them often.

Teacher Resources

Field Trip Ideas

1. Walk to a nearby field to find dandelion greens and other treats for the gerbils.

2. Visit a pet store to purchase the gerbils or gerbil supplies.

Classroom Visitors

1. Invite a veterinarian to visit the classroom and check the gerbils.

2. Invite a scientist who studies rodents to visit the class, and tell about his or her work.

Children's Books

Albert, E. R. (1994). *Alejandro's Gift*. San Francisco, CA: Chronicle Books.

Henrie, F. (1980). *Gerbils*. New York: Franklin Watts.

Petty, K. (1989). *Gerbils*. New York: Gloucester Press.

Ulrich, T. (1971). *Applemouse*. New York: Farrar, Straus & Giroux.

Wildsmith, B. (1987). *Squirrels*. Oxford: Oxford University Press.

Adult References

Bossert, H. T. (1990). *Folk Art of Asia, Africa, Australia, and the Americas*. New York: Rizzoli.

Child Study Association of America. (1969). *Pets and More Pets, Read-to-Yourself Stories of the City*. New York: HarperCollins.

Cole, J., and Calmenson., S. (1990). *Miss Mary Mack and Other Children's Street Rhymes*. New York: Morrow Junior Books.

The Encyclopedia of Gerbils. (1980). Neptune City, NJ: T.F.H. Publications.

Gudas, R. (1986). *Gerbils: Everything About Purchase, Care, Nutrition, Diseases, Breeding and Behavior*. Woodbury, NY: Barron.

Ostrom, M. (1980). *The T.F.H Book of Gerbils*. Neptune City, NJ: T.F.H. Publications.

Pope, J. (1987). *Taking Care of Your Gerbils*. New York: Franklin Watts.

Robinson, D. G. (1984). *Gerbils*. Neptune City, NJ: T.F.H. Publications.

Shuttlesworth, D. E. (1970). *Gerbils and Other Small Pets*. New York: Dutton.

Weber, W. J. (1979). *Care of Uncommon Pets: Rabbits, Guinea Pigs, Hamsters, Mice, Rats, Gerbils, Chickens, Ducks, Frogs, Toads and Salamanders, Turtles and Tortoises, Snakes and Lizards, and Budgerigars*. New York: Henry Holt.

Fish

Terms, Facts, and Principles (TFPs)

Characteristics

1. Fish are animals that live in water, breathe through gills, and have a skeleton inside their body.

2. Fish are cold blooded (their bodies usually stay at the same temperature as the water around them.)

3. Fish have fins, which help them to move in the water.

4. Fish use their fins for braking and steering. Fins help the fish to "stand still" in the water.

*5. Most fish have a swim bladder, a sac inside their body that is filled with air. The swim bladder helps keep fish from sinking or floating to the surface of the water.

*6. By varying the amount of air in its air bladder, a fish can adjust its body weight to equal the weight of water its body has displaced. The effect of this is to make the fish have almost no weight at all—it neither floats nor sinks, but remains suspended at whatever level it desires.

7. A fish's body is covered with a protective coat of scales. These scales usually overlap each other.

*8. Internal fish parts include the brain, spine, kidney, mouth, gills, heart, stomach, air bladder, and intestines.

9. External fish parts include eyes, nostrils, gill cover, lateral line, spiny dorsal fins, soft dorsal fin, pectoral fin, ventral fins, scales, anal fin, and tail fin.

10. Fish sometimes move by expelling water from their gills, which propels them quickly for a brief period.

*11. Fish breathe oxygen. They use the small amounts of oxygen dissolved in the water, absorbing it into their blood through their gills.

*12. If the oxygen in the water becomes used up, the fish cannot breathe.

13. Fish vary in color; some are colorful, some have little color, and some are almost transparent.

*14. Fish's colors may blend into their natural surroundings to protect them from their enemies.

15. Fish vary in size, shape, and texture. They may be long, thin, fat, flat, round, short, bumpy, or smooth.

16. Fish do not sleep. They rest for only short periods of time and keep their eyes open.

Kinds of Fish

17. Aquarium fish are not miniatures or babies of larger fish. They are types of fish that are small.

18. There are many kinds of fish. Each kind of fish has a different name, such as molly, goldfish, angelfish, guppy, and so on.

19. Some fish are hatched from eggs; others are born live.

20. Some fish live near the surface of the water, some stay in the middle of the tank, and others swim at the bottom of the aquarium.

21. Some fish swim together in groups called *schools*, other fish live alone.

22. Some fish live in warm water; others live in cold water.

23. Some fish live in salt water; others live in fresh water.

Environment

24. An aquarium is a place to keep fish.

25. Rocks and other objects on the aquarium bottom are replications of natural habitats.

26. Fish kept in a classroom usually live in a fishbowl or aquarium.

27. A fishbowl must have its water changed often to keep oxygen levels high for the fish to breathe.

28. Aquariums have an aeration system to circulate the water to renew oxygen and filter out waste products.

29. It is difficult or impossible for fish to live in polluted water.

30. Aquariums have a filter system to reduce waste in the water and filter out chemicals that are harmful to the fish over time.

31. Fish require water that is a certain temperature in order to live (usually between 72° to 86°).

32. Some aquariums have heaters to keep the temperature at the correct level. They have thermometers to let people know the temperature of water.

33. Most fish need periods of light and dark to live.

34. Most aquariums have an artificial light to supplement the natural light in the room.

*35. Proper care of an aquarium includes maintaining the filtration, aeration, heating, and lighting systems for the fish.

36. Aquascaping is the decorating of the aquarium floor and interior with plants, rocks, and gravel.

Study and Care

37. People often enjoy keeping fish as pets at home, school, or work.

38. Scientists who study fish are called *ichthyologists*.

39. A marine aquarist is a person who tries to reproduce the natural habitat for fish within a contained home aquarium.

40. Care of fish includes feeding them, keeping the water fresh and clean, and watching for and treating a variety of diseases that may occur.

41. For fish to be healthy it is important not to overfeed them and not to overcrowd the tank.

Activity Ideas

Aesthetic

1. Colorful Fish

Provide paper to be used on a table or easel on which you have drawn the outline of fish. Place pictures of aquarium fish on nearby walls or on the table for children to observe. Encourage the children to color their picture using crayons, markers, or watercolor paints. Invite the children to use multiple mediums and to mix them on each picture.

To Simplify:
● Provide a single coloring medium for the children.

To Extend:
● Have the children cut out their finished work for display. Add paper for the children to tear and glue as another medium to try.

2. Gluing Scales

Cut out fish shapes and place them on a table along with sequins, colorful paper scalelike shapes (paper circles made with a paper punch also make good scales), and white glue or glue sticks. Direct the children to decorate their fish using the materials provided.

Hint for Success:
● Do this activity after the children have observed live fish. Have the children look at the fish by shining small flashlights on them through the glass to see how the light reflects off the scales.

3. Fish Magic

Create props that will allow the children to take on the persona of fish as they participate in activities. This can be done in a variety of ways depending on

time, materials, and effort. Old T-shirts can be painted or decorated with markers to serve as a colorful body for the children as they play "fish." Paper bag vests also serve equally as effective although slightly more cumbersome. If making vests, small colored paper plates or cupcake paper liners can be attached to serve as fish scales. Fins can be attached by folding a large flexible paper plate in half allowing a half-inch middle section to secure it to the paper vest. Teachers can involve children in most or all of these steps. Talk with the children about the colors they are using and any patterns or designs in their painting. Upon completion, these can be shared in the pretend play activities to help the children act out "being" fish.

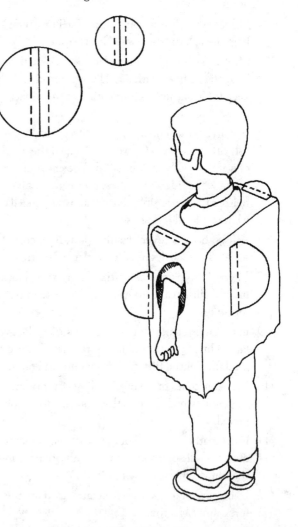

4. Fish Dance

Prepare for this activity by making fin-shaped paddles using colored pieces of paper plates that have been cut as illustrated here. Tape these fins to a tongue depressor to serve as the handle. You may wish to attach colored crepe paper strips to the fins to get a flowing effect. Select music that is calm and slow as an accompaniment to the children as they dance or move around the room pretending to be fish, using the fins for movement. Invite children to wear the T-shirts they created in the "Fish Magic" activity above.

Hints for Success:
● Tape record the bubbling sounds from the fish tank in the classroom or use a tape of other water sounds.

5. Fish Tank Backgrounds

Show children some examples of commercially prepared fish tank background scenes. Commonly these include plants, rocks, and fish and may have a variety of colors. Explain that today each child will have a chance to make his or her own scene. Provide the children with pieces of paper that match the size of the back of your aquarium. Lay out the backgrounds from which children may choose as well as the items provided for decoration (markers, crayons, colored pencils, watercolor paints, etc). Have the children work in a place where they can see the fish tank. Display the children's backgrounds on the walls or alternate them behind the aquarium for the children and fish to look at.

Affective

1. A Fish Out of Water

Obtain a copy of the book *A Fish Out of Water* by Helen Palmer (1989). This is a story about what happens when a child feeds his goldfish too much. It provides a great vehicle for discussion about what is real and what is pretend in the story about fish. After reading and discussion, ask the children to generate rules to follow to keep fish in good health. Write the children's ideas on a large sheet of paper and post them near the fish tank.

2. Caring for Fish

Introduce this activity by reading *A Fish Out of Water* by Helen Palmer (see the description above). Make an assignment for one person to feed the fish each day. Check the bowl or tank to make sure it is operating properly. Have the child help you read the instructions on the fish food container to find out how much food the fish need for each day and how often they need to eat. Once the fish are fed, have the child check the water temperature and make sure the filter, pump, and light are working. Record each child's findings on a chart or clipboard stored nearby. Children may also enjoy providing a verbal description of the fish's behavior and physical condition for you to record. At the end of the week, involve the children in the cleaning of the fish tank, including draining the water, transferring the fish, scrubbing the sides and rocks, cleaning the filter, and so on.

3. Aquascaping

Gather the following materials: fish stencils, fishing line, aquarium gravel, plastic aquarium plants, construction paper string, glue, and markers. Collect or ask the children to bring shoe boxes from home to use in this project. All these items will be used to represent fish tanks. Have children draw or trace fish shapes, rocks, and plants and cut them out. Encourage them to glue some of their objects to the box or suspend them with string or fishing line from the top of the pretend tank. Allow each child to design his or her own box. As a finishing touch, use spoons, hands, and Popsicle® sticks to move the gravel into desired places on the bottom. Have children describe their work and how a fish would live and move in the fish tank. Have them describe what part of the decorated tank the fish would like best.

To Simplify:
- Provide precut materials for the children to use.

To Extend:
- Show children how to view their creations from a variety of directions by cutting windows in the sides of the box.

Cognitive

1. Fish Sort

Make a variety of fish shapes out of paper and color them with markers or, instead, cut out pictures of fish or purchase small plastic fish to use for this activity. Place all the fish in a shoe box in the middle of a table. This will serve as the classroom aquarium. Provide several small boxes (individual aquariums) for the children to use for sorting. Encourage them to select a fish out of the aquarium box and place it in one of the smaller boxes with fish that share some likeness with it. Encourage children to tell why they chose to put a fish in a certain box. Fish may be sorted by likeness in color, shape, fins, and so on.

Hint for Success:
- Use a variety of fish shapes and colors so the fish can be sorted and classified in a variety of ways. Cover paper fish with clear adhesive paper or laminate them to preserve them for more than one use.

To Simplify:
- Use fewer varieties of fish or have children match identical fish.

To Extend:
- Have children sort the fish using multiple criteria at the same time (such as size and color, or shape and color). Another option is to have children sort the fish using criteria related to fish behavior rather than physical characteristics, such as the ones that swim the fastest. They will need to make judgements based on what has been learned from observation and from other activities.

2. Fish Count I

Depending on the number of fish, size of the tank, and the activity level of the fish, this may be a simple or a challenging activity. Put a chart near the tank listing each child's name and a space by the names to record how many fish children think are in the tank each day. Begin with a small number of fish in the tank and increase the number over time. Numbers may also vary due to live births or deaths of fish. Encourage the children to count the fish each day and to record their answers next to their names. Have the children examine the tank from as many sides as possible. Ask them whether this makes counting easier or more difficult. Record each child's final count. Compare the children's answers. If their answers vary, ask them how they could resolve the differences. Try out the children's ideas. Encourage them to check their answer and to recount to see if they count the same number each time.

Hint for Success:
- Children may not have reached the understanding of one-to-one correspondence. For this reason they may not be counting accurately. Repetition of this activity is fine as it builds children's development of number concept and usefulness.

To Simplify:
- Have small, cut-out fish for the children to use in counting. For every fish they count have them tape one paper fish to the outside of the aquarium.

3. Fish Count II

This is a good follow-up to the "Fish Count I" activity described above. Create several "fish tank" scenes, using pictures of fish glued to large sheets of blue paper (fish hobby magazines are good picture sources). Make sure to use fish varieties that might really be found in a classroom or home aquarium. Group some fish and spread others out in each scene. Invite children to estimate how many fish are in the aquarium. Write down each child's prediction. Invite them to count the fish aloud to determine which estimates were closest to the actual number.

To Simplify:
- Use five or fewer fish on each paper.

To Extend:
- Help children create verbal story problems to describe the various groupings of fish on the papers. Write their ideas on another page attached to each scene.
- Invite children to use numeral stamps to create an equation to match the fish groupings in each aquarium.

4. Fish Tank Experiments

Watching Fish. Display an aquarium in a prominent place in the classroom. If possible, place it in an area where children can comfortably move around to

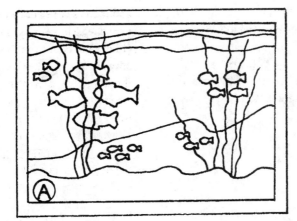

Count the Fish in Each Picture

Name

Ⓐ   Ⓑ   Ⓒ

more than one side for observation. Invite children to move their chairs so they can sit up close and watch for a long period of time. Provide magnifying glasses, small flashlights, and books with pictures of the types of fish in your aquarium. Encourage children to find pictures of the fish and to look for more information.

To Simplify:

● Provide individual pictures of the kinds of fish that are in your aquarium. Have children point out the real fish that match the fish in the pictures.

To Extend:

● Have children record (via dictation or their own writing) some of the information they found out about each fish from the books provided. Post their observations near the fish tank.

Tank Volume. Children may be curious about how much water an aquarium holds. Prior to introducing the activity, collect as many one-gallon milk jugs as correspond to the volume of your fish tank. Begin by putting an aquarium in a empty water table next to one empty gallon milk jug. Keep the others out of sight for now. Ask the children how many milk jugs it will take to fill the tank. Record their estimates. (Most classrooms will have tanks for ten to twenty-five gallons.) Beginning with the smallest estimate, involve the children in filling each of the containers and pouring them into the aquarium. Count as each is added. Have children compare their estimates with the actual number it took to fill the tank. Later, reverse the process, emptying the tank. See if the number remains the same.

What Grows in a Tank. Fill a small tank with water and set it near a window or in direct sunlight. Have the children monitor the tank and look for changes in the tank. Add magnifying glasses to the area and have discussions with the children about algae growth.

5. Fish Bladder

Children are often fascinated that fish appear to suspend themselves in the water at any level they choose. Collect several small objects children could put in water. Make sure some are things they are likely to see in a fish tank (such as sand, rocks, pebbles, plants, structures, and so on). Extend traditional sink and float activities by using clear plastic oblong fishing bobbers found in most fishing tackle shops to show how air captured in an object can cause the object to float below the water's surface. The bobbers come in a variety of sizes and make a good representation of a fish's swim

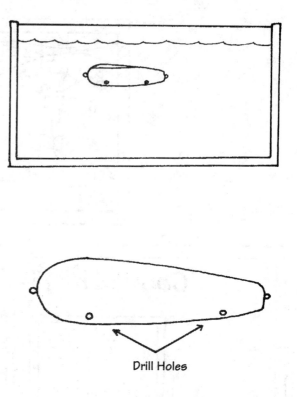

Drill Holes

bladder (air sack). By putting two small holes in one side and allowing a little water to collect within the bobber, it can be made to float below the surface. This will allow for children to experiment with varying the level at which the object floats in the water.

To Extend:

● Give children acrylic paints to use to paint their bobbers like fish. Plastic fin shapes can be attached to these using a hot glue gun or other water-resistant glue if desired.

6. Filters

Fish tanks use a variety of filtering systems to clean the water. These can be duplicated in several ways. The most common filter types are gravel filters, sponge filters, and charcoal filters. In advance of the children's arrival, gather filter materials such as cotton batting, sponges, gravel, and charcoal. Knee-high nylon stockings or sieves filled part way with one of these materials will serve as an actual filter for the children to use. Begin by having each child select a filter material to put in a stocking or sieve. Next, mix soil, sand, and water in a bucket. Pour water through the filter and collect the water that passes through in another bucket. Repeat this procedure, periodically checking to see how the clarity of the water has changed. Later have the children take apart their filters to see all the "waste" that was collected.

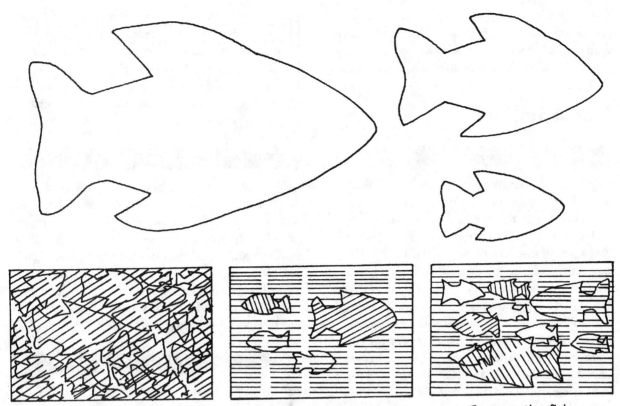

Cut out fish shapes.   Paste shapes to background.   Trace on other fish.

7. Camouflaged Fish

Gather the following materials in advance of the children's arrival:

> sheets of newspaper, both black and white and the comic pages
>
> large pieces of cardboard, at least 2 feet by 3 feet (the sides and bottoms of grocery boxes work well for this)
>
> construction paper of varying colors, including black and white sheets
>
> markers
>
> scissors
>
> fish-shaped templates or tracing forms as needed
>
> transparent tape

Cover one side of each cardboard sheet with the newspaper. Make some of these black and white, some colored, and some a combination of both. Cut out fish shapes of different sizes from the newspaper and the construction paper. Securely tape four or five fish shapes at varying angles on each of the cardboard sheets. Make sure some shapes stand out; make others blend into the background. Also, draw one or two fish shapes on the newspaper among the other paper fish.

After these materials have been prepared, work with the children in a group. Explain that you will be showing them some underwater scenes in which fish are camouflaged to blend in with their surroundings. Show the "fish scenes" one at a time. Have children point out all the fish they see in each scene. Count them. Invite one or more of the children to look very closely at the sheet to see if any fish were missed.

To Simplify:

● Make the fish easy to see by contrasting colored construction paper against black and white newsprint.

To Extend:

● Increase the difficulty of the task by placing like-colored fish against the various backgrounds or use fish made out of like-colored newspapers simply outlined on the page. Have children estimate how many fish are on a particular sheet, then ask one child to count the fish aloud as the children point them out.

8. Selecting Fish for the Room

Bring fish books such as those recommended in the adult reference section into the classroom for children to look through. Identify types of fish available that would fit well together in the same tank. Have the children select the kinds of fish they want for the aquarium. (You will have to decide in advance what quantity to purchase.) If possible, combine a field trip to a fish store with the purchase of new fish. Workers in the store can provide the children with additional information about each type of fish selected. Have aquarium books available so that older children can research the fish further.

Construction

1. Fish Collage

Ahead of children's arrival, gather 8" x 10" sheets of clear adhesive paper, art tissue paper, fish-shaped cutouts no bigger than three inches long, and one-half-inch-wide strips of black construction paper. Take the backing off of the adhesive paper and place it on the table, sticky side up. Assist each child in putting the black strip around the perimeter of the paper to serve as the edge of the tank (this will also prevent the paper from rolling up while the child is working). Ask the children to place fish shapes, tissue paper pieces, cut plant shapes, and so on on the paper. When they are finished, take the backing off of another piece of paper and place it, sticky side down, over the picture. Press the two sticky sides together. Trim edges to get rid of any overlap and either display by taping the pictures to a window or suspend them from the ceiling so that children can examine them from both sides.

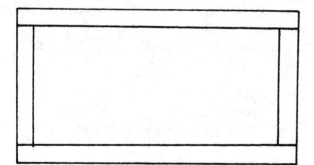

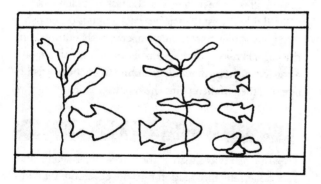

2. Texture Fish

Prior to the children's participation, cut out fish shapes that are approximately 6" x 4". Paste tissue paper or crêpe paper on each fish shape. Allow the glue to fully dry. Provide the children with small paint brushes and water. By "painting" on the paper, the color will run or bleed, mixing the colors and coloring the fish. Children may also glue sequins to the fish shape to act as scales. Hang these fish from the ceiling for the children to appreciate using string or fish line.

3. Pop Bottle Fish Tank

Gather sixteen-ounce plastic pop bottles, one per child, aquarium gravel, a funnel, small plastic fish and small plastic plants. Take off the labels so that most of each bottle is clear. Have each child place two handfuls of aquarium gravel in his or her bottle using a funnel. Next have the children pour water into their bottles. Allow children to select two or three small plastic fish and plants to add. Tighten the cap on each bottle and label it with the child's name.

4. Construction Paper Fish

This is a good activity to help children with their cutting skills. Draw a fish shape outline on construction paper. Have the children cut out the fish. You may wish to include fish that require varying degrees of cutting skill. The simplest shapes are rounded ones with few protrusions; the most difficult will have sharp corners and multiple curves.

To Simplify:
● Precut the most difficult parts. Draw double lines around the outline about a half-inch apart and have the children cut between the lines.

To Extend:
● Have the children draw their own outline from a fish stencil made from cardboard or plastic, then cut it out.

Language

1. Learning Fish Names

Make a fish chart on posterboard. Draw fish, cut out fish pictures from magazines, or photocopy fish illustrations and place these on the chart. Label each kind of fish below the appropriate pictures. Post this chart somewhere in the room for children to examine. Spend time with children during the day looking at the fish. Tell children the name of each fish and help them pronounce the names.

2. "Fishful" Fantasy

Leo Lionni's fanciful tale *Fish Is Fish* (1970) provides a perfect opportunity for children to explore the notion of story line while letting their imaginations run free. First, get a copy of *Fish Is Fish* from a bookstore or library. Make several paper booklets from construction paper folded in half and bound in the center with staples, like a book. Create a cover page that says "A Fish Story" by _____ (insert child's name here later). Make a second page that says "There are extraordinary things in the world." On a third page write "Like what?" Four or five blank pages should follow. Have on hand markers and crayons. Set these materials aside for the moment. Now, gather the children in a group. Read the story at least one time through. Talk with the children about what the fish imagined life was like beyond the pond. Consider reading the story a second time, with children listening more closely for specific details. Afterwards, explain to the group that they will get a chance to create their own "fish" story. This one will use the same story line as Leo Lionni's tale, but will be about what the fish in your aquarium might imagine life to be like beyond their tank. Give children the booklets and markers to use for this purpose. Encourage them to dictate or write their own stories and to illustrate them as they choose.

Hint for Success:

● Children benefit from generating a list of potential characters for their stories, such as the guinea pig in the next classroom, or ants on the sidewalk, or birds in the trees. Other inanimate items the fish might wonder about could also be included.

To Simplify:

● Create a group story to which several children contribute ideas during a circle time.

● Have each child create a single illustration; then put all the children's pictures together into one whole book.

To Extend:

● Focus on the notion of dialogue between two characters, a fish in the aquarium and a child at school. Have children alternate each character's words on every other page.

3. Fishy Solutions

Nancy Coffeit's book *Tom's Fish* (1994) presents a fishy dilemma children will enjoy. Read the book to the children. On another day tell children you will read the story again. This time their job is to listen for all the different reasons people thought Tom's fish was swimming upside down. Go through the pictures and text from start to finish. Ask children to generate a list of reasons people had for the "upside down fish." Record the children's ideas on a large piece of easel paper, review them, and post them near the library corner. On another day, after reading the story, have the children bend over from the waist, looking at the world between their legs. Ask them to describe the "upside down world" they see. Record these observations on paper and display the list near the library corner too. Talk with the children about what Tom's fish might have seen in his "upside down" position.

4. Fish Relatives—Big, Bigger, Biggest

Make fish shapes in a variety of sizes, shapes, colors, and textures. Begin by asking children to sequence the fish shapes by size. Use the words big, bigger, biggest, small, smaller, and smallest to describe the fish. Ask children to show you the fish that corresponds to each of these descriptive words. Expand the activity by introducing other properties such as color or texture. Invite children to describe each fish in comparison to the others.

To Simplify:

● Focus on asking children to find the fish that corresponds to a particular adjective. For instance, "Find the shiniest fish" or "Show me a fish that is thinner than this one."

To Extend:

● Give children a certain number of fish to put in order and to describe. After a sequence has been established, introduce another fish. Ask children to find a place for it and use a variety of words to describe it in relation to those already there.

● Another option is for each child to be assigned a fish or to make a fish of his or her own. Comparisons could be made with each child keeping track (verbally or on paper) of the words used to describe his or her fish according to a variety of properties.

Tom's Fish

Big	Widest	Funny	Shiny
Bright	Darkest	Heaviest	

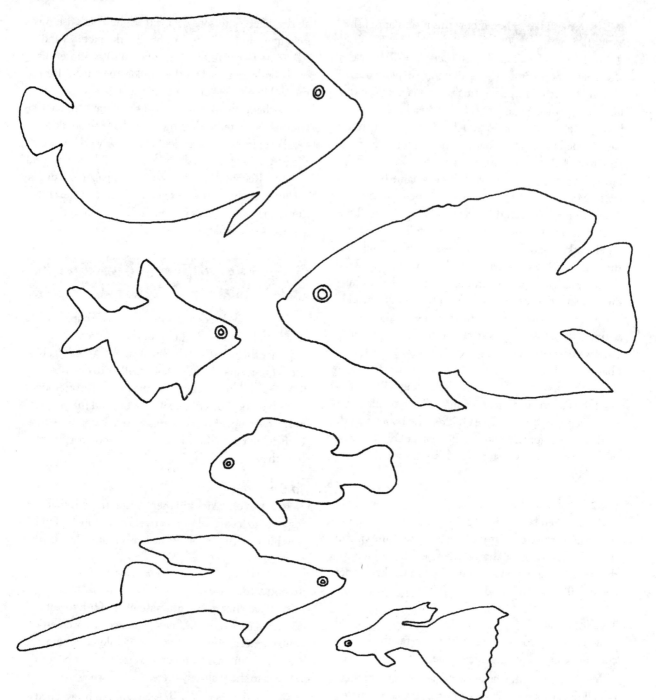

Physical

1. Fish Skeleton

Materials needed are construction paper, scissors, glue in small squeeze bottles, and toothpicks. Create an outline of a fish skeletal system using the illustrations provided here. Make one or more per child. Show children how to outline the bones of the fish with the glue. Have them place toothpicks on the glue to represent the bones.

2. Paddles

Using wire hangers and nylon stockings, simple paddles can be created very inexpensively. Bend the hanger to look like a teardrop or egg shape. Bend the hook to make a loop handle. Wrap the handle with tape for safety. Pull a nylon stocking over the shaped wire and tie it at the handle. The children can use these to hit a ball suspended from the ceiling, or a yard or sponge ball that is untethered. Point out how it feels when the paddle is moved through the air. Ask the children to feel the air resistance as the paddle moves through the air. Discuss with the children how this is similar to fish fins in the water.

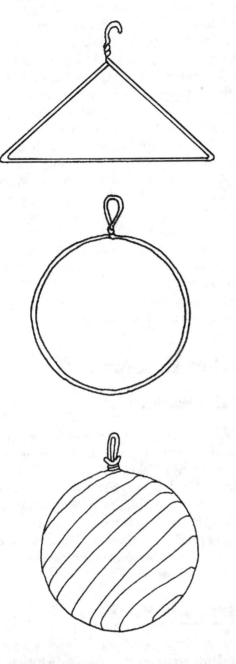

Provide the children with construction paper and help them work to tear the paper in the shape of a fish. Arrange the fish on paper and glue them in place. Other colors and paper may be used to make parts such as the fins and eyes of the fish. Add "torn paper" rocks, plants, and other objects to the picture as well.

Pretend Play

1. Fish Store

Either purchase a variety of plastic fish or make paper fish for children to use in their play. This can become a central activity for supplying many of the fish products needed in the other activities which are going on in the room. Include such things as shoe boxes for aquariums, straws for tubing for filters, paper on which children can draw plants and rocks, gravel and small pebbles, plastic fish, and plastic wrap to cover box aquariums. Have the children make suggestions for other materials to add to the store. Invite children to make signs and other advertisements for sale items. Encourage the children to take on the roles associated with running a fish store.

2. Plastic Fish in the Water Table

Fill the water table or a plastic tub with about three or four inches of water. Put plastic fish in the water and provide small fish nets for the children. Have the children try to scoop out each of the fish and put them in a secondary tank or series of fish bowls, as if they were supplying the fish with new homes.

3. Fish TV

Involve the children in setting up a housekeeping area in the classroom in which an aquarium will be used as part of the furnishings. Have them make the decisions about where to put all of the furniture so the aquarium is easily visible. Ask children where the aquarium could be placed so that it can be seen from all of the places in the "house." It will be important to have a sturdy shelf, table, or other object to serve as the support base for the aquarium. Help the children to include awareness of the fish and aquarium as a part of their play in the house area.

3. Flipper Feet

This is a stretching activity. Gather the children in a circle and talk about fish body parts. Have the children sit on the floor with their legs out in front of them. Ask them to point their toes up in the air and then down toward the middle of the group. Have the children hug their legs up close to their bodies and then straighten them out on the floor. Encourage the children to stretch each part of their bodies as you name the body parts. Cards can be made to show the child what body part to move by drawing the body part with a fin attached to each.

Social

1. Fish Mobiles

Involve all of the children in this activity to make a fish mobile. Materials needed will include fishing line or string, one-fourth-inch dowels, and fish-shaped cutouts. Provide each child with a fish shape to be decorated, colored, or painted. Give children plenty of opportunities to make choices about the materials they use and the final outcomes they create. Be sure to display these with the children's names on their fish so they recognize the results of their own efforts and those of the other children in the class. Suspend the fish from the dowel. Be sure to space the fish along the dowels using different lengths of line for each fish.

2. School of Fish

Make fish name tags for the children in the class. Read the story *Swimmy* by Leo Lionni (1973) and discuss how some fish stay together in groups for safety. Encourage the children to watch the fish in the aquarium and see if there are any fish that are staying near each other. During the day tell the children that everyone is going to move together in a "school." As children are going to meals, outdoors, or through other transitions, have them move in concert. Set up a course for the children to follow as they move around in a "fish school."

3. Tracing Fish

Prepare ahead of the children's arrival a table covered with a large sheet of butcher paper and assorted fish stencils. Encourage the children to trace as many fish shapes as they can on the paper, to the point that the fish overlap and cover each other. Involve the children in coloring all of the fish in the picture.

To Simplify:
● Prepare individual sheets of paper so the children can work on their own school of fish or work with a friend.

To Extend:
● Give children crayons to use in coloring the fish. Later, paint over the fish with a very light blue watercolor paint. This will only affect the parts of the paper that have been uncolored, representing water.

4. Go Fish

Make your own game cards of matching pairs of fish, using pictures and names of real aquarium fish. The game is played by spreading all of the cards face down on the table or floor. Each participant then selects five cards from the group. Holding these cards so that other participants cannot see them, the players take turns from right to left. When it is a player's turn he or she may ask any one of the other players if they have a card that matches one he or she is holding. If the child who receives this request has a match, then he or she must pass over the card. If not, the child who was asked responds by saying "go fish." The child whose turn it was then selects one card from the middle. The object of the game is to make matches of fish types. Pairs are created and they are placed face up in front of the player to whom they belong. This process continues until all cards are matched up. This is a fun way for children to practice saying the names of the fish, while they practice taking turns and following simple rules.

Teacher Resources

Field Trip Idea

1. Locate a nearby pet store that deals with fish and aquarium supplies. Divide children into small groups so that adults can easily talk with them about the fish they are seeing. Involve as many parents as are available to participate. Take children through the area where the fish tanks are set up for people to purchase fish. If possible, have someone from the store talk about size of tanks, types of fish, food, and care.

Classroom Visitors

1. An aquarist is a person who raises fish as a hobby and tries to recreate the fish's natural habitat in an aquarium. Ask him or her to bring tools to show how water is changed, medicines are given, and water quality is checked as well as to talk about fish.

2. Invite parents who have aquariums to visit the classroom. Often parents within the groups have fish tanks in their own homes or have taken care of fish in the past. Ask some of these parents to come and sit near the aquarium to talk with the children about the fish they see. Also, ask them to talk with the children about what they like about having fish.

Children's Books

Coffelt, N. (1994). *Tom's Fish*. San Diego: Harcourt Brace Jovanovich.

Ehlert, L. (1990) *Fish Eyes: A Book You Can Count on*. San Diego: Harcourt Brace Jovanovich.

Keats, E. J. (1972). *Pet Show!* New York: Macmillan.

Lionni, L. (1989). *Swimmy*. New York: Knopf Books for Young Readers.

Lionni, L. (1970). *Fish Is Fish*. New York: Pantheon.

Palmer, H. (1989). *A Fish Out of Water*. New York: Beginner Books.

Pfister, M. (1992). *The Rainbow Fish*. New York: North-South Books.

Adult References

Bauman, E. (1991). *The Essential Aquarium*. New York: Crescent Books.

Loiselle, P. V., and Baensch, H. A. (1991). *Marine Aquarist Manual*. Morris Plains, NJ: Tetra Sales.

Van Ramshorst, J. D. (1978). *The Complete Aquarium Encyclopedia of Tropical Freshwater Fish*. Morris Plains, NJ: Chartwell Books.

Backyard Animals

Little Miss Muffet sat on a tuffet, eating her curds and whey.

Along came a spider and sat down beside her,

And . . .

A group of children are with a teacher outside on the playground. Heidi excitedly exclaims, "Look, a spider!" Chris moves to step on the little creature. Manuel cries out, "Stop! Don't kill it!" The teacher holds Chris back and says to the group, "Let's watch." She then encourages the children to look at the spider, count its body parts and legs, and observe its movements. Eventually some children start looking for its web.

Outside, Lorna carries an earthworm in her hands. Bridget yells, "Lorna, put that worm down. It's gonna bite you!" Lorna carefully turns the worm over, looking for its teeth.

On Tuesday, Mr. Rademacher brings to the program a toad he found on a walk with his dog. As he holds the toad for the children to see, a parent leading her child into the classroom watches from a distance for a few minutes. She moves closer and remarks that she has never seen a toad this close before. She gently touches the toad and encourages her son to do the same. He refuses, but stays nearby as teacher, parent, and other children touch and talk about the toad.

Spiders, earthworms, frogs, and toads are animals commonly found outside in urban, suburban, and rural environments. Although they are small, these creatures have much to teach us about animal life and the interdependence of all living things on earth.

Purpose

This unit on "Backyard Animals" is based on two beliefs. First, spiders, earthworms, frogs, and toads are ideal creatures for people to study. There are many harmless varieties to which children have ready access. These animals can be observed in their natural habitats without elaborate preparation or precautions, and children can be taught to learn about their behavior through unobtrusive observation and careful handling. Moreover, spiders, earthworms, frogs, and toads are interesting. Their characteristics and behaviors are distinctive and provide insight into the wonders of nature. Second, because of their small size, children can literally hold a spider, earthworm, frog, or toad in the palms of their hands. This provides a perfect entree into talking to children about the sanctity of life and their own role in the ecological scheme of things.

With these ideas in mind, this unit has been designed to give children many opportunities to explore their "backyard" environments firsthand. The TFPs for each mini-theme focus on the physical characteristics of the animals as well as the behaviors that characterize them. Children are encouraged to discover these characteristics and behaviors for themselves through observation, experimentation, enactment, and symbolization. Our hope is that children will come away from their experience with a sense of wonder and appreciation for these tiny wild animals with whom we share the world.

Implementation

"Backyard Animals" is divided into three mini-themes: "Spiders," "Earthworms," and "Frogs and Toads." For convenience, they are presented in an order we think reflects the ease of access children and teachers might have to live specimens. Spiders are found everywhere—inside, outside, all year round. Earthworms are more easily discovered during warm weather months. They can be found in the country or the city, as long as there is a place where children can dig in the soil. Frogs and toads are the most elusive creatures included in this unit, but even they can be located with a bit of quiet hunting in a city park, a suburban garden, or a rural glade. This sequence of mini-themes may or may not suit your needs. Therefore, it is not absolute. The mini-themes in "Backyard Animals" can be carried out in any combination. Some possibilities are listed here:

Option One:

Week 1:	Spiders
Week 2:	Earthworms
Week 3:	Frogs and Toads
Week 4:	Comparing the Animals Studied in This Unit

Option Two:

| Weeks 1 and 2: | Spiders |
| Weeks 3 and 4: | Insects |

Option Three:

Weeks 1 and 2:	Frogs and Toads Common to the Local Environment
Week 3:	Frogs and Toads Found in a Distant or Exotic Environment
	Or
Week 3:	Amphibians Other Than Frogs and Toads
	Or
Weeks 3 and 4:	Additional Animals Found in or Around Ponds

Option Four:

| Weeks 1 and 2: | Earthworms |
| Weeks 3 and 4: | Snakes |

Spiders

Terms, Facts, and Principles (TFPs)

General Characteristics

1. Spiders are arachnids. Spiders are not insects.
2. Arachnids have four pairs of segmented legs and bodies that are divided into two sections. Insects have six legs and three body segments.

3. Spiders have eight legs, a body divided into two segments, and silk-producing spinnerets.

4. Spiders have a hard outer body covering with joints in the legs so they can bend.

5. The body segments of a spider are the cephalothorax (combined head and thorax) and the abdomen.

6. The eyes, mouth, and stomach of a spider are located in the cephalothorax. The legs are also connected to this body part.

7. Most of a spider's senses are in its legs.

8. Spiders have fangs at the tip of each jaw and pedipalps alongside each jaw. The fangs contain a poison that is strong enough to kill insects; the pedipalps assist in feeling and also aid in holding prey.

9. Most spiders have eight simple eyes. Some species have fewer than eight (2, 4, or 6).

10. Spiders cannot see well at all.

11. Spiders molt as they grow; they shed their outer skeleton or cuticle.

12. Silk is produced in the abdomen and is spun out through spinnerets at the end of the abdomen.

13. Spiders use silk to make nests, cocoons, or webs for trapping insects.

14. There are different types of spiders; they vary in size and in color.

Spider Webs

15. The web of a spider performs several functions:

    a. The web is an extension of the spider's senses. A spider can feel vibrations through its threads and therefore be aware of prey or an enemy.

    b. The web protects the spider from some enemies by entangling them or slowing down their approach.

    c. The web can catch insects over a larger area than a spider could cover simply by walking.

16. Web builders wait to trap flying insects.

17. Once a spider catches its prey in the web, the spider wraps it in silk, making it helpless.

18. Each species of web-building spiders makes a particular kind of web.

Additional Interesting Facts

19. Female spiders lay eggs that are protected by an egg sac made of silk.

20. The baby spiders that hatch from the eggs are called spiderlings.

21. Wandering spiders walk along the ground and hunt crawling insects. They do not build webs.

22. Most spiders live for one year or less.

23. Spiders help humans by eating insects that are harmful to plants.

*24. Some spiders are poisonous to people. However, only a few spider varieties have poison strong enough to harm humans.

25. People should avoid touching a spider unless they know that it is not a kind that is harmful.

26. When picking up a spider, it is important to be careful not to crush or harm it in any way.

Activity Ideas

Aesthetic

1. Spider Songs

Sing the following songs with children throughout the week during circle times, outdoors on the playground, as the children pretend to be spiders, or while they wait for turns to get a drink or wash their hands.

♫ "Spider Spinning"
Words by Donna Howe
Tune: "Frère Jacques"

> Spider spinning, spider spinning,
> On her web, on her web,
> Waiting for a fly, waiting for a fly,
> Say goodbye,
> Goodbye fly.

"Spider Spinning" presents the children with new words to a familiar tune. To teach the children the song, first sing it once for the children to hear. Second, explain to the children that you are going to sing the song again. This time when you sing, they are to listen for what the spider is doing or where the spider is spinning. Sing the song; then ask the children to tell you what the spider is doing or where it is spinning. Next, invite the children to sing along with you. By now the children should find it easier to sing the song themselves.

♬ **"Eensy Weensy Spider"**

The eensy weensy spider

Went up the water spout.

Down came the rain and washed the spider out.

Out came the sun and dried up all the rain,

And the eensy weensy spider went up the spout
again.

The teeny, tiny spider

Went up the water spout.

Down came the rain and washed the spider out.

Out came the sun and dried up all the rain,

And the teeny, tiny spider went up the spout
again.

The hugey, woogey spider

Went up the water spout.

Down came the rain and washed the spider out.

Out came the sun and dried up all the rain,

And the hugey, woogey spider went up the spout
again.

Give children the opportunity to play with volume
and pitch, while also singing about spiders. Sing the first
verse in a moderate volume and pitch. Then, vary the
size of the spider while also changing the pitch. Change
to a quiet volume and higher pitch for the second verse.
For the final verse of the song, sing about the "hugey,
woogey" spider using a loud volume and a lower pitch.

To Simplify:

● Teach the first part of the song to the children.
Sing this several times the first day of the spider unit. As
children become more familiar with the song, teach the
variations of spider sizes and "voices" to go along with
each.

To Extend:

● Add a tempo change to the song. For the teeny,
tiny spider, sing very quickly to create a fast tempo. For
the hugey, woogey spider, sing in a slower, plodding type
of a tempo.

● Have children think of alternate adjectives to
describe spider sizes.

Additional resources for songs about spiders:

"Anansi" by Bert Simpson and Raffi on *Raffi: the Corner
Grocery Store*. A & M Records, Inc., Hollywood,
CA, 1979.

"Spin, Spider, Spin" by Patty Zeitlin and Marcia Berman
on *Spin, Spider, Spin*. Educational Activities, Inc.,
Freeport, NY, 1974.

2. Paint a Web

This activity should be implemented once the children have had several chances to observe spider
webs. As children paint the structural parts of a spider
web, they will be developing familiarity with the artistic
element of line. To prepare for this activity: a) cover the
art table with newspaper, b) set out smocks for the children, c) put white liquid tempera paint in small containers, in easy reach of each child, and d) post pictures of
spider webs where children can see them (see page 425).

Begin by demonstrating how to use a paint brush
to create a line on the paper with a light sweeping
motion. Next, show children how to add sweeping lines,
each connected to the first one to give the impression of
a spider's web. After you remind the children that varying species of spiders make webs that differ from one
another, invite them to create their own interpretation
of a spider web. Give each child black construction
paper and a small paint brush. Encourage everyone to
experiment with a variety of brush strokes.

To Simplify:

● Use white chalk rather than paint.

To Extend:

● With the children, look at drawn or painted illus-
trations of spider webs in children's picture books.
Potential titles might include Margaret Graham's *Be
Nice to Spiders* (1967), Gerald McDermott's *Anansi the
Spider: A Tale from the Ashanti* (1972), and Eric Carle's
The Very Busy Spider (1989). Compare how each illus-
trator has used the artistic element of line to create spi-
der webs.

Affective

1. Spider Snacks

For this activity, children will create their own spi-
der-like snack. Provide the children with pretzel
sticks (legs), small cheese balls (thorax and cephalothorax), and chopped nuts (eyes). Give each child a plate
for a "work space," show them the materials and invite
them to create spiders. Once the children believe their
spiders are finished, they can eat their creations!

Recipe for cheese balls (makes enough for 10 to 12
servings):

Mix 2 packages (8 ounces each) cream cheese, 3/4
cup shredded white cheese (Swiss, Monterey jack, moz-
zarella), 1 cup shredded sharp cheese, 1 tablespoon
Worcestershire sauce. Give each child enough to make a
spider's thorax and cephalothorax. Offer children a

Garden Spider Web

Tangled Web

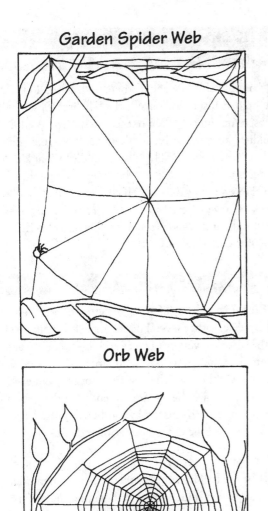

Orb Web

Spiral Web

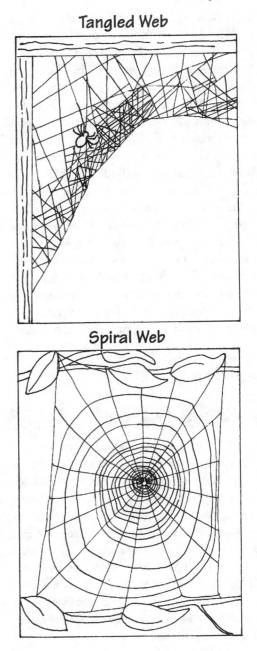

choice of poppy seeds, sesame seeds, or chopped parsley in which to roll their spider bodies if they desire.

Hints for Success:

● Provide each child with a 12" square of waxed paper at his/her place, so the cheese doesn't stick to the table.

● The cheese works best when it has been allowed to warm to room temperature for at least 30 minutes after shredding and before combining.

To Simplify:

● Create the thorax and cephalothorax yourself; invite the children to attach eight pretzel stick legs and eight raisin eyes.

To Extend:

● Have the children help prepare the cheese balls.

2. Me as Spiderperson!

This activity will give the children a chance to imagine themselves looking different from their "usual" selves. Prepare for the activity by cutting out oval-shaped head pieces (about six inches long) and round body pieces (about nine inches in diameter) from a variety of colors of construction paper. Also, cut out many human eyes, legs, and arms (at least eight each for every child) from magazine pictures; put some of each body part in several pie pans so the children can have easy access to them. In addition, have markers available for children to use in adding finishing touches to their pictures. Provide children with glue in small bottles or glue sticks and 11" x 18" pieces of construction paper.

Introduce the activity to the children by showing them the materials. Tell them: "Imagine what it would be like to be a spider with eight eyes, eight legs, and two body parts. Today you will use the paper pieces, legs, and eyes to create a picture of yourselves as spiders." Let each child choose a piece of 11" x 18" paper and a head oval and a body circle. Instruct the children to choose eight eyes and glue them onto the head piece (the oval). They can use the markers to make fangs, mouths, and whatever else they would like on their faces. After the children have glued on their eyes, direct them to select eight arms/legs and glue these also to the head section (the cephalothorax). Once the children think their faces are complete, direct them to add the thorax portion to the spider bodies. When completed, invite each child to name his or her spider picture, such as "Spider Amelia."

Cognitive

1. Beautiful Spiders

This activity will give the children an opportunity to learn about some varieties of spiders and the webs they weave. Many informational books about spiders contain detailed photographs or illustrations of these creatures, such as *Amazing Spiders* by Claudia Schnieper (1989), *Spiders* by Barrie Watts (1991), *The Spider* by Margaret Lane (1983), *The Fascinating World of Spiders* by Maria Angels Julivert (1992), and *Spiders* by Kate Petty (1990). Make several of these books available to the children in the library area. Read a selected text with a group of children. As children make comments and ask questions, talk about what they have observed and look for information in the book to answer their questions.

To Simplify:

● Become familiar with the texts of the informational books. With the children, focus on the pictures and talk with them about ideas from the text that are obvious within the pictures.

To Extend:

● As children observe spiders and webs indoors and outdoors, refer them to the informational books on spiders to look up answers to questions they might have.

● Post a paper in the book area and the spider observation area labeled, "Interesting Facts About Spiders." After children tell something they have learned, write their comments on the paper, along with their names.

2. Spider, Where Do You Live?

To teach children about where spiders live, look for spiders inside and outside the building. Observe the webs, reminding children not to touch them. As the children study the webs, ask them questions such as: What is on the web? Where is the spider? What kind of spider is it? How are these webs alike? How are they similar? How are they different? If children find a spider that is not on a web, ask them to look for a web in the area, or consider if the spider could possibly be a type that does not spin a web.

3. Spider or Insect?

To help children differentiate between insects and spiders, gather several plastic models (or pictures) of both. Choose a variety of types and sizes of the creatures. Invite the children to look at and touch the insects and spiders. Ask them to tell what they notice about each figure. Encourage the children to put all of the spiders in one pile and all the insects in another. Ask them how they could tell the difference between them.

Hint for Success:

● If the children aren't sure of how to differentiate the insects and spiders, remind them that the spiders have two body parts and eight legs, while insects have three body parts and six legs.

To Simplify:

● Count the legs and body parts with the children to help them do the sorting.

To Extend:

● While outdoors, look for crawling creatures. Encourage the children to identify which ones are spiders, which ones are insects, and which ones don't fit either category. It would be helpful to take a creature identification book outdoors as a reference. Helpful resources are: *The Bug Book* by Hugh Danks (1987), *Golden Book of Insects and Spiders* by Laurence Pringle (1990), and *Spiders* by Gail Gibbons (1993).

4. How Many Legs?

Give the children practice recalling information about spiders with this counting activity. Materials needed are stamp pads (preferably with washable ink), white paper, and crayons or thin markers. Invite the children to make spiders. Ask the children to recall how many body parts spiders have. Direct them to create the body parts by pressing their thumb first onto the ink pad and then onto the paper. Encourage the children to count the parts (the thorax and the cephalothorax) as they are made. Next, have the children tell you how many legs spiders have. Tell them to use the markers or crayons to draw the eight legs onto the spider's body parts. Again, have the children count the legs as they are drawn.

To Simplify:
● Have a large spider model available for the children at the table so they can count the number of legs on the model and compare that with the number of legs on their spider.

To Extend:
● Encourage the children to make multiple spiders and to count the cumulative numbers of body parts and legs.

● Have children make insects, differentiating them from the spiders by counting the total number of parts.

Construction

1. Construct a Spider

Once the children have observed several varieties of live spiders, looked at pictures displayed on the walls, and viewed illustrations of spiders in books, give them several opportunities to create their own representations of spiders. Since spiders vary greatly from one another in size, shape, and color, provide the children with an interesting array of materials for creations. As they are working, encourage the children to recall the number of body sections, legs, and eyes spiders have. Materials children could use include:

a. Modeling dough and pipe cleaner spiders: Provide pipe cleaners and different colors of modeling dough (brown, red, gray, yellow, and orange).

b. Styrofoam spiders: Here you will need large and small Styrofoam balls as well as pipe cleaners or toothpicks.

c. Construction paper spiders: Gather together scraps of construction paper, scissors, glue, and markers.

d. Natural spiders: Make these with twigs, acorns, leaves, pine needles, small stones, grass, and weeds. Stick parts together with a mixture of white glue and paste (equal amounts of each).

2. Stuck on You

To prepare for this activity, mix 1 teaspoon of white tempera paint with one of cup white glue and pour the mixture into small squeeze bottles. Cut many small insect shapes out of paper or get pictures of insects from magazines. Give each child a glue bottle and a piece of dark-colored construction paper (dark enough so the white glue will show when dry). Demonstrate how to squeeze glue from the bottle slowly, drawing web-like lines across the paper. Encourage children to connect the lines together as a spider would in making a web. After the web is finished, invite the children to glue the insect pictures onto the web.

To Simplify:
● Provide glue bottles in which a very small hole has been pricked in the top. This will reduce the flow of the glue, making it easier for children to control.

To Extend:
● Give the children toothpicks to press onto the glue lines to make a "raised" web.

Language

1. Interactive Statements

Display pictures of spiders on the walls of the classroom. Give children an opportunity to attach meaning to print by posting a relevant statement or question near each one. Post a blank piece of paper nearby as well. As children participate in activities throughout the room, draw their attention to the pictures and the written remarks. Encourage children to write a response to each item or dictate a response to an adult. Examples of such statements or questions related to spiders are:

Where is the spider in this picture?

Which spider picture do you like the most? Why?

How many insects did this spider catch in its web?

How do you think this spider built its web?

2. Busy Spider Character Recall

While the children are together for a circle time, show them Eric Carle's *The Very Busy Spider* (1989). Tell them to listen carefully to all the animals that talk to the very busy spider as you read the book. When finished, ask the children to recall the animals. (They do not have to name the animals in order.) As the children call out, write their ideas on a large piece of newsprint paper posted nearby. Check to see if the list is complete by going through the book again, making sure no animals are left out and this time emphasizing the order.

To Simplify:

● Name an animal and ask the children to say "yes" or "no" as to whether it appeared in the story. Repeat until all the characters have been identified.

To Extend:

● Provide flannelboard figures of the animals and a flannel board for the children to use to put the animals in order in the library corner. Offer the book as a reference for children to check as needed.

3. Anansi Stories

Several folktales have been written about a spider named Anansi. In some, the spider is a trickster; in others he is very wise. Collect several stories about Anansi and read one each day to the children. As each story is read, help the children to pay particular attention to the character of Anansi. At the end of each tale, ask the children to describe Anansi. Prompt their discussion with questions such as "Would you like to have this Anansi as a friend? Why or why not?" Keep a record of the children's ideas by writing them down on a large piece of paper. Make one chart for each story. After several of the tales have been told, compare two or more of the stories. For instance, ask the children which story they enjoyed the most and why they liked it or ask them to describe the story that was funniest or scariest or most exciting.

Suggestions for Anansi stories include *Anansi* by Brian Gleeson and illustrated by Steven Guarnaccia (1992); *Anansi and the Moss-Covered Rock* (1988) and *Anansi and the Talking Melon* (1994) retold by Eric Kimmel and illustrated by Janet Stevens; Gerald McDermott's *Anansi the Spider: A Tale from the Ashanti* (1972); and *Frances* Temple's *Tiger Soup: An Anansi Story from Jamaica* (1994).

To Simplify:

● Select two stories in which the Anansi character is portrayed similarly. Focus on differences in plot between the two stories.

To Extend:

● Compare two of the Anansi stories at a time. Talk with the children about how Anansi was portrayed in each one. Ask them to generate a list of adjectives to differentiate one from the other.

● Ask children to tell what lesson they think the story could be teaching listeners.

Physical

1. Handle with Care

As spiders are being gathered for indoor observation, teach the children how to collect and handle them in a careful manner. Demonstrate how to hold a paper or plastic cup under a spider and gently tap it into the container. It is best to let the spider lower itself into the container as it holds onto its silk thread. Sometimes it is possible to hold a larger clear plastic container (with air holes in the top) under the web of a spider, catching the spider with part of its web in this temporary home.

Hint for Success:

● Provide the children with plastic spiders to gently tap into containers before trying to briefly capture live ones.

2. Prey Wrapping

This activity will give children an opportunity to practice their eye-hand coordination. Provide the children with a variety of plastic flying insect models, as well as white string or yarn (the spider's silk). Invite the children to wrap the string around and around the insect as a spider would do to its prey.

3. Spider Fang Pickup

After talking with the children about how spiders catch their prey, have children pretend that tweezers are spider fangs. Encourage them to pick up small plastic insect models or pictures with their tweezer fangs. This activity provides fine motor skill practice while enabling children to simulate spiders catching prey.

To Simplify:

● Use tongs as the fangs with larger insect models.

To Extend:

● Have the children use chopsticks as their pretend spider fangs. Teach them to hold the chopsticks as illustrated.

4. Oh, What a Tangled Web We Weave!

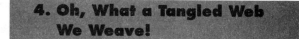

In this activity, children will make webs that could be hung on a wall or in a window. Provide the children with white yarn, white glue in small squeeze bottles, and waxed paper. First, direct the children to create connected spider web-like lines with glue on the paper.

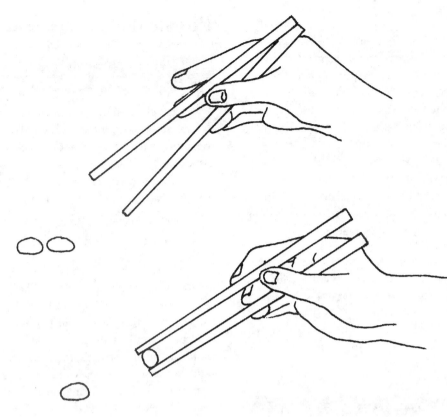

Then, have them press yarn into each glue line. Let the glue dry. Once the glue is dry, lift the yarn from the paper and hang the webs on the walls or windows for all to see.

To Simplify:
● Apply the glue for the children. Have them focus only on pressing the yarn onto the glue.

To Extend:
● Once the webs are complete, invite children to make a copy of their yarn shape on paper using crayons or markers.

Pretend Play

1. Spider Moves

Conduct this activity in a large open space in the classroom or outdoors after children have observed several spiders moving over their webs, up walls, or across the ground. Tell children that they are going to pretend to move like the spiders you describe. Move with them as you describe the following:

a. Pretend to be spiders on a web. Imagine you are hiding on the edge of your web. Suddenly the web starts to bounce. Here comes an insect—it's caught! You gingerly tiptoe across the silk threads until you reach the prey. You gobble it up!

b. You are jumping spiders. You have just been discovered in a person's house, on the bed. This person doesn't like spiders on his/her bed. Quickly you jump away to safety!

c. Now, you are all spiders on the wall. You hug your bodies close to the wall (the floor or ground). Reach with your legs and pull your bodies up the wall.

Hint for Success:
● Encourage the children to think of others kinds of spiders or scenarios they would like to pretend.

To Simplify:
● Repeat each scenario two or three times.

To Extend:
● Encourage children to work together in pairs to move as spiders (two body parts, eight legs!).

2. Shed Your Cuticles!

In this activity the children will pretend they are like growing spiders, shedding their outer skeletons or cuticles to allow their bodies to grow larger. Prior to the children's involvement, gather several pillowcases or large sacks. Set these aside for a moment. Explain to the children that as spiders grow, they shed their outer body covering, which is called the cuticle. Tell children they are going to pretend to be growing spiders, shedding their old cuticles. Direct each participating child to select a "cuticle" (one of the cases or sacks) and crawl inside with his/her head sticking out of the opening. Encourage the children to make their bodies small by tucking in arms and legs so they will fit inside the cuticle. Once all spiders are inside their cuticles, tell them it is time to pretend to be growing spiders, meaning they will wiggle their ways slowly out of their old cuticles. Make the pillow cases and sacks available to the children throughout this mini-theme, so they can continue to pretend to be growing spiders as desired.

Hint for Success:

● Have actual spider cuticles to show the children. Often these can be obtained from pet stores that sell tarantulas.

Social

1. Where Are You, My Prey?

To prepare for this group game, either draw a huge spider web on an asphalt/concrete section of a playground or sidewalk or use tape to create a web on a large floor space or place a clothesline on a grassy area in the shape of a web. Invite some children to pretend to be spiders and others to be insects. Encourage the insects to crawl or "fly" around the area until they become "stuck" on the web. The "spiders" will then walk along, carefully following the web lines until they reach an insect. Once the spider comes to the insect, the insect is free to leave the web. Continue, with children trading roles when they wish. Remind the spiders to be careful to keep their feet on the web lines so they don't "fall off." Remind the insects that once their feet touch the web, they are stuck.

To Simplify:

● In advance, lay a few plastic models of insects on the lines of the web. Encourage the children to walk along the web as spiders and gather the insects. Remind the spiders to move along the web without bumping into any of their "spider mates."

To Extend:

● Tell the insects to be very quiet on the web. Also, explain that they may wiggle their bodies, but their feet are "stuck" on the web. Instruct the spiders to close their eyes (or wear plastic glasses with plastic wrap taped around the lenses to obscure the "spiders'" vision) and feel their way around the web until they find an insect.

Once all the insects are found, insect and spider people can switch roles if they so desire.

2. Lilting Elephants

For the children to play this group game, first teach them the following song. Each two lines is sung to the tune of the first two lines of "Twinkle, Twinkle Little Star."

> One elephant went out to play,
> out on a spider's web one day
> She(he) had such enormous fun
> that she (he) called for other elephants to come.

After the children are familiar with the words of the song, explain how to play the game.

Have the children form a large circle. Choose one child to go to the center of the group and pretend to be an elephant (using some pantomime motions) having enormous fun on a spider's web. Encourage all of the children to sing the song. As the words "She/he called for another elephant to come" are sung, the elephant in the middle picks a second child to be an elephant. The second child joins the first in the middle of the circle as the group sings "Two elephants went out to play . . ." and so on. The second elephant chooses a third child to be an elephant as the last line of the song is sung. Sing the song again, increasing the number of elephants each time it is repeated. Continue until all the children are in the spider web.

Hint for Success:

● At first, limit the number of "elephants" on the web to four or five. As the web becomes "full," send the elephants back to the circle so more elephants can play on the web. Once children understand how to play the game, include greater numbers of elephants on the web.

Teacher Resources

Field Trip Ideas

1. Arrange a field trip for the class to visit someone's home, possibly a home with a basement or cellar, garage, and a front or back yard. The purpose of the visit would be to find places in and around the house where there are spiders or spider webs. When a spider or web is found have children write where it was found and draw a picture of it. If there is a web, note the kinds and numbers of insects on the web. Either have spider resource books at the home or back at school for children

and adults to use to find out the names and descriptions of the spiders found.

2. Some pet stores sell spiders for pets. Ask your local pet store if spiders are stocked and if it would be possible for your class to come visit. When at the store, ask store personnel to describe what each arachnid available is like as a pet, what each type eats, and what care it requires.

Classroom Visitors

1. Ask someone who has a spider as a pet to bring it into the class for a visit. Ask your visitor to describe what it is like to have this creature as a pet and how he or she cares for the spider.

2. Invite a person who knows from experience how spiders eat insects that would harm plants in a garden or field.

Children's Books

Carle, E. (1984). *The Very Busy Spider*. New York: Putnam Publishing Group.

Craig, J. (1990). *Amazing World of Spiders*. Mahwah, NJ: Troll Associates.

Danks, H. (1987). *The Bug Book*. New York: Workman Publishing.

Gibbons, G. (1993). *Spiders*. New York: Holiday House.

Gleeson, B. (1992). *Anansi*. New York: Simon and Schuster Books (audiocassette also available).

Graham, M. B. (1967). *Be Nice to Spiders*. New York: HarperCollins.

Hawcock, D., and Montgomery, L. (1994). *Bouncing Bugs: Spider*. New York: Random House.

Julivert, M. A. (1992). *The Fascinating World of Spiders*. New York: Barron's Educational Series.

Kimmel, E. A. (1988). *Anansi and the Moss Covered Rock*. New York: Scholastic.

Kimmel, E. A. (1992). *Anansi Goes Fishing*. New York: Holiday House.

Kimmel, E. A. (1994). *Anansi and the Talking Melon*. New York: Holiday House.

Lane, M. (1983). *The Spider*. New York: Dial Books for Young Readers.

Lovett, S. (1991). *Extremely Weird Spiders*. New Mexico: John Muir Publications.

McDermott, G. (1972). *Anansi the Spider: A Tale from the Ashanti*. New York: Henry Holt.

Parsons, A. (1990). *Amazing Spiders*. New York: Alfred A. Knopf.

Petty, K. (1990). *Spiders*. New York: Franklin Watts.

Pringle, L. (1990). *Golden Book of Insects and Spiders*. Racine, WI: Western Publishing.

Schnieper, C. (1989). *Amazing Spiders*. Minneapolis: Carolrhoda Books.

Temple, F. (1994). *Tiger Soup: An Anansi Story from Jamaica*. New York: Orchard Books.

Watts, B. (1991). *Spiders*. New York: Watts.

Adult Resources

Levi, H. (1969). *Spiders and Their Kin*. Racine, WI: Western Publishing.

Earthworms

Terms, Facts, and Principles (TFPs)

General Characteristics

1. Earthworms are cylindrical shaped, segmented animals (annelids) that live in the soil.

2. Earthworms have a mouth (no teeth), a headed end and a tailed end (the head is more pointed than the tail).

3. Earthworms have no ears, eyes, legs or skeleton.

*4. The area around the earthworm's mouth is called the prostomium.

*5. The clitellum is an enlarged glandular area that looks like a band going around each earthworm's body. (This body part is important for mating.)

Earthworm Behaviors

6. Earthworms burrow in the soil.

7. Earthworms move by waves of muscular contractions traveling along the body.

*8. On each segment of the worm's body are two tiny "bristles" called setae. These help the worm to move and allow the worm to cling to the sides of its burrow as it moves out to get food.

9. Earthworms eat leaves, decaying matter, rotting plants, dead animals and soil.

10. Earthworms actually eat their way through dense, hard-packed earth, and excrete the displaced material in small, dark piles called worm castings. Worm castings are a combination of the nutrients of all the foods worms eat. They are a type of enriched soil.

11. Earthworms come to the surface of the ground when their tunnels are flooded.

12. Earthworms breathe through their skin. They must stay moist or they will die.

*13. Each earthworm has both male and female internal body parts. When two worms mate, the pairs reciprocally fertilize each other.

14. Earthworms hatch from small eggs cases, called cocoons, as tiny white worms.

*15. In the winter, worms dig below the frost line and hibernate (sleep) until the ground becomes warmer.

16. There are many species of earthworms which vary in size and color from one to another.

Benefits

17. Worms help the soil in several ways:

   a. Worms eat dead plants and animals.

   b. Worms enrich the soil by excreting worm castings.

   c. Worms burrow in the soil, which loosens the soil particles and allows air and water to enter the ground.

   d. Worms carry rich soil from deep in the ground up to the earth's surface. This causes the surface soil to be replenished over time.

18. Because of the benefits worms bring to the soil, farmers and gardeners value earthworms.

19. Earthworms are a food choice of many different creatures, such as birds, shrews, moles, snakes, turtles, fish, and frogs.

Activity Ideas

Aesthetic

1. Wormy String Painting

This activity is best carried out after children have seen earthworm trails in sand or soil. To prepare for this activity, you will need clothespins, construction paper, tempera paint, and several pieces of yarn cut into approximately eight-inch lengths. Cover the art table with newspapers and have smocks available for the children. Provide a selection of colors of tempera paints poured into pie tins from which the children may choose. Clip clothespins to the ends of the yarn for the children to hold (or tape the yarn to the end of a pencil or short dowel). Give each child a piece of construction paper. Show the children how to pick up the yarn by holding onto the clothespin. Next, gently dip the yarn into the container of paint and then carefully lift the paint-filled yarn from the paint and drag it along the paper. Note how the line that is created may resemble an earthworm's trail across the ground. Invite the children to try the string painting.

Hint for Success:
● Caution children to move the paint-filled yarn slowly, so the paint doesn't spatter onto others' artwork.

To Simplify:
● Offer only two colors of paint to the children from which to choose.

To Extend:

- Cut a variety of yarn lengths from 5" to 15".

- Vary the thickness of the yarn and/or string used. Invite children to try the different strings as they paint. Ask them to choose which type they like using best.

2. Worm Colors

Provide the children with smocks, watercolor paints, small paint brushes, individual containers of water, and white construction paper. Demonstrate how to dip the paint brush into the water, onto a paint color, and then onto the paper. Show how drawing the brush across the paper will create a line that may resemble an earthworm. Direct the children to create these lines on their paper as they wish. Encourage them to make worm lines in whatever color and length they like.

To Simplify:

- Provide the children with commercially available watercolor "crayons." Show them how to dip the end of the crayon in the water and then onto the paper to create the worm-like lines.

- Give children chalk and dark-colored construction paper. Invite them to use the chalk to make the "wormy" lines.

To Extend:

- Invite the children to surround their "worms" with colors they believe the earthworms would like.

3. Wormsical, Musical Elements

🎵 **The Itsy, Bitsy Earthworm**
Tune: "Eensy Weensy Spider"

> The itsy bitsy earthworm went burrowing through the ground.
> Down came the rain and the worm was almost drowned.
> Out came the sun and dried up all the rain.
> Then the itsy bitsy earthworm went burrowing again.

Incorporate hand motions: finger wiggle on "itsy bitsy," throat clutch on "almost drowned," and other actions similar to those used while singing "Eensy Weensy Spider."

> The huge gigantic earthworm went burrowing through the ground.
> Down came the rain and the worm was almost drowned.

> Out came the sun and dried up all the rain.
> Then the huge gigantic earthworm went burrowing again.

Use this simple tune to emphasize the musical elements of volume and pitch. Sing the first verse very quietly. Sing the second verse more loudly. As an alternate approach, sing the first verse in a high-pitched voice. Sing the second verse using a deeper pitch.

4. Earthworm Monotony

Teach children new words to this familiar tune, while introducing the musical element of tempo. Vary the tempo (speed) each time you sing the verse. Children will enjoy the "tongue twister" aspect of repeating the same word so many times in so many ways.

🎵 **Earthworm Monotony**
Tune: "Twinkle, Twinkle, Little Star"

> Earthworm, earthworm, earthworm, earthworm.
> Earthworm, earthworm, earthworm, earthworm.
> Earthworm, earthworm, earthworm, earthworm.
> Earthworm, earthworm, earthworm, earthworm.
> Earthworm, earthworm, earthworm, earthworm.
> Earthworm, earthworm, earthworm, earthworm.

Affective

1. A Snack Fit for Worms!

Though there are many differences between earthworms and people, both eat some types of plants. Worms love to live in gardens where they can find a fresh supply of decaying leaves, roots, and stems. Tell the children this information as you also let them know that they are going to make a snack fit for worms (and people). In advance, bring in a selection of salad vegetables, such as a few varieties of lettuce, carrots, and celery. Have available two salad bowls, as well as tools children can use to help prepare the vegetables (vegetable peeler and paring or plastic knives). Direct the children to first help with the salad by washing the vegetables in the sink. Then, invite children to choose a vegetable to prepare for the salads. Show children how to use a vegetable peeler to peel the carrots. Put the outer peelings in one bowl—this will be the worms' salad. Have them continue to shave the carrot with the peeler into the other bowl. Instruct the children how to tear off the outer leaves of a lettuce head as well as any wilted portions of the lettuce; these go in the worms' salad. Show them how to tear the other leaves into smaller bite-sized pieces for their salad. Give the children paring knives or plastic knives to cut the celery. Again, any brown spots or ends and possibly the celery leaves should go to the worms' salad; the other parts are for the children's salad. Once everything is prepared, serve the people's salad at the next meal with favorite salad dressings, and take the earthworms' salad outdoors to feed to the worms. Choose an "earthy" spot that is shady and moist.

To Simplify:

● Omit the knives, limit the children to peeling carrots and tearing lettuce leaves.

To Extend:

● Invite the children to bring in a favorite salad item from home to add to the worms' and children's salads.

2. Feed the Worms

Help children discover the pleasures of work by having them take responsibility for saving any plant food leftovers from meals. These could include vegetables as well as fruits and grains (crackers, bread, cereal). Provide a plastic container to be kept in the classroom at meal times. Above the container, post a pictograph of types of leftover foods that would be appropriate for the earthworms (see below). Choose a spot of earth on the school grounds away from the main play traffic. Assign a child each day to take the container of food outside during outdoor time and empty it into the worms' feeding place.

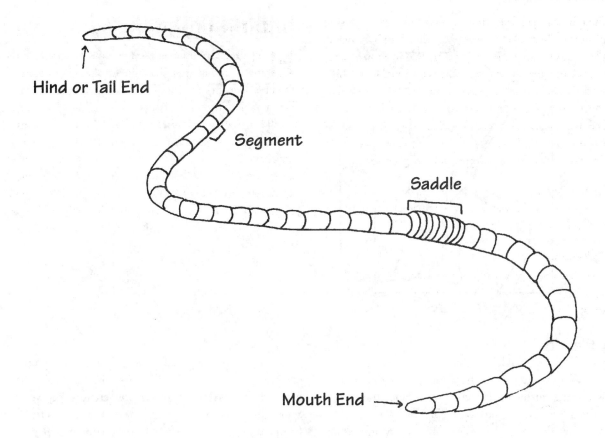

Hind or Tail End

Segment

Saddle

Mouth End →

3. The Early Bird Catches the Worm!

In this activity the children will have the opportunity to make their own tasty worm treat (it's great fun if you are pretending to be a hungry robin!). To prepare for the activity, gather a set of 1/4, 1/2, and 1 cup measuring cups, as well as smooth peanut butter, honey, powdered milk, a mixing bowl, a mixing spoon and waxed paper. Tell the children that they are going to work on preparing a snack to eat—peanut butter dough earthworms. Direct one child to measure 1/2 cup of peanut butter and scoop it into the mixing bowl. Have another child pour 1/4 cup of honey in with the peanut butter. Two children can each put one cup of powdered milk into the mixture. Invite the children to take turns mixing the dough with a mixing spoon. Give each child a scoop of the dough. Invite everyone to roll and shape the dough into earthworm shapes and then pretend to be a bird eating a tasty breakfast.

To Simplify:

● Have each ingredient measured out in advance. Invite the children to take turns pouring or scooping the materials into the mixing bowl and then mixing the dough.

To Extend:

● Provide each child with a plastic knife as they are forming their earthworms. Direct them to use the knife to create the worm's segments.

Cognitive

1. Earthworm Facts

To prepare for this activity, dig up some large earthworms or buy some at a bait store. Place the worms in a dishpan containing moist soil or worm bedding. Cover the pan of worms with cheesecloth to help keep the soil darkened and moist until the activity begins. Invite the children to look at the earthworms. Encourage them to gently pick up the earthworms, feel their skin, watch how they move, and even look for their mouths. On a piece of paper, write down the children's discoveries. As the children look at the earthworms and make comments, give them information about the earthworms. Have available a large picture of an earthworm with the body parts labeled as well as children's reference books about earthworms so it will be convenient to look up answers to questions that arise.

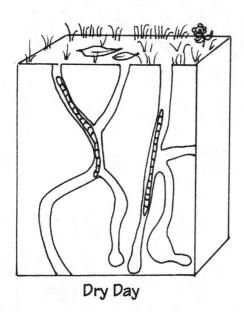

Dry Day

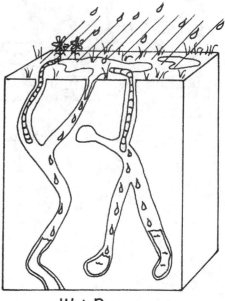

Wet Day

To Simplify:

● Guide the children's discoveries. Encourage them to look for various parts of the worm, such as the mouth (usually the earthworm moves its "head" first; therefore that is the end where the mouth is). Also have them watch how the earthworm moves, even though it has no legs, by stretching out and pulling in.

To Extend:

● Have the children continue to add earthworm facts to the discovery sheet as they learn more about the creatures over the week.

2. It's Raining!

In order to demonstrate for the children what happens to earthworms when it rains, take a few plastic gallon jugs of water to a grassy area outdoors. Mark off a small section of grass with a round plastic hoop or a nylon rope. (The actual shape of the area is not important to the activity, but make it approximately one to two feet in diameter.) Pour the water all over the area inside the rope or hoop—children can help. Wait about an hour. Then gather the children on the dry section of grass around the wet area. Watch the earth and look for earthworms. Ask the children why they think the earthworms came out of their tunnels (or why they didn't come out of their tunnels!). Listen to their answers. Explain to the children that when it rains, water fills up the earthworms' tunnels and the earthworms come up on top of the ground so they can breathe. They are not able to breathe when they are under water. If they stayed under the ground in the water-soaked tunnels, they would die.

To Simplify:

● While you are outside, bring hand-drawn pictures of a cross section of earth with earthworm tunnels—one where the soil is dry and the other where it is very wet. Show children the tunnels and the earthworms in the first picture and compare it with the second in which the tunnels are full of water and the earthworms are approaching the top of the earth to get out of the wet tunnels.

To Extend:

● Take children outside after a rainstorm and look together for earthworms. Ask questions such as "Where are the earthworms?" and "Why are they on the sidewalks and on the streets?"

3. Favorite Habitats

The purpose of this experiment is for the children to discover where earthworms prefer to live. In advance, choose four or five areas on the outdoor playground from which to collect earth samples. Areas to choose include sand, dry soil, moist soil, a garden, under a stone, under grass. Write down each area chosen on a separate piece of paper. You also will need a large piece of black plastic (about 4' x 4'), a bucket, a shovel, a clipboard, pencil, and paper.

Gather the children and go to the first collection area. You (or another adult) will be responsible for the digging; the children will be the gentle earthworm finders and counters. Dig up a shovelful of earth and dump it onto the piece of plastic. Direct children to gently sift their fingers through the sample to find the earthworms. Have them put the earthworms into the bucket. Once

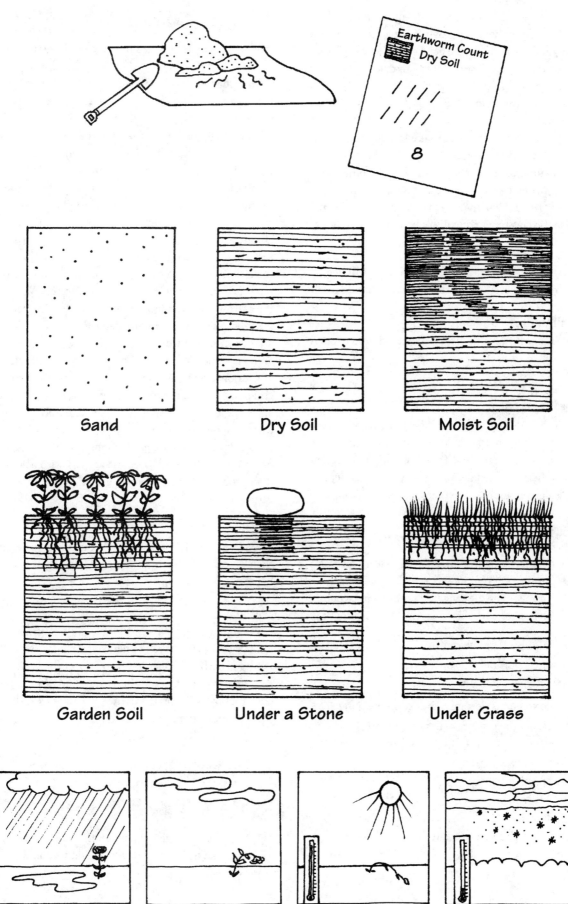

Earthworm Count
Dry Soil

8

Sand

Dry Soil

Moist Soil

Garden Soil

Under a Stone

Under Grass

Rainy

Dry

Hot

Cold

all the worms have been found, count them with the children. Either have the group count aloud or make a mark for each worm on the appropriately labeled paper; write down the total count for the sample, too. After the count is done, carefully return the soil and earthworms to where they were found. Repeat this process for each sample area.

Once each of the earth sample areas has been counted, compare the total counts. Ask the children which sample of earth had the most earthworms. Why do they think that was so? Record their answers on a piece of paper. Save the results in a folder for reference inside the classroom naturalist laboratory.

Hint for Success:
● A simple drawing of the sample area will help children more easily make sense of the counting results.

To Simplify:
● Choose only one area of the playground to study each day.

To Extend:
● Repeat the process on several different days: after a rainy day, during a dry spell, on a hot day, on a cold day, etc. Compare the count of worms for each sample area on the different days. To aid the children in comparing their results, draw a picture symbol that depicts the "soil type" and the weather.

4. Sleeping Earthworms

One interesting way for children to learn factual information is to incorporate these ideas into songs. In the following song, the tune "Frere Jacques" has been used to teach about earthworms hibernating.

♫ Sleepy Earthworms
Words: Grace Spalding
Tune: "Frère Jacques"

> Earthworms sleeping, earthworms sleeping,
> Under the ground, under the ground,
> Waiting for spring, waiting for spring,
> Sleep, sleep, sleep,
> Sleep, sleep, sleep.

To Extend:
● Invite children to create additional verses filled with "earthworm facts."

5. Dry/Wet

This activity is designed to enhance children's observation skills as well as their understanding of earthworm behavior. In a medium-sized, shallow rectangular pan, place two paper towels (one wet, the other dry). Leave a 4" space between the two paper towels. Show children how you have set up the pan with the paper towels. Explain that they are to put about five earthworms in the space between the two towels. Before doing so, ask children to predict what they think the worms will do when they are placed in the pan—will they move to the dry paper or to the wet paper? Ask children to give a reason for their answers. Write down the children's responses on a piece of paper. Now direct the children to place the earthworms in the middle section of the pan between the two paper towels. Watch the earthworms for a few minutes. Ask the children to describe what the worms are doing as they move. Why do they think the worms are moving? Write the children's comments down on a paper. Reread the children's predictions and their current observations. Have the children compare the two. Repeat the activity to see if another group of worms will do the same thing or something different. Again, write down the children's predictions before placing the earthworms in the pan and their observations afterwards. End the activity with a group discussion of what children have learned about the earthworms.

To Simplify:
● Observe the earthworms. Ask children to describe their observations without first predicting what would happen.

To Extend:
● Vary this experiment by seeing if the worms prefer light or dark paper. Use the same rectangular pan with light and dark wet paper towels (or cover the bottom of the pan with wet paper toweling and then place light construction paper on top of the toweling on one half of the pan and dark paper on the other side).

Construction

1. Worm Compost Box

This project will give the children the opportunity to create an indoor or outdoor habitat for the earthworms as well as learn about composting.

Materials Needed:

Shallow wooden box made from exterior grade plywood (2' x 2' x 8") with holes drilled in the bottom for drainage and 1" feet to prop up box

Tray to go under box if kept indoors

Shredded paper, cardboard, or leaf mold

Peat moss (optional) (commercially made worm bedding is also available)

Buckets and large spoons to mix the bedding material with water

Piece of cheesecloth large enough to cover the surface of the soil

Red wiggler worms—about 1 pound

Water

Food leftovers: vegetables, grains, and fruits (beware—fruit leftovers inside will attract fruit flies)

Procedure:

1. One day in advance, set out about two gallons of water to mix into the worm bedding.

2. With the children, fill the bucket about half full with the dry bedding material. Mix in the water until the bedding material is moist but not soaked (if the material is too wet the worms will drown). Give the children turns stirring the mixture.

3. Once the bedding material is moist, pour it into the wooden worm box.

4. Repeat steps 2 and 3 until the worm box is half full of bedding material.

5. Gently place the worms on top of the bedding material. Watch to see what they do.

6. Put food leftovers on the top of the bedding. If these are left on top of the bedding, children can peek under the food periodically to see if the worms have been coming to the surface of the bedding material to eat the food. Sometimes the worm burrows can be seen even if the worms cannot.

7. Keep the bedding material moist. If the worms' home becomes dry or too wet, the worms will die. Cover the worm box with a piece of cheesecloth to help darken the box and hold in some of the moisture.

Hint for Success:

● This worm box can be kept inside. However, the warm, moist environment that has been created for the worms will attract other creatures (such as insects). Keeping the box in a shady spot outdoors may be a better place if it is to be used over an extended period of time.

2. A Home Fit for a Worm

While the earthworms are visiting the classroom, it is important for children and adults alike to prepare a safe, comfortable place for them to live. Before the children arrive, prepare a worm "house." First, find a container that will hold worms and soil. A heavy cardboard box or plastic storage container that is about 4" high, 2-1/2' long and 1-1/2' wide will work well. Drill small holes in the bottom of the container for drainage of excess water. Prepare a lid for the container; use either the plastic container's lid with a large hole cut in the center and covered with cheese cloth or use just a large piece of cheese cloth. Find a large tray or something similar to place under the container to catch excess water as it drains out. Explain to the children that while the worms are inside the classroom away from their natural home, they will need a moist, dark, safe soil home. Direct the children to tear newspaper into small, thin strips. Mix the newspaper strips in a large bucket 1/2 to 3/4 filled with soil (peat moss or soil from the yard). Pour enough water into the soil and newspaper to get the mixture moist, but not wet (or the worms will drown). Put this special worm "bedding" into the house. Fill a spray bottle with water to keep next to the worms' home so children and adults can keep it damp. Add either earthworms from your garden or playground or red worms from a bait shop (approximately 50 worms). Sprinkle cornmeal over the top of the soil surface as the worms' food. Grain and vegetable leftovers from meals or snacks can be placed on top of the surface, also. Direct children and adults to gently use their hands or a small curved shovel to find the worms.

3. Rollin', Rollin', Rollin'

This activity should be implemented after the children have had several opportunities to look at live earthworms. First, ask the children to recall what they noticed about the earthworms. Provide them with reddish-brown colored modeling dough. Invite them to create earthworms by rolling the dough back and forth between the palms of their hands or with their palms on a table. Have them roll the dough until it is the same width as an earthworm. Provide plastic knives so the children can cut the modeling dough to earthworm length. Direct them to work with the ends of their modeling dough worms to make them like real earthworm "heads" and "tails." Ask children what they remember about the earthworm's skin—how it felt and how it looked. Invite them to make their modeling dough earthworms look like that. Encourage the children's creative efforts. Note the various features of the earthworms they create, as well as the unique ways in which they represent these creatures!

To Simplify:
● Have live earthworms available for the children to look at as they create their own.

To Extend:
● Provide a darker brown modeling dough for the children to use as earth. Encourage them to make tunnels and burrows for their modeling dough worms.

Language

1. Shhhh! Listen Very Carefully!

Listening is an important language skill. Explain to the children that this will be a listening activity. Remind them that earthworms have tiny pairs of bristles, called setae, on just about every segment of their bodies. The setae help the worms to move and burrow in their tunnels. Put an earthworm on a piece of construction paper. Tell the children they must be very, very quiet to hear the sound of the setae "scratching" along the paper as the earthworm moves. Listen. Have the children describe what they hear as the earthworm moves.

2. Rhyming Worm Words

This humorous game is a good way to give children practice creating rhymes and to emphasize word articulation.

To carry it out, tell the children they are going to play a rhyming game with you. You will say a word to them, they are to think of a word to rhyme with yours. Demonstrate what you mean by giving them an example, such as "wiggle rhymes with squiggle." Then, sing the two words over and over to the tune "Open, Shut Them" (or another tune they may enjoy). Now, let the children attempt to think of a word to rhyme with a word you give them. After a pair of rhyming words is determined, sing them once again to the tune. Repeat this a few times.

♫ Examples (Sing to the first four lines of "Open, Shut Them.")

    wiggle—squiggle

    worms —squirm

    belly—jelly

    coil—soil

    burrow—furrow

    tunnel—funnel

    trail—tail

To Simplify:
● Provide children with both rhyming words. Have them first repeat the rhyming words without the tune; then sing the rhyming words to a familiar melody.

To Extend:
● Write down favorite pairs of rhyming words and post them in a place everyone can refer to during song times. Ask the children to create their own pairs of rhyming words.

3. Worm Discovery Diaries

This activity will give the children the opportunity to see their ideas written down in words. Fill a three-ring notebook with blank paper. Label the cover of the book to say Earthworm Discovery Diary. Have this notebook available to the children wherever they are working with earthworms. Introduce the book during a time all the children are gathered together. Let them know that one way people remember things they learn is to write their ideas on paper. Show the children the notebooks and tell them where the notebooks will be kept. Tell the children that as they learn something about earthworms and talk with an adult, the adult will write what they say in the notebook. Invite children to draw illustrations of their work if they want to do so.

Hint for Success:
● You may want to have a notebook for each area of the classroom in which the children are working with worms. Examples include: the science table, the pretend play naturalist area, and one more for outside.

To Simplify:
● Have one notebook for the group to use at the area where the live earthworms are kept.

To Extend:
● Periodically enter what the children have dictated into your word processor. Make photocopies of the printouts together with the children's illustrations. Provide this published version in the book area for the children to read with adults. Add to this book throughout the week. If possible, make a copy to send home with the children.

● Combine the information to create an earthworm news bulletin to send home.

Physical

1. Bend and Stretch

This activity will give the children a chance to stretch their bodies in a variety of ways. Remind the children that earthworms have no arms or legs; they move their bodies by shrinking up and stretching. In this activity everyone is going to pretend to stretch and then shrink up like earthworms. Start the movements by having the children watch you and copy what you are doing. Tell the children what to do as you are modeling the stretches. Stand up. Slowly move your shoulders straight up in a shrugging motion, then down. Repeat this a few times. Next, stretch one arm out to the side (watch to not bump the person by your side!). Gently move your hand straight back towards your shoulder, then out again—reach way out, then back in again. Repeat this with the other arm. Also try stretching your arms straight up over your head and back to your shoulders, then in and out in front of your body. Lie down on the floor. Stretch your whole body lengthwise as long as you can, with your arms reaching beyond your head.

Bring your whole body back into a tight ball. Turn over and try this lying on your tummy. Ask children, "Is your body moving ahead or backwards at all?" As you cool down, discuss children's answers to your query.

To Simplify:

● Introduce one or two stretching activities each day.

To Extend:

● Invite the children to make suggestions about how to stretch their bodies. Let them be the leaders and show the rest of the group what to do.

2. Burrowing Cutting Practice

This activity provides children with scissors practice that is fun, too. Here they will use scissors to cut through paper, pretending an earthworm is burrowing through the ground. Prior to the children's arrival, make earthworm burrows on paper using a brown marker. Vary the width of the burrows as well as how straight or curved they are (see page 441).

Hints for Success:

● Start with burrows 3" wide. Gradually offer children narrower burrows until they are cutting along a line.

● When adding curves to the path, begin with rounded ones, then introduce right angles, which are more difficult to cut accurately.

To Simplify:

● Encourage the children to follow the cutting paths with their fingers before cutting.

To Extend:

● Invite the children to draw their own earthworm burrows to cut out.

3. The Worms Go In, The Worms Go Out

This lacing activity will give the children an opportunity to practice eye-hand coordination. Prior to the children's participation, draw thick, curving lines on brown cardboard. These represent worm burrows. Punch holes along the line with a hole puncher, about 3/4" apart. Make several of these, varying the "burrow paths" children are to follow. Have on hand several brown and oxblood-colored shoelaces, with one end tied into a knot larger than the holes in the cardboard. Tell the children to use a shoelace to pretend a worm is burrow-

ing in and out of the holes in the card. Show them how to push the plastic tip of the shoelace up through one hole and down through the next. Continue in this way until the entire burrow is filled.

To Simplify:

● Have the burrow lines go straight across the cardboard.

To Extend:

● Create curved burrow lines. Have the children use shoelaces in different widths as they try more worm burrow cards.

● Number the burrow holes. Have the children follow the numbers as they burrow their worm through the holes.

Pretend Play

1. Earthworm Naturalist— Earthworm Activities

In this activity the children will have the opportunity to pretend to be naturalists. As naturalists, the children will study earthworms, learning about their characteristics, the places they live, and what foods they prefer. Some of these observations are best implemented outdoors; others could be set up inside in a pretend play laboratory.

To set up the laboratory, several items should be prepared in advance.

a) Prepare a work table for the children, large enough to hold the worms' home and space for the children to carry out experiments.

b) Set out a variety of recording tools for the children to use: charts, books, construction paper, pencils, markers. Set these on or by the table so the children will have easy access to the materials. (Some specific suggestions on how to use these materials are found throughout this chapter. See, for example, "Worm Discovery Diaries" on page 440.)

c) Provide observation tools, such as magnifying lenses and an earthworm viewing apparatus: To create this special apparatus, place a rectangular mirror flat on the table. At each end of the mirror, place a rectangular wooden block to support a rectangular piece of clear plastic, which is the same size as the mirror (glass could also be used with older children). This viewing apparatus will make it possible for the children to watch the worm as it moves on top of the plastic and to see its underside that is reflected on the mirror.

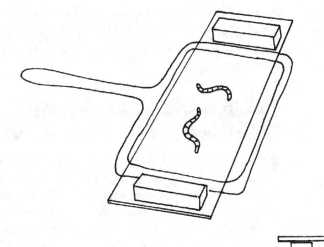

d) Make available paper towels and a spray bottle filled with water. Remember, an earthworm's skin must be kept moist for it to stay alive. Caution the children about spraying too much water since this could cause the worms to drown.

e) Have available a temporary worm habitat (see "A Home Fit for a Worm!" on page 439). Provide live earthworms for the children to study. Dig up approximately 50 earthworms. Again, the children could be part of the collection process. (Earthworms can also be purchased at bait shops.)

Offer children laboratory coats, clipboards, and additional magnifying lenses as dress-up clothes and props. Invite children into the naturalists' laboratory.

2. Gardener: Friend of the Earthworms

This activity could be implemented indoors in the water table or other large rectangular tub or else outdoors on the playground. Prepare a pretend garden for the children by pouring soil into the water table or large tub. Add a few rocks, plastic earthworms, and possibly a few small, "weedy" looking plastic plants (or use actual weeds from outdoors with roots). Gather plastic gardening tools for the children to use: trowels, small rakes, a watering can, and a bucket for collecting weeds and rocks. Also, have available flower or vegetable seeds, pictures and labels for each kind of seed attached to a Popsicle® stick, gardening gloves, and sun hats. Explain to the children that they will have the opportunity to pretend to be gardeners. Gardeners and earthworms, in a sense, work together to make a fertile environment for plants to grow. Instruct the children to pretend to be gardeners by digging up the soil, raking out the rocks and pulling weeds, planting seeds, and watering the ground. As the gardeners find earthworms in the soil, remind them to be careful with the worms and gently put them back into the soil. It is to the gardener's advantage to be gentle with the earthworms found in the soil as he or she is digging.

To Simplify:

● Start the garden area with just a few materials, such as soil, seeds, and rakes. Each day, introduce a few new materials to the area, teaching the children how to use each item as it is introduced.

To Extend:

● Create a real garden outdoors in which the children care for plants in cooperation with the earthworms.

3. Kitchen Area with Compost Box

A simple pretend compost box can be created for a make-believe kitchen area. Fill a cardboard box with cut up pieces of brown and/or gray yarn (the worm bedding). Add plastic earthworms (these can be purchased at a bait shop—without hooks!). Encourage children to place food scraps in the worm box as they pretend to prepare meals or clean up after pretending to eat.

Social

1. Worms in the Rain

After a rainstorm, go outside for a walk with buckets half full of soil. Have children walk in groups of two or three, one bucket of soil per group. Explain to the children that if the earthworms are on the sidewalk when the sun comes out, they will dry out and die. They also could get stepped on as people walk down the sidewalk. Direct the children to pick up the earthworms and put them in the soil-filled buckets. When all the earthworms are picked up, have each group of children decide on a safer outdoor place to take the earthworms. Once a decision is made, have children pour out the earthworms and soil in the safe place they chose.

To Simplify:

● Have only one bucket for the adult to hold as the children pick up the worms.

To Extend:

● Before the earthworms are freed, have the children work together to count them. Find out how many worms the whole class saved from drying out.

2. Worm Around the Classroom

Gather all the children together in a large group area. Teach them the following song to the tune of "Hey, Ho, Nobody Home." Sing the first three lines to the tune of the first three lines of "Hey, Ho, Nobody Home." Line 4 below repeats line 1 of "Hey, Ho."

> Worm, worm, worm, worm,
> Go around and round and round.
> Worm, worm, worm, worm,
> Go around and round.

Once the children are familiar with the song, direct them to stand up and hold hands. Tell the children that as a group, you are all going to sing the song and walk around in a circle. Do this by first circling left and then circling right. Now, direct the children to let go of hands and follow you as you walk around the classroom. Sing the song together as you walk. End the activity by coming back to the large group area, form a large group circle, and sing:

> Worm, worm, worm, worm,
> Go around and round and round.
> Worm, worm, worm, worm,
> Now it's time to sit down.

Have everyone sit down.

To Simplify:

● As the group is singing the song, walk around in the large group area only.

To Extend:

● Invite the children to take turns being the leader

of the group as everyone walks around the classroom.

● Once the children are familiar with the activity, try singing the song outdoors, winding around the play yard as you sing.

3. Cooperative Worm Habitat Mural

In advance, prepare a bulletin board in the classroom that depicts a cross section of earth. Include a brown section on the bottom to represent soil on which earthworm burrows have been drawn and an open section for the plants above the soil (see page 445). Introduce the bulletin board on the first day the unit starts. Tell the children that over the next week, they are going to work together to create a large picture of earthworms and their home. Then each day as the children learn about earthworms and their habitat, encourage them to add items to the mural. Examples of items to be added to the mural are:

a) **Earthworms:** Draw earthworm shapes on paper. Invite the children to cut out the earthworms and then tape or glue them to the mural in a place they believe the earthworms belong.

b) **Grass:** Give the children 3" to 5" strips of green construction paper. Show them how to use scissors to cut fringes in the paper to resemble grass. Have the children glue or tape the grass to the top of the soil.

c) **Trees:** Either provide children with tree shapes to cut out or large paper tree parts (trunk, branches, and leaves) to put together on the mural. Also have brown, "dead" leaves for the children to place on the top of the soil level as worm food.

d) **Flowers:** Give children a variety of colors of paper to use to create their own flowers with markers and scissors. Either provide them with stems and leaves or provide green paper for the children to again create their own.

f) **Predators:** Draw bird, snake, toad, turtle, and mole shapes for the children to cut out and place on the mural as they desire. Children can choose to have the earthworms hiding from the predators or place them in a spot where the predators might catch them for a meal.

g) **Rocks:** Children can freely cut out rock shapes, draw their own rocks to cut out, or cut out shapes of rocks an adult has drawn.

Choose one item for the children to work on at a time. Place the materials on a table near the mural site, so children can work on the cooperative project as they

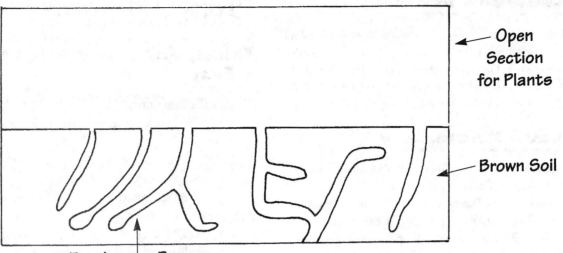

Open Section for Plants

Brown Soil

Earthworm Burrows

desire. As the week goes along, frequently bring the children's attention to the mural and talk about how they have worked together to create the artwork. On one section of the mural, place a large piece of paper for all the children to use to "sign" their name to the mural.

To Simplify:
● Have the materials already made for the children to tape or glue onto the bulletin board.

To Extend:
● Encourage the children to think of additional items they believe are still necessary to complete this cooperative project.

Teacher Resources

Field Trips

1. Bait shops may have a variety of live worms for sale, as well as plastic worms to be used for catching fish. Call ahead to a local bait store to find out if the store is large enough for your group of children to visit. (If it isn't, you could tell parents where the store is and encourage them to take their children to the store at their convenience.) Also, ask if the bait shop sells live worms. Find out if someone from the store could talk with the children about the different kinds of worms for sale, where the worms come from, and how the workers care for the worms.

2. If your area has a nature center, find out if there is someone who could take the children on a walk that would focus on earthworms—looking for different places the worms would live and finding

animals that possibly eat earthworms for meals. Ask the person to discuss with the children how earthworms are helpful to the environment.

3. If there is a nature area by your school, take the children on a walk. Look for earthworms under piles of leaves and under rocks. Find out what other creatures live near the earthworms. Divide children into groups and ask an adult to accompany each group. Ask each adult to record on a piece of paper what the children in her/his group have discovered on their walk. When everyone is finished walking, gather the children in a group and discuss what they found.

Classroom Visitors

1. Invite a naturalist to come to the classroom to talk about earthworms: their habitats, their care, and how earthworms are helpful to humans and other creatures and plants.

2. Have a fishing enthusiast talk with the children about using live earthworms or plastic earthworms as bait. Investigate questions such as: Which bait is best for catching fish? How does the person get the worms used for fishing? Possibly have the person prepare and cook a fish for the children to taste.

3. Arrange for a gardener to talk with the children about how earthworms are essential for healthy plants. Ask what the gardener does to care for the worms in his or her garden.

Children's Books

Dunrea, O. (1989). *Deep Down Underground*. New York: Macmillan.

Jennings, T. (1990). *Earthworms*. New York: Watts.

Watts, B. (1991). *Keeping Minibeasts: Earthworms*. New York: Franklin Watts.

Adult References

Appelhof, M. (1982). *Worms Eat My Garbage*. Kalamazoo, MI: Flower Press.

Cohen, R., and Tunick, B. P. (1993). *Snail Trails and Tadpole Tails*. St. Paul, MN: Redleaf Press.

Kalman, B. (1992). *Squirmy Wormy Composters*. New York: Crabtree.

Frogs and Toads

Terms, Facts, and Principles (TFPs)

General Characteristics

1. Frogs and toads are leaping amphibians; they have no tails.

2. Amphibians are cold-blooded animals with scaleless skin that can live on land or in water.

3. Frogs and toads have short, round bodies and large heads with bulging eyes.

4. Frogs and toads begin life in eggs. These are laid in a jelly-like mass on the water's surface.

5. Tadpoles hatch from the eggs.

6. Tadpoles live in water; have round heads and bodies and a tail, but no legs. They swim using their tails. As tadpoles grow, they lose their tails and grow legs.

7. Tadpoles have gills for breathing under water; the gills are replaced by lungs as the tadpole matures into a frog or toad.

8. Frogs and toads have lungs, but they can also breathe through their skin.

*9. The process of a frog or toad changing in form from egg to tadpole to frog is called metamorphosis.

10. Frogs and toads must breathe air to live.

11. Frogs and toads have short front legs and long back legs.

12. The long back legs enable frogs and toads to jump.

13. Webbed feet help frogs to swim.

14. Frogs have smooth, moist skin; toads have drier, bumpy skin.

15. Many frogs live in or near ponds, marshes, lakes or slow-running streams with vegetation. Some frogs live in trees.

16. Toads habitats are more terrestrial in habit than frogs—they live mainly on the land. (Technically, toads are also frogs.)

Frog and Toad Behaviors

17. Frogs and toads eat a variety of insects, worms, and vegetation; larger frogs may eat small birds and young snakes.

18. Frogs catch their food by shooting out their long, sticky tongues and catching insects.

19. Frogs and toads are the food of several animals, such as snapping turtles, several kinds of birds (heron, owls, hawks), snakes, and raccoons.

20. Frogs and toads vary in size and color from one species to another.

21. In the winter, frogs burrow down into the mud to hibernate (sleep) until spring.

22. Frogs and toads make a variety of noises, especially during the mating season. Sometimes, frogs and toads can be identified by the type of sound they are making. Some examples:

    a. Bullfrog: jug-o-rum or brr-uum

    b. Green frog: sounds like the twang of a banjo string

    c. Pickerel frog: low-pitched croaking that sounds like snoring

    d. Northern Chorus frog: short, rasping trill, similar to the sound made by a person running a fingernail over a comb

    e. Spring Peeper: bird-like pee-eeep sound

    f. American toad: w-a-a-a-ah, sounds like a sheep's bleat

Frogs, Toads, and People

23. People who study frogs and toads as well as other animals are called zoologists.

24. Frogs and toads must be handled in a gentle fashion to keep them safe. Because frogs tend to be faster and longer jumpers than toads, toads are easier to handle.

Activity Ideas

Aesthetic

1. Colorful Frogs

This activity will give the children an opportunity to experiment with color as they also learn that frogs vary greatly from one another in their colorings, depending on their species. Draw large frog shapes on white construction paper (see page 448 for models). Give the children watercolor paints in various shades of green, red, orange, yellow, tan, and brown. Demonstrate to the children how to dip the paintbrush first into the water, then onto the paint chip, and finally onto the frog shape. Encourage children to paint their frogs in colors that are pleasing to them.

Hint for Success:

● Display pictures of various frog types in the classroom for the children to use as a reference for their artistic creations. Provide a variety of live frogs for the children to observe as well.

To Simplify:

● Use poster paints in lieu of watercolors. Provide children with frog-shaped paper made from large sheets of easel paper.

To Extend:

● Encourage children to draw lines on their frog shapes before starting to paint; they can use the lines as guides in making their frogs a combination of several colors.

2. Sponge and Tear Art

Denise Fleming is an artist who portrays the natural world through sponge painting and construction/tissue paper illustrations. This activity will give children a chance to do the same. Obtain a copy of one of *In the Tall, Tall Grass* (1991) and/or *In the Small, Small Pond* (1993). Read one or both of these books to the children. Give them a chance to look closely at the illustrations. Encourage them to find the frogs and toads as they examine the pages. Point out how the artist has used sponges and paint as well as torn paper to make pictures. Offer similar materials for children to use at the art table. Support their efforts with no pressure to create any particular kind of scene.

To Simplify:

● Draw the children's attention to only one of the art styles used. Provide like materials with which they may work.

To Extend:

● As the children look at the pictures, draw their attention to the theme of the artist's illustrations. Encourage them to recreate that theme in their own work. Make it easier for children to explore the artist's techniques by focusing on particular elements such as how the grass is shaped or how animals bodies are depicted with different sizes of sponges.

3. Rocky Frogs and Toads

Collect a variety of fist-sized rocks: some flat, some round, some bumpy, some smooth. Mix tempera paint in a range of colors: some bright, some dull, some neutral, some colorful. Cover a table with newspaper and place the paint in small containers within easy reach of the children. Put a short brush in each container. Make some of the paintbrushes thin-tipped, others wide. Provide smocks for the children and wear one

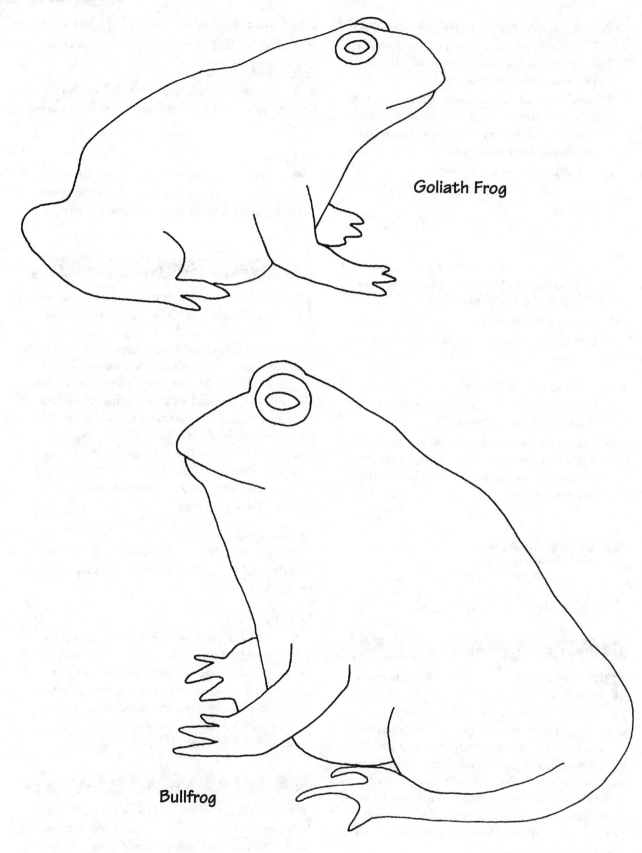

Goliath Frog

Bullfrog

yourself. Post a number of frog and toad pictures in the area nearby. Tell children to select a rock and paint it to look like a frog or toad. Enjoy!

To Simplify:

● Reduce the number of children who participate in the activity at one time.

● Provide sponges instead of brushes. This will be messier, but easier for children to handle.

To Extend:

● Prior to beginning this activity, have the children go outside and select their own rocks, looking for frog- or toad-like shapes.

4. Amphibious Song

Teach the "Frog Pond Song" to the children one part at a time. As children become familiar with the various parts, divide the group into four sections. Have children in group #1 start by singing Part 1 all the way through, one time, by themselves. Tell the other children to remain quiet for the moment; explain that you will signal for them to begin singing their own parts at the appropriate time. Ask group #2 to sing Part 2, as group #1 sings its part through again. Next, have group #3 enter the singing as groups 1 and 2 repeat their parts. Finally, have group #4 join the singing by adding Part 4. Repeat the entire song with all groups two or three times.

♫ "Frog Pond Song"

Words by Janet Brock and Grace Spalding
Tune: "Fish and Chips and Vinegar"

Part 1:

Mos-qui-toes, mos-qui-toes, mos-qui-toes.

Part 2:

1 Bullfrog, 2 bullfrogs, 3 bullfrogs, 4 bullfrogs,
5 bullfrogs, 6 bullfrogs, glub, glub, glub, glub.

Part 3:

Don't throw your muck in my frog pond, my frog
    pond, my frog pond.
Don't throw your muck in my frog pond,
My frog pond's clean.

Part 4:

Fish and frogs and dragonflies, dragonflies, dragon-
    flies,
Fish and frogs and dragonflies, live in my pond.

Hints for Success:

● Assign an adult or child leader to each group to help its members know when to enter the round.

● Tape record the children's singing so they more easily hear the effect of the four parts being sung simultaneously.

Affective

1. Frog Lacing

The purpose of this activity is for children to gain mastery in using age-appropriate tools. To prepare, gather four to six blunt-ended, plastic sewing needles and cut one-yard lengths of medium-weight yarn (enough so each child will have two or three yarn pieces). Also, trace the shapes illustrated below onto white posterboard.

Cut out enough shapes for each child to receive two that are identical. Punch holes around the edge of each shape, about 1/2" apart, to serve as lacing holes. Thread the yarn onto the needles. Tie the two ends of each yarn piece together in a knot that is larger than the punched holes so the yarn won't pull through as the children sew. Give each child two shapes to lace together, as well as a needle and yarn. Demonstrate as you explain to the children how to put the needle up through one hole, down through the next, and so on, around the frog or toad shape, until the animal is completely laced. Assist children in tying off the end of one length of yarn and beginning another if one piece is not long enough to completely lace the shape.

Hint for Success:

● Provide the children with markers or crayons to decorate their frogs or toads while they are waiting for a turn to begin lacing.

To Simplify:

● Have the children sew only one frog or toad. Also, tie the end of the yarn to the starting hole so the yarn will not pull through the holes as the children sew.

To Extend:

● Once the children have laced all but 5 or 6 holes, have them stop lacing for a few moments and stuff their toads or frogs with tissue paper, old stockings, or crumbled-up strips of newspaper. This will give their amphibians some form.

● Lace the frog shapes onto a larger lily pad shape. The lily pad should have holes that correspond to the holes in the frog shapes.

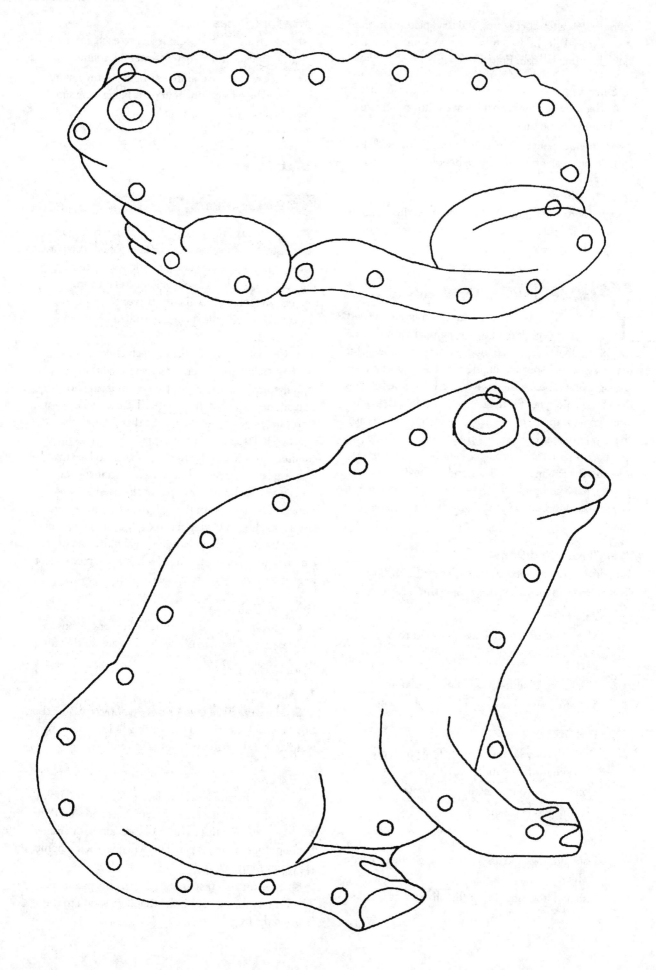

2. Toad Talk

This activity requires a live toad, easel paper, and markers. Show children the toad either by holding it gently or placing it in a clear container in which it has air to breathe and room to move. Ask the children to help you create a list of words describing what the toad looks like and how it behaves. Write these in large print on the easel paper as the children say them.

> Toad Talk
> hopping
> brown
> bumpy
> soft
> quiet
> spots

Next, go back over the list. Have children find or show ways in which they share some of the same characteristics used to describe the toad. Say things like: "You said the toad was bumpy. Show me a place on your body that is bumpy." "This toad has brown spots. Show me a brown spot on you." "This toad jumps. Show me how you can jump."

To Simplify:
● Focus on visible characteristics and body parts; for instance, "This toad has eyes. Show me your eyes."

To Extend:
● Ask each child to describe his or her physical characteristics and actions. Next, have the children compare their lists with the toad descriptions generated by the group.

3. Tidy Toads

This activity is aimed at helping children gain competence in maintaining their environment. Prior to cleanup time, announce to children that today they will become tidy toads, whose job it is to keep their environment clean. Remind children that all living creatures need a clean, safe environment in which to live. When cleanup begins, the children will hop from place to place, cleaning up the room. Carry out this plan, reminding children to "hop" about as they put materials away.

Hint for Success:
● Sing this song as the children become Tidy Toads:

♫ **Tidy Toads**
Words: Grace Spalding
Tune: "Skip to My Lou"

> Tidy toads, cleanup the room,
> Tidy toads, cleanup the room,
> Tidy toads, cleanup the room,
> Keep our habitat clean.

Cognitive

1. Tadpole to Frog, Part I

The materials for this activity include factual books about frog metamorphosis, such as *From Tadpole to Frog* by Wendy Pfeffer (1994) and *Frog* by Moira Butterfield (1992). Also, display large pictures of each phase of a frog's development (see page 452).

As an introduction to the activity, show the pictures first (not in any order) during circle time. Tell children that the story you are about to read will tell them the true sequence. Explain that you will ask them to put the pictures in order showing how a frog develops after you complete the book. Next, read one of the books about frog metamorphosis. When you are done, ask the children to study the pictures. Ask questions such as "How did the frog's life begin? What happened next?" and so on, until the children have sequenced the pictures. When they think they are finished, talk through the order they chose. Ask if they think the order is the same as the one described in the book. Make any changes in the arrangement that the children suggest. Then look through the book again. Tell the children to watch the order of the pictures as you look at the pages. If they notice something they would like to change in their ordering of the frog's metamorphosis, have them verbally point it out.

2. Tadpole to Frog, Part II

Make three or four smaller sets of pictures similar to those used in "Tadpole to Frog: Part I." Give each child a set of pictures and ask him or her to put the pictures in order to show how a frog develops from egg to adult. When each child is finished, have him or her compare the ordering of the pictures to the sequence depicted in the books presented.

Hint for Success:
● Attach seven circles or squares of Velcro® to a strip of posterboard. Put the other side of the Velcro® on the backs of the frog development pictures. This will

help keep the pictures from sliding around as the children are working.

To Simplify:

● Start with fewer pictures, such as 1) the egg, 2) tadpole with no legs, and 3) frog. Add more pictures as the children gain confidence in seriating them.

To Extend:

● Ask the children to explain why they ordered the pictures as they did. Once they have accomplished this, read the book a second time, with the children pointing to their pictures as each phase is mentioned by the author.

3. On Land, in Water

*G*ive children an opportunity to observe live frogs and toads. First, obtain two separate aquariums with tightly fitting screen covers. Prepare one for a toad with soil inside and another one for a frog that would live in the water. Fill the frog's aquarium about 1/4 or 1/3 full of water. Place two or three rocks carefully in the water. Make sure these are big enough and stacked in such a way that the frog can walk out of the water. Also, leave enough room in the water for the frog to swim. Live-water plants in the water could make the frog feel more comfortable, as they provide camouflage. Provide

the frog with insects found around the habitat from which it came. In the toad's aquarium, place about 2 or 3 inches of garden soil hopefully with a few earthworms and insects. Lay a few leaves on top of the soil to help hold in moisture as well as provide a hiding place for the toad. Mist the soil with water to keep it moist. Keep the frog and toad in the tanks for only a few days (less than one week), because it is difficult to encourage a grown frog or toad to eat in captivity.

Put the aquariums in an area of the classroom where the children can easily view the frog and toad. It would be best to have them on a table so children would have room to draw or write observations of the creatures. The first day the frog and toad are in the room, encourage children to watch them. The second day, ask them to describe what they notice about the two amphibians: how they move, their colorings, their skin, and so on. Have the children compare the features of the frog to those of the toad. How are they similar? How are they different? On another day, give the children paper and other materials they will need to draw pictures of each animal. Put these together in book form to keep at the frog/toad table (either stapling pages together or punching holes in the papers and keeping them together in a three-ring notebook). Invite children to look at each other's pictures and add more pictures to the books as they continue their observations.

Hint for Success:
● Have nearby factual information books about frogs and toads for the children's reference. (Several suggestions are listed in the bibliography at the end of this mini-theme.)

To Simplify:
● Introduce only one amphibian to the room at first. Add the second after the children have had a day or two to observe the first one.

To Extend:
● Find frog or tadpole eggs, or tadpoles for the water environment. (Tadpole "growing kits" are commercially available at some toy stores.) These will require more water as well as water plants and/or bloodworms for the tadpoles to eat. Encourage the children to observe the eggs or tadpoles each day and note any changes they see. Keep a written record of what the children say about the creatures. Post this list by the aquarium. Also, invite the children to draw a picture each day of the eggs or tadpoles as a way to record their development.

4. Camouflage Collage

The purpose of this activity is to teach children about ways frogs and toads hide themselves from predators. In advance, cut out pictures of frogs and toads from magazines. Gather a variety of nature materials, such as leaves, twigs, and tree seeds. Give each child a piece of white paper, glue, and a glue-spreading paddle. Direct everyone to choose a frog or toad picture and paste it on his or her paper. Draw the children's attention to how easy it is to see the frog or toad on the white background. If the frog were outside, a hungry heron, snake, or raccoon could quickly spot the little creature and eat it for lunch. Invite the children to hide their frogs or toads with the leaves, twigs, or seeds by gluing the nature items on their paper.

Hint for Success:
● Have a model of a frog predator on the table as children camouflage their frogs and toads.

To Simplify:
● Use leaves that children can dip into glue and then stick to their paper, thus omitting the glue paddles.

To Extend:
● Cut out pictures of brightly colored frogs. Have children choose the kinds of materials necessary to camouflage those creatures.

Construction

1. Leaping Frog Habitat

This activity would be appropriate as a follow-up to "Rocky Frogs and Toads" (see page 447). To prepare, collect enough shoeboxes so that each child has one. Gather nature materials such as rocks, soil, leaves, acorns, pine cones, twigs, and moss. In addition, provide children with blue or green cellophane and possibly small plastic plants. Place the materials in separate plastic containers on a table covered with newspaper and talk about the variety with children. Invite them to use their boxes in creating a home for the frogs or toads they have made during this mini-theme. Have children choose either a water habitat or a soil habitat, and encourage them to arrange the materials they select in a way that would make their frogs or toads feel comfortable.

Hint for Success:
● Line the boxes with plastic to help prevent soil from leaking through the bottom.

2. Mysterious Toads

Gather a variety of natural items, including pine cones, twigs, rocks, maple tree seeds, acorns, and tree bark. Cut 6" squares of cardboard to serve as bases for the children's constructed items. Also, mix 1/2 cup of paste with 1 cup of glue and pour the mixture into small, open containers; put a spreading paddle in each container. Show children the materials available. Invite them to use the materials to construct a frog or a toad in whatever way they like.

3. Frog Food

This is a cooking activity in which the children use cheese dough to create insects. Later, the children will pretend to be frogs and toads and eat them. Assemble the following ingredients:

> 1 cup grated sharp cheddar cheese
>
> 1 stick softened margarine
>
> 1 teaspoon salt
>
> 1 cup all-purpose flour

Preheat the oven to 350°. Combine the first three ingredients and cream. Add flour and mix thoroughly. Roll in a ball and wrap tightly in plastic wrap. Refrigerate 30 minutes. (Makes enough for 16 tablespoon-size servings.) Provide each child with a 12" square piece of waxed paper to use as a work space. Explain to the children that they are to create insects from the dough. Give each child a small amount of dough and almond slices for wings. After the children have finished their insects, bake their dough creations on an ungreased cookie sheet until golden, about 15 to 20 minutes. Cool, then eat. Yum! (These can be stored in a cookie tin for three to four days.)

Hint for Success:

● As the children are beginning their insects, help them recall information, such as how many legs an insect has or how many body parts. Provide some insect pictures nearby to which the children can refer.

Language

1. Wordless Frog Adventures

Children enjoy the adventures of the frog created by Mercer Mayer in the "A Boy, a Dog, and a Frog" series. Several titles are listed in the resource section of this mini-theme. Make one or more of these available to the children in the library corner. Once they have had a chance to look at the books on their own, invite children to create words to go with a story. Go through one of the books page by page, talking through the adventure.

To Simplify:

● Ask children to identify who is in each picture and what action is taking place.

To Extend:

● Ask children to provide dialogue for the characters. Record their ideas on paper, one sheet per child. Children may complete one or more pages depending on their interests and abilities. If children are able, encourage them to record their ideas in their own versions of writing.

2. Frog Chorus

Refer to the Terms, Facts, and Principles for this mini-theme. Note the different sounds frogs make (page 447). Use the outlines provided to create paper representations of a bullfrog, a Spring Peeper, and an American toad. Make enough for each child in the group to have one of the three varieties.

Gather the children in a group. Explain that today they will be a frog chorus. That is, they will sing together like frogs. Give some children the bullfrog symbols and tell them they will make a deep "jug-o-rum" sound. Give some children the Spring Peeper pictures and explain that their sound will be a shrill peep. Give the rest of the children the American toad cutouts, describing the sound they make as a "w-a-a-a-ah" noise, much like a sheep's bleat. Have each group of children practice making their sounds separately. As the group leader, you should have all three pictures. Keep them face down, only showing one at a time. As you show a picture, the designated group makes the corresponding sounds. Eventually have two, then all three groups making sounds simultaneously. Following this practice session of sounds without any tune, invite children to accompany you in making their sounds to a simple tune the group knows well.

Hint for Success:

● To make them easier to hold, tape each of the leader's symbols to a tongue depressor. Make the cues to start and stop dramatic so children can more easily follow them. The signal to start should be a strong motion with the symbol facing toward the children. The signal to stop should be a sweeping motion downwards as the symbol is placed face down.

American Toad

Pickeral Frog

Spring Peeper

Green Frog

Bullfrog

Toad

Toad

Bullfrog

Toad

Toad

To Simplify:

● Have all the children pretend to be one kind of frog at one time. As they become comfortable, introduce a second sound for everyone to make together.

To Extend:

● Make the role of the leader more significant. Have children enter the song on cue, with only one group sounding at a time for brief segments of a song. Emphasize the importance of watching for the leader's signals. Eventually, have children take on the role of leader.

3. Amphibious Sound Patterns

This is an excellent follow-up to the "Frog Chorus" activity (see page 454). Using several copies of the same images used to depict bullfrogs, Spring Peepers, and American toads, have children select four or five with which to create a line of pictures. Invite children to read their symbols by making the sounds associated with each, in the order in which they appear.

As children become proficient, increase the number of symbols used in a single line, the variety of frogs/toads, or the number of lines in each child's pattern. A few additional frog/toad varieties are provided here.

4. Frog Fantasies

Read one of the following books to the children: *The Vingananee and the Tree Toad: A Liberian Tale* by Verna Aardema (1988), or *Ma'ii and Cousin Horned Toad: A Traditional Navajo Story* by Shonto Begay (1992). Once the children are familiar with the story you have chosen, tell them you are going to read it again. This time they are to listen for characteristics of the toad. In discussion following your reading, write children's ideas on a large piece of easel paper. Once it is finished, read the list back to the group. Ask children to determine whether each feature of the toad character from the book is true of real toads or is pretend.

To Simplify:

● Have the children find the toad in the illustrations of the book.

To Extend:

● Have children tell how they know the various characteristics are real or pretend.

● Read both stories. Then, ask children to compare the two toad portrayals.

Physical

1. Leaping Frogs

Set up this jumping activity in a large open space, indoors or outdoors. Create obstacles over which the children must jump; the obstacles should represent a plant, a log, a lily pad, and a pond of water. For instance, plastic plants poked into the ground could be one obstacle, long wooden blocks or tree branches could represent the log, a circle of green felt material could be the lily pad, and a blue towel or blanket could symbolize the pond. Place the props apart from one another, in a line or a circle. Explain to the children that they are to pretend to be frogs, jumping over each obstacle.

Hint for Success:

● Have the children move in one direction. Use arrows taped to the floor or numbered traffic cones placed next to each obstacle to help children identify the direction and order in which they are to jump.

To Simplify:

● Have the children try only one jump each day. Add more obstacles over time.

To Extend:

● Before carrying out this activity, read *Jump, Frog, Jump!* by Robert Kalan (1981). Later, introduce the jumping course to the children. Tell them to pretend to be the frog from the story, getting away from hungry predators. Say "Jump, frog, jump!" as they go over each obstacle.

2. Catch that Insect!

For this targeting activity, buy several party blow toys that have a rolled up tube of paper that shoots out when a person blows on the mouthpiece. Make sure each child can have his or her own. On the walls around the classroom, tape many flying insects, some higher than children's eye level, some lower, and some at the children's eye level. Invite the children to pretend they are frogs and the blow toys are their tongues. Tell them to hop around the room until they see an insect. When they see an insect they should reach out their "tongues" to catch it. As an insect is touched, the child can hold it in his or her free hand. Direct the "frogs" to keep catching insects until there are no more left on the walls.

3. Spray Bottle Frog Tongues

This is an enjoyable targeting activity best implemented in the outdoor environment. To prepare, fill several spray bottles with water. Draw insect shapes with permanent markers on large, plastic buttons (available at fabric or department stores). Lay the buttons around the ground on the play yard. Direct children to find the "insects" outside and "catch" them with their pretend spray bottle tongue. Explain to children that the insects are caught once they are wet.

To Simplify:
- Draw large insect shapes on the sidewalk for children to "catch" with their spray bottle tongues.

To Extend:
- Encourage children to pick up the insect buttons once they are "caught," then place the insect buttons again around the playground for others to catch.

Pretend Play

1. Tabletop Habitat

To prepare for this make-believe activity, gather the following materials: either two dishpans, a divided water table, two water tables, or a roasting pan in a water table; damp sand; plastic frog and toad models; rocks; plant materials, such as small logs, short branches, leaves, twigs, and bark; plastic animal models, such as turtles, fish, insects, and birds; and plastic people. Each day of the week add materials to the simulated frog or toad habitat. Encourage children to manipulate the frog and toad models as if they were alive. To set up the activity:

Day 1: Pour water into one container (either one dishpan, one water table, or the roasting pan, placed in an empty water table).

Fill the other container with sand (if you are using the roasting pan, place the sand around the outside of the roasting pan to represent land around a pond).

Invite the children to use the frogs to swim, splash, and hop in the water and the toads to hop, walk, and burrow in and around the sand.

Day 2: Add rocks and logs or branches to the habitats.

Day 3: Add plants, leaves, and other plant materials.

Day 4: Add other animals, such as turtles, fish, insects, and birds.

Day 5: Add people.

To Simplify:
- Only use one habitat at a time.

To Extend:
- Invite the children to create their own frog/toad habitats in the sand outdoors.

2. Frog and Toad Naturalist

In the "Earthworms" mini-theme, a pretend play naturalist's laboratory is described (see page 442). Adapt the materials in the laboratory so that frogs and toads are the creatures being studied.

Social

1. Great Blue Heron and the Frogs

This outdoor activity is based on the game "Hide and Seek." Explain to the children that in real life, frogs and toads are eaten by several different kinds of animals; one of the predators is the Great Blue Heron. While in or around the water, frogs watch carefully for any other creatures that might be approaching. If they sense danger, they quickly hop away. In this game, one child at a time will have a turn to be the Great Blue Heron. The other children will be the frogs. To start the game, the child who is to be the Great Blue Heron will pretend to be asleep. As he or she sleeps, the "frog" children will hop away and hide in a place they think is safe. To signal to the Heron that the frogs are "ready" (meaning they have found hiding places), ask the children to make frog croaking noises until the Heron starts to move. The "Heron" child can either walk or pretend to fly around the area looking for frogs to eat. When the heron finds a frog, he or she will gently tap him or her. The first frog caught will be the next Great Blue Heron.

2. How Do I Love Thee? Let Me Count the Ways

The purpose of this activity is for children to hear one another's ideas and to recognize similarities and differences among their opinions. Have a live toad for them to observe and touch. Encourage children to study the toad's body as you hold it: touch the skin and feel the bumps, study its eyes, and watch the toad hop or walk across the floor. As the children observe the toad, ask them to describe what they like best about the toad. As the children make comments, paraphrase what they say: "Talbot, you like the toad's bumpy skin" or "Carrie, you notice the gold coloring of the toad's eyes." Note similarities in the children's observations: "Nishan, you think the toad is funny as it hops on the floor; Meghan is laughing also. You are both enjoying the toad's movements." Also acknowledge differences in opinions: "Michelle thinks the toad's bumps are fun to look at; Michael likes the smooth skin of the frog better." Have another adult or child write down the children's names on a large piece of paper along with their comments. As children discuss the toad, talk about ways their opinions are the same, as well as different.

3. Musical Lily Pads

This game is a "frog" version of "Musical Chairs." To prepare for the game, cut large lily pad-shaped leaves from green felt (about 1' in diameter). Place these in a circle in a large, open space. Choose a selection of "bouncy" recorded music the children enjoy. Explain to the children that they are to pretend to be frogs swimming around the pond. As they are swimming, you will play music. When the music stops they are to hop onto a lily pad. Each time the music stops you will remove one lily pad. After each time the music stops, the frog who doesn't have a lily pad to hop onto will go "hibernate" (sleep) until spring (or when the game starts again!). Reserve a hibernating area in one portion of the group area. When only one frog remains on a lily pad, start the game over.

To Simplify:

● Play the game without removing any lily pads.

To Extend:

● Take away the lily pads one at a time each time the music stops. Have the children find a way to share the lily pads with one another, until all are "crowded" onto the final lily pad.

Teacher Resources

Field Trips

1. Find a shallow pond in your area that would be convenient to visit as a group. Go to the pond ahead of time to make sure the area is safe for the children: easy access, shallow edges, etc. Ask as many volunteers as possible to accompany the group. Talk with the volunteers in advance about your goals for the children during their visit to the pond. Ask volunteers to guide children in moving slowly and quietly around the pond so as not to scare the wildlife. Have everyone watch for frogs and toads at the water's edge, look for tadpoles or frog/toad eggs near the water's surface, and search the water's surface for frog heads peeking out of the water. Frogs also may be seen sitting on rocks or logs in or by the water.

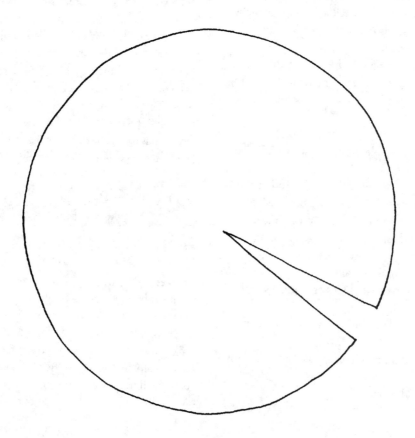

Remind parents to send children in long pants and long-sleeved shirts for bug and nettle protection, as well as waterproof boots or shoes that can get muddy! Arrange for them to put insect repellent on their children before leaving on the trip to the pond.

2. If there is a nature center in your area, find out what resources they have related to frogs and toads. Ask the naturalist to give the children a tour of the grounds, directing their attention to frogs, toads, and their habitats.

Classroom Visitors

1. Invite a person who specializes in amphibians to talk with the children and bring live amphibious creatures for the children to see.

Children's Books

Aardema, V. (1988). *The Vingananee and the Tree Toad*. New York: Puffin Books.

Begay, S. (1992). *Ma'ii and Cousin Horned Toad: A Traditional Navajo Story*. New York: Scholastic.

Bernard, G. (1979). *Common Frog*. New York: G. P. Putnam's Sons.

Butterfield, M. (1992). *Frog*. New York: Simon & Schuster.

Chinery, M. (1991). *Life Story: Frog*. Mahwah, NJ: Troll Associates.

Clarke, B. (1990). *Eyewitness Juniors: Amazing Frogs and Toads*. New York: Alfred A. Knopf.

Cole, J. (1980). *A Frog's Body*. New York: Morrow.

Cristini, E., and Puricelli, L. (1984). *In the Pond*. New York: Scholastic.

Fichter, G. (1993). *Turtles, Toads, and Frogs*. Racine, WI: Western Publishing Company.

Fleming, D. (1991). *In the Tall, Tall Grass*. New York, Henry Holt and Company.

Fleming, D. (1993). *In the Small, Small Pond*. New York, Henry Holt and Company.

Florian, D. (1986). *Discovering Frogs*. New York: Scribner's.

Fowler, A. (1992). *Frogs and Toads and Tadpoles, Too*. Chicago: Childrens Press.

Hirschi, R. (1992). *Hungry Little Frog*. New York: Dutton.

Kalan, R. (1981). *Jump, Frog, Jump!* New York: Scholastic.

Kalman, B., and Everts, T. (1994). *Frogs and Toads*. New York: Crabtree Publishing Company.

Kepes, J. (1961). *Frogs Merry*. New York: Pantheon.

Lobel, A. (1976). *Frog and Toad All Year*. New York: HarperCollins.

Lobel, A. (1970). *Frog and Toad Are Friends*. New York: HarperCollins.

Lobel, A. (1972). *Frog and Toad Together*. New York: HarperCollins

Mayer, M. (1967). *A Boy, a Dog and a Frog*. New York: Dial Books for Young Readers.

Mayer, M. (1969). *Frog, Where Are You?* New York: Dial Books for Young Readers.

Mayer, M. (1971). *A Boy, a Dog, a Frog and a Friend*. New York: Dial Books for Young Readers.

Mayer, M. (1974). *Frog on His Own*. New York: Dial Books for Young Readers.

Pallotta, J. (1990). *The Frog Alphabet Book*. Watertown, MA: Charlesbridge, 1990.

Parker, N. W., and Wright, J. R. (1990). *Frogs, Toads, Lizards, and Salamanders*. New York, Scholastic.

Pfeffer, W. (1994). *From Tadpole to Frog*. New York: HarperCollins.

Sabin, F (1982). *Wonders of the Pond*. Mahwah, NJ: Troll Associates.

Taylor, B. (1992). *Pond Life*. New York, Dorling Kindersley.

Adult Resources

Behler, J. L. (1988). *Audubon Society Pocket Guides: Familiar Reptiles and Amphibians, North America*. New York: Alfred A. Knopf.

Behler, J. L. (1992). *The Audubon Society Field Guide to North American Reptiles & Amphibians*. New York: Alfred A. Knopf.

Jennings, T. (1985). *The Young Scientist Investigates: Pond Life*. Chicago: Childrens Press.

Parker, S. (1988). *Eyewitness Books: Pond and River*. New York: Alfred A. Knopf.

Reid, G. (1987). *Pond Life*. New York: Golden Press.

Stidworthy, J. (1990). *Nature Club: Ponds and Streams*. Mahwah, NJ: Troll Associates.

Cats

Pussy cat, Pussy cat, where have you been?

Four thousand years ago, the ancient Egyptians domesticated cats. Since then cats have been a source of companionship and delight for humans. First brought into human surroundings because of their abilities as hunters, cats served their early human friends by keeping the rodent populations in granaries and homes under control. Later, cats grew to be admired for their beauty, physical agility, and independence. Today, cats are among the most popular pets in the world. Most children have experienced a cat firsthand. They have had opportunities to observe, touch and wonder at the grace of real cats.

Purpose

This unit has been designed to respond to the natural interest that children seem to have in cats, both domestic and wild. Here are opportunities to explore the familiar and the exotic, the known and the mysterious. An understanding of the needs and habits of domestic cats will help children become better pet owners, with a sense of responsibility for those animals who depend upon them for care. Because few of us are likely to have firsthand experience with wild cats, the zoo is suggested as a potential field trip, for that is probably the only place where most children can see these animals. The reader will note, however, that a field trip is the only place where zoos are mentioned in this unit. Because we wish to stress the natural habitat of these beautiful creatures, we do not advocate the creation of pretend zoos or circuses or other captive wild cat settings. Instead, we urge you to create with your children replicas of natural environments in which to explore wild cats. It is our hope that this unit will help your children develop an appreciation for all creatures, domestic and wild, and to begin to consider the impact that humans are having on life on our planet.

Implementation

The "Cats" unit is divided into three mini-themes: Cats—An Introduction, Domestic Cats, and Wild Cats.

The material within these mini-themes may be used in several ways. A three- or four-week cat unit could be planned around the sequence presented here, with general introductory cat activities followed by specific emphasis first on domestic and then on wild cats. A second option would be to include cat activities in a theme dealing with animal life in general. Alternatively, the general or domestic cat activities could be incorporated into a unit on "Pets." (See *Teaching Young Children Using Themes*, 1991.) Finally, the wild cat activities could be integrated into a thematic unit related to the environment and ecology.

Introduction to Cats

Terms, Facts, and Principles (TFPs)

1. Cats are mammals that have long, powerful bodies with somewhat rounded heads. They have fur and their feet are padded.

2. Mammals are warm-blooded animals, with fur, who give birth to live young; the young are nursed by their mothers.

3. Cats have facial whiskers (special tough hairs) that protect their eyes and help them to feel their way as they move in the dark.

4. Cat tongues are very rough, with tiny barbs on them which are useful for cleaning meat from bones.

5. Cats have very well-developed senses of hearing and smelling.

*6. Cats have very good vision and can see in darkened areas much better than people can.

7. Spongy pads of thick skin cover the bottoms of cat feet; these cushions help cats to move quietly.

8. Cats can retract (pull in) and extend their claws for protection and grasping.

9. Cats have long tails that help them to balance when climbing, jumping, and running.

*10. Cats have several types of fur: the outer fur is made up of long, stiff guard, or primary, hairs; the inner fur is soft and short.

11. Cats are carnivorous predators; they hunt and catch other animals for food.

*12. Cats often make many hunting attempts that are unsuccessful.

13. Cats spend a lot of time sleeping, probably to conserve energy so that they do not need more food than they can catch.

14. Cats communicate with one another, with other animals, and with human beings in a variety of ways: sounds, body signal, and scent.

*15. Cats commonly communicate with each other by means of scents that are released from scent glands on the forehead, around the mouth, and near the base of the tail.

*16. A cat rubs its forehead, mouth, or tail against objects and so marks them with its scent.

*17. Only cats and a few other animals can detect the scents cats leave on things.

18. Mother cats take care of their babies by feeding, protecting, and cleaning them, and teaching them how to take care of themselves.

19. Young cats practice hunting skills during play as they stalk, pounce, and strike.

Activity Ideas

Aesthetic

1. Claw Scratch Art

Provide the children with 9" x 12" drawing paper, assorted crayon colors and lots of black crayons. Direct the children to color the paper with varied swatches of crayon color. Then, demonstrate how to cover the entire paper with heavy black crayon and direct the children to imitate this process. Provide nails or pointed toothpicks and tell the children to pretend that these represent the extended claws of a cat. Use the points to scratch through the black crayon to reveal the colors underneath. Encourage the children to draw simple designs or to write their names with the "claws."

To Simplify:
● Provide paper already crayon colored. Invite the children to simply do the scratching part of the activity.

To Extend:
● Encourage older children to draw cat pictures with the "claw."

2. Fantastic Felines

You will need plastic squeeze bottles for this activity. Catsup or shampoo bottles will work, or you may wish to invest in the purchase of wider-mouthed squeeze bottles that are much easier to fill. Make the paint by mixing equal parts flour, salt, and water; color by adding liquid paint or food coloring (as part of the water measurement) or dry tempera powder. Put the paint into the squeeze bottles, using a funnel and a pushing stick if using narrow-necked bottles. Because there is no preservative in the mixture, it does not keep well in an enclosed container (mold forms quickly). Use it the same day it is mixed, or refrigerate the paint overnight and allow it to warm up before using it the next day. Cut some cat shapes from heavy construction paper or tagboard. Have children put on paint smocks and push up their sleeves; give them each a cat shape and direct them to place their names on the back. Invite children to squeeze the paint onto the cats as they desire. You may wish to caution them that the paint spreads out, so it is best not to place paint too close to the edge of the shape. The most wonderful thing about this paint is that the colors maintain their purity even if one color is touching or on top of another; in other words, you can squeeze yellow paint into the middle of a black paint circle and the yellow remains yellow! The effects are beautiful. The high salt content also creates a sparkling effect. These pictures should be dried flat and will take some time to set.

To Simplify:
● Provide really large cat shapes for younger children to use.

To Extend:
● Have children mix the paint and fill the bottles themselves, and/or get them involved in cutting their own shapes.
● Suggest that children use the paint to create spots or stripes.

3. Fine Felines

Gather a collection of cat pictures (use calendars, magazines, posters) for display in your classroom while discussing cats. These may be domestic or wild cats. If the pictures include humans, be sure to include people of varied ages, races, and genders. Use cues such as "Tell me what you see in this picture" or "I wonder what the cats are doing in this picture" or "Show me something that you like in this picture."

Obtain art prints of cats to add to the aesthetic quality of your classroom. These are sometimes available on loan from public libraries. Consider the following:

Jean-Leon Gerome, *Tiger and Cubs*, 1800s
Edward Hicks, *The Peaceable Kingdom*, c. 1830
Currier and Ives, *The Little Pets*, 1800s
Henri Rousseau, *The Sleeping Gypsy*, 1897

Encourage the children to view and discuss the pictures throughout the week.

4. Fur Fun

Cut some cat shapes from cardboard or tagboard. Gather a selection of fur-like fabric bits and provide glue. Invite the children to use the fur pieces to cover the cat shapes.

To Simplify:
● Use only one large cat shape and create a classroom cat for display during the unit.

To Extend:
● Add additional materials so that children can create eyes, whiskers, and so on, for their cats.
● Invite children to draw and cut their own cat shapes.

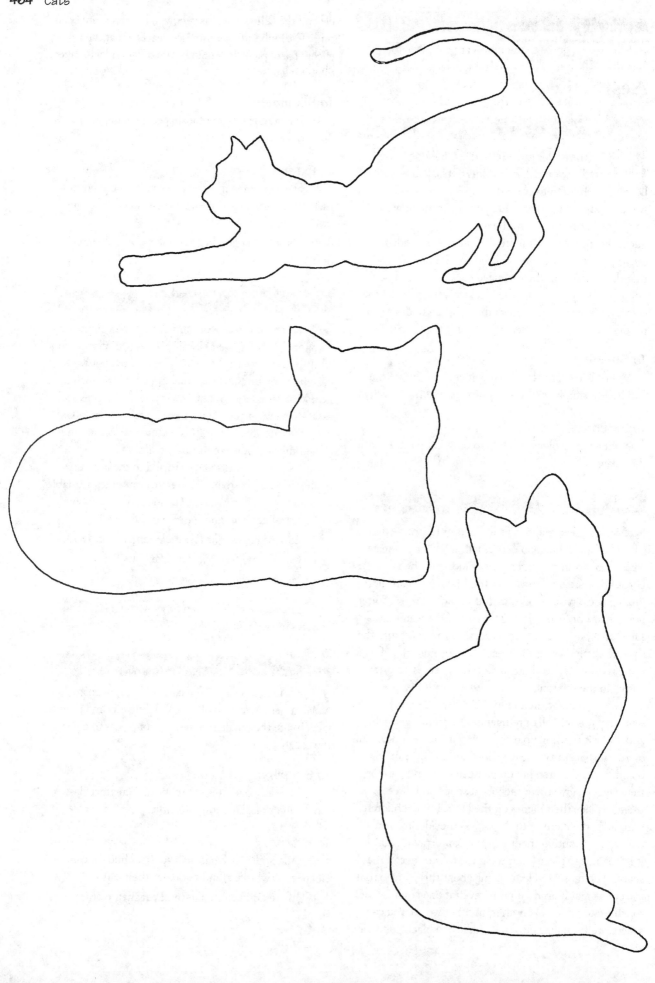

5. Paw Prints

Cut some sponges to resemble cat paws. Provide thick paint in shallow containers such as cake pans or pie tins and an assortment of paper. Encourage the children to dip a sponge in the paint and apply it to paper with a dabbing motion to create "paw prints." Remind children to press firmly and lift the sponge carefully to avoid smudging the paw shape and to use each sponge in only one color throughout the activity to keep the paint colors clear.

To Simplify:
● Use only one paint color.

To Extend:
● Suggest that children draw scenes of places that a cat might visit to accompany the prints.

● Use long strips of paper (shelf paper works well) and suggest that children use the paint paws to create a story, using a different color to represent each cat character. These stories may also be written out as dictated by the children and attached to the pictures.

Affective

1. Cat Tastes

Provide a "catty" snack assortment for children to try. Include small pieces of tuna fish and cooked chicken and milk to drink. Encourage the children to try each of the "catty" foods and to decide which they prefer.

To Simplify:
● Introduce only one kind of cat food per day and omit asking children to express preferences. Encourage children to try each food, even if it is not a familiar item.

To Extend:
● Create a graph of the favorite choices and see which is most popular with the group.

2. Pretty Kitty

Gather some hand mirrors or set this activity up near a large mirror so that the children can look at their faces. Encourage the children to do so and to describe how they look. Tell children to focus on their own facial features and on those of their friends. Notice how each has the same features (eyes, nose, mouth, and so on), but that each person also looks different. Tell the children that you are going to help them to change their faces so that they look like cats. Use face paint to draw whiskers on children's faces. While you are drawing, talk about real cat whiskers (they are stiff hairs; they help cats to maneuver in the dark and protect their eyes). Encourage children to admire their "Pretty Kitty" faces in the mirrors and to see if they look more alike or more different now that they all have whiskers.

3. Wear a Cat

Declare one day during the theme as "Wear a Cat Day." Encourage the children to wear an article of clothing that has a cat motif or that calls to mind certain cat features such as stripes, spots or a fuzzy collar. Tell children how "purrfectly" wonderful they look. Do provide some cat stickers or badges that you have prepared for any children who do not have "catty" clothes. This is a good time to carry out some of the cat behavior activities such as "Claw Scratch Art," "Listen, Cat!," and "Balance Beam Walk" (see pages 463, 466, and 470).

Cognitive

1. Eye/Paw/Tail Match

Cut several pairs of eye, paw, and tail shapes from a variety of colored or patterned papers. Arrange some of these randomly on a table and invite a child or two to explore them. Suggest that they find pairs that match or find a "set" that belongs together. If a set is formed, ask a child to explain how the pieces are alike.

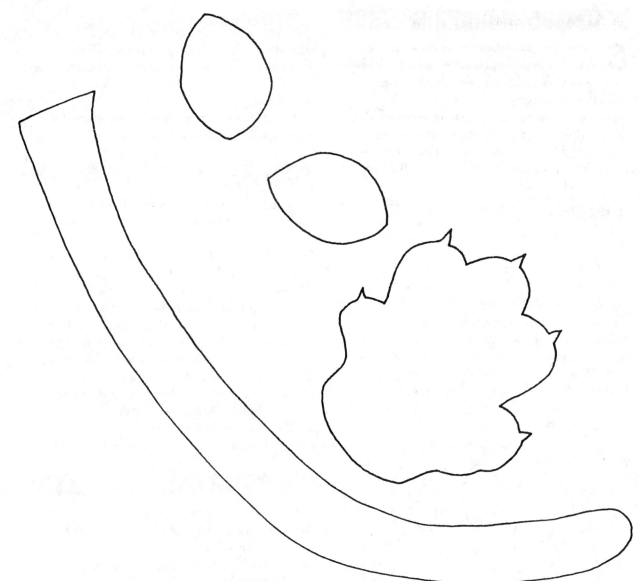

To Simplify:
- Begin with only one cat body part, such as eyes, and direct children to find exact matches.

To Extend:
- Add additional pieces to be sorted.

2. Listen, Cat!

Tell the children that cats have very good hearing and that you are going to give them an opportunity to find out if they can also hear well. First, tell them that they are mother cats and one of their kittens is lost. Direct the children to close their eyes and listen carefully, then to point to the source of a very quiet sound. Once all eyes are closed and the children are listening, move slowly around the group and make a very quiet mewing sound. Wait and see if anyone has detected the

sound and pointed at you. If so, praise their great listening, and tell them what caring mother cats they are. If not, mew a little louder. Remind the children not to peek. Next, tell the children that they are hungry cats and they are going to listen for a mouse. Repeat the eye closing; this time make a soft squeaking sound.

To Simplify:
- Use a bell as the sound source and/or divide the physical space in half, asking children something like "Did the sound come from the window side of the room or the door side?"

To Extend:
- Make it into a game by giving children an opportunity to be the kitten or the mouse. Think of other sounds that a cat might listen for and try to identify the source of these as well.

3. Mice Are Nice

Carry this activity out after the children have learned something about how and what cats eat. Gather an assortment of animal pictures. Ask the children to look through the pictures and to identify animals that a cat might eat. Be sure to include prey for both domestic and wild cats: mice, varied birds, rabbits, antelope, deer, zebra, and so forth. Ask the children to tell you which cat might hunt for a particular animal.

4. Mouse Paint

Read *Mouse Paint* by Ellen Stoll Walsh (1989), a story about some mice who fool a cat by playing in paint. Provide lots of white paper mice; red, blue, and yellow paint in small containers; small brushes; empty containers; and small spoons. Invite children to try mixing their own mouse paint colors with which to paint the paper mice. Ask the children to tell you how they created the new colors.

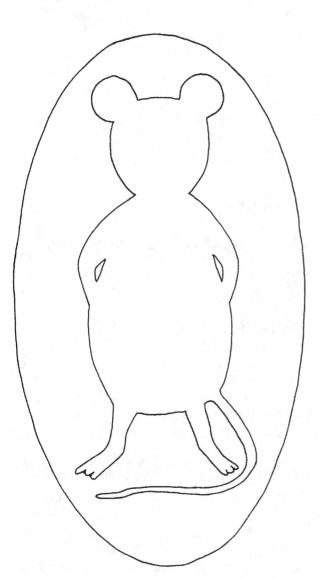

5. Scent Match

Prepare a set of containers that contain various aromas; you should have two of each scent. Some suggestions for scent cans include: orange juice, peppermint extract, lemon extract, cinnamon, baby oil, perfume, liquid soap, and fabric softener (avoid harsh, unpleasant, or potentially harmful materials). Place cotton balls saturated with the scent into sealed containers with a few holes punched into the lid of each. Plastic film canisters work well. (Place a foil cover under the lid to prevent loss of scent if there will be a delay between preparing and using these. Remove foil before beginning the activity with the children.) Begin by discussing the superior sense of smell that cats possess. Then, invite the children to use their sense of smell to try and match identical scents.

Hint for Success:

● Demonstrate how to wave your hand over the container and bring the scent to your nostrils rather than touching the container to your nose. Encourage children to imitate this technique. At first, use scents that are easily distinguished or familiar. As children gain experience, the differences in scents can be made more subtle and less familiar.

To Simplify:

● Present one scent to a child and assist him or her in smelling it. Then present two choices, one of which matches and one of which is very different. Have the child indicate the one that matches the first scent.

● Begin with only two or three pairs of scents and add more as children are successful.

To Extend:

● Show children pictures or give them real objects related to the scent. Have them match a scent to its original source.

Construction

1. Cat Mask

This activity is best carried out after children have had numerous opportunities to observe real cats and to see pictures of a variety of cats. There should be lots of cat pictures in the area as the children are working on this project. Provide paper plates with pre-cut eyeholes, scissors, construction paper, short (3 to 5 inches) white pipe cleaner pieces, glue, markers, tongue depressors, and masking tape. Invite the children to use the materials to construct cat masks of their own design. Fasten a

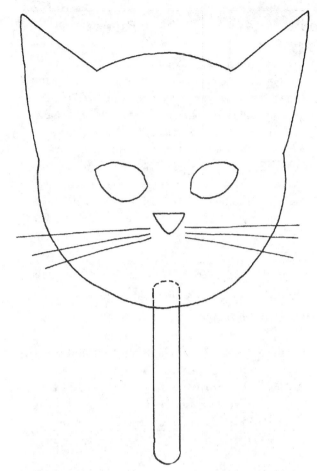

tongue depressor handle on each mask with tape so that it may be held up in front of the child's face.

2. Ears Up

Provide staplers, four-inch construction paper squares in cat colors, and sturdy paper or tagboard strips (2" x 24"). Assist each child in bending a strip into a headband to fit his or her head. Once the headband is completed, the child may cut cat ears of her own design and attach them to the band. Encourage the children to wear their "cat ears" as they portray cats in pretend play situations.

Hints for Success:
● Be sure to staple so that the staple ends are pointed away from the child's head to prevent hair snags.

● If a child requires assistance with the stapler, place your hand on the stapler and have the child push down on your hand.

To Simplify:
● Prepare the headbands ahead of time. The children will then only need to cut or tear the ears which can be fastened to the band with paste or tape.

To Extend:
● The children could also wear lengths of braided yarn or rope "tails" to complete the cat look. You could braid these ahead of time or assist the children in cutting, twisting, and tying their own tails. Pin the tails to children's waistbands.

3. Feline Face

Prepare construction paper shapes ahead of time by cutting various sized triangles (heads, ears, noses) and ovals (eyes). Put these shapes, paste, and markers on a table for the children's use. Invite the children to select materials to create cat faces of their own design. Add toothpicks or short white or gray pipe cleaners for whiskers if desired.

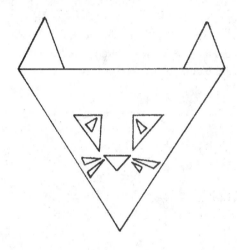

Language

1. Cat Vocabulary in Motion

Prepare some cards printed with words that relate to cat movement for a reading and movement activity. Some suggested words include: *pounce, prowl, leap, jump, stretch, curl, bound, hurdle, spring, vault, bounce.* Read the word cards to the children and ask them to demonstrate the action. After you have done this a few times, present the cards randomly without saying the words, and ask the children to first read and then act out each word. Vary the number and complexity of the words to suit the children with whom you are working.

2. Cloudy

Prepare a recording chart with three columns labeled: *morning, afternoon, night.* Obtain a copy of Deborah King's delightful book *Cloudy* (1990), a story about a cat's day. Before you read it to the children, tell them to listen carefully to the things that Cloudy does

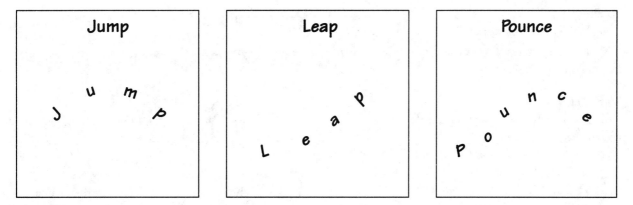

and to try and decide what time of day these things are happening. After reading, have the children recall an event and the time of day. Record their suggestions on the prepared chart. After listing the ideas that they remembered, go through the book and fill in any missed events.

Hint for Success:

● If children recall events that are not in the story, try reflecting that "You thought of something else that a cat might do. The author didn't put that in the book about Cloudy. Maybe you can tell us something that is in the book."

To Simplify:

● Prepare cards with Cloudy's actions printed on them ahead of time. After reading the story, use these cards to help the children recall events; use tape to place them on the chart.

To Extend:

● Prepare a large mural paper with the corresponding *morning*, *afternoon*, and *night* sections and suggest that the children draw pictures of Cloudy in appropriate activities for the different sections.

3. Here Comes the Cat!

American author Frank Asch has collaborated with Russian artist Vladimir Vagin to create a bilingual book, *Here Comes the Cat!* (1989). Before reading this book to your group, tell the children that it is a story about a mouse town and that the mice seem to be very excited because the cat is coming. Ask the children to tell their ideas about why the mice might be so excited. Read the book and ask if any of their predictions were accurate or if the author fooled them. Discuss the probability of this story actually happening and why it could or could not.

Note: For teachers in multi- or bilingual classrooms, substitute an appropriate language(s) for the Russian. It might also be possible to create your own version of this story in the appropriate language(s) with magazine pictures.

4. Illustrated Cat Vocabulary

Ask the children to think of words that describe cats in motion. On 12" x 18" pieces of easel paper write one word at the top of each using simple block letters. Encourage the children to describe ways to make the letters in the word illustrate or correspond to the motion.

Carry out the children's instructions as best you can. Try more than one approach for each word. If the children are able, invite them to experiment with creating their own "illustrated" words.

5. Rhymes with Cat

Prepare a book cover and pages for a classroom book before presenting this activity. The book pages should have plenty of blank space for drawing and the following words printed at the bottom of each page:

"_____ rhymes with cat."

You should have at least one page for every child in the group. The book cover should be of a sturdy or laminated paper and should feature a title and class name. A cat-shaped book adds to the fun but is not necessary. During a group time, ask children to think of words that rhyme with cat. Write and post these so that the children can see them. Tell the children that you have book pages available for a class "Rhymes with Cat Book." Direct each child to draw a picture of a rhyming word (from the list or another that wasn't mentioned) on her/his page and to write the word on the blank line at the bottom. Assemble all of the finished pages in the binder and make the new book available for the children to read and share.

To Simplify:
- Write the words yourself.
- Provide pictures of cat rhyming words for children to paste on their book pages.

To Extend:
- Ask the children to write simple rhymes to accompany their illustrations.

Physical

1. Balance Beam Walk

Use a low or high balance beam and encourage the children to walk gracefully and quietly across "like a cat." Direct the children to jump lightly off at the end and to land softly on their feet.

To Simplify:
- Use a wide (8-inch) board that is resting flat on the floor.

To Extend:
- Place some tape Xs on the floor and direct the children to jump from the end of the beam onto one X and then to gracefully leap from one X to another "like a cat."

2. Walk on Cat's Paws

Prepare some foot pads for the children to wear as they practice walking softly like cats. These may be made of foam rubber, plastic air-filled bubble packing material, or Styrofoam. Use shoelaces or strong string to tie them onto the bottoms of children's shoes. Encourage the children to practice walking softly so that they make no noise while walking on cat's paws.

Pretend Play

1. Night Vision

The purpose of this activity is to provide opportunities for children to take on the role attributes of a cat and to act out an interpretation of that role. You will need access to a large space that can be darkened. A hallway or unused office may serve this purpose. Designate a space near the entry as "home." This may be accomplished by using a tape line or by spreading an old blanket on the floor. Collect some "mice" or other cat prey. Use cat-toy mice or make some mice from two-inch pieces of a paper towel roll with yarn or string tails. A flashlight may be handy, too. It is best to play with no more than four or five children at a time. Take the children into the space so that they may see it with the lights on. Explain to the children that they are going to have a chance to pretend to be cats and to practice hunting in the dark. Tell them that most cats have very good night vision and are able to find and catch prey with very little light. Remind them that cats are very quiet hunters; they move slowly and softly until they are close to their prey and then they pounce on it. Point out the "home" space where cats will go with their prey. Show them the prey and then take them out of the space.

When the children are not in the space, place the mice (be sure to have at least one mouse for each hunter) in the room. Spread them out against the walls and away from the home space. Then, invite the children to enter the room. Direct them to get down on all four paws (crawl) and to close their eyes before entering the hunting ground. Tell them that you will lead them in to hunt and that they should keep their eyes closed until you tell them to open them. Lead the children in slowly. Have them open their eyes and wait for a brief time before beginning to hunt. This will help them to adjust to the dark and will prevent spotting of prey when the door is opened to admit them. Allow the "cats" to hunt. Direct successful hunters to take their prey "home" and to sit still and hold their catch while the others continue to hunt. The flashlight may be used to give quick glimpses of the space if children have too much difficulty in locating prey. After the hunt, talk about how difficult it was to see with so little light. Collect the mice for the next hunt.

To Simplify:

● This is probably too intense an experience for most very young children. If you think that your children are up to it, do it with only two hunters at a time.

To Extend:

● Children may like to construct their own mice using cardboard tubes, string, felt, or paper pieces.

2. Pretend You're a Cat

Share *Pretend You're a Cat*, an active book full of animal movements by Jean Marzollo and illustrated by Jerry Pinkney (1990), with the children. As you read, encourage the children to perform the varied movements described in the book. After trying a few movements, let the children take a rest and ask if any of the other animals do movements that resemble those of the cat. Continue with as many animals as you wish.

Social

1. Class Survey

Prepare some survey sheets for the children to use. If possible, also provide clipboards with pencils attached. Encourage the children to interview classmates and to record the results of their survey. If your children are not familiar with classroom surveys, model this process by taking your own survey, either during a self-selected activity time or during a large group situation:

> "Today, I am going to take a survey of the class to find out how many people like gray cats. Here is my survey sheet. (Read the sheet to the children.) I will begin by asking Jonah. Jonah, do you like gray cats? Jonah says that he *does* like gray cats. I will make a mark on my paper here in the yes column to record what Jonah said. (Continue with other children in the class)
>
> . . . Now, I have surveyed the class. That means that I have asked each person to tell me how he/she feels about gray cats. I will tally, or add up, the responses. I have ___ marks in the yes column and ___ marks in the no column. Now I know that ___ people in our class do like gray cats and ___ people do not like gray cats."

Classroom Survey

Do you like _____?

YES   NO
_____

totals   _____   _____
                 yes   no

Survey by _____

date _____

(sample survey form)

To Simplify:

● Provide an assortment of surveys with specific questions already printed. Some possible questions: Do you like cats? Do you like black cats? Do you like kittens? Do you like calico cats? Children then need only record yes/no responses with check marks or any other mark of their choice.

To Extend:

● Provide open-ended survey sheets. Children can fill in their own questions and record more complex responses.

2. Paw Twister

Prepare a playing surface according to the following directions. Use an old sheet or a plastic tablecloth or shower curtain. Cut a piece three feet square and divide it into several sections. Draw a cat paw in each section. Use red, blue, and yellow permanent markers for the paws. Make two spinners or prepare two dice as choosers. One chooser should indicate color and the other should indicate "front paw-arm" or "rear paw-leg."

Invite a few children at a time to play the Paw Twister game. One child will be designated as caller and two will stand on the playing surface. The caller uses the choosers (dice or spinners) to determine a body part and color for each player in turn. The player then places the called body part on the called color and leaves it there. As more directions are issued, the children will be all

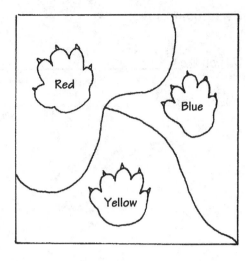

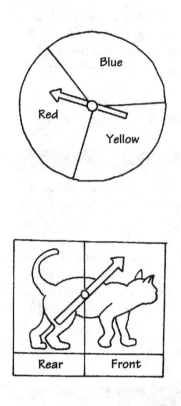

twisted up! Encourage the two players to help each other by moving to make room or by offering ideas to help find a place.

To Simplify:

● Play with only one player at a time.

To Extend:

● Add "left" and "right" to the paw choosers and direct children to move the corresponding body part. If using right and left directions, be sure that the children are able to correctly identify these. If needed, use a red-inked rubber stamp to stamp the appropriate hand to indicate "right red paw." Never use right and left directions unless you are able and willing to ascertain that the children are using the named side. Avoid reinforcing incorrect labels with a physical movement.

● Prepare a larger playing surface and play with three or four players.

3. Stalking Prey

Discuss with the children the methods that cats use to obtain food. Most cats stalk or sneak up on animals they are hunting. In order to be successful, a cat must do this very quietly so that its prey does not know the cat is there. Tell the children that they will have an opportunity to practice stalking. Show them a special badge or cat symbol that the stalker will wear (this could be a very simple circle of cardboard with a cat sticker, attached to a string that is worn around the neck). Tell the children that you will give this badge to a child who will then try to "catch" someone without being detected. When the "stalking cat" reaches the "prey," the prey is caught when the stalker gently touches her/his elbow. Stress the importance of being gentle with friends—no one is *really* going to be eaten! Remind all of the children that they may have a turn sometime during the day if they wish. Also tell them that you will be choosing people quietly so no one will know who is stalking. Remember, children can only be caught as prey once.

Once children are engaged in the day's activities, approach one child and quietly slip the stalker badge over her head. When that child has caught someone, take the badge and wait until the children are again involved in the day's activities before selecting the next "stalker." Continue until all children have had an opportunity to try stalking. When a child spots the stalker, he should look at the stalker and quietly shake his head to let the stalker know that she or he has been spotted already and other prey must be sought. (It helps to give each child who is caught a sticker to wear so that he or she is not caught again. Anyone wearing a sticker may not be stalked. Any child who does not wish to participate may also be protected from stalking in this way.) It may help you to keep a list of stalkers and prey to make selection of new stalkers easier and fair. This will be especially helpful if the game is continued on more than one day.

Teacher Resources

Field Trip Ideas

1. Plan a trip to a local animal shelter for a tour of the facility and an opportunity to look at the cats and kittens.

Classroom Visitors

1. If a visit to an animal shelter isn't feasible, perhaps the shelter will bring in some feline visitors for your class to meet.
2. Invite a cat owner to visit your classroom with a cat or kitten. If possible, arrange to have the children see how the cat is groomed by the owner.

Children's Books

Asch, F. (1989). *Here Comes the Cat!* New York: Scholastic, Inc.

DeBourgoing, P. (1992). *Cats: A First Discovery Book.* New York: Scholastic, Inc.

Hirschi, R. (1991). *Where Do Cats Live?* New York: Walker Publishing.

King, D. (1990). *Cloudy.* New York: Putnam.

Kostelnik, M. (1991). *Teaching Your Child Using Themes.* Glenview, IL: GoodYearBooks.

Marzollo, J. (1990). *Pretend You're a Cat.* New York: Dial Books for Young Readers.

Parsons, A. (1990). *Amazing Cats.* New York: Knopf Books for Young Readers.

Walsh, E. S. (1989). *Mouse Paint.* San Diego, CA: Harcourt Brace Jovanovich.

Teacher Resources

Clutton-Brock, J. (1991). *Cat.* New York: Knopf Books for Young Readers.

Schultz, J. L., and E. Teal. (Spring, 1993) "The Truth About Cats" in *Animal Watch.* New York: ASPCA.

Taylor, D. (1989). *The Ultimate Cat Book.* New York: Simon and Schuster.

Domestic Cats

Terms, Facts, and Principles (TFPs)

1. Domestic cats are cats that people keep as pets.
2. People who own cats are responsible for providing them with food, shelter, attention, and medical care.
*3. Human beings first tamed cats almost five thousand years ago.
4. Some domestic cats live indoors all of the time; some are allowed to spend part of their time outside.
5. Each cat has unique, individual needs for attention and affection.
6. Within its own territory, a cat will establish favored spots for particular activities such as sleeping, playing, and grooming.
7. A cat needs 16 to 18 hours of sleep a day.
8. A cat spends up to one third of its waking time in grooming.
*9. Scientists believe that although cats have excellent vision, they are unable to detect color. The world looks black, white, and gray to a cat.
*10. There are more than 100 types, or breeds, of domestic cats. Some of these are: Calico, Siamese, Tabby, Persian, and Abyssinian.
*11. Each type, or breed, of domestic cat has particular physical characteristics that differentiate it from others. Characteristics include: body and head shape, color, length of fur, shape of eyes.
12. Adult male cats are called toms; adult females are called *queens*; and baby cats are called *kittens*.
*13. Kittens are totally dependent upon their mothers for about twenty days; they gradually grow more able to care for themselves and are able to leave their mothers at about six weeks of age.
14. A cat can make many different sounds, and these sounds have various meanings:
   - A meow can be a friendly greeting, a sound of curiosity, or may mean that a cat is hungry.
   - Purring usually means that a cat is happy.
   - A hiss or growl usually means that a cat is angry or scared.
15. Cats also use body signals to communicate:
   - A happy cat usually lies on its chest with its eyes half closed and its ears upright.

- Cats that want to play often roll over on one side and wave a paw in the air.
- An angry or frightened cat will swish its tail from side to side, arch its back, flatten its ears, and puff up its fur.

*16. A person who loves cats is called an *ailurophile*.

Activity Ideas

Aesthetic

1. Cats in Verse

Select some poetry that relates to cats to read to the children. Some possibilities from *Sing a Song of Popcorn: Every Child's Book of Poems*, edited by Beatrice S. deRegniers (1988), include: "I Have a Lion" by Karla Kuskin, "My Cat, Mrs. Kick-a-chin" by John Ciardi, and "The Mysterious Cat" by Vachel Lindsay.

To Simplify:
- Choose a familiar nursery rhyme such as "Pussy Cat, Pussy Cat, Where Have You Been?" instead of contemporary poetry.

To Extend:
- Encourage the children to illustrate one of the poems.

2. Cat's View

Explain that cats probably are unable to see colors; therefore, everything looks black, white, or gray to cats. Invite the children to work together to create a "cat's view" mural for display in the classroom. Provide a large white background paper; white, black, and gray paint, paper, fabric, and markers; pencils; cotton balls; glue and scissors for children to use as they create the mural. Suggest that they create black, white, and gray pictures of simple everyday objects such as a ball, a tree, flowers, cars, or houses. Add a title such as "Seen by a Cat . . ." and display your "Cat's View" for all to admire.

3. K-I-T-T-Y

Substitute cat words in the old favorite song, "B-I-N-G-O."

♫ K-I-T-T-Y

Tune: "B-I-N-G-O"

There was a family* had a cat,
And Kitty was her name-Oh!
K-I-T-T-Y, K-I-T-T-Y; K-I-T-T-Y,
And Kitty was her name-Oh!
Repeat, substituting hand claps for letters, i.e.,
   X-I-T-T-Y;
X-X-T-T-Y; X-X-X-T-Y; X-X-X-X-Y; X-X-X-X-X.

* You may wish to substitute children's names for "family" or to select different people (grocer, teacher, farmer, etc.) as cat owners.

To Extend:
- Write K-I-T-T-Y on a chalkboard or wipe-off board, erasing and substituting an X for a letter each time the song is sung.
- You may prefer to prepare a set of letter cards with one letter each on one side and an X to represent a clap on the other. Five children can assist in holding and turning the cards at the appropriate moment.

4. Musical Cats

Read to the children from T. S. Eliot's *Old Possum's Book of Practical Cats* (1967). Repeat these poems over several days until children are familiar with the words and cadence. Once children have had opportunities to hear the poem(s) several times, play some of the music from the overture to the Andrew Lloyd Webber's musical *Cats*. Listen for fast and slow rhythms; loud and quiet. Challenge children to choose the music for a particular poem by playing two or three selections and asking them to identify the one that the composer wrote for the poem. You can then play the selection with words and music to allow the children to compare their ideas with those of the composer.

Affective

1. Favorite Cats

Prepare a graphing chart with pictures of various cat breeds. Allow each child to initial the column representing his or her favorite cat.

To Simplify:
- You may wish to provide plain, small stickers with children's names on them to be used as markers instead of initials. If the chart is lined with spaces that just accommodate the stickers, the finished graph may be easier to read.

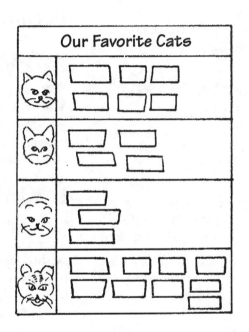

Our Favorite Cats

Floor Graph

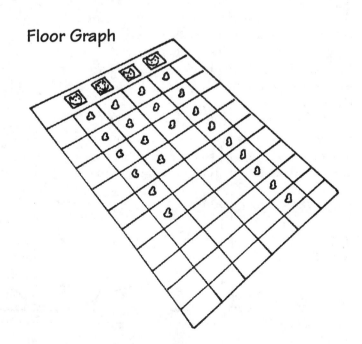

To Extend:

● Encourage children to tell the reasons for their choices. These could be recorded on individual papers for use in personal cat books.

● Do a floor graph as a total group experience. Divide a large piece of fabric or plastic (a shower curtain will do) into a minimum of six rows and columns (the columns should be wide enough to record 8 to 10 votes). You will also need large cat pictures to place at the beginning of each row. Children may mark their choices on a floor graph in a variety of ways: give each child a kitty-cat counter or other plastic counter to place on the graph; prepare a set of small paper plates with a child's name on each to be used for this and other graphing activities; use the children's name cards from your writing center.

2. Kitty Sandwiches

Provide snack items that children can prepare independently. Gather cat-shaped cookie cutters or make some from stiff cardboard using the templates offered below, soft bread, and something to spread on the bread (soft cream cheese, apple butter, cheese spread, peanut butter or tuna salad*). Direct the children to cut their own kitty shapes from the bread and to fix and enjoy their own kitty sandwiches for a snack.

*A simple and healthy tuna salad may be made using water-packed tuna, a dash of lemon juice, diced celery, and low-fat salad dressing or plain yogurt.

3. Lap It Up

Allow the children to try eating like cats. Provide a soft food such as frozen yogurt, apple sauce or pudding. Place some newspaper on the floor. Place each child's snack serving in a low bowl and put it on the paper so that children can try eating with their tongues. A piece of tape on the bottom of each bowl helps to hold the bowl in place and reduces the number of cats who try to use their paws to hold the dishes (a rather un-catlike behavior). In addition to the snack food, serve water in a separate bowl for each "cat."

Cognitive

1. Breed Books

Gather a few books that illustrate and describe some of the many varieties of domestic cats. Have these available for the children to examine frequently during the unit on domestic cats. Your local library will probably have satisfactory books for this purpose.

2. Calico Cat Prints

You will need some simple rubber stamps and a variety of stamp pad colors for this activity. Cut some cat shapes from white paper and select two stamps and two colors to create some simple models to help explain the idea of patterning to the children. Prepare two models that illustrate simple patterns:

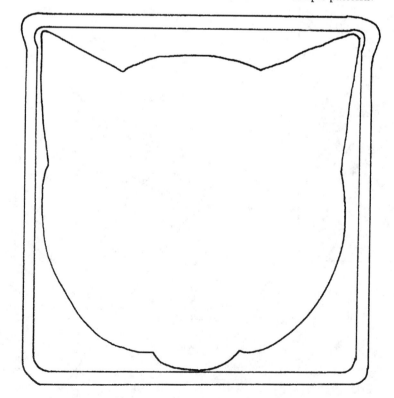

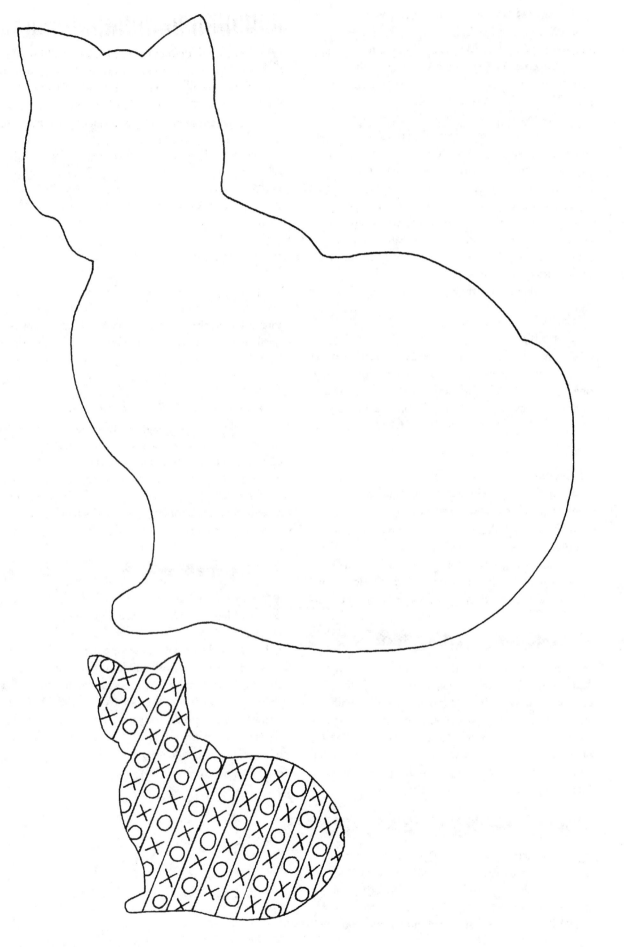

Model 1: Use an alternating pattern (a-b-a-b-a-b) such as red O, black X, red O, black X; repeat this to cover the entire cat in rows of the pattern.

Model 2: Use a slightly more complicated pattern (a-b-b-a-b-b-a-b-b) such as one blue O; two green Xs; one blue O; two green Xs.

Also prepare a single strip of each pattern to use in introducing the idea of patterns. Begin this activity by showing the sample pattern strips to the children and explaining the idea of patterning—repeating a design in a particular order. Next show the children how you have used your patterns to decorate the cats creating calico cats. Allow the children to select two stamps and two colors and to design their own pattern on a strip of paper. Once they have demonstrated an understanding of the patterning process, provide the cat shapes and encourage them to use their patterns to create their own calico cats.

To Simplify:

● Limit the number of choices available by creating the patterns using one color or one shape. Provide only one color stamp pad and a variety of shapes or provide multiple stamps with an identical shape and a variety of stamp pad colors. Also, demonstrate a simple a-b-a-b-a-b pattern.

To Extend:

● Challenge the children to use more complex patterns with multiple colors or shapes.

● Once the children have demonstrated an understanding of patterning, use fabric squares in place of rubber stamps. Cut several colorful fabrics into equal-sized pieces. Direct the children to arrange the fabric bits in patterns and to glue them into place on their calico cats.

3. Calico Cats Revisited

Once your children understand the notion of patterning, provide large paper and a big cat template cut out of sturdy cardboard for them to trace. Challenge them to think of a way to decorate the cats with repeated patterns. Provide scissors, markers, paints, wallpaper or fabric scraps, glue, space, and time. If a separate tail is cut, it can be fastened to the cat with a paper brad so that the tail can move.

4. Cat Trading

For this activity you will need lots of differently colored cat counters (these are commercially available plastic objects shaped like cats), prizes (cat stickers are one possibility), and a die. Prepare a set of small (5" x 5") game boards with three sections marked

on each: red, yellow, and green. Explain to the children that they will be playing a trading game with three rules:

1) Three red cats may be traded for one yellow cat.
2) Three yellow cats may be exchanged for one green cat.
3) Three green cats may be traded for a prize.

Add that as they play the game, children will be placing their cats on the game board to help keep track of them. Each player will have turns to roll the die. To play, the die is rolled and a number of red cats corresponding to the number rolled is given to the player. These red cats are placed on the child's game board in the red section. The player then can either trade three red cats for a yellow (if she/he rolled a three or higher) or wait until the next turn to roll the die and receive additional red cats to trade. Play continues in this fashion, following the trading rules above. Play continues until all children have collected three green cats and traded for a prize.

To Simplify:

● Require only two cats for each trade.

● Make circles on the game board on which cats are placed. A child will know she is ready to trade when all circles of a color are occupied by a cat.

To Extend:

● Require five (or any number of your choosing) cats for each trade.

5. Kitty Bingo

Prepare some bingo boards with K-I-T-T-Y as the only letters. Give a board and some markers to each child. Also prepare a set of letters (several of each letter: k, i, t, t, y) to be drawn and read to the children by the caller. Before playing, ask children to identify the lines that spell out "kitty" on their boards; remind them that these are the lines that they are trying to fill. Direct the children to cover only one space at a time as the caller reads the letters drawn. The first child(ren) to complete a "kitty" line wins and calls out "Kitty!"

T	K	I	T	Y
K	I	T	T	Y
I	T	T	Y	K
Y	T	I	K	T
K	Y	K	T	I

To Simplify:

● For younger children, provide only a strip with a single "Kitty" word. If the children are paying attention, they should all win!

To Extend:

● For more experienced children, include other letters to be called on the boards.

6. Meet the "Cat"!

This activity should be carried out late in the unit after the children have had many opportunities to see and learn about cats. It is an enjoyable way for the children to let you know what they have learned. Arrange for a visit by a non-cat (a dog, guinea pig, bunny, lizard, or any other non-feline animal). During a large group situation, tell the children that you are expecting a cat visitor in the classroom. Announce the visitor in a firm voice, "Here's the cat!" When the visitor enters, the children will undoubtedly be anxious to tell you that it is not a cat. Pretend to be confused and ask them to tell you why they think that this "cat" is not a cat. Repeat or paraphrase each of their ideas, but continue to act as though you think that this is a cat until they convince you otherwise. Congratulate them on their knowledge and thank them for their help. Do be sure to accurately identify your visitor before it leaves.

7. Silhouette Classification

Prepare materials for this game ahead of time. You will need a few game boards and accompanying pieces. The game boards will feature rows and columns. Each column will have a cat silhouette at the top. Each row will have a color patch on the left side. The game pieces will be a set of identical silhouettes in each of the colors. You will need a set of pieces for each board. Demonstrate how to place a piece in the matching row and column; for instance, the blue silhouette of the jumping cat belongs in the box where the blue row and the jumping cat silhouette column intersect. Once a child understands the game, allow him or her to complete the game board.

Hint for Success:

● When first attempting this activity, it sometimes helps if a child concentrates on one row at a time. Suggest that pieces be sorted into color piles before playing and that one color at a time be placed on the board.

To Simplify:

● Reduce the number of rows and columns on each game board.

To Extend:

● Expand the number or rows or columns or make the discriminations more subtle to make the game more challenging.

Construction

1. Cat Puzzles

Provide the children with large (8 1/2" x 11") cat pictures to color as desired with markers and crayons. Glue these onto sturdy poster board or tagboard and cover with clear adhesive vinyl (optional). Direct the children to cut the pictures into six or eight pieces to create their very own cat puzzles. Provide storage envelopes to hold the pieces.

To Simplify:

● Draw cutting guidelines on the backs of the puzzles ahead of time to help the children know where to cut and to assure more easily assembled puzzles later.

To Extend:

● Children may prefer to draw their own cats before the coloring step.

2. Double Cats

Provide dark construction paper (9" x 12") in a variety of colors, white crayons, and white school glue in squeeze bottles. Direct the children to draw very simple cat outlines on the paper with the crayons. Once the cat is drawn, direct everyone to use the glue to trace over the crayon, forming a thick outline of the cat. Set these aside to dry overnight. Once the glue is firmly set, you are ready to double your cats by using them as the base for crayon rubbings. Provide lightweight white paper (also 9" x 12") and unwrapped crayons. Show the children how to lay the thin paper over the glue outline. Next, ask them to rub over the cats with the side of a crayon, creating a second version of the same drawing. Display your double cat prints in pairs throughout the classroom.

Hint for Success:

● It is helpful to use masking tape to hold the papers in place while doing the rubbing.

Red				
Yellow				
Blue				
Green				

Language

1. Cat Care

Provide pre-made booklets for the children to write and illustrate. Tell the children that they can draw pictures of cats (or use rubber stamps or stickers) and write something about how to take care of cats. Suggest that they may write something about feeding, grooming, veterinary visits or any other important aspects of cat care that they wish to include. Use the finished booklets in the pretend play area or display in the story corner.

2. Cookie's Week

Read about Cindy Ward's mischievous cat Cookie in *Cookie's Week* (1988). Before reading the story, tell the children to listen carefully to all of the trouble that Cookie causes so that they can tell you some of the things that happened. After reading, review some of the things that Cookie did and have the children tell you what resulted from these actions. For instance: "Tell me what happened when Cookie fell in the toilet." After recalling Cookie's adventures, discuss with the children what they think were the reasons for Cookie's actions— was she trying to make a mess of the house? It would also be fun to think of some other cat actions and possible results (the cat jumped up on the counter where the lemon pie was cooling, the cat played with the ball of knitting yarn, the cat tried to catch the goldfish).

To Simplify:
● Limit the discussion to the events in the story.

To Extend:
● Provide paper and markers for children to illustrate their own ideas of what Cookie did on Sunday.

3. Feathers for Lunch

Before reading Lois Ehlert's *Feathers for Lunch* (1990), ask the children to listen carefully so that they can tell you why the cat has so much trouble catching his lunch. During the first reading, read only the main text. After reading, discuss the things that birds can do that cats cannot. Also talk about the bells on the cat's collar. Distribute wrist bells to the children and have them put them on. Reread the book, including the bird names and sounds, directing the children to shake their "cat bells" after each bird is presented.

4. If I Had a Wondercat

After reading Betsy Everitt's *Frida, the Wondercat* (1990), provide blank book pages and a cover titled "If I Had a Wondercat." Direct the children to prepare pages for the book with illustrations of their very own Wondercat and the remarkable things that it can do. To accompany the pictures, have the children either write or dictate a brief description of their cat's abilities. Add the finished book to your reading corner.

5. Three Little Kittens

Prepare one mother cat and three kitten masks for child use. Invite four children at a time to assist you in reciting the poem of the "Three Little Kittens Who Lost Their Mittens." This could also be done by using individual finger puppets instead of masks.

Physical

1. Cat Cookery

Select a nutritious cat-related recipe from *The Beatrix Potter Country Cookery Book* (1981) or *Peter Rabbit's Cookery Book* (1986) for the children to prepare and sample. Consider "Tabitha Twitchit's Roly-Poly Pudding, Without Tom Kitten" or "The Brown Bread That Tom Kitten Didn't Want to Eat," both related to *The Tale of Tom Kitten*. Easy individual versions of Roly-Poly Pudding may be made by using refrigerated biscuit dough spread with softened low-fat margarine and sprinkled with raisins or currents, other dried fruit and a touch of honey and cinnamon. Roll them up and bake as directed on the package. Be sure to include a reading of this appropriate Beatrix Potter story either before preparing your recipe or while it bakes.

2. Cat Play

Gather a selection of actual cat toys (soft cloth mice, balls, etc.) for use in throwing and catching games. Yarn balls may be used if other cat toys are not easily obtained. Provide baskets or tubs into which these may be tossed from a throwing line (a length of yarn placed on the floor and secured with tape). Throwing activities could also take place outdoors with a mouse target placed on a wall or fence. The yarn balls or other soft toys may also be used for catching practice. While the children are engaged in these activities, encourage them to do some jumping like "cats at play."

3. No Thumbs

Gather several pairs of child-sized gloves (ask parents to send them to school if possible). Assist children in putting the gloves on, but do not have them put their thumbs into the thumb slots. Instead, push the thumb slot into the glove, and have the children tuck their thumbs against the palms of their hands inside the gloves. Explain that cats do not have opposable thumbs like humans, and that it is much more difficult to do things without thumbs. Provide some challenges for the children to try in their thumb-less state. Ask them to try catching and throwing soft balls; manipulating tools such as scissors, pencils, and paper punches; or assembling puzzles.

Pretend Play

1. Cats at Home

Add stuffed cats and cat accessories to your housekeeping area. You may wish to provide a cat basket, litter box, and dishes, as well as brushes, toys, and empty food containers. Encourage the children to take care of the cats, offering gentle handling and remembering to provide food and water on a regular basis. Also remind them that cats require lots of rest and should be allowed to sleep for part of the day.

2. Cat Clinic

Set up a veterinary office that specializes in cat care. Provide stuffed cats; medical equipment and supplies such as stethoscopes, hypodermics, cotton balls, a scale, and white coats; cat carriers; cat care booklets; a telephone; appointment book; cat food and toys. Encourage the children to take on the roles of cat owners and veterinarians. As you visit the clinic yourself, be sure to introduce and reinforce accurate cat care information.

3. Cat Shop

Set up a pet store that specializes in cats and cat supplies. Provide stuffed cats, cat carriers, cat dishes, cat food containers, cat toys, cash register, phone. Encourage children to assume roles of shop workers and customers. Stress that an important task for the workers is to care for the cats and to instruct owners in how to care for their new pets.

Social

1. Cats for a Day

If your tolerance for fun and confusion is high, plan a Cat Day. Invite the children to BE cats for all or part of the day. Use "ears and tails" that children or you have made, and add whiskers to each "cat face." Encourage the children to move on all fours and to communicate with each other using purrs and meows. Call attention to the use of cat body language as well. This is a great time to try activities such as *Lap It Up* (page 476), *Catnaps*, and *No Thumbs*. You may also wish to add a "perch" from which cats may observe the room. A low climber or horizontal ladder fitted with cushions and a landing mat for descending works well for this. Do be sure to have an area in the classroom set aside for "human activity" for children whose interest wanes after a brief time.

2. Catnaps

Explain to the children that cats spend a lot of time resting and sleeping and that sometimes they take short naps. People call short naps like these cat naps. After a very active play period or toward the end of a long day, suggest that the children might like to try a cat nap. Provide lots of blankets, floor space, and a quiet atmosphere. Direct children to work with each other to form a comfortable bed and to curl up for a catnap. Add some soft music, and you may find that there are many sleeping cats!

3. Colorful Classroom Calico

Provide a large cat shape of sturdy paper or cardboard. Opportunities to refer to a photo of an actual calico cat will enhance this activity. Gather a variety of cloth scraps (parents may be willing to contribute to this effort), scissors, and glue. Encourage each child to participate in the creation of a beautiful classroom calico cat for display in the classroom.

Teacher Resources

Field Trip Ideas

1. A local pet shop may be willing to host your class or bring in a visiting cat or kitten.

Classroom Visitors

1. Some veterinarians specialize in the care of cats. If you are able to locate one in your area, arrange a visit for your class. The vet will undoubtedly be able to offer much interesting information about the needs of domestic cats.

2. Invite classroom parents to bring in the family pet for a brief visit. Parents are able to show their pet and explain its needs in a manner appropriate to their children. Ask the parent to demonstrate how to handle, pet, brush, trim nails. Also take this opportunity to look carefully at the cat, noticing body shape, facial features such as whiskers and eyes, and body language.

Children's Books

Abercromie, B. (1990). *Charlie Anderson*. New York: Macmillan Children's Book Group.

Doherty, Berlie. (1989). *Paddiwack and Cozy*. New York: Dial Books for Young Readers.

deRegniers, B. S. (1988). *Sing a Song of Popcorn: Every Child's Book of Poems*. New York: Scholastic, Inc.

Ehlert, Lois. (1990). *Feathers for Lunch*. San Diego, CA: Harcourt Brace Jovanovich.

Eliot, T. S. (1990). *Mr. Mistoffelees with Mungojerrie and Rumpelteazer*. San Diego, CA: Harcourt Brace Jovanovich.

Eliot, T. S. (1967). *Old Possum's Book of Practical Cats*. San Diego, CA: Harcourt Brace Jovanovich.

Emerson, A. (1980). *Peter Rabbit's Cookery Book*. New York: Frederick Warne & Co.

Everitt, B. (1990). *Frida, The Wondercat*. San Diego, CA: Harcourt Brace Jovanovich.

Felder, D. G. (1989). *The Kid's World Almanac of Animals and Pets*. New York: Pharos Books.

Herriot, J. (1984). *Moses the Kitten*. New York: St. Martin's Press.

Jessel, C. (1991). *The Kitten Book*. Cambridge, MA: Candlewick Press.

Lane, M. (1991). *The Beatrix Potter Country Cookery Book*. Middlesex, England: Frederick Warne & Co.

Lobel, A. (1985). *Whiskers and Rhymes*. New York: Morrow Junior Books.

Royston, A. (1991). *See How They Grow: Kittens*. New York: Dutton Children's Books.

Ward, C. (1988). *Cookie's Week*. New York: Putnam Publishing Group.

Yolen, J. (1993). *Raining Cats and Dogs*. San Diego, CA: Harcourt Brace Jovanovich.

Adult Resources

Caravan, J. (1991). *An Identification Guide to Cat Breeds*. New York: Gallery Books.

Loxton, H. (1985). *Caring for Your Cat*. New York: Arco Publishing.

Wild Cats

Terms, Facts, and Principles (TFPs)

1. Wild cats are strong and graceful, and many have beautiful fur.

*2. Wild cats live in many different kinds of places. They are found in more places on earth than any other group of mammals.

3. Wild cats vary in size, coloring, and habitat.

*4. Wild cats are described by scientists as *big cats or small cats*. These groups are determined by the ability to roar, not by size. *Big cats* are able to roar; *small cats* do not roar.

*5. Many *small cats* are larger in size than some big cats.

*6. Big cats include: lions, tigers, leopards, and jaguars.

*7. Some small cats are: lynx, puma (or cougar), ocelot, snow leopard, clouded leopard, bobcat, serval, and African wildcat.

8. Wild cats are carnivores; they eat meat.

9. Wild cats use their excellent eyesight and hearing to hunt for food.

*10. Mother wild cats take very good care of their young. They feed and protect them and teach them how to hunt for food.

*11. Once cats are grown, they establish their own hunting territories and live by themselves.

12. Most cats stalk, or sneak up on, their prey and quickly jump and kill by grabbing the back of the neck or the throat.

*13. The cheetah is the fastest of all land animals and does not stalk its prey. Instead, a cheetah chases and catches its food.

*14. Lions are the only big cats that live and hunt in groups. These groups are called *prides*. Each member of a pride has a special job when hunting. Some lions scare the prey and chase it toward the other lions who are waiting to catch it.

*15. Leopards are the smallest of the big cats. They are the best at stalking prey. After a kill, a leopard usually drags its food up into a tree to keep it safe from other animals.

16. Some cats have special coloring that enables them to more easily stalk their prey without being seen. Leopards and jaguars are the spotted big cats. Tigers are striped big cats. No two tigers have the same stripe pattern.

*17. Tigers, jaguars, and some small cats like water and will swim or catch food in water.

18. Many wild cats have been killed because some people like to use their beautiful skins for coats.

*19. As people want more land, big cats and many small cats are becoming endangered because their habitats are threatened.

Activity Ideas

Aesthetic

1. Beautiful Cats

Be sure to find pictures of these beautiful creatures with which to beautify your room during the "Cat" unit. Include books with photographs. Take time every day to admire one or more of these beautiful cats. After children have had some time to view the various cats, plan additional activities related to the Beautiful Cats.

2. Big and Little Cats

Here is a song that will help children learn how scientists classify big and little cats. Pictures of the various big and little cats make a fine addition to this song. The children could each hold a cat picture and display it as their group is mentioned in the song.

♫ **Big Cats**
Tune: "Ten Little Indians"

> Lions, tigers, leopards, jaguars.
> Lions, tigers, leopards, jaguars.
> Lions, tigers, leopards, jaguars.
> Four big cats can roar. ROAR!
>
> They may mew or they may snarl.
> They may purr or they may growl.
> They can make a lot of noise,
> But little cats can't roar. Mew!

A simpler, alternate version of this song follows:

♫ One big, two big, three big cats,
> Four big, five big, six big cats,
> Seven big, eight big, nine big cats,
> Ten big cats can roar. ROAR!

One little, two little, three little cats,
Four little, five little, six little cats,
Seven little, eight little, nine little cats,
Ten little cats can't roar.

3. Down on the Plain

You and your children are sure to enjoy singing "Down on the Plain" to the same tune as Raffi's song "Down By the Bay." (The original song can be heard on "The Raffi Singable Songs Collection," distributed by A&M Records, Inc., Hollywood, CA.)

♫ Down on the Plain
Tune: "Down By the Bay"

Down on the plain, where the lions roar,
Back to my home, I'll go no more.
For if I do, my Dad will complain:
Why are all the bees hiding in the trees,
Down on the plain?

Down on the plain, where the lions roar,
Back to my home, I'll go no more.
For if I do, my Dad will complain:
Why is all the honey dripping on the bunny,
Down on the plain?

Add your own rhyming words for more fun!

4. Painting with Lion Tails

For this activity, you will need to prepare some "lion tails" (a length of tan or brown yarn with a bunch of shorter yarn strings tied on one end). Also provide tempera paint in shallow containers, construction paper, and smocks. Encourage the children to paint by dipping a "tail" into the paint and then applying it to the paper. Point out the lines that are created and how the colors blend when they are mixed.

To Simplify:
● Use only one color of paint.

To Extend:
● Provide large sheets of yellow or tan paper, pencils and scissors. Suggest that children first draw a lion shape, cut it out and use that for their painting surface.

Affective

1. How Do They Feel?

Read Judy Allen's and Tudor Humphries' thoughtful book *Tiger* (1992). It is about a village, a tiger, and a very special hunter. The story has a surprise ending that should not be revealed to the children in advance. After reading, talk with the children about the various characters in the book and how they were feeling during different parts of this story. Include the Hunter; the boy, Lee; the father; the uncle; the other villagers and the tiger in your discussions. (See "Find the Site," as a follow-up activity.)

2. My Favorite Cat

Provide a variety of wild cat photos or figures. Allow the children to explore these as well as an assortment of books about wild cats. Toward the end of the unit, encourage each child to select his or her favorite wild cat and provide opportunities during large group times for children to tell about their choices. Encourage each child to tell something that she/he has learned about that cat and why it is a favorite.

3. This Is My Territory

Tell the children that cats usually identify and mark their own territory and that other cats do not intrude. By marking their territory, cats let other cats know the space and hunting rights are reserved; this lessens the possibility of conflict. Young cats seek unmarked territory to claim as their own. Provide opportunities for children to mark off their own "territory" during the cat unit. This could be done by using floor tape to define individual spaces in the block area: children can take blocks to their own "territory" and construct as they wish. Another way to help children to experience this sense of personal space (territory) would be to use carpet squares for individual spaces during large group situations. Children could also mark their own territory at the snack or lunch table by creating individual place mats.

Cognitive

1. Find the Site

Several days before presenting this activity, quietly take some pictures of your children during the day at school. You can take these indoors or outside. Take the photos in as unobtrusive a way as possible. Pay special attention to your location for each photo; take notes if needed to help you remember. Have these photos developed, mount them in clear protective folders, and wait. When you are ready to carry this out, read *Tiger* by Judy Allen and Tudor Humphries. After discussing the story, ask if the children were surprised by the ending. Tell them that you have also done some "hunting" with your camera and that they were the prey. Display your "trophies"—the photos—and allow the children to view and discuss them. Gather the photos and tell the children that you have a challenge for them: they are to try to discover where you were when you took each picture. Remind them that they will have to try and visualize where the camera was, not just find where they are in the photo. There are a variety of options, and you will have to decide how best to structure this part of the experience for your children:

a. Take photos of individuals and have each child take his or hers and look for the site. When found, the child may leave the photo at the site until all the sites have been found.

b. Direct the children to work together in small teams to decide where each photo was taken. Give each team one photo with which to work and direct them to leave the photo at the agreed-upon site. They can then check and move these as needed until they are satisfied.

c. Number and mount each photo separately and place each on a clipboard with a pencil attached. Also mark each camera site with a letter posted in some fashion. Give each child a numbered paper to attach to the clipboards and allow them to individually seek out the site of each photo in turn and to record the letter that identifies the site on the paper.

After the children have completed their hunting, walk them through your path showing them where you actually were for each photo. Have them compare their ideas to the actual site.

2. How Big Is a Big Cat?

Use the life-size tiger head illustration from Julia Finzel's storybook *Large as Life* (1991) to help your children begin to appreciate how large these big cats really are. Since this illustration is also featured on the dust jacket, it could be removed from the book and used on a magnet board for some activities related to measuring or counting. Prepare lots of life-size ladybug pictures and attach each one to a tiny bit of magnetic tape. Predict how many ladybugs will be needed to cover the tiger's eye or ear. How many will be needed to form a line across the tiger's entire face? With the children, measure and cut a length of narrow paper (shelf liner will do) that is as long as a tiger (6 or 7 feet). Use orange and black paint stripes or alternating strips of orange and black construction paper to color the large paper to resemble a tiger's coat. Comment frequently as the children are working that it takes a very long time to decorate such a big piece of paper—tigers are very big, indeed!

3. Losing Ground

Do this activity as a large group experience. Prepare a three-foot-square space on the floor with tape, and direct the children to sit outside of the space. Gather an assortment of small wild animal figures that represent potential cat prey. Talk with the children about the decreasing natural habitat available to wild cats because of the needs of people for more land, and tell them that they are going to pretend to be hunting cats in the space that you have marked out. Spread the animal figures in the space and select one child to be the first "cat" to stand in the space. Tell the "child-cat" to bend over and collect some "food" when you say "Hunt." After the child has successfully captured an animal, ask if it was easy or difficult to get food (it should be easy). Add another child to the space and repeat the Hunt and the easy-difficult question. Continue to add children and to repeat the hunt until it is no longer possible for the children to bend and hunt without interfering with each other and the food supply is diminished. Discuss with the children what they think happens when too many predators attempt to hunt in a limited space.

4. Wild Cat Habitats

You may use the jungle and plain habitats that the children create as construction projects to carry out this activity, or you can create habitats with tree figures, foil rivers, and water holes on a sheet or in another limited space. You will also need wild cat figures, other wild animal figures, blocks or buildings, cars, trains, and airplanes. Place appropriate figures in the jungle (tigers, leopards, elephants, snakes, orangutans, birds) and on the plain (lions, cheetahs, zebra, antelope, giraffes). Allow children to use the space and to manipulate and play with the animal figures. On another day, add houses, cars, roads, railroads, and airports and decrease the space available to the animals. Discuss with the children what happens when the animals lose space to make way for people.

Construction

1. Cat Construction

Provide small and large paper plates, varied colors and sizes of construction paper, scissors, markers, glue, tape, yarn, pipe cleaners, and lots of time and space. Encourage the children to design and construct a cat of their own choosing. Place some cat photos nearby and suggest that the children look at these to determine what body parts their cats might require.

2. Create a Jungle*

Cover a table with a large piece of paper. Provide varied shades of green and brown construction paper, paper towel tubes, green and brown yarn, scissors, glue, tape. Encourage the children to use these materials to create a jungle setting. If available, place jungle pictures nearby to provide inspiration. Demonstrate how to fringe paper to form grass; suggest using the yarn to make vines; add paper leaves to the tubes to make trees. This activity may take more than one day. Enjoy!

3. Plainly Beautiful!*

Begin this activity just like the jungle creation, but add blue paper or foil for a watering hole and yellow and tan paper for dried grass, and limit the number of tubes available for trees. Suggest longer grass, low bushes, and rocks for this landscape.

* **Note:** Both the plains and jungle constructions may be placed on the floor or left on a table and used with appropriate animal figures for lots of cat play.

Language

1. Cat Hunt

Gather the children into a circle at group time and tell them that you are all going on an imaginary cat hunt, similar to the familiar Bear Hunt. Ask for suggestions about the kind of wild cat you should look for. Once a cat is selected, use facts about the cat to guide you in creating the hunt. Direct the children to repeat each line of the chant after you.

Sample chant:

We're going on a cat hunt.
Looking for a Lion *(Hand to eyes)*
Pack a lunch *(Pack)*
Wear a safari hat *(Put hat on)*

Bring a camera *(Hang camera around neck)*
Are you ready?
Let's go!
First, we cross the river, *(Swimming motion)*
Through the mud, *(Press palms together)*
Through the tall grass, *(Rub hands together)*
To the plain.
I see a lion!
He looks hungry!
Better get home!
Through the grass, *(quickly: Rub hands)*
Through the mud, *(Press palms)*
Cross the river, *(Swim)*
Safe at home!
Did you get a picture?
I forgot.

2. "Down on the Plain" Book

After introducing the song "Down on the Plain" (see page 484), ask the children to think of rhyming words. You may want to start them off by asking for words that rhyme with specific words such as *cat* or *snake*. Write these suggested word pairs down on a large sheet of paper and post near the writing center. Provide large (12" x 18") paper with *Why* printed in the upper left corner and *down on the plain?* printed at the bottom of each page. Suggest that the children complete a page with words and a drawing to add to the book. Sing the song with the child-created words frequently and keep the book in your reading area. Some of the rhymes that children have created are found on page 484.

3. Somewhere in Africa

Somewhere in Africa, by Ingrid Mennen and Niki Daly (1992), offers an opportunity for the children to compare their lives to that of a boy who lives in a city in Africa. Ashraf has never seen a lion, but he is interested in them and enjoys reading about them in books. Share this story with the children and suggest that they listen for things that Ashraf does that are similar to the things that they do. Write a "letter to Ashraf" (this may be a group letter or done individually) telling about your town and some of the things that you like to read about.

4. Tiger Environments

Read *Tiger Trek* by Ted Lewin (1991) and *Tigress* by Helen Cowcher (1990). Focus on the animals that are present in the tigers' environments in both books.

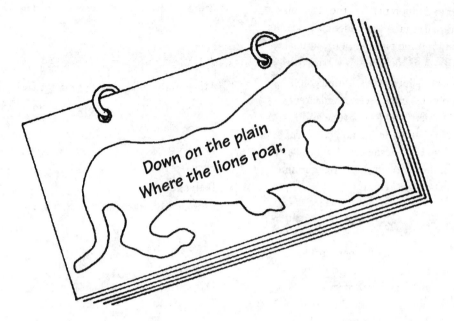

Down on the plain
Where the lions roar,

Back to my home
I'll go no more.

2

For if I do,
My dad will complain,

3

Why

down on the plain?

4

How are they similar and different? Ask the children to think about other animals that a tiger might see near its home. If possible, obtain some pictures of the animals that are mentioned in these books and compare them to animals with which the children are familiar in their own environments. Build on this activity by revisiting these books another time and contrasting with the animals present in the environment of a domestic cat such as Deborah King's *Cloudy*.

To Simplify:

● Select just one of the books and discuss the animals that are mentioned

To Extend:

● Provide pictures of animals from both domestic and wild cat environments and have the children sort them into groups.

5. Way Down in the Jungle

Share this fun chant with your children. Introduce it by reciting the first two lines with the accompanying gestures and direct the children to repeat the lines and movements with you. Add the next two lines, repeat, and then do the first four lines. Continue adding two lines at a time until the entire chant has been done.

> Way down in the jungle (*Stoop down and hold hand to shade eyes*)
> Where nobody goes,
> There's a big striped tiger,
> And he's washing his toes.
>
> He goes "Ooh," (*Dip one hand in "water"*) "Ah" (*then other*)
> "Ooh," (*Dip one foot*) "Aahhh" (*then other*)
> The big striped tiger
> As he washes his toes.
>
> Wallee-ah-chee (*Pound on chest—ape*)
> Goochy-goochy-goo (*Wiggle like snake*)
> Wallee-ah-chee (*Pound on chest*)
> Goochy-goochy-goo (*Wiggle*)
> Wallee-ah-chee (*Pound on chest*)
> Goochy-goochy-goo (*Wiggle*)
>
> The big striped tiger
> As he washes his toes!
> YEAH! (*Spread arms out in front*)

Physical

1. Cheetah Chase

Prepare cloth strips out of an old sheet or other discarded material. These should be four to six inches wide and about eighteen inches long. Invite the children to play a chasing game. Designate a few players to be cheetahs, and tell the others that they are the cheetahs' prey. Give each prey animal a cloth strip and direct everyone to place one end in a back pocket or into a waistband so that it sticks out when they run. In order to catch the prey, a cheetah must grab the cloth strip. Designate a safe place for prey to hide or rest; they may not be caught while in the safe place. Captured prey should sit down until a new game begins. Be sure to give all of the children opportunities to be both cheetah and prey.

2. Leopard Leaps

This activity may take place either outdoors or indoors. Outdoors, you may use playground climbing equipment if you feel that it is safe for jumping. For indoor play, you will need: a large space, a gym mat for safe landings, and a jumping platform such as a small climber. If a variety of safe heights is available, this will add to the interest. Tell the children that leopards are very good jumpers and that they are going to try some Leopard Leaps. Encourage children to practice jumping down from a height. Show them how they can land softly on their feet by bending their knees and using arms for balance. Mention that leopards can jump easily from heights and that they use their tails to help them to balance and land gracefully. Encourage children to try gradually higher jumps. Praise success and effort.

3. Spots and Stripes

Prepare yellow and orange cat shapes of construction paper. Provide small pieces of black construction paper, scissors, round paper punches, and glue. Direct the children to cut thin stripes for tigers or to punch out spots for leopards and to apply them carefully to the appropriately colored cat figures with glue. Display your finished spotted and striped cats in a jungle bulletin board setting.

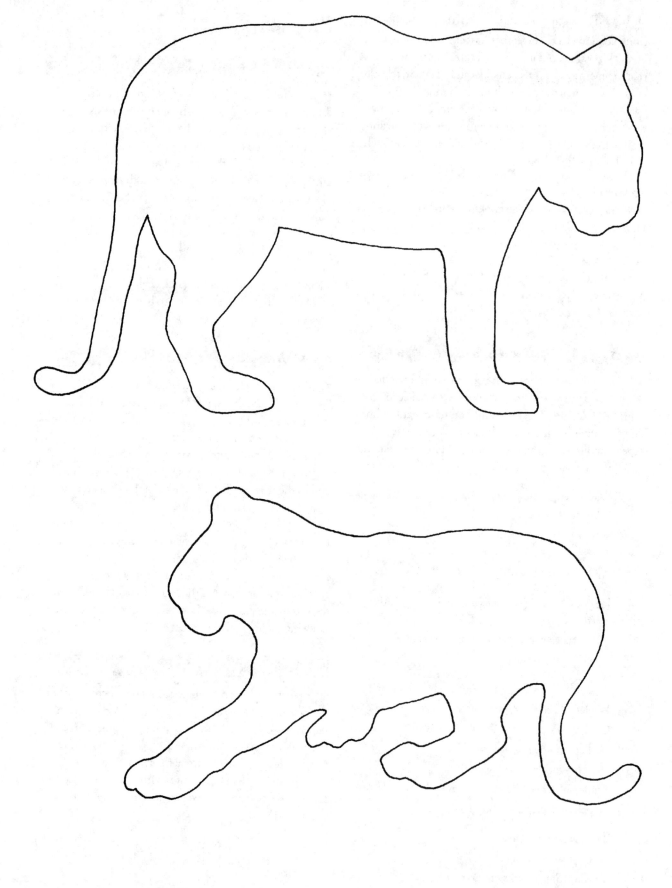

Pretend Play

1. Camera Safari

Create a jungle mural as a backdrop for this pretend play setting. It should include trees, ferns, and vines. A green cloth draped overhead will add to the jungle feeling. Add camping equipment such as sleeping bags, dishes, canteens, backpacks, logs for a fire, binoculars, cameras, a compass, walkie-talkies, maps, sunglasses, and hats. Encourage the children to set up camp, look for wild cats and other animals, and to take photos of those that they see.

To Simplify:
● The adult sets up the camp, providing fewer material choices. Children use the materials to explore, take photos, and camp.

To Extend:
● Children could help you to create the background mural, construct trees from large cardboard cylinders and green construction paper, create yarn vines, etc.

● Add clipboards and pencils for recording animals observed.

Social

1. Lion Hunt

This activity should take place outdoors or in a gym. Before playing, explain to the children that lions are the only cats that hunt in groups. Sometimes a few lions scare the prey and chase it toward the others who capture it. Designate one side of the yard or gym as the safe place to which the prey will escape. Select several children to be prey and tell them that their task is to escape from the lions. The remaining children (4–8) may be lions. Tell the lions to decide who will scare (the chasers) the prey and who will capture (the hunters) them. Place the chasers on the far side of the "plain" (playing space). Place the prey in the middle of the plain to graze. Give each prey animal a strip of cloth that is approximately 6" x 18" and that resembles a prey animal (for example black and white striped cloth for zebras or tan for antelope) to place in a back pocket or waistband. Explain that the hunters will try to grab the cloth. A prey animal is caught when a hunter has the cloth, and the prey must immediately sit down. Place the hunters between the prey and the safe place. They should lie down low so that they are not easily seen by the prey as they graze.

Once all animals are in place, the hunt can begin. The prey animals should pretend to be eating grass until frightened by the chasers. Once frightened, the prey run toward the safe place and try to elude capture; i.e., reach the safe place with their cloth still attached. If they reach safety, they are free to graze another day. The hunters should lie quietly until the prey run toward them. When the prey start to run, the hunters should spring up and try to capture a cloth strip. The chasers should agree on a signal and all run toward the prey when the signal is given. A loud roar is appropriate. The hunt ends when all prey animals are either safe or caught. The hunt may be repeated with the children switching roles if desired.

2. Papier-Mâché Cat

Prepare a large "cat" frame of sturdy cardboard. Ask the children to work together to cover it with strips of newspaper dipped into wallpaper paste. Use large pieces of balled-up paper to add roundness where desired. Tape these in place and cover with more paper and paste. Allow to dry for several days. Decide with the children what kind of cat it is to be. Here is a grand opportunity for a class vote. Ask for suggestions, write them down on a large sheet of paper divided into columns, and allow each child to record a preference by writing her/his name in the corresponding column. Once the cat is thoroughly dry, provide paints in the appropriate colors, brushes, smocks and clean-up

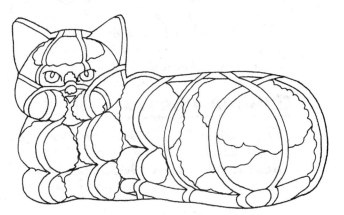

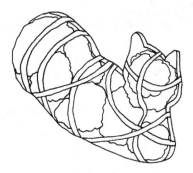

supplies. Encourage the children to again work together to complete the class cat. The finished cat may be named by another round of voting if desired. It should be prominently displayed with pride.

3. Lioness, Lioness, Where's Your Cub?

Y ou will want a small lion cub figure, stuffed animal or picture for this activity. Have the children sit in a circle with their hands behind their backs. Tell the children that this game requires lots of cooperation. They will be trying to fool the lioness into thinking that they are hiding the cub. Select one child to be the lioness and direct this lioness to either go to another part of the room or to cover her/his eyes. Quietly give the cub figure to another child to hide behind her/his back. The lioness is called back by all of the children chanting "Lioness, Lioness, Where's Your Cub?" The lioness has three chances to guess where the cub is hidden. Encourage the children to keep the secret as the lioness tries to guess where the cub is hidden.

Teacher Resources

Field Trips

1. If your local zoo has a good variety of wild cats that are appropriately housed with adequate space and respect, schedule a visit for your class. With advance notice, the zoo may provide a person to give your children a behind-the-scenes look at how the cats are provided with food, medical attention, and exercise.

Children's Books

Allen, J., and Humphries, T. (1992). *Tiger*. Cambridge, MA: Candlewick Press.

Cowcher, H. (1993). *Tigress*. New York: Scholastic.

Finzel, J. (1991). *Large as Life*. New York: Lothrop, Lee & Shepard.

Goss, L. and C. (1989). *The Baby Leopard (An African Folktale)*. New York: Bantam Books.

Hadithi, M. (1990). *Lazy Lion*. London: Hodder and Stoughton.

Lewin, T. (1990). *Tiger Trek*. New York: Macmillan.

Mennen, I., and Daly, N. (1990). *Somewhere in Africa*. New York: Dutton Children's Books.

Simon, S. (1991). *Big Cats*. New York: HarperCollins.

Zoobooks, published by Wildlife Education Ltd., San Diego, California:

> *Big Cats*, March, 1992; Volume Nine, Number Six
>
> *Cheetahs*, August, 1990; Volume Seven, Number Eleven
>
> *Lions*, June, 1989; Volume Six, Number Nine
>
> *Little Cats*, October, 1988; Volume Six, Number One
>
> *Tigers*, July, 1992; Volume Nine, Number Ten

Adult References

Ashby, R. (1990). *Jane Goodall's Animal World: Tigers*. New York: Macmillan.

Brockman, A. (1986). *Lions and Tigers*. Mahwah, NJ: Watermill Press.

Lavine, S. A. (1987). *Wonders of Tigers*. New York: Dodd, Mead.

Petty, K. (1991). *Tigers*. New York: Gloucester Press.

Ryden, H. (1983). *Bobcat*. New York: G. P. Putnam's Sons.

Dogs

Old McDonald had a farm,
E I E I O.
And on this farm he had a dog.
E I E I O.

O ld McDonald has a dog and so do lots of other people. Dogs are a pervasive feature of human society—in homes, in neighborhoods, and in communities at large—dogs are everywhere. Tall dogs, short dogs, fluffy ones, scruffy ones, pure breeds, mixed breeds, quiet dogs, bouncy dogs, young pups, older dogs, friendly dogs, aggressive dogs—dogs come in all shapes, sizes, and temperaments. Thus, wherever children go they are likely to come in contact with dogs of many kinds. How positive those contacts are is related, in part, to how much children know about dogs and what kinds of experiences children have had with these animals.

Purpose

Ranging from excitement to fear, children have varying reactions to dogs.

Amalia loves dogs. Every time she sees one she's eager to hug it, pet it, or urge the dog to fetch.

Roberto has a different reaction. Whenever a dog comes in view, he retreats behind the nearest adult. Roberto wants nothing to do with dogs and considers all dogs dangerous.

Nathan has had few encounters with dogs other than seeing them on television or in the movies. However, he is sure he would like a dog of his own someday.

When the police officer brings her canine partner to the classroom, the children are invited to pet the dog. Allison announces, "Okay, but just on the tail end, not on the teeth end."

Elizabeth's mother reports that when Elizabeth gets excited she sometimes plays too rough with their new puppy. Her actions cause the animal to yelp or seek refuge under the bed. "She still has a lot to learn about dogs," her mom says.

In reality, all children have much to learn about dogs—what they are like, how they behave, and ways in which dogs and people relate to one another. This unit was written to expand children's understanding of dogs and to teach children safe, positive ways to interact with them. It was also created with the understanding that some children (and adults) view dogs warily, while others find them enticing or delightful.

Implementation

There are three mini-themes in this unit about dogs: "Dogs as Pets," "Working and Helping Dogs," and "Wild Dogs." Focusing on domesticated dog behaviors, characteristics, and needs, "Dogs as Pets" enables children to explore the concept of dogs within a familiar context. It is the most basic of the three mini-themes and is especially suited for preschoolers and children who have had limited experience with dogs.

Learning about pet dogs serves as an excellent foundation for introducing the notion that many dogs do work. Such dogs play important roles in people's lives beyond giving pleasure. The "Working and Helping Dogs" mini-theme includes common canine helpers children might see on the street such as police dogs and guide dogs for the visually impaired or physically disabled. It also features other kinds of herding, pulling, and tracking dogs with which children might be less familiar, but whose behavior is interesting and meaningful to them. This mini-theme also offers children chances to think about the value of work and the importance of helping as well as to explore people's needs both similar and different from their own.

The mini-theme "Wild Dogs" is best suited to children thoroughly familiar with the concept of dogs. These activities take children beyond the boundaries of day-to-day experience and encourage them in learning about other members of the family canidae—foxes, wolves, dingoes, and coyotes. We included this content to counteract the negative wild dog stereotypes to which children are frequently exposed through fairy tales and folktales. It is also designed to help children develop an appreciation for wildlife and its value to the planet. There are two different ways to approach the "Wild Dog" mini-theme. If wild dogs are part of the environment in which children live, take advantage of that proximity. Focus your examples on whatever wild species children might see or hear about in their community. On the other hand, if there are no wild dogs in the vicinity, emphasize that domestic dogs have instincts and responses much like their wild relatives. Build on children's knowledge of domestic dogs to make wild dogs relevant. In both cases, the challenge of this portion of the unit is that wild dogs tend to be shy of humans and are not readily seen in nature. Even at zoos, if wild dogs are kept in a simulated natural habitat, they often stay out of sight of visitors. Consequently, educators will be dependent on photographs and models to communicate information to children about foxes, wolves, dingoes, and coyotes. These conditions make the wild dog mini-theme more appropriate for children of elementary age than for preschoolers.

Finally, since children build concepts through firsthand experiences, numerous activities involving real dogs are integrated throughout the unit. In order to maximize the benefits of these encounters between children and dogs the following guidelines are recommended when canine visitors come to the program.

1. Display many pictures of dogs in the classroom to familiarize children with different kinds of dogs. Make sure to select paintings and photographs that represent dogs of varying breeds, sizes, and colors.

2. Give children opportunities to practice interacting with dogs, using toy animals.

3. Invite owners of "child friendly" dogs to visit the playground or classroom with their pets. Prior to the visit, discuss with the owner what you would like the dog and owner to do.

4. Alert parents that a dog visitor will be coming to the program. Ask them to contact you if their child might be uncomfortable with such a visit.

5. Explain to children in advance what the dog will be like (such as big or small, excited or quiet, in the room or on the playground, and so on).

6. Offer simple directions to children about what they should do when the dog arrives. Examples include: talking quietly, allowing the dog to sniff, asking the owner if it's all right to touch the dog.

7. Find a way for children not yet comfortable with dogs to feel safe during the visit. Watching the dog through a classroom window or holding an adult's hand are comforting strategies.

8. Avoid forcing children to approach or touch an animal if they do not wish to do so.

Keeping these simple guidelines in mind will do much to increase your pleasure and that of the children as you explore the wonderful world of dogs. Besides implementing this unit in the sequence presented here, suggested options for developing a dog theme are listed below.

Option One:

Week 1:   Pet Dog Characteristics and Behaviors

Week 2:   Dogs in People's Homes

Week 3:   Puppies

Option Two:

Week 1:   Pet Dogs—What They Are Like and How They Behave

Week 2:   Pet Dogs—Caring for Your Pet

Week 3:   Working and Helping Dogs—The Work They Do

Week 4:   Training Dogs for Home and Work

Option Three:

Week 1:   Dogs and People at Home

Week 2:   Dogs and People on the Job

Week 3:   Dogs and People in the Wild

Option Four:

Week 1:   Dogs in Stories

Week 2:   Dogs in Real-Life

Dogs as Pets

Terms, Facts, and Principles (TFPs)

General Characteristics

1. Dog are carnivorous (meat-eating) mammals that human beings keep as pets.

2. Pets are animals that are lovingly kept, primarily for fun and companionship.

3. Dogs vary in size; body build; fur-type; coloring; ear, head, and tail shape.

4. A breed of dogs is a group of dogs related by descent from common ancestors. Dogs within a given breed share visibly similar characteristics.

5. Dog breeds differ from one another in size, strength, stamina, aggressive tendencies and training potential.

6. Some dogs are one breed. Some dogs are a mixture of breeds.

7. Dogs and people have many body parts that have similar names and functions. Dogs have some body parts that are unique to them.

8. Dogs' fur helps to keep them dry and warm.

9. Dogs have claws that help them grip things.

10. Dogs have strong jaws and teeth for tearing, grinding, and chewing.

11. To cool off when hot, dogs pant by opening their mouths and letting their tongues hang out. Sometimes saliva will drip from their tongue.

12. Dogs have five senses: seeing, hearing, smelling, tasting, and touching.

13. Hearing and smelling are the senses dogs rely on the most.

14. Dogs respond to touch. They can easily differentiate between gentle and rough touches, loving and harsh touches.

15. Dogs use their senses to find out things: Is that person a stranger or someone I know? Is this place safe? Where is food? Who's that calling?

16. Most dogs have tails that they use for balance and for communicating.

17. Dogs move in various ways. They walk, run, jump, swim, dig, sit, and lie down.

18. Dogs make a variety of sounds. They bark, yap, whine, cry, howl, sneeze, cough, pant, and snore.

19. Dogs communicate through body movements and sounds.

a) When dogs want to play, they often wag their tails and lean their bodies and front paws forward. People can respond to these invitations by throwing a ball or other dog toy for the dog.

b) The lips on dogs often curl back and show teeth. Sometimes this expression is almost like a smile and shows the dog is happy.

c) A dog's eyes show emotions. When a dog is happy its eyes are bright.

d) Staring with large open eyes may imply fear. When a dog is afraid, it shows its teeth, growls or barks, sets its ears back, and stiffens its body. It is best for people not to approach or corner a frightened dog.

e) When a dog is upset, its ears and tail are held high while looking right at the person or animal.

f) A dog's tail also shows its emotions. It is held in a curled position while playing. While eating, the tail drops down. When the dog is threatened or worried, it holds its tail high. If a dog is insecure, it drops its tail between its legs. It is best for people not to corner an insecure dog, shout, or make sudden movements.

g) Dogs greet each other by sniffing and making sounds. Dogs greet people in the same way. It is best for people to respond by letting the dog sniff them and by avoiding any sudden movements.

20. People should observe dogs carefully to figure out what they are communicating.

*21. When people meet dogs they don't know, they should ask the owner what is the best way to act with the dog. If no owner is in sight, it is best to avoid strange dogs.

Dogs in People's Homes

22. Dogs are social animals. They form relationships with people and other dogs to gain protection, companionship, and satisfaction of their physical needs.

23. Dog care includes:

a) regular feeding

b) regular grooming with a special brush

c) daily exercise

d) providing toys for playing and chewing

e) a clean bed

f) medical care

g) shelter

h) love

24. Dogs that are not properly cared for—those that are abused or teased—may bite and/or become mean, mistrustful, and timid.

*25. Some types of dog training include obedience and agility.

*26. Obedience training involves teaching the dog to follow commands such as sit, come, heel, stay, and down. In this way dogs are taught to come when they are called, to sit, to stay in a particular place or position, and not to jump on people.

*27. Agility training involves teaching the dog to go through tunnels, jump over hurdles, walk over a raised balance beam, and other similar tasks and skills.

28. Some dog owners teach their dogs to play or do tricks such as fetching (retrieving items such as balls, Frisbees®, or other objects), sitting up or rolling over.

29. Dogs should wear collars with identification tags. These tags indicate who to contact in case the dog is lost.

30. Doctors who provide medical care for dogs and other animals are called veterinarians. Owners should take their dogs to visit a veterinarian once a year for a checkup and shots; when they are sick, injured, or pregnant; for neutering; and for the treatment of fleas and worms.

31. People may get a dog by purchasing one, receiving one as a gift, or adopting one from a dog shelter or humane society.

Puppies

32. Young dogs are called puppies.

33. Puppies are dependent on their mothers and their owners for nourishment and protection.

34. Young dogs have very sharp teeth. As the puppies play together they learn how to control their bites.

35. Mother dogs carry their young inside their bodies for 9 weeks.

36. Puppies are born sightless, deaf, and vulnerable.

37. The average size of a litter of puppies is 5, but may vary from 1 to 12.

Caring for Puppies

38. Puppies love to chew. Sometimes they chew objects that are unsafe. Dog owners must watch their puppies carefully to ensure that they do not hurt themselves by chewing on unsafe items.

39. Keeping a dog in a puppy crate is one way to ensure the dog's safety while the owner is away. Puppies treat their crate as their territory. Puppies feel safe in a crate, but should have many opportu-

nities to leave the crate to eat, go to the bathroom, exercise, and play.

40. House-training is the process of teaching dogs to urinate and defecate outdoors and signaling when they need to go.

41. Puppies usually urinate and/or defecate shortly after waking up and after eating. They should be taken outside at these times.

42. Puppies need many chances to learn new things. Sometimes they make mistakes. When this happens, a gentle correction and additional training is necessary. When puppies do what people want, praise is essential so they will try again.

Activity Ideas

Aesthetic

1. Canine Sing-Along

Here is a familiar tune that can be adapted to help children become more familiar with various dog breeds and canine characteristics.

♫ Dog Breed Musicale
Words by Grace Spalding
Tune: "How Much Is That Doggie in the Window?"

How much is that Dalmatian in the window?
The one with the big black spots.
How much is that Dalmatian in the window?
I do hope that Dalmatian's for sale.
How much is that Saluki in the window?
The one with the long fluffy tail?
How much is that Saluki in the window?
I do hope that Saluki is for sale.
Ideas for other verses:
Dachshund with the short, short legs.
Collie with the long, soft fur.
Bulldog with the short, short nose.

To Simplify:
● Focus on only one breed of dog each day.
● Sing about one certain body part, such as tails, comparing them from breed to breed.
● Make available pictures of different dog breeds so the children are able to visualize how they look.

To Extend:
● Ask the children to suggest dog breeds and distinguishing characteristics to use in creating new verses.

2. Pup Paints

To prepare for this activity, trace, then cut out several dog shapes from large and medium-sized pieces of easel paper. Use the templates provided here as samples. Enlarge them by using an overhead projector to project an image on a wall, then trace each one in the desired size. Make sure to represent a variety of breeds of dogs as well as sizes of dogs. Prepare paints for the children (tempera paints, fingerpaints, or watercolors). As the children come to the activity, invite them to choose a dog shape on which to paint. Encourage them to color their dogs as they desire, with or without spots, in actual dog colors or any color of their choosing.

Hint for Success:
● Implement this activity at the easel or on a table. If the children are working around a table, remove the chairs so they can be standing while they paint. Many children find that standing while painting gives them more room to maneuver their arms, making it easier to control the paint on the paper.

To Simplify:
● Trace the dog shapes onto the paper for the children to paint, but do not cut them out. This will reduce the potential problem of having the dog's legs tear as children paint.

To Extend:
● Invite the children to trace their own dog shapes on the paper before beginning to paint.

Affective

1. Canine Care

This activity gives children an opportunity to gain pleasure from the experience of work. Provide children with several grooming tools, such as dog brushes, combs, empty dog shampoo bottles, as well as stuffed dogs, dog bowls, dog food containers, leashes, and collars. Talk with the children about the care that dogs need and how people can help them. Demonstrate how to gently brush a dog. Explain to the children that by talking in a quiet, gentle tone of voice, the dog feels more at ease as you work with it. Encourage the children to use the various tools to care for the dogs.

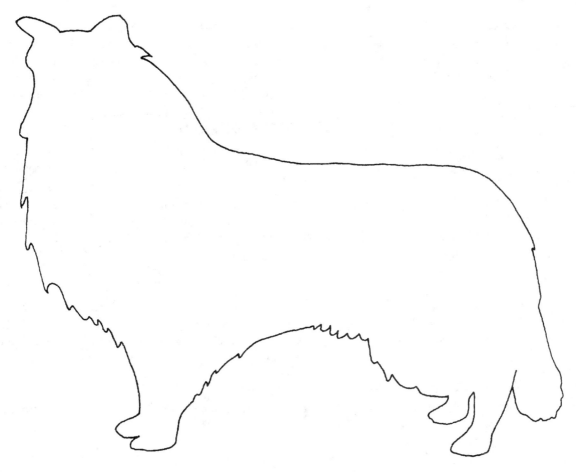

To Simplify:

● Introduce the children to one tool at a time. Demonstrate how to use the tool; then let the children try it.

To Extend:

● Teach one child a day how to use one new tool. Designate this child as the "head dog groomer" whose job it is to teach the other dog groomers how to use the tool.

2. Let's Go for a Walk!

In the pretend play area, have available for the children several sizes of stuffed dogs to choose from along with collars and leashes (ribbons with Velcro® fasteners or small plastic chains work well as make-believe collars and leashes). Invite children to care for their dogs by taking them for a walk so the dogs will have a chance to get some exercise.

To Simplify:

● Put the collars and leashes on the dogs for the children before the youngsters' arrival.

To Extend:

● Provide children with paper, scissors, and a stapler to use in making their own collars for the dogs.

3. Friendly Dog Visit

Before the dog unit is introduced, ask if any of your families has a pet dog who could be a gentle visitor in the classroom or on the playground. From those families who respond, invite some to come in, one at a time, during a circle time or outdoor play period. Structure each visit by asking the person who brings the dog in to be prepared to talk about how the family takes care of the dog, or to demonstrate ways to groom the dog, or to show things the dog can do. As much as possible, have the child owner talk about the dog and specific things he or she does with and for the dog. Also consider asking an owner to bring his or her dog to play on the playground with the children. Find out what outdoor activities the dog likes that the children can participate in, such as throwing a ball or frisbee, or taking it for a walk on a leash.

Hints for Success:

● An alternate source of animals can be found by calling the local Humane Society or Animal Rescue League. Such organizations often have public education programs that include friendly dog visitors.

● Greet the dog and his or her adult owner out of sight of the children, before introducing the animal to the group. This will give you an opportunity to make an initial assessment of the dog's temperament and the owner's ability to handle the dog safely.

To Simplify:

● For children who are not familiar or comfortable with dogs, make toy stuffed dogs available for several days in the classroom as well as pictures of dogs for everyone to see. Use these materials to introduce children to the idea of having a dog in their midst. Be sure that the first dogs to visit are smaller than the children and have a calm, friendly temperament.

To Extend:

● Prior to the visit, talk with the children about some of the things they expect to see during the dog's time in the classroom. Record their responses on a piece of chart paper and post it in the classroom. After the visit, ask children to describe the dog and what they noticed about its appearance and behavior. Help children compare their observations with what they thought they would see.

4. Identification Tags

Prepare for this activity by cutting moderately heavy paper (posterboard or tagboard) in a variety of shapes, such as bones, hearts, circles, or rectangles, approximately 4" x 6". Also, have available a list of the children's addresses and telephone numbers for reference. Explain that today children will have a chance to make identification tags similar to those worn by pet dogs. Invite the children to choose a shape out of which to make their own tag. Ask them to supply important identifying information such as their name, where they live, and their telephone number. If necessary, refer to the address list to help children recall such information. Assist the children either by taking their dictation or by supporting them as they attempt to write the information on their own. When the children have completed their identification tags, cover them with clear adhesive paper so they are more durable. Punch a hole in the top of the name tag with a paper punch. Have children wear their identification tags by attaching them to their clothes with a large safety pin or by hanging them on a "collar" made of ribbon or yarn.

Hints for Success:

● Determine how important it is that children actually know their address and phone number. If teaching that information seems critical, supplement this lesson with other address and telephone number activities provided in this volume. Some of each can be found in the "Communication" unit and in the "Safety" unit.

● An alternative is to use this activity as a way to tell children what their address and telephone numbers are.

● A third alternative is for children to tell you whatever they can about where they live and for the adult to write the information as described by the children, disregarding the need for particular street addresses.

To Simplify:

● Have each child make a mark or select a sticker to place on his or her tag for easy identification. Write the other identifying information based on children's dictation.

To Extend:

● Encourage children to read each other's identification tags.

Cognitive

1. Dog Seriation

Prepare for this activity by drawing or tracing pictures of several dogs. Vary certain attributes from picture to picture, such as the number of spots, length of tail, size of dog, short ears straight up to long ears hanging down. Encourage children to explore the pictures. Ask them to tell you what they notice about them. Create a story about the dog pictures to pique children's interest in seriating them. For example, tell children that there was a dog show in which many prizes were awarded. Invite children to choose the prize categories and then order the dogs as to first place, second place, and so on.

To Simplify:

● Use only a few pictures and limit the number of criteria to be considered. For example, have three pictures of dogs that vary in size or provide three dogs each obviously varying in the number of spots on his/her coat.

To Extend:

● Use photographs of real dogs—some of the same breed, some of varying breeds. This will expand the number of potential criteria available for children to consider. A second option is to provide pictures of dogs maturing from puppyhood to adulthood. Ask children to put these in order from youngest to oldest.

2. Dog Biscuit Matching

Collect toy stuffed dogs of varying sizes. Bring to the classroom small-, medium-, and large-sized dog biscuits. Invite the children to match the dog biscuits to the dogs by size. Ask them to explain why they gave the dogs the biscuits they did.

To Simplify:
● Use obviously large and small animals and large and small biscuits.

To Extend:
● Add additional items to pair with the dogs: dog dishes, rawhide bones, collars, or leashes.
● Make the differences among the sizes less obvious.

3. Reading Dogs' Signals

Collect a number of photographs or magazine pictures of dogs, some at play, some showing aggression, and some showing fear. Make three "dog faces" as illustrated, using sandwich-sized paper plates. Label one happy, one fearful, one upset. Keep a copy of TFP 19 with you and refer to it as necessary while you talk with the children.

Explain to the children that dogs communicate with each other and with people through their body stance and sounds. Have the children look at the pictures and describe what they see. Point out a picture in which the dog is bowing, front down, back up and tail wagging. This is an invitation to play. In a picture where the dog's head and body are lowered and the tail tucked under the body, the dog is showing fear. Tell the children that if they see a dog in this position to stay away. Dogs that are scared may bite. A dog that is upset will hold its ears and tail high and look straight at a person. Also show a picture demonstrating this and tell children to stay away from a dog looking like this. Ask children to look carefully at all the pictures and put them in piles below the "dog face" that best depicts what the dog is communicating.

4. Painful Partings

The purpose of this activity is to give children opportunities to discuss death in a safe, comfortable environment and to provide them with accurate information about it. Two books that deal with the death of a pet dog are *I'll Always Love You* by Hans Wilheim (1985)

Happy Dog

Insecure Dog

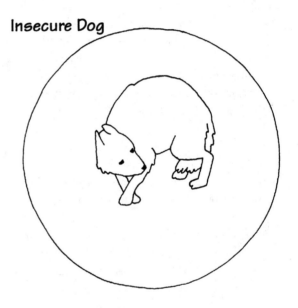

Upset Dog

and *The Accident* by Carol Carrick (1976). You needn't wait for a child to actually experience the death of the family dog to broach this subject with the group. In fact, there is evidence that children benefit when they have opportunities to discuss death in day-to-day circumstances rather than waiting for a crisis to occur. Select one of these books and read it to children in small groups or at circle time. Follow up by asking straightforward questions such as, "What happened in this story?" "How did _____ feel when his dog died?" "What does it mean to die?" Carry out a discussion with children in accordance with the following guidelines (Kostelnik, Stein, Whiren, and Soderman, 1993).

Guidelines for Talking to Children About Death

1. Use appropriate vocabulary when discussing death and dying. Use the words dead and died. Avoid euphemisms such as passed away, lost, or gone away. Children are literal in their understanding and are confused by these latter terms. Death is not like anything else. It is not like sleeping, or resting, or lying still, or going away on a trip. No other words in the English language mean exactly the same as dead and died.

2. Describe death in terms of familiar bodily functions. Point out that when an animal dies all normal body functions stop: the heart stops beating, the lungs stop breathing, the eyes stop seeing, the stomach stops working, there is no thinking, no feeling, no sleeping, no eating, no more emotions.

3. Explain why the death occurred, giving children accurate information. Eventually, children ask, "Why did he/she die?" In these circumstances it is best to answer as truthfully as possible. For instance, if an animal dies because it is too sick to live any more, say this. Then move into talking about the idea that its body was so ill that its lungs stopped breathing, its heart stopped beating, and so forth. It helps to explain that all living things get sick sometimes, but mostly they get better. However, there are times when they are so terribly sick their body cannot function anymore and then they die. Similar statements can be made about death from an accident. When talking to children in these circumstances, help them differentiate between mortal injury and the everyday bumps and bruises from which we all recover.

4. Answer children's questions about death matter of factly. Help children understand better the details of death by responding calmly to their queries. Accept their questions nonjudgmentally. Answer simply and honestly. Remember, too, that children learn through repetition so they may ask the same questions several times. Each time they hear the answer, they add a new fragment of information to their store of knowledge.

5. Acknowledge and accept children's varying reactions to death. Some children will be intrigued by the story and ask numerous questions or ask to hear it again and again. Others will hardly seemed fazed by the animal's death and will quickly move on to other activities in the classroom. These are normal reactions and should be respected.

Hint for Success:

● The book *Lifetimes* by Bryan Mellonie and Robert Ingpen (1983) gives a simple, matter-of-fact explanation of life and death that is useful to children exploring this concept.

To Simplify:

● Read the story and discuss it with the children.

To Extend:

● After reading the story, help children write an experience story about their reactions to the animal's death. In addition, take advantage of looking at and discussing dead insects, earthworms, or other small animals such as birds that you might find outdoors. For instance, tell the children, "The earthworm is dead. Look at its body—it isn't moving, it isn't breathing, it's all dried up. That means it is dead." If a classroom pet dies, this will be an important time to talk about death and dying. Again, invite the children to look at the dead animal. Notice what has changed about the pet: not moving, not breathing, heart has stopped beating, the body is stiff—the pet is dead. Encourage the children to take part in preparing the pet for "burial." They could possibly help dig a hole in which to bury the animal or prepare a cardboard box for the animal's body by decorating it. Be sure to explain that these rituals are for the benefit of the living; the dead animal will have no knowledge of the children's preparations. If it is possible to bury the animal on the school grounds, gather the children together for this. Let them help fill up the hole or make a marker for the grave with a rock. Let the parents know that the pet has died and that the children were involved in the discussion about death and the burial of the animal.

Construction

To give the children an opportunity to create a dog, provide them with modeling dough made in a realistic-looking dog color (such as black, brown, white, or yellow). Add extra materials, such as various lengths of plastic tubing or wooden dowels for legs, small pieces of vinyl or soft plastic for ears (some pointed, some oblong), and various lengths of yarn for tails. Allow the children to explore the materials, then ask them to think of a way to use these materials to create a dog. Have them consider what kind of dog they would like to make: small-, medium-, or large-sized; what color; what kind of ears; and so on. When they are completely finished, ask each child to name his or her dog. Provide a name tag with the name of the dog and its owner.

Hint for Success:

● The value of this activity to children is the linkage between their own mental image of a dog and the tangible product they create. Realism from an adult perspective is not necessary. Asking children to picture a dog in their minds and then create it using the materials available is a good way to get the activity started. Many children like to have access to reference books as a way to remind themselves of certain aspects of the dog they have in mind. Such materials can be useful to children as long as they are treated as potential resources, not as required models.

At the woodworking table, have available for children a variety of wood pieces, small carpet pieces, nails, hammers, and saws. Remind children that some families keep their dogs outside. When dogs stay outside for a long length of time, it is important for them to have a safe, dry place to sleep. Encourage the children to use the materials at the workbench to create such a place.

To Simplify:

● Provide wood glue to use instead of nails or carry out the activity in the block area with wooden blocks, toy dogs, small blankets, and pillows.

To Extend:

● Ask children to think of other items dogs might need in their safe places. Assist children in getting the materials they need to construct these items as well.

Language

To carry out this activity get a battery-operated or windup alarm clock with a loud ticking sound and a loud alarm. Gather the children in a circle. Introduce this activity by reminding children that dogs have a keen sense of hearing and can often hear sounds that humans cannot hear or have a harder time distinguishing. Explain that today children will be like dogs, listening for hard-to-hear sounds. Pass the clock around the circle and let each child hold it up to his or her ear to hear the ticking sound. Set the alarm to go off in about three minutes. Tell the children that you will hide the clock in the classroom while their eyes are closed. Their job is to try to find the clock by listening for the ticking sound. At the end of three minutes the alarm will go off to provide a further clue to the clock's location. Repeat this procedure throughout the day. Let the children take turns hiding the clock.

To Simplify:

● Set the alarm to go off in a few seconds so the children are locating the clock by the alarm's sound.

To Extend:

● Use a clock with a softer alarm and ticking sound. As a further variation, invite a dog to visit the class and demonstrate the dog's keen sense of hearing using a dog whistle which the children will not be able to hear, but the dog will.

Invite the children to generate a list of words they would use to praise a puppy or dog. Begin by thinking of the good things the animal might do, such as coming when called, jumping down when told to do so, or walking by one's side. Ask children what they might say in these circumstances and record their answers on a large piece of easel paper which will remain posted in the classroom. Refer to this list whenever a canine visitor is expected or as children carry out pretend play activities in which they are dogs or dog owners.

To prepare for this activity, draw a chart on a large piece of construction paper or posterboard titled "Caring for Dogs." Under the title, divide the chart into two vertical sections, one headed "Mother Dog" and the other, "People."

Caring for Dogs	
Mother Dog	People

Obtain a copy of the book, *My Puppy Is Born* by Joanna Cole (1991) or *The Puppy Book* by Camilla Jessel (1991). During a circle time or a small group time, gather the children together and tell them you are going to read them a book about puppies being born. Before you start to read, give the children a "listening job." Tell them to remember what things the mother dog did to care for the puppies and what things the people did to care for the puppies. Consider giving half the children the job of listening for the dog-caring items, and the other half of the group, the people-caring items. Read the book. Afterwards, ask the children to tell you the ways the mother dog cared for the puppies. Write this on the chart. Do the same for the "people caring for the puppies" column. When finished, read the children's responses back to them. Refer back to the book to check if there are any other ways the people or mother dog cared for the puppies that weren't mentioned. Praise the children for working hard at listening and remembering.

Physical

1. Different Strokes

This game is a variation of Simon Says. Prior to introducing it, gather enough stuffed toy dogs so that there is one for each child and one for the game leader. Keeping the toys temporarily out of sight, gather the children in a circle and conduct a discussion about the appropriate ways to touch a dog. Use words like stroking, patting, scratching, and rubbing to describe the gentle, loving touches dogs enjoy. Next, give each child a toy dog and have them try the different kinds of touches the group had generated. Finally, make a game out of these motions by having the leader call out different touches either by prefacing the direction with the words, "Simon Says," meaning the group imitates the action, or omitting "Simon Says," meaning the group should ignore the leader's directions. Emphasize to the children that it is their job to listen very carefully and follow what the leader directs when saying "Simon Says." React with good humor when children are fooled and continue the game with everyone participating. Examples of directions might include: "Simon says, rub your dog's belly," "Simon says, scratch your dog's ears," "Simon says, pat your dog's head."

To Simplify:
● Use the words "Simon Says" with every direction.

● Ask the leader to model the action every time Simon Says to do something and for the leader to freeze when giving a direction in which "Simon Says" has been omitted.

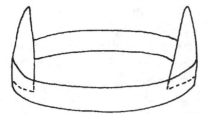

To Extend:
● Speed up the pace of the directions.

2. Dog Ear Cutouts

To prepare for this activity, draw several shapes of dog ears on a piece of paper. Vary the shapes in terms of cutting difficulty (see illustration). Invite children to cut out the shapes.

To Simplify:
● Make the space between the lines at least two inches wide so children will have an easier time following the cutting path.

To Extend:
● Provide the children with strips of construction paper that are one inch wide; tape or staple the ears to the strips so the children can wear the ears in a headband fashion.

Pretend Play

1. Housekeeping with Dogs

Add materials to the housekeeping area so that children can pretend they are caring for a dog at home. Provide toy dogs, dog collars, dog food bowls, a little dry dog food in small resealable containers, dog toys, and dog biscuits. As children play in the area, encourage them to feed, walk, talk to, and play with their dogs.

2. Dog Supply Store

Incorporate a dog supply store within the classroom. Supply items such as dog collars of various sizes, several types of dog biscuits, canned as well as dry dog food, dog grooming items, dog toys, leashes, and stuffed dogs in a variety of sizes and colors. Establish roles for the children: customer, inventory keeper, cashier, manager. Provide name tags, clipboards, dress up clothes, purses, wallets, and cash registers to help children choose and identify the various roles. As children recognize a need for dog items in the housekeeping area, send them to the dog supply store to purchase what is necessary.

To Simplify:
● Limit the amount of materials available to the children until they are familiar with their use. Gradually add materials to extend their play.

To Extend:
● Arrange for the delivery of several "new" items to the store. Acquaint children with the jobs workers might have to perform in relation to the delivery, such as sorting out and packaging like materials for sale (classification activity), organizing items in order of size to help customers find what they need more easily (seriation activity), and conducting an inventory of various products for sale (counting and recording activity).

3. Dog Shelter

Create a dog shelter in the pretend play area by setting up boxes in rows along the walls. Line the boxes with newspaper. In each box put a dog bowl, a water dish, a few dog toys, and a toy dog. Have available on some additional shelves extra bowls and newspaper, dog biscuits, dog food, dog toys, and blankets. Tell children that the area is now a dog shelter. This is a place where people bring their animals if they can no longer care for them or if they find a lost animal. People who work in the facility care for the dogs until a new home can be found. When people decide they want a new pet, a place they can go to choose one is the dog shelter. At the shelter, there are many jobs for people to do: office worker, dog walker and exerciser, dog feeder, tour guide for people looking for a new pet, and cage cleaners. Support children as they take on these roles or the roles of people looking for a pet.

To Extend:

● Suggest that children think of a name for each dog.

● Children may also write an information sheet about each animal, listing details such as the dog's name, the dog's age, and what kind of food the dog likes to eat.

Social

1. Dog Pets

B efore a dog visitor comes to your room, talk with the children about how to approach and touch a dog. Use a toy dog to demonstrate how to walk slowly toward the dog and how to allow the dog to sniff before petting it. Talk to the dog in a quiet voice using the dog's name. Touch the dog in a gentle way, petting the fur. Divide the children into pairs. Give each pair a toy dog with which to practice. Have the children take turns being the owner of the dog and the person who is approaching it. Encourage each child to ask the pretend owner if he or she can pet the dog. Tell the pretend owners to provide appropriate instructions. Make sure each child gets a chance to play both human roles.

2. How Could You Help?

P resent the children with several situations in which a dog needs care. These could be shown in pictures or demonstrated with toy dogs and props. For example, a stuffed toy dog with tangled fur, a dog with an empty water bowl or food dish, a dirty dog, a dog with no collar or identification tags, a dog sleeping outside on cement, a wet dog, and a dog chewing on an electrical cord (or something else that could hurt the dog). Ask the children to identify the problem for the dog and then suggest a way that they could help.

To Simplify:

● Carry out this activity with toy dogs and props. Have available objects the children can choose from to help the dogs, such as a grooming brush, a bag of dog food, water, soap, a dog collar, a pillow or blanket, a towel, and a rawhide bone. Ask the children to choose one of the objects and then show how they could help the dog using that object.

To Extend:

● Discuss with the children ways they have helped pet dogs at home or dogs who have visited your classroom.

Teacher Resources

Field Trips

1. If there is a dog sheltering facility close by, call ahead to see if school visitors are welcome. If so, schedule a time to visit. Tell children before the trip that they will be going, provide guidelines to follow at the shelter such as, keep hands out of cages and use quiet voices.

2. Ask a veterinarian in your area if it would be possible for the class to visit the clinic. Visit the clinic in advance to check out space—is there enough room at the clinic for the whole class to move around and see the various rooms of the clinic? Talk with the receptionist or veterinarian about what you would like the children to see at the clinic and information someone at the clinic could talk with the children about on their visit. Some clinics have a "live-in" pet that a veterinarian could use to demonstrate a physical examination. If this is not possible, arrange for the children to see the different rooms and tools veterinarians use in their practice. Ask for someone from the clinic to guide the tour.

3. Call a local chapter of the American Kennel Club, a dog breeder or dog trainer to gather information on dog shows that may possibly be occurring in your area. As many of these are scheduled on weekends, inform families of the times and arrange to meet at the site. Prepare an observation sheet to guide children's attention at the show. Some examples of observation items include:

Draw a picture of your favorite dog at the show.
What about this dog made it your favorite?
Which dog had the longest fur?

Which dog had the most interesting name?

Describe one dog you saw.

Describe one thing you saw a dog do.

Describe one thing you saw a person do with a dog at the show.

Classroom Visitors

1. Ask a dog breeder to talk about characteristics of the specific breed he or she works with, how he or she cares for the dogs, and what he or she does to help a new owner prepare for having a puppy in their home.

2. Have a veterinarian describe ways children could help keep their own dogs healthy and safe—taking the dog for a walk, exercising the animal, knowing which foods to feed the dog and which foods to avoid, remembering to "puppy proof" the house by not leaving toys out that the dog could chew up, and so on. The vet might also demonstrate on a stuffed or live dog what she/he does for a routine examination, demonstrating tools used and describing what she or he looks for while checking the animal.

3. Ask a dog groomer to bring a dog and to demonstrate what she or he does to keep dogs neat and clean.

Children's Books

Adamoli, V. (1992). *The Love of Dogs*. New York: Smithmark.

Brown, M. (1990). *Arthur's Pet Business*. New York: Little, Brown.

Brown, R. (1987). *Our Puppy's Vacation*. New York: Dutton Children's Books.

Burton, J. (1991). *See How They Grow: Puppy*. New York: Lodestar Books.

Carrick, C. (1976). *The Accident*. Boston: Houghton Mifflin.

Cole, J. (1991). *My Puppy Is Born*. New York: Morrow Junior Books.

Hansard, P. (1994). *Wag, Wag, Wag*. Cambridge, MA: Candlewick Press.

Harper, I., and Moser, B. (1994). *My Dog Rosie*. NY: The Blue Sky Press.

Herriot, J. (1989). *The Market Square Dog*. New York: St. Martin's Press.

Jessel, C. (1991). *The Puppy Book*. Cambridge, MA: Candlewick Press.

Khalsa, D. (1987). *I Want a Dog*. New York: Clarkson N. Potter.

Mayer, M. (1985). *Just Me and My Puppy*. Racine, WI: Western Publishing.

Mellonie, B, and Ingpen, R. (1983). *Lifetimes*. New York: Bantam Books.

Seligson, S., and Schneider, H. (1987). *Amos, The Story of an Old Dog and His Couch*. New York: Little, Brown.

Selsam, M., and Hunt, J. (1981). *A First Look at Dogs*. New York: Walker and Company.

Wilheim, H. (1985). *I'll Always Love You*. New York: Crown Books for Young Readers.

Adult References

Caras, R. (1992). *The Roger Caras Dog Book*. New York: Dorset Press.

Clutton-Brock, J. (1991). *Eyewitness Books: Dog*. New York: Alfred A. Knopf.

Fox, M. (1992). *Understanding Your Dog*. New York: St. Martin's Press.

Morris, D. (1986). *Dogwatching*. Crown Publishers.

Sayer, A. (1989). *The Complete Book of the Dog*. New York: Gallery Books.

Secord, W. (1992). *Dog Painting 1840–1940: A Social History of the Dog in Art*. Suffolk, England: Antique Collector's Club.

Taylor, D. (1990). *The Ultimate Dog Book*. New York: Simon and Schuster.

Tortora, D. (1983). *The Right Dog for You*. New York: A Fire Side Book.

Working and Helping Dogs

Terms, Facts, and Principles (TFPs)

1. Working dogs are dogs trained to help people in particular ways.

2. Some breeds of dogs are traditionally used as working dogs, other dogs sometimes are trained as working dogs.

3. Because of their characteristics, particular dogs are well suited for doing specific kinds of work.

4. Working dogs do many different kinds of work.

5. Some dogs do work primarily by guiding people, animals or objects (herding dogs, sled dogs, leader dogs).

6. Some dogs do work primarily by using their sense of smell (tracking dogs, police dogs, rescue dogs).

7. Some dogs do work primarily by hearing and seeing (guard dogs, watch dogs, helping dogs for visually or hearing impaired people).

*8. Some dogs do work primarily by carrying things, fetching things, or pushing on things (helping dogs for people who have limited mobility). These dogs are sometimes called companion dogs.

*9. Some dogs do work primarily by letting people hold them and pet them. These dogs are sometimes described as therapy dogs.

10. Holding or petting a dog sometimes makes people feel good.

*11. Some dogs with easygoing personalities do their work by visiting people who are elderly, sick, feeling lonely or sad, or who are not able to leave their homes.

12. Working dogs are trained by people to do their jobs.

13. People teach dogs specific commands.

14. Commands are key words or gestures that tell the dog what to do.

15. In addition to obedience commands, working dogs learn commands that are specific to their job.

16. Working dogs and the people in their lives practice to master the working commands.

17. The types of commands taught to the dog relate directly to the job the dog is expected to do.

18. Some working dogs are also pets.

Activity Ideas

Aesthetics

1. Frame That Dog

To prepare for this activity, gather magazine pictures of various dogs typically used as working or helping dogs.

Examples of working dogs to use for this activity:

Herding dogs
Old English Sheepdog
Shetland Sheepdog
Puli
Welsh Corgi
Collie
Border Collie
Bearded Collie
Australian Shepherd
German Shepherd
Australian Cattle Dog
Belgian Sheepdog
Bouvier Des Flandres
Beauceron
Draft dogs (meant for pulling carts or sleds)
Alaskan Malamute
Siberian Husky
Zamoyed
Bernese Mountain Dog
Police dogs
Boxer
Doberman Pinscher
Rottweiler
German Shepherd

Giant Schnauzer

Akita

Bull Mastif

Diving dogs (who dive for lost fishing gear and fish that have wescaped the trawl)

Portuguese Water Dog

Water Rescue dogs

Newfoundland

Guide Dogs for the Blind

German Shepherd

Labrador Retriever

Golden Retriever

Provide 8-1/2" x 11" sheets of construction paper in varied colors and glue sticks or glue in small squeeze bottles. In advance, cut out strips of colored construction paper 1 to 2 inches wide. Make some 9 inches long and others 11-1/2 inches in length. These strips will become the frame children create for their art work.

Cover a table with newspaper and lay the pictures on the table so they can be easily viewed by the children. Invite the children to choose a few dog pictures that they like. Tell them to arrange the dog pictures on their pieces of construction paper in a way that pleases them. (Advise children to keep their pictures away from the edges of the paper so parts of their creation will not be covered by the frame.) Next, have children actually glue their pictures on to the paper. When children have finished using the glue, show them how to glue the frame-strips to the edges of the collage to create a framed effect (see illustration). After the pictures are complete and the glue is dry, ask children whether they would like to hang their collages on the wall at school or take them home.

To Simplify:

● Place only a few pictures on the table at a time. Provide paste instead of glue.

To Extend:

● Encourage children to design and cut out their own frames from construction paper. Offer children scissors with which to cut pictures of their own choosing from magazines.

2. Song for the Working Dog

Children enjoy the repetitive melody of Woody Guthrie's "Pick It Up," which is available on the audiotape *Woody's Grow Big Songs* by Woody and Arlo Guthrie (Warner Bros. Records, 1992). Take that familiar tune and insert words to draw children's attention to the varied work some dogs do.

♫ **Working Dog Song**
Words by Laura Stein
Tune: "Pick It Up" by Woody Guthrie

For the Companion Dog:
Dropped my keys, pick them up, pick them up.
Dropped my keys, pick them up, pick them up.
Dropped my keys, pick them up, pick them up.
And put them back on my lap.
For the Leader Dog:
Crossing the street, keep me safe, keep me safe.
Crossing the street, keep me safe, keep me safe.
Crossing the street, keep me safe, keep me safe.
And stay right by my side.
For the Therapy Dog:
I want a friend, play with me, play with me.
I want a friend, play with me, play with me.
I want a friend, play with me, play with me.
or just sit on my lap.
For the Guard Dog:
Guard my house, be alert, be alert.
Guard my house, be alert, be alert.
Guard my house, be alert, be alert.
And don't let strangers in.

To Simplify:

● Teach one verse of the song at a time. As each type of working dog is introduced in the classroom, sing the verse of the song that describes that dog.

To Extend:

● Once the children are familiar with the song, encourage them to be songwriters. Have them think of other ways working dogs help people and fit the children's ideas into the tune.

Affective

1. Blue Ribbon Winner!

Post pictures of working dog at shows or with their ribbons in the classroom where children can easily see them. Engage the children in a discussion about how working and helping dogs are trained. Explain that sometimes dog owners take their dogs to shows so other people can see the dogs work and so the dogs can earn points to show they know how to do their jobs. Dogs who do well and complete the tasks they are assigned are given trophies or ribbons for their efforts.

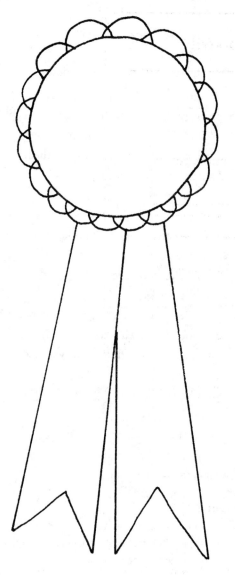

Set up a "show" area for the children in which each one gets a ribbon for demonstrating and completing a particular skill/job such as smell matching, finding hidden items, racing, jumping over a hurdle or long jump, carrying out climbing or fetching tasks. Create ribbons out of construction paper or satin ribbon (see illustration). Write the child's name and the name of the completed task. Present the ribbon to the child after he or she has finished the job.

Hint for Success:

● Make sure each child gets a ribbon upon completion of the task regardless of how well she or he performs a given job. Reinforce children for their hard work and persistence in completing each task.

To Simplify:

● Limit the number of skill areas addressed to two or three at a time. Offer simple tasks with only a few steps from beginning to end. Allow the children to choose one skill they would like to carry out.

To Extend:

● Offer children the materials with which to create their own ribbons, such as 1-inch-wide satin ribbon, construction paper, scissors, glue, stapler, and fabric markers. Also, expand the number of tasks necessary for children to complete a task.

2. Classroom Workers

Create a job chart for the classroom that includes tasks to correspond with the jobs that working dogs do. Such a chart might include a person who gets things for people who need them (the fetcher), a person who comforts people in distress (the comforter), a person who leads the group from one place to another (the guider), a person who turns the lights off and on (the switcher), a person who makes sure doors are open and closed as appropriate (the door guard). Each day assign or allow different children to choose a job. Make sure every child gets a turn to do something before anyone gets a second turn. Fashion a chart on which the jobs are listed along with a picture symbol to illustrate each one and on which children's names can be posted. Two options for making such a chart are illustrated.

If you have never used a job chart before, introduce it to the children by talking about the importance of work and the need for classroom workers. If you have used a job chart in the past, explain to children that you have created a new one that involves jobs similar to those carried out by working dogs. Assure children that everyone will get a turn to do a job. Have the children take turns selecting and carrying out jobs for the day.

Hint for Success:

● Create badges, using pictures of working dogs, for children to wear that correspond to the jobs on the job chart. This will remind each worker and others in the classroom about who is responsible for each job. Also, remain alert for children assigned to a job who have had no opportunity to carry it out. Create such opportunities as necessary.

To Simplify:

● Remind and assist children in carrying out their jobs.

To Extend:

● At the end of each day, ask each classroom worker to evaluate the work experience in terms of how he or she felt about it and who he or she helped throughout the session.

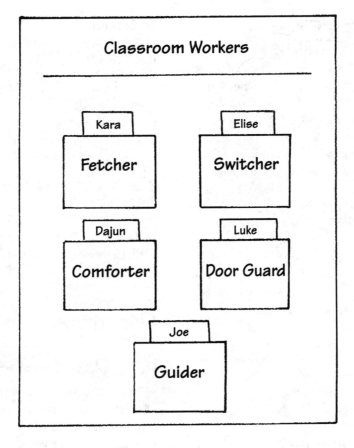

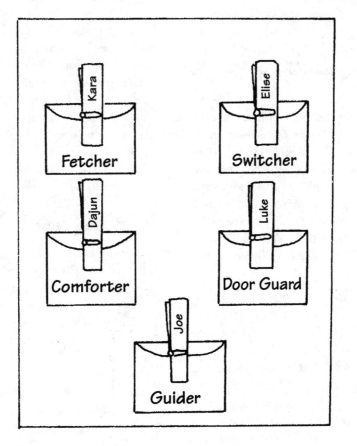

3. Comfort Puppies

The purpose of this activity is to teach children a simple coping skill—how to gain comfort from a soothing object. Prepare for the activity by collecting four or five toy dogs that are soft and cuddly. Show the dogs to the children and explain that these dogs have a special job in the classroom—they will be the children's "comfort puppies." Explain that whenever anyone feels sad or lonely, he or she can select a favorite comfort puppy with which to sit in a quiet, comfortable place. As a group, talk about where the puppies will be kept, how a puppy should be held, and what kind of voice children should use when they are with the puppy. Write the children's ideas on a piece of paper and post the guidelines in a "comfort puppy area." Place the puppies in an easily accessible spot and invite children to get the puppies whenever they have the need for them.

To Simplify:
- The teacher will present two or three guidelines for how the comfort puppy is to be used; the children will use the puppy as they need it.

To Extend:
- Ask the children to be on the lookout for anyone in the classroom who may need to hold a comfort puppy. Encourage children to help a distressed classmate by getting a puppy and asking the unhappy child if he or she would like to hold it.

4. Tracking Feelings

Once at least a few children have had the experience of holding the comfort puppy, have them talk about their feelings—why they needed comfort and how it felt to hold the puppy. Write down each child's ideas in a "feelings" book made from pieces of construction paper folded in half, then stapled together at the folded edge to create a binding. Keep this book close to the comfort puppy area so the children's feelings can be written down as they express them. Periodically, read through the book with the group as a whole or with individual children.

Cognitive

1. Scent Smelling

To prepare for this activity, create scent containers by taking small plastic containers with covers and putting small amount of scented materials in them (i.e.,

orange peel, lemon peel, garlic, onion). Make two or three of each different scent type. Direct children to sniff the various containers and match the scents that are the same. Explain to the children that this is how some dogs do their work. Hunting dogs and police dogs, for example, use their keen sense of smell to follow a scent until they find what they are looking for. Examples include hunting dogs and police dogs.

To Simplify:
- Use scents that are very familiar to the children, and easily differentiated.

To Extend:
- Use scents that are more similar to one another and harder to discriminate.

Construction

1. Sleds and Carts

The purpose of this activity is for the children to create their own versions of sleds or carts for make-believe working dogs to use in doing their work. Gather cardboard boxes in a variety of sizes, plastic or wooden wheels that can be attached to the boxes, lengths of rope to be tied onto the boxes for pulling, markers or crayons for decorating or labeling the carts and sleds. Explain to the children that some dogs help people by pulling supplies in carts when traveling on dry ground or sleds when traveling over snow and ice. Set the materials out in a large open space indoors on newspaper or outdoors. Then invite the children to look at the materials and think of ways they could use them to create a sled or cart for working dogs to use (these could be for either toy dogs or children pretending to be dogs). Encourage the children to make the carts and sleds, giving assistance as necessary.

2. Dog Dough Faces

To carry out this activity you will need flour, salt, oil, water, 4-inch aluminum tart pans, a knife, a bowl, a cookie sheet, a fork, a rolling pin, smocks for the children and yourself, and access to an oven. You will also need pictures of various working and helping dogs in action. Select pictures that represent a variety of dog breeds and types. Gather the materials and show them to the children. Explain that today each child will get to make a helping or working dog's face out of dough. After having all the children wash their hands, use the following recipe for every eight children.

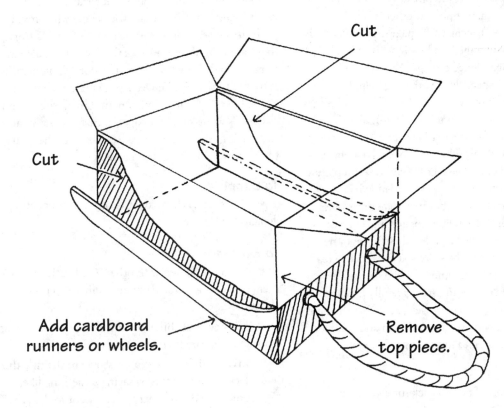

Cut

Cut

Add cardboard
runners or wheels.

Remove
top piece.

2 cups flour

3/4 cup ice water

1/2 teaspoon of salt

With the children, measure the flour and salt into a bowl. Add the oil a drop or two at a time and work it into the mixture with a fork. Stop adding oil when the mixture resembles coarse oatmeal. Next, add the water a bit at a time. Blend the mixture with fingers, adding more water as needed to form a ball of dough. Gather the dough into a ball. Knead for 10 minutes. Divide the dough into eight evenly sized balls. Roll each ball into a 6-inch circle. Place each circle on an inverted tart pan. Pinch features with fingers and attach other features with extra bits of dough. When attaching extra dough pieces rub a little water on the base and the dough piece so they will stick to one another better. Place the inverted tart pans on cookie sheets and bake in a 250° oven for 6 to 8 hours. Ask the children to make a label for their helping/working dog, identifying its name or its type, and the name of the artist/owner. Display these canine works of art for everyone to enjoy.

Hints for Success:

● Give children plenty of opportunities to partici-pate in the mixing as well as in the final molding of the dog faces.

● Reserve some extra dough so children have enough with which to make facial features such as eye-brows and noses.

To Simplify:

● Make up the dough in advance. Have the children begin this process by rolling out the dough, then making their dog faces.

To Extend:

● Provide food coloring mixed in "doglike" colors children can use to paint their dog faces before they place them in the oven. Darker colors work best because the paints will "fade" as they bake. After the faces are cool, the adult can coat them with water soluble polyurethane (applied with a brush) to preserve them "forever".

Language

1. Helpmates

Use a narrative picture book to assist children in gaining a better understanding of what it means to help. Possible selections include *My Buddy* by Audrey Osofsky (1992), a story about a boy who has muscular dystrophy. Buddy is his dog. Buddy has the special job of helping the boy do many tasks. Another is *Newf* by Marie Killilea (1992), a children's picture book about a Newfoundland dog, alone on a beach, who finds a hungry kitten in an abandoned cottage. The story tells of their friendship—especially how the dog helps feed, comfort and protect the kitten. A third, *The Shepherd Boy* written by Kristine L. Franklin (1994), tells the story of Ben, a Navaho shepherd boy, and his sheepdogs, White Eye and No Tail. What the boy and dogs must do to keep the sheep safe is the focus of this colorful picture book. Select one of these stories to read aloud. Before you begin, remind children that help sometimes takes the form of rescuing, defending, comforting, or assisting. Dogs are capable of providing all of these forms of help. Tell the children that in the story you are about to read, one character needs help. Other characters provide help. The children's job is to listen carefully to figure how who needs help, who gives help, and what the help involves. Read the book you have chosen and conduct the discussion as described in your introduction.

To Simplify:

● Read the story. Then go back through the book, page by page, with the children. Identify ways in which the dog helps the other main character with whom it comes in contact.

To Extend:

● Ask half the children to listen for what kind of help the boy (or kitten or lamb) needed. Have the other half of the group listen for what the dogs do to be helpful. When the story is over, ask both groups to recount what they heard. Write the children's ideas on chart paper, periodically reading their words back to them to clarify what was said and to summarize the main points of the story.

● Read the two books. Then have the children compare the kind of help Buddy provides with the kind of help Newf gives or the help provided by White Eye and No Tail. Discuss what is similar and what is different about their behavior.

2. Words for Carl

Alexandra Day has written several books about a Rottweiler named Carl who has the special job of helping to care for his family's child. Select any of the following "Carl" books, including: *Good Dog, Carl* (1991), *Carl's Afternoon in the Park* (1991), *Carl Goes Shopping* (1989), and *Carl Goes to Day Care* (1993).

Make the book you selected available to children in the book area several days before initiating this activi-ty. Announce to the children that today they will become authors. Authors are the people who provide words to a story. *Carl's Afternoon in the Park* is a story that has no words, but each of them will have a chance to make up their own words to the story. Conduct the activity as a whole group exercise, giving each child a chance to tell about one picture in turn. Write down the children's words on chart paper so that everyone can see the words as they are written. Read back to the group their "story" after it has been completed.

To Simplify:

● Ask each child to identify one object or action depicted on a page.

To Extend:

● Provide children with other "Carl" titles and ask them to create a dictated or personally written story about them.

● Have several children write about the same "Carl" story and compare their writings.

● Invite children to create a sequel to the title they had selected. Prompt this by saying something like, "What did Carl do the next time he went to the park?"

3. If I Had a Helping Dog

Begin by asking children to think about work they do at home or at school. Invite them to imagine what it would be like to have a dog by their side to help them carry out that work. Ask them to describe in what ways a dog might be able to help them. Write down each child's ideas as he or she says them on a separate sheet of construction paper. Invite children to create an illustration to accompany their ideas. Later, read each child's ideas to the whole group, or have the descriptions available for the children to read on their own or with an adult in the book area.

To Simplify:

● Provide pictures of dogs helping people for children to examine. Have each child select one picture to talk about. Ask children what they see in the picture—what kind of help is needed, what is the dog doing to help? Write the children's comments on a piece of paper above or below the picture they selected.

To Extend:

● Encourage children to use their own form of writing to record their ideas.

Physical

1. Heeling Trials

Explain to children that heeling is a process whereby dogs learn to follow closely at their owner's side. When a dog heels, he or she is to follow the owner and move as the owner moves. For example, when the owner stops, the dog stops; when the owner runs, the dog runs; when the owner turns, the dog turns. Talk about why this skill would be an important one for a helping or working dog to learn.

This exercise will require two children to work together, one as the leader/owner, the other as the follower/dog. Divide the children into pairs and have the children in each pair stand side by side. The "dog" is to watch the "owner" and move as he or she moves. Encourage leaders to walk, then stop; run, then slow down to a walk; go straight forward, turn around and go in the opposite direction. The dog is to stay right by the owner's side, in a sense mirroring each movement. Start the game by having the teacher call off directional commands: walk (heel), run, stop, turn around, slow. Once the children grasp the idea of the game, have the owner take charge deciding the commands. Give the children a chance to switch the leader and follower roles.

To Simplify:

● Practice the commands as a whole group. Have the children stand in a line and tell them to listen to your directions. Work in unison until the children demonstrate an understanding of each command. Next, have children try the game in pairs, following directions called out by the teacher.

To Extend:

● Make each round of the game last at least three minutes. Child "dogs" will have to maintain their attention to successfully mirror their owner. Another option is to have the "dog" move on all fours at the owner's side. This will require both children to adjust their movements to one another.

2. Endurance Trials

Create a circular course on which children can run in a large safe area indoors or outdoors. Make the track wide enough (approximately 10 feet or more if possible) so the children can safely get around each other. Clearly mark the course using masking tape and/or traffic cones. When the children arrive, show them pictures of dogs pulling sleds full of supplies. Explain that sled dogs often have to pull their loads and run for long distances as they do their work. The ability to sustain this kind of physical activity over time is called endurance. Working dogs build up their endurance by practicing. Tell the children that today they will have a chance to practice building their endurance. This will involve running around the track several times in a row. Have the children run in groups of at least four or five at a time—this adds to the fun and motivation to keep going. Tell children to run until they are tired. Time the children's first efforts. On another day, have children run the same number of laps plus one or add 30 seconds to the time during which they are to run. Use a bell to signal the start and the stop of the endurance trial.

Hint for Success:

● In one segment of the course suspend a balloon or pom-pom ball suspended by yarn or light string which children can tap in passing to mark the completion of each lap. Count the laps out loud and cheer the children on to keep them going. Approximately nine minutes of sustained running provides excellent aerobic exercise. Gradually work children up to this level of endurance through daily practice. Build their endurance through encouragement; avoid competition or rigid expectations.

To Simplify:

● Begin with short increments of running, for instance two times around the track or one minute of running. Gradually increase the number of laps or minutes.

To Extend:

● Add interest to the activity by giving the children something to pick up and carry each time they make another round. Have the carried item get progressively heavier and larger, but also soft, so the child will not get hurt if he or she falls while carrying it. For example, on lap 1, the child will carry a scarf; lap 2, a tennis ball; lap 3, a soccer ball; lap 4, a basketball; lap 5, a backpack; lap 6, a backpack filled with balls.

● On another day, add large plastic hula hoops face-down somewhere along the track. Have the children move through the hoops by jumping or hopping when they get to this part of the course.

Pretend Play

1. Canine Corps

Set up a police station which includes dogs who help people find things they have lost and who use their sniffing skills to find concealed items. Provide caps and badges for the police officers. Make available toy dogs, leashes, dog dishes, and dog beds for the canine corps. Add telephones, paper and pencils, maps, walkie-talkies, and a table for the police to use in locating missing people or objects. A steering wheel with a few chairs set up behind can serve as a police car. Help children take on the roles of police officers, dogs, and people needing help as they play in this area.

2. Working Dogs at Home

Set up the housekeeping area to include dogs to help the people who live there. Add a child-sized wheelchair (available on loan from some medical supply companies or from a pediatric medical unit), child-sized crutches, glasses made with several layers of plastic wrap for the lenses, and mittens with the thumb sewed to the finger section for children to wear. Suggest that children use these props to take on the roles of household members whose movements are restricted in some way. Other children may play the role of dogs who must help their human family carry out such daily tasks as making meals, answering the telephone, caring for the baby, and so on.

3. Dog School

Remind children that working dogs and helping dogs require special training. Often they learn their commands and how to do their work at a dog school. With the children, set up an area of the classroom which contains elements of a house and another area which includes simple hurdles and obstacles. Post pictures of helping and working dogs in action. Add leashes, collars, toy stuffed dogs, pretend dog food, water bowls, and biscuits to use as rewards. Provide some training manuals—both real ones and ones created by the children. Suggest that some children pretend to be trainers, some children pretend to be dogs, and some children pretend to be owners or prospective clients learning how to work with their helping animals. Support children as they play out this scenario.

Hint for Success:
● Make these pretend play props available after children are familiar with the concept of helping/working dogs and after they have participated in some of the training activities described in this segment of the unit.

To Simplify:
● Give children stuffed, toy dogs to use as the dog trainees rather than relying on children to take on that role.

To Extend:
● Add money and a cash register so clients can pay for the services they receive.

Social

1. Leader May I?

This adaptation of the well-known children's game "Mother May I?" will give children an opportunity to learn about and practice signals typically used to train dogs. It will also give them a chance to play together in a group. In this game a person signified as the leader stands at one end of the play yard (initially, the adult should be the leader to model the role for the children). All other players (the dogs) stand at the opposite end of the yard in a line facing the leader. The leader's job is to call out a command that the players must follow. The commands are "Sit" (child crouches low to the ground in a squatting position), "Down" (child lays prone on the ground, hands forward, face looking toward leader), "Come" (child walks on two feet slowly toward leader), "Hurry" (child walks on two feet quickly toward leader), and "Stay" (child freezes in position). One at a time, each dog asks, "Leader May I?" and the Leader then responds with a command which all the dogs obey until the leader says "Stay." Each round of the game continues until all the dogs have moved to the leader's side. At the end of the round, another child becomes the leader.

To Simplify:
● Only use the commands "Stay" and "Come" until children become familiar with the game.

To Extend:
● Using all the commands, have children carry out the game with the "dogs" moving on all fours rather than upright on two feet.

2. Lost and Found

This game is similar to "Hide and Seek." The purpose is to give children a chance to work together to find a hidden classmate. To introduce the game, remind children that one way dogs help police officers in their work is finding lost people. Children may choose the role of police officer, police dog, or lost person. Once the roles have been chosen, the police officers and dogs will gather together, hiding their eyes at the "police station" (any designated spot will do for this). The missing persons will find a place to hide (either singly or in a group).

Once the missing persons are hidden, someone should call out "Come find us!" Police officers and dogs search together until all missing persons are found. When the game is repeated, children may switch roles.

3. Leader Dog Walk

This activity requires children to work together cooperatively. Prior to the children's participation, make or collect the following items: two or three child-sized life jackets (these will be used to approximate a leader dog harness), and plastic or cardboard eye glasses with lenses made from several layers of plastic wrap or wax paper. These glasses should fit easily over children's eyes, allowing in light but causing them to have restricted vision. Create an obstacle course indoors or outside using three or four soft obstacles (such as traffic cones or plastic hoops laid on the ground).

Show children the obstacle course and let them walk through it. Next divide the children into pairs. Remind children of the work that leader dogs do. Explain that one child will pretend to be a leader dog and one child will pretend to be a person with limited vision. Give each child the corresponding props. Have the child pretending to be the dog get down on all fours wearing his or her life jacket. Show the other child how to hold onto the "dog" by grasping a piece of the life vest. Have the dog and person maneuver through the obstacle course. The "dog's" job is to keep the person from running into or tripping over the obstacles. After a time, let the children switch roles.

Hints for Success:

● Remind the dogs not to talk and the person wearing the glasses not to peek.

● Encourage the pair to move slowly through the course.

To Simplify:

● Allow the pair to move through the obstacle course with both persons standing upright. Then redo the course with the "dog" on all fours. Also, allow the "dog" to talk as a way to further help his or her person until the pair is more comfortable with the course.

To Extend:

● Increase the complexity of the course and the differences among the obstacles.

Teacher Resources

Classroom Visitors

1. Have a trainer demonstrate skills she/he has taught a dog and show children some techniques used to train a dog. Also, ask the person to discuss the value in training a dog and some various jobs a dog can be trained to do.

2. Invite an officer to have a police dog find a missing teacher, tennis ball, or possibly food hidden in the classroom. The officer could talk about his/her relationship with the dog, how she/he works to train the dog and how the dog helps him/her on the job.

3. Ask a person with a helping dog to describe and show how the person helps the dog and how the dog helps the person. Have her or him discuss how life is made easier because of the dog.

4. In some farming communities, people use dogs to assist them in gathering and moving herds of animals. If this is true for your area, find out if it would be possible for the farmer to visit the children on the playground to demonstrate what the herding dog does to help out. Sometimes this can be shown by having the dog herd a group of ducks to simplify the visit. Another idea would be to arrange a field trip to the farm so the children could watch the dog at work.

5. Call local nursing homes to find out if they have a Therapy Dog program. If so, ask if it would be possible for the children to visit on a day that the dogs come to the home. Talk with children in advance about guidelines for their behavior. It will be important that they are very quiet as the dogs are doing their work, so the dogs are not distracted by the children. If it is not possible for the children to visit the nursing home when the dogs are there, find out if the dogs could possibly visit the children's classroom with their owners. Have the dogs' owners talk about the job that the dogs do and why people feel that the dogs help. Find out if the dogs could sit with the children to give the children the opportunity to experience how it feels to have a calm dog sit on their lap or by their side.

Children's Books

Day, A. (1991). *Carl's Afternoon in the Park.* New York: Farrar, Straus & Giroux.

Day, A. (1991). *Good Dog, Carl.* New York: Simon & Schuster.

Day, A. (1989). *Carl Goes Shopping.* New York: Farrar, Straus & Giroux

Day, A. (1993). *Carl Goes to Day Care.* New York: Farrar, Straus & Giroux.

Day, A. (1990). *Carl's Christmas.* New York: Farrar, Straus & Giroux.

Day, A. (1993). *Carl's Masquerade.* New York: Farrar, Straus & Giroux.

Franklin, K. L. (1994). *The Shepherd Boy.* New York: Macmillan.

Hill, E. (1987). *Where's Spot?* New York: Putnam Publishing Group.

Killilea, M. (1992). *Newf.* New York: Putnam Publishing Group.

Krulik, N. (1990). *Animals on the Job.* New York: Scholastic.

Osofsky, A. (1992). *My Buddy.* New York: Henry Holt and Company.

Paulsen, G. (1993). *Dogteam.* New York: Delacorte Press 1993.

Rosen, M. J. (1993). *Kid's Best Dog Book.* New York: Workman Publishing.

Adult References

Sayer, A. (1989). *The Complete Book of the Dog.* New York: Gallery Books.

Wild Dogs

Terms, Facts, and Principles (TFPs)

1. A wild dog lives apart from people and must find its own food and shelter.

2. Wild dogs can be found in many regions of the world: in forests, on the plains, in deserts, in the mountains, on the tundra.

3. There are approximately 35 kinds of wild dogs, such as wolves, foxes, coyotes, dingoes, and African wild dogs.

4. A group of wild dogs is called a pack.

5. A pack of wild dogs is like a family.

6. Every member of the pack has a place or rank.

*7. Each pack has a leader (alpha), which is usually the largest and strongest member. Often there is an alpha male and an alpha female.

*8. Most of the time, pack members are subordinate to the leader and will do what the leader wants them to do.

9. Most wild dogs hunt for their food in packs.

*10. Those wild dogs that hunt in packs are sociable, meaning they develop relationships with the other animals in their pack and remain with their pack for much of their lives.

11. Some species of wild dogs are solitary hunters, such as the fox.

*12. Wild dogs are carnivores, meaning they eat meat (other animals).

13. Wild dogs are fast runners.

*14. When wild dogs hunt, they chase and run down their prey.

*15. Types of prey wild dogs eat include mice, rabbits, squirrels, beavers, ducks, geese, fish, deer, elk, moose, caribou, musk-oxen, and bighorn sheep.

16. The wolf is the largest of all wild dogs.

*17. The wolf is the ancestor of all domestic dogs.

18. Dogs in the wild establish an area for hunting and sleeping. This area is called a territory.

19. A wild dog's sleeping place is referred to as the den. The den could be a cave, a hollowed-out place in the ground, or a hollow log.

20. Wild dogs guard their den carefully to keep it safe and for themselves.

21. The den is the place where the mother wild dog gives birth to her pups and provides a safe place for the pups to stay until they are older.

22. Most adults in the pack cooperate in raising the young, sometimes helping to find food and fighting to protect the pups.

23. Wild dogs make several kinds of noises: they howl, bark, growl, whine, and squeak.

24. Wild dogs tend to bark as a warning if they are surprised by something at the den.

25. Grown wild dogs growl when feeling challenged by another wild dog; wild dog pups growl while they play.

26. When wild dogs are playing, feeding, or just feeling good they may whine or squeak.

27. Wolves and coyotes howl to locate each other when separated. They may also howl as a warning to other wolves or coyotes or just for fun.

Activity Ideas

Aesthetic

1. Paw Print Stamps

Prepare for this activity by first making paw print stamps. Create the stamps by cutting four small (fingernail size) circles and one larger one from a thick piece of cardboard or a dry flat sponge. Glue these on a small block of wood to resemble a paw print, as illustrated above. Pour a thin covering of tempera paint (any color) on top of four damp sponges, each of which has been placed in a pie tin with the paint side facing up. Demonstrate for the children how to press the paw pad stamp into the painted sponge and then onto the construction paper to make a print. After this introduction, give each child a piece of 12" x 18" construction paper. Encourage them to make prints on their papers in a like fashion. Explain that when wild dogs walk over damp ground or through water and then onto a dry surface, they leave prints similar to the ones the children have just made.

To Simplify:

● Limit the paint to one color. Make sure the blocks fit easily into the palms of children's hands.

To Extend:

● Give children long pieces of paper on which they can make prints individually or in a collective manner. Display these end-to-end, creating an effect of paw prints going around the classroom walls.

● Have the children help you make the paw print stamps. Add further challenge by using different block sizes to simulate paw prints of varying sizes of wild dogs.

● Use natural-looking paint colors to represent paw prints on rocks, in earth, on moss, or in sand. Discuss the kinds of wild dogs whose prints might be found in such places.

● Talk about the use of color as a way artists convey information to an observer (such as many prints might signify a pack; prints strung out along the page might look like a lone wild dog on the run; big prints and little prints together might signify a family of wild dogs). Invite child artists to show their paw prints to another child or adult. Have that observer describe the message he or she thinks the artist is trying to convey about wild dogs through the picture created. Help the artists record the many different ideas people express about their pictures.

2. Countryside Traveler

Two books that capture the beauty of the countryside as seen through the eyes of foxes are *The Fox*, written by Leith Douglas Morton (1989), and *Red Fox Running* authored by Eve Bunting (1993). Select one of these stories and either show it or read it to the children. If you choose to focus on the lovely illustrations, let children examine them closely before reading the text. If you choose to emphasize the beauty of the words, be careful to preserve their rhythm. In either case, focus on the mood created by the author and/or illustrator. Talk with the children about that mood—was it loud or quiet, fast or slow, happy or sad? Discuss how the children reached their conclusions.

Hint for Success:

● The emphasis in this activity is on aesthetic appreciation. Avoid making comments or asking children questions that would cause them to focus primarily on the facts of either book.

To Simplify:

● Ask children to point out or describe their favorite part of the book.

To Extend:

● If you choose *The Fox*, ask children to find the fox in each illustration.

● As an alternative, ask children what the fox is seeing in each picture (this will help children focus on the details in the paintings).

● *The Fox* has a bilingual text. Point out the Japanese text to the children, comparing the shape and flow of the words to their English counterparts on the same page.

● If your selection is *Red Fox Running*, ask children to describe what they see in the illustrations or to identify all the movement words used by the author to depict the fox's actions.

Affective

1. Home Packs

In a note home to parents, ask for group pictures of children's families. Individual pictures of more than one family member will also be suitable for this activity. Make sure each child's family is represented by at least two family members besides the child himself or herself. Conduct a discussion around the following questions: What similarities are noticeable among family members in each child's picture? What differences are evident in the photos? Begin by focusing on easily identifiable characteristics such as hair, eye, and skin color; body shape; facial expressions; clothing. Next, talk about other signs of being in the same pack such as touching, living in the same household, shared activities, and expressions of affection. Record the children's ideas on paper for future reference. Later in the day, or on the next day, review the children's ideas about their family photos. Then explain to the children that they will have a chance to look for similarities and differences among wild dog families using some of the same ideas. Begin with the idea that members of a dog pack tend to look similar to one another. Show children pictures of several dog packs. Ask them to look for and point out similarities between the wild dogs. (For resources, there are many books about wolves, foxes, and coyotes available commercially and in libraries. Refer to the resource section of this unit for some suggestions.) Eventually, invite the children to look for signs beyond physical appearance that might signal that certain dogs belong to the same pack.

To Simplify:

● Focus on physical attributes only.

To Extend:

● Have the children create a book made from pieces of paper stapled together. Title the book: *Members of My Pack*. Invite each child to glue his or her family picture in the book or draw his or her own family. Review with children their responses to the following questions: "What similarities are noticeable among family members in each child's picture?" "What differences are evident in the photos?" Write the children's responses down exactly as they are stated and read them back to each child for verification.

2. Wild Dog Banners

Many early childhood activities are carried out by having children participate in small groups. For the duration of the "Wild Dog" mini-theme divide the children into small groups according to wild dog families—red wolves, gray wolves, red foxes, coyotes, and dingos. Then move into the following exercise to give children a chance to talk about themselves and to recognize commonalities between themselves and others.

Day One: Have children make banners designating the wild dog family to which they belong. Prior to the children's arrival, make one large (at last 36 inches across) outline of a wolf, a fox, a coyote, and a dingo—these will serve as banners for the groups. Gather a variety of art materials such as crayons, markers, glue, glitter, magazine photos of wild dogs, and tape. Cut out small pictures of wild dogs representing each of the four categories listed above—one for each child in your class. Put the wild dog pictures in a bag. Ask each child to select one, sight unseen. Help children identify the wild dog they pulled from the bag and have them find the others in the class in the same group. Provide each small group with the art materials and the wild dog outline that corresponds to their wild dog family. Give children time to create a banner for their wild dog family that includes the names of its human members as well as its wild dog family name.

Day Two: Ask each wild dog family member to introduce himself or herself to the other members of his or her wild dog family. Tell children to describe themselves physically and to talk about things they like to do in the classroom and at home. Ask other small group members to repeat some of the information each child offered in his or her introduction. (Some of this information should be recorded on the back of that group's banner.)

Day Three: Ask each child to talk about something he or she likes to eat. Write down the children's ideas. Read the comments back to the small group. Ask the children to identify similarities among people's favorite foods. Talk about the fact that the people in their group are just like the animals in a wild dog family; they are not exactly alike but they have many things in common.

Days Four and Five: Repeat the process as described for Day Three; simply vary the topic of conversation: children's favorite colors, what children do at bedtime, favorite games or classroom activities.

Hint for Success:

● Use these same small group designations for other small group activities carried out during the week, not just the activities described here. This will help children develop common bonds through participation in like activities.

3. Leader of the Pack

This activity will give each child an opportunity to take on a leadership role in the classroom. Explain to the children that wild dogs often live in groups called packs. Within a pack at least one dog is viewed as the leader. The other wild dogs follow their leader. Designate a child as "Leader of the Pack" for a day or part of a day. Provide a badge for the leader to wear to help the other children identify who is in charge. The badge could be a picture of a wolf or coyote on a paper circle suspended on a necklace of yarn or string. The pack leader makes decisions and assigns responsibilities to other children. These decisions might include assigning seats for snack; choosing a story, song, or game; taking charge of special cleanup tasks such as table washing, sweeping, or straightening an area. The pack leader might also be the person to perform other special tasks such as doing the weather report or taking messages to other parts of the building during his or her time in the role.

Hint for Success:

● During this mini-theme, make sure every child gets a turn at being the pack leader.

To Simplify:

● Confine the leadership role to one particular job.

To Extend:

● Assign two pack leaders at a time, one boy and one girl (usually a wolf pack has an alpha male and an alpha female). They will have to figure out a way to share the leadership responsibilities. Support them as they work out how to do this during the day.

Cognitive

1. Who's in the Pack?

Gather sketches or pictures of several wolves, foxes, and coyotes singly, in pairs, and in groups. Lay these out on a table. Tell the children to look at the pictures and tell you what they notice. Explain that members of a wild dog pack often share similar characteristics. Invite the children to choose one picture of a solitary wild dog. Then have them look at the other pictures and put together all the wild dogs that might join their first pick in a pack. When the children are finished finding pack members, ask them to describe what is the same about all those dogs. Next, select any wild dog picture the child did not use in his or her grouping. Ask, "Why is this dog not part of the pack?" Wait for the child's response. Invite the child to insert or eliminate this wild dog from his or her pack.

Hint for Success:

● There are no "wrong" answers in this activity. The purpose is for children to articulate the similarities and differences that they perceive and to create their own criteria for grouping the animals.

To Simplify:

● Choose pictures of wild dogs with easily discernable characteristics, For example, select pictures of gray wolves, red wolves, and coyotes.

To Extend:

● Once children have identified a pack of animals, mix the pictures together again. Repeat the activity, asking children to create a new and different pack.

2. Number Packs

For this counting activity, gather a number of wild dog models, including both adults and cubs or kits. Pictures or drawings of wild dogs and their young could also be used (see page 522). Put the wild dogs together in packs, adult dog(s) with young cubs or kits. Vary the number of adults and young in the groupings. Show the children the packs of wild dogs, asking them, "Which pack has more?" and "Which pack has less?" "Do any of the packs have the same number of wild dogs?" After children have had a chance to answer your queries, ask, "How did you know?" Listen to the children's answers and paraphrase what they say. Invite the children to count the animals in each set with you. Write down numerals to represent each group. After the wild dogs have been counted, review the information: "When we

counted the dogs, we decided this pack had ___, this pack had ___, and so on. Now which pack do you think has the most wild dogs? Show me a pack which has less?" Repeat the process of counting and comparing as you periodically reformulate the packs.

Hints for Success:

● Small open boxes could be used as dens or territories and as a means of separating the various groupings of wild dogs.

● Use words such as more, less, the same as, most, and least, as well as the numeral names as you interact with the children.

To Simplify:

● Help the children compare the numbers of wild dogs by taking the animals out of the dens and lining them up in rows. "Now look at the families. Which one has more?" Give children many chances to experiment.

● Work with number combinations of five or less or ask children to compare only two groups at a time.

● When working with more than two groups, make the differences very obvious—ten in one group, five in another, two in the last.

To Extend:

● Encourage the children to take turns changing the number of animals within each family. Have them work with each other to compare and count the numbers of wild dogs in each group.

● Work with group numbers higher than five and compare more than two groups at a time.

3. Death in the Wild

Part of understanding how wild dogs live is understanding that they are born, they live, and then they die. Their lives also involve killing other living things for food. Use any of the following children's books to introduce the topic of life and death in the wild to the children in your group.

Gray Fox by Jonathan London (1993)

The Eyes of Gray Wolf by Jonathan London (1993)

Red Fox Running by Eve Bunting (1993)

The Seasons of a Red Fox by Susan Saunders (1991)

Wolf Island by Celia Godkin (1993)

Follow the same guidelines for discussing life and death in the wild with children as those described in "Painful Partings" (see page 501).

Construction

1. Make Prey

Wild dogs are carnivores, meaning they eat meat. Their meals may consist of animals such as mice, squirrels, rabbits, fish, birds, beavers, marmots, moose, elk, deer, mountain sheep, bison and caribou. Put plastic wolf models at the playdough table and invite the children to create food for them to eat. Talk about features of the various kinds of prey (such as a small body and a long, thin tail for mice; the large body, long legs and large antlers of a moose; scales and fins of the fish; the long fluffy tail of a squirrel). Encourage children to choose an animal and then create it with the modeling dough. Demonstrate ways to roll the dough back and forth on the table to make long, thin tails; poke small holes using fingers to create eyes or mouths; gently pull one small part of the dough in a pinching motion to make a snout; ball up the dough between two hands to create a body. Watch as children create and positively acknowledge their constructive efforts, "Arthur, you found a way to flatten the modeling dough to make the bird's wing! Great!"

To Simplify:
- Post pictures of the prey animals around the area for the children to look at as they create.

To Extend:
- Add supplementary materials to the activity such as pipe cleaners (for tails or antlers), beads (for eyes), yarn pompons (for rabbit tails), etc.

2. Safe Place Outside

Have available a variety of natural materials such as leaves or straw as well as other potential make-believe items such as large hollow blocks and a dark-colored blanket. Pretend with the children that they are a pack of wolves and that the outdoor play yard is their territory. Have them choose a safe place in which to create a den. Suggest that the "wolves" figure out what they will need to make their den comfortable and safe from other animals (including people!). Have the children build the structure they have in mind using the materials available.

To Simplify:
- Provide children with sleeping articles that people would use (such as a pillow or blanket).

To Extend:
- Have the children create more than one den to accommodate more than one family of wild dogs.

3. In the Woods

In this activity, the children will create a forest habitat for wild dogs. Prior to the children's participation, gather an assortment of construction paper and tissue paper (include various shades of green, brown, red, and gray) and paper tubes. Provide these items along with scissors, yarn, colored pipe cleaners tape, glue, crayons, and markers. A variety of natural items such as pine straw, small stones, or sand could also be included. Use the bottom of a large cardboard box as a base for the forest. Ask the children to describe what a wild dog's home would be like in the woods. What kinds of things would the wolves need to eat? What things would they use to make a home? Have pictures or books available for children to look at so they can see the vegetation and wildlife common to forests. Tell the children that they will have the opportunity to create a pretend forest home for wild dogs. Show them the variety of materials available. If the base is quite sturdy, add some rocks to be glued in place to create a possible den site. Use the completed forest as a prop for children's play with wolf figures.

To Simplify:
- Create the base of the forest habitat in advance. Ask the children to add natural items they have gathered outdoors to complete their wild dog forest habitat.

To Extend:
- Provide modeling dough or clay for the children to make forest items or creatures.
- Have the children think about wolves in the winter, when the weather is cold and snow is on the ground. Ask, "What would the wolves' winter habitat look like?" Have the children create another habitat to show what life might look like for the wolf in the midst of a cold winter.

Language

1. Sounds of the Wolf

Recordings of wolf sounds are available on CD or cassette tape. For this listening activity, obtain a copy of one of these and play it for the children. Ask them how they feel as they listen to the sounds. What do the sounds make them think of or what do they "see" in their minds as they listen? Invite children to count and describe the different kinds of wolf sounds they hear. At the end, suggest that children imitate some wolf sounds. Conduct this portion of the activity after they have heard the tape or CD at least once without interruption.

Hint for Success:

● One source of wolf recordings is a company called NorthSound (North Word Press, Inc., P. O. Box 1360, Minocqua, WI 54548; phone: 1-800-336-5666). Examples of recordings are *Jazz Wolf*, *The Contemporary Wolf*, *Classical Wolf*, and *Wolf Talk*.

2. Legendary Wild Dogs

In some legendary stories wild dogs, such as coyotes, foxes, or wolves, are depicted as helpful and wise creatures. Examples of these legends are: *Fire Race: A Karuk Coyote Tale* by Jonathan London (1993), *Magic Dogs of the Volcanoes* by Manlio Argueta (1990), and *Dream Wolf* by Paul Goble (1990). The wise coyote and fox in *Fire Race* work with the other animals to steal fire away from the "yellow jackets" so their people will be warm in the winter. This is a legend of the Karuk people, a Native American tribe. The *Magic Dogs* (or cadejos) protect the people of the El Salvadoran villages from danger and misfortune. This book is written in both Spanish and English and is one of the many stories of El Salvador about the Magic Dogs who in folklore play an important part in protecting people. *Dream Wolf* is a legend of the Plains Indians in which a wolf helps two children who have wandered away from their families find their way back. Select one of these books to read to the children. Have them listen for ways the wild dogs were helpful or wise. Record the children's ideas on a large piece of easel paper where children can refer back to them. Compare the ideas represented in these stories with those represented in fictional stories about wolves such as "The Three Little Pigs" or "Little Red Riding Hood."

To Simplify:

● Focus on only one story at a time.

To Extend:

● Have the children compare the stories of the various cultural groups. Talk with children about the similarities and differences among the stories.

3. Coyote Contrasts

Coyote is a fantasy figure common to North American Indian mythology. At times he is portrayed as trickster or fool; at other times, he is hero, helper, or teacher. In this activity, children will have a chance to explore character development in a story by examining the contrasting depictions of the mythical coyote. You will need at least two different versions of a story about coyote. These can be found in children's picture books or read-aloud story books such as *The Tale of Rabbit and Coyote* by Tony Johnston (1994), *And It Is Still That Way* by Byrd Baylor (1988), or *Coyote: A Trickster Tale from the American Southwest* by Gerald McDermott (1994). In addtion, have available a large piece of chart paper divided in half and a thick-tipped, dark marker. Introduce the activity with a discussion of real coyote behavior. Talk about the fact that people sometimes make up stories about animals which mix fact and fiction. Tell the children you will be telling them two such stories about a coyote. Ask the children to listen carefully to how the coyote acts in each story. Read or simply tell one of the two stories. Afterwards, ask the children to describe the coyote based on what you have read. Write their descriptions on one side of the chart paper. Repeat this process with the second story. Contrast the two different characterizations of coyote.

To Simplify:

● Read one story per day. Record children's descriptions and contrast them each time or skip the contrasts and focus only on the individual characterizations used by the storytellers chosen.

To Extend:

● Go back over the stories and ask children to contrast the fictional accounts of the coyote with their understanding of coyote behavior in the wild. Talk about the elements of actual coyote behavior that served as the basis for the storyteller's characterization.

4. Wild Dog Study Center

In this activity children will use books and other written materials as references to find out factual information about wolves. Set up a "Wild Dog Study Center" in the library area or the writing center of the classroom. Such a place should hold a variety of writing materials including different kinds of paper, markers, crayons, pencils, pens, and a working typewriter or computer (depending on the age of your children and available resources). It should also contain several factual wild dog books written for children as well as narrative picture books in which wild dogs are portrayed realistically. (A list of such books is available at the end of this mini-theme.) Some books should be ones you have read to the group while others may be new to the children. Supplement these items with photographs of wild dogs, posters, and pamphlets.

Introduce the "Wild Dog Study Center" by asking children to generate a list of what they know about wild dogs. Using chart paper and a marker, write down the children's ideas as they say them. Next, ask children what questions they have about wild dogs and what new things they would like to know about them. Make a list of the children's queries. Post both lists in the "Wild Dog Study Center." Talk to the children about how they might begin to answer their questions using the resources available in the room. Have each child identify a question he or she will try to answer. Support children while they carry out their research. As children come across facts that interest them or that answer their questions, record this information. Such recording could involve taking the children's dictation or having the children draw pictures, or having the children write the information in their own form of writing. Post these "facts" on single strips of paper within and nearby the "Wild Dog Study Center." Periodically, review what children have found out and what they still want to discover.

Hint for Success:

● Some natural history or wildlife programs in communities can provide pelts or actual stuffed animals for the children to examine.

To Simplify:

● Use as reference books only ones you have read to the group out loud so children will be familiar with their content in advance.

● Pair more experienced readers with less experienced ones as co-investigators searching for the answer to a particular question.

● Alternately, have the whole group work on the same two or three questions for a day. Address different questions throughout the week.

To Extend:

● Expand children's use of references to include people and places. Invite a visitor who knows about wild dogs to the classroom. Have the children interview this person using some of the questions they had generated earlier.

● Arrange for children to visit a wild life center or natural history museum where they could have firsthand experiences observing wild dogs or talking to the experts who work there.

5. Caring Communications

Introduce this activity by explaining to the children that wild dogs are sometimes misunderstood because people don't know a lot about them. One way children can help wild dogs is to find out true things about them and communicate those facts to others. Based on their participation in the "Wild Dog Study Center," suggest that children write a letter to someone in their family or to someone in their community whose job it is to protect nature and wildlife. In their letter they are to tell the person some of the things they think are important for people to know about wild dogs. In creating these letters children can dictate to adults or more experienced children, or they can use pictures and/or their own form of writing.

Physical

1. Follow the Wild Animal Prints

Prepare for this activity by drawing or stamping animal foot tracks (such as rabbit, mouse, or deer) on squares of paper. Make several squares of each animal

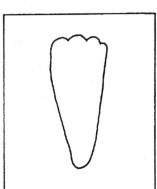

Rabbit

Mouse

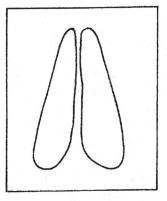

Deer

type (20 to 40 per animal works well). Place the tracks in trails around the play yard before the children go outdoors. Have the trail go around trees, under the climber, down the slide, over rocks, etc. Before the children go outside, let them know that the prints are all over the playground. Their job is to follow the tracks, wherever they go. Remind children how important following tracks can be. This is one way wild dogs find their food.

Hint for Success:

● Hide pictures of sample prey at various places along the trail for the children to find.

2. Wolf Race

Wolves are known to be fast runners. They run together to catch their prey. To have the children learn about this, while also getting physical exercise, organize a running game outside. Choose a stuffed toy animal or puppet to represent the prey (this could be just about any outdoor animal such as a mouse, squirrel, rabbit, duck, moose, deer). One child will run with the prey while the other children (limit the number to four or five) will be the wolf pack. Have the "prey" run off first to try to escape the wolf pack. Tell the wolf pack to run together to catch the prey. The child who catches the prey could choose to keep running or hide the animal from the wolf pack. (Once one member of the wolf pack gently touches the prey, it is caught.) Start the game again, encouraging the children to change roles, if they so desire.

Pretend Play

1. Wolf Packs

This outdoor activity works best after children have acquired some basic information about how wolves live and interact with one another in packs. In advance of the children's participation, prepare wolf tails for them to wear by attaching a one foot length of furry material to a belt that can be fastened around the waist. Also, make wolf-type ears by cutting ear shapes out of construction paper, covering them with clear adhesive paper and then taping the ears onto a plastic headband that the children can wear. Invite the children to wear the tails and ears outside on the playground so they can pretend to be a pack of wolves. Remind them to remain in their pack as they engage in a variety of outdoor activities. This may require some negotiation as individual members of the pack develop different ideas about what they want to do.

Hint for Success:

● The children could help the adult make the ears. (Refer to the "Dog Ear Cutouts" activity on page 505.)

To Simplify:

● Limit the wolf packs to three children at most. Encourage them to stay together for some portion of the outdoor time, playing the typical games with which they are familiar. Do not require the children to engage in these activities verbally.

To Extend:

● Expand the wolf packs to five or more children at a time. Encourage the children to engage in physical activities such as running together, rolling on the ground, or finding a safe place to curl up and rest as a group.

● Ask the children to determine who will be the alpha dogs in their pack. Once children are chosen for the alpha roles, they get to lead the pack for some portion of the outdoor time. These roles may be alternated among the children at different times or on subsequent days.

2. Wolf Tag

This is an outdoor pretending game. Before the game begins, ask the children to choose to be prey or wolf. Because wolves hunt in packs and sometimes run after a group of animals that could be prey, multiple children could pretend to be wolves, as well as the prey. Explain to the children that the purpose of the game for the wolves is to catch an animal (prey) to eat. The purpose of the game for the prey is to find a place to get away from the wolves and not be eaten. Designate a "home base" for the prey. This is the place where the prey will be safe and can no longer be caught by the wolves. For safety's sake, the wolves will gently tag the prey to catch it. Once the wolves have tagged the prey, or the prey have escaped the wolves, the players will exchange roles, and the game will continue.

Hint for Success:

● Have the children practice "tagging" one another in advance of actually playing the game. Emphasize the importance of gentle touches that will not really hurt anyone.

To Simplify:

● Let just four children play wolf tag at a time with an adult. Two children will be the wolves and two children will be the prey.

To Extend:

● Encourage children to move as the animals they have chosen. As wolves, running on "all fours"; as prey, the children will have to decide what animal they are and then move as that animal would: hop like a rabbit, scurry like a mouse, leap as a deer, fly like a duck.

Social

1. Pack Mates

Obtain or take photographs of each child in the class. Display these together on a classroom wall or bulletin board. Label this space "Our Classroom Pack." Next to each child's photograph, post a blank sheet of paper. Tuck a corner of the paper under the photo so it is evident which paper goes with which picture. During a circle time, invite the children to look at the pictures and tell them the title of the display. As you point to the pictures, ask them to name each child. As children say the names, write them on the corresponding papers. Next, go back through the photos, one at a time. Ask the children to tell you something about this particular classroom friend—what he or she looks like or what he or she likes to do. Write this information under the child's name. Repeat this process, until everyone has been described. Throughout the week, as children look at the photos, ask them to find their own information sheet. Also, have them point to other children by name and read for them or have them read the information that is there.

Hint for Success:

● This activity works best when the materials are at the children's eye level.

To Simplify:

● Print the children's names next to their pictures as detailed above. Put a piece of Velcro® near each name. Make available, in an envelope attached to the wall, a corresponding set of names printed in a similar fashion, each with a small piece of Velcro® on the back. Tell the children to remove these names and match them to the pack members' names and pictures on display.

To Extend:

● Tell children that throughout the week they should be thinking of additional descriptors for the members of their pack. As children identify new information, add it to the identification sheet by the particular child's name. A good strategy is to designate certain children for the group to find out about each day. Announce this at the beginning of the session; record what children find out at the day's end. Cover the entire group by the end of the unit.

2. Fox, Fox, Where's Your Prey?

Adapt the well-known game "Doggy, Doggy, Where's Your Bone?" to "Fox, Fox, Where's Your Prey?" Direct the children to sit in a circle together. Select one child to be the fox. This child sits in the middle of the circle and pretends to be asleep with his/her eyes closed. Hide the "prey" behind one of the children. Lead the whole group in saying, "Fox, fox, where's your prey? Someone came and took it away. Wake up, fox!" At this point the "fox" wakes up and tries to guess behind which child the prey is hiding. The "fox" gets three chances to guess where its prey is. After the three guesses or after the child has found the prey, the child holding the prey gets to have a turn being the fox. Repeat until each child has had a turn being the fox.

Hint for Success:

● Provide the child who is the fox with a fox ear headband. Make the prey be a picture of an animal such as a mouse or rabbit, glued onto cardboard for durability.

3. Cooperative Paw Prints

Create life-sized wild dog paw prints by gluing pieces of dry sponge (as described in "Paw Print Stamps" on page 519) on the outside tops of shoe box lids. After the glue has thoroughly dried, turn the lids over and insert two pieces of elastic across the middle of the lid from one short side to the other. Knot the ends of the elastic on each side so they are secure. This will allow children to strap the lids on their stocking feet with the sponge paw prints facing downward.

Implement this activity in a large open area or outdoors. Get a long sheet of mural paper, moderately thick tempera paint mixed in jelly roll pans (large enough to insert the shoe box lids, one color per pan), soapy water, and paper towels for cleanup. Show children how to put the paw print lids on their feet, step into the paint, and then step onto the paper. Tell children to walk down the paper one or two at a time, making wild dog prints as they go. In this way each child will contribute to the final product. Hang the finished paw prints for everyone to see. Congratulate children on their group effort. After the prints have been on display for several days, take the paper down and cut it into pieces so each child can have a part of this cooperative project to take home.

Hints for Success:

● This activity works best with just one or two colors of paint. Keep one set of lids for each color.

● Encourage children to help their friends as they step from the paint to the paper, due to the slippery nature of the paint.

● Teachers who wish to use these paw prints for more than one activity have found that plastic lids from large-sized coffee cans can be substituted for the shoe box lids. The plastic paw print lids are washable and are reusable.

To Simplify:

● Have children put the paw prints lids on their hands rather than their feet, making the activity easier to manage.

To Extend:

● Give children an opportunity to work together making the paw print lids.

4. Wild Dog Follow the Leader

During outdoor time have one child be the pack leader as a group of children follows slightly behind. Whatever action the leader starts, the group must follow (such as jumping, walking in a silly fashion, arms swinging from side to side). Switch leaders often so each children can have a turn leading the group.

Teacher Resources

Field Trips

1. Visit a local zoo to view wild dogs. Once there, compare the wild dogs to other animals determining how they are similar and different.

Classroom Visitors

1. Invite a wildlife specialist to describe the work he or she does to protect the habitats and lives of wild dogs. Possibly have the person talk with the children about ways they could also help.

2. Tales of wild dogs are common to many cultures. Through your local library, museum or cultural center, find out if there are any experienced storytellers who would be able to visit your classroom and tell stories about wild dogs to your children.

Children's Books

Argueta, M. (1990). *Magic Dogs of the Volcanoes*. San Francisco: Children's Book Press.

Baylor, B. (1988). *And It Is Still That Way*. Santa Fe, NM: Trails West Publishing.

Brett, J. (1988). *The First Dog*. New York: Harcourt Brace Jovanovich.

Bunting, E. (1993). *Red Fox Running*. Boston: Houghton Mifflin.

Goble, P. (1990). *Dream Wolf*. New York: Macmillan.

Godkin, C. (1993). *Wolf Island*. New York: W. H. Freeman.

Hogrogian, N. (1971). *One Fine Day*. New York: Macmillan.

Johnson, F. (1977). *Foxes*. Washington, DC: National Wildlife Federation.

Johnston, T. (1994). *The Tale of Rabbit and Coyote*. New York: Putnam Publishing Group.

Lepthien, E. (1991). *A True Book: WOLVES*. Chicago: Childrens Press.

Ling, M. (1991). *Amazing Wolves, Dogs & Foxes*. New York: Knopf Books for Young Readers.

London, J. (1993). *The Eyes of Gray Wolf*. San Francisco: Chronicle Books.

London, J. (1993). *Fire Race: A Karuk Coyote Tale*. San Francisco: Chronicle Books.

London, J. (1993). *Gray Fox*. New York: Viking Children's Books.

McDermott, G. (1994). *Coyote: A Trickster Tale from the American Southwest*. New York: Harcourt Brace Jovanovich.

McKissack, P. (1992). *Flossie and the Fox*. New York: Dial Books for Young Readers.

Milton, J. (1992). *Wild, Wild Wolves*. New York: Random House Books for Young Readers.

Morton, L. D. (1989). *The Fox*. Flagstaff, AZ: Northland Publishing.

Murphy, J. (1989). *The Call of the Wolves*. New York: Scholastic.

Reed, E. D. (1988). *Coyote Tales from the Indian Pueblos*. Santa Fe, NM: Sunstone Press.

Spier, P. (1961). *The Fox Went Out on a Chilly Night*. New York: Doubleday.

Tejima. (1987). *Fox's Dream*. New York: Putnam Publishing Group.

Wexo, J. B. (1993). "Wild Dogs." Zoobooks 10 (4). San Diego, CA: Wildlife Education, Ltd.

Wexo, J. B. (1989). "Wolves." Zoobooks 6 (4). San Diego, CA: Wildlife Education, Ltd.

Wolpert, T. (1990). *Wolves for Kids*. Minocqua, WI: NorthWord Press, Inc.

Adult References

Field, N., and Karasov, C. (1992). *Discovering Wolves*. Middleton, WI: Dog-Eared Publications.

Patent, D. (1990). *Gray Wolf, Red Wolf*. Boston: Houghton Mifflin.

Savage, C. (1988). *Wolves*. San Francisco: Sierra Club Books.

Simon, S. (1993). *Wolves*. New York: HarperCollins.

Turbak, G. (1992). *Twilight Hunters: Wolves, Coyotes & Foxes*. Flagstaff, AZ: Northland Publishing.

Curricular Domains

Aesthetic

Developmental Focus

Enjoyment
Stimulation
Insight
Satisfaction

Ultimate Goal

For children to integrate feeling, thought, and action within art, music, and other sensory experiences to achieve pleasurable, personally meaningful ends.

Intermediate Objectives

The following objectives lead to the ultimate goal.

Children have opportunities to:

1. increase their familiarity with varying forms of art and music;

2. develop familiarity with the basic elements of art (line, form, color, texture, space, and composition);

3. develop familiarity with the basic elements of music (musical sounds, melody, volume, rhythm, pitch, tempo, beat, and harmony;

4. use tools and techniques related to art and music to achieve a desired aesthetic effect;

5. reflect upon and talk about their observations and reactions related to their aesthetic experiences;

6. contribute to the aesthetic environment of the school;

7. demonstrate appropriate behaviors related to aesthetic appreciation;

8. recognize their own strengths as artists and musicians;

9. gain pleasure from a variety of sensory experiences with no other goal in mind.

Affective

Developmental Focus

Trust
Autonomy
Initiative
Industry
Self-concept
Self-esteem

Ultimate Goal

For children to feel lovable, valuable, and competent.

Intermediate Objectives

The following objectives lead to the ultimate goal.

Children have opportunities to:

1. learn that school is safe, predictable, interesting, and enjoyable;

2. engage in affectionate relationships beyond the family;

3. identify the characteristics and qualities that make each of them unique;

4. explore similarities and differences among people to gain personal insight;

5. practice self-help skills (such as dressing and pouring);

6. independently begin and pursue a task;

7. make choices and experience the consequences of personal decisions;

8. develop mastery in using age-appropriate materials and tools (pounding tools, writing implements, cutting tools, computers, tape recorders, record players, typewriters, etc.);

9. complete a task they have begun;

10. gain awareness of personal emotions;

11. learn to accept both positive and negative emotions as a natural part of living;

12. become familiar with the situational circumstances that influence personal emotions;

13. learn how to act deliberately to affect their own emotions;

14. understand the concept of possession and ownership;

15. value their own gender, culture, and race;

16. increase their knowledge, understanding, and appreciation of their own cultural heritage;

17. develop cross-gender competencies of various kinds;

18. experience the pleasure of work;

19. keep trying in situations that are difficult for them;

20. learn how to recover from setbacks;

21. evaluate themselves positively.

Cognitive

Developmental Focus

Perception

Physical knowledge

Logical mathematical knowledge

Representational knowledge

Critical thinking skills

Conventional social knowledge

Ultimate Goal

For children to integrate knowledge and experiences as they construct new or expanded concepts.

Intermediate Objectives

The following objectives lead to the ultimate goal.

Children have opportunities to:

1. attend to particular sensory stimuli while ignoring extraneous stimuli;

2. develop finer degrees of sensory acuity;

3. coordinate their use of the senses;

4. learn about the attributes of objects;

5. develop concepts related to objects and events;

6. recognize or construct relationships among objects and events through the process of comparing (perceiving likenesses and differences and discovering incongruities in a systematic manner);

7. recognize or construct relationships among objects and events through the process of classification (grouping according to perceived similarities and differences);

8. recognize or construct relationships among objects and events through the process of seriation (sequencing according to the magnitude of a particular characteristic);

9. recognize or construct relationships among objects and events through the process of patterning (repeating a particular configuration and discovering inconsistencies);

10. construct a concept of number invariance (conservation and one-to-one correspondence;

11. construct a concept of quantity (counting, working with equal and unequal sets, association a number of objects with a numeral, measurement);

12. develop a concept of time;

13. develop a concept of space;

14. attach meaning to symbols in the environment;

15. learn how to define problems and set their own goals;

16. learn information-gathering techniques (questioning, experimenting; observing, consulting);

17. develop and practice a repertoire of strategies for remembering;

18. develop strategies for analyzing objects and events;

19. apply current knowledge to make inferences or predictions;

20. learn how to review and summarize what they have experienced;

21. learn how to evaluate their experiences (monitor, establish standards, verify);

22. develop perspective-taking skills (determining how objects or events are perceived from more than one point of view);

23. use the scientific method (observe, hypothesize, predict, test out, evaluate);

24. integrate decision-making skills (observe, infer, define, generate alternatives, analyze, select a solution, implement, evaluate);

25. become aware of their own thought processes;

26. learn about the natural world;

27. learn about the interdependence of all things in the world;

28. learn about history, folklore, and traditions relevant to them;

29. acquire factual information that is interesting and useful to them;

30. recognize and use diverse sources of information.

Construction

Developmental Focus

Iconic representation

Ultimate Goal

For children to translate mental images into tangible products that represent their own interpretation of an object or event.

Intermediate Objectives

The following objectives lead to the ultimate goal.

Children have opportunities to:

1. engage in a wide range of experiences from which to draw their interpretations;

2. interpret events and reconstruct them in tangible ways;

3. use diverse approaches to represent objects or events:

   a) represent a single object or event using different materials or techniques;

   b) represent different objects and events using one material or technique;

4. interact with classmates to collaboratively construct a representative object.

Language

Developmental Focus

Listening skills
Receptive language
Expressive language
Writing
Reading

Ultimate Goal

For children to interpret accurately the communications of others as well as communicate more effectively themselves.

Intermediate Objectives

The following objectives lead to the ultimate goal.

Children have opportunities to:

1. learn how to use and interpret nonverbal messages accurately;

2. learn appropriate attending behaviors (looking at speaker, waiting for own conversation turn, responding meaningfully to oral and visual cues);

3. learn how to interpret interpersonal verbal messages accurately;

4. improve memory skills related to nonverbal, oral, and written messages;

5. practice listening for content, details, sequence, and sound;

6. extract and interpret relevant content from auditory information presented to them;

7. increase their receptive vocabulary;

8. experiment with language sounds, rhythm, volume, pitch, and words;

9. expand their ability to use words to represent knowledge, events, ideas, imaginings, and perceptions;

10. increase their repertoire of verbal strategies;

11. recognize and use humor as a means of communication;

12. expand their ability to present ideas to others coherently;

13. seek out book experiences for pleasure and information;

14. use their prior knowledge to make sense of literary experiences;

15. become familiar with the elements of the story in order to gain increased pleasure and meaning from literary experiences (setting, characters, detail, plot, main idea, sequence, mood, etc.);

16. attach meaning to print;

17. explore the mechanics and conventions of reading and writing;

18. express themselves in their own form of writing.

Physical

Developmental Focus

Physical development:

Body awareness

Gross-motor development

Fine-motor development

Physical health

Ultimate Goal

For children to achieve mastery of the environment through improved body control and to develop attitudes, knowledge, skills, and behaviors related to maintaining, respecting, and protecting their bodies.

Intermediate Objectives

The following objectives lead to the ultimate goal.

Children have opportunities to:

1. gain confidence in using their bodies;

2. develop awareness of the location of their own body parts;

3. develop spatial awareness (understanding of personal and general space and direction);

4. engage in a variety of activities that require balance;

5. engage in activities that require coordinated movements;

6. sustain a vigorous motor activity over time in order to develop endurance;

7. engage in a variety of activities that require flexibility;

8. engage in motor activities that require agility;

9. use their whole bodies in appropriate activities to strengthen muscles and muscle groups;

10. develop fundamental motor skills such as jumping, hopping, throwing, kicking, striking, running, or catching;

11. coordinate finger, finger-thumb, and eye-hand movement;

12. control the movement of their bodies in relation to objects;

13. use their bodies to move or change objects;

14. develop a positive attitude about their bodies;

15. learn how to keep their bodies clean;

16. learn how to keep their bodies fit;

17. learn and practice good nutritional habits;

18. learn appropriate safety procedures for school, home, and neighborhood;

19. discriminate good and poor health and safety practices;

20. learn how to apply health and safety knowledge in making choices in daily life.

Pretend Play

Developmental Focus

Imitation

Role-playing

Symbolic play

Dramatization

Ultimate Goal

For children to integrate meaning derived from their experience with knowledge and skills from all developmental domains as they create roles or scenarios.

Intermediate Objectives

The following objectives lead to the ultimate goal.

Children have opportunities to:

1. mimic in their play behaviors they have seen or experienced;

2. use their bodies to represent real or imaginary objects or events;

3. assign symbolic meaning to real or imaginary objects using language or gestures;

4. take on the role attributes of beings or objects and act out interpretations of those roles;

5. create play themes;

6. experiment with a variety of objects, roles (leader, follower, mediator), and characterizations (animal, mother, astronaut, etc.);

7. react to and interact with other children in make-believe situations;

8. dramatize familiar stories, songs, poems, and past events;

9. integrate construction into pretend play episodes.

Social

Developmental Focus

Social skills
Socialization

Ultimate Goal

For children to develop successful patterns of inter-action as well as internal controls and pro-social values.

Intermediate Objectives

The following objectives lead to the ultimate goal.

Children have opportunities to:

1. develop play skills (how to join a group at play, how to make suggestions, how to take suggestions, how to deal with unpleasant social situations and the emotions associated with them, how to play productively alone);
2. develop friendship skills (how to constructively initiate, maintain, and terminate interactions and relationships);
3. learn how to negotiate conflicts in democratic ways (compromising, voting, bargaining);
4. develop empathy for others (recognize others' emotions, respect others' emotional responses);
5. become aware of similarities and differences in opinions, points of view, and attitudes;
6. perceive adults as sources of gratification, approval, and modeling;
7. learn how to control antisocial impulses;
8. learn how to delay gratification;
9. learn how to conform to reasonable limits set upon behavior, play space, use of materials, or the types of activities in which they are involved;
10. identify the reasons for classroom rules;
11. learn how to be cooperative (work with others toward a common goal);
12. learn how to be helpful (share information or materials, give physical assistance, offer emotional support);
13. distinguish acceptable classroom behavior from unacceptable classroom behavior;
14. use their knowledge of appropriate behavior in one circumstance to determine appropriate conduct in another circumstance;
15. develop awareness and concern for the rights and well-being of others;
16. learn approved behaviors related to social customs;
17. develop an appreciation of the family compositions, traditions, values, ethnic backgrounds, and cultures of others;
18. develop a sense of responsibility for the environment.

Themes List

Themes Teachers Use

Art and Artists

Visual Arts
Performing Arts
Usable Arts

The Human Body

The Body and Its Parts
The Senses
Bodies in Action: Mobility and Immobility

Food

Food and Food Preparation
Where Food Comes From
How the Body Uses Food

Safety

Vehicle Safety
Fire Safety
Personal Safety

People Living Together

People Playing
People Working
People Living in Communities

Communication

Interpersonal Communication
Print Media
Communication Through Visual Media

Math Connections

Grouping and Patterning
Parts and Wholes
Geometric Exploration

Science and Scientists

The Process of Science
Science in the Everyday World

Trees

Trees as Plants
Variety and Changes in Trees
Tree Gifts

Classroom Pets

Rabbits
Gerbils
Fish

Backyard Animals

Worms
Spiders
Frogs and Toads

Cats

Introduction to Cats
Domestic Cats
Wild Cats

Dogs

Dogs as Pets
Working Dogs
Wild Dogs

Teaching Young Children Using Themes

Self-awareness

Families

Friends

Pets

Living in homes

Clothing

Dental health

Vehicles

Exploring space

Plants

Insects

Wild birds

Bears

Water

The sky

Rocks

Machines

Dinosaurs

Music makers

Storytelling

Writers

Number and numerals

Measuring

Stores

Activities Index

Aesthetic

Aiken Drum, 53
All the Colors of the Rabbits, 378
Amphibious Song, 449
Around It Goes, 182
Artful Movement, 77
Artist Performers on the Wall, 29
Artists' Tools, 35
Artplay, 183
Artwork, 196
Arty Shapes, 279
Beat It, 259
Beautiful Beads, 35
Beautiful Cats, 484
Beautiful Sounds, 63
Beautiful Wood Products, 363
Big and Little Cats, 484
Body Band, 52
Bread Day, 63
Brilliant Art Pictures, 151
Canine Sing-Along, 497
The Car Song, 136
Cats in Verse, 474
Cat's View, 474
Chalk, Stencils, and Templates, 346
Children's Block Prints, 362
Clap Those Hands, 53
Classroom Art Photos, 242
Claw Scratch Art, 463
Colorful Fish, 408
Colorful Frogs, 447
Colorful Tunes, 259
Community Portraits, 208
Countryside Traveler, 519
Create a Movement Dance, 77
Creative Dancing, 29
Design a Magazine Cover, 242
Discard Art, 105

Down on the Plain, 485
Earthworm Monotony, 433
Everyone's a Critic, 259
Fantastic Felines, 463
Far and Near, 280
Find the Pattern, 260
Fine Felines, 463
Finger Paint on Me, 162
Fire Paintings, 151
Fish Dance, 408
Fish Magic, 408
Fish Tank Backgrounds, 408
Flat or Not?, 280
Flower Beds, 208
Frame That Dog, 508
Fur Fun, 463
Garden Wash, 105
Gentle Dance Touching, 162
Gerbil Food Designs, 396
Gerbil Pictures, 396
Gluing Scales, 408
Gourd Shakers, 92
Graph Crafts, 295
How Does Your Garden Grow?, 260
Hue View, 260
I'm Forever Blowing Bubbles, 295
Interesting Stuff, 35
The Joy of Play, 183
K-I-T-T-Y, 474
Leader of the Band, 225
Leaf Castings, 346
Lines, Lines, Lines, 19
Magazine Art, 242
Make a Picture with Safety Colors, 136
Make It a Gerbil Song, 396
Making Flower Arrangements, 36
Making Styrofoam Prints, 17
Mosaic Art, 270
Musical Cats, 474

Musical Director, 250

Musical Glasses, 314

Notes in Order, 260

Options in Song, 250

Paint a Web, 424

Painting with Lion Tails, 485

Paint to Stop and Go Music, 136

Paint with Feet, 29

Paint with What?, 19

Paw Prints, 465

Paw Print Stamps, 519

The Peanut Butter and Jelly Chant, 118

Peels Appeal, 118

Playing with Light, 314

Please Pass the Senses, 118

Popping Corn, 64

Pressure Points, 53

Puff, 313

Pup Paints, 497

The Rabbit Hop, 378

Rabbit Rhymes and Finger Plays, 378

The Rest of the Picture, 280

Rocky Frogs and Toads, 447

Round and Round, 270

Scarecrow Faces, 225

Scrap Iron, 314

Scrapwork, 195

Shape Hunt, 280

Sharing Our Snack with a Rabbit, 378

Shaving Cream Squish, 64

Sign a Song, 226

Silent Song, 226

Sing About Color, 18

Sing About Work, 196

Sing-Along, 208

Sing with Me, 52

Sing with Me, 207

Smell-and-Taste Party, 91

Smell This Modeling Dough, 64

Song for the Working Dog, 509

Songs Around the Campfire, 151

Spice Up Your Space, 92

Spider Songs, 423

Sponge and Tear Art, 447

A Style of Painting, 19

Sweet Wood Sounds, 363

This Is a Performance, 29

This Is My Body, 161

Top to Bottom, 118

Tour of Art, 17

Tree Art, 333

Tree Lines, 346

Tree Part Painting, 334

Tree Trough, 334

Un-Handed Art, 77

Up, Up, and Away!, 295

Vegetable Fun, 63

Walk Around the Garden, 105

What a Hat!, 36

What's Missing?, 270

Who Wants to Touch?, 162

Word and Mouth Collage, 226

Wordplay, 182

Worm Colors, 433

Wormsical, Musical Elements, 433

Wormy String Painting, 432

You Inspire Me, 18

Affective

All About Me, 271

All of Me, 271

Aquascaping, 409

Auction, 228

Back in Place, 281

Birthday Rings, 347

Blue Ribbon Winner!, 509

Call Me, 229

Canine Care, 497

Caring for Fish, 409

Carrot Cake, 380

Cat Tastes, 465

Chewy Things from Home, 398

The Choice is Yours, 39

Classroom Workers, 510

Comfort Puppies, 512

Community Members Collages, 209

Complete My Collage, 271

Computer Drawing, 20

Cover-Up Bingo, 137

Designing My Own Clothes, 40

Do You Like This Taste?, 65

The Early Bird Catches the Worm!, 435

Favorite Cats, 474

Favorite Flavor Chart, 65

Feed the Worms, 434

Find the Shapes on Me, 281

Fire Hazard Spotter Badges, 152

A Fish Out of Water, 409

Friendly Dog Visit, 499

Frog Lacing, 449

Getting the Job Done, 197

Help Wanted Ads, 242

Home Fire Escape Route, 152

Home Food Inventory, 105

Home Food Preference Interviews, 93

Home Packs, 520

How Do They Feel?, 485

How to Choose?, 379

How Was Your Day?, 229

I Am a Problem Solver, 315

I Am a Scientist, 298

I Can Be a Creative Performer, 29

I Can Care for the Gerbils, 397

I Can Decide, 20

I Can Say No, 162

I Don't Like It, 251

I Have an Address, 151

I Like It Like That, 93

I Like You, 162

Identification Tags, 500

I'm a Fire Hazard Spotter, 152

I'm an Artist, 20

It's Done Now, 19

It's My Turn, 230

It's Up to Me, 251

I Want a Hug, 163

Kitty Sandwiches, 476

Lap It Up, 476

Leader of the Pack, 521

Leading Us On, 208

Let's Go for a Walk!, 499

Light Up My Life, 315

Like Me, Not Like Me, 381

Make a Game, 183

Matching Skin and Eye Color, 54

Me and the Gerbil, 397

Me as Spiderperson!, 425

ME Magazines, 242

Messing Around, 297

Mood Sort, 260

Music of My Family, 30

My Bathing Suit, 162

My Crossing Story, 138

My Family Does It This Way, 163

My Favorite Cat, 485

My Favorite Crop, 105

My Favorite Grain, My Favorite Fruit, 121

My Hands Can Feel, 65

My News Story, 251

My Right, My Left, 78

My Usable Family Art, 37

Parts Make a Whole Salad, 271

People I Like to Touch, 163

People Patterns, 261

Personal Exercise Plan, 77

Personal Paper Inventory, 363

Planning for Healthful Eating, 119

Play Favorites, 183

Port-a-Kit, 298

Portrait Session, 242

Pretty Kitty, 465

A Puzzle of My Own, 270

Pyramid Plan, 120

Quiet Movement, 78

Rabbit Greeting Cards, 379

Recycling Tree Products, 364

The Safe Thing to Do, 152

Safety Captain for Today, 136

Same and Different, 54

Shapely Tags, 281

Sign Your Name, 230

A Snack Fit for Worms!, 433

Sound Emotions, 316

Spider Snacks, 424

Stock Exchange, 209

Symbolic Trees, 363

Telephone Number Memory, 163

That's Cool, 19

This Is Me, 54

This Is My Territory, 485

Tidy Toads, 451

Toad Talk, 451

Taste Tests, 364

Tracking Feelings, 512

Trail Mix, 184

Tree Crowns, 334

Tree Photo Ops, 348

Tree Seed Names, 335

Trees Like Me, 335

TV Time, 251

The Way I Like to Move, 30

Wear a Cat, 465

What Comes First?, 261

Wild Dog Banners, 520

Workcheck, 197

A Worker Am I, 196

Wrapping Rap, 92

Writing Portfolio, 242

Cognitive

Above or Below?, 304

Adopt a Class Tree, 348

All About Rodents, 400

All Fall Down, 299

Animals on Parade, 261

The Art Sorting Game, 40

Balancing Act, 303

Ball Blast, 316

Ball Guess, 184

Baseline, 211

Beautiful Spiders, 426

Blowing in the Wind, 319

Boy Bodies/Girl Bodies, 56

Breed Books, 476

Bunches and Bunches of Bunnies, 382

Buying/Selling Art, 21

Calico Cat Prints, 476

Calico Cats Revisited, 478

Camouflage Collage, 453

Camouflaged Fish, 413

Card Games, 184

Cat Trading, 478

Collection Box, 304

Comics in Order, 243

A Commercial Pause, 252

Condensation Sensation, 300

Counting Gerbils, 401

Days Gone By, 210

Death in the Wild, 522

Describe a Structure, 282

Dog Biscuit Matching, 501

Dog Seriation, 500

Do You Hear What I Hear?, 384

Drop by Drop, 302

Dry/Wet, 438

Earthworm Facts, 435

Eclectic Electric, 320

Estimating Jar, 272

Exits, Exits Everywhere!, 154

Eye/Paw/Tail Match, 465

Fact or Fiction?, 382

Fancy Fabrics, 262

Favorite Habitats, 436

Favorite Toy, 186

Filters, 412

Find a Solid, 282

Find Details in Art, 21

Find the Site, 485

The Fire Alarm Signal, 154

Fire Hazards, 154

Fire Is Useful, 153

Fires Start Anywhere, 154

Fish Bladder, 412

Fish Count I, 410

Fish Count II, 410

Fish Sort, 410

Fish Tank Experiments, 410

Flash!, 321

Food Book Extension, 109

Food Riddles, 94

Food Source Sorting Game, 107

Gerbil Numbers, 401

Gerbil Patterns, 401

Getting Ready for Fire Safety, 153

Good Vibes, 319

Halves and Half Not, 272

Hazard Hunt, 154

Heart Throbs, 56

Homey Shapes, 282

How Big Is a Big Cat?, 486

How Could You Tell?, 65

How Do You Eat It? Collage, 122

How Long Will It Take to Dry?, 40

How Many Legs?, 426

How Would It Be?, 57

How Would You Use It?, 40

Incomplete Pictures, 272

Is It True?, 318

It's Raining!, 436

Jillions of Ways to Move, 79

Kitchen Chemistry, 320

Kitty Bingo, 478

Leaf Logs, 352

Leafy Graphs, 349

Let's Work It Out, 209

Life in the Desert, 402

Lifework, 200

Listen, Cat!, 466

Listen to Me!, 230

Location Search, 243

Look, Touch, Record, 298

Losing Ground, 486

Magnetic Attractions, 318

Magnetic Mates, 318

Make the Difference, 79

Measure by Measure, 335

Measure the Edge, 282

Meet the "Cat"!, 479
Memories, 199
Mice Are Nice, 467
Mood Match, 231
Mouse Paint, 467
Movement Directions, 80
My Senses Book, 66
Nose to Knows, 94
Number Packs, 521
Observing the Gerbils, 399
Of the People, For the People, By the People, 213
On Land, in Water, 452
Other Ways to Move, 809
Our School, 199
Page Count, 243
Painful Partings, 501
The Parts of the Whole, 121
Peek-a-Boo Pictures, 272
People Patterns, 213
Photo Sort, 243
Play Teaching, 186
Playmates, 185
Plumb the Depths, 299
Prediction Walk, 302
Private Parts, 164
Protection Plus, 67
Put It There, 263
Rabbit Lineup, 382
Reading Dogs' Signals, 501
Roll and Race, 300
Sawdust Counting, 365
Scent Match, 467
Scent Smelling, 512
Schoolwork, 199
Searching for the Pyramids, 121
See It, Smell It, Feel It, 384
Selecting Fish for the Room, 413
A Sensory Walk, 67
Seriating Brushes, 20
Seriating Textures, 66
Shape Walk, 282
Should I Accept the Ride?, 138
Silhouette Classification, 479
Singles, Pairs, and Multiples, 56
Sleeping Earthworms, 438
Slide It, 301
Smell and Tell, 66
Solutions to the Problem, 316
Solve a Movement Problem, 80
Something in Common, 30

Sort Them Out, 263
Sorting Touches, 163
Sound as a Bell, 321
Spider, Where Do You Live?, 426
Spider or Insect?, 426
Sticks, Sticks, Sticks, 336
Straight as an Arrow, 319
Supporting Roles, 336
Tadpole to Frog, Part I, 451
Tadpole to Frog, Part II, 451
Temperature Trials, 321
Texture Tubs, 66
There's Music in the Air, 320
Tiny Kangaroos?, 399
Tree Bingo, 352
Tree Census, 337
Tree Chart Grouping, 365
Tree Detectives, Part I, 364
Tree Detectives, Part II, 365
Tree Part Chart, 336
Tree Part Comparisons, 348
Tree Part Examination, 335
Tree Part Groupings, 349
Tree Seed Count-Up, 353
Tree Silhouettes, 349
Tree Tags, 365
Trucks, Trains, Ships, and Planes, 107
Twinkle, Twinkle Traffic Light, 138
Uprooted Discoveries, 336
Useful Props, 30
Voice Predictions, 252
Watch Us Work, 40
Water, Water Everywhere, 299
We Do It Together, 213
Weighing Rabbit Food, 382
We Like to Eat, 211
We've Got Class, 264
What Are Vehicles?, 138
What a Surprise, 67
What Came First?, 107
What Happened to That?, 107
What's a Bone Like You Doing in a Joint Like This?, 55
What's My Rule?, 94
What's Similar?, 21
What's Up?, 336
What Would Happen If?, 164
Who's in the Pack?, 521
Wild Cat Habitats, 486
Will They Eat It?, 400
Wood Samples, 352

Construction

All the Ships at Sea, 231

Amazing Gerbil Maze, 404

Assembly of People, 58

Boats from Trees, 366

Blocks in Order, 264

Box Town Buildings, 243

Build and Tell, 284

Building Digestive Systems, 122

Build with Wet Sand or Snow, 68

Cases and Places, 109

Cat Construction, 487

Cat Mask, 467

Cat Puzzles, 479

Character Art, 252

Construct-a-Play, 186

Construct a Spider, 427

Construction Paper Fish, 414

Cookbooks, 95

Cornhusk Wreaths, 95

Cover Me Up, 164

Crazy Word Creations, 274

Create a Jungle, 487

Creating a Mask, 30

Currant Bun-nies, 386

Design a TV Camera, 252

A Dog for Me, 503

Dog Dough Faces, 512

Double Cats, 479

Ears Up, 468

Fans of Mine, 304

Feline Face, 468

Fish Collage, 414

Forest in a Box, 353

Frog Food, 454

Funny Halves, 274

Gear Boards, 274

Geometric Sculptures, 284

Gerbil Nests, 402

Gerbil Toys, 402

Hear Ye!, 214

Hidden Ingredient Detectors, 124

A Home Fireplace, 156

Home, Sweet Home, 503

A Home Fit for a Worm, 439

Homes Designed for Everyone, 41

I Can Make My Own Usable Art, 41

In the Woods, 523

I See the Light, 323

Leaping Frog Habitat, 453

Make a Movement Path, 81

Make-a-Toy, 187

Make Prey, 523

Making Rabbit Ears, 384

Making Seat Belts, 139

Mask Play, 186

A Microphone of My Own, 253

My Art Portfolio, 22

My Moving Body Parts, 81

My Own Exit Sign, 156

My Own Kind of Gerbil, 402

My Own Kind of Vehicle, 139

My Own Mobile, 21

My Own Private Sign, 164

My Own Telephone, 154

My Own Wrapping Paper, 42

My Parachute, 304

My Puppet Character, 31

Mysterious Toads, 454

My Touch-Tone Phone, 68

My Trusted Person, 165

No-Talk Block Structures, 231

On the Border, 265

Our Class Vehicle, 139

Painted Toast, 95

Paper Gliders, 321

Paper Towel Trees, 338

Papier-Mâché Creations, 243

Pattern Walls, 265

People Trees, 338

Plainly Beautiful!, 487

Playground Plotting, 214

Pop Bottle Fish Tank, 414

Post Office Box, 244

Potholder Designs, 42

Puppet Folk, 253

Rabbit Hutches, 386

Rollin', Rollin', Rollin', 439

Safe Place Outside, 523

Safety Helmets, 139

Sandwich Books, 109

Scenery for a Performance, 31

Schoolhouse, 200

Seed Collage, 353

Sensory Tubes, 109

Shadow Puppets, 322

A Shape of My Own, 282

Silent Cooperation, 232

Site Visit, 214

Sleds and Carts, 512
Solid Shapes, 284
Stick Houses, 366
Stuck on You, 427
Terrific Towers, 284
Toothbrush Test Kits, 124
Tree Stars, 353
Vibrating Strings, 323
We'll Eat It Up, We Love It So, 58
What Moves You?, 57
Wood Construction, 22
Wood Sculptures, 366
Working Together, 200
Worm Compost Box, 438
Yarn Bubbles, 22

Language

Add-On Song, 58
Adjectives Under the Arbor, 338
All the Better to See You with, My Dear, 68
Amphibious Sound Patterns, 456
Anansi Stories, 428
An Artist's Story, 42
And Bunny Was Her Name, Oh . . ., 387
Anybody Got a Word Match?, 59
Art Messages, 23
"Ask the Scientists," 306
A Backwards Story, 306
Book of Hugs, 165
Bump-a-Deedle, 31
Busy Spider Character Recall, 427
Buy This!, 253
Caring Communications, 525
Cat Care, 481
Cat Hunt, 487
Cat Vocabulary in Motion, 468
Class Newspaper, 244
Classroom Work Songs, 202
Cloudy, 468
Come to Our Play, 31
Community Clues, 215
A Complete Joke, 59
Cookie's Week, 481
Counting Out Games, 187
Coyote Contrasts, 524
Crazy Words, 274
Don't Touch!, 82
Down Around the Corner, 111
"Down on the Plain" Book, 487

Do You Hear What I Hear?, 503
Family Food Completion Stories, 112
Feathers for Lunch, 481
Fish Relatives—Big, Bigger, Biggest, 415
"Fishful" Fantasy, 415
Fishy Solutions, 415
Five Brave Firefighters, 156
Food Group Books, 125
Foods Grab-Bag, 96
Food Talk Around the World, 125
Frog Chorus, 454
Frog Fantasies, 456
Good Pup Words, 503
Haiku, 265
Help! There's a Fire, 158
Helpmates, 513
Here Comes the Cat!, 469
Hot or Cold?, 307
If I Had a Helping Dog, 514
If I Had a Wondercat, 481
Illustrated Cat Vocabulary, 469
Interactive Statements, 427
Interview a Firefighter, 158
I Spy! Part I, 306
I Spy! Part II, 323
I Want It Too, 166
I Wonder as I Wander, 323
Learning Fish Names, 414
Legendary Wild Dogs, 524
Letter to a Friend, 232
Little Blue, Little Yellow, 22
The Little Red Hen and the Grain of Wheat, 200
Little Red Riding Hood, 216
Mama's Secret, 165
May I Ride?, 141
Mommy/Daddy Work, 202
Musicplay, 188
My Artist's Badge, 42
My Dance Has Meaning, 31
My Gerbil Book, 404
My Own Touching Story, 166
My Shadow, 323
Name That Tree, 355
Oh, Dear!, 112
One Part of the Picture, 274
On the Air, 253
Our Gerbil Story, 404
Pen Pals, 215
Place That Word, 274
Plane Message, 245

Poetry for Scientists, 324
Press Conference, 253
Rabbit Care Guides, 387
Rabbit Communication, 387
Rebus Recipes, 97
Recipe Files, 112
Rhymes with Cat, 469
Rhyming Play, 188
Rhyming Worm Words, 440
Rima de Chocolate/Chocolate Rhyme, 97
Safety Color Game, 141
A Safe Way to Cross Streets, 141
Sell It to Me!, 245
Shapely Letters, 284
Shape Story, 285
Shape Talk, 285
Sharing Day, 232
Shhhh! Listen Very Carefully!, 440
Show Me a Story, 82
Signal Flags, 233
Simple Pleasures, 366
Skinnamarink, 69
Smell Talk, 69
Something Is Missing, 274
Somewhere in Africa, 487
Sounds of the Wolf, 523
Sound Vibrations, 70
Stories in Action, 82
Story Patterns, 265
Story Time, 32
The Tale of Peter Rabbit, 388
Talk About Talk, 82
Talking with Artists, 23
Tastes in Nursery Rhymes, 97
Telephone Game, 236
Telling Fire Stories, 158
Tell Me a Story, 216
Things We Learned About Fire and Fire Safety, 158
This Is Braille, 69
Three Little Kittens, 481
Tiger Environments, 487
Touching Pictures, 165
Touch Talk, 339
Tree Biographies, 355
Tree Echoes, 339
Tree Encyclopedias, 355
Tree Facts and Fiction, 340
Tree Haiku, 355
Tree Letters, 367

Tree-Nut Butter Recipes, 367
Tree Nut Narratives, 367
Vehicle Safety Rebus, 141
Way Down in the Jungle, 489
What Comes Next?, 266
What Do You Know?, 59
What Is Fire?, 156
What's This For?, 42
Who Takes Care of the Puppy?, 503
Wild Dog Study Center, 524
Wood Collections, 125
Wordless Frog Adventures, 454
Words for Carl, 514
Words That Tell About Gerbils, 404
Worm Discovery Diaries, 440
Writing Labels, 42
You Are Invited!, 23

Physical

Action Patterns, 266
Act Out a Stretching Poem, 32
As Still as a Statue, 25
Attractive Creatures, 325
Balance Beam Walk, 470
Ball Play, 190
Bend and Stretch, 441
Blow Up, 325
Boat Float, 325
Braille Letters, 236
The Bumps Tell Us, 236
Burrowing Cutting Practice, 442
Catch That Insect!, 456
Cat Cookery, 481
Cat Play, 481
Cheetah Chase, 489
Clean Up Your Community, 217
Cutting Out Signs, 143
Dance Game, 32
Different Strokes, 504
A Disarming Game, 84
Dog Ear Cutouts, 505
Endurance Trials, 515
Energy and Growth Exercise Song, 126
Everybody's Song, 60
Exercise Show, 254
Eyes Closed Movement, 72
Feather Touches, 167
Firmly Rooted, 341
Fish Skeleton, 416

Flipper Feet, 417
Follow the Leader, 216
Follow the Wild Animal Prints, 525
Food Tracings, 99
Fresh Fish, 307
Funny Walks, 84
Going Lots of Ways, 84
Grinding, Shaking, and Churning, 114
Grinding Grains, 113
Ha Ha, This-a-Way, 203
Handle with Care, 428
Happy Hat, 307
Heeling Trails, 515
Hopscotch Jumping, 85
Hop to It, 390
How Do You Sit?, 254
A Hutch for Us, 390
It's a Puzzlement, 275
Keep Our Balance, 308
Lace a Shape, 285
Leaf Stencils, 356
Leaping Frogs, 456
Leopard Leaps, 489
Leveraged "Pull Out," 308
Light Touch, 70
Log-istics, 341
Make a Magnet, 324
Modeling Dough Cut-Ups, 275
Movement in Order, 266
Movement Sounds, 72
Move Those Hands and Arms, 83
Move to the Shape, 285
Moving Through a Maze, 405
My Lungs Can Fill Up, 60
Mystery Wax Resist, 23
Nesting Toys, 266
Newspaper Fold and Roll, 245
Newspaper Toss, 245
No Thumbs, 482
Nutty Tools, 359
Oh, What a Tangled Web We Weave!, 428
On the Line, 203
Over, Under, In Between, 286
Paddles, 416
Paint a Tree, 356
Paper Tearing, 417
Parachute Listening Games, 71
Pass a Hand Hug, 166
Plucking Out the Seeds, 113

Pottery, 43
Pour and Tell, 276
Prey Wrapping, 428
Puzzling Trees, 340
Ready, Set, Action, 32
Rhythm Sticks, 368
Rig-a-Jig-Jig Game, 167
The Right Way to Hold a Gerbil, 404
Rip It Up, 245
Robot Parade, 59
Rubber Band Designs, 25
The Sandwich Game, 100
Sawdust Sculptures, 368
Shearing Rabbits, 380
Shelling, Peeling, Stripping, Boning, 114
Show a Touch, 166
Slab and Slip Clay Method, 44
Slab Patterns, 25
Spider Fang Pickup, 428
The Sports Page, 246
Sportsplay, 190
Spots and Stripes, 489
Spray Bottle Frog Tongues, 457
Squeezing Orange Juice/Making Lemonade, 368
Stop, Drop, and Roll, 158
Stop and Go Movements, 143
The Tail Game, 84
Tong Transfer, 276
Tools of the Trade, 100
Tops and Bottoms, 276
Tossed Salad, 100
Touch and Run, 166
Trace the Path Your Food Takes, 126
Track and Field, 189
Tree Bark Rubbing, 356
Tree Tag, 341
Tunnel Crawling, 405
TV Snacks, 254
Using Hand Signals, 143
Using Weaving Tools, 44
Walk Fast in a Fire Drill, 158
Walk on Cat's Paws, 470
Water Relay, 341
What's a *Pas de Deux?*, 33
Wolf Race, 526
The Worms Go In, The Worms Go Out, 442
Wrap It, Roll It, Eat It Up, 100
Wrap It, Snap It, 100

Pretend Play

Apple Orchard, 342

Architect's Office, 46

An Artist's Studio, 26

Audiologist/Optometrist, 73

Bakery, 46

Birthday Party, 236

Box Town, 245

Bubble Dance, 308

Camera Safari, 491

Camping Around the Fire, 159

Canine Corps, 515

Carpenter Shop, 369

Catalog Order Desk, 246

Cat Clinic, 482

Cats at Home, 482

Cat Shop, 482

Community Services, 217

Costume Shop, 276

The Cottontail Household, 391

Crossing a Pretend Street, 145

Doctor's Office, 60

Dog School, 516

Dog Shelter, 505

Dog Supply Store, 505

Earthworm Naturalist—Earthworm Activities, 442

Exercise Spa, 85

Figure Play, 191

Fire Engines Go, 158

Fish Store, 417

Fish TV, 417

Five-and-Ten-Cent Store, 266

Five Senses Museum, 309

Food Story Corner, 115

Frog and Toad Naturalist, 457

Fruit and Seed Store, 342

Galloping Away, 85

Gardener: Friend of the Earthworms, 443

Home Proud, 218

Housekeeping with Dogs, 505

I Am Lost, 167

Imagine and Move, 85

International Cuisine, 218

Kitchen Area with Compost Box, 443

Let's Play Bakery, 72

Life in a Gerbil Cage, 405

Mini-Firefighting, 159

Newsstand, 146

Night Vision, 470

Nutritionist's Office, 128

Operator, 236

Our Art Gallery/Museum, 26

Our Little Street, 145

Our Science Center, 308

Our Show, 33

Outdoor Art Picnic, 26

Pack and Wrap Shop, 286

Paper Factory, 267

Parts and Wholes Restaurant, 276

Pet Shop, 391

Pet Store, 405

Pizza Parlor, 114

Plastic Fish in the Water Table, 417

Play School, 203

Poster Shop, 369

Post Office, 237

Preparation Pantomimes, 101

Pretend and Real, 327

Pretend Play Ideas, 190

Pretend the Story, 33

Pretend You're a Cat, 471

Produce Stand, 114

Puppet Production, 255

Push and Pull, 325

Rabbit Charades, 391

Raking Leaves at Home, 359

Repair Shop, 277

Riding in a Pretend Car, 145

Sensory Restaurant, 72

Shadow Climbing, 341

Shadows on the Wall, 326

Shadow Stage, 326

Shady Picnic, 369

Shape Bookstore, 286

Shed Your Cuticles!, 429

Sign Shop, 286

A Special Family Member, 85

Spider Moves, 429

Store Survey, 217

Swimming Together, 167

Tabletop Habitat, 457

Thrift Shop, 60

Tree Artists, 359

Tree Orchard/Nursery/Arboretum, 359

TV at Home, 254

TV Meteorologist, 254

TV Studio, 33

Usable Art Store, 45

We Are Firefighters, 159
What Has It Done for You Lately?, 128
What's That For?, 101
Which "Weigh" to the Check Out?, 101
Wolf Packs, 526
Wolf Tag, 526
Working Dogs at Home, 516
Workplaces, 203
You're On!, 255

Social

Are You Satisfied?, 219
A Baby's Body, 61
Barn Raising, 369
Body Tracing with a Friend, 60
Books for Babes, 287
Bubble, Bubble, Pop!, 309
Busy People, 86
Can I Hug You?, 168
Caterpillar Over the Mountain, 86
Catnaps, 482
Cats for a Day, 482
Celebrations, 219
Charades, 237
Circle Band, 287
Class Rainbow, 277
Classroom Signals, 237
Class Survey, 471
Class Telephone Directory, 171
Clean Up the Mess!, 327
Cold Garden Soup, 102
Colorful Classroom Calico, 482
Comics by Partners, 247
Commercial Team, 255
Cool Cat!, 193
Cooperation Cafe, 102
Cooperative Food Chain, 129
Cooperative Games, 191
Cooperative Paw Prints, 527
Cooperative Tree Mural, 359
Cooperative Tree Web, 369
Cooperative Worm Habitat Mural, 444
Critic's Choice, 256
Crop-and-Livestock-Pizza Vendors, 115
Did You Ever See a Lassie?, 33
Dog Pets, 506
Don't Play with Matches Song, 159
Do the Parts Make a Whole?, 277
Family Play, 191

Feeding My Friends, 101
Fish Mobiles, 418
Food for All the People of the World, 130
Forest Bed Collage, 344
Fox, Fox, Where's Your Prey?, 527
Friendly Musical Squares, 167
Friendly Portraits, 26
Friendly Touches, 168
Friendship Circle, 287
From Farm to Market, 115
From Generation to Generation, 220
Go Fish, 418
Great Blue Heron and the Frogs, 457
Group Mural, 159
Hand Trees, 343
Hello in Many Languages, 238
Help!, 220
Help Me Walk, Please, 74
Hokey Pokey, 288
Homework, 204
How Could You Help?, 506
How Do I Love Thee? Let Me Count the Ways, 457
I Want to Play!, 192
If You're Friendly and You Know It, Say Bonjour, 238
Keeping Our Gerbils Safe, 406
Leader Dog Walk, 517
Leader May I?, 516
Let's Name It, 27
Lilting Elephants, 430
Lion Hunt, 491
Lioness, Lioness, Where's Your Cub?, 491
Lost and Found, 516
Make Juicy Pops, 74
Me and My Shadow, 328
Musical Lily Pads, 458
Mystery Line Up, 268
Name Bingo, 239
Naming Our Gerbils, 405
911 Reminders, 159
Oh My, No More Pie!, 129
Opinion Poll, 247
The Other Half, 278
Our Class Quilt, 46
Our Escape Route, 159
Our Next Feature, 247
Pack Mates, 527
Papier-Mâché Cat, 491
Parents, Please Help, 171
Passenger Pull, 147

Pass the Shoe Game, 268
Paw Twister, 471
Play Break, 191
Playful Choices, 193
Production Song, 115
Rabbit Garden Mural, 392
Red Light/Green Light, 146
Reflections, 328
Riding Tricycles Safely, 147
School of Fish, 418
Searching for Rabbits, 392
Silent Directions, 239
Social Seniors, 218
Soft as a Bunny, 393
Stalking Prey, 472
Sticky Group Collage, 26
Teamwork, 204
Tell Me, 268
This One's for You, 27
A Tisket, A Tasket, 34
Tower Topple, 309
Town Trees, 369
Tracing Fish, 418
Tree Salad, 369
Tree Search, 361
Tree Shadows, 343

Tree Treasure Hunt, 361
Try to See Me in the Dark, 74
Turn-Taking with Gerbils, 406
Two in the Boat, 86
Two-Way Cookies, 328
Use It, 220
The Way You Are, 240
Weaving Together, 46
We Made Paper!, 46
We Meet Something Special, 85
We Share, 219
We Write a Senses Story Together, 74
What a Great Audience!, 34
What Are the Rules on Our Trip?, 146
What in the World?, 309
Where Are You, My Prey?, 430
Wild Dog Follow the Leader, 528
Work-a-Day World, 204
Working People, 204
Worldwide Trees, 360
Worm Around the Classroom, 444
Worms in the Rain, 443
Yesterday and Today, 219
You, Too, Can Be a Scientist, 310
You Look Very Different, 33